The Anthropology
of Infectious Disease

THEORY AND PRACTICE IN MEDICAL ANTHROPOLOGY AND INTERNATIONAL HEALTH

A series edited by

Susan M. DiGiacomo
University of Massachusetts, Amherst

Editorial Board

H. Kris Heggenhougen
Harvard University
Cambridge, Massachusetts

Daniel E. Moerman
University of Michigan, Dearborn

R. Brooke Thomas
University of Massachusetts, Amherst

International Advisory Board

Joan Ablon, George Armelagos, Hans Baer, Peter Brown, Xòchitl Castaneda, Deborah Gordon, Xòchitl Herrera, Thavitong Hongvivatana, Judith Justice, Montasser Kamal, Charles Leslie, Shirley Lindenbaum, Margaret Lock, Setha Low, Harriet Ngubane, Mark Nichter, Duncan Pedersen, Tom Ots, Nancy Scheper-Hughes, Merrill Singer

Founding Editor

Libbet Crandon-Malamud [†]

Volume 1
Hippocrates' Latin American Legacy: Humoral Medicine in the New World
George M. Foster

Volume 2
Forbidden Narratives: Critical Autobiography as Social Science
Kathryn Church

Volume 3
Anthropology and International Health: Asian Case Studies
Mark Nichter and Mimi Nichter

Volume 4
The Anthropology of Infectious Disease: International Health Perspectives
Edited by Marcia C. Inhorn and Peter J. Brown

This book is part of a series. The publisher will accept continuation orders which may be cancelled at any time and which provide for automatic billing and shipping of each title in the series upon publication. Please write for details.

The Anthropology of Infectious Disease

International Health Perspectives

Edited by

Marcia C. Inhorn

and

Peter J. Brown

Emory University
Atlanta, Georgia

GORDON AND BREACH PUBLISHERS
Australia • Canada • France • Germany • India • Japan • Luxembourg
Malaysia • The Netherlands • Russia • Singapore • Switzerland

First published 1997
Second printing 2000

Amsteldijk 166
1st Floor
1079 LH Amsterdam
The Netherlands

British Library Cataloguing in Publication Data

The anthropology of infectious disease : international
    health perspectives. – (Theory and practice in medical
    anthropology and international health ; v. 4)
    1. Communicable diseases 2. Medical anthropology
    I. Inhorn, Marcia C.   II. Brown, Peter J.
    306.4'61

    ISBN 90-5699-556-1

In memory of *Libbet Crandon-Malamud*

founding editor
of this medical anthropology book series

CONTENTS

INTRODUCTION TO THE SERIES

Theory and Practice in Medical Anthropology and International Health seeks to promote works of direct relevance to anthropologically informed international health issues, practice, and policy. It aims to bridge medical anthropology—both biological and cultural—with international public health, social medicine, and sociomedical sciences. The series' theoretical scope is intentionally flexible, incorporating the most current advances in social science theory, while its topical breadth ranges from specific issues to contemporary debates to practical applications informed by current anthropological theory. The distinguishing characteristic of this new series is its emphasis on cultural aspects of medicine and their links to larger social contexts and concrete applicability of the anthropological endeavor.

ACKNOWLEDGMENTS

The seeds of this volume were planted in 1992, when a group of anthropologists working on domestic and international infectious disease problems convened at the 91st Annual Meeting of the American Anthropological Association to present their current work in a session entitled "The Anthropology of Infectious Disease." We thank those anthropologists, some of whose work is presented in this book, as well as the additional contributors who have joined this project. Bringing a large edited volume to fruition is a laborious and time-consuming endeavor. We appreciate the patience of all the authors, as well as their exceptional responsiveness in the process of review and revision.

We are indebted to copyeditors Donna Horne and Holli Levinson. Donna saw this volume through multiple stages of revision and expertly brought the chapters together stylistically and on computer. Holli willingly picked up where Donna left off, and saw the book through to final publication. We also want to thank Erin Finley for her excellent job on the index. We are grateful to Emory University, which has provided institutional support for them, as well as a fine academic home for us.

Finally, we thank our families: our spouses Kirk and Betsy, and our sons Carl, Nico, Patrick and Thomas. They provide us with continuing love and support and make us happy after our day's work as medical anthropologists.

CONTRIBUTORS

Karabi Bhattacharyya, Sc.D. is a medical anthropologist and a research officer at the Academy for Educational Development, 1255 23d St., NW, Washington, DC 20037. She has conducted fieldwork in South Asia and Sierra Leone focusing on women's and children's health issues. Her interests include the household production of health and participatory research.

Peter J. Brown is professor of anthropology at Emory University, where he also holds an appointment in the School of Public Health. He is editor in chief of the journal *Medical Anthropology*. His research interests include anthropological aspects of malaria, obesity, tuberculosis and Alzheimer's disease. He is currently preparing a monograph on the history of malaria and its eradication in Sardinia, Italy. His work has been supported by the School of American Research and the Emory University Research Committee.

Kimberly A. Buss is an epidemiologist and biostatistician who has served as a research assistant in the Department of Epidemiology, School of Public Health, University of California, Berkeley. Currently, she is a medical student at the University of California, Davis. Her research interests include international public health and primary care.

Sara H. Cody is a physician completing her residency in internal medicine at Stanford University Hospital. She completed this work as part of an MD thesis requirement while a medical student at Yale University School of Medicine. She plans to work in international health and medical anthropology after completing her training.

Jeannine Coreil is a professor in the Department of Community and Family Health at the University of South Florida. Her research interests include international health, maternal and child health, comparative healing systems, and the effects of household and family organization on health. She has conducted fieldwork in Haiti, Costa Rica, the Dominican Republic, Rwanda, Uganda and the United States.

Paul Farmer is an anthropologist and a physician specializing in infectious disease. For over a decade, he has conducted his research and clinical practice in rural Haiti, where he works for the community-based organizations mentioned in his chapter. In the United States he divides his time between Harvard Medical School and the Brigham and Women's Hospital.

William R. Harrison did doctoral studies in anthropology at the University of Arizona. He is a medical anthropologist and a trained electron microscopist. His research interests include paleopathology, contagion beliefs, death, and racial issues in organ transplantation.

Marcia C. Inhorn is associate professor of anthropology, Department of Anthropology, Emory University. Her medical anthropological research interests include women's health, reproduction, international health, infectious disease and stigma. She is the author of two books on infertility in Egypt, one of which won the Society for Medical Anthropology's Eileen Basker prize for outstanding research in the area of gender and health.

Karina Kielmann completed a masters degree in medical anthropology at McGill University looking at medical and media discourses on AIDS and prostitution in Africa. She has earned a doctor of science in international health at The Johns Hopkins School of Public Health. Her research interests lie in understanding the social, economic and political contexts of sexual and reproductive health risks of low-income women in India, Kenya and Tanzania.

Carol Shepherd McClain is a lecturer in the Medical Anthropology Program at the University of California, San Francisco. She works in the University of California Office of Research and Laboratory Affairs. Her research interests include ethnomedicine, cultural studies of biomedicine and technology, and race and ethnicity.

Cristina G. Monte is a researcher at the Instituto Conceitos Culturais in Brazil.

Dorothy S. Mull is an associate professor of psychiatry at the Texas Tech University School of Medicine, El Paso. Her PhD is from Yale and she holds an MA from the University of Cambridge, England. Her publications have focused on maternal and child health in the developing world.

J. Dennis Mull, a Harvard-educated physician-anthropologist, is professor and chair of the Department of Family Medicine at Texas Tech University in El Paso. He has written extensively on international health issues and has directed major health projects in Pakistan, Mexico and the Middle East.

Marilyn K. Nations is currently a member of the Department of Social Medicine, Harvard University Medical School and director of Harvard's Center for the Study of Culture and Medicine in Fortaleza, Brazil, as well as a visiting professor of the Federal University of Ceara, Department of Social Medicine.

Mark Nichter is a professor of anthropology at the University of Arizona. He specializes in the anthropology of health and development as well as ethnomedicine. Dr. Nichter has conducted research on several infectious diseases in South and Southeast Asia. He is the author of *Anthropology and International Health: South Asian Case Studies*, as well as more than 20 articles in the field of medical anthropology.

Diego Salazar is on the faculty of the School of Public Health at the University of Chile. He has conducted research on the ethnoecology of dengue fever in the Dominican Republic. His current research involves working with the World Health Organization on studies of adolescent sexuality and prevention of sexually transmitted diseases.

Norbert L. Vecchiato obtained a PhD in anthropology from the University of California, Los Angeles. He has conducted medical anthropological fieldwork on illness behavior, traditional medical practices, and infectious disease transmission among the Sidama of southern Ethiopia. He has taught in the Anthropology Departments at California State, Northridge and California State University, Los Angeles.

Linda A. Whiteford is professor of anthropology and graduate program director in the Department of Anthropology at the University of South Florida. Her research interests include infectious diseases, gender and the environment. She has conducted research in Mexico, the Dominican Republic, Ecuador and the United States.

Part One

Anthropologies

CHAPTER 1

Introduction

Marcia C. Inhorn and Peter J. Brown

INTRODUCTION

As the year 2000 approaches, a large portion of the world's population still suffers from, and struggles against, diseases caused by infectious agents. Indeed, at the dawn of the new millennium, infectious diseases remain *the* major cause of death worldwide, and are an incalculable source of human misery and economic loss. The Institute of Medicine's recent, ominous report, *Emerging Infections: Microbial Threats to Health in the United States* (1992), outlines the daunting number and variety of microbial threats to human health. More infectious pathogens exist than ever before, and, given the current state of preventive and therapeutic knowledge, the vast majority of these infectious disease threats are likely to persevere well into the twenty-first century (Institute of Medicine 1992).

Indeed, the committee charged with writing the Institute of Medicine report focuses on what it calls the "trouble ahead" – namely, the emergence, and re-emergence, of serious infectious disease problems. These problems comprise four basic categories. First, a host of "new" infectious diseases have been identified during the past two decades, and they are affecting more and more people every year. AIDS, caused by the human immunodeficiency virus (HIV), provides the most sobering global example of this class of new emergent infections. There are numerous examples of other new infectious diseases that have been shown to be lethal, despite their more limited geographic scope than HIV. Diseases such as *Hantavirus* pulmonary syndrome, Legionnaires' disease, and the widely publicized Ebola hemorrhagic fever can be included in this category.

The second category of threats includes a number of "old," well-known infectious diseases – once considered by many to be "under control" – that have increased in incidence beyond all expectations during the past two decades. The two primary examples of these re-emergent infectious diseases are malaria and tuberculosis. Not surprisingly, both of these diseases also provide excellent examples of what happens when microbial agents become resistant to mainstay therapeutic drugs and what happens when public health control measures slacken or break down altogether. The re-emergent infectious disease category includes many other examples, some of which, such as dengue, cholera, and measles, will be described along with malaria and tuberculosis in this volume. Taken together, the numbers of infectious disease agents in these first two categories are quite impressive: seventeen forms of bacteria, rickettsiae, and chlamydiae, twenty-seven forms of viruses, and eleven forms of parasites (both protozoans and helminths) and fungi (Institute of Medicine 1992). All the scientific evidence suggests that these are not merely newly *identified* forms of disease, but actually new species of pathogens that have evolved through natural selection, often because human behavior has changed the ecological context.

The third category includes microbial agents that are the likely causes of some widely occurring chronic diseases whose precise etiology had previously remained obscure. Two salient examples of such diseases are peptic ulcer (and possibly stomach cancer), which appears causally linked to previous infection with the *Helicobacter pylori* bacterium, and cervical cancer, many cases of which seem causally linked to previous exposure to a sexually transmitted pathogen, the human papillomavirus (HPV). Although not listed in the Institute of Medicine's report, many other non-infectious conditions, such as tubal infertility described in Chapter 7 of this volume, also share an underlying infectious etiology. The important point here is that morbidity and mortality from some chronic diseases may actually be caused by infectious agents, so that prevention efforts must target the earlier infectious causes.

The final category of "trouble ahead" identified in the Institute of Medicine report involves the introduction of infectious disease agents into previously unaffected populations. Throughout history, the introduction of infectious diseases to "virgin" populations with no immunities to the disease has caused untold human suffering and massive mortality. Indeed, McNeill (1976) has tied such epidemics to the collapse of New World civilizations. Nevertheless, it is impossible to build impenetrable epidemiologic borders between populations, so that constant surveillance and political willingness to protect populations proactively from new diseases (while justly and humanely treating infected people) will remain an important challenge for the future. In this regard, the notion of infectious disease "traffic" – a term coined by virologist Stephen Morse (1993) in reference to the movement of infectious disease agents to new species or new individuals – is significant. Indeed, Morse, who is not a behavioral scientist, recognizes that human beings are often unwittingly responsible for infectious disease traffic through, for example, ecologically disruptive agricultural practices or various culturally prescribed methods of water impoundment and storage. As he concludes in his book on *Emerging Viruses*:

> Viral traffic, often abetted by human actions, is the major factor in viral emergence. Because human activities are often involved in emergence, anticipating and limiting viral emergence is more feasible than previously believed. Basically, people are creating much of the viral traffic, even though we are doing it inadvertently. We need to recognize this and learn how to be better traffic engineers (Morse 1993:210).

Given the role of human behavior in infectious disease traffic, it seems only logical that anthropologists, as professional observers and interpreters of human behavior in its social and cultural context, play a significant role in global efforts to curb infectious disease problems.

This volume on *The Anthropology of Infectious Disease* is dedicated to four simple propositions: first, that infectious diseases are profoundly important to all human societies for the reasons outlined above; second, that anthropologists, particularly medical anthropologists with interests and experience in international health, should therefore study these diseases; third, that these anthropologists should share their research findings in cross-disciplinary dialogues and collaborative efforts with people in biomedical sciences and international public health who are working to stop the spread of infectious diseases; and fourth, that these anthropological research findings should be seriously considered by biomedical scientists and international public health personnel. Although these propositions may appear simple and even self-evident, they have been met with variable reception in both anthropology and international public health circles. Why might this be so? To answer this question, one must first take a look back at the history of infectious disease research in international health, before examining the role of anthropologists in that history.

LOOKING BACK: THE HISTORY OF INFECTIOUS DISEASE RESEARCH AND CONTROL IN INTERNATIONAL HEALTH

Although infectious diseases have once again gained the spotlight, the history of infectious disease research and control during the modern, post-World War II era of international health has generally been inglorious. Without a doubt, there are some well-deserved success stories – including the global eradication of smallpox (to be described in this volume), the elimination of poliomyelitis from the Western hemisphere, and the substantial reduction in childhood killers like diphtheria and measles in the Western industrialized countries (AMA Council on Scientific Affairs 1996). In general terms, however, this fifty-year period has been characterized by: (1) the scientific neglect of both major and minor infectious diseases, leading to numerous "scientific blind spots" in our understanding of infectious disease threats; (2) missed opportunities for basic and applied research that may have improved public health interventions; (3) an overzealous emphasis on eradication of certain priority infectious diseases, mixed with often feeble attempts to control others; (4) a general "mood of complacency," or a critically low awareness of and concern about infectious diseases, except among a handful of infectious disease specialists (Institute of Medicine 1992); and (5) the underdevelopment of a global infectious disease surveillance and public health infrastructure to deal with epidemics. These historical characteristics, in turn, have affected how anthropologists have – or have not, in most cases – contributed to infectious disease research and control programs.

International health efforts to understand and control infectious disease problems harken back much longer than fifty years – at least to the turn of the twentieth century, when the discipline of Tropical Medicine emerged to help cope with the diseases of colonizing groups, including military forces, and, to a lesser extent, colonized labor forces (Brown 1976; Curtin 1989; Warren 1990). However, modern international health programs are largely a post-WWII phenomenon linked to the foreign policy aims of Western industrialized nations, who continue to use health aid as a part of attempts to gain or maintain national political loyalties in the post-colonial era.

Some of the neglect of infectious disease in international health circles during this period is certainly linked to disappointments regarding disease eradication programs, particularly the failure of malaria eradication during the 1950s and 1960s. As described by Warren (1990), the concept of eradication of a major human disease may have originated with the Rockefeller Foundation, which set as its major goal in 1913 the eradication of hookworm, the so-called "germ of laziness," in the southern United States. Although the Rockefeller campaign to eliminate hookworm infection from the U.S. (as well as fifty-two other countries where the campaign was carried out) was a failure, this did not prevent the foundation from attempting to eradicate another disease, yellow fever, from the Western Hemisphere. Again, this campaign was unsuccessful, but the concept of disease eradication remained in tact. Undaunted, Rockefeller Foundation officers worked with World Health Organization (WHO) officials to initiate a global campaign to eradicate malaria in 1955. This campaign lasted for seventeen years and was responsible for eliminating malaria from large areas of the world, including the United States and Europe (see Chapter 5 of this volume). However, malaria eradication was never even remotely complete due to the development of resistance to both insecticides and drugs, as well as the impossibility of controlling malaria-carrying mosquitoes in their native African habitat (Warren 1990). Thus, WHO decided to terminate the effort – or, at least, to redefine the goal to malaria control – after spending approximately four billion dollars. Following malaria program termination, malaria has re-emerged in some parts of the world in massive proportions.

Although the subsequent eradication of smallpox was an absolute and unprecedented success – the world was declared officially free from smallpox on December 9, 1979 – the failure of malaria eradication (as well as programs that had preceded it) had taken its toll in the international public health community. As described by Warren (1990:149), "there was a major backlash, not only against the concept of eradication of disease but against direct, targeted (vertical) attempts to improve health in the developing world." As part of this backlash, the international health community renounced the high-technology, "engineering" approach to solving infectious disease problems through drugs, vaccines, and insecticides. The decline of the vertical disease-oriented approach was linked to the growth of international health's Primary Health Care (PHC) revolution of the late 1970s. But there was a negative consequence in that the rise of PHC succeeded in further marginalizing the many serious, but underappreciated infectious disease problems that had never been targeted for eradication.

With the concept of eradication all but eliminated from international public health discourse by the 1970s, few of the international health agencies were interested in tackling what appeared to be insurmountable infectious disease problems in the developing world. As a result, WHO remained the sole – and seriously underfunded – force in international infectious disease research and control. Specifically, WHO responded to the demands of public health leaders from sub-Saharan Africa that the organization increase its prioritization of infectious disease work. In 1975, WHO initiated the Special Program for Research and Training in Tropical Diseases (TDR), with the following statement: "The recent enormous extension of knowledge in the biomedical sciences has as yet hardly begun to be applied to the problems of tropical diseases where methods of control and treatment have scarcely changed in the past 30 years." Through its TDR program, WHO hoped to terminate the old colonial tradition in tropical medicine, where European experts would go "to the field" for short periods of time. The emphasis instead was on self-reliance through the training of researchers in the countries where tropical diseases were endemic. However, given the huge number of tropical disease problems present in the developing world and WHO's limited funds for TDR (raised outside the regular WHO budget, but with an average annual level of twenty-five million dollars), WHO restricted its TDR program to six "priority" diseases. Five of these – filariasis, leishmaniasis, malaria, schistosomiasis, and trypanosomiasis – were parasitic. Only one – leprosy – was bacterial. The soil-transmitted helminths (or intestinal "worms" to be described in Chapter 9 of this volume) were left out despite their global prevalence; essentially, WHO recognized that control first required fundamental (and expensive) improvements in environmental sanitation and water supply.

Soon after, a few philanthropies joined WHO in attempting to curb infectious, primarily parasitic, diseases. The Edna McConnell Clark Foundation initiated an innovative schistosomiasis research program, later extended to include trachoma. In 1977, the Rockefeller Foundation started the "Great Neglected Diseases" program, which involved many of the important infectious diseases of the developing world as well as the hemoglobinopathies related to malaria (Warren 1990). In the early 1980s, the MacArthur Foundation began a five-year program, the Biology of Parasitic Diseases, while Burroughs Wellcome initiated fellowships in the Molecular Biology of Parasitic Diseases (Warren 1990).

These programs resulted in many basic scientific advancements in the biology, diagnosis, treatment, and prevention of parasitic diseases during the 1970s and 1980s (Warren 1990). But these programs were small compared to other major international public health efforts. More important, the programs never focused on bacterial and viral illnesses. This was a crucial oversight, because studies from the late 1970s and early 1980s revealed that bacterial and viral infections are the leading causes of death for individuals of all ages in the developing world (Grant 1983; Walsh and Warren 1979; Walsh 1988). Of particular concern are diarrheal diseases (and associated dehydration and malnutrition) and acute respiratory infections (ARIs), which continue to be the major killers of children in developing countries.

Recognition of the importance – and neglect – of deadly bacterial and viral childhood illnesses forced a policy shift in international health circles. Namely, the 1980s initiative known as "Child Survival" defined the next phase of infectious disease research. UNICEF's declaration of "A Children's Revolution" in 1983 fit in with the overall mission of PHC, which aimed in part to improve the health of the world's children by controlling the major causes of childhood morbidity and mortality. Diarrheal diseases and acute respiratory infections (ARIs) were therefore targeted for intervention. Similarly, six vaccine-preventable childhood diseases – diphtheria, pertussis, tetanus, measles, poliomyelitis, and tuberculosis – became the focus of a joint WHO/UNICEF program, known as the Expanded Programme on Immunization (EPI). Indeed, WHO, although maintaining its TDR parasite control activities on a shoestring budget, became a major force in the field of children's infectious diseases, developing separate programs for the control of diarrheal diseases, ARI, and what came to be known simply as the "EPI diseases."

Child Survival created an important opening in the world of infectious disease, by moving research and control activities "beyond parasitology" (Warren 1990). However, infectious diseases themselves were never the major focus of Child Survival, as they were in the TDR program. Thus, the Child Survival initiative did not serve to generate concern for other, non-"priority" infectious diseases of childhood – nor for infectious diseases in a more general sense.

As of this writing, Child Survival is no longer the leading initiative in international health, although organizations like WHO and UNICEF retain their focus on children. Newer international health activities are women-centered, in part because of the realization that child survival depends largely on the health and well-being of mothers. Generally speaking, these women-centered initiatives do not have an explicit infectious disease agenda – even though reproductive tract infections and the infectious complications of childbirth and abortion represent major problems for women around the world.

Rather, infectious disease research in international health today revolves around AIDS and the opportunistic infections, such as tuberculosis, that are AIDS-related. Without question, AIDS is *the* disease of international concern today, as it has been for the past decade. This has led some observers, frustrated with an AIDS-exclusive focus in international infectious disease research, to speak sardonically of an internationally funded "AIDS industry" in Africa and other parts of the developing world. Nonetheless, the focus on AIDS has been extremely important. Not only has it sparked interest in – and initiatives for – other emerging infectious diseases, but it has served to unseat the kind of complacent attitudes toward infectious disease problems that have hampered international health work over its fifty-year history.

Today, the Centers for Disease Control and Prevention (CDC) and WHO are attempting to address AIDS and other emerging infectious disease threats in the U.S. and beyond. Their strategy – first outlined in the CDC's 1994 report, *Addressing Emerging Infectious Disease Threats: A Prevention Strategy for the United States*, then adopted on an international level by WHO – involves the prioritization of four areas of activity. These activities, if successfully carried out, could have far-reaching implications for the understanding and control of all infectious diseases.

The first priority is strengthening infectious disease surveillance activities. As noted in the Institute of Medicine report, this will involve the formation of global consortia to promote detection, prompt investigation, and monitoring of emerging infections and the factors influencing their emergence. Specific objectives include monitoring trends of antimicrobial resistance, investigating food- and water-borne outbreaks, and studying animal reservoirs and vectors associated with human disease agents (Inhorn 1995). This attempt to improve surveillance is being closely linked with the campaigns for global eradication of polio and for elimination of measles from the Americas, making maximum use of existing networks of collaborating laboratories (LeDuc 1996).

The second priority is applied research, in which attempts will be made to integrate laboratory science, biotechnology, and epidemiology with public health practice (Inhorn 1995). Among the research activities to be undertaken are vaccine efficacy studies, laboratory studies of diagnostic techniques for identifying new pathogens, studies of the economic impact of emerging infections, and, most important to anthropologists, studies of the behavioral factors that contribute to microbial emergence and affect individual risk of infection.

The third priority is prevention and control. Because most infectious disease problems are not manageable through vaccination alone, attempts will be made to define and institute practical public health measures which rely heavily on the effective dissemination of information, including to the public. Currently, CDC is in the process of strengthening its communications related to infectious diseases through free electronic dissemination of a new journal, *Emerging Infectious Diseases*, as well as its *Morbidity and Mortality Weekly Report* and other CDC publications.

Finally, a fourth priority involves strengthening public health infrastructure. Breakdowns of public health infrastructure have been deemed crucial to the re-emergence of infectious disease problems such as tuberculosis and cholera. Thus, the goal here is to improve the physical infrastructure, such as public health laboratories, and to train infectious disease professionals in countries around the world.

The ultimate goal of this four-pronged strategy is to be able to anticipate and prevent infectious diseases rather than having to react with expensive and possibly ineffectual containment measures. Although CDC and WHO officials recognize that such actions cannot guarantee protection against future, pathogen-caused "disasters," they argue that "a strengthened epidemiological and microbiological defense will surely afford better protection and ensure prompt response to the microbial challenges that lie ahead" (Berkelman, Pinner, and Hughes 1996).

LOOKING BACK: THE HISTORY OF INFECTIOUS DISEASE RESEARCH IN ANTHROPOLOGY

But the question remains: Where does anthropology fit in this history, including the most recent attempts to deal with emerging infectious diseases? Looking back over fifty years, it is possible to discern an anthropology of infectious disease – or, perhaps more accurately, anthropo*logies* of infectious disease, since no single paradigm or approach can be said to characterize this work. However, this anthropological history of research on infectious disease is even more fragmentary and inchoate than the international health efforts described above. Moreover, it is largely restricted to the last twenty years, as reflected in the review of studies contained in Chapter 2. Indeed, in a 1990 editorial retrospective in the *American Journal of Public Health*, anthropologist-physician Frederick Dunn lamented the relative dearth of culturally oriented behavioral research on infectious disease. "It is fair to say," he states, "that studies of human behavioral, social, and cultural factors have not been prominent in the long history of research on communicable disease transmission, control, and prevention, even though it is generally recognized that some of these factors did attract the attention of the earliest epidemiologists" (Dunn 1990:141).

Although anthropology's disciplinary roots can be traced to the turn of the twentieth century, anthropological work on infectious disease did not begin until the 1950s. With the rise of modern, post-WWII international health, anthropologists were soon invited to join these efforts in various capacities. As described by Foster (1982) in his retrospective on anthropology and international health, the years of 1950 and 1951 stand as milestones. In 1950, WHO hired its first anthropologist (Cora DuBois, whose appointment lasted only one year), and the Rockefeller Foundation hired Edward Wellin, still an anthropology graduate student at Harvard University, to undertake research on typhus control in southern Peru. In 1951, Benjamin Paul was invited to join the faculty at the Harvard School of Public Health, an appointment that lasted until 1962.

Paul's tenure at Harvard was particularly significant, for it was there that he produced his classic edited volume, *Health, Culture and Community* (Paul 1955). From the perspective of infectious disease research in anthropology – and medical anthropology more generally – Paul's book was highly significant. Several of the sixteen case studies in the book dealt with community reactions to vertically imposed infectious disease control programs. Among the case studies were Wellin's work on typhus and water boiling in Peru (Wellin 1955); Hsu's study of community reaction to a cholera epidemic in southwestern China (Hsu 1955); and the Hanks's study of diphtheria immunization in a Thai community (Hanks and Hanks 1955). (For additional description of these studies, see Chapter 2.) These studies presaged the future role of many anthropologists in infectious disease work and in international health work more generally: namely, to serve as cultural interpreters and "troubleshooters," who were brought into projects to anticipate, or to provide post-hoc explanations of, negative community responses.

Although the Paul book was notable for its infectious disease orientation, there was relatively little other significant anthropological work being done on infectious disease during the 1950s, a lacuna which lasted well into the 1970s. As described by Dunn:

> By the 1950s and 1960s social and behavioral scientists – and epidemiologists employing some of the methods of the social and behavioral sciences – were beginning to change and broaden perspectives in chronic non-infectious disease research. Through those years, however, only a very few sociomedically oriented studies were undertaken of communicable diseases... Even through the 1970s, however, reports on social or behavioral factors in communicable disease transmission or control were mostly anecdotal (Dunn 1990:141).

The relative lack of anthropological participation in infectious disease research during this period is reflected most poignantly in the fact that smallpox eradication, a major collaborative effort between the scientific and public health communities during the 1970s, was accomplished with virtually no anthropological input (see Chapters 2 and 4 for further details).

It was not until the creation of WHO's TDR program in the mid-1970s that the impetus and monies for social science research on infectious diseases clearly emerged. WHO, through TDR, began to support substantial field-based studies of malaria, schistosomiasis, and the other TDR "priority" diseases; these field studies included specific agendas for behavioral research by anthropologists and human geographers, as well as research on the economic impact of parasitic disease by economists. Among the most significant of the examples of this kind of WHO-promoted behavioral research were the extensive observational studies of human water contact (and, to a much lesser extent, defecation behavior) in relation to schistosomiasis transmission. (These schistosomiasis transmission studies, which were carried out mostly by medical geographers but also by anthropologists, are reviewed in Chapter 2, as well as in Brown and Inhorn [1990].)

Largely as a result of the TDR initiative and the international health community's renewed interest in infectious disease problems, the anthropology of infectious disease was given new life by the end of the 1970s. Studying infectious disease was no longer considered an unusual or pedestrian pursuit for anthropologists, especially those identifying themselves as belonging to the newly emerging subdiscipline of medical anthropology. Indeed, many of those anthropologists choosing to study infectious disease problems did so through traditional anthropological channels, conducting their fieldwork with anthropological (as opposed to international health agency) funding. In 1980, at the 79th Annual

Meeting of the American Anthropological Association, a group of these anthropologists met in a small symposium to address the potential role of anthropology in infectious disease research. Together, they formed a "Working Group on Anthropology and Infectious Disease," defining as their research platform "the broad area which emphasizes the interactions between sociocultural, biological, and ecological variables relating to the etiology and prevalence of infectious disease" (Brown 1981:7).

The year of 1980, when the working group first met, marks something of a watershed for the anthropology of infectious disease. Compared to the previous thirty years, the period from 1980 forward has been a research boom period, with more anthropological research on infectious disease than even before. There appear to be four major reasons for this veritable flurry of activity.

First, the subdiscipline of medical anthropology has come of age, attracting more and more cultural and biological anthropologists interested in issues of human health and illness. As the ranks of medical anthropology have grown (to more than 1,500 members of the Society for Medical Anthropology as of this writing), so have the numbers of anthropologists interested in pursuing infectious disease research agendas – either through traditional anthropological routes of solo fieldwork or through participation in agency-funded, collaborative health development projects. This does not mean that infectious disease research is one of the major foci of medical anthropology; in the conclusion of Chapter 2, which is a major review of the literature first published in the *Annual Review of Anthropology* in 1990, we bemoan the relative abandonment of infectious disease research on the part of many medical anthropologists as they have moved into other domains of empirical research and critical theory. Nonetheless, as reflected in the research presented in this volume, a significant minority of medical anthropologists, particularly those working outside the academy as applied researchers in international health development projects, have continued to pursue infectious disease research agendas. Such individuals convene at anthropological meetings, like the symposium on "The Anthropology of Infectious Disease" held in 1992 at the 91st Annual Meeting of the American Anthropological Association, which provided the springboard for this edited volume. They are active disseminators of their research findings through reports written for international health agencies, as well as through publications intended for both anthropological and public health audiences. And they continue to meet and communicate through the mails and over the Internet as members of the Society for Medical Anthropology's "International

Health and Infectious Disease Study Group" (IHIDSG), the outgrowth of the 1980s working group described above. In other words, although anthropologists interested in infectious disease are by no means a dominant force in the discipline of anthropology as a whole or in its medical anthropology subfield, they nonetheless see themselves as a loosely linked collectivity with basic and applied research interests of paramount importance.

Second, many of these anthropologists have been drawn into infectious disease research because of the 1980s Child Survival initiative, which has provided one of the major impetuses for an anthropology of infectious disease. Essentially, Child Survival, with its focus on diarrhea, ARI, and immunization for the EPI diseases of childhood, has opened up numerous research opportunities for anthropologists interested in infectious disease problems. Diarrhea and oral rehydration therapy (ORT) have been particularly well studied from a cross-cultural and hence comparative perspective, as reflected in Kendall's 1990 review of the literature (Kendall 1990), as well as the 1988 special issue of *Social Science & Medicine* (Vol. 27, No. 1) devoted entirely to anthropological studies of diarrheal illness. (It is interesting to note that five of the contributors to that special issue are also contributors to this volume.) Although anthropological studies of ARI and the EPI diseases are more recent (reflecting the later starting dates of the WHO/UNICEF programs in these areas), a significant amount of rich ethnographic work has nonetheless been carried out on these topics, as reflected in Chapters 8, 11 and 12 of this volume, as well as in a recent review of vaccination studies in the Third World (Nichter 1995) and a 1994 special issue of *Medical Anthropology* (Vol. 15, No. 4) devoted to ARI. (Again, four of the contributors to that special issue are also contributors to this volume.) Because Child Survival is an outgrowth of PHC, anthropological research in all of these areas reflects the entrance of large numbers of medical anthropologists into PHC – both as participants in community-based PHC projects and as outside evaluators/critics of those projects (Coreil and Mull 1990).

Third, anthropologists have also been drawn into infectious disease research in large numbers as a result of the global AIDS pandemic. Those anthropologists who study AIDS – domestically and internationally – now represent a significant force in the profession. The American Anthropological Association has a Task Force on AIDS, and the AAA's Society for Medical Anthropology has an "AIDS and Anthropology Research Group" which is hundreds of members strong. AIDS has been the topic of numerous papers and special sessions at

annual meetings of anthropologists over the past decade. And, perhaps
most impressive, the published anthropological research literature on
AIDS has truly proliferated. Chapter 2 of this volume summarizes
some of this research (as does Brown, Inhorn, and Smith [1996]), and
Chapters 13 and 14 provide excellent exemplars of internationally
based studies. The full scope of both the domestic and international
research on AIDS truly becomes apparent, however, in the impressive
bibliography on AIDS and anthropology put together by Bolton and
Orozco (1994).

Finally, AIDS has generated anthropological interest in other
emerging infections – especially, but not limited to, those infectious
diseases such as tuberculosis which are AIDS-related. Tuberculosis has
been particularly well studied by anthropologists, as reflected in
Chapters 10 and 14 of this volume, as well as in the session on
"Cultural Factors in Tuberculosis Prevention and Treatment" held at
the 93rd Annual Meeting of the American Anthropological Association
in 1994. That same year, the president of the American Society of
Tropical Medicine and Hygiene invited a group of anthropologists,
organized by Barry Hewlett and Joan Koss, to present a panel of
research findings about cultural and social factors related to tropical
infectious diseases.

Other emerging and re-emerging infectious diseases are also on the
research agenda of anthropologists, whose interests in some cases
predate the CDC/WHO global initiative described above. For
example, several of the studies of (re)emergent infections included in
this volume were carried out in the late 1980s and early 1990s, before
the 1994 global initiative was launched. Furthermore, soon after the
initiative began, anthropologists convened to discuss their possible
contributions to the global effort to understand and control these
diseases. At the 94th Annual Meeting of the American Anthropological
Association held in Washington, D.C., in 1995, a group of anthropologists participated in a session on "Emerging and Reemerging Infectious Diseases: Sociocultural and Biocultural Approaches."

LOOKING FORWARD: FUTURE DIRECTIONS IN INFECTIOUS DISEASE RESEARCH IN ANTHROPOLOGY AND INTERNATIONAL HEALTH

It would appear from this history that the anthropology of infectious
disease is here to stay and is perhaps even at its most robust historical

moment as the new millenium approaches. However, we must not become overly sanguine. Much more has yet to be done in infectious disease research and control on every level. As the global Emerging Infections initiative takes off, now is a prime time for anthropologists to seize new opportunities – not only to enlarge significantly the research agenda, but to build interdisciplinary bridges in ways heretofore untried.

Here, we propose five overarching recommendations for future research in the anthropology of infectious disease. (For an impressive list of more specific recommendations on infectious disease research topics, see Sommerfeld [1995].) Quite intentionally, we have organized this volume in sections that reflect these recommendations, for it is our belief that the anthropological research on infectious disease contained in this volume is "cutting edge" and thus presages these future directions.

Recommendation One: Undertake the Anthropologies of Neglected Infectious Diseases

As revealed in WHO's *International Classification of Diseases*, the variety and complexity of infectious agents and the diseases they produce is impressive. Yet, few of these infectious diseases have been well studied, a problem that reflects the long international health history of disease "prioritization" and the subsequent marginalization of all but a few privileged disease categories. Unfortunately, anthropologists' infectious disease studies tend to reflect fashions and funding opportunities in international health. Thus, anthropologists by fiat or by choice have focused rather narrowly on what, in the grand scheme of things, are a relatively small number of infectious disease problems. For example, in this volume, eleven infectious disease problems are explored in some depth, and the anthropological literature on a limited number of other infectious disease problems is briefly reviewed in Chapter 2. Frankly, few other infectious disease problems – of either major or minor importance – have received serious anthropological consideration. This anthropological neglect extends even to some of the "priority diseases" – such as trypanosomiasis (African sleeping sickness, American Chagas disease), leishmaniasis, filariasis, leprosy, and polio – targeted in the TDR and Child Survival initiatives. On a most basic level, anthropologists need to cast their research nets more widely to begin studying some of these lethal and disfiguring conditions, as well as the many infectious agents whose disease toll may include, *inter alia*, pain and suffering, short- and long-term disability, and social stigma. In addition, we need to examine these infectious diseases as they manifest themselves in different cultural and ecological settings, for causal factors, cultural models of individual risk, and community responses may vary widely. Although anthropologists have made a good beginning in their understanding of diseases such as malaria, tuberculosis, and measles, many more diseases remain to be studied wherever they occur. Indeed, there are many anthropolo*gies* of infectious diseases yet to be undertaken – of different diseases, in different settings, by anthropologists of different theoretical and methodological persuasions. Exploding the restrictive boundaries of our inquiry must be our most basic charge.

Recommendation Two: Reconstruct Infectious Disease Histories

Looking back in time, the plague pandemic of the mid-1300s and the influenza pandemic of the early 1900s – both of which claimed thousands of human lives – demonstrate the potential danger of uncontrolled infectious diseases and alert us to the importance of history in contemporary understandings of infectious disease threats. As new infectious diseases appear on the horizon and old ones return in sometimes frightening proportions, we are forced to ask: Why now? This is an historical question that raises multiple issues of anthropological concern – about why new infectious diseases agents evolve, about why epidemics occur at particular historical moments in particular places, and about why public health measures to combat infectious diseases are (or are not) implemented over time. As virologist Stephen Morse (1993:viii) puts it, "Despite our wish to anticipate emerging diseases, we cannot foretell the future. What we can do is to draw the best inferences possible from past experience; for this, history can be a valuable guide."

As demonstrated in this volume, historically oriented anthropologists have much to contribute to the writing of infectious disease histories on multiple levels – including the biological history of disease evolution, the cultural history of human response to epidemics, and the critically oriented, political economic history of public health measures to eradicate or control infectious diseases. In the future, anthropologists need to consider the historical forces underlying the epidemiologic transition – or the shift from infectious to chronic disease mortality in the developed countries of the West. More important, we need to evaluate critically why large proportions of the human population in developing countries have yet to experience this transition as they cope with *both* infectious and chronic disease mortality simultaneously. Furthermore, this evaluation will entail a discussion of why the epidemiologic transition seems to be "reversing" in the West as new infectious diseases emerge with frightening rapidity.

Recommendation Three: Employ Methodological Triangulation

For anthropologists to become more useful members of multidisciplinary teams devoted to infectious disease research, it is imperative that we become much more explicit about the logic and usefulness of the ethnographic research methods we employ. Although we use the term "ethnography" to refer to both the methodological process and written product of our cultural anthropological research, there is no single ethnographic method, as there is no single theoretical paradigm that dominates the field. We see this multiplicity of theories and methods as an important strength, rather than a weakness, of anthropology in general and medical anthropology in particular. To build on that strength, however, it is essential to identify some consensus on commonly used ethnographic field methods, as has been attempted by Plattner (1989) in the AAA's widely read *Anthropology Newsletter.* There also needs to be more discussion within anthropology about the strengths and weaknesses of methods, the standards for recognizing persuasive evidence, and the complementarity of methods. Anthropologists can better contribute to interdisciplinary research on infectious disease when they are able to identify how the anthropological data collected through such means as in-depth interviews and participant observation will complement other sources of information.

Denzin (1970) has described methodological triangulation in social science as combining the strengths of multiple methodological approaches – like in-depth interviews, direct observation, and surveys – while simultaneously minimizing the weaknesses of these approaches – like observer effects. In medical anthropological research on infectious disease, this type of triangulation might best be considered when combining ethnographic and epidemiological methods, as exemplified in Chapter 7 of this volume. In the future, researchers should design other "qualitative case-control" studies of epidemiologic phenomena to better understand why populations engage in high-risk behaviors. The use of multiple methods in a research project also allows for the comparison of the methods themselves, and this provides an important service to the discipline. Chapter 8 of this volume, which assesses the advantages and disadvantages of traditional versus "rapid" and "focused" ethnographic interview methods in the study of ARI, is a fine example of this type of work.

In summary, we recommend the strategy of methodological triangulation for two reasons. First, by using complementary methods – for example, from ethnography and epidemiology – the validity and completeness of explanations of human behavior can be enhanced in infectious disease research efforts. When the use of multiple methods results in conflicting analyses, the goal of triangulation is to refine the methodological tools to reduce the discrepancies. The strategy of triangulation implies a cooperative stance between the "advocates" of different methods or theories; it also implies that there is little to be gained in having fixed conclusions based on single methodologies, especially when these intellectual stances are based on personalistic biases. Second, a commitment to both methodological and theoretical triangulation will make medical anthropologists more valuable colleagues in multidisciplinary research teams. We believe that the political-economic approaches in medical anthropology described below will be better understood and appreciated by infectious disease collaborators when offered in the spirit of methodological triangulation.

Recommendation Four: Enrich Infectious Disease Ethnography

As CDC and WHO launch the global Emerging Infections initiative, much mention is made of human behavior – not only as one of the six broad factors responsible for infectious disease emergence, but also as something that must be "changed" in order to achieve infectious disease prevention and control. Yet, in the Institute of Medicine report that helped to spawn this initiative, human behavior is decontextualized from any larger sociocultural or political-economic context, and human behavioral change, as an explicit strategy to help achieve infectious disease control, is not included in the four-part CDC/WHO agenda for dealing with emerging infections outlined above.

Anthropologists, as professional "participant observers" who consider behavioral observation to be a key element of their methodological tool kit, have much to contribute to future behavioral studies of infectious disease risk factors. This includes microsociologically oriented studies of individual risk behavior (such as when a woman steps into a schistosome-infected canal in order to collect water for cooking), as well as macrosociologically oriented studies of population-based risk behaviors (such as when poor homesteaders in Brazil clear a section of the rain forest to open it up for farming). Anthropologists are behavioral scientists *par excellence*, who are trained to record and describe human behavior in field-based settings.

But anthropologists have much more to contribute to infectious disease studies by helping to explain *why* people behave as they do. This is what good anthropological ethnography is all about – interpreting human behavior by understanding the human rationales for that behavior. Indeed, such understanding is of critical importance for the design of culturally appropriate and effective public health interventions. For example, in the efforts to combat growing problems of antibiotic resistance in pathogens, there is a need for more research on the pharmaceutical practices of people, including the use and misuse of drugs, the role of media in promoting the use of particular medicines, and the cultural perceptions of antibiotics. There is a dearth of studies combining fine-grained behavioral research – for example, observational studies of how medicines are actually dispensed at pharmacies or used in people's homes – with interview research on the cultural ideas and beliefs about how medicines work. Indeed, another method that needs to be added to the aforementioned strategy of triangulation is the elicitation through discourse analysis of "cultural models" (Shore 1996), or the cognitive schema that people use to think and talk about phenomena, such as medicines or infectious diseases themselves. For example, elicitation of cultural models might reveal that some infectious diseases induce fear – even panic – in populations, while others do not; some infectious diseases are simply more frightening and stigmatizing than others. Although the individual interview-based elicitation of explanatory models of illness has become widespread in clinically applied medical anthropology, there is a need to utilize this powerful method in population-based infectious disease research as well.

Enriching the explanations of health behaviors through descriptions of the cultural ideas and beliefs surrounding those behaviors should be an important contribution of medical anthropology to infectious disease research. In so doing, anthropologists can demonstrate the salience of culture for public health programs in infectious disease that attempt to induce behavioral change.

Recommendation Five: Provide Political-Economic Context

Medical anthropologists have taken a leading role in adding the political-economic dimension to research on infectious disease. Indeed, the final section of this book provides three excellent examples of this type of work. We believe that widening the scope of analysis beyond the narrow biomedical frame is a vitally important contribution of medical anthropology to infectious disease research. Yet, as mentioned in the methodological triangulation section above, this political economic contextualization must not be offered with an "us versus them" attitude.

To date, many of the political-economic (or political ecological) studies of infectious disease have made a strong general argument about macrosociological factors involved in changing disease frequencies (e.g., Turshen 1980). There is an important need, however, for research demonstrating in very specific terms and places *how* ecological changes and disruption have been influenced by political-economic policies. The particular linkages between political economy and disease transmission are likely to be played out through two mechanisms – the local economic market and the cognitive processes of individual decision making in the context of scarce resources. Because the role of political-economic factors in infectious disease transmission is often not sufficiently recognized, arguments for political-economic contextualization will become much more persuasive when medical anthropologists begin to demonstrate the linkages between macrosociological pressures and microsociological processes.

Indeed, medical anthropologists studying infectious diseases need to build more sophisticated models which link three levels of analysis: biological outcomes experienced on the individual level, cultural processes affecting social groups, and political-economic conditions affecting regions or nations. Some important work in this regard has been done by biocultural anthropologists in a special issue of *Human Organization* on "Agrarian Transformations and Health" (Leatherman and Gordon 1994), in the edited volume *Disease in Populations in Transition* (Armelagos and Swedlund 1990), and in a 1992 Wenner-Gren conference on "Political Economic Perspectives in Biological Anthropology." The development of models linking biology, culture, and political economy should be an important goal in the future anthropology of infectious disease.

THE ORGANIZATION OF THIS BOOK

These five recommendations for future research on the anthropology of infectious disease are also reflected in the five major sections of this volume. The section headings – Anthropologies, Histories, Methods, Ethnographies, and Political Economies – are plural because no single theoretical paradigm or methodological orientation encompasses all of this work. We have grouped these case studies, all of which describe an infectious disease problem in a particular historical or cultural context, in broad categories based on their epistemological approach. Note that we did *not* organize the volume by biomedical criteria, like the type of pathogen or the route of infection. Rather, we have combined these chapters into sections based on their outstanding strengths in describing either the history of an infectious disease problem and its control, methodological approaches to studying infectious diseases, ethnographic descriptions of the cultural context of infectious disease problems in particular places, or the larger political-economic contexts which put people at risk of infection.

The introductory section, including this essay, refers to the anthropologies of infectious disease. This essay has described medical anthropological approaches to the study of infectious disease and how they have changed over time. Given the growing importance of infectious diseases at the present historical moment, it makes sense to survey the history of research that has brought us to this present volume, and also look ahead to the future. Chapter 2 is a review of the literature, reprinted from the *Annual Review of Anthropology*, that provides an overview of research examples about a wide range of infectious diseases. A major focus of the chapter is how culturally prescribed behaviors either increase or decrease the risk of infectious disease transmission.

Part Two – Histories – provides three examples of diachronic analyses of disease and culture. The first case demonstrates the contribution of paleopathology to infectious disease research. Harrison (Chapter 3) describes a case of Valley Fever identified in a human skeleton with severe bone lesions uncovered in an archaeological excavation in Arizona. Microscopic examination of stained thin sections of bone from this 750-year-old male revealed infection with the cocci fungi that cause Valley Fever. Although this finding is interesting in itself as the oldest documented case of this fatal fungal infection in a Native American, the actual analysis goes much further, highlighting issues of race,

stigma and the social epidemiological distribution of Valley Fever.
Harrison argues that groups at high epidemiologic risk for Valley
Fever are disadvantaged on many fronts and therefore have more
exposure to the "dangerous dirt" carrying the cocci fungi. The second
case in this section is about smallpox, one of the most famous diseases
in history and the only infectious disease to be globally eradicated.
McClain (Chapter 4) provides a cultural history of smallpox and its
eradication, beginning with the traditional cultural responses to the
disease through variolation techniques and ending with the contemporary scientific and technological debates about the post-eradication
destruction of the two remaining laboratory samples of the smallpox
virus. Her look at "culture," therefore, is two-pronged: the cultural
beliefs of peoples who have historically suffered from smallpox, and the
beliefs of the virologists who, as biotechnological "cultural insiders,"
now control the virus. Important cultural themes emerge from the
ethical debate about the destruction of the virus stock. The third
example concerns a disease that the WHO targeted but failed to
eradicate. Brown (Chapter 5) traces the cultural history of malaria
control efforts from early in this century to the postwar heyday of
eradication and finally to the current resurgence of the disease,
particularly its chloroquine-resistant varieties. This historical analysis
suggests that cultural, rather than parasitological or entomological,
factors are the primary cause of the current resurgence. These cultural
factors include "ideological resistance," a consequence of the military
metaphors of the early eradication campaigns that later caused a
precipitous decline in anti-malaria efforts.

Part Three – Methods – demonstrates the advantages of methodological triangulation in medical anthropological work on infectious
disease. These case studies combine qualitative and quantitative
methods, analysis of individuals and households, and analytical epidemiology and ethnography. In a study of the mosquito-borne disease
dengue fever, Coreil and colleagues (Chapter 6) demonstrate the utility
of the household as the unit of analysis for health studies. They argue
that there are particular advantages to an analytical strategy that
describes the variations within households (e.g., based on gender and
age) and between households (e.g., based on social class and living
conditions), rather than an analysis that assumes that individuals are
all independent actors. Their study is truly triangulative, combining
the research strategies of mapping, survey research, and direct observation to understand a dengue outbreak in one Dominican community.
The study therefore generates important background information

regarding the feasibility of community participation in disease control efforts. The combination of ethnographic and epidemiological methods is well exemplified in Inhorn and Buss's study of tubal-factor infertility among poor urban Egyptian women (Chapter 7). Although the synergistic power of combining epidemiology and ethnography has been recognized before (Janes, Stall and Gifford 1986), this study shows how many of the most salient categories for epidemiological analysis can be generated from ethnographic interviews. Furthermore, by using ethnographic and political-economic contextualization to widen the scope of the analysis, the "anthropologist-epidemiologist" is able to identify and explain epidemiologic risk factors – like exposure to harmful procedures within the biomedical system – that are usually neglected in epidemiologic studies. In the last chapter of this section, Bhattacharyya (Chapter 8) shows how the use of multiple social science methods can be used to examine the validity and reliability between those methods. This comparative methodological study, based on fieldwork about cultural factors related to ARI in West Bengal, introduces the reader to the variety of methodologies available to social scientists – from structured survey instruments (KAP) to focused ethnographic study to participant observation – and their strengths, weaknesses, and requirements. This type of comparison yields a fruitful analysis of the question of qualitative versus quantitative methods; it is not a question of one or the other, but rather what combination is best suited for the needs of a particular research agenda.

Part Four – Ethnographies – includes four excellent examples of how medical anthropologists examine ethnomedical health cultures and the way ethnomedical beliefs influence health-seeking behavior and clinical treatment of some important infectious diseases. Vecchiato (Chapter 9) focuses on the relatively neglected disease of intestinal parasitism in Southern Ethiopia. This study provides a classic ethnomedical description of native theories of causation, categorization, diagnosis, and traditional modes of treatment of intestinal illnesses. For example, in this population, "digestive worms" are thought to be a necessary part of normal physiological functioning. Vecchiato not only points out the importance of these health beliefs but also discusses their practical implications for the implementation of a helminthic disease control program currently ongoing in the region. It is important to remember that the people engaged in international health activities also have their own cultural beliefs and values, and that problems of communication and cooperation can emerge when there is a disjuncture between those cultural beliefs and the local ethnomedical system.

Nichter (Chapter 10) offers an excellent example of this phenomenon in a detailed ethnographic description of the native illness terms for respiratory problems, including tuberculosis, in the Philippines. Using methods developed in linguistics and cognitive anthropology, he analyzes the semantic domains of illness categories and shows how these native terms do not correspond with the labels in the *International Classification of Diseases.* The poor overlap between these two types of disease labels represents a cultural challenge to effective TB prevention and control; it is not simply a question of translation. In Chapter 11, Mull reports on ethnomedical beliefs surrounding the treatment of measles, including measles associated with diarrhea and dehydration, in Pakistan. While measles is a minor childhood disease in the West, it remains a major killer in the developing world, in large part because chronic malnutrition makes recovery from the measles infection more difficult. Cultural beliefs about the Sitala goddess, previously associated with smallpox, as well as traditional beliefs about hot and cold illnesses, have a significant impact on the clinical management of measles and its associated diarrhea. It is obvious how important these ethnomedical features are to local mothers, and how local disease categories influence the acceptability of clinical treatments, like ORT in the case of diarrhea. Also, for better or for worse, a new class of unlicensed practitioners are sought out by mothers for treatment of measles in this setting. In the final example of research on local health culture and its influence on infectious disease management and control, Cody and colleagues (Chapter 12) examine the differences in maternal and professional cultural knowledge of ARI in Pakistan. One of the most salient aspects of this research is its dual focus on the behaviors of local biomedical practitioners, as well as the mothers of sick children. In an era of growing antibiotic resistance of the pathogens causing ARI, patterns of health seeking and treatment are important; it is striking in this case how poor families are steered by physicians into purchases of a panoply of medicines to treat a single ARI episode. Better understanding of the knowledge and behaviors of practitioners as well as mothers should provide a key element in the improved efficiency and effectiveness of basic health services. It is critical that medical anthropologists continue to do research on how ethnomedical beliefs and practices affect the acceptability of public health interventions. But, as the cases in this section so aptly demonstrate, it is also essential that anthropologists focus their attention on the ethnomedical beliefs and practices of local professional health care workers, both biomedical and traditional.

Finally, Political Economies is the focus of Part Five, even though a sensitivity to political and socioeconomic factors can be found in virtually every case study in this volume. Based on fieldwork in Kenya, Kielmann (Chapter 13) provides a critical analysis of the cultural and political-economic underpinnings of concepts such as "prostitution" and "risk" as they are used in AIDS prevention discourse. The process of blaming the victim for disease is both a social and political-economic issue, and the case of blaming "prostitutes" for the spread of HIV in Central and East Africa is an excellent case in point. Based on a detailed analysis of the cultural context of and economic constraints on individual Kenyan women's lives, Kielmann challenges the culturally loaded category of "prostitute" and demonstrates how the continuing AIDS epidemic needs to be seen in a broader macrosociological context. In Chapter 14, Farmer pushes further the political-economic analysis of the AIDS epidemic in Haiti that is found in his excellent ethnography, *AIDS and Accusation* (Farmer 1992). Linking personal experience to political context, Farmer demonstrates the political-economic dimensions of gender and poverty, while at the same time offering a powerful indictment of the depoliticization of standard epidemiological analyses of AIDS. By offering a political-economic analysis from the viewpoint of Haitian peasants, Farmer shows how anthropological research can be applied to local empowerment and the development of community control over local health education. Finally, in a masterful description of epidemic politics surrounding an outbreak of cholera in Brazil, Nations and Monte (Chapter 15) show how the victims of a disease, if they happen to be poor and powerless, may be blamed for the disease by the wider community, including the politically powerful biomedical community. In this case study of the social responses to a cholera epidemic – one that is related to the lack of adequate water and sewer infrastructure – important themes of scapegoating and conspiracy emerge. Here, the anthropologists are able to give voice to the experience of those living through the epidemic, powerfully representing their feelings of stigmatization in the context of severe political-economic inequality.

We hope that all five of these kinds of anthropologies of infectious disease will add to our understanding of ongoing and emerging infectious disease problems. More important, we hope that such knowledge will assist in the design of effective interventions to reduce the human suffering caused by infectious disease.

REFERENCES

American Medical Association Council on Scientific Affairs. 1992. Epidemic Infectious Disease Risks: Striving for Perspective. Journal of the American Medical Association. 275(3):181.

Berkelman, R.L., R.W. Pinner and J.M. Hughes. 1996. Addressing Emerging Microbial Threats in the United States. Journal of the American Medical Association. 275(4):315–317.

Bolton, R. and G. Orozco. 1994. The AIDS Bibliography. Arlington, VA: American Anthropological Association.

Brown, E.R. 1976. Public Health in Imperialism: Early Rockefeller Programs at Home and Abroad. American Journal of Public Health. 66(9):897–903.

Brown, P.J. 1981. Cultural Adaptations to Endemic Malaria in Sardinia. Medical Anthropology. 5:313–39.

Brown, P.J. and M. Inhorn. 1990. Disease, Ecology, and Human Behavior. *In* T.M. Johnson and C.F. Sargent, eds. Medical Anthropology: A Handbook of Theory and Methods. Pp. 187–214. New York: Greenwood Press.

Brown, P.J., M. Inhorn and D.J. Smith. 1996. Disease, Ecology, and Human Behavior. *In* C.F. Sargent and T.J. Johnson, eds. Medical Anthropology: A Handbook of Theory and Methods (second Edition). Pp. 183–218. Westport, CT: Praeger.

Coreil, J. and J.D. Mull. 1990. Anthropology and Primary Health Care. Boulder, CO: Westview Press.

Curtin, P.D. 1989. Death By Migration. Cambridge: Cambridge University Press.

Denzin, N.K. 1970. The Research Act. Chicago: Aldine.

Dunn, F.L. 1990. Human Behavior and the Communicable Diseases of Childhood. American Journal of Public Health. 80(2):141–142.

Farmer, P. 1992. AIDS and Accusation: Haiti and the Geography of Blame. Berkeley and Los Angeles, CA: University of California Press.

Foster, G.M. 1982. Applied Anthropology and International Health: Retrospect and Prospect. Human Organization. 14(3):189–197.

Grant, J. 1983. The State of the World's Children 1984. Oxford: Oxford University Press.

Hanks, L.M. and J.R. Hanks. 1955. Diphtheria Immunization in a Thai Community. *In* B. Paul, ed. Health, Culture and Community: Case Studies of Public Reactions to Health Programs. Pp. 155–185. New York: Russell Sage Foundation.

Hsu, F.L.K. 1955. A Cholera Epidemic in a Chinese Town. *In* B. Paul, ed. Health, Culture and Community: Case Studies of Public Reactions to Health Programs. Pp. 135–154. New York: Russell Sage Foundation.

Inhorn, S. 1995. Emerging Infections are Major Public Health Problem. Wisconsin State Laboratory of Hygiene Results 4:2–3.

Institute of Medicine. 1992. Emerging Infections: Microbial Threats to Health in the United States. Washington D.C.: National Academy Press.

Janes, C.R., R. Stall, and S.M. Gifford, eds. 1986. Anthropology and Epidemiology: Interdisciplinary Approaches to the Study of Health and Disease. Dordrecht: D. Reidel Publishing Company.

Kendall, C. 1990. Public Health and the Domestic Domain: Lessons From Anthropological Research on Diarrheal Diseases. *In* J. Coreil and J.D. Mull, eds. Anthropology and Primary Health Care. Pp. 173–195. Boulder, CO: Westview Press.

Leatherman, T.L. and A. Gordon. 1994. Introduction. Human Organization (Symposium on Agrarian Transformations and Health) 53(4): 345.

LeDuc, J.W. 1996. World Health Organization Strategy for Emerging Infectious Diseases. Journal of the American Medical Association. 275(4):318–320.

McNeill, W.H. 1976. Plagues and Peoples. Garden City, NY: Doubleday.

Morse, S.S. 1993. Emerging Viruses. New York: Oxford University Press.

Nichter, M. 1995. Vaccinations in the Third World: A Consideration of Community Demand. Social Science and Medicine. 41(5):617–632.

Paul, B.D., ed. 1955. Health, Culture and Community: Case Studies of Public Reactions to Health Programs. New York: Russell Sage Foundation.

Shore, B. 1996. Culture in Mind: Cognition, Culture, and the Problem of Meaning. Oxford: Oxford University Press.

Sommerfeld, J. 1995. Emerging and Resurgent Infectious Diseases: A Challenge for Anthropological Research. Paper prepared for the 94th annual meeting of the American Anthropological Association. Washington D.C. Nov. 15–18, 1995.

Swedlund, A.C. and G.A. Armelagos. 1990. Disease Populations in Transition. New York: Bergin and Garvey.

Turshen, M. 1980. The Political Ecology of Disease in Tanzania. New Brunswick, NJ: Rutgers University Press.

Walsh, J.A. 1988. Establishing Health Priorities in the Developing World. Boston: Adams Publishing Group.

Walsh, J.A. and K.S. Warren. 1979. Selective Primary Health Care: An Interim Strategy for Disease Control in Developing Countries. New England Journal of Medicine. 301:967–974.

Warren, K.S. 1990. Protecting the World's Children: An Agenda for the 1990s. Lancet. 1: 659.

Wellin, E. 1955. Water Boiling in a Peruvian Town. *In* B. Paul, ed. Health, Culture and Community: Case Studies of Public Reactions to Health Programs. Pp. 71–103. New York: Russell Sage Foundation.

CHAPTER 2

The Anthropology of Infectious Disease

Marcia C. Inhorn and Peter J. Brown

INTRODUCTION

Diseases caused by infectious agents have profoundly affected both human history and biology. In demographic terms, infectious diseases – including both great epidemics, such as plague and smallpox, which have devastated human populations from ancient to modern times, and less dramatic, unnamed viral and bacterial infections causing high infant mortality – have likely claimed more lives than all wars, noninfectious diseases, and natural disasters taken together. In the face of such attack by microscopic invaders, human populations have been forced to adapt to infectious agents on the levels of both genes and culture. As agents of natural selection, infectious diseases have played a major role in the evolution of the human species. Infectious diseases have also been a prime mover in cultural transformation,

Reproduced, with permission, from the **Annual Review of Anthropology,** Volume 19, © 1990, by Annual Reviews Inc.

We express appreciation to Frederick L. Dunn, who reviewed and revised earlier drafts of this manuscript and whose interests in theoretical, methodological, and applied issues in the anthropological study of infectious disease have been an inspiration. M. C. I. thanks Nelson H. H. Graburn and James Anderson for reviewing an early draft of the manuscript, and P. J. B. thanks Eric Johnson for bibliographic assistance.

as societies have responded to the social, economic, political, and psychological disruption engendered by acute epidemics (e.g. measles, influenza) and chronic, debilitating infectious diseases (e.g. malaria, schistosomiasis). Today, the global epidemic of acquired immune deficiency syndrome (AIDS) provides a salient example of the processes underlying infectious-disease-related cultural transformations. As many of the examples cited in this review illustrate, human groups have often unwittingly facilitated the spread of infectious diseases through culturally coded patterns of behavior or through changes in the crucial relationships among infectious disease agents, their human and animal hosts, and the environments in which the host-agent interaction takes place.

Thus, infectious diseases provide a rich area for anthropological research, with contributions to be made from all of anthropology's subdisciplines. Indeed, because the study of infectious disease is an intrinsically biocultural endeavor, the "anthropology of infectious disease" described here must be a holistic one, in which traditional subdisciplinary boundaries are irrelevant. Infectious disease problems are both biological and cultural, historical and contemporary, theoretical and practical. Because the relevant research requires the synthesizing theoretical framework of general anthropology, it cannot be subsumed by medical anthropology. Note the range of anthropological and public health literature cited in this review.

Simply defined, infectious diseases are those caused by biological agents ranging from microscopic, intracellular viruses to large, structurally complex helminthic parasites (see 33 for a classification of infectious disease agents, including viruses, bacteria, fungi, parasites, and several classes of intermediate forms, as well as their routes of transmission). The variety and complexity of infectious agents – in terms of their biological characteristics, their reproductive strategies, and their modes of transmission – are impressive (35). The classification of this tremendous diversity forms part of the subject of the World Health Organization's (WHO's) *International Classification of Diseases*, now in its ninth revision (224). These disease categories provide a standard mode of scientific discourse in biomedicine, where "diseases" are considered as clinical entities with pathological underpinnings, while "illnesses" are more closely linked to a patient's perceptions and behaviors. As is generally recognized by medical anthropologists, however, biomedicine is only one type of culturally constructed medical system (100, 101).

It is important to note that infection with a specific agent does not necessarily result in disease. This progression depends upon a number of intervening variables, including the pathogenicity of the agent, the route of transmission of the agent to the host, and the nature and strength of the host's response (23, 193). All of these factors, in turn, are affected by the natural and social environments in which the agent and host are juxtaposed; in some cases, the environment may promote the transmission of the agent to the host, while in other cases it may limit or even prevent such transmission. Critical characteristics of the environment result largely from sociopolitical influences; thus, many infectious diseases, such as tuberculosis, are rightly considered "social diseases" (57, 217).

The American Anthropological Association's Working Group on Anthropology and Infectious Disease defined the anthropological field of infectious disease as the "broad area which emphasizes the interactions between sociocultural, biological, and ecological variables relating to the etiology and prevalence of infectious disease" (26:7). This review uses the same definition, examining anthropological works on infectious disease (including those by scholars in related disciplines whose methods or theoretical frameworks are anthropological in nature) and classifying them for heuristic purposes according to their primarily biological, ecological, or sociocultural orientation.

BIOLOGICAL APPROACHES

Microevolutionary Studies

From an evolutionary perspective, infectious diseases have probably been the primary agent of natural selection over the past 5000 years, eliminating human hosts who were more susceptible to disease and sparing those who were more resistant. Individual biological factors that conferred protection from a specific disease could eventually be selected for in the human populations living where the disease was endemic. Thus, as first suggested by Haldane (102), humans adapted to infectious disease at a most basic level – the level of the gene (5, 6).

Over the past 40 years, anthropologists and human geneticists have been testing the hypothesis that specific genotypes may confer immunity or resistance to infection. Such hypotheses have also been suggested to help explain relatively common genetic conditions that may be adaptive in one context and maladaptive in another. Allison (4) was the first to suggest that the heterozygous condition known as sickle-cell trait (i.e. inheritance of the gene for the common form of hemoglobin from one parent and the sickling hemoglobin S from the other) appeared with greater frequency in regions of Africa where life-threatening *Plasmodium falciparum* malaria was present. This association led Allison to hypothesize that hemoglobin S, when present in the heterozygous state, conferred resistance to death from malaria. Although this hypothesis has been a prominent textbook example for two decades, the statistical correlation between malaria prevalences and sickle-cell gene frequencies in West Africa has only recently been systematically confirmed (70). Moreover, while there is significantly higher malaria mortality among children who are homozygous sicklers than among homozygous normals, differences in parasite densities among individuals of the two genotype groups have not been determined (159).

In a classic anthropological work that followed Allison's, Livingstone (158) related the widespread distribution of the sickle-cell trait in West Africa to specific factors of cultural evolution: namely, the introduction of iron tools and subsequent swidden agriculture. He argued that the diffusion of the new technology led to increased sedentism, horticultural production, and deforestation, effectively increasing the available breeding grounds for *Anopheles gambiae*, the major mosquito vector. These changes allowed falciparum malaria to become established as an endemic disease among settled, West African agricultural societies and as a selective agent for the sickle-cell allele (158, 160). Through analysis of data from 60 African communities, Wiesenfeld (221) demonstrated that populations most reliant on root and tree crops (the Malaysian agricultural complex) created the most malarious environments; this would lead to greater selective advantage for heterozygous individuals, who enjoy protection from malaria death yet are not at risk of death from sickle-cell anemia (the condition of homozygous sicklers).

More recently, other hemoglobin abnormalities have been identified (161) that appear to confer resistance to malaria, including glucose-6-phosphate-dehydrogenase (G6PD) deficiency, thalassemia, and hemoglobins Hb^C, Hb^E, and Hb^F. Similarly, it has been argued that the Duffy blood group negative genotype, characteristic of most African and US blacks, provides a high level of protection from *Plasmodium vivax*, a more benign strain of malaria (164). In an examination of fava bean consumption and its relation to malaria in the G6PD-deficiency-endemic, circum-Mediterranean area, Katz & Schall (136) have suggested that the combination of nonexpressed gene and consumption of fava beans (the "gene–bean interaction") may protect heterozygous females from malaria death. This may be viewed as an excellent example of the "coevolution" of genes and cultural traits, which, in combination, offer substantial protection from disease (135), although in this case, G6PD-deficient males may suffer potentially fatal hemolytic crises of favism (32).

Other studies tentatively linking infectious diseases to genetic traits and cultural factors have recently emerged. For example, Blangero (18) studied the relationship among helminthic zoonoses, the P2 allele of the P blood group system (which is hypothesized to confer resistance to these zoonoses), and subsistence practices involving animal husbandry. He has shown that high frequencies of the P2 allele occur in populations manifesting heavy dependence on and contact with domesticated livestock. In a different context, Meindl (174) has hypothesized that, for European populations with a long history of pulmonary tuberculosis and high frequencies of cystic fibrosis, carriers of the recessive gene for cystic fibrosis may have increased resistance to tuberculosis.

Conversely, anthropologists helped to demonstrate that the hepatitis B surface antigen (HBsAg) was not part of the genetic endowment transmitted from parents to offspring. Rather, the clustering of the antigen observed in families was due to both horizontal (i.e. person to person) and vertical (i.e. mother to infant) infectious transmission (20–22) – a finding made, in part, through participant observation of family life in New Hebrides (51, 52). These discoveries played a role in the successful development of a hepatitis B vaccine.

Macroevolutionary Studies

Macroevolutionary studies of infectious disease attempt to reconstruct epidemiological patterns of disease transmission among prehistoric and historic human populations. The broad aims of this research are two-fold: (a) to establish the antiquity and evolution of various infectious diseases in human populations through examination of prehistoric osteological and, in some cases, soft-tissue evidence; and (b) to contextualize these findings to the physical and cultural circumstances of the human populations involved.

Paleopathology has contributed significantly to the understanding of the prevalence and spread of infectious diseases in human populations. Simply defined, paleopathology is the study of disease in prehistoric populations through examination of skeletal and tissue remains, coprolites, and when available, works of art (1, 130). Because some infectious diseases leave their marks on the human skeleton and flesh, examination of these remains has allowed researchers to describe the disease patterns of prehistoric populations and to establish relative chronologies.

Paleopathological reconstructions utilizing skeletal and tissue remains have been attempted for infectious diseases including tuberculosis (34, 181), leprosy (179), and American (203) and African trypanosomiasis (151). Studies of the kidneys of Egyptian mummies have yielded evidence of schistosomiasis (191); and coprolite studies, utilizing dried fecal remains found in or near prehistoric camps and shelters, have provided valuable insights on the epidemiology of intestinal helminthiases in prehistoric populations (40, 69, 191, 201, 205, 206).

Paleopathology has had a particularly decisive role in the debate over the antiquity and origin of syphilis in the Old and New Worlds. Using osteological evidence, paleopathologists have argued that human venereal syphilis originated in the Americas and was transported to Europe and then to other human habitats by European colonists and explorers, including, as Crosby (45, 46) has argued, Christopher Columbus's crew. This conclusion is based on abundant evidence of syphlitic skeletal material from pre-Columbian remains discovered in the New World (43, 93, 94, 179, 181, 200, 222) and the distinct absence of pre-Columbian, Old World skeletal material with any of the treponemal stigmata (223). Nevertheless, other reconstructions of the history of syphilis based on contemporary and historical knowledge of the treponemal diseases have been put forward (39, 99, 119–122); these have been well summarized by McNeill (172) and Wood (223).

In addition, paleoepidemiological reconstruction of infectious disease patterns in prehistoric and early historic human populations has been undertaken through ethnographic analogy – that is, examination of disease patterns in contemporary isolated hunter-gatherer populations followed by extrapolation of these findings into the past. First suggested by Dunn (58) and Polunin (196), this approach has been advocated subsequently by a number of scholars (16, 17, 40, 95, 185). Basing their theses largely on serological evidence collected from contemporary hunter-gatherer groups, they hypothesize that, because of their small numbers, mobility, and relative isolation from other groups, ancient hunter-gatherers were relatively free from the acute, epidemic infectious diseases that later took their toll on more advanced agrarian societies. Many acute infectious diseases require large numbers of susceptible individuals to support their chains of transmission, which are characterized by brief and rapid stages of infection. In early food-foraging groups, populations of no more than 200–300 persons would not have been large enough to sustain such a chain of transmission; if introduced, these acute infections would have run their courses and then died out. From the standpoint of natural selection, pathogens that live in a long-term commensal relationship with the host (e.g. the agents of typhoid, amoebic dysentery, trachoma) and those that persist periods of time outside the final host or vector (e.g. the agent of schistosomiasis) would have been favored, and infections like measles, which spreads rapidly and immunizes a majority of the population in one epidemic, would have been rare or absent.

A number of scholars (5, 40, 55, 56, 82, 171, 195) have gone beyond this original proposition to describe the coevolution of human culture and infectious disease, basing their arguments largely on knowledge of population size and density and their impact on infection. Humans made a rapid cultural transition from small, isolated groups of hunter-gatherers to small, scattered villages of farmers, to large, preindustrial and then industrial cities, marked by aggregates of people living in close proximity. This cultural transition profoundly affected the nature of infectious disease patterns by (a) changing the degree of contact between humans and animals, either directly or via arthropod vectors, and (b) altering the size of human aggregations and the communications and movement within and between them. Thus, the contagious epidemic diseases, which would not have had a large enough population base to affect hunter-gatherers or even small farming villages, would eventually decimate populations in urban centers.

Likewise, the clearing of land for cultivation, the domestication of animals, the increase in sedentism, and the concomitant problems of human and animal waste removal, all of which occurred during the agricultural revolution of Neolithic and Mesolithic periods, provided ideal conditions for many of the helminthic and protozoal parasites (5). The health consequences of this transition from food foraging to food production have been topics of considerable attention, as seen in the important collection *Paleopathology at the Origins of Agriculture* (42). Twelve of the eighteen case studies in this collection report substantial increases in infection rates from the time of early hunter-gatherers to early farmers (41). Research from both the Old and New Worlds shows a repeated pattern of decreased stature, higher infant mortality, and increased physiological stresses indicative of malnutrition, character-istic of populations during the Neolithic revolution. Such a pattern indicates the strong synergistic relation between chronic malnutrition and infectious disease morbidity and mortality (207). It should be noted, however, that the intensification of agricultural systems, whether in the past or present, shows no direct linkage with increased infectious disease rates (41, 112).

In addition, a number of scholars, primarily medical historians, have examined the effect of infectious diseases on civilizations during historical periods (for numerous examples of these works, see 24). Utilizing texts and other primary and secondary sources, they have chronicled the impact of such infectious diseases as the plague (53), typhus (226), cholera (202), malaria (105), and smallpox (115), for better and for worse, upon state-level societies and populations. In the most comprehensive treatment of this theme, McNeill (172) argues that epidemics have played an active role in the expansion of empires throughout history, as state-level societies introduce endemic childhood diseases into smaller and simpler societies, causing massive population losses and subsequent socioeconomic disorganization. The depopulation of North and South American Indian societies by epidemic infections brought from Europe by colonizers and from Africa by slaves (8, 91, 138, 149, 186, 187) provides a salient example of McNeill's point: Infectious diseases accelerated the conquest, subjugation, and acculturation of tribes and chiefdoms.

McNeill's model requires the recognition that a universal aspect of history has been the "confluence of disease pools." Owing to rapid transportation, we now live in a single epidemiological world system – despite striking differences in the distribution of disease and death between the poor societies of the Third World and affluent nations, an important theme in a number of recent analyses (14, 171). Kunitz (150) and McKeown (170) have also concluded that socioeconomic change has had a greater impact on improvement of health and diminution of infectious diseases than has the introduction of (and innovation in) clinical medicine.

ECOLOGICAL APPROACHES

Theoretical Models

Most anthropological research on infectious disease has been ecological, focusing on the interaction between agent and host within a given ecosystem. Disease ecology, as the discipline is often called (33), owes much to the pioneering work of the medical geographer May, who in his classic volume *The Ecology of Human Disease* (167) formalized the role of the environment – both physical and sociocultural – in the study of infectious disease problems. May constructed a model that treated physical environment, disease pathogens, human hosts, and the cultural practices employed by these hosts as separate factors in an interactive process. In this view, disease expresses a temporary maladjustment between human hosts and their environment. Using examples from his own research in Asia, May demonstrated how transmission of malaria in North Vietnam and hookworm in China were affected by specific environmental and cultural patterns. In the North Vietnamese case, he showed how lowland housing types, which were transplanted without modification to the highlands, were responsible for the higher rates of malaria among lowland-to-highland migrant populations, whose ground-level dwellings exposed them to low-flying mosquito vectors. Native hill peoples, on the other hand, had adjusted to the malaria threat by constructing stilted houses with living quarters above the mosquito's 10-foot flight ceiling. Likewise, in China, May showed how rates of hookworm infection depended upon the environments within which individuals worked: While rice growers who worked in fields of mud mixed with nightsoil (raw human feces) were usually and often seriously infected, silkworm farmers who spent their days on ladders tending to mulberry leaves were not.

Following May's lead, a number of scholars delineated models of the interactions among infectious disease agents, human hosts, and the environment. Audy (10, 11) whose major work focused on the roles of human behavioral and environmental factors in the transmission of scrub typhus (9), broadened his approach to disease etiology by incorporating the notion "insults" into his model. Insults were defined as physical, chemical, infectious, psychological, or social stimuli that adversely affected an individual's or population's adjustment to the environment. Audy viewed both health and disease as states in an individual's dynamic relations with the environment: Measuring either one depended upon identifying the multiple positive and negative insults and their cumulative effects. Moreover, exposure to a pathogen was a necessary but not sufficient cause of disease; the progression from exposure to disease depended in part on the health of the exposed person, which, given an individual's vulnerability to a complex of insults, was never a constant.

Audy introduced the concept of insults in an attempt to overcome the limitations of a pathogen-specific approach to disease. Dunn (68) developed the even broader concept of "causal assemblages" – complexes of environmental, host-biological, and host-behavioral factors that must be considered when studying disease etiology or attempting to control disease spread. In his early work with Malaysian aboriginal groups, Dunn (59, 61) showed how both environmental factors (e.g. altitude, temperature, soil type, presence of scavenging animals) and human behavioral factors (e.g. subsistence strategies, housing types, community mobility) significantly affected rates of parasitic infection. He later demonstrated the important implications of this model in the design of effective disease control programs (60, 62–64, 66).

In a radical departure that she has labeled the "political ecology of disease," Turshen (217) has argued that "bourgeois empiricist" models of disease causality, such as those described above, are little more than accretions to the basic epidemiological triad of agent, host, and environment – a model that is inadequate because it fails to consider the ultimate causes of disease, which she holds are economic, social, and political. In her own study of infectious disease and related health problems in Tanzania, Turshen argues that the continued focus on the former triad is the ultimate cause of scholarly failures to elucidate why epidemics occur at certain historical moments or why eradication of a specific infection does not ensure prevention of illness. She favors a Marxist construction of the causes of poor health, which focuses on modes and factors of production and changing social relations seen from the perspective of colonialist and neocolonialist history. This approach has also been influential in medical geography (131), as well as in the development of "critical medical anthropology" (211).

Research Examples in Disease Ecology

Much of the recent empirical work in disease ecology has been, in fact, political-economic, if not explicitly Marxist in orientation, in that it focuses on the untoward consequences of ecologically ill-advised development schemes. It concerns the so-called "developo-genic" diseases, the consequence of environmental disruptions caused by large-scale, internationally sponsored projects (123). Dubos (54, 55) was among the first to note that all technological innovation, whether industrial, agricultural, or medical, upset the balance of nature; the sensible goal was thus not to maintain the balance of nature but to change it to the benefit of as many plant and animal species (including humans) as possible.

Unfortunately, many of the development schemes of the past and present have been neither balanced nor beneficial. As Hughes & Hunter (123) point out in their comprehensive review of development projects and disease in Africa, few of the projects initiated on that continent over the past two centuries have been undertaken within a preconceived ecological framework. They include in their survey programs of agricultural, industrial, and infrastructural change, as well as resulting population relocations, all undertaken in the name of progress. As they note, development projects of dam construction, land reclamation, road construction, and resettlement in Third World countries have probably done more to spread infectious diseases such as trypanosomiasis, schistosomiasis, and malaria than any other single factor.

The life-threatening blood fluke infection schistosomiasis (bilharziasis) provides a trenchant example of the unforeseen health consequences of ecological disruption caused by development schemes. As Heyneman (110, 111) notes, schistosomiasis is probably the fastest spreading and most dangerous parasitic infection now known. The rapid spread of this disease is almost entirely due to programs of water resource development involving the construction of high dams, man-made lakes and reservoirs, and irrigation canals (50, 110, 111, 208). These waterways have provided an ecological "free zone" for the snails that are the intermediate host of the schistosomal parasites. As the snail population has spread throughout Africa and parts of the Middle East, Asia, South America, and the Caribbean, so have schistosomiasis infections, which are acquired when larval parasites, released in the water from snail vectors, penetrate immersed human skin. Today, 200–300 million people worldwide are estimated to be infected (134), and new "epidemics" of the disease occur following the expansion of waterways in areas of the world where the parasite and vector live. For example, Kloos and coworkers (140, 141, 144, 145, 147) have described the expanding distribution of schistosome-transmitting snail populations and escalating rates of human infection following government-sponsored creation of large, irrigated farming estates in the Awash Valley of Ethiopia. In neighboring Sudan, the disease cycle was established within a few years of the start of the Gezira scheme, a large-scale, irrigated cotton project south of Khartoum (83, 98, 147), which was also responsible for an increased prevalence of malaria in this region (98). In Nigeria, the prevalence of schistosomiasis soared following construction of a low-earth dam providing perennial access to a large body of infective water – an increase that was likely to continue, researchers predicted, given government plans to build more dams in the area (198).

Subtler ecological changes may also be associated with increases in infectious disease. For example, Chapin & Wasserstrom (37) have shown how increased pesticide use in the intensive production of cotton in both Central America and India resulted in a serious resurgence of malaria because of the rapid evolution of insecticide-resistant strains of *Anopheles* mosquitoes. Similarly, the severe epidemic of typhoid fever in Mexico in 1972–73 was the result of overuse of the powerful antibiotic chloramphenicol for ailments such as the common cold; this change in disease ecology brought about rapid selection for chloramphenicol-resistant strains of the typhoid fever bacterium (218).

SOCIOCULTURAL APPROACHES

Human Behavior and Infectious Disease Transmission

Theoretical Models

As we have argued elsewhere (33), any anthropological study that hopes to shed light on the etiology and transmission of infectious disease must ultimately adopt both a macrosociological perspective – of the kind advocated by Turshen (217) and exemplified in much of the work on disease ecology and development – and a microsociological perspective. We have defined the latter as the study of the individual manifestations of culturally prescribed behavioral patterns, which are seen as risk factors (or, in some cases, limiting factors) for the contraction of infection (33).

The critical links between human behavior and infectious disease transmission have been recognized for more than a century, when, during an epidemic of cholera in London, differential rates of infection were linked by early epidemiological investigators to varying drinking patterns of factory workers (212). Since then, numerous anthropologists and other behavioral scientists (3, 60, 62, 64–67, 109, 176, 184, 195, 204, 210) have noted the importance of understanding culturally prescribed and proscribed behavioral practices and their effect on the transmission of infectious disease agents.

The impetus for this orientation in anthropology owes much to the pioneering work of Alland (3), who used evolutionary theory to examine how cultural behaviors could enhance human hygiene and health. Utilizing concepts from mathematical modeling, Alland used the term "minimax" to refer to cultural practices that minimize the risk of disease and maximize the health and welfare of the group.

However, as both Roundy (204) and Dunn (60, 62, 64) have suggested, not all human behavior is adaptive in the evolutionary sense, since many culturally prescribed patterns of behavior actually promote infectious disease spread. Roundy (204) has called such disease-promoting patterns of behavior "hazards." In his model, human behavior can affect disease transmission in four areas: (a) exposure to the agent, (b) shedding of the disease agent from an infected human host, (c) creation of man-made habitats in which the transmission cycle can be completed, and (d) diffusion of the transmission system from one place to another.

Dunn's (60, 62, 64) model of health-promoting and health-demoting behaviors is perhaps more useful on a methodological level. Dunn classifies all health-related behaviors along two axes: deliberate vs nondeliberate and health-promoting or maintaining vs health-demoting. He conceptualizes four major categories of individual or group health-related behaviors: (a) deliberate, consciously health-related behavior that promotes or maintains health; (b) deliberate behavior that contributes to ill health or mortality; (c) behavior not perceived to be health related that nevertheless enhances or maintains health; and (d) behavior not perceived to be health related that contributes to ill health or mortality. He notes that each of these categories of behavior may be further divided along a third axis: the perspectives of "insiders" (the populations at risk) as opposed to "outsiders" (members of the health-care community).

Research Examples

The role of human behavior in increasing or limiting transmission can be demonstrated for virtually every infectious disease. Dunn (60), for one, has applied his classificatory scheme to the study of behavioral factors in filariasis transmission. In more recent works, he has outlined theoretical and methodological considerations in the study of behavioral risk factors for trachoma (66), human arboviral infections (67), and four of the five parasitic infections (schistosomiasis, filariasis, American and African trypanosomiasis, and malaria) targeted by the United Nations (UN), the World Bank, and WHO for 20-year research and control programs (62, 64).

Nations (184) has recently summarized some of the behavioral factors that affect infectious disease transmission, including dietary customs, child care patterns, religious practices, migration patterns, agricultural techniques, kinship relations, and traditional medical treatments. However, as Nations notes, observational studies of disease-related behaviors – and, more important, anthropological studies that "make sense" of these behaviors in a broader cultural context – are few, considering the tremendous potential for this type of research.

Kuru and cannibalism   Perhaps the best-known example of anthropological involvement in an infectious disease problem involves the case of kuru, a neurological degenerative condition found in the remote eastern highlands region of New Guinea among the Fore (157). A multidisciplinary team of anthropologists, neurologists, pathologists, and epidemiologists eventually discerned that this lethal condition was due to an infectious agent — a "slow virus" acquired through behavioral practices associated with cannibalism (124). Anthropologists provided clinicians detailed information regarding subjects' reports of the preparation and consumption of the flesh and organs of deceased relatives (157). Adult women suffered the highest kuru infection rates, since it was their responsibility to prepare corpses for consumption. As Lindenbaum (157) notes, following the imposition of Western law and a subsequent government-monitored ban on cannibalism, disease incidence plummeted, thus indirectly supporting the etiological role of cannibalism in kuru's transmission.

Steadman & Merbs (215), however, have questioned the association between kuru and cannibalism, noting that researchers in the New Guinea highlands never actually witnessed an act of cannibalism. These authors suggest that Fore mortuary practices were more likely the crucial behavioral variable, permitting transmission of the deadly virus via cuts and sores on the hands of the women preparing dead bodies for burial.

Malaria and cultural adaptation   Anthropologists interested in cultural adaptations to disease have focused their attention upon malaria, a parasitic infection thought to have killed more people than any other named disease (159). Genetic adaptations to this disease have merited particular interest, and malariologists have recognized the important role of human behavior in malaria control (see the bibliography in 213). Wood (223) summarizes many of the studies of cultural practices, most of them nondeliberate, that may limit transmission in areas where malaria is endemic. These include the use of alkaline laundry soaps that destroy mosquito breeding sites, clothing styles that serve as mechanical barriers to biting insects, the use of malodorous traditional pesticides and insect repellents, and seasonal migrations away from mosquito vectors. Empirical evidence for the efficacy of such practices is generally lacking, however. Brown (27) has also argued that the combination of nucleated settlement pattern and inverse transhumance (flock movement to high elevations in summer) served to reduce exposure to malaria in Sardinia and to explain its social epidemiological distribution. These and other traditional behaviors based on the folk theory of miasma probably had preventive effects. Behavioral adaptations to malaria in other cultural contexts include fava bean consumption in the Mediterranean (135, 136), traditional medicines in Nigeria (75, 76), and the use of thick blankets and netting in Africa (163).

Echinococcosis and companion dogs   Echinococcosis (hydatid disease) is a life-threatening parasitic infection transmitted from domesticated livestock to dogs to humans. Hence, it occurs in areas of the world where humans, dogs, and livestock (primarily sheep) live in close association. The Turkana of Kenya and the neighboring tribes of southwestern Ethiopia are highly infected. Medical anthropologists and geographers (89, 90, 92) working in this region have provided rich reports of the interactions between humans and their dogs. Of particular interest from the standpoint of echinococcosis transmission are the women's "nurse dogs," which are specially trained to lick and clean children who have just defecated; in so doing, these nurse dogs disseminate infective parasitic eggs throughout the domestic environment and to their young charges. In addition, potentially infective dog feces are highly valued among the Turkana as a traditional medicinal and cosmetic substance, which is used to dress wounds, ward off evil spirits, and protect women's skin from the damaging effects of their heavy layered necklaces (90). Unfortunately, the Turkana and other highly infected tribes in this region do not associate their often lethal disease with dogs, dog feces, or the hydatid cysts they observe in their livestock (92); this situation makes preventive cultural adaptations to the disease less likely.

Schistosomiasis and water contact   Schistosomiasis is a water-based parasitic disease in that water plays a major role in the developmental life cycle of the parasite and in its transmission to humans. Because of the importance of water contact in schistosomiasis transmission, WHO (225) has advocated and supported numerous water-contact studies throughout the world. The extensive single investigation of water-contact behavior was carried out in Egypt, where Farooq and associates (77–80) performed elaborate observational studies of the daily social, occupational, and religious uses of water in a Nile Delta village. They noted that schistosomiasis was more prevalent among Muslims than among Christians, presumably owing to the frequent Islamic practice of *wudu*, or ritual ablution before prayer. Since then, a number of other investigators in Africa have studied how individuals became infected through water-contact activities (47, 72, 84, 142, 143, 146, 192). Much less attention has been paid to ways individuals infect water through urination and defecation into waterways. Cheesmond & Fenwick (38) showed that excretory behaviors in an area of the Gezira, Sudan, served to diminish the chances of schistosomiasis transmission. Namely, they observed that excretory episodes occurred in sites far removed from bodies of water, privacy being a more important consideration than proximity to water for purposes of ablution.

Sexually transmitted diseases (STDs) and labor migration   The crucial role of human behavioral factors in the dissemination of sexually transmitted diseases (STDs) has been known for hundreds of years and is a reason why these conditions were dubbed "social diseases." However, the need for social scientific studies of the behaviors placing individuals at risk from STDs – of the sociocultural determinants and consequences of those behaviors – has only been recognized recently. This need has been made more urgent by the appearance of AIDS during the past decade (13, 81, 97, 127, 176). Prior to the recognition of AIDS as a widespread problem in sub-Saharan Africa, a number of behaviorally oriented researchers working in that region (7, 15, 49, 173, 197, 219) noted the roles of rural-to-urban migration and prostitution in the transmission of STDs, primarily gonorrhea. The typical pattern of transmission included the following components: Young men from rural tribal areas – areas plagued by political upheaval, unemployment, rapid modernization, and the uneven distribution of economic opportunities – migrate to cities, where they make up the clientele of prostitutes operating from bars, brothels, dance-halls, and the street. These prostitutes, who face the same economic pressures as the males and are mostly young (aged 15–30), rural-born, uneducated, unmarried (often as the result of abandonment by nonreturning migrant husbands), and highly mobile, constitute the major reservoir of sexually transmitted infection. The risk of STD transmission is even further increased when men migrate to isolated labor camps and mines where, characteristically, a small number of prostitutes have sexual relations with a large number of men (155). Upon accumulating sufficient wealth, these men return to their natal towns and villages, where they infect their regular sex partners, usually their wives, who may be rendered infertile as a result of STD-induced reproductive pathology. This triad of migration, prostitution, and STD has been recognized in other areas of the nonindustrialized world as well (106, 133, 175, 183, 199). It is impossible to overemphasize the impact of this cycle of STD transmission on the serious sociomedical problem of infertility in these populations (169).

AIDS and sexual behavior The above-described pattern of STD transmission is also responsible in large part for the rapid spread of AIDS in sub-Saharan Africa and is a primary reason why the epidemiological profile of AIDS in Africa is radically different from that in the United States (81, 97, 155). In Africa (a) the infected population comprises primarily heterosexuals, (b) prostitution plays a dominant role in the transmission of the human immunodeficiency virus (HIV), and (c) the epidemiology of the disease is largely explained by economic influences on male labor migration patterns (155). In the United States, on the other hand, early cases of the disease were reported almost exclusively among gay and bisexual men in New York City and San Francisco (48). Since the early 1970s, these urban epicenters had already had a high prevalence of STDs among gay and bisexual populations, especially among the more sexually active men in the so-called "fast lane" (97, 148). When AIDS appeared in the United States in the early 1980s, an initial reaction to the epidemic in the gay community was denial; the severity of the AIDS epidemic was deemphasized in the interest of preserving the sexual values and institutions that represented the successful political struggles of gay liberation (97, 209). Among these institutions, bathhouses (and the sexual behaviors they encouraged) particularly facilitated the transmission of STDs, including HIV, in urban gay centers (209). By the mid-1980s, however, many gay and bisexual men began to modify their sexual behavior, especially by reducing the number of casual partners (36); the extent of this behavioral change toward "safe sex" is remarkable.

Ethnomedical Beliefs Regarding Etiology, Diagnosis, and Cure

Research Needs

Although behavioral studies of the kind cited above can provide useful information on infectious disease transmission, they are nevertheless limited in their utility if they do not proceed beyond the observational level. As Dunn (62:503) has cautioned in his discussion of schistosomiasis and water contact, "A further series of studies ... will be needed in each situation to specify why people behave as they do, where and when ... Any effort to change human behavior must rest on such studies." Dunn's call for anthropological studies that answer the all-important "why" question – by identifying the social, cultural, and psychological correlates of human behavior relating to infectious disease, including indigenous beliefs about etiology, diagnosis, and cure – has been reiterated by a number of other anthropologists (33, 97, 109, 184).

Nation's (184) recent survey of the literature revealed that ethnomedical studies of lay recognition, etiology, and treatment of infectious diseases are even rarer than behavioral studies, in part because of the entrenched belief in the biomedical community that indigenous beliefs and practices are irrelevant to the problem at hand. Yet, information of this sort is of the utmost importance in ensuring the success of public health efforts.

Research Examples
The need for such information becomes clear in the literature on ethnomedicine and infectious disease, a number of examples of which are included here.

Diarrhea and folk beliefs   In her study of indigenous beliefs surrounding infant diarrhea in northeastern Brazil, Nations (184) argues that traditional "folk beliefs," disdained by the epidemiologists and biomedical practitioners working in this area, could not be more relevant to controlling this widespread problem. These beliefs, she demonstrates, are intimately tied to epidemiological issues, such as (a) underreporting of infant mortality, (b) detection of morbidity and establishment of accurate attack rates, (c) identification of high-risk populations, (d) identification of behavioral risk factors, and (e) generation of testable analytical epidemiological hypotheses. These issues are apart from that raised by frustrated physicians, of why more children with severe diarrhea and dehydration are not brought to physicians sooner, when the chances of saving them are greater. Nations concludes that the beliefs of poor Brazilian mothers regarding the recognition, etiology, and treatment of childhood diarrheal illnesses are the key to this problem.

Another example of the importance of ethnomedical beliefs for the successful treatment of an infectious disease is provided by the work of Kendall and coworkers (137) in Honduras. They showed that diarrhea thought to be caused by the folk illness *empacho* was consistently *not* treated with oral rehydration therapy, since *empacho* was thought to warrant a purgative cure.

Dracunculiasis and contaminated water   Dracunculiasis (guinea worm disease) is a parasitic disease characterized by the presence of long adult worms in subcutaneous tissues, usually of the leg. When infected individuals steps into waterways, the female worms vomit their eggs into the water via small ulcerations on the infected individual's skin (114). If water fleas, the intermediate host of the parasite, are present they become parasitized and transmit disease to humans, who ingest them while drinking. Dracunculiasis is, in fact, the only infectious disease that could be completely eliminated if all populations living where the parasite is endemic were provided with – and used – safe drinking water (113). Because of the importance of water in the transmission cycle, dracunculiasis has been targeted by a number of international agencies, including the UN, WHO, and the World Bank, as the primary focus of their International Drinking Water Supply and Sanitation Decade (1981–90) (152). However, studies (74, 220) carried out in villages in Ghana and Nigeria – where the disease has been called the "annual festival of agony" – showed that, despite eradication efforts, few individuals thought the disease was preventable or were aware of the mode of transmission of the parasite through contaminated drinking water. Rather, the disease was attributed to heredity, transmission through soil or blood, person-to-person contact, or even the god of smallpox (2). In addition, efforts to prevent secondary infections in dracunculiasis ulcers, a significant cause of absenteeism in schools and agricultural settings throughout West Africa (126, 188), were hampered by local methods of treatment, some of which exacerbated the dracunculiasis wounds or prevented healing (73, 74).

African trypanosomiasis and brush removal   Another example of the need for ethnomedical studies revolves around African trypanosomiasis, or "sleeping sickness." In the 1930s and 1940s, the British colonial government attempted to rid the tribal Hausa peoples of northern Nigeria of the often fatal disease through efforts by biomedical personnel to explain the nature of the disease, its transport by flies, and the necessity of controlling it by slashing brush near streams to eliminate fly breeding areas. But, as Miner (178) explains, the Hausa refused to believe that brush was related to the illness, which they attributed to spirit possession. The control program was eventually carried out by force, and the Hausa were convinced to slash the brush once a year, thereby virtually eliminating the disease. But, when asked later why they cut the brush, the Hausa replied that they were forced to do so, and many people wanted to discontinue the practice. In short, the biomedical connection among brush, flies, and sleeping sickness never successfully replaced the Hausa's indigenous beliefs about the etiology of the illness.

Malaria and traditional medicines and foods   Other researchers working among the Hausa have examined traditional means by which they have coped with malaria. Etkin & Ross (75, 76) have identified 31 antimalarial plant medicines used by either herbal specialists or the general population. Some of these medicinal plants have been shown to change the oxidation–reduction status of red blood cells, a physiological condition known to impede development of the malaria parasite (71). Furthermore, parasitological tests of extracts of these traditional medicines, using a mouse model of malaria, showed that three of the substances were highly effective cures. Similarly, in China, a promising compound, artemisinin, extracted by chemists from a traditional antimalarial treatment (*quing hao*, or "green herb," related to *Artemisia annua*), has recently been identified (139). Such biochemical evaluation of native ethnopharmacopoeias for the effectiveness of antimalarial treatments, which has its historical roots in the discovery of quinine, has gained added significance with the evolution of chloroquine-resistant strains of the disease. In addition, in dietary studies from Liberia, Jackson, who has examined Liberian mothers' folk classification of malaria symptoms (128), has hypothesized that regular cassava consumption may curtail parasite growth and development in humans, because of the minute amounts of lethal cyanide contained in traditional cassava foods (unpublished manuscript).

Trachoma and ethno-ophthalmological practices Trachoma, the leading cause of preventable blindness in the world, is a bacterial eye disease whose transmission is highly dependent on individual and community hygiene (for a comprehensive review of social factors relating to trachoma transmission, see 165, 166). Medical anthropologists working in rural Egypt where the disease is endemic have examined the behaviors that place individuals at risk of trachoma (153) and described the traditional beliefs and practices surrounding eye disease in general and trachoma in particular (177). Millar & Lane (177) showed that Egyptian villagers had a complex repertoire of "ethno-ophthalmological" practices to treat trachoma, including mineral substances applied to the eyelids, surgical curettage of the inner surfaces of the eyelids with a razor blade, and blood-letting from the temples to let the "bad blood" out of the inflamed eyes. These practices can all be traced to earlier literate medical systems in Egypt, dating back in some cases to Pharaonic times. Lane & Millar argued that decisions to use traditional or biomedical treatment depended more on the individual's status in the family or community than on belief in traditional-vs-biomedical etiologies of the disease (154). As a result, individuals with less social status, particularly adult women and children, were more likely to receive less highly valued traditional remedies – despite their elevated risk of trachoma and (among women) blindness.

Local Responses to Infectious Disease Control Programs

Given the small size of the discipline of anthropology, its contributions to international health and disease control programs have been significant (216). In their early role in such efforts, anthropologists served as cultural interpreters and "troubleshooters," who were brought into programs following negative community responses. Anthropologists demonstrated that public health interventions succeeded first by being acceptable to the public. This was especially important in international programs, where recognition of differences in community organization, cultural values, and preexisting health beliefs was critical. Paul's edited volume, *Health, Culture, and Community* (189), provided important case studies of community reactions to health programs, most of which involved infectious disease prevention or control.

Thus, part of the early anthropological contribution to infectious disease control programs involved identifying social and cultural "barriers" to local-level acceptance of innovations. For example, a cholera vaccination program in China, following epidemics in the 1940s (117, 118), was hindered by the fact that villagers had their own ideas, both "scientific" and "magico-religious," about the cause of the outbreak; for most villagers, prevention did not involve acceptance of an injection. Similarly, in Bang Chan, Thailand, only a handful of villagers availed themselves of diphtheria immunization, because the channels of communication used by public health workers never reached the majority of the rural populace (103). Heggenhougen & Clements (107) have summarized more recent applied anthropological work on the effective delivery of immunizations. Of particular interest is the "checklist" of reasons for low immunization coverage developed by Brown (25); it includes behavioral attributes of both the participating population and health providers.

Following initial anthropological activity in international health programs, Foster, who had much experience in such work (85–87), warned of the danger of inappropriately blaming "culture" for failures caused instead by the attitudes and behaviors of health care planners and providers (85). This recognition was based in part on Polgar's (194) insightful analysis of "four fallacies" afflicting international public health endeavors: (a) the fallacy of empty vessels; (b) the fallacy of the separate capsule; (c) the fallacy of the single pyramid; and (d) the fallacy of interchangeable faces. Such critical questioning of the intellectual premises underlying both biomedicine and the organization of health care probably played a role in the development of "critical medical anthropology." The tradition of ethnography applied to the critical analysis of international health programs is best exemplified by the recent work of Justice in Nepal (132).

Theoretically, the ultimate goal of infectious disease control programs is the reduction of disease transmission to the point where the disease organism becomes eradicated. Such an outcome has been achieved for only one disease – smallpox – through a coordinated, global effort completed in 1978 (116). This remarkable accomplishment of international public health involved minimal anthropological expertise – namely, Morinis's assessment of the flow of smallpox case-detection information in rural markets in India (180). Toward the end of the eradication effort, Foster & Deria (88) developed a culturally acceptable method of case isolation among Somalian pastoralists by adapting a traditional technique used for sick camels.

Yet, control programs aimed at reduction of a single disease identified by outsiders can meet with resistance from local populations. Various programs to eliminate hookworm (63, 85, 87, 125) and malaria (105) appeared, from the people's point of view, too concentrated on a seemingly minor health problem. In the tea plantations of Ceylon, the Rockefeller Foundation's 6-year program to eliminate hookworm through treatment and installation of pit latrines was a failure. Far from being grateful to public health workers, tea pickers actively opposed the program because of its dull routine and focus on what they deemed an unimportant problem (190). Likewise, a malaria control program using insecticide spraying in Surinam met resistance from local populations; reasons for the reluctance ranged from fear of the insecticide and its effects on animals and local gods to disbelief about the relationship between mosquitoes and malaria (12). More recently, MacCormack (163), who has worked in malaria control activities in Africa, has encouraged the treatment of traditional sleeping nets with residual insecticides.

In addition to direct participation in malaria control programs, some anthropologists have focused on the demographic, economic, and cultural effects of successful malaria control in such locations as Mexico (108), Sardinia (29), Sudan (98), and Sri Lanka (31). Brown (28) has described this approach as the anthropology *of* disease control, since these researchers view health improvements as the result of outside influences on social and cultural change. This approach contrasts with the application of anthropological knowledge *in* disease control programs. An example of the latter approach is provided by the work of Gordon (96), who examined the causes and local perceptions of the vector-borne disease dengue fever in an urban area of the Dominican Republic. As part of a mixed-strategy intervention program, Gordon's survey demonstrated significant changes in people's explanatory models of dengue, although such changes were not accompanied by a reduction of sources for the mosquito vector, *Aedes aegypti*.

Widespread medical anthropological interest in primary health care (PHC) (19) – including such key strategies as oral rehydration therapy (44) – is, in fact, aimed primarily at the reduction of infectious disease morbidity and mortality. Because PHC requires more community participation and adaptation of culturally acceptable and affordable health technologies than did the older, vertically oriented disease control strategies, this is an area where anthropological research contributions will be especially critical.

CONCLUSION: THE IMPORTANCE AND LEGITIMACY OF INFECTIOUS DISEASE RESEARCH IN MEDICAL ANTHROPOLOGY

Anthropological studies of infectious diseases comprise an impressive literature characterized by a broad range of theoretical paradigms and research methodologies. We have examined this rich body of research, categorizing it according to three basic orientations – biological, ecological, and sociocultural. Note that research related to the interaction of humans and infectious disease agents is not limited to medical anthropology. Indeed, this subject requires discussion of classic research questions in biological anthropology, archaeology, cultural ecology, ethnomedicine, and applied anthropology in international health. A focus on infectious disease requires us to bridge the gap between the cultural and biological subfields and to return to a holistic perspective.

Nevertheless, there are four reasons why medical anthropologists in particular should pay increased attention to infectious disease research. First, infectious diseases have acted throughout human history as important agents of selection for both biological and behavioral characteristics of the species. Second, the distribution of infectious diseases is significantly influenced by human actions that affect ecology, since infectious agents make up an important part of that ecology. As such, culturally coded behaviors provide critical clues for understanding the social epidemiology and potential control of such diseases. Third, infectious diseases represent the most important cause of suffering and death in societies traditionally studied by anthropologists. The origins of this suffering must be analyzed from both micro- and macro-sociological perspectives, including the political-economic one. And, finally, applied medical anthropologists must be equipped to work within the biomedical paradigm if they hope to be effective in improving infectious disease control programs or health care delivery. This does not imply, however, that they should be limited to that paradigm.

In recent years, many medical anthropologists have abandoned the research directions described in this review. Concepts such as adaptation to disease, while still prominent in teaching texts (168), are receiving less than adequate attention from researchers. Even worse, the charge has been made that medical anthropologists who utilize biomedical categories (e.g. the diseases described above or epidemiological concepts) have been "coopted" by the intellectual hegemony of Western biomedicine. This accusation by critical medical anthropologists has three basic elements: (1) that because all reality – including the processes of sickness and health – is socially constructed, biomedicine is predicated upon culturally limited assumptions about fundamental categories like "causation" and "disease"; (2) that diseases are only the proximate causes of human suffering, since the ultimate etiologies involve political and economic inequality (the so-called "political economy of health"); and (3) that the institution of biomedicine itself functions to maintain social inequalities. These criticisms, which are not altogether new, have merit; but they do not contradict the basic findings of the literature described here, which does not advocate an unquestioning acceptance of biomedicine.

In fact, anthropological research in infectious disease reemphasizes the long-standing claim of medical anthropology that culture "manufactures" disease in two ways. First, societies actively change their ecology so as to increase or decrease the risk of particular diseases. Second, culture provides a theoretical system for understanding – and attempting to manipulate through medicine – the diseases that cause human suffering and death. As students and interpreters of societies and cultures, anthropologists cannot afford to ignore the infectious diseases, because coping with them is a universal aspect of the human experience.

NOTES

1. Ackerknecht, E. H. 1953. Paleopathology. In *Anthropology Today: An Encyclopedic Inventory*, ed. A. L. Kroeber, pp. 120–26. Chicago: Univ. Chicago Press.

2. Akpovi, S. U., Johnson, D. C., and Brieger, W. R. 1981. Guinea worm control: testing the efficacy of health education in primary care. *Int. J. Health Ed.* 24:229–37.

3. Alland Jr., A. 1970. *Adaptation in Cultural Evolution: An approach to Medical Anthropology.* New York: Columbia Univ. Press.

4. Allison, A. C. 1954. Protection afforded by sickle-cell trait against subtertian malarial infection. *Br. Med. J.* 1:290–94.

5. Armelagos, G. J. and Dewey, J. R. 1970. Evolutionary response to human infectious diseases. *BioScience* 157:638–44.

6. Armelagos, G. J., Goodman, A., and Jacobs, K. H. 1978. See Ref. 162, pp. 71–84.

7. Arya, O. P., Nsanzumuhire, H., and Taber, S. R. 1973. Clinical, cultural, and demographic aspects of gonorrhoea in a rural community in Uganda. *Bull. WHO* 49:587–95.

8. Ashburn, P. M. 1947. *The Ranks of Death: A Medical History of the Conquest of America.* New York: Coward-McCann.

9. Audy, J. R. 1968. *Red Mites and Typhus.* London: Athlone Press.

10. Audy, J. R. 1971. Measurement and diagnosis of health. In *Environmental: Essays on the Planet as a Home*, eds. P. Shepard, D. and McKinley, pp. 140–62. Boston: Houghton-Mifflin.

11. Audy, J. R. and Dunn, F. L. 1974. Health and disease. In *Human Ecology*, ed. R. Sargent, pp. 325–43. New York: North Holland.

12. Barnes, S. T. and Jenkins, C. D. 1972. Changing personal and social behaviour: experiences of health workers in a tribal society. *Soc. Sci. Med.* 6:1–15.

13. Barton, T. 1988. Sexually-related illness in Eastern and Central Africa: a selected bibliography. In *AIDS in Africa: The Social and Policy Impact*, eds. N. Miller and R. C. Rockwell, pp. 269–91. Lewiston, NY: Edwin Mellen Press.

14. Basch, P. F. 1978. *International Health.* New York: Oxford Univ. Press.

15. Bello, C. S. S., Elegba, O. Y., and Dada, J. D. 1983. Sexually transmitted diseases in northern Nigeria: five years' experience in a university teaching hospital clinic. *Br. J. Vener. Dis.* 59:202–5.

16. Black, F. L. 1975. Infectious diseases in primitive societies. *Science* 187:515–18.

17. Black, F. L. 1980. See Ref. 214, pp. 37–54.

18. Blangero, J. 1982. The P blood group system: genetic adaptation to helminthic zoonoses. *Med. Anthropol.* 6:57–69.

19. Bloom, A. and Reid, J. 1984. Introduction (Anthropology and primary health care in developing countries). *Soc. Sci. Med.* 19:183–84.

20. Blumberg, B. S. 1982. Hepatitis B infection and human behavior. *Med. Anthropol.* 6:11–19.

21. Blumberg, B. S. and Hesser. J. E. 1975. Anthropology and infectious disease. In *Physiological Anthropology*, ed. A. Damon. pp. 260–94. New York: Oxford Univ. Press.

22. Blumberg, B. S., Sutnick, A. I., London, W. T., and Melartin, L. 1972. Sex distribution of Australia antigen. *Arch. Intern. Med.* 130:227–31.

23. Brachman, P. S. 1985. Transmission and principles of control. In *Principles and Practice of Infectious Diseases*, eds. G. L. Mandell, R. G. Douglas Jr., and J. E. Bennett, pp. 103–6. New York: Wiley. 2nd ed.

24. Brothwell, D. and Sandison, A. T. 1967. *Diseases in Antiquity: A Survey of the Diseases, Injuries and Surgery of Early Populations.* Springfield. IL: Thomas.

25. Brown, J. E. 1983. Low immunization coverage in Yaounde, Cameroon: finding the problems. *Med. Anthropol.* 7:9–18.

26. Brown, P. J. 1981. Working group on anthropology and infectious disease. *Med. Anthropol. Q.* 12:7.

27. Brown, P. J. 1981. Cultural adaptations to endemic malaria in Sardinia. *Med. Anthropol.* 5:313–39.

28. Brown, P. J. 1983. Introduction: anthropology and disease control. *Med. Anthropol.* 7:1–8.

29. Brown, P. J. 1983. Demographic and socioeconomic effects of disease control: the case of malaria eradication in Sardinia. *Med. Anthropol.* 7:63–87.

30. Brown, P. J. 1986. Cultural and genetic adaptations to malaria: problems of comparison. *Hum. Ecol.* 14:311–32.

31. Brown, P. J. 1986. Socioeconomic and demographic effects of malaria eradication: a comparison of Sri Lanka and Sardinia. *Soc. Sci. Med.* 22:847–59.

32. Brown, P. J. 1993. Favism. In *The Cambridge History and Geography of Diseases*, ed. K. Kiple. pp. 722–724. Cambridge: Cambridge Univ. Press.

33. Brown, P. J. and Inhorn, M. C. 1990. Disease, ecology, and human behavior. In *Medical Anthropology: A Handbook of Theory and Method*, eds. T. M. Johnson, C. F. Sargent. Westport, CT: Greenwood Press. In press.

34. Buikstra, J. E., ed. 1981. *Prehistoric Tuberculosis in the Americas.* Evanston, IL: Northwestern Univ. Archeol. Program.

35. Burnet, M. and White, D. O. 1972. *Natural History of Infectious Disease.* Cambridge: Cambridge Univ. Press. 4th edn.

Anthropology of Infectious Disease 57

36. Centers for Disease Control. 1987. Self-reported changes in sexual behaviors among homosexual and bisexual men from the San Francisco City Clinic cohort. *Morbid. Mortal. Week. Rep.* 36:187–89.
37. Chapin, G. and Wasserstrom, R. 1981. Agricultural production and malaria resurgence in Central America and India. *Nature* 293:181–85.
38. Cheesmond, A. K. and Fenwick, A. 1981. Human excretion behaviour in a schistosomiasis endemic area of the Geizira, Sudan. *J. Trop. Med. Hyg.* 84:101–7.
39. Cockburn, T. A. 1961. The origin of the treponematoses. *Bull. WHO* 24:221–28.
40. Cockburn, T. A. 1971. Infectious diseases in ancient populations. *Curr. Anthropol.* 12:45–62.
41. Cohen, M. N. 1987. See Ref. 104, pp. 261–83.
42. Cohen, M. N. and Armelagos, G. J., eds. 1984. *Paleopathology at the Origins of Agriculture.* New York: Academic.
43. Cole, H. N., Harkin, J. C., Kraus, B. S., and Moritz, A. R. 1955. Pre-Columbian osseous syphilis. *Arch. Dermatol.* 71:231–38.
44. Coreil, J. and Mull, J. D., eds. 1988. Anthropological studies of diarrheal illness. *Soc. Sci. Med.* 27:1–118.
45. Crosby Jr., A. W. 1969. The early history of syphilis: a reappraisal. *Am. Anthropol.* 71:218–27.
46. Crosby Jr., A. W. 1972. *The Columbian Exchange: Biological and Cultural Consequences of 1492.* Westport, CT: Greenwood Press.
47. Dalton, P. R. and Pole, D. 1978. Water-contact patterns in relation to *Schistosoma haematobium* infection. *Bull. WHO* 56:417–26.
48. Darrow, W. W., Gorman, E. M., and Glick, B. P. 1986. See Ref. 81, pp. 95–107.
49. D'Costa, L. J., Plummer, F. A., Bowmer, I., Fransen, L., and Piot, P. et al. 1985. Prostitutes are a major reservoir of sexually transmitted diseases in Nairobi, Kenya. *Sex. Transm. Dis.* 12:64–67.
50. Desowitz, R. S. 1981. *New Guinea Tapeworms and Jewish Grandmothers: Tales of Parasites and People.* New York: Norton.
51. Dickie, E. R. 1979. *Family behavior and the transmission of hepatitis B virus in Malo, New Hebrides: ethnology, ethnography and epidemiology in the study of the natural history of disease.* PhD Thesis. Univ. Penn., Philadelphia.
52. Dickie, E. R., Knight Jr., R. M., and Merten, C. 1982. Ethnographic observations on child care and the distribution of hepatitis B virus in the nuclear family. *Med. Anthropol.* 6:21–36.
53. Dols, M. W. 1977. *The Black Death in the Middle East.* Princeton: Princeton Univ. Press.

54. Dubos, R. 1959. *Mirage of Health: Utopias, Progress, and Biological Change.* New York: Harper & Row.

55. Dubos, R. 1965. *Man Adapting.* New Haven, CT: Yale Univ. Press.

56. Dubos, R. 1968. *Man, Medicine, and Environment.* New York: Praeger.

57. Dubos, R. and Dubos, J. 1952. *The White Plague: Tuberculosis, Man and Society.* Boston: Little, Brown.

58. Dunn, F. L. 1968. Epidemiological factors: health and disease in hunter-gatherers. In *Man the Hunter*, eds. R. B. Lee and I. DeVore, pp. 221–28. Chicago: Aldine.

59. Dunn, F. L. 1972. Intestinal parasitism in Malayan aborigines (Orang Asli). *Bull. WHO* 46:99–113.

60. Dunn, F. L. 1976. Human behavioural factors in the epidemiology and control of *Wuchereria* and *Brugia* infections. *Bull. Public Health Soc. Malay* 10:34–44.

61. Dunn, F. L. 1977. Secular changes in Temuan (Malaysian Orang Asli) settlement patterns, subsistence, and health. *Malay. Nat. J.* 31:81–92.

62. Dunn, F. L. 1979. Behavioural aspects of the control of parasitic diseases. *Bull. WHO* 57:499–512.

63. Dunn, F. L. 1983. The sociomedical component in the epidemiology and control of parasitic infections. Presented at *Workshop on Intestinal Parasitism*, WHO and Anambra State Univ., Enugu, Nigeria.

64. Dunn, F. L. 1983. Human behavioural factors in mosquito vector control. *SE Asian J. Trop. Med. Public Health* 14:86–94.

65. Dunn, F. L. 1984. Social determinants in tropical disease. In *Tropical and Geographical Medicine*, eds. K. S. Warren and A. A. F. Mahmoud, pp. 1086–96. New York: McGraw-Hill.

66. Dunn, F. L. 1985. Sociomedical contributions to trachoma research and intervention. *Rev. Infect. Dis.* 7:783–86.

67. Dunn, F. L. 1988. Human factors in arbovirus ecology and control. In *The Arboviruses: Epidemiology and Ecology*, ed. T. P. Monath, pp. 281–90. Boca Raton: CRC Press.

68. Dunn, F. L. and Janes, C. R. 1986. See Ref. 129, pp. 3–34.

69. Dunn, F. L. and Watkins, R. 1970. Parasitological examinations of prehistoric human coprolites from Lovelock Cave, Nevada. *Univ. Calif. Arch. Res. Facil. Rep.* 10:176–85.

70. Durham, W. H. 1983. Testing the malaria hypothesis in West Africa. In *Distribution and Evolution of Hemoglobin and Globin Loci*, ed. S. J. Bowman, pp. 45–72. Dordrecht: Elsevier.

71. Eaton, J. W., Eckman, J. R., Berger, E., and Jacob, H. S. 1976. Suppression of malaria infection by oxidant-sensitive host erythrocytes. *Nature* 264:758–60.

72. Edungbola, L. D. 1980. Water utilization and its health implications in Ilorin, Kwara State, Nigeria. *Acta Trop.* 37:73–81.

73. Edungbola, L. D. 1984. Dracunculiasis in Igbon, Oyo State, Nigeria. *J. Trop. Med. Hyg.* 87:153–58.

74. Edungbola, L. D. and Watts, S. J. 1985. Epidemiological assessment of the distribution and endemicity of guinea worm infection in Asa, Kwara State, Nigeria. *Trop. Geog. Med.* 37:22–28.

75. Etkin, N. L. and Ross, P. J. 1982. Malaria, medicine, and meals: plant use among the Hausa and its impact on disease. In *The Anthropology of Medicine: From Culture to Method*, eds. L. Romanucci-Ross, D. E. Moerman, and L. R. Trancredi, pp. 231–59. New York: Praeger.

76. Etkin, N. L. and Ross, P. J. 1982. Food as medicine and medicine as food: an adaptive framework for the interpretation of plant utilization among the Hausa of northern Nigeria. *Soc. Sci. Med.* 16:1559–73.

77. Farooq, M. 1966. Importance of determining transmission sites in planning bilharziasis control: field observations from the Egypt-49 project area. *Am. J. Epidemiol.* 83:603–12.

78. Farooq, M. and Mallah, M. B. 1966. The behavioural pattern of social and religious water-contact activities in the Egypt-49 bilharziasis project area. *Bull. WHO* 35:377–87.

79. Farooq, M., Nielsen, J., Samaan, S. A., Mallah, M. B., and Allam, A. A. 1966. The epidemiology of *Schistosoma haematobium* and *S. mansoni* infections in the Egypt-49 project area. 2. Prevalence of bilharziasis in relation to personal attributes and habits. *Bull. WHO* 35:293–318.

80. Farooq, M. and Samaan, S. A. 1967. The relative potential of different age-groups in the transmission of schistosomiasis in the Egypt-49 project area. *Ann. Trop. Med. Parasitol.* 61:315–20.

81. Feldman, D. A. and Johnson, T. M., eds. 1986. *The Social Dimensions of AIDS: Method and Theory*. New York: Praeger.

82. Fenner, F. 1980. See Ref. 214, pp. 7–26.

83. Fenwick, A., Cheesmond, A. K., and Amin, M. A. 1981. The role of field irrigation canals in the transmission of *Schistosoma mansoni* in the Gezira Scheme, Sudan. *Bull. WHO* 59:777–86.

84. Fenwick, A., Cheesmond, A. K., Kardaman, M., Amin, M. A., and Manjing, B. K. 1982. Schistosomiasis among labouring communities in the Gezira irrigated area, Sudan. *J. Trop. Med. Hyg.* 85:3–11.

85. Foster, G. M. 1976. Medical anthropology and international health planning. *Med. Anthropol. Newsl.* 7(3):12–18.

86. Foster, G. M. 1982. Applied anthropology and international health: retrospect and prospect. *Hum. Org.* 41:189–97.

87. Foster, G. M. and Anderson, B. G. 1978. *Medical Anthropology*. New York: Wiley.

88. Foster, S. O. and Deria, A. 1983. Smallpox eradication in Somali nomadic encampments: the search for a culturally acceptable method of case detection, case isolation, and outbreak control. *Med. Anthropol.* 7:19–26.

89. French, C. M. and Nelson, G. S. 1982. Hydatid disease in the Turkana District of Kenya. II. A study in medical geography. *Ann. Trop. Med. Parasitol.* 76:439–57.

90. French, C. M., Nelson, G. S., and Wood, M. 1982. Hydatid disease in the Turkana District of Kenya. I. The background to the problem with hypotheses to account for the remarkably high prevalence of the disease in man. *Ann. Trop. Med. Parasitol.* 76:425–37.

91. Friedlander, J. 1977. Malaria and demography in the lowlands of Mexico: an ethno-historical approach. In *Culture, Disease, and Healing: Studies in Medical Anthropology.* ed. D. Landy, pp. 113–19. New York: Macmillan.

92. Fuller, G. K. and Fuller, D. C. 1981. Hydatid disease in Ethiopia: epidemiological findings and ethnographic observations of disease transmission in southwestern Ethiopia. *Med. Anthropol.* 5:293–312.

93. Goff, C. W. 1953. New evidence of pre-Columbian bone syphilis in Guatemala. In *The Ruins of Zaculeu Guatemala*, eds. R. B. Woodbury and A. S. Trik, pp. 312–19. Richmond, VA: William Byrd Press.

94. Goff, C. W. 1967. Syphilis. See Ref. 24, pp. 279–94.

95. Goldstein, M. S. 1969. Human paleopathology and some diseases in living primitive societies: a review of the recent literature. *Am. J. Phys. Anthropol.* 31:285–93.

96. Gordon, A. J. 1988. Mixed strategies in health education and community participation: an evaluation of dengue control in the Dominican Republic. *Health Educ. Res.* 3:399–419.

97. Gorman, E. M. 1986. See Ref. 129, pp. 157–72.

98. Gruenbaum, E. 1983. Struggling with the mosquito: malaria policy and agricultural development in Sudan. *Med. Anthropol.* 7:51–62.

99. Hackett, C. J. 1963. On the origin of the human treponematoses (pinta, yaws, endemic syphilis and venereal syphilis). *Bull. WHO* 29:7–41.

100. Hahn, R. A. 1984. Rethinking "illness" and "disease." *Contrib. Asian Stud.* 18:1–23.

101. Hahn, R. A. and Kleinman, A. 1983. Biomedical practice and anthropological theory: frameworks and directions. *Annu. Rev. Anthropol.* 12: 305–33.

102. Haldane, J. B. S. 1949. Disease and evolution. *La Ric. Sci.* 19:68–76.

103. Hanks, L. M. Jr. and Hanks, J. R. 1955. See Ref. 189, pp. 155–85.

104. Harris, M. and Ross, E. B. 1987. *Food and Evolution: Toward a Theory of Human Food Habits.* Philadelphia: Temple Univ. Press.

105. Harrison, G. A. 1978. *Mosquitoes, Malaria and Man: A History of the Hostilities since 1880.* New York: Dutton.

106. Hart, G. 1974. Social and psychological aspects of venereal disease in Papua New Guinea. *Br. J. Vener. Dis.* 50:453–58.

107. Heggenhougen, K. and Clements, J. 1987. *Acceptability of Childhood Immunization: Social Science Perspectives.* London: London Sch. Trop. Med. Hyg. Eval. Plan. Cent. Health Care.

108. Heinrich, M. 1985. The anthropology of malaria control. *Cent. Issue Anthropol.* 6:27–40.

109. Hesser, J. E. 1982. Studies of infectious disease in an anthropological context. *Med. Anthropol.* 6:1–10.

110. Heyneman, D. 1971. Mis-aid to the Third World: disease repercussions caused by ecological ignorance. *Can. J. Public Health* 62:303–13.

111. Heyneman, D. 1984. Development and disease: a dual dilemma. *J. Parasitol.* 70:3–17.

112. Hodges, D. C. 1987. Health and agricultural intensification in the prehistoric valley of Oaxaca, Mexico. *Am. J. Phys. Anthropol.* 73:323–32.

113. Hopkins, D. R. 1982. Guinea worm disease – a chance of eradication? *World Health Forum.* 3:434–35.

114. Hopkins, D. R. 1983. Dracunculiasis: an eradicable scourge. *Epidemiol. Rev.* 5:208–19.

115. Hopkins, D. R. 1983. *Princes and Peasants: Smallpox in History.* Chicago: Univ. Chicago Press.

116. Hopkins, D. R. 1988. Smallpox: ten years gone. *Am. J. Public Health* 78:1589–95.

117. Hsu, F. L. K. 1952. *Religion, Science and Human Crises: A Study of China in Transition and Its Implications for the West.* London: Routledge.

118. Hsu, F. L. K. 1955. See Ref. 189, pp. 135–54.

119. Hudson, E. H. 1962. Villalobos and Columbus. *Am. J. Med.* 32:578–87.

120. Hudson, E. H. 1963. Treponematosis and anthropology. *Ann. Intern. Med.* 58: 1037–48.

121. Hudson, E. H. 1965. Treponematosis and man's social evolution. *Am. Anthropol.* 67:885–901.

122. Hudson, E. H. 1972. Diagnosing a case of venereal disease in fifteenth century Scotland. *Br. J. Vener. Dis.* 48:146–53.

123. Hughes, C. C. and Hunter, J. M. 1970. Disease and "development" in Africa. *Soc. Sci. Med.* 3:443–93.

124. Hunt Jr., E. E. 1978. See Ref. 162, pp. 84–100.

125. Hunter, S. S. 1985. Historical perspectives on the development of health systems modeling in medical anthropology. *Soc. Sci. Med.* 21:1297–1307.

126. Ilegbodu, V. A., Kale, O. O., Wise, R. A., Christensen, B. L., and Steele Jr., J. H. et al. 1986. Impact of guinea worm disease on children in Nigeria. *Am. J. Trop. Med. Hyg.* 35:962–64.

127. Inhorn, M. C. 1986. Genital herpes: an ethnographic inquiry into being discreditable in American society. *Med. Anthropol. Q.* 17:59–63.

128. Jackson, L. C. 1985. Malaria in Liberian children and mothers: biocultural perceptions of illness vs clinical evidence of disease. *Soc. Sci. Med.* 20:1281–87.

129. Janes, C. R., Stall, R., and Gifford, S. M., eds. 1986. *Anthropology and Epidemiology: Interdisciplinary Approaches to the Study of Health and Disease.* Dordrecht: Reidel.

130. Janssens, P. A. 1970. *Paleopathology: Diseases and Injuries of Prehistoric Man.* London: Baker.

131. Jones, K. and Moon, G. 1987. *Health, Disease and Society: A Critical Medical Geography.* London: Routledge & Kegan Paul.

132. Justice, J. 1986. *Policies, Plans, and People: Foreign Aid and Health Development.* Berkeley: Univ. Calif. Press.

133. Kalm, F. 1985. The two "faces" of Antillean prostitution. *Arch. Sex. Behav.* 14:203–17.

134. Katz, M., Despommier, D. D., and Gwadz, R. W. 1982. *Parasitic Diseases.* New York: Springer-Verlag.

135. Katz, S. H. 1987. See Ref. 104, pp. 133–59.

136. Katz, S. H. and Schall, J. 1979. Fava bean consumption and biocultural evolution. *Med. Anthropol.* 3:459–76.

137. Kendall, C., Foote, D., and Martorell, R. 1984. Ethnomedicine and oral rehydration therapy: a case study of ethnomedical investigation and program planning. *Soc. Sci. Med.* 19:253–60.

138. Kiple, K. F. and King, V. H. 1981. *Another Dimension to the Black Diaspora: Diet, Disease and Racism.* Cambridge: Cambridge Univ. Press.

139. Klayman, D. L. 1989. Weeding out malaria. *Nat. Hist.* 10/89:18–27.

140. Kloos, H. 1977. *Schistosomiasis and irrigation in the Awash Valley of Ethiopia.* PhD Thesis. Univ. Calif., Davis.

141. Kloos, H. 1985. Water resources development and schistosomiasis ecology in the Awash Valley, Ethiopia. *Soc. Sci. Med.* 20:609–25.

142. Kloos, H., Higashi, G. I., Cattani, J. A., Schlinski, V. D., and Mansour, N. S., et al. 1983. Water contact behavior schistosomiasis in an Upper Egyptian village. *Soc. Sci. Med.* 17:545–62.

143. Kloos, H., Higashi, G. I., Schinski, V. D., Mansour, N. S., and Polderman, A. M. et al. 1980–81. Human behavior and schistosomiasis in an Ethiopian town and an Egyptian village: Tensae Berhan and El Ayaisha. *Rural Afr.* 8–9:35–65.

144. Kloos, H. and Lemma, A. 1977. Schistosomiasis in irrigation schemes in the Awash Valley, Ethiopia. *Am. J. Trop. Med. Hyg.* 26:899–908.

145. Kloos, H., Lemma, A., and Desole, G. 1978. *Schistosoma mansoni* distribution in Ethiopia: a study in medical geography. *Ann. Trop. Med. Parasitol.* 72:461–70.

146. Kloos, H., Polderman, A. M., Desole, G., and Lemma, A. 1977. Haematobium schistosomiasis among seminomadic and agricultural Afar in Ethiopia. *Trop. Geogr. Med.* 29:399–406.

147. Kloos, H. and Thompson, K. 1979. Schistosomiasis in Africa: an ecological perspective. *J. Trop. Geogr.* 48:31–46.

148. Kotarba, J. A. and Lang, N. G. 1986. See Ref. 81, pp. 127–43.

149. Krech III, S. 1978. Disease, starvation, and Northern Athapaskan social organization. *Am. Ethnol.* 5:710–32.

150. Kunitz, S. J. 1983. *Disease Change and the Role of Medicine: The Navajo Experience.* Berkeley: Univ. Calif. Press.

151. Lambrecht, F. L. 1967. See Ref. 24, pp. 132–51.

152. Lancet. 1983. After smallpox, guineaworm? *Lancet* 1 (8317):161–62.

153. Lane, S. D. 1987. *A biocultural study of trachoma in an Egyptian hamlet.* PhD Thesis. Univ. Calif., San Francisco.

154. Lane, S. D., Millar, M. I. 1987. The "hierarchy of resort" reexamined: status and class differentials as determinants of therapy for eye disease in the Egyptian delta. *Urban Anthropol.* 16: 151–82.

155. Larson, A. 1989. Social context of human immunodeficiency virus transmission in Africa: historical and cultural bases of East and Central African sexual relations. *Rev. Infect. Dis.* 11:716–31.

156. Learmonth, A. 1988. *Disease Ecology: An Introduction.* Oxford: Basil Blackwell.

157. Lindenbaum, S. 1979. *Kuru Sorcery: Disease and Danger in the New Guinea Highlands.* Palo Alto, CA: Mayfield.

158. Livingstone, F. B. 1958. Anthropological implications of sickle cell gene distribution in West Africa. *Am. Anthropol.* 60:533–62.

159. Livingstone, F. B. 1971. Malaria and human polymorphisms. *Annu. Rev. Genet.* 5:33–64.

160. Livingstone, F. B. 1976. Hemoglobin history in West Africa. *Hum. Biol.* 48:487–500.

161. Livingstone, F. B. 1985. *Frequencies of Hemoglobin Variants: Thalassemia, the Glucose-6-Phosphate-Dehydrogenase Deficiency, G6PD Variants, and Ovalocytosis in Human Populations.* New York: Oxford Univ. Press.

162. Logan, M. H. and Hunt, E. E. Jr., eds. 1978. *Health and the Human Condition: Perspectives on Medical Anthropology.* North Scituate, MA: Duxbury Press.

163. MacCormack, C. P. 1984. Human ecology and behaviour in malaria control in tropical Africa. *Bull. WHO Suppl.* 62:81–87.

164. Martin, S. K., Miller, L. H., Hicks, C. U., David-West, A., and Ugbode, C. et al. 1979. Frequency of blood group antigens in Nigerian children with falciparum malaria. *Trans. R. Soc. Trop. Med. Hyg.* 73:216–18.

165. Marx, R. 1988. Sociomedical aspects of trachoma. *Acta Ophthalmol. Suppl.* 183.

166. Marx, R. 1989. Social factors and trachoma: a review of the literature. *Soc. Sci. Med.* 29:23–34.

167. May, J. M. 1958. *The Ecology of Human Disease.* New York: MD Publications.

168. McElroy, A. and Townsend, P. K. 1989. *Medical Anthropology in Ecological Perspective.* Boulder, CO: Westview Press. 2nd edn.

169. McFalls Jr., J. A. and McFalls, M. H. 1984. *Disease and Fertility.* Orlando: Academic.

170. McKeown, T. 1979. *The Role of Medicine: Dream, Mirage, or Nemesis?* Princeton: Princeton Univ. Press.

171. McKeown, T. 1988. *The Origins of Human Disease.* Oxford: Blackwell.

172. McNeill, W. H. 1976. *Plagues and Peoples.* Garden City, NY: Doubleday.

173. Meheus, A., De Clercq, A., and Prat, R. 1974. Prevalence of gonorrhoea in prostitutes in a Central African town. *Br. J. Vener. Dis.* 50:50–52.

174. Meindl, R. S. 1987. Hypothesis: a selective advantage for cystic fibrosis heterozygotes. *Am. J. Phys. Anthropol.* 74: 39–45.

175. Menke, H. E. 1978. Sexually transmitted diseases in Surinam: observations and thoughts. *Br. J. Vener. Dis.* 54:215–17.

176. Millar, M. I. 1987. Genital chlamydial infection: a role for social scientists. *Soc. Sci. Med.* 25:1289–99.

177. Millar, M. I. and Lane, S. D. 1988. Ethnoophthalmology in the Egyptian delta: an historical systems approach to ethnomedicine in the Middle East. *Soc. Sci. Med.* 26:651–57.

178. Miner, H. 1960. Culture change under pressure: a Hausa case. *Hum. Org.* 19:164–67.

179. MÁller-Christensen, V. 1967. See Ref. 24, pp. 295–306.

180. Morinis, E. A. 1980. Tapping the flow of information in a rural region: the example of the smallpox eradication program in Bihar, India. *Hum. Org.* 39:180–84.

181. Morse, D. 1967. See Ref. 24, pp. 249–71.

182. Morse, D. 1969. The origin of treponematosis. *Proc. Peoria Acad. Sci.* 2:27–34.

183. Morton, R. S. 1974. Venereal diseases in Bangladesh. *Br. J. Vener. Dis.* 50:64–67.

184. Nations, M. K. 1986. See Ref. 129, pp. 97–123.

185. Neel, J. V. 1970. Lessons from a "primitive" people: do recent data concerning South American Indians have relevance to problems of highly civilized communities? *Science* 170:815–22.

186. Neel, J. V., Centerwall, W. R., Chagnon, N. A., and Casey, H. L. 1970. Notes on the effect of measles and measles vaccine in a virgin-soil population of South American Indians. *Am. J. Epidemiol.* 91:418–29.

187. Neel, J. V. 1982. Infectious disease among Amerindians. *Med. Anthropol.* 6:47–55.

188. Nwosu, A. B. C., Ifezulike, E. O., and Anya. A. O. 1982. Endemic dracontiasis in Anambra State of Nigeria: geographical distribution, clinical features, epidemiology and socio-economic impact of the disease. *Ann. Trop. Med. Parasitol.* 76:187–200.

189. Paul, B. D., ed. 1955. *Health, Culture, and Community: Case Studies of Public Reactions to Health Programs.* New York: Russell Sage Foundation.

190. Philips, J. 1955. The hookworm campaign in Ceylon. In *Hands Across Frontiers: Case Studies in Technical Cooperation*, eds. H. M. Teaf Jr. and P. G. Franck. pp. 265–305. Ithaca: Cornell Univ. Press.

191. Pike, A. W. 1967. See Ref. 24, pp. 184–88.

192. Polderman, A. M. 1979. Transmission dynamics of endemic schistosomiasis. *Trop. Geogr. Med.* 31:465–75.

193. Polednak, A. P. 1987. *Host Factors in Disease: Age, Sex, Racial and Ethnic Group, and Body Build.* Springfield, IL: Thomas.

194. Polgar, S. 1963. Health action in crosscultural perspective. In *Handbook of Medical Sociology.* eds. H. E. Freeman, S. Levine, and L. G. Reeder, pp. 397–419. Englewood Cliffs, NJ: Prentice-Hall.

195. Polgar, S. 1964. Evolution and the ills of mankind. In *Horizons of Anthropology*, ed. S. Tax, pp. 200–11. Chicago: Aldine.

196. Polunin, I. V. 1967. See Ref. 24, pp. 69–97.

197. Plorde, D. S. 1981. Sexually transmitted diseases in Ethiopia: social factors contributing to their spread and implications for developing countries. *Br. J. Vener. Dis.* 57:357–62.

198. Pugh, R. N. H. and Gilles, H. M. 1978. Malumfashi endemic diseases research project, III. Urinary schistosomiasis: a longitudinal study. *Ann. Trop. Med. Parasitol.* 72:471–82.

199. Rajan, V. S. 1978. Sexually transmitted diseases on a tropical island. *Br. J. Vener. Dis.* 51:141–43.

200. Reichs, K. J. 1989. Treponematosis: a possible case from the late prehistoric of North Carolina. *Am. J. Phys. Anthropol.* 79:289–303.

201. Reinhard, K. J. 1988. Cultural ecology of prehistoric parasitism on the Colorado Plateau as evidenced by coprology. *Am. J. Phys. Anthropol.* 77:355–66.
202. Rosenberg, C. E. 1962. *The Cholera Years*. Chicago: Univ. Chicago Press.
203. Rothhammer, F., Allison, M. J., Nunez, L., Standen, V., and Arriaza, B. 1985. Chagas disease in pre-Columbian South America. *Am. J. Phys. Anthropol.* 68:495–98.
204. Roundy, R. W. 1978. A model for combining human behavior and disease ecology to assess disease hazard in a community: rural Ethiopia as a model. *Soc. Sci. Med.* 12:121–30.
205. Samuels, R. 1965. Parasitological study of long-dried fecal samples. *Mem. Soc. Am. Archaeol.* 19:175–79.
206. Sandison, A. T. 1967. See Ref. 24, pp. 178–83.
207. Scrimshaw, N. S., Taylor, C. E., and Gordon, J. E. 1968. *Interactions of Nutrition and Infection*. Geneva: WHO Monogr. Ser. 57.
208. Scudder, T. 1973. The human ecology of big projects: river basin development and resettlement. *Annu. Rev. Anthropol.* 2:45–61.
209. Shilts, R. 1987. *And the Band Played On: Politics, People, and the AIDS Epidemic*. New York: St. Martin's Press.
210. Sigerist, H. E. 1943. *Civilization and Disease*. Ithaca: Cornell Univ. Press.
211. Singer, M. 1989. The limitations of medical ecology: the concept of adaptation in the context of social stratification and social transformation. *Med. Anthropol.* 10:223–34.
212. Snow, J. 1936. *Snow on Cholera: Being a Reprint of Two Papers by John Snow, M. D.* New York: Common wealth Fund.
213. Sotiroff-Junker, J. 1978. *A Bibliography on the Behavioural, Social, and Economic Aspects of Malaria and Its Control*. Geneva: WHO.
214. Stanley, N. F. and Joske, R. A. 1980. *Changing Disease Patterns and Human Behaviour*. London: Academic.
215. Steadman, L. B. and Merbs, C. F. 1982. Kuru and cannibalism? *Am. Anthropol.* 84:611–27.
216. Trostle, J. 1986. See Ref. 129, pp. 59–94.
217. Turshen, M. 1984. *The Political Ecology of Disease in Tanzania*. New Brunswick, NJ: Rutgers Univ. Press.
218. van der Geest, S. 1984. Anthropology and pharmaceuticals in developing countries. *Med. Anthropol. Q.* 15:59–62.
219. Verhagen, A. R. and Gemert, W. 1972. Social and epidemiological determinants of gonorrhoea in an East African country. *Br. J. Vener. Dis.* 48:277–86.

220. Ward, W. B., Belcher, D. W., Wurapa, F. K., and Pappoe, M. E. 1979. Perception and management of guinea worm disease among Ghanaian villagers. *Trop. Geogr. Med.* 31:155–64.

221. Wiesenfeld, S. L. 1967. Sickle-cell trait in human biological and cultural evolution: development of agriculture causing increased malaria is bound to gene-pool changes causing malaria reduction. *Science* 157:1134–40.

222. Williams, H. U. 1932. The origin and antiquity of syphilis: the evidence from diseased bones. *Arch. Pathol.* 13:779–814, 931–83.

223. Wood, C. S. 1979. *Human Sickness and Health: A Biocultural View.* Palo Alto, CA: Mayfield.

224. World Health Organization. 1977. *Manual of the International Statistical Classification of Diseases, Injuries, and Causes of Death.* Geneva: WHO. 9th rev. edn.

225. World Health Organization. 1979. Workshop on the role of human/water contact in schistosomiasis transmission. *WHO TDR/SER-HWC/79.3.*

226. Zinsser, H. 1935. *Rats, Lice, and History: Being a Study in Biography, Which, After Twelve Preliminary Chapters Indispensable for the Preparation of the Lay Reader, Deals with the Life History of Typhus Fever.* New York: Little, Brown.

Part Two

Histories

CHAPTER 3

Dangerous Dirt: Paleopathology of Valley Fever and the Biopolitics of Race

William R. Harrison

INTRODUCTION

This chapter discusses the role of paleopathological techniques in resolving a debate about the antiquity of a fungal disease, cocci-dioidomycosis (cocci), common to certain regions within the southwestern United States. Coccidioidomycosis is gaining recognition as a significant disease entity, affecting immunocompromised hosts in such numbers that the Centers for Disease Control now list it as one of the indicators for active AIDS. Furthermore, people are immigrating to cocci-endemic zones from nonendemic regions in great numbers. There is a pattern of differential severity of infection apparently breaking down along "racial" lines, with Native Americans suffering far more morbidity and mortality than Anglo-Americans in the Southwest. The history of this disease in prehistoric human populations is important in the explanation of these peculiar distribution patterns noted in modern populations suffering from cocci. The problems of disease demographics have confounded biomedical researchers making use of laboratory and clinical models.

An integrated approach, considering biological, sociocultural, political-economic, and human behavioral issues seems likely to afford a greater degree of current control over this disease. Nearly one hundred years of intensive research have not produced a biological explanation for differential rates of infection. The resulting body of research has noted social, behavioral, and political-economic factors, but generally only as side issues. In the few instances where overt emphasis has been given to a factor other than biology (e.g., occupation patterns), no effort has been made to integrate other factors. The total body of knowledge about the exposure models, infective processes, morbidity patterns, and mortality associated with cocci clearly calls for an integrative analysis. While much is now known about the fungus, its requirements and pathogenic nature, the lack of understanding about its relationship to humans in antiquity has left us ignorant of the causes of cocci's peculiar distribution among populations in the southwestern United States.

This chapter will present a brief history of the enigma surrounding cocci's relationship with humans throughout antiquity, and the ensuing debates among researchers. Next, a review of the role of paleopathology in understanding modern infectious diseases will be presented. This will be followed by detailed reviews of the fungus's pathogenic properties, human disease response, and current epidemiology. A case of paleomycosis will then be presented, followed by a discussion of the implications for directing future investigations into the causal factors involved in cocci's distribution. The issue of "race" and racial biology will then be examined. Finally, a case will be made for an integrationist paradigm in the investigation of distribution patterns of severe coccidioidomycosis.

THE ARGUMENT

Over the last fifty years, a discussion of the odd distribution of cocci arose between members of an informal collaborative network, the Cocci Study Group. Between sessions focusing on antigenicity, intranasal challenges, antifungal medications and cocci in nonhuman primates, the study group members argued over the age of cocci as a human pathogen. Essentially two camps arose, one holding to the view that cocci had long been associated with humans, the other that the fungus was a new cause of human disease. In both cases, the two groups argued from positions weakened by the absence of data. Technically, cocci can only be diagnosed by the direct demonstration of either the fungus or antibodies to it. Without either of these, cocci cannot be ruled in.

Those favoring the new-pathogen model held that since there was no incontrovertible evidence for cocci in the archaeological record, we must conclude that cocci had not been associated with humans until recently. The position that cocci was new could also account for the severity of disease observed in Native Americans, since these groups would not have a long history of exposure (in general, the longer the duration of a relationship between pathogen and its host population, the less severe the disease). The logic of this position is flawed by the erroneous assumption that absence of proof constitutes refutation.

The other group argued that there had not been significant change over time in the environment where cocci is found today. Given the constancy of environmental conditions, the fungus seemed likely to have been present for a long period of time. Another aspect of this group's position was that evidence suggestive of cocci had been found in the bones of nonhuman mammals associated with human archaeological contexts. This demonstrated that the fungus was at least present in the southwestern desert areas where pre-Columbian Native Americans such as the Hohokam lived. The position of this group was that proof of the fungus's long standing pathogenicity to humans would eventually be found. Their conviction was eventually borne out through paleopathology.

Once the question of cocci's antiquity as a human affliction had been settled, the previously academic debate took on an applied focus. The demonstration that cocci was an ancient human pathogen makes implausible the position that Native Americans are severely affected in greater numbers because of a biological naivete; some other factor had to be looked for. In order to generate hypotheses for what this factor might be, one needs to understand what this fungus is, how it lives, and how it produces disease.

PALEOPATHOLOGY

Paleopathology is the study of disease in ancient human remains. Inhorn and Brown (1990) present paleopathology as a technique used to fulfill at least one of two broad aims of the macroevolutionary study of infectious disease. Specifically, they state that macroevolutionary studies seek to "establish the antiquity and evolution of various infectious diseases in human populations through examination of prehistoric osteologic and, in some cases, soft-tissue evidence" and to "contextualize these findings to physical and cultural circumstances of the human populations involved" (Inhorn and Brown 1990:93). Paleopathology makes use of mummified or skeletal materials in order to reconstruct disease histories for the individual or groups being examined. Patterns of trauma, nutritional behaviors, neoplasia, genetic disorders, and infectious disease all fall within the scope of paleopathology. The evidence may be found by simple visual examination of tissues, or with light or electron microscopy, by serological testing or advanced DNA replicative techniques and molecular analyses.

Paleopathology has been important to the understanding of a variety of human infectious diseases, including tuberculosis, schistosomiasis, leprosy, and others. Indeed, a review of a textbook of skeletal paleopathology (Ortner and Putschar 1985) indicates that paleopathologists have found human skeletal evidence of prehistoric infections including tuberculosis, leprosy, treponemal infections, brucellosis, echinococcosis, and sarcoidosis in various skeletal populations from around the world. Soft tissue from mummies has revealed the presence of schistosomiasis, blastomycosis and trypanosomal infection (Inhorn and Brown 1990). Zimmerman (1990) reported the identification of schistosomal infection in the liver of a 3200-year-old Egyptian mummy, and concluded that mummified livers could provide prehistoric health and nutritional data in many instances.

In a recent commentary on the role of paleopathology in examining the transatlantic transmission of infectious diseases, Jarcho (1990) suggested that, besides treponemal infections, influenza, malaria, and yellow fever may be amenable to paleopathologic investigations. Ortner and colleagues examined the applicability of DNA and immunoglobulin analyses to ancient human skeletal materials in order to more precisely document the presence and distribution of infectious disease in antiquity (Ortner, Tuross, and Stix 1992).

In all of these cases, paleopathology has detected the presence of the disease in prehistoric populations. By contributing to the understanding of where the modern forms of these diseases came from, paleopathological data has allowed the development of theories of disease evolution. Some rely on analogies between prehistoric populations and modern hunter-gatherer societies (cf. Dunn 1968), while others have gone on to suggest that diseases and human hosts co-evolved (cf. Mckeown 1988). These theories may help in understanding the development and spread of new infectious diseases in modern populations.

An example of the critical role played by paleopathology in the investigation of the antiquity and origins of certain diseases comes from the case of venereal syphilis. Researchers have argued over the origins of syphilis, whether it developed in the Old World or in the New, if it traveled from one to the other and when, or if, it developed simultaneously in both. While there is abundant evidence of treponemal infection in both Old and New World prehistoric and historic skeletal remains, pre-Columbian New World remains show signs associated with venereal syphilis while Old World remains from the same time show signs which, it is argued, are indicative of nonvenereal syphilis. The conclusion is that venereal syphilis appears to have arisen in the New World and been taken back to the Old World by Columbus's crew. This has led some to call venereal syphilis the true "Montezuma's Revenge."

DISTRIBUTION, REQUIREMENTS, AND LIFE CYCLE OF THE FUNGUS

The fungus which causes cocci, *Coccidioides immitis*, is predominantly found in areas called the "Lower Sonoran Life Zone," a geographical classification characterized by an arid climate, with a mean temperature of 70 degrees Fahrenheit. These areas are further characterized by the presence of saguaro and prickly pear cacti, ocotillo, creosote bushes, and palo verdes. The fungus itself was first identified in soil samples taken from the San Joaquin Valley in 1932 (Stewart and Meyer 1932) and its range of endemicity is now known to extend from the western United States to Argentina, covering an area of approximately 40 degrees north to 40 degrees south. The organism has been found in Washington, California, Texas, Nevada, Utah, New Mexico, Mexico (Sonora, Baja California, Coahuila, Colima, and Chihuahua), Honduras, Guatemala, Venezuela, Argentina, and Bolivia. The distribution of the organism is far from uniform, varying with geographic and climatologic differences and varying within "appropriate" environmental regions.

There are areas within the broad endemic range which are more endemic than others. Even within endemic "hot spots" there is considerable variation in distribution of the fungus. In one study of soil from the land associated with a single private home, 23 samples were negative while one sample produced great fungal yields in culture (Ajello et al. 1956). This one sample was taken from a desert squirrel nest, a common location since the organism is often found in association with rodent burrows.

In general, the fungus is found in relatively hostile environments. It is able to tolerate temperatures of up to 42 degrees centigrade, and it grows well in humidities ranging from 10% to 95%. While the fungus has never been directly observed in the soil, it is often grown from soil samples. Observations of the fungus grown in laboratory environments from soil samples are thought to hold true for the organism in its natural state. It is most commonly isolated from soils which are fairly alkaline. It tolerates salt quite well, and is often grown from soils associated with marine fossils. The fungus is especially associated with soils high in boron salts.

Coccidioides immitis migrates in the soil by extending tendrils up or down in the earth; its depth varies from immediately subsurface to 30 centimeters deep depending upon season[1] (Egeberg and Ely 1956). Egeberg and Ely (1956) argued that the high heats associated with the dry periods (up to 125 degrees Fahrenheit) provide a sterile environment for the fungus to grow in during the wet season by burning off all potentially competing microorganisms. Interestingly, after experiencing a markedly wet rainy season in 1992, the incidence of Valley Fever in Arizona increased by several hundred percent.

The fungus can be described as doubly bi-phasic. The organism takes on two forms in each of its two life phases. The first phase, the saprobic, is observed in laboratory cultures, and is presumed to be the form found in the natural environment, where it lives as a saprophyte, consuming dead organic material in the soil; the second phase, the parasitic, finds the fungus in a living host.

The morphology of the fungus in the saprobic phase is a tangled mass of white fibers called mycelia. These mycelia consist of a linked chain of viable, barrel shaped spores (arthroconidia) or ovoid spores (chlamydospores) interspaced with thin-walled structures devoid of any cellular material, called null cells. The spores, also called hyphal cells, may have up to four nuclei each. The null cells are extremely fragile and break easily when the soil is disturbed. The arthroconidia are then freed from the mycelial mass to float in the air, and be inhaled by a host.

The most common exposure scenario places the victim in immediate proximity to the released arthroconidia, although many cases have been recorded involving people infected outside the endemic area. Pappagianis and Einstein (1988) report a series of cases brought about by inhalation of spores which traveled 400 miles from Kern County, California to northern California. The more typical pattern of infectious challenge, a cloud of arthroconidia floating in the air after a local soil disturbance, makes coccidioidomycosis an occupational hazard for people such as agricultural workers, construction laborers, and archaeologists who inhale the spores while excavating (Pappagianis 1988, Werner 1974, Werner and Pappagianis 1973, Werner et al. 1972).

Once an arthroconidium has been inhaled and lodges itself in the lung, the second (parasitic) phase of life begins with the "rounding up" of the arthroconidium. The barrel-shaped arthroconidium changes shape, becoming round in a process called spherulation, which occurs within 48 hours after inhalation (Sun et al. 1986). This is followed by a process of cell division which results in the production of large, multi-nucleate spherules. Eventually the spherule undergoes septation, with division and the eventual production of uninucleate endospores. In time, the amount of endospores becomes too great and the wall of the spherule ruptures releasing the entire load of endospores into the lung. The endospores are not released singly, but rather in packets which are roughly 10 microns in size. The rupture and release is associated with the beginnings of the host response, as macrophages rush to the site of the release. The macrophages engulf the endospores, but often die without inactivating them. The endospores mature to become spherules, multichambered round structures with a double layered cell wall. Endospores are produced in the spherules, and the spherule eventually ruptures releasing the endospores and the cycle repeats itself. When the host dies, residual endospores and spherules tend to revert to the saprophytic phase and begin to form mycelial masses again.

HISTORY OF THE DISEASE

The disease now known as coccidioidomycosis[2] was first reported by Alejandro Posada in 1891 in a 36-year-old Argentine cavalryman. At this time, the condition was described as "mycosis fungoides with protozoa" (Posada 1892a, 1892b). It is interesting to note that the term "mycosis fungoides" was used to refer to a neoplastic skin condition that looked like mushrooms, and not to a fungal etiology as it was not until later that microscopic fungi were implicated in human disease.

The second and third reported cases of coccidioidomycosis, the first in the United States, involved natives of the Azores who had come to California to work on farms in the San Joaquin Valley (Thorne 1894; Rixford 1894), an area now known to be highly endemic for the disease. The mysterious organism producing the disease, observed as a nonmotile enucleate sphere and thought to be a dermatitis-producing protozoan, was named *Coccidioides immitis* (*Coccidioides* means coccidia-like, while *immitis* means not mild) in 1896 (Rixford and Gilchrist 1896). Early attempts to isolate the organism failed as cultures from infected spleen and pleura became contaminated with a white mold, which was only recognized as the pathogenic organism itself in 1932 (Stewart and Meyer 1932).

Fairly recently, an intensive effort began at a number of research sites, with the goal of producing a vaccine against coccidioidomycosis. Many variations of the vaccine have been produced, and a number of controlled trials have been conducted, but with little success after nearly thirty years of labor (cf. Pappagianis et al. 1993).

MODERN DISEASE AND PATHOLOGY

The inhalation of spores may produce no noticeable effect, or a generally benign respiratory infection, but in some cases the organism may disseminate in the host, producing severe pathology and even death. Very rarely, infection results from a puncture wound, with a direct inoculation of contaminated soil. There are also instances of exposure to the fungus occurring with no exposure to soil. Veterinarians have been known to contract Valley Fever during autopsies of horses who died from the disease. Medical students, microbiologists and mycologists have also contracted the disease directly from culture plates. An anecdotal account tells of a traveler stopped for a short layover in Phoenix. He never left the airport, and so was never exposed to desert air that had not gone through an air conditioning system. His half-hour stay in Phoenix was enough for him to develop a case of Valley Fever. Still other anecdotes tell of museum artifacts carrying spores to locales as diverse as London, Paris, and Hong Kong.

It seems that this organism is variable in all aspects of its existence, and this holds true in terms of human infection. Salkin (1980) reports that exposure can have several different outcomes: exposure with no infection; infection without disease; and infection with disease. In the first scenario, the host is exposed to the fungus, but through an adequate immune response or through organism incompetence, no infection ensues. Naturally, such incidents are hard to quantify since no infection means no immune markers of infection and we are left with no measures to directly assess the absence of infection.

When infection results from exposure, we may encounter either overt disease or asymptomatic infection. The latter state accounts for nearly 60% of all infections. In such cases, the disease is diagnosed fortuitously, during laboratory examinations to rule out other syndromes. This portion of the infected population usually produce self-diagnoses of bad colds or influenza.

The remaining 40% of those infected experience disease with clinical symptoms. The severity of the disease varies, ranging from benign and self-limited to progressive, body-wide, and fatal. By far the most common clinical picture is one of a series of vague respiratory and general complaints, including: malaise, fatigue, chronic productive cough, pneumonia, arthralgia, red bumpy skin eruptions (erythema nodosum or multiforme or toxic erythema), fever, and hemoptysis (which indicates erosion of a pulmonary blood vessel). If headaches occur they may indicate involvement of the meninges (Bronnimann and Galgiani 1989).

In very rare cases (roughly 4% of the total number of infections resulting in clinical disease), the pathogen spreads beyond the boundaries of the lung, either by direct confluence of infected areas or by hematogenous dissemination. When the fungus does spread beyond the lungs, the brain, bones, and skin are most commonly affected (Bronnimann and Galgiani 1989). Severe infection is often found in immunocompromised hosts, making this disease especially important in the face of AIDS and increasing numbers of transplant procedures with subsequent immunosuppression. The work of Graham et al. (1988) demonstrates the problems of coccidioidomycosis in AIDS patients.

Coccidioidomycosis engenders two forms of immune response. The primary line of defense is cell mediated (i.e., lymphocytes) and the second response is humoral (i.e., circulating antibodies). Since AIDS is marked by inversions of T and B cell ratios (cf. Kovacs et al. 1984), we would expect that AIDS patients are at greater risk for severe disease. Graham and colleagues' work supports this position. Their report claimed greater levels of organisms, lesions and higher levels of antibodies in AIDS patients with disseminated coccidioidomycosis when compared to matched victims of the disseminated disease who did not have AIDS. Indeed, AIDS patients often presented with extremely high titers of antibodies as well as very severe anatomic symptoms. This is not surprising since the B-cell population, responsible for the production of the antibodies in question, is not influenced to the extreme that T cells are in AIDS (Graham et al. 1988).

In another line of investigation, the works of Kirkland and Fierer (1983) and Sun et al. (1986) demonstrate the dose dependent aspect of *C. immitis* infection in different inbred species of mice. The evidence suggests that lethality is more a function of dose than species, although mice from a species specifically bred for resistance to the infection fared better than mice from a species specifically bred for susceptibility. High doses (10^4) of arthroconidia in intranasal challenges caused more extensive infection more rapidly than low doses (10^3) of the pathogen.

DIFFERENTIAL RATES OF INFECTION AND DISEASE SEVERITY: EPIDEMIOLOGIC ISSUES

Two particularly problematic aspects of cocci are the lack of demographic uniformity among victims and differential rates of severe disease. Many authors have commented on apparent racial or ethnic differences in both infection and disseminated disease (cf. Ampel, Weiden, and Galgiani 1989; Pappagianis 1982, 1988; Sievers 1974; Flynn et al. 1979; Johnson 1982; Drutz 1980). Most of these authors suggest that the explanation for these observed differences lies in inherent differences in racial biology. Sievers, however, suggests that (unspecified) external environmental factors are responsible rather than host biology (Sievers 1974). Ampel and associates conclude by affirming that "the most prudent course is to consider that certain individuals, such as blacks, Hispanics, or Filipinos, may be more likely to develop severe infection" and that once diagnosed, these patients need to be "followed closely for any evidence of disseminated disease" (Ampel, Weiden, and Galgiani 1989:898). While this position can lead to better standards of patient care, it does not address the prevention-relevant question of why certain groups are more likely to become more seriously ill. The idea that there is racial variation leads to speculation about what biological mechanisms may be responsible. While none have published the results of such speculation, informal discussions have focused on factors associated with highly visible differences. One speculation was that melanin precursors might present a favorable biochemical environment for the fungus. Since melanin is a compound responsible for dark skin, the presence of more melanin (hence melanin precursors) in darker people would then explain high infection rates. Another line of rumination focused on nasopharyngeal structure. Nasopharyngeal mucous traps airborne particles like fungal spores, so certain structural variations (for example broad nostrils) might let more of the fungus get into the lungs in the first place. Neither of these models has been tested, nor even considered seriously, but they have been entertained at clinical conferences.

There are elements of the germ theory which posit that recently established host-parasite relationships manifest more severe pathology and that as the relationship endures, the severity of pathology is ameliorated either by the pathogen becoming less lethal or the host becoming more tolerant of infection. This would suggest that the most recent immigrants to an endemic area would have the greatest incidence of severe disease, while the populations living in the region for the greatest period of time would have the lowest numbers of severe disease. It is true that African Americans and "Filipinos" are newer to the endemic zone than Caucasians; higher ratios of both disease (13.7 and 175.5 times greater respectively) and severe disease (23.3 and 191.4 times greater respectively) are found in the former groups than in the latter (Sievers 1974). However, Native Americans, who have been in the endemic zone the longest, also have substantially higher ratios (3.4 more cases and 5.6 times more severe cases) than white Americans. This aberration in distribution, with the longest residents being more seriously affected, suggested to some that cocci is a relatively new human pathogen (cf. Fink 1985). The ensuing debate surrounding the antiquity of the disease proved to be resolvable using paleopathological techniques.

Because cocci produces skeletal lesions which in some instances resemble those of tuberculosis (Long and Merbs 1981), researchers were unable to unequivocally demonstrate cocci in human skeletal remains from the southwestern United States or any other region. Fink (1985) argued that the fungus was present in prehistoric Arizona, in the regions populated by Hohokam, Sinagua, and Anasazi Indians, based on the presence of distinctive cauliflower type lesions found in dog pelves excavated from prehistoric sites (these lesions are pathognomic for cocci in dogs), but he could not address the likelihood of human infection. In the case of cocci, the question of antiquity remained unresolved because of a lack of evidence rather than negative evidence. Ortner and Putschar (1985) commented that, at the time, there was no documented skeletal proof of prehistoric human fungal infection. This changed in 1991 with the publication of the report documenting a case of paleococcidioidomycosis (Harrison, Merbs, and Leathers 1991) found after an intensive paleopathological examination of a human skeleton with severe, unexplained lesions.

In 1981 at the site of Chavez Pass in northern Arizona, a group of archaeology students at a summer excavation found a skeleton with massive lesions, affecting the skull, shoulder blades and collar bones, the bones of both legs and the right foot (Harrison, Merbs, and Leathers 1991). A careful analysis of the skeletal remains was undertaken, using radiologic and microscopic analyses. X-rays were taken of the entire skeleton, and thin sections of bone were removed from

several sites for staining and microscopic examinations. The thin
sections from this approximately 750-year-old male skeleton demonstrated the presence of the fungus in the bone. The fungus was found
in its parasitic form distributed throughout the bone in a pattern which
strongly suggests hematogenous spread and discounts the possibility of
post mortem contamination (some spherules were found in Haversian
Canals, for example, suggesting they had been carried by the blood).

This pathogenic fungus has therefore been a parasite to human
hosts in the endemic zone for quite some time. Since the ideal model

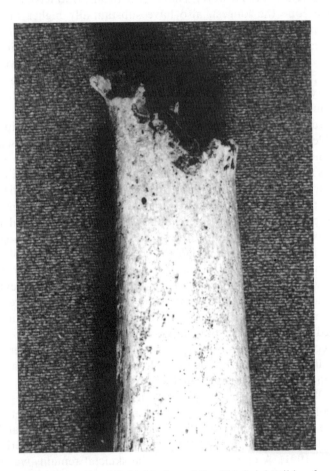

Figure 3.1   Coccidioidal lesion of the distal right tibia of
an Anasazi Indian skeleton.

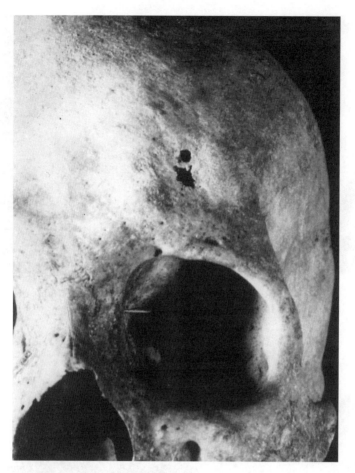

Figure 3.2 Coccidioidal lesion of the left frontal of
an Anasazi Indian skeleton.

of host-parasite relationships proposes that mortality rates (and severity of disease) are reduced over time, one would expect that *C. immitis*
would be less severe in people who had been in the endemic area for
the longest time, i.e. Native Americans. However, as noted, Native
Americans suffer three to five times more cases of severe disease than
white Americans (Sievers 1974).

The possibility that the fungus has undergone radical changes in its
pathology promoting capacity has to be considered. We know that the

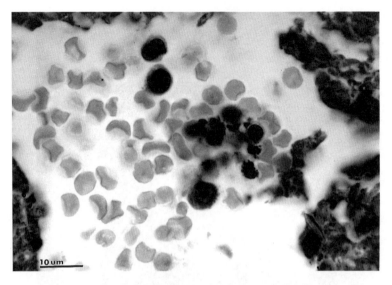

Figure 3.3   Red and white blood cells from the right talus of
an Anasazi Indian skeleton.

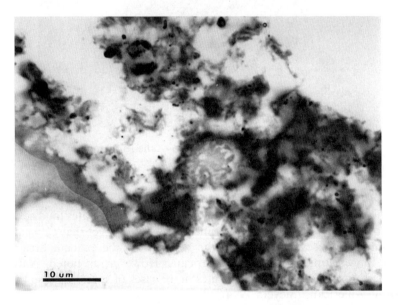

Figure 3.4   Spehrulating endospore from the right talus of
an Anasazi Indian skeleton.

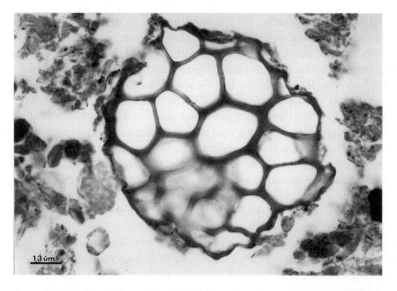

Figure 3.5 Spherule from the right talus of an Anasazi Indian skeleton.

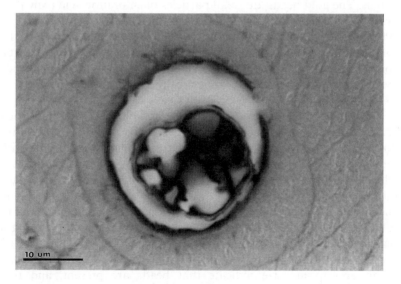

Figure 3.6 Spherule lodged in a Haversian Canal, right radius from the right talus of an Anasazi Indian skeleton.

immunological aspects of *C. immitis* are extremely complex (cf.
Catanzaro, Spitler, and Moser 1975). However, it is also very well
characterized. Antigens in the fungus stimulate lymphocytes and
initiate the production of immunoglobulins. The immunoglobulins are
found in the serum, while the lymphocytes are, of course, cellular
components of blood. Fortuitously, the same skeleton that revealed
evidence of Valley Fever also provided intact red and white blood cells,
including lymphocytes. This meant that studies could be conducted to
compare the immunologic nature of the fungus 750 years ago with that
of the modern fungus. A scanning electron microscopic study was
undertaken to determine whether antigenic changes had occurred in
the fungus over the last three-quarters of a millennium.

After extracting lymphocytes from the skeleton by washing, the
cells were exposed to either a mixture of colloidal gold beads mixed
with a commercially produced antigen or colloidal gold beads alone.
This procedure was repeated with cells from two modern donors, one
who was known to have had cocci, and the other who had not been
infected.

The antigen, spherulin, is derived from spherules grown in laboratories, and is used in skin tests to see if one has been exposed to the
fungus. The gold beads are small particles of chlorauric acid ($AuClO_4$)
made in the laboratory. The diameter of the beads ranges from 2.5 to
500 nanometers, depending upon the temperature and acidity of the
solutions being used to make the beads. Since these factors can be
controlled in the laboratory, the researchers can know what size beads
they have made. The beads are chemically sticky, and can be adhered
to a variety of chemical probes, in this case spherulin.

Once the beads and the antigen have combined, a sample of each
of the three groups of cells (skeleton, negative donor, and positive
donor) are added to an aliquot of the mixture and allowed to react with
the antigen–bead complex. Another sample from each group of cells is
allowed to react with gold beads alone. This is done in order to rule
out nonspecific binding reactions, which may occur if the beads are
chemically sticky enough. After the reaction, each sample is filtered to
catch the cells, and the filters are prepared for examination using a
scanning electron microscope. The microscope's beam will reflect off
the gold beads more brightly than off the cell itself. Thus, bright flashes
of an appropriate size indicate that beads are present, and that
something has made them stick.

In this case, the cells from the negative donor took up neither the gold
beads mixed with spherulin, nor the gold beads alone. The positive

donor cells took up only the gold beads mixed with spherulin. This indicated that the gold beads were not binding to just any cell, but only to sensitized cells and only in the presence of spherulin. According to the controls, the test was both sensitive and specific. The skeletal cells were examined last, and were found to have taken up the gold bead spherulin complex, but not the gold beads alone. This result suggested that the diagnosis of coccidioidomycosis in the skeleton was accurate, and that the fungus's antigenic composition had not changed dramatically in seven centuries. Since antigenic shift had not occurred, the higher rates of cocci found in Native American could be attributed to neither the newness of the fungus (it was ancient) nor to significant changes in the chemical nature of the fungus. The results of the paleoimmunologic inquiry meant that some other factor was at play, and that researchers had to reach beyond traditional disciplinary boundaries and embrace an approach which considered both human biology and human culture. One of the more significant questions that needed to be addressed was the concept of "race" as a scientific (biological) construct.

RACE AND RACIAL BIOLOGY

Race is a complex issue. Many people, both scientists and lay people, seem to regard the existence of different races as a biological fact. On careful reflection, however, race seems more like a scientifically endorsed social fact. A number of authors have critically examined the concept of "race" recently, and find it is a construct fraught with problems.

Race is not a new issue for anthropologists, as noted by Armelagos in a 1994 address. Among the central themes in his address, Armelagos comments upon the racist and typological underpinnings of early scientific formulations of the racial concept, a history of bias and preference which lent itself to eugenics and which still influences health care issues in America today. He further points out that race was not an independent construct, but rather one which mixed physical markers (skin and hair qualities), behavioral features (laziness, diligence), and the quasi-psychophysiological constructs of humoral type (sanguine, phlegmatic, etc).

He further argues that racial classification is typological and static, and that explanations generated by appeals to race (and presumably fundamental biological differences between races) are tautological. The cocci argument is a classic example of this: different races are affected differently because of racial differences; these inherent racial differences are what predispose certain races to particular afflictions or conditions. Armelagos notes that changing terminology (from race to "ethnic group" or "population") does not help since the fundamental theme remains the same.

This obviously bears on the applicability of race as a research tool. The use of race as an integral component of theoretical models is dubious, not only because of the weakness of the construct itself, but also because of the unacknowledged agendas which so often underlie its invocation.

Armelagos's 1994 commentary is paralleled by reviews in other disciplines, including public health and transplant science. A recent edition of *Public Health Reports* was largely devoted to issues of race in public health. In the introductory editorial, Warren and colleagues (1994:5) conclude that "race as assessed in public health surveillance is a social measure, [and] biological or genetic references, or both, should be made with extreme caution." Hahn and Stroup (1994) point out that the use of the term race is plagued by questions of validity, definition, terminological variability, and diversity in popular understanding. Williams, Lavizzo-Mourey, and Warren (1994) reviewed a variety of social science dictionaries and texts, and found that: (a) there has been chronological inconsistency in the connotation of race; and (b) that most social science disciplines view race as a biologically unfounded, scientifically untestable social construct, developing out of social response to phenotypic variation among humans.

Williams, Lavizzo-Mourey, and Warren (1994) suggest that by making the differences objective fact rather than subjective impression, scientific support for biological bases of racial difference preserves the social status quo. If human group (racial) variation is biologically based, then the social responses to it are deemed to have a valid basis. This position lends itself to the development of patterns of differential action and attitudes towards members of various races, which Williams, Lavizzo-Mourey, and Warren (1994) define as racism. This form of racism has a long history in America, and is even codified in the Constitution of the United States, where paragraph 3, section 2, article 1 indicates that for "taxation and political representation, black slaves would be counted as three-fifths of a person, and Indians would not be counted at all" (Williams, Lavizzo-Mourey, and Warren 1994:29). These authors further suggest that a subtle conflation of race and racism occurs frequently, with far-ranging results, many of which affect health status.

Race seems to be a nebulous concept, which is poorly defined, hard to operationalize and not a reliable (i.e., uniformly replicable) measure.

All too often, science attempts to rely on this loose construct as a variable in models explaining disease distribution and patterns of mortality. The end result is often what one finds in cocci, a generalized statement that some races are more at risk, but with no explanation and little hope for finding one: By looking beyond race, acknowledging and critically examining factors such as socioeconomic status, scientists have a greater chance of finding casual factors in disease distribution.

The position that race is a "real" (i.e., scientific) construct is essential to the work of authors like Zachary (1993) who contend that, for example, African-American and white Americans are inherently incompatible in terms of a variety of anatomical and physiological variables, hence the reported difficulties in matching organ donors and recipients across the two populations. This position is significant when administrative decisions need to be made about allocation of limited resources such as donated organs. Perhaps no area of biomedical research is more concerned with race than organ transplantation. Issues of racial biology are especially important in kidney transplantation; some early works can be read to suggest that there were correct and defective models of kidney function, and the correct model, which responds "properly" to sodium levels, is found in "White" kidneys. The defective model, which responds "improperly" to sodium levels is found in "Black" kidneys (Guyton et al. 1972). Some feel that the implication of Guyton's work is that such things as biologically distinguishable White and Black organs exist, that they are incompatible, and that exchange across racial lines is biologically unsound (Livingstone 1993).

Williams, Lavizzo-Mourey, and Warren (1994) point out, as do many others, that science does not operate in a social vacuum. In order for the business of science to go on, scientists need money, and projects which are in concordance with prevailing social themes and ideologies are more likely to be funded than those standing in opposition to them. In order to survive in its current incarnation in the United States, science must furthermore be socially responsive. One way to justify itself is by providing excuses which allow society to skirt responsibility for unpleasant events like disease. While certain groups may suffer a greater burden of a particular illness, like cocci, society obviously cannot be held accountable if there is a scientific, biological reason for this. Racial variation, genetic predispositions, and the like, can absolve society from any blame. Indeed, society is credited with exercising altruism and benevolence by expending resources to find the scientific way to right the wrongs of biology which leave some populations disproportionately at risk.

This seems to have been the route cocci research has followed since the early years of the twentieth century. The paleopathologic evidence of infection in early Native Americans undermines the argument for a purely biological basis of differential rates of severe disease. The apparent racial pattern may well be accounted for in terms of social and cultural factors. A strictly biomedical, laboratory-based, clinically directed research approach has failed to account for cocci's current differential rates of severity. Sievers (1974), Huberty (1963), and Johnson (1981) stand out in the cocci literature because they look beyond biological factors and examine alternative (behavioral) factors in the causal chain leading to severe coccidioidomycosis. Unfortunately, the bases of these alternative factors remain largely hypothetical, unexamined empirically. The only token foray into social factors and severe infection is found in Sievers' (1974) article; he does mention that poverty associated with reservation life may lead to housing conditions enhancing exposure to fungus-laden dust and dirt.

Integration of these hitherto disparate bodies of knowledge addressing biological and nonbiological factors shows (in part) how future research needs to be developed. It can also point out simple interventions which could immediately reduce the incidence of severe disease.

AN INTEGRATIONIST MODEL AND THE ROLE OF ANTHROPOLOGY

An integrated approach, like that ideally associated with biocultural medical anthropology, attempts to understand biological aspects of disease in light of additional factors such as human behavior and associated patterns of environmental manipulation; social and cultural factors such as ethnic relations, religion and science, and nonbiomedical concepts of health and illness; and political-economic relationships within existing hierarchies of power and control of economic resources.

In the case of coccidioidomycosis, one notices that the groups at risk for severe disease are those typically regarded as disadvantaged on many fronts. The Native American groups who have been studied, Apache, Pima, and Papago (Tohono O'odham) of central and south central Arizona, tend to live in conditions which Sievers suggested were impoverished and harsh, with many avenues for enhanced environmental exposure to the fungus (1974). Anecdotal evidence suggests that some of these groups may engage in ritual practices encouraging exposure to the fungus. Specifically, the Tohono O'odham are reported to engage in ritual geophagy, a behavior which all but assures exposure to high doses of the fungus in a fashion which could not be better suited to respiratory contamination.

At a cocci study group meeting, a discussion arose between this author and several leading figures in coccidioidal research. The topic worked around to "racial predilections" for serious disease, and the medical experts were explaining how it was that race might predispose one to severe infections. The point was made that those deemed to be most at risk, "dark skinned people," tend to work out of doors in the endemic zone, often doing manual labor involving extensive contact with potentially contaminated soil. The medical experts, once confronted with this point, commented that it had taken long enough for someone to say this bluntly. Of course, they said, what was to be done with this newly acknowledged perspective remained to be seen, but it was certainly an important point. The conversation then went back to the diagnostic potential of a new chitin-protein compound that had been recently isolated. The tight inquisitive focus of the medical mycologists and molecular biologists in the example above is what has led them to the advances they have made to date, including the understanding of the fungus's life cycle and requirements, the nature of the immune response and dose-related morbidity and mortality. It may also be what has kept them from making headway in understanding why certain groups are stricken with severe coccidioidomycosis in disproportionate numbers.

Future studies to more fully understand the behavioral and cultural mechanisms associated with severe coccidioidomycosis are needed. Such studies will need to integrate techniques and theories gleaned from current medical and biological research and ethnographic, economic and cognitive inquiries associated with anthropology.

Medical researchers, without anthropological input, would likely continue to look for purely biological bases of differential infection and severity. This would necessarily entail looking for purely biological answers to the problem, an approach which is apparently inadequate. They would likely overlook the contribution of social factors such as class-associated employment patterns or housing that does not adequately prevent contact with contaminated soil.

At the same time, anthropologists need the biomedically derived data to guide their own studies. If anthropologists approach the problem from a perspective emphasizing behavioral or cultural factors to the exclusion of biology, they will miss critical aspects of the fungus and its pathogenic pathways, such as the loading dose or the seasonality of the fungus's position in the soil (predicting when more intensive interventions would be necessary). Without biomedical input, the anthropologists might well emphasize the necessity for large-scale social interventions which might prove unfeasible. By combining biomedical and anthropological data and techniques, a realistic model for preventive interventions can be developed, such as the one detailed below.

It has been shown that severity of disease in the laboratory setting is directly related to the amount of fungus inhaled in the initial challenge. The lower the number of organisms breathed in, the less severe the disease, all other things being equal (Kirkland and Fierer 1983). Thus it seems that controlling exposure would likely ameliorate the problem of extreme morbidity and mortality in the groups felt to be classically at-risk. This control would not need to rely upon the still unproven vaccine, but could come in the form of things as simple as education about the fungus, its relation to the soil, and how interaction with the soil means interaction with the fungus. It could rely on technologies as simple as masks or even wet bandannas worn over the nose and mouth when working with contaminated soil.

It must be made clear that such an intervention has not been tested, and that this model is only presented as an example of an ideal integrationist approach to the problem. This approach is integrationist because it combines theories, methodologies, and data derived from divergent theoretical and disciplinary concentrations to produce a new, synthetic framework to control exposure. None of these remediations address the underlying issues of advantage and disadvantage, but they represent a significant improvement over either continuing the historically futile search for racially founded biological bases of blame or embarking on sociocultural investigations ignoring the fact that human behavior occurs in interaction with biological as well as symbolic elements of the surrounding environment.

NOTES

1. During the dry season, the fungus tends to live deep below the surface while in wet periods it is immediately adjacent to the soil surface (Egeberg and Ely 1956).
2. Coccidioidomycosis is also known as Valley Fever, San Joaquin Fever, Desert Fever, and Desert Rheumatism.

REFERENCES

Ajello, L., R. E. Reed, K. T. Maddy, A. A. Budurin, and J. C. Moore. 1956. Ecological and Epizootiological Studies on Canine Coccidioidomycosis. Journal of the American Veterinary Medical Association 129:485–490.

Ampel, N. M., M. A. Wieden, and J. N. Galgiani. 1989. Coccidioidomycosis: Clinical Update. Review of Infectious Diseases 11:897–911.

Armelagos, G. J. 1994. The Concept of Race, Racism and Anthropology. A Paper Presented at the Plenary Session of the sixty-third meeting of The American Association of Physical Anthropologists.

Beaman, L., E. Benjamini, and D. Pappagianis. 1983. Activation of Macrophages by Lymphokines: Enhancement of Phagosome–Lysosome Fusion and the Killing of *Coccidioides immitis*. Infection and Immunity 39(3):1201–1207.

Bronnimann, D. A. and J. N. Galgiani. 1989. Coccidioidomycosis. European Journal of Clinical Microbiology of Infectious Diseases 8(5):466–473.

Catanzaro, A., L. E. Spitler, and K. M. Moser. 1975. Cellular Immune Response in Coccidioidomycosis. Cellular Immunology 15:360–371.

Dunn, F. L. 1968. Epidemiologic Factors: Health and Disease in Hunter-Gatherers. *In* Man the Hunter. R. B. Lee and I. DeVore, eds. Pp. 221–228. Chicago: Aldine.

Egeberg, R. O. and A. F. Ely. 1956. *Coccidioides immitis* in the Soil of the Southern San Joaquin Valley. American Journal of the Medical Sciences, February, 151–154.

Fink, T. M. 1985. Coccidioidal Bone Proliferation in the Pelvis (*Os coxa*) of Canids. *In* Health and Disease in the Prehistoric Southwest. C. F. Merbs and R. J. Miller, eds. Pp. 324–339. Tempe, Arizona: Arizona State University Press.

Graham, A. R., R. E. Sobonya, D. A. Bronnimann, and J. N. Galgiani. 1988. Quantitative Pathology of Coccidioidomycosis in Acquired Immunodeficiency Syndrome. Human Pathology 19:800–806.

Guyton, A., T. Coleman, A. Cowley, K. Scheel, R. Manning, and R. Norman Jr. 1972. Arterial Pressure Regulation: Overriding Dominance of the Kidneys in Long-term Regulation and in Hypertension. The American Journal of Medicine 52:584–594.

Hahn, R. A. and D. F. Stroup. 1994. Race and Ethnicity in Public Health Surveillance: Criteria for the Scientific Use of Social Categories. Public Health Reports 109:7–15.

Harrison, W. R., C. F. Merbs, and C. R. Leathers. 1991. Evidence of Coccidioidomycosis in the Skeleton of an Ancient Arizona Indian. Journal of Infectious Diseases 164:436–437.

Huberty, G. 1963. An Epidemic of Coccidioidomycosis. American College Health Association 12:131.

Inhorn, M. C. and P. J. Brown. 1990. The Anthropology of Infectious Diseases. Annual Review of Anthropology 19:89–117.

Jarcho, S. 1990. Transatlantic Transmission of Infectious Diseases: The Applicability of Paleopathology. Bulletin of the New York Academy of Medicine 66:660–663.

Johnson, W. M. 1981. Occupational Factors in Coccidioidomycosis. Journal of Occupational Medicine 23:367–374.

Kirkland, T. N. and J. Fierer. 1983. Inbred Mouse Strains Differ in Resistance to Lethal *Coccidioides immitis* Infection. Infection and Immunology 40(3):912–916.

Kovacs, A., D. N. Forthal, J. A. Kovacs, and G. D. Overturf. 1984. Disseminated Coccidioidomycosis in a Patient with Acquired Immune Deficiency Syndrome. Western Journal of Medicine 140:447–449.

Livingstone, I. 1993. Renal Disease and Black Americans: Selected Issues. Social Science and Medicine 37(5):613–621.

Long, J. C. and C. F. Merbs. 1981. Coccidioidomycosis: A Primate Model. *In* Prehistoric Tuberculosis in the Americas. J. E. Buikstra, ed. Pp. 69–83. Northwestern University Archaeological Program, Scientific Papers Number 5. Evanston, Illinois: Northwestern University.

Maddy, K. T. 1957. Ecological Factors in the Geographic Distribution of *Coccidioides immitis*. Journal of the American Veterinary Association June:475–476.

McKeown, T. 1988. The Origins of Human Disease. Oxford: Blackwell.

Ortner, D. J. and W. G. J. Putschar. 1985. Identification of Pathological Conditions in Human Skeletal Remains. Washington, D.C.: Smithsonian Institution Press.

Ortner, D. J., N. Tuross, and A. I. Stix. 1992. New Approaches to the Study of Disease in Archaeological New World Populations. Human Biology 64:337–360.

Pappagianis, D. 1988. Epidemiology of Coccidioidomycosis. *In* Current Topics in Medical Mycology. M. R. McGinnis, ed. Pp. 199–238. New York: Springer Verlag.

Pappagianis, D. 1982. Coccidioidomycosis. *In* Occupational Mycoses. A. Di Salvo, ed. Pp. 13–28. Philadelphia: Lea and Febiger.

Pappagianis, D. and the Valley Fever Vaccine Study Group. 1993. Evaluation of the protective Efficacy of the Killed *Coccidioides immitis* Spherule Vaccine in Humans. American Review of Respiratory Diseases 148:656–660.

Posada, A. 1892a. Ensayo Anatomopatologico sobre una neoplasia considerada como micosis fungoidea. Anales del Circulo Medico Argentino 15(8): 481–497.

Posada, A. 1892b. Un Nuevo Caso de Micosis Fungoidea con Psorospermia. Anales del Circulo Medico Argentino 15(9):585–596.

Reed, R. E. and J. Converse. 1966. The Seasonal Incidence of Canine Coccidioidomycosis. American Journal of Veterinary Research 27(19): 1027–1030.

Rixford, E. and T. Gilchrist. 1896. Two Cases of Protozoan (coccidioidal) Infection of the Skin and Other Organs. Johns Hopkins Hospital Report 1:211.

Rixford, E. 1894. A Case of Protozoic Dermatitis. Occidental Medical Times 8:704–707.

Salkin, D. 1980. Classification of Coccidioidomycosis. *In* Coccidioidomycosis. D. A. Stevens, ed. Pp. 133–138. New York: Plenum Press.

Sievers, M. L. 1974. Disseminated Coccidioidomycosis among Southwestern American Indians. American Review of Respiratory Disease 109:602–612.

Smith, C., R. Beard, H. Rosenberger, and E. Whiting. 1946. Effects of Season and Dust Control on Coccidioidomycosis. Journal of the American Medical Association 132(14):833–838.

Stewart, R. and K. F. Meyer. 1932. Isolation of *Coccidioides immitis* (Stiles) from the Soil. Proceedings of the Society for Experimental Biology and Medicine 29:937–938.

Sun, S. H., G. T. Cole, D. Drutz, and J. Harrison. 1986. Electron Microscopic Observations on the *Coccidioides immitis* parasitic cycle *in vivo*. Journal of Medical and Veterinary Mycology 24:183–192.

Thorne, W. 1894. A Case of Protozoic Skin Disease. Occidental Medical Times 8:703.

Warren, R. C., R. A. Hahn, L. Bristow, and E. S. H. Yu. 1994. The Use of Race and Ethnicity in Public Health Surveillance. Public Health Reports 109:4–6.

Werner, S. 1974. Coccidioidomycosis Among Archaeology Students: Recommendations for Prevention. American Antiquity 39:367–369.

Werner, S. and D. Pappagianis. 1973. Coccidioidomycosis in Northern California: An Outbreak among Archaeology Students Near Red Bluff. California Medicine 119:16–29.

Werner, S., D. Pappagianis, I. Heindl, and A. Mickel. 1972. An Epidemic of Coccidioidomycosis among Archaeology Students in Northern California. New England Journal of Medicine 286(10):507–512.

Williams, D. R., R. Lavizzo-Mourey, and R. C. Warren. 1994. The Concept of Race and Health Status in America. Public Health Reports 109:26–41.

Zachary, A. 1993. The Genetics of Race. Transplantation Proceedings 25:2397.

Zimmerman, M. R. 1990. The Paleopathology of the Liver. Annals of Clinical and Laboratory Science 20(6):301–306.

CHAPTER 4

A New Look at an Old Disease: Smallpox and Biotechnology

Carol Shepherd McClain

The confluent smallpox – invented perhaps as the cruellest remedy for human vanity...

Lawrence Durrell, *The Alexandria Quartet*

INTRODUCTION

Smallpox was probably the most devastating of human afflictions, if one measures devastation by sheer numbers killed. It was also one of the oldest of deadly human pathogens, probably making its appearance earlier than three thousand years ago somewhere in Africa or Asia. The first direct record of its presence dates to Pharonic Egypt, where the mummified remains of three royal personages bearing smallpox-like lesions have been discovered. Ramses V died of what was probably

Reprinted from **Perspectives in Biology and Medicine**, Volume 38, Number 4, Carol Shepherd McClain, ©1995 by the University of Chicago. All rights reserved.

I am grateful to Professors Fred Dunn, Peter Brown, and Marcia Inhorn for helpful comments on earlier drafts of this essay. I owe special thanks to Dr. Joseph Esposito of the CDC, who patiently and freely shared with me his expert knowledge of variola virus. Any inaccuracies that may remain are my own.

smallpox in 1157 B.C. The face of Ramses shows the characteristic pustular lesions of smallpox, although they are distorted and flattened because of the mummy's great age and the cosmetic preparations used for embalming in ancient Egypt. The virus itself, however, has never been identified from Ramses remains (Esposito 1993, personal communication; Hopkins 1983).

In the millennia since Ramses V, smallpox killed hundreds of millions of people in an unbroken chain of human-to-human transmission. The lives of uncounted others who survived its attack were transformed by disfigurement and blindness. The last naturally-occurring case of smallpox was diagnosed on October 26, 1977 in Somalia. That case brought to completion a decade-long global campaign, orchestrated by the World Health Organization to eradicate smallpox.

An accidental laboratory release of the virus that causes smallpox resulted in the world's last death from smallpox in Birmingham, England in 1978. The Birmingham episode was the final smallpox tragedy and sobering proof that live smallpox virus is among the most lethal of laboratory biohazards.

Since the early 1980s, smallpox virus stocks have been confined to maximum containment storage at two laboratories: the Centers for Disease Control and Prevention in Atlanta and the Research Institute for Viral Preparations (RIVP) in Moscow. These stocks are the only known source of stored virus; any other repository would be viewed by virologists as a malevolent violation of the WHO's recommendation to maintain strict consolidation of all smallpox viral stocks. Scientists at the two labs have sequenced the DNA of strains of the virus to archive its genetic code. The DNA sequences constitute unique genetic "fingerprints" that could identify the virus should it somehow return in the future. Now that the smallpox DNA sequences are stored on computer disks, a debate that began among a few virologists in the late 1970s about whether and when to destroy the remaining stocks of smallpox virus has resurfaced, sparking renewed and intense interest in the biomedical community.

What questions does the new knowledge of the virus pose and what significance do the questions have, not only for the fate of the smallpox virus itself, but, by extension, for how biomedical scientists frame public discourse on fundamental issues of society and health? This chapter approaches these questions from an anthropological stance, viewing current research on the smallpox virus, and biotechnology more generally, as a cultural enterprise. The biotechnology revolution of the past twenty years has created new levels of understandings of human pathogens and their interactions with human hosts. Some of this technological armamentarium has been brought to bear on unlocking the secrets contained in the genetic codes of viruses and other micro-organisms. But like other novel technologies, the knowledge gained and applications permitted by the technology have raised difficult questions that could not have existed before the technology was perfected. The difficulties arise in two ways: when a new technology threatens or challenges traditional social relations and shared expectations among biomedical scientists, who must in turn make adjustments to accommodate the technology; and when unexpected and possibly costly social consequences attend the technology.

The juxtaposition of the disease smallpox and biotechnology exemplifies these dilemmas in a particularly meaningful way. As a kind of anthropological case study, the smallpox virus debate illustrates biomedicine's reshaping of itself in response to the new knowledge and technical capabilities made possible by biotechnology. But as a case study, the smallpox virus debate must also include as context the historical and cultural significance of epidemic smallpox, one of the great destroyers of human lives and cultures. Without the cultural history of smallpox as a backdrop, the emotional and moral intensity of the present dispute cannot be fully appreciated. I will present an overview of this cultural history before outlining the dilemma of whether and when to kill the remaining stocks of smallpox virus.

THE SMALLPOX VIRUS

The virus that causes smallpox – variola virus – is a member of a genus of viruses called orthopoxviruses. Orthopoxviruses belong to the poxvirus family, the largest and most complex of all viruses and the only viral family whose virions can, under proper illumination, just be seen with an ordinary light microscope. Certain features of variola virus made it uniquely susceptible to eradication. Most significantly, it infected only humans. It could not be introduced or reintroduced to humans from an animal vector, as is the case, for example, with malaria and yellow fever. Also, no other species of animals constituted a reservoir for the virus, as is true of a number of viral hemorrhagic fevers, such as Lassa virus and probably Ebola virus.

Smallpox was also vulnerable to eradication because of its clinical peculiarities. Virtually all persons infected with variola virus exhibited the characteristic signs of smallpox, the horribly disfiguring pustules – sometimes so thick they were described clinically as "confluent" – that developed over the entire body, particularly the face and extremities. Survivors, immune for life, bore the scars of previous infection. There were no carriers. The rare subclinical and inapparent infections were confined to those who either had survived an earlier attack or had been vaccinated. Further, only smallpox victims in the most obvious stage of their illness – the pustular rash – could transmit the virus. In the prodromal stage of infection, smallpox victims might have been prostrate with fever and toxemia, but they could not transmit the disease to others until the rash erupted. It was just this feature of smallpox – the unmistakable appearance of its victims – that health workers seized advantage of during the later stages of the worldwide smallpox eradication campaign of the 1960s and 1970s. Eradication strategists had figured out that surveillance and containment of active cases were more effective than mass vaccination in controlling outbreaks. By showing photographs of smallpox victims wherever they went, fieldworkers were able to ferret out cases of smallpox that would otherwise have been missed and vaccinate susceptible contacts. Everyone recognized the characteristic rash, even those who could not read.

Vaccination interrupted the transmission of the virus; it conferred full protection for up to ten years and a lifelong immune priming. During the global eradication campaign, surveillance and containment, combined with vaccination, prevented infectious cases from becoming outbreaks and outbreaks from spilling over to nonimmune populations. When an active case was reported, health workers isolated the index case and vaccinated all contacts, beginning with those in the immediate household and, wave-like, extending outward until all persons with possible contact with the index case had also been vaccinated. A discovery of one smallpox victim might result in hundreds or thousands of vaccinations. Vaccination broke the chain of human-to-human infection and eventually rid the world of the disease.

There are two pathologic varieties of variola virus: variola major virus and variola minor virus. Variola major was deadlier. It caused more severe symptoms and in populations long familiar with the disease, it killed about 25% of its victims. In "virgin soil" populations, the name given populations exposed to smallpox for the first time, the case fatality rate surpassed 50% (Dobyns 1983; Fenner et al. 1988; Hopkins 1983). Variola minor's case fatality rate was one percent or less. Although variola minor was first identified pathologically and clinically in the nineteenth century, it was not until the late 1970s, when the explosive development of recombinant DNA technology allowed the physical mapping of viral genomes, that strains of variola minor could be distinguished from those of variola major (Esposito, Nakano, and Obijeski 1985). The great smallpox epidemics on all continents were caused by highly virulent strains of variola major virus.

SMALLPOX: THE LIVED EXPERIENCE

At the close of the twentieth century, smallpox is far removed from not just the lives but even the imaginations of most of the world's people. Smallpox is so thoroughly a disease of the past that today's medical students no longer study it and could probably not identify a case of smallpox if they saw one. But smallpox was endemic in the Old World and among the great epidemics that decimated nonimmune populations in North and South America in the wake of European exploration. The first – and most violent – smallpox pandemic in the New World descended within a few years of Cortez' first landing and lasted from 1520 to 1524. Epidemics returned periodically, usually after the birth of sufficient numbers of children to present a newly susceptible host population. There were at least 41 smallpox epidemics among native North Americans from 1520 to 1898, and probably others that went unrecorded and so remain lost to history (Dobyns 1983:15). Not only were there massive loss of life and human suffering on a scale hard to imagine, but we will never know the full extent of cultural discontinuities that must have ensued in the wake of successive epidemics. Historical demographers today debate not whether smallpox was a major cause of hemispheric depopulation, but such fine points as the appearance and magnitude of smallpox epidemics in different regions of the Americas and at different times (Crosby 1992:277–278; Roberts 1989:1245).

Europeans traveling to the New World were less susceptible to smallpox than the indigenous peoples they encountered. Their resistance stemmed not from natural immunity, which does not exist at all in the case of smallpox. During the centuries of European exploration and colonization, Europe itself was an endemic home of smallpox. In eighteenth-century Europe for example, smallpox regularly killed 200,000 to 600,000 yearly (Joklik et al. 1993). The European traders, soldiers, merchants, and colonists who came through New World epidemics seemingly untouched had themselves undergone "trial by smallpox" (Crosby 1993:1009) from having survived the scourge as children. In the endemic regions of the Old World – Asia, India, North

Africa, Europe – infants and children were the most susceptible. Most living adults had already survived smallpox and were immune to further attacks. Smallpox was so common that some tenth century physicians concluded that it was a normal childhood experience (Dixon 1962:188). In sixteenth century Europe and later, when smallpox ravages were at their worst, mortality was highest among children. In the last years of the eighteenth century in London and Glasgow, nine out of ten small-pox deaths occurred in children under the age of five years (Hopkins 1983:74). Although children were primary victims of smallpox in en-demic areas, adults who somehow escaped infection during childhood numbered as much as 20% of smallpox victims. Abraham Lincoln is a famous American case in point. Lincoln was suffering from prodromal smallpox while delivering the Gettysburg address on November 19, 1863. His rash appeared two days later (Fenner et al. 1988:240).

CULTURE AGAINST SMALLPOX

Variolation

Variolation was perhaps the most effective preventive technique ever devised by traditional medical systems (Hughes 1963). Specialist practi-tioners inoculated the pustular substance from an active case of smallpox into a nonimmune person. The usual result was a mild infection and many fewer pustules than in naturally acquired smallpox. Inoculation tech-niques differed. The favored method in India and Africa, and later in Europe and North America, was cutaneous inoculation. Variolators inoculated a small amount of smallpox material from scabs or fresh pustules into the skin, usually of the arm, by a variety of techniques. Techniques which implanted the virus deeply enough to enter the blood-stream probably resulted in a more severe reaction than methods in which the surface of the skin was only punctured or scratched. Chinese variola-tors blew powdered smallpox scabs into the nostrils of nonimmune persons, thus introducing the virus by the normal respiratory route. Why variolation in general, and nasal insufflation in particular, did not result in fully virulent smallpox has never been fully answered. Some medical historians have suggested that smallpox virus stored in scabs became attenuated through aging. Virologists tested the viability of smallpox virus in scabs obtained from Afghani and Ethiopian variolators in the 1970s. They found that none of the smallpox virus survived longer than two years (Fenner et al. 1988:1174). The variolators themselves claimed that for best results, it was necessary to replenish their supplies yearly with fresh scabs. (Variolation differed from vaccination in that it introduced live, unattenuated smallpox virus into a susceptible person to achieve immunization. Vaccination imparted a different, but closely related virus that produced an immune reaction to the smallpox virus.)

Variolation preceded vaccination by hundreds of years, perhaps by a millennium or more. It saved uncounted lives over the centuries and bestowed lifelong immunity on those who received it. But it was not risk-free. Variolation was known to sometimes induce smallpox so severe as to take the life of the inoculee. Contagion was an even greater danger of variolation. Unless isolated, the recently variolated individual was fully infectious and could spread smallpox to others by the normal respiratory route. Smallpox contracted from a variolated individual was as virulent as smallpox caught from a naturally acquired case. In many areas, people recognized contagion enough to know that isolation was necessary to protect nonimmune persons. When variolation was not accompanied by isolation, smallpox outbreaks could and did follow. Such outbreaks occurred as late as 1973 in Afghanistan and 1976 in Ethiopia. Although there remain gaps in our understanding of the history and practice of variolation, the evidence in hand suggests that it was independently invented in different cultures, since its practice was widespread in Asia and Africa. It was only in the early eighteenth century that variolation became accepted in Europe and North America after much initial skepticism.

Smallpox Deities

If variolation was the most effective weapon against smallpox in the empirical realm, the elaboration of smallpox deities was a potent spiritual defense. Smallpox deities allowed people facing the chaos of an epidemic to make sense of the disaster and place it in a comprehensible and ordered universe. Neither was variolation – and later, vaccination – incompatible with smallpox deities. The strict Western separation between science and religion finds little concurrence elsewhere in the world. Cultures which attribute spiritual and moral agency to disease base such defenses as prevention and treatment on supernatural and magical as well as empirical measures.

Few diseases were so frightening that they inspired cultures to construct deities that were at once responsible for sending the pestilence and for curing it. Smallpox was foremost among these diseases, and was perhaps unique in that specific deities associated predominantly if not exclusively with smallpox were found in all major regions of the Old World. Smallpox goddesses were both feared and worshipped throughout China and India, and displayed benign as well as malevolent features. In West Africa, a smallpox god existed alongside medical specialists who were believed to be able to prevent as well as call forth the disease (Imperato and Traore 1979; Quinn 1979). Africans took their smallpox gods to Brazil during the slave trade. There the cults adapted to new cultural settings, but they still made smallpox spiritually if not physically bearable (Hopkins 1983).

Of all the smallpox cults, we know most about those in South Asia through ethnographic and historical accounts. The Indian goddess of smallpox, Sitala, occupied one of a number of middle ranks in the vast Hindu pantheon. Her domain was geographically broad and her history dates at least to the twelfth century. In village India, Sitala was the object of community-wide worship on her special day of the year and in pilgrimages. She was also propitiated in household ceremonies, particularly in the spring – the start of the hot, dry smallpox season.

In research conducted more than a decade before the eradication of smallpox in India, Pauline Kolenda (1982) found in Sitala a master image of smallpox as a hot, angry, unpredictable, and deadly mother. Sitala, as Mother Pox, not only caused smallpox, she was the pox itself. When appeased, flattered with offerings, and cooled with fragrant baths, she withheld her rage and spared her devotees. When angered, she retaliated by bringing smallpox, especially to children. She settled on the bodies of her victims, "burning" them with fever and pustules. To lure Mother Pox away from household children, village women enticed her with temporary abodes, like pots of water with fresh and pleasing offerings placed on rooftops for her to enjoy while cooling herself. Treatment was designed to induce her to leave the sick child. Taking care not to insult her, mothers led her out of the sickroom and to the doorway of the house with offerings of bathing vessels and cool foods and favors. From there she was further enticed to cool places beyond the village outskirts.

The domain of Sitala extended beyond smallpox, contoured in part by place and time (Bang 1973). She had many names; in south India, she was known as Mariamman, the goddess of all pustular disorders. In northern India, she was, in her benevolent aspect, the guardian of village children and the giver of good fortune. Although there are many variations in rituals connected with the goddess, she was foremost Sitala "the cool one" (Wadley 1980). Her enduring association with "coolness" invokes the hot-cold dichotomy important to Hindu concepts of health and disease. The hot-cold opposition remains central to a number of non-Western medical traditions and it was fundamental to the humoral theories predating cosmopolitan medicine. According to this conceptualization, optimum health rests on a balance between hot and cold states or qualities. In India, the excess of heat produced by smallpox – in the form of fever, prostration, and fulminating pustules – was given meaning through the image of Sitala's rage. Conversely, the ambivalence of the goddess, perhaps representing the symbolic ambivalence of women in Indian culture, was readily expressed through the capricious and deadly power of smallpox.

What happened to the world's smallpox deities after the disease was eradicated? Ralph Nicholas, writing in 1981 about smallpox in Bengal, ten years after the region was free of the disease, observed that rural villagers still put on Sitala's annual spring worship "with as much splendor and celebration as each village can manage" (Nicholas 1981:21). People accepted that smallpox was a contagious disease transmitted from an infected to a susceptible person. But rural Bengalis still revered Sitala as the "mother of the village" who "takes away the fear of smallpox." In classic functionalist tradition, Nicholas found a deeper moral and cathartic effect underlying the yearly celebratory praise of Sitala. He saw in the collective ritual a release of mounting anxieties connected with factional strife and economic want and a simultaneous reaffirmation of community values.

As smallpox waned, other dimensions of Sitala's multiple qualities assumed greater significance. Sitala the goddess of good fortune and Sitala the protectress of children are old powers that still define her. Elsewhere, she has become symbolically identified with other diseases. In Madras, South India, for example, as Mariamman, the goddess has been appropriated by traditional curers to help them cope with tuberculosis (Egnor 1984).

Vaccination

Mainstream America in the late twentieth century is accustomed to thinking of vaccination as a routine part of health care, particularly for children. We tend to forget that it is also a cultural invention designed to protect against devastating disease, just as were variolation and smallpox deities. The vaccine against smallpox is live vaccinia virus, a close relative of variola virus. Only a small number of vaccines in use today are live unattenuated viruses of a species different from the one causing the disease in question. Vaccinia virus and variola virus have considerable antigenic overlap. Vaccinia is unusual in another respect. It is one of only two viral vaccines that pre-date mid-twentieth century medical technology (rabies vaccine is the other, developed by Pasteur in 1885). All of the other viral vaccines in use today could not have been developed before post-World War II advances in medical research. A partial exception is yellow fever vaccine, which was developed and tested just prior to World War II. American troops during World War II were vaccinated against both yellow fever and smallpox (White and Fenner 1986).

The smallpox vaccine dates back two centuries, to 1796. In that year the English physician Edward Jenner first demonstrated to the medical community the principle of vaccination, originally called "cowpoxing." Local farmers knew from empirical observation that milkmaids infected with cowpox, a mild disease in humans, never became infected with smallpox. Jenner took the critical next step, experimentally introducing cowpox material into the arm of a local boy and then deliberately inoculating the youth with smallpox. The boy did not fall ill. Jenner later demonstrated that immunity could be transferred from one person to another by arm-to-arm inoculation of material taken from the site of the vaccination. Jenner's discovery took place half a century before the emergence of the germ theory of disease and 100 years before experimental proof of the existence of viruses in 1898. Only with the advent of the electron microscope in the mid-twentieth century could the actual structure of viruses be seen.

Without preserved samples, we cannot trace viral evolution back in time other than by speculation. No such samples have survived from Jenner's time so we have no way of knowing if the poxvirus material used by Jenner was the cowpox of today. Contemporary virologists consider that possibility unlikely. Some speculate that the original vaccine material was a vanant of cowpox that progressively evolved into vaccinia after many arm-to-arm passages, or that present day vaccinia is a hybrid of cowpox and smallpox (Baxby 1977). What is known for certain is that current vaccinia vaccine strains are different by DNA analysis from cowpox virus and indeed from all other naturally-occurring poxviruses that have been studied.

CAN SMALLPOX RETURN?

The WHO certified the world free of smallpox on December 9, 1979. At the same time, concerns that had been expressed previously reemerged about the fate of stocks of variola virus in laboratories around the world. Since 1976, the WHO had been trying to reduce the number of laboratories holding variola virus specimens. Its goal was to restrict the virus to a small number of collaborating centers with maximum containment facilities. The number of laboratories with variola virus stocks declined from 75 in 1975 to 18 in 1977, and in 1981 the WHO recommended that only the CDC in Atlanta and the RIVP in Moscow preserve smallpox samples. Since 1984, variola virus stocks have been restricted by international agreement to these two high-security laboratories.

Even before the eradication of smallpox, virologists discussed possible ways smallpox might be reintroduced. Could there occur an accidental release of variola virus, or worse, a deliberate release? Some laboratories might unknowingly retain variola virus, so that an inadvertent release would be an accident waiting to happen. Although the possibility of such an accident is remote, it is not trivial. On March 23, 1979, staff microbiologists at the Viral and Rickettsial Disease Laboratory at the California State Department of Health Services discovered twelve ampules of variola virus whose existence was unrecorded. The lab thought it had destroyed all its variola virus in 1976. The twelve ampules were autoclaved the same day they were discovered (CDC 1979).

The danger of smallpox infection from burials in church crypts or other entombed smallpox victims has received serious attention in the medical literature (Baxter, Brazier, and Young 1988; Zuckerman 1984). A related concern is the possibility of accidental infection from previously frozen viruses. Recently, scientists at NPO Vector, a Russian biotechnology company with a high-security laboratory, mounted an expedition to a mass smallpox gravesite in northeast Siberian permafrost, but discovered no viable virus. The human tissue samples recovered were too badly damaged to identify smallpox virus because the area had alternately frozen and thawed as the permafrost advanced and receded over the past century and more. The team plans to return to the site and continue its research (Esposito 1993, personal communication).

During the eradication campaign, smallpox workers worried that an animal poxvirus like monkeypox could mutate into a variola-like virus. Monkeypox is a zoonotic infection which in humans is nearly indistinguishable from smallpox. Its primary natural hosts are monkeys and squirrels in the forests of Zaire. In Zaire from 1970 to 1986, 33 of 404 recorded cases of human monkeypox virus infections were fatal (Joklik et al. 1993:1225). Although these figures seem alarming, research on monkeypox virus has shown that it quickly loses its virulence after transmission from one person to another, and it has not been observed to persist past five human-to-human transmissions. Also, the majority (78%) of recorded introductions of monkeypox virus into human populations have failed to result in a single secondary case (Jezek and Fenner 1988:109), further evidence of its low transmissibility in humans. Other studies have been undertaken to determine if a variola-like virus could be derived from monkeypox virus by spontaneous mutation. In these analyses, investigators used a DNA mapping technique to examine the genomes of 18 orthopoxviruses, including variola virus and monkeypox virus. The results confirmed the absolute distinctiveness of true variola and the other viruses. The investigators concluded that spontaneous mutation of monkeypox virus to variola virus is genetically impossible (Dumbell and Kapsenberg 1982; Esposito, Nakano, and Obijeski 1985).

Few people stay awake at night worrying about a reappearance of smallpox from laboratory accidents, long-dead smallpox victims, or mutations of animal poxviruses. But the possibility of the malevolent use of smallpox is quite real to the U.S. Government. Although the former Soviet Union stopped vaccination in 1986, the Pentagon routinely vaccinated U.S. military recruits until March of 1990 (Peterson 1993, personal communication). This was 13 years after the global eradication of smallpox, and nearly two decades after both the United States and the Soviet Union, along with over 50 other nations, signed the 1972 Biological Weapons Convention renouncing the use of such weapons. The Army's directive was not the result of a shift in military intelligence. The Pentagon still worries that a terrorist group or a hostile foreign government could possess long-concealed stocks of variola virus. The cessation of routine vaccination was instead a result of the Pentagon's concerns over its dwindling stocks of vaccinia-immune globulin (VIG). Prepared from the plasma of recently vaccinated persons, VIG is used to treat side effects of vaccination, which, although rare, can be life-threatening. Smallpox vaccination can cause generalized vaccinia and other serious complications, particularly in immunosuppressed individuals; those infected with HIV are an important case in point. In any program of mass vaccination, such as the vaccination of military recruits, there are bound to be a small number of such complications. The Pentagon needs sufficient quantities of VIG to run its vaccination program. Although it has stopped vaccinating, the Pentagon is rebuilding its VIG stocks by recruiting paid volunteers to accept smallpox vaccination and then extracting VIG from their blood. When the stocks are replenished, the Pentagon may revisit its decision (Peterson 1993, personal communication). The threat of smallpox is still so real to the Pentagon that it continues to vaccinate certain active duty personnel under circumstances involving hostile governments or "terrorist" groups. At this writing, only Israel continues to vaccinate its troops against smallpox.

Despite continued U.S. military preoccupation with smallpox, it would not be a good offensive weapon. The vaccine is highly effective, easily administered, and its production and distribution can be accelerated if needed. Nor can smallpox be targeted; since most people are susceptible (routine vaccination of civilian populations has long ceased throughout the world) there is no way to be sure it will infect only the intended victims.

DILEMMAS OF A TECHNOLOGY

An ad hoc WHO Committee on Orthopoxvirus Infections, made up of virologists from around the world, including virologists who were deeply involved in the smallpox eradication campaign, agreed in December of 1990 that all remaining stocks of variola virus should be destroyed. They set December 31, 1993 as the target date. The group also recommended destruction of all recombinant bacterial plasmids containing variola virus DNA sequences, or clones, with the proviso that "an expert technical committee, established by the WHO, is satisfied that sufficient sequence information is available and serious scientific objections have not been raised" (Mahy, Esposito, and Venter 1991:578).

By 1991 the CDC had assembled an international team to sequence the Bangladesh 1975 strain of variola virus, a highly virulent Asian variola major virus. The team worked with cloned variola virus DNA. The sequencing was completed in 1993 and the order of the 186,102 base pairs identified and archived on computer tape. The Russian scientists worked in parallel. Collaborators at the RIVP and NPO Vector completed the sequencing of a 1966 Indian strain of variola major. The CDC and Russian scientists are working together at the time of this writing to sequence the Garcia 1966 strain of variola minor Alastrim virus from South America. Next on the CDC's list are the highly virulent 1970 Congo strain from Africa, and a 1977 Somalia strain (from the last naturally occurring case of smallpox). A small part of the Congo strain is being sequenced at a poxvirus laboratory at the University of Oxford in England (Esposito 1993, personal communication).

Concurrent with the sequencing work, the esoteric debate over whether the remaining stocks of variola virus should be destroyed has expanded and intensified (Joklik et al. 1993; Mahy et al. 1993; Siebert 1994). The points of difference and the unstated assumptions underlying them together raise fundamental questions about the conduct of biomedical research and about prevailing biomedical paradigms. One disagreement focuses on a scenario of deliberate release of concealed smallpox stocks by terrorists or a hostile government. Proponents of destruction point out that extinguishing the remaining known live smallpox viral stocks would send a clear message to any terrorist group or government working secretly with smallpox that such activity is "punishable by national and international authorities, and that the mere possession of such virus is criminal" (Mahy et al. 1993:1223). Opponents of destruction counter that destroying the known stocks of variola virus does little to lessen the threat of smallpox from another potential source. Possible sources are corpses of smallpox victims buried in permafrost, unrecognized and unidentified smallpox virus specimens existing in laboratories somewhere in the world, and a recombination of the monkeypox virus genome with a variola virus gene (Joklik et al. 1993:1225). A recombinant monkeypox virus or vaccinia virus with smallpox-like virulence could happen deliberately or accidentally. The merits of the arguments aside, the possibility of an unintended escape of viable smallpox virus from any of these sources is virtually eliminated by simple vaccination of all researchers and laboratory workers who might possibly come into contact with the virus. Vaccination of laboratory employees working with orthopox-viruses is a precaution already widely practiced (CDC 1991).

The technologies of DNA sequencing and recombinant DNA which could permit the creation of viral chimeras not found in nature forces scientists to debate and grapple with such questions as, "Could there be a re-creation of smallpox or a new creation of a hybrid virus with all the virulence of smallpox?" Further, because scientists supported by public funds are expected and encouraged to publish their work in the open literature, controlling the uses to which the research is put takes on new significance. The virologists who have sequenced the genome of the smallpox virus have begun publishing the sequences (Massung 1994). A future researcher might use this information to recreate variola virus DNA. Further, although the use of cloned variola virus DNA fragments are tightly controlled by the WHO, which requires registration of all such clones, unregistered transfers could happen. Although poxvirus DNA is not infectious, a future researcher could create a virulent virus by co-infecting cells with variola virus DNA simultaneously with live vaccinia virus or monkeypox virus. The current debate focuses on whether the published sequence information could or might result in the re-creation of smallpox or a new poxvirus lethal to humans. But it is the development of the technology that permitted the sequencing in the first place, together with the ethical requirement that the fruits of publicly supported research be shared openly, that have created this unique dilemma. Are the sequencers of variola virus prepared to withhold publication to prevent the possibility, however remote, of a return of smallpox? Is the biomedical community prepared to generalize from this example and hold secret the results of future research that might have harmful consequences or be used unethically? Should research that might result in the ability to create new lethal pathogens be stopped? Should it instead be placed under restrictions similar to "classified" research on nuclear weapons? The destruction of smallpox viral stocks is not just a question of what to do with a few hundred frozen specimens of an otherwise extinct virus. Its ramifications, not yet fully explored, challenge some of biomedicine's most cherished values and traditions.

Over the past few decades, remarkable advances in molecular biology have reinforced and expanded a reductionist trend in biomedical conceptualizations of disease processes. Publicly funded research has followed suit, as attested to by biomedicine's big-science Human Genome Project. The idea of DNA as the Master Molecule (Keller 1985:154) lies at the base of the argument of proponents for the destruction of the remaining smallpox specimens. The "central dogma" of molecular biology asserts that

> DNA--RNA--protein. In other words, there is a one-way flow of information between these molecules, a flow that gives historical and ontological primacy to the hereditary molecule. It is this that underlies the sociobiologists' 'selfish-gene' arguments that, after all, the organism is merely DNA's way of making another DNA molecule; that everything, in a preformationist sense that runs like a chain through several centuries of reductionism, is in the gene (Lewontin, Rose, and Kamin 1984:58).

The WHO first recommended the destruction of remaining small-pox virus in 1986, on the rationale that the existence of smallpox virus DNA clones obviated the need for storing the intact virus. A majority of virologists surveyed at the time favored postponing destruction until a library of cloned smallpox virus from a number of different smallpox strains could be assembled (Henderson 1987). The WHO's subsequent 1990 recommendation for destruction called for extending the delay until December 1993, pending completion of the sequencing of at least three smallpox DNA strains. The reasoning behind both of WHO's recommendations – that all future scientific questions about smallpox virus can be answered by information contained in its DNA – reflects the power of the master molecule paradigm. This conviction, when added to the universal revulsion inspired by smallpox, makes the argument for its destruction particularly forceful.

It is from within the biomedical community itself, however, that anti-reductionist assertions are gaining momentum. Opponents of destruction want another reprieve, of up to ten years, for the smallpox virus (Jokiik et al. 1993). The retentionists' strongest claim is that only the intact virus can answer questions about how the virus interacts with cells in the living human host and what are the mechanisms of its pathogenicity. Joseph Esposito, Director of the WHO Collaborating Center for Smallpox at the CDC, has said "we still haven't discovered a vulnerable point, an Achilles' heel, in the virus, nor do we understand how the virus overcomes the body's cellular defenses. Should a similar virus ever emerge again in a situation where we could not ethically use the (smallpox) vaccine, such as in an AIDS epidemic area, we would be poorly prepared to eradicate it" (Szpir 1993:527).

The study of the details of pathogenesis of the smallpox virus requires the complete virus. As stated by another microbiologist, "the mechanisms whereby viruses cause disease – and the subtle variations in the disease process – are as much a black box today as when first described, despite advances in cloning and expression of viral genes *in vitro*" (Howard 1993:134). Disagreement persists over whether experiments with whole smallpox virus in suitable animal models is possible, and an animal model, such as a transgenic mouse, has not yet been developed. Humans are the only natural host of smallpox virus, and as the proponents of destruction rightly point out, deliberate infection of humans with smallpox virus would never be morally defensible. Other poxviruses, after all, can be studied in animals, and the smallpox virus DNA could be used as a reference should a new poxvirus emerge in the future that might be virulent in humans. On the other hand, should not the smallpox virus be preserved until such time as new, more integrative, methodologies for studying virus-host interactions are developed?

The question of preserving smallpox specimens has still other dimensions, which become clearer if the implications of disease eradication are more fully explored. Two other human diseases are close to eradication, dracunculiasis (guinea-worm disease) and polio. Should the pathogens responsible for these diseases also be preserved? The nematode that causes dracunculiasis cannot remain viable in a frozen state; it can only live in its human host. How then could its preservation as a living form be morally accomplished (Mahy 1993:132)? Should repositories be set up in selected laboratories for preserving other disease-causing viruses, bacteria, protozoa, and so forth when they appear close to extinction in the wild? Repositories of traditional varieties of rice and maize have been established in various countries to preserve their genetic uniqueness, but unlike human pathogens, these life forms benefit humanity in their natural states. Can the cost of maintaining growing numbers of repositories of extinct human pathogens be justified against the resource needs for urgent research on other infectious diseases currently plaguing millions, such as tuberculosis, malaria, and AIDS?

The dilemmas made explicit by the debate over the survival of variola virus will continue as new information and technological advances challenge the culture of biomedicine. Meanwhile, the fate of variola virus itself remains undetermined. On September 9, 1994, the WHO Ad Hoc Committee on Orthopoxvirus Infections reaffirmed its 1986 and 1990 recommendations to destroy all remaining stocks of variola virus (WHO 1994). It set the date for June 30, 1995. The Committee recommended that cloned DNA fragments of variola virus genome should be retained, and identified two international repositories for the storage, distribution, and monitoring of the cloned material – the CDC in Atlanta and the Russian State Research Center of Virology and Biotechnology in Koltsovo. The clones may not be sent to laboratories working with other poxviruses (WHO 1994). Part of the rationale for the decision for destruction is that the scientific conception of eradication is absolute and includes not only the elimination of the disease but the complete removal of its causative agent. At this writing, however, an eleventh hour reprieve has been granted by the Executive Board of the WHO and the date for destruction of the smallpox virus has been postponed again, perhaps indefinitely (Altman 1995; Maurice 1995).

CONCLUSION

I have attempted to show in this essay how an anthropological framing of the smallpox virus debate both enlarges the field of analysis and sheds light on the biomedical research enterprise as a cultural system. First, the premises and assumptions underlying the debate cannot be understood without a broad appreciation of the cultural history of smallpox as an epidemic disease. I use the term "cultural history" intentionally, for smallpox had no existence other than as a catastrophic human disease and was one of the great natural challenges to human cultural adaptation and resilience everywhere. The substance and significance of smallpox's cultural history are traced in texts produced by anthropologists, historians, archeologists, physicians, public health experts, and cultural demographers, a small portion of which I have drawn upon here. The smallpox virus debate is impoverished unless placed in this encompassing context. Second, anthropology is uniquely situated to interpret biomedicine and biomedical research as a cultural system (Lock 1988:3; Rhodes 1990). As "cultural insiders" and practitioners, virologists claim authority over the production and dissemination of knowledge about the smallpox virus, the maintenance and laboratory manipulations of the virus, and its ultimate survival. Virologists govern themselves professionally by adhering to the cultural norms and sanctions surrounding scientific research that require, among other things, openly sharing research results at conferences and in peer-reviewed scientific journals. The "cultural outsider" view provided by anthropology makes explicit the unstated standards, rules, norms, and values of the cultural system within which the smallpox virus debate is embedded. It thus accentuates emerging discontinuities such as those described in this essay – the challenges that advances in biotechnology present to traditional research ethics and practice, the power of the master molecule paradigm to determine what research questions are asked, and the cost and ethical implications of storing human pathogens that are extinct in the wild.

The irony of the smallpox debate cannot be overlooked. Many species of plants and animals have been eradicated by human activity, and with the expansion of humans into new habitats, the "unintended" destruction of other life forms has reached alarming proportions. Yet a community of scientists is agonizing over whether and when to destroy a captive virus that for millennia brought only misery and death to humans the world over. Most virologists, when pressed, will hesitate to even characterize a virus as a true form of life, since it is metabolically inert and requires a host in which to replicate itself. But the mere contemplation of destroying smallpox viral stocks, which could be achieved by simple autoclaving of existing specimens, raises issues central to biomedicine's view of the world, a few of which have been raised here. It transcends the immediate concerns of virologists and microbiologists and it foreshadows other dilemmas to come as biotechnology continues to advance dilemmas that, although created by biotechnology, flow outside its boundaries into other arenas of social and cultural significance.

REFERENCES

Altman, L. K. 1995. Lab Samples of Smallpox Virus Win a Last-Minute Reprieve. New York Times, January 19, 1995.

Bang, G. G. 1973. Current Concepts of the Smallpox Goddess Sitala in Parts of West Bengal. Man in India 53(1):79–104.

Baxby, D. 1977. The Origins of Vaccinia Virus. Journal of Infectious Diseases 136(3):453–455.

Baxter, P. J., A. M. Brazier, and S. E. J. Young. 1988. Is Smallpox a Hazard in Church Crypts? British Journal of Industrial Medicine 45:359–360.

Centers for Disease Control (CDC). 1979. Destruction of Variola Virus Stock – California. MWWR 28(15):172.

Centers for Disease Control (CDC). 1991. Vaccinia (Smallpox) Vaccine. Recommendations of the Immunization Practices Advisory Committee (ACIP). MMWR 40: No.RR-14.

Crosby, A. W. 1992. Summary on Population Size before and after Contact. *In* Disease and Demography in the Americas. John W. Verano and Douglas H. Ubelaker, eds. Washington, D.C.: Smithsonian Institution Press.

Crosby, A. W. 1993. Smallpox. *In* The Cambridge World History of Human Disease. Kipple, K., ed. Cambridge: Cambridge University Press.

Dixon, C. W. 1962. Smallpox. London: J. and A. Churchill, Ltd.

Dobyns, H. 1983. Their Number Become Thinned: Native American Population Dynamics in Eastern North Americ & Knoxville: University of Tennessee Press.

Dumbell, K. R. and J. G. Kapsenberg. 1982. Laboratory Investigation of Two "Whitepox" Viruses and Comparison with Two Variola Strains from Southern India. Bulletin of the World Health Organization 60:381–387.

Egnor, M. T. 1984. The Changed Mother or What the Smallpox Goddess Did When There Was No More Smallpox. Contributions to Asian Studies XVIII:24–45.

Esposito, J. J., J. H. Nakano, and J. F. Obijeski. 1985. Can Variola-like Viruses be Derived from Monkeypox Virus? An Investigation Based on DNA-Mapping. Bulletin of the World Health Organization 63(4):695–703.

Fenner, F. 1987. Can Smallpox Return? World Health Forum 8:297–304.

Fenner, F., D. A. Henderson, I. Arita, Z. Jezek, and I. D. Ladnyi. 1988. Smallpox and its Eradication. Geneva: World Health Organization.

Foege, W. H. 1979. Should the Smallpox Virus be Allowed to Survive? New England Journal of Medicine 300(12):670–672.

Henderson, D. A. 1982. The Deliberate Extinction of a Species. Proceedings of the American Philosophical Society 126(6):461–471.

Henderson, D. A. 1987. Stocks of Variola Virus. American Journal of Public Health 77(2):238–239.

Hopkins, D. R. 1983. Princes and Peasants: Smallpox in History. Chicago: University of Chicago Press.

Howard, C. 1993. The WHO Recommendation to Destroy All Smallpox Stocks Should Not be Enacted without Delay. Reviews in Medical Virology 3:133–135.

Hughes, C. C. 1963. Public Health in Non-Literate Societies. In Man's Image in Medicine and Anthropology. Iago Galdston, ed. New York: International Universities Press.

Imperato, P. J. and D. Traore. 1979. Traditional Beliefs about Smallpox and Its Treatment in the Republic of Mali. In African Therapeutic Systems. Z. A. Ademuwagun et al., eds. Waltham, Massachusetts: Crossroads Press.

Jezek, A. and F. Fenner. 1988. Human Monkeypox. New York: Karger.

Joklik, W. K., B. Moss, B. N. Fields, D. H. L. Bishop, and L. S. Sandakhchiev. 1993. Why the Smallpox Virus Stocks Should Not Be Destroyed. Science 262:1225–1226.

Keller, E. F. 1985. Reflections on Gender and Science. New Haven: Yale University Press.

Kolenda, P. 1982. Pox and the Terror of Childlessness: Images and Ideas of the Smallpox Goddess in a North Indian Village. In Mother Worship. James J. Preston, ed. Chapel Hill: University of North Carolina Press.

Lewontin, R. C., S. Rose, and L. J. Kamin. 1984. Not in Our Genes: Biology Ideology and Human Nature. New York: Pantheon Books.

Lock, M. 1988. Introduction. In Biomedicine Examined. M. Lock and D. R. Gordon, eds. Boston: Kluwer Academic Publishers.

Mahy, B. W. J., J. W. Almond, K. I. Berns, R. M. Chanock, D. K. Lvov, R. F. Pettersson, H. G. Schatzmayr, and F. Fenner. 1993. The WHO Recommendation to Destroy All Smallpox Stocks Should Be Enacted Without Delay. Reviews in Medical Virology 3:131–132.

Mahy, B. W. J., J. J. Esposito, and J. C. Venter. 1991. Sequencing the Smallpox Virus Genome: Prelude to Destruction of a Virus Species. American Society of Microbiology News 57(11):577–580.

Mahy, B. W. J. et al. 1993. The Remaining Stocks of Smallpox Virus Should Be Destroyed. Science 262:1223–1224.

Massung, R. F., L. Liu, J. Qi, J. C. Knight, T. E. Yuran, A. R. Kerlavage, J.M. Parsons, J. C. Venter, and J. J. Esposito. 1994. Analysis of the Complete Genome of Smallpox Variola Major Virums Strain Bangladesh-1975. Virology 201:215–240.

Maurice, J. 1995. Virus Wins Stay of Execution. Science 267:450.

Nicholas, R. W. 1981. The Goddess Sitala and Epidemic Smallpox in Bengal. Journal of Asian Studies XLI (1):21–43.

Quinn, F. 1979. How Traditional Dahomian Society Interpreted Smallpox. *In* African Therapeutic Systems. Z. A. Ademuwagun et al., eds. Waitham, Massachusetts: Crossroads Press.

Rhodes, L. 1990. Studying Biomedicine as a Cultural System. *In* Medical Anthropology: A Handbook of Theory and Method. T. Johnson and C. Sargent, eds. Westport, Connecticut: Greenwood Press.

Roberts, L. 1989. Disease and Death in the New World. Science 246:1245–1247.

Siebert, C. 1994. Smallpox is Dead. Long Live Smallpox. New York Times Magazine, August 21, Pp. 30–37.

Stone, R. 1994. Smallpox is Dead. Long Live Smallpox. New York Times Magazine. August 21, 1994, pp. 30–37.

Szpir, M. 1993. No Stock in Smallpox Virus. American Scientist 81:526–527.

Wadley, S. S. 1980. Sitala: The Cool One. Asian Folklore Studies 1:33–62.

White, D. O. and F. Fenner. 1986. Medical Virology. Third edition. New York: Academic Press, Inc.

World Health Organization (WHO). 1994. Scene is Set for Destruction of Smallpox Virus. WHO Office of Information. Press Release WHO/54, 9 September 1994.

Zuckerman, A. J. 1984. Paleontology of Smallpox. The Lancet V II. for 1984, No. 8417/8, December 22/29.

CHAPTER 5

Culture and the Global Resurgence of Malaria

Peter J. Brown

INTRODUCTION: EMERGING INFECTIONS AND FEAR

Some new diseases cause strong social reactions of fear – like ebola hemorrhagic fever and AIDS. Some old diseases – like cholera and plague – recently thought controlled and relegated to the domain of historians, have reappeared, bringing back age-old fears of contagion and the diseased "other." Pessimistic visions of the future predict the "coming plagues" and the end of the current antibiotic era. In spring 1995 an outbreak of deaths from ebola virus in a remote part of Africa brought a considerable amount of fear to the United States and Europe. Ebola is fearsome because it is so unknown, so virulent and so dramatic, striking adults in previously good health. Emerging and resurgent infectious diseases are fearsome because they highlight the limits of our advanced biomedical technology. Without the protections of biomedicine, these diseases threaten the health of people in wealthy nations like the U.S.

Historical change is not a uniform process. The historical decline of overall mortality in Europe and the U.S. (known as the demographic transition) has been shown to involve a change in causes of mortality from infectious to chronic disease (McKeown 1979; Omran 1971). These transformations, in turn, appear linked to dramatic changes in fertility and have been used as models for improving health worldwide (Cleland and Hill 1991). But for most of the world still living in extreme poverty the epidemiological transition has never occurred; there has not been much of an antibiotic era to end. Indeed, the undeniable evolution of resistant strains of old diseases like malaria and tuberculosis is short-circuiting the standard modernist discussion of health and development.

The current public health concern with emerging and resurgent infectious diseases must be understood in the modern global context. Both rich and poor nations now find themselves in what the historian McNeill has called a "single disease pool" (McNeill 1976). Much of the interest (and funding) in international health and research on the changing epidemiology of infectious diseases has been generated because these are a direct threat to the health of people in the affluent developed world (Lederberg 1992).

The goal of this chapter is to offer a simple and specific model of culture that can be used in the generation of hypotheses about the role of human behavior in improving or exacerbating health problems. In this paper, I will use a historical lens to show how much of the scientific and political discussion about emerging and resurgent infections has emphasized the disease pathogens, has deemphasized the role of human behavior in creating these new epidemiological trends, and has underemphasized human empowerment to improve health conditions. This is the result, I think, of neglecting the political-economic dimensions of the relationship between culture and disease.

This paper will focus on malaria for three reasons: first, and most important, malaria continues to be an enormous and intractable health problem; second, world public health policy has changed significantly in recent history, particularly with the reconfiguration of World Health Organization policy from malaria eradication to control; and finally, the resurgence of malaria represents a significant challenge to social scientists and is associated with a recent call for a scientific paradigm shift in malaria research.

THE CURRENT MALARIA PROBLEM

During the 1980s and 1990s, the problem of malaria throughout the world has been getting worse. Malaria prevalence has increased and the geographical range of the disease, particularly its chloroquine-resistant strains, has expanded. Current United Nations statistics indicate that malaria is the only major disease, other than AIDS, that has been steadily spreading in the 1980s and 1990s (Liisberg 1991; Brown 1992). This current situation is very disturbing for two reasons. First, this resurgence reverses the historical trend of decreasing malaria morbidity and mortality over the past fifty years, especially after the global malaria eradication effort in the late 1950s and 1960s. Second, the current technological and political-economic contexts throughout the world make the future of malaria control look particularly grim.

The poor prognosis is generally linked to the twin problems of resistance – anopheline mosquito resistance to insecticides and plasmodium parasite resistance to chloroquine. Mosquito resistance to insecticides means that there are fewer (and more expensive) options available for malaria vector abatement and control. This development is the result of evolution, since public health and agricultural uses of insecticides created an environment that resulted in the natural selection of genetic strains of mosquitoes unaffected by the toxins. Insecticide resistance has led to an "arms race" between chemical weapons of mosquito control and genetic adaptation of the mosquitoes themselves. Chloroquine resistance refers to the product of a similar evolutionary process where a genetic strain of malaria parasite that is able to circumvent the chemoprophylactic and therapeutic actions of the predominant antimalarial drug of the postwar period has been selected for and has consequently expanded its geographic distribution throughout the world. Chloroquine resistance means that it is more difficult, less reliable and more expensive to prevent or treat malaria. To an extent, chloroquine resistance is an important concern for international travelers, maybe even more so than for people living in endemic areas, because travelers expect to have the resources to prevent, or at least treat, malaria.

To focus attention on these problems, the World Health Organization (WHO) held a global summit on malaria in 1992 (Brown 1992). The public discussions surrounding this conference were remarkably different from similar summits in the past. The negative tone, to be sure, reflects the serious and growing problems of resistance and the fact that there are no clear technological solutions to them. In this regard, much hope has been pinned to the development of a malaria vaccine, the imminent arrival of which was announced two decades ago. In the meantime, the public health community has been obliged to keep "waiting for the vaccine": This is, in fact, the title of a recent collection on malaria (Targett 1991) that is distressingly reminiscent of Beckett's existentialist play "Waiting for Godot," in which the long awaited title character never arrives. An equally important factor in the negative tone of the last malaria summit is the effect of worldwide economic difficulties, often linked to World Bank policies of structural adjustment, that make it less than financially feasible for developing countries in malarial zones to continue past levels of financial support for anti-malaria efforts (Bello 1994). For a variety of historical reasons discussed below, malaria has lost its one-time status as a special target for international health and development funds.

The new and negative tone of the 1992 summit is remarkably different from the optimistic tenor of earlier WHO meetings on malaria – especially in the heady days of the global eradication campaign from 1955 to 1972 (Brown 1992). Gone is the spirit of progress, of technological solutions, of difficulties and triumph from the field. Gone is an emphasis on human agency and the notion that with sufficient effort and expertise, malaria would become merely a disease of the past, like smallpox. In contrast, the current discussions of malaria resurgence tend to place the disease in the active voice and thereby depict humans as passive victims. In the new discourse the emphasis is on the craftiness of the parasite which has become immune to medicines and on the dangerous spread of anopheline mosquitoes, which have become invincible to insecticide weapons. In short, the resurgence of malaria has been generally blamed on the biology of the "bugs."

This paper focuses on *cultural* factors in the current resurgence of malaria. I will use the holistic conception of culture to remind us that both insecticide resistance and chloroquine resistance are largely the products of, and reactions to, human activities like agricultural practices or migration. It is also important to remind ourselves that the continuation of brutal poverty and hunger in much of the world is undoubtedly linked to large numbers of unnecessary deaths from malaria. Finally, I want to suggest that another kind of resistance – ideological resistance – is playing a role in the current resurgence of malaria. I will argue that the public health community became trapped in the military metaphors of the postwar eradication era, and when victory became impossible (symbolized by a redefined global strategy from eradication to control), ministries of health throughout the world abandoned, or at least neglected, anti-malaria activities. At the same time, vertically organized, single-disease control programs did not fit the policies of integrated services and community participation characterized by the Primary Health Care (PHC) movement.

THE CONCEPT OF CULTURE

Culture is the single most important "orienting concept" in anthropology (Homans 1967), and an ironic consequence of its centrality is the fact that its definition is not always explicit. The concept of culture refers to learned patterns of thought and behavior characteristic of a social group. This conceptualization is extremely broad, since it incorporates material factors – like economic systems and patterns of socio-economic organization – as well as important non-material factors in human activities – like ideas, beliefs, and values. To a large extent, culture provides the behavioral and interpretive "software" that people use to organize their experiences and make them meaningful. Culture provides both the habitual behaviors and the common sense ideas and values that people use on a daily basis; as such, cultural knowledge and expectations are "taken for granted" from the actor's point of view. Anthropological analyses contend that culturally coded behaviors and beliefs become more visible and apparent when seen in a cross-cultural comparative framework.

Because cultures are interdependent and patterned systems, a change in one part of a culture will likely result in corresponding changes in other parts. As such, cultural systems are never static; they always change (albeit at inconsistent rates) over historical or evolutionary time. Cultural change can occur because of invention or, much more commonly, the borrowing of cultural traits from other groups (not always voluntarily). Anthropologists argue that the direction of cultural change is predicated on the fact that, in general, cultural patterns of behavior and thought have been *adaptive* mechanisms that improve the likelihood of survival and reproduction. Therefore, cultures tend to be "in fit" with their ecological context (which, in fact, might be significantly shaped by cultural behaviors). When cultural patterns are not adaptive, for example, when they exacerbate problems of disease morbidity and mortality, it is important to explain why this is the case (Edgerton 1992). An important factor for understanding maladaptive cultural change, particularly in complex societies divided by social class and ethnicity, is that a change that may be beneficial for some people may be maladaptive for others. As such, political power and access to resources are important processes and determinants of culture change, and it becomes important to answer the question of who benefits from a particular change – and who loses.

The materialist model of culture developed by Harris (1979) divides culture into three interdependent layers: economy, social organization, and ideology. The material foundation of a cultural system is the economic mode of production, which includes the technology and the population size that the productive economy allows and requires. While all levels of a cultural system are constrained by ecological context, it is this first level that has the most intimate connection to the ecology. Contingent on the first layer is the pattern of social organization, including a variety of social variables like socioeconomic stratification and political power. The third layer, contingent on the social structure, is the ideology or belief system, including ideas, values and beliefs, both sacred and secular. Most anthropologists believe that ideology is an extremely important part of culture, in part because it rationalizes and reinforces the economy and social structure. Ideology enables people to make sense of their world and to share their common world view which is communicated through symbols. A culture is an integrated system; a change in one part causes changes in other layers. This materialist model, to be used in this analysis of malaria, specifies the direction of causation in cultural change from the economy to the social structure to the ideology.

This broad concept of culture has important implications for understanding historical change in arenas like international health policy. This is because western institutions, like international health agencies, have their own cultures characterized by particular economic constraints, social organizations and belief systems (Justice 1986). The cultural beliefs of the international health community are reflected not only in the behaviors and policies of the agencies, but in their discourse as well. Similarly, the interactive and holistic concept of culture has value in understanding the ebb and flow of malaria rates. The global resurgence of malaria is not merely due to biological resistance in the parasite and its mosquito vector, but more importantly results from human cultural practices in all three levels of the model described above. To a large extent, cultural practices determine the disease ecology of a population (Brown and Inhorn 1990). While economic variables that have an effect on ecology probably have the most direct influence on disease ecology, it is important to recognize that cultural activities linked to all three levels can influence the social epidemiological distribution of a disease.

HISTORICAL BACKGROUND: THE RISE AND FALL AND RISE OF MALARIA

Malaria is a very old disease – much older than the human species. Plasmodium species infect a wide variety of animals and there is much evidence that the pathogen has co-evolved with particular mosquito vectors. For example, in colder climates where mosquitoes cannot breed year-round, *Plasmodium vivax* triggers malaria relapses at the beginning of the warm season to re-infect the new generation of disease vectors (Bruce-Chwatt 1980). In the course of human cultural evolution, however, malaria became widespread only after the invention of agriculture some ten thousand years ago. The landmark research of Livingstone (Livingstone 1958) demonstrated how in West Africa during the Iron Age, people transformed their ecology through slash and burn horticulture; consequently, they increased the density of *Anopheles gambiae* mosquitoes, which subsequently turned to humans as the primary source of blood feasts, thereby spreading malaria. In other words, human cultural evolution, in the form of a new economic system, changed the disease ecology and increased the pace of genetic evolution. The disease became such an important cause of death – as it still is today – that it was responsible for the evolution of elevated gene frequencies for the sickle-cell trait and the duffy negative antigen (Durham 1991).

There are many historical accounts of malaria and the history of malaria eradication efforts (Harrison 1978; Oaks, Mitchell et al. 1991; Najera-Morrondo 1991; Key 1991). My purpose here is to provide an outline of the historical changes in cultural factors affecting malaria and its control. The best documented case about the history of malaria is in Europe, particularly Italy, partly because of the early work by Jones (1908) and Celli (1933), and partly because of the superb historical work of Bruce-Chwatt and DeZulueta (1980) on the progress and success of malaria eradication in this zone. More recently, the work of Litsios (1996) has carefully documented the changing malaria policies of international health agencies.

In Italy, malaria was thought to have been caused by bad air that exuded from swamps in the form of *miasma*. Throughout Europe there was no standardization of the nosological classification of malaria, however, until the eighteenth century; before that, "malaria" was called by a variety of local names, like *ague* in Britain or *intemperie sarda* on the island of Sardinia. Most of Europe, particularly the southern zones, was characterized by a temporal pattern of periodic fevers during the late summer and early fall, linked to the seasonal life cycle of anophelines in temperate climates. A minority of areas, like the Andalusian plains of Spain, were affected by sporadic epidemics of malaria (Hackett 1937). Later it was recognized that these zones were characterized by "anophelism without malaria." Although malaria is often thought of as a so-called "tropical" disease typical of a colonial holding, it was historically found as far north as Siberia and Korea, and was a major problem in the Upper Mississippi Valley in American pioneer days (Ackerknecht 1945; Harrison 1978). In endemic malarial zones in Europe, malaria was commonly recognized as having costs in diminished economic production.

In 1639, Jesuit missionaries brought back to Europe chincona bark from South America, where it was a traditional treatment for fevers. Use of the drug in its bark form met a mixed reception, in part because of serious problems in quality and therapeutic consistency, and in part because it was expensive and associated with the religious order (Duran-Reynals 1946). Nevertheless, malaria treatment with chincona represented an early success in scientific medicine. After 1820 when the alkaloid quinine was identified as the active ingredient in the "Jesuit's bark," use of the drug for malaria treatment became widespread. The nineteenth-century discoveries of the etiology of malaria form a fascinating chapter in the history of science, as recently described by Desowitz (1991). In 1880, Laveran, a French colonial military officer, first identified live parasites in blood taken from a feverish soldier in Algeria. In 1898, Italian malariologists led by Grassi documented the transmission of human malaria in anopheles mosquitoes (Cozzani 1972). Probably because they published in Italian, these scientists did not receive proper scientific credit for this major discovery. Rather, in 1902, Sir Ronald Ross received the Nobel Prize for showing that culex mosquitoes transmitted malaria in birds.

The discovery of the anopheline etiology of malaria opened up the possibility of preventing the disease. Before the development of chemical insecticides in the 1930s, malaria prevention emphasized relatively expensive ecological changes like swamp drainage or improvement of housing with screens (Celli 1933; Hackett 1937). Land reclamation schemes made sense because of cultural beliefs that malaria was, in essence, a disease of rural poverty and therefore required interventions of agricultural development. Before DDT, anti-mosquito efforts for malaria reduction used arsenic-based larvicides like Paris Green or the widespread (but ineffective) fumigations with the same toxins. In addition, the common use of quinine in some areas like Italy around the turn of the century resulted in impressive decreases in malaria mortality, although such chemotherapeutic campaigns had little effect on total prevalence.

It is important to recognize that in the late nineteenth century malaria spontaneously disappeared from Northern Europe. In an unrecognized classic of human ecological research, *Malaria in Europe: An Ecological Study*, Hackett (1937) described this spontaneous decline (the spread of anophelism without malaria) in terms of changing agricultural crop choices (to sugar beets) and housing patterns (keeping cows in the basement), resulting in a decline in the density of anthropophilic anopheline populations and an increase in zoophilic mosquitoes. Hackett's sensitive use of human ecological reasoning was impressive (and in fact presaged new malariological approaches of the 1990s), but this kind of approach had little or no role after World War II, during the heyday of global eradication efforts.

Two technological discoveries by Americans during World War II completely changed the character of malariology and international health itself. Both DDT and chloroquine were developed as part of the U.S. war effort, due to the major role malaria played in the war (especially in the Pacific theater after the Japanese invasion of the Philippines effectively stopped quinine from reaching American markets). The scientific search for chloroquine represents one of the most concerted and labor-intensive scientific projects in history (Coatney 1963). The predominance of military metaphors for anti-malaria efforts, and military patterns of social organization in anti-malaria programs, clearly fit with the predominant cultural models of the time (The military development model of anti-malaria technology continues today through basic scientific work for the development of a vaccine.).

Armed with the new weapon of DDT, malariologists began to talk about the eradication of their foe. After success in Panama and Brazil and an expensive failure-turned-success pilot project in Sardinia, the international health community argued that malaria eradication using residual insecticides was technically feasible. More importantly, they argued that time was of the essence, because the mosquito vectors ultimately would become resistant to the weapon of DDT. It was argued that a substantial but time-limited investment in the total elimination of malaria would be cost effective because it would remove an age-old obstacle to economic development and therefore pay dividends in perpetuity (Pampana 1963).

The arguments were convincing, and in 1955 at the eighth World Health Congress, a Global Program for the eradication of malaria was announced. The global eradication campaign was to take eight years beginning in 1958 and to cost about 25 cents per year per person (about $519 million over the first five years) (Oaks et al. 1991). Eradication campaigns based on the use of insecticides and larvicides were begun in all regions of the world, except sub-Saharan Africa. Throughout the 1960s malaria eradication campaigns resulted in impressive declines in malaria morbidity. But there were also an incredible number of technical and administrative problems that plagued these programs and made the goal of eradication seem to be more and more illusory. The eradication plans had almost no provision for scientific research; it was assumed that technical solutions were already at hand. Consequently, when difficulties arose due to either anopheline variations or ecology, scientific answers were most often not available. In fact, Desowitz reports that as a public health graduate student in the 1960s, he was advised *not* to take an interest in malaria, because there was no future in that disease (1991).

Was the goal of global malaria eradication simply a hype – a sales gimmick for funding agencies and ministries of health? Given the incredible ecological complexity and diversity of the disease, wasn't eradication an impossible dream? Certainly, the historical failure of malaria eradication (in all WHO regional zones except Europe) must be seen in light of the remarkable success of the smallpox eradication campaign (described in Chapter 4 of this volume), particularly because the global campaigns overlapped. In retrospect, it seems clear that some of the biological characteristics of the smallpox virus (no vector, vaccination available, clear symptomology) made global eradication more feasible than malaria eradication. At the time, it was widely recognized that malaria eradication was more ambitious and had more technical barriers to overcome. But, perhaps more importantly, in the culture of the time it was believed that there were indeed technical solutions to all problems that might be encountered.

Interestingly, the "global" malaria eradication campaign never really developed any plan for the most malarious continent – Africa. WHO expert committees debated this issue at length, since a temporary cessation of malaria transmission in endemic areas would mean that adults would lose their acquired immunities to malaria, and a later re-introduction of malaria would result in epidemics and high mortalities. They argued that unless there was a solid commitment of economic funds and political will to sustained anti-malaria efforts, it was unwise, and even immoral, to design an eradication intervention. During the same time, however, more limited malaria control efforts in parts of Africa using residual insecticides had significant impact, leading to a decrease in overall malaria prevalence, especially in urban areas (Packard 1986).

In 1969, the WHO revised its malaria strategy and encouraged control in places where eradication was not feasible. The strategy of control was not time-limited but was aimed at the decrease and eventual elimination of unnecessary malaria mortality and then morbidity.

The strategy of malaria control was somewhat more difficult to understand and a lot more difficult for funding agencies and ministries of health to get excited about. In the mid-1970s, funds for malaria control activities were drying up. DDT was banned in the U.S., and by 1982 its production was stopped altogether. After the 1978 Alma Ata conference on Primary Health Care, the responsibility for malaria control activities in many countries was shifted away from technical experts to basic health care workers (Litsios 1996; Justice 1986).

The global resurgence of malaria is not something that suddenly happened in the 1980s and 1990s. The resurgence was predicted at the beginnings of the eradication campaign. In fact, the idea that there was a historical and time-limited opportunity to "once and for all" defeat malaria because of the effective tools of DDT and chloroquine was an important part of the selling of the eradication concept within the scientific community. Despite enormous decreases in malaria at the beginning of national malaria eradication campaigns in regions like South Asia, malaria prevalence has been on the rise for the past fifteen years. During the same period, funding for malaria control activities and training has been shrinking (Sharma 1986). During the 1980s, USAID was the primary supporter of scientific research on malaria and over half of that financial support was earmarked for the development of a malaria vaccine. Even with the vaccine research, only about 5 percent of USAID's annual expenditures for health programs were aimed at malaria (Desowitz 1991).

In hindsight, it is clear that the 1980s represent the decade of the spread of plasmodium resistance to chloroquine and anopheline resistance to DDT and other insecticides. It is also clear that the major reasons for this changing epidemiological situation during the 1980s were not only the breakdowns in massive public health programs for malaria, but other more mundane human cultural activities.

THREE LEVELS OF CULTURE IN MALARIA RESURGENCE

All three levels of cultural systems described earlier have played a role in the historic resurgence of malaria. The cultures involved include both the "native" cultures of the areas with endemic malaria (mostly in the developing world), but also the cultures of the donor countries and the international health organizations themselves. Since both types of cultures are human constructions, the emphasis here is on recognizing the role of both conscious and unconscious patterns of thought and behavior (and funding) that have had epidemiological repercussions.

Although the role of human behavior in the transmission and the resurgence of malaria is so important, the literature on this topic is rather limited. The WHO/TDR bibliography on behavioral, social and economic aspects of malaria and its control (Sotiroff-Junker 1978) is now outdated, although there have been some social science collections on malaria since (Wessen 1986; Gomes 1993; Nakajima 1991). Moreover, some of the sociocultural and behavioral research is not well designed, and little of it has had practical implications for malaria control programs. While these facts have been recognized by Dunn (1979), the problem has been succinctly summarized by Prothero, a leader in this area of research:

> Of the three related elements in human malaria (parasite, vector and human being) the third has received insufficient attention, time and competence in its study. Levels of generalization are accepted concerning the human element which would not be tolerated in respect to the parasite and vector (Prothero cited in Rajagopalan 1986).

It is my contention that some of these difficulties result from the lack of an overarching paradigm of how human behavior and culture are patterned. The materialist model of culture can be helpful in this regard.

Economic and Demographic Variables

Economic production systems have an important impact on ecology. Production systems, particularly those related to agriculture, are the primary mechanisms by which people have changed the face of the earth. Agricultural practices have been implicated in the historic spread of malaria, and they play a central role in its resurgence today (Wessen 1972). Irrigation has been a common mechanism for the intensification of agriculture, and it has often resulted in increased opportunities for mosquito breeding and increased malaria prevalence. A good example of this has been the history of agriculture and malaria in the Gezira scheme of Sudan (Gruenbaum 1983) as well as in Swaziland (Packard 1986). The resurgence in both of these cases occurred without the appearance of chloroquine resistance in the malaria parasite or insecticide resistance of the vectors.

Of particular note is the modern use of pesticides in agriculture. Chapin and Wasserstrom (1981, 1983) have presented some convincing evidence that the over-use of pesticides in cotton production in India and Central America has created an ecological context in which many insects, including anopheline mosquitoes, have become insecticide resistant. This analysis met serious objections from malariologists like Bruce-Chwatt and Sharma (Sharma 1986). Chapin and Wasserstrom's argument is that the resurgence of malaria may be related to poorly designed and administered DDT spray campaigns – for example, in India where local DDT production was unreliable and sufficient supplies were not available. Nevertheless, the evolution of insecticide resistance requires exposure to insecticides. To my knowledge, there is no evidence from any place in the world that demonstrates that insecticide resistance in malaria vectors is the result of public health activities. The amount of insecticide used in malaria eradication and control is extremely small compared to the amount of pesticides used in agriculture. In general, the "green revolution" varieties of cereal crops require more pesticides than older varieties. On the other hand, farmers feel forced to use insecticides to minimize crop loss and, more importantly, to minimize insect damage that lowers the market value of the product. After all, consumers demand "perfect" fruits and vegetables, and it is only possible to grow them in sufficient quantities using chemicals. Chapin and Wasserstrom advocate the use of "integrated pest management" for addressing these problems, but there is no evidence that such a solution is feasible given market demands.

The evolution of insecticide resistance represents an increasing expense to anti-malaria programs. Not only has it required an escalation of insecticides used (and newer insecticides are much more expensive than the old DDT), but it has also set the ecological stage for increased loss of life due to malaria and other vector-borne diseases. In other words, the use of newer insecticides is part of an "arms war" between the mosquitoes and people; as older weapons become less effective and the supply of new weapons becomes less dependable, the threat of becoming defenseless against a new malaria strain or vector becomes more costly.

Literature about the economic costs of malaria emphasizes the hidden costs of endemic malaria making an area uninhabitable or inaccessible for agricultural production. There is little or no evidence that this is the case, at least in the context of high population pressure and low economic opportunity. High risk of contracting malaria, for example, does not slow gold mining in holoendemic areas of the Amazon (Sawyer 1993), nor does it stop the establishment of new farms in Paraguay (Conly 1975); the risk of malaria simply adds to the overall personal costs of seeking a livelihood. In this regard, Brown has developed a contrast between the microparasitic demands of endemic malaria and the macroparasitic demands of traditional labor contracts in Sardinia (Brown 1987). The high risk of malaria, however, can lead to economic strategies involving seasonal migrations, allowing use of malarious areas while families are maintained at another location. A number of studies in Thailand (Sighanetra-Renard 1993), Colombia (Sevilla-Casas 1993), and Africa (Prothero 1965) have documented the role of such population movements in spreading or re-introducing malaria to an area. Labor migration thus plays a significant role in linking previously discrete epidemiological zones.

Road-building is a common aspect of modernization that can also reduce ecological isolation and has been implicated in the spread of malaria. In situations such as the Highlands highway in Papua New Guinea or the various trans-Amazon highways, anopheline vectors have been shown to spread, sometimes by exploiting the ecological niche of the disturbed zone of the highway itself, and sometimes by being moved long distances by truck (Wessen 1972). In general, modern transportation, especially jet travel, has made the age-old idea of epidemiological borders obsolete (Bruce-Chwatt 1979).

Land utilization patterns are also implicated in urban malaria. For example, recent outbreaks on the island zones in greater Bombay appear to be related to continuation of major building projects and poor control of ground water, despite existing legislation that requires ground water control at construction sites (Kamat 1996).

Social Factors

There has been little written about social factors in the modern resurgence of malaria. This is because the focus of public health, and malariology in particular, has been narrowly fixed on the parasite and the mosquito vector. The bigger picture has been neglected – namely, that increased rates of malaria *morbidity*, although directly influenced by changes in the parasite and vector, are more directly caused by human behaviors. Those behaviors are both related to individual culturally coded patterns and larger-scale sociological phenomena including the political-economic level. At the same time, higher levels of malaria disease and *mortality* are linked to lack of access to sufficient medical care and appropriate anti-malaria medication. Access to these resources is linked to social stratification, both within and between countries. By telling the individual story of one pregnant woman with malaria, Desowitz (1991) does an excellent job emphasizing the human dimensions of suffering from malaria and the fundamental fact that most malaria-related deaths throughout the world could be avoided if people had enough economic resources and access to sufficient medical care for adequate treatment of severe cases. Today, as in the recent past, most malaria deaths are unnecessary. Similarly, malaria mortality fits into a larger infectious disease and malnutrition matrix that is predominantly characterized by conditions of poverty.

In this regard it can be argued that a major reason for the resurgence of malaria is the worsening problem of poverty throughout the world. Increasing poverty is the result of increased social stratification both within and between nations. As such, the phenomenon of poverty is of masked by aggregate macroeconomic statistics like GNP, often used in World Bank studies to deny the worsening economic situation and its social and medical repercussions (O'Rourke 1994). During the 1960s and 1970s, on a global scale, there was indeed a significant decrease in the number of people throughout the world living in conditions of abject poverty; for example, in Latin America the proportion of families living below the poverty line decreased from 51 to 40 percent between 1960 and 1970 (Bello 1994). Bello (1994) has argued that much of this economic growth reflected the policies of liberalism and containment resulting in significant World Bank investment in Third World countries during this period. But the situation has changed remarkably in the past fifteen years. Largely because of the "debt crises" of the 1980s and the World Bank policies of structural adjustment loans, the conditions of the rural poor in the developing world have become worse and worse. Structural adjustment loans – new borrowing to pay the debt on old loans, but contingent on the imposition of austerity measures in the domestic economy – have clearly added to the misery of the poor. There is little evidence, however, that these policies hurt the elites of developing countries. As Desjarlais and colleagues point out:

> Given that one-fifth of the world's population – an estimated one billion people – lives in abject poverty, the current global economic slowdown, which is projected to continue, bodes ill ... Though the farms of Asia, Africa, and Latin America produce more than half of the grain harvested in the world, at least half a billion people in those regions lack enough food to eat, and thus live with chronic energy deficiencies ... About 15 million people die each year of hunger, and malnutrition affects the lives of 24% of the global population each day (Desjarlais et al. 1995:19).

Increased social stratification and poverty exacerbate the problems of malaria and its associated mortality in four ways. First, they mean that large portions of the world's population live in inadequate housing where they get no protection from anophelines. In fact, substandard housing provides ideal resting places for anthropophilic anopheline vectors (Oaks et al. 1991). Second, the undernutrition associated with poverty plays a major role in malaria mortality, especially in children. Third, poor sanitation and drainage control in poor areas increases anopheline densities. This is especially the case in Third-World urban areas where malaria was once thought to be largely controlled. The expansion of urban malaria is directly linked to poor living conditions. Finally, poverty means that people do not have adequate health care. They do not have sufficient resources to access anti-malarial drugs, or there is a tendency to use inadequate doses (Foster 1991). Undertreatment of malaria with a small and limited course of chloroquine is caused by the lack of economic resources of malaria victims and not simply the lack of appropriate medical advice. These poverty-related medical practices play a significant role in the evolution and spread of chloroquine-resistant strains of plasmodium.

The relationship between poor health and economic underdevelopment is a common theme in International Public Health, usually to justify disease control as an "economic investment in health" (Bryant 1969). There is a large literature on this topic, but there is little or no solid evidence to demonstrate that malaria causes poverty. On the other hand, it seems clear that in both historical and contemporary contexts, poverty plays a major role in increasing malaria – and especially malaria mortality (Packard 1996).

Ideological Factors

A centrally important part of culture, ideology, also plays a role in the modern resurgence of malaria because of its influence on changing health policies. Ideologies about health are communicated through symbols and metaphors used in discourse. There has been a major change in the way that malaria is discussed in the 1990s as compared to the postwar era of eradication. This change in metaphors and discourse style is not a trivial matter, because it is closely linked to the decline in public funding for anti-malaria efforts. The collapse of ongoing anti-malaria public health programs consequently plays an important role in resurgence (Sharma 1986). The change in discourse and the choice of symbolic depictions of anti-malaria efforts is not a direct cause, but rather a reflection, of changing ideas of policy makers in the international health community.

In the postwar heyday of malaria eradication, military metaphors predominated in the discourse on malaria. Military concepts and terms included: "campaigns," "strategies," the "weapon" of DDT, the "enemy" of malaria, and constant monitoring of progress in "wiping out" the enemy. The final stages of an eradication campaign were called "mopping up" exercises. The key to success in this war against malaria was organization, particularly the hierarchical or vertical chain of command that has characterized all central disease control operations (Pampana 1963; Bruce-Chwatt 1980). Although the key to victory is seen in the logical and systematic use of superior weapons by a well-managed and disciplined army of malaria eradication workers, the explanation of defeat is not simply the lack of those features. All competitions, including wars, are lost because the "enemy" was better at the game.

The military ideology in malaria control has been predominantly entomological, and at the beginning of the eradication era, work was almost exclusively aimed at the mosquito vector. Because residual insecticides were the weapon of choice, mosquitoes became the primary enemy. An important function of the military metaphor was to convince funding agencies, particularly the WHO, of the necessity and "winability" of the war against this terrible enemy (Bruce-Chwatt 1979).

In the eradication days, the discourse on the evil enemy of malaria was therefore surrounded by hyperbole, and the anticipated benefits of malaria eradication were over-sold. But economic development did not "naturally" follow the demise of malaria in previous endemic areas like Sardinia and Sri Lanka. This problem has been studied by a variety of social scientists (Conly 1975; Brown 1986; Packard 1996; Wessen 1986; Sub-Saharan Africa Program 1991).

The military metaphor was a natural one because malaria had been such a serious problem in the colonial armed forces stationed overseas (Curtin 1989). The fight against malaria in the colonies, as described by Harrison (1978), was largely the responsibility of military authorities, and the development of new anti-malaria technologies was accomplished by military researchers from nonmalarial countries like the U.S. and Britain. Malaria control had played a key role in the allied victory in the second world war, a conflict in which hospitalizations due to parasitic disease outnumbered battle casualties more than three-to-one in both southern Europe and the Pacific (Oaks et al. 1991).

The military metaphor was also a key rhetorical devise for convincing the ministries of health from all over the world to make malaria eradication a high priority for the WHO from 1955 to 1957. It was argued that the time to launch the all-out attack on the enemy of malaria was *immediately*, while the forces of health had superior weapons of insecticide and medicine. There was a warning that if ministries of health waited too long, or if there was insufficient political will to achieve total victory, the enemy would learn to resist the weapons of DDT and chloroquine. These metaphors and this argument were effective, and malaria eradication became one of the highest priorities of the WHO countries from 1957 though the 1970s. The central symbolic theme was that the war against malaria could be won; eradication was possible even if the enemy was great.

But the military metaphor was also a trap. The negative aspect of using the military metaphor was not clearly recognized until 1972 when, after considerable debate, WHO redefined the goal of eradication to one of control for some areas of the world. This redefinition signaled a practical realization that eradication was neither a feasible nor prudent goal for some endemic areas and that progress had to be measured against reasonable standards of first reducing malaria mortality, then morbidity, and finally total eradication. This redefinition meant something else for people who had been previously convinced by the military metaphor. It meant defeat, or at least a massive retreat. It was a declaration that the "War on Malaria" could not be won in the foreseeable future and that funding for malaria control would be chronic and continual rather than a one-time, all-out battle. It should also be noted that in the United States, this corresponded to a time of cultural and political change when the military was not revered and there was widespread public discourse, mostly surrounding the Vietnam war, that not every war was "winnable."

Ideological resistance occurred when people, particularly ministries of health, who had been stuck in the military metaphors for understanding malaria, faced the redefinition of malaria control strategies. They saw defeat, and withdrew attention and funding for anti-malaria activities. Within the international health community, malaria became a low prestige disease, associated with an inglorious past. It should be noted that the decline in funding and attention to malaria control activities during the seventies also corresponded to the rise of the Primary Health Care model in international health. Primary Health Care, as originally envisioned, was based on the completely different metaphor of community participation and "health for the people," and its ideology viewed the vertical organization of disease eradication programs as neocolonial anachronisms (Mull 1990). Because PHC activities included both prevention and the delivery of basic health services, malaria control activities could be subsumed under the community-based programs. This strategy makes logical sense – in particular, the presumptive treatment of childhood fevers with anti-malarials was very effective in reaching the first goal of decreasing malaria mortality (and overall child mortality) in hyperendemic areas. But for malariologists of the old school – veterans of the global eradication war – the fact that anti-malaria activities were subsumed under the clinical programs of PHC seemed like a form of humiliation. In these ways, malariology and anti-malaria public health activities have significantly declined in prestige, policy importance, and most importantly, public health funding.

SUMMARY

The modern global resurgence of malaria cannot be understood as the result of actions or activities of crafty bugs – whether plasmodium or anopheline mosquitoes. Biological changes in the bugs of malaria are largely their response to human actions. Those actions have changed the ecological context in which the disease and its vectors have continued to evolve. These human activities are *cultural*; they involve learned patterns of thought and behavior that have wide influence on the actions of both individuals and groups.

There is an advantage to a broad view of culture in which the material underpinnings of agricultural production and population play an important role in epidemiological change. Moreover, previous discussions of the resurgence of malaria have ignored a basic observation that poverty – especially rural poverty and childhood undernutrition – plays a central role in the continuation of high mortality rates from this disease. Finally, adding to the list of resistance associated with the resurgence of malaria, is the *ideological resistance* that characterized the reaction to the entrapment in the military metaphors of the eradication epoch. Ideological resistance has played a role in the precipitous declines in funding for anti-malaria activities.

There is no denying that the current outlook for malaria control is grim. There are no new technologies on the horizon that could give humans the upper hand again in a war against malaria. But this fact misses the point. The political and public health discourse should not be about "victory" against the disease, but rather it should be about preventing unnecessary human suffering and death. The recent Institute of Medicine report on emerging infections described in Chapter 1 is a landmark volume in the history of malaria research, and it contains some encouraging news for anthropologists interested in malaria research. The volume is important not only as an elegant state-of-the-art compendium, but also for emphasizing three facts: the ecological variations (paradigms) of malaria transmission; the importance of the distinction between malaria infection and disease in the development of policy and programs; and finally, the importance of social and behavioral factors – on what this paper has called cultural factors – in malaria transmission.

REFERENCES

Ackerknecht, E. 1945. Malaria in the Upper Mississippi Valley, 1760–1900. New York: Arno Press.

Basch, P. F. 1990. Textbook of International Health. New York: Oxford University Press.

Bello, W. 1994. Dark Victory: The United States, Structural Adjustment, and Global Poverty. London: Pluto Press (in association with Institute for Food and Development Policy).

Brown, P. 1992a. Gloomy Prognosis for Malaria 'Summit'. New Scientist 136:10.

Brown, P. 1992b. Malaria Summit Demands Plans Before Cash. New Scientist 136:4.

Brown, P. 1992c. The Return of the Big Killer. New Scientist 136:30–37.

Brown, P. J. 1986. Socioeconomic and Demographic Effects of Malaria Eradication: A Comparison of Sri Lanka and Sardinia. Social Science and Medicine 22(8):847–861.

Brown, P. J. 1987. Microparasites and Macroparasites. Cultural Anthropology 2:155–171.

Brown, P. J., M. C. Inhorn, and D. G. Smith. 1996. Disease, Ecology and Culture. *In* Medical Anthropology: A Handbook of Theory and Method (second edition). C. Sargent and T. Johnson, eds., *in press*. New York: Greenwood.

Bruce-Chwatt, L. J. 1979. Man Against Malaria: Conquest or Defeat. Transactions of the Royal Society of Tropical Medicine and Hygiene 73:605–617.

Bruce-Chwatt, L. J. 1980. Essential Malariology. London: Heinemann Medical.

Celli, A. 1933. The History of Malaria in the Roman Campagna. London: John Bale, Sons and Danielson.

Chapin, G. and R. Wasserstrom. 1981. Agricultural Production and Malaria Resurgence in Central America and India. Nature 293(5829):181–185.

Chapin, G. and R. Wasserstrom. 1983. Pesticide Use Malaria Resurgence in Central America and India. Social Science and Medicine 17:273–290.

Coatney, G. R. 1963. Pitfalls in a Discovery: The Chronicle of Chloroquine. American Journal of Tropical Medicine and Hygiene 12:121–128.

Conly, G. N. 1975. The Impact of Malaria on Economic Development: A Case Study. Washington, D.C.: Pan American Health Organization.

Cozzani, E. 1972. La Sardegna al Vincitore della Malaria – Giovanbattista Grassi. Cagliari: Editrice Sarda Fossataro.

Curtin, P. D. 1989. Death by Migration: Europe's Encounter with the Tropical World in the Nineteenth Century. Cambridge: Cambridge University Press.

Desjarlais, R. and A. Kleinman. 1995. World Mental Health: Priorities and Problems in Low-Income Countries. New York: Oxford University Press.

Desowitz, R. S. 1991. The Malaria Capers. New York: W.W. Norton and Company.

DeZulueta, J. and L. J. Bruce-Chwatt. 1980. The Rise and Fall of Malaria in Europe; A Historico-Epidemiological Study. Cambridge: Oxford University Press.

Dunn, F. L. 1979. Behavioral Aspects of the Control of Parasitic Diseases. Bulletin of the World Health Organization 57:527–534.

Duran-Reynals, M. L. 1946. The Fever-Bark Tree: The Pageant of Quinine. Garden City, New York: Doubleday.

Durham, W. H. 1991. Coevolution: Genes, Culture, and Human Diversity. Palo Alto, California: Stanford University Press.

Edgerton, R. B. 1992. Sick Societies: Challenging the Myth of Primitive Harmony. New York: Free Press.

Foster, S. F. 1991. The Distribution and Use of Antimalarial Drugs: Not a Pretty Picture. *In* Malaria: Waiting for the Vaccine. G. A. T. Targett, ed. Pp. 123–140. Chichester and New York: John Wiley and Sons.

Gomes, M. 1993. Economic and Demographic research on Malaria: A Review of the Evidence. Social Science and Medicine 37(9):1093–1108.

Gruenbaum, E. 1983. Struggling with the Mosquito: Malaria Policy and Agricultural Development in Sudan. Medical Anthropology 7(2):51–62.

Hackett, L. H. 1937. Malaria in Europe: An Ecological Study. New York: Oxford University Press.

Harris, M. 1979. Cultural Materialism: The Struggle for a Science of Culture. New York: Random House.

Harrison, G. 1978. Mosquitoes, Malaria and Man: A History of Hostilities since 1880. New York: E.P. Dutton.

Homans, G. C. 1967. The Nature of Social Science. New York: Harcourt, Brace and World.

Inhorn, M. C. and P. J. Brown. 1990. The Anthropology of Infectious Disease. Annual Review of Anthropology 19:89–117.

Jones, W., R. Ross., and R. Ellet. 1908. Malaria: A Neglected Factor in the History of Greece and Rome. Naples: Dethen and Rocholl.

Justice, J. 1986. Policies, Plans and People: Culture and Health Development in Nepal. Berkeley: University of California Press.

Kamat, V. 1996. Personal communication.

Key, P. J. 1991. Malaria: Challenges for the 1990s. In Malaria: Waiting for the Vaccine. G. A. T. Targett, ed. Chichester and New York: John Wiley and Sons.

Liisberg, E. 1991. The World Malaria Situation. World Health 9:5.

Litsios, S. 1996. The Tomorrow of Malaria. New Zealand: Pacific Press.

Livingstone, F. B. 1958. Anthropological Implications of Sickle Cell Gene Distribution in West Africa. American Anthropologist 60:533–562.

McKeown, T. 1979. The Role of Medicine: Dream, Mirage, or Nemesis. Princeton, New Jersey: Princeton University Press.

McNeill, W. H. 1976. Plagues and Peoples. New York: Doubleday.

Mull, J. D. 1990. The Primary Health Care Dialectic: History, Rhetoric, and Reality. In Anthropology and Primary Health Care. J. Coreil and J. D. Mull, eds. Pp. 28–48. Boulder, Westview.

Najera-Morrondo, J. A. 1991. Malaria Control: History Shows It's Possible. World Health 9:3–4.

Nakajima, H. 1991. Breaking the Fatal Cycle of Transmission. World Health 9:2–4.

Oaks, S. C. and V. S. Mitchell. 1991. Malaria: Obstacles and Opportunities. Washington, D.C.: National Academy Press.

Omran, A. R. 1971. The Epidemiologic Transition. Milbank Memorial Fund Quarterly 49(4):509–538.

O'Rourke, P. J. 1994. All the Trouble in the World. New York: Atlantic Monthly Press.

Packard, R. C. and P. J. Brown. 1997. Introduction: Malaria and Development. Medical Anthropology 17: in press.

Packard, R. M. 1986. Agricultural Development, Migrant Labor and the Resurgence of Malaria in Swaziland. Social Science and Medicine 22(8): 861–868.

Pampana, E. 1963. Textbook of Malaria Eradication. London and Oxford: Oxford University Press.

Prothero, R. M. 1965. Migrants and Malaria. London: Longmans.

Rajagopalan, P. K., P. Jambulingam, S. Sabesan, K. Krishnamoorthy, S. Rajendran, K. Gunasekaran, and N. P. Kumar. 1986. Population Movement and Malaria Persistence in Rameswaram Island. Social Science and Medicine 22(8):879–886.

Sawyer, D. 1993. Economic and Social Consequences of Malaria in New Colonization Projects in Brazil. Social Science and Medicine 37(9): 1131–1136.

Sub-Saharan Africa Program, American Academy for the Advancement of Science. 1991. Malaria and Development in Africa: A Cross-Sectional Approach. Washington, D.C.: American Association for the Advancement of Science (under cooperative agreement with the U.S. Agency for International Development).

Sharma, V. P. and K. N. M. Mehrotra. 1986. Malaria Resurgence in India: A Critical Study. Social Science and Medicine 22(8):835–846.

Sighanetra-Renard, A. 1993. Malaria and Mobility in Thailand. Social Science and Medicine 37(9):1147–1154.

Sotiroff-Junker, J. 1978. A Bibliography on the Behavioural, Social, and Economic Aspects of Malaria and Its Control. Geneva: World Health Organization.

Targett, G. A. T. 1991. Malaria: Waiting for the Vaccine. London School of Tropical Medicine and Hygiene, First Annual Public Health Forum. Chichester and New York: John Wiley and Sons.

Wessen, A. F. 1972. Human Ecology and Malaria. American Journal of Tropical Medicine and Hygiene 27:658–663.

Wessen, A. F. 1986. Resurgent Malaria and the Social Sciences. Social Science and Medicine 22(8):III–IV.

Part Three

Methods

CHAPTER 6

The Household Ecology of Disease Transmission: Dengue Fever in the Dominican Republic

Jeannine Coreil, Linda Whiteford, and Diego Salazar

THE ECOLOGY AND EPIDEMIOLOGY OF DENGUE FEVER

Dengue fever is caused by a virus that is injected into human hosts by several species of mosquito vectors which breed in clean, cool water. Unlike malaria-carrying mosquitoes which reproduce in pools of sunlit water such as ponds and marshes, dengue vectors prefer urban, domestic breeding environments such as household water containers and human-made receptacles in which rain water collects. Dengue is most prevalent in Southeast Asia, where a series of epidemics have occurred since the 1970s. In the Americas, dengue is transmitted primarily by the *Aedes aegypti* mosquito from one infected human host to another. The disease is characterized by fever, chills, headache, ocular pain, skin rash, and other symptoms. The after effects are very debilitating and may include prolonged fatigue, depression, weakness, and inability to work. Although rarely fatal, repeat infections can lead to life-threatening conditions such as dengue hemorrhagic fever or dengue shock syndrome, particularly in children.

Dengue is one of the leading causes of pediatric morbidity and mortality in tropical and subtropical areas (Halstead 1980). Most Caribbean countries have confirmed cases of dengue since 1985, although the largest number of cases in the Americas have been reported in Brazil, Colombia, Mexico, and Puerto Rico. In recent years the number of reported cases has increased markedly, causing increased concern among public health officials that the disease could easily reach epidemic proportions in large cities (Gordon 1989).

To date there are no immunological methods to control the disease. Prevention programs have focused largely on source control through insecticide spraying and alteration of water conditions, that is, reduction in the number of *Aedes aegypti* which breed to maturity, as well as other protective methods such as use of chemically treated bednets. The failure of national vector control programs to reduce the incidence of dengue fever has led health planners to take a closer look at community and household level interventions to control the disease.

Background to the Research Project

Concern over the marked increase in dengue fever cases in Latin America during the 1980s led to the establishment of the "Integrated Community-Based *Aedes aegypti* Control Program" under the sponsorship of the Rockefeller Foundation and Johns Hopkins University. Designed to include both research and training goals, the program emphasized the incorporation of social science and community development perspectives in the formulation of new approaches to address the challenge of dengue fever in the Americas. The Dominican Republic was one of the countries targeted for research on dengue because of the magnitude of the problem there. Surveys in the Dominican Republic reported high endemicity for dengue fever with antibody rates of approximately 70% in children younger than 10 years old (Tidwell et al. 1990). Funding for the authors' study in the Dominican Republic (Whiteford and Coreil 1991) was secured through this program. The objectives of the study were to: (1) conduct an ethnography of dengue fever, (2) describe the household ecology of *Aedes aegypti*, and (3) identify culturally acceptable approaches to community participation in dengue control.

The conceptual framework that guided the research was first presented in a session organized for the 1990 meetings of the American Anthropological Association entitled "The Household Ecology of Disease Transmission." The session brought together papers dealing with the household environment as a context for investigating family adaptation to infectious disease. Several of the papers focused on dengue fever as a case example of disease transmission within the household context, as does this chapter.

The notion of disease transmission refers to the epidemiologic model of specific pathways through which human hosts are exposed to infectious disease agents, and in this case we are interested in those pathways that are structured and mediated by the household environment. Such a view examines the household as constituting multiple, interacting systems including biological, physical, social and cultural dimensions, all of which articulate in a microlevel ecological system. Stated briefly, our approach narrows the traditional biocultural ecological perspective of medical anthropology to a much smaller sphere of human activity, the domestic group (Wilk 1991).

Ecological studies in medical anthropology have largely focused on macrolevel systems in which the unit of analysis is a large population or whole societies interacting with and adapting to environmental factors such as geography, climate, natural resources, fauna and flora, and disease pathogens (McElroy 1990). Even when a microlevel perspective is identified, analytic units are relatively smaller population aggregates such as a common mating pool, town, or ethnic group (Moore et al. 1980). When yet a lower level of analysis is undertaken, the focus usually shifts to the individual organism as the locus of disease processes. In this chapter, we present a model for studying the *household* as a microlevel system which links the individual to larger systems at the community and societal levels (Dewalt and Pelto 1985), one we refer to as *the household ecology of disease transmission*.

We begin by reviewing different traditions of research on the household as a unit of analysis for understanding health conditions and disease control. The concept of household is herein differentiated from the family in that it encompasses the physically bounded setting for everyday activities such as eating, sleeping, and washing for a group of people who share a dwelling, whereas the family refers to a system of social relationships defined by kinship rules, role expectations, and functional goals (Wilk and Netting 1984). Although we address family relations in discussing the social environment of the household, we view the family as conceptually distinct from the household. In reviewing the traditions of research on the household and health, we draw upon work shaped by various disciplines including economics, family studies, human development, and anthropology.

Next we present a model for studying the household ecology of dengue fever which may serve as a template for microlevel research on other infectious diseases. In particular, the model has utility for household-level studies of vector-borne diseases, water-borne diseases, and health conditions linked to domestic water and sanitation. We then illustrate the application of the model to a study of dengue fever in an economically disenfranchised urban neighborhood of the Dominican Republic. This is followed by a discussion of the utility of a household ecology perspective for anthropological research on infectious disease, noting the need to examine links between the household and larger spheres of influence, particularly in the design of intervention programs.

THEORETICAL ORIENTATIONS FOR STUDYING THE HOUSEHOLD AND HEALTH

The Household in Anthropological Research

Since the 1970s research in cultural anthropology has increasingly focused on the household as the basic unit for studying culture change and adaptation, with greater attention to issues of intracultural variation and within-community differences in belief and behavior (Netting, Wilk, and Arnould 1984; Pelto and Pelto 1975). In hierarchical systems of human social organization, the household is conceptualized as the first level of aggregate groups linking individuals to higher-order systems at the levels of community, region, nation, and world system (Dewalt and Pelto 1985). To a large extent, household level studies have focused on decision processes within the domestic group as a framework for understanding patterns of behavior, that is, for predicting the choices that individuals and families make within a range of alternative courses of action and given a delimited set of knowledge and resources.

Anthropological studies of the household have focused largely on economic decision-making in relation to agricultural production, gender and labor relations, income distribution, household budgets, and the organization of domestic activity systems (Wilk 1989). Traditionally, anthropological studies have tended to treat the household as a unitary entity, with little attention to subsystems operating within the domestic sphere. This is particularly true of medically oriented household studies, in which horizontal differentiation within the household has not been well developed, except perhaps within the field of nutritional anthropology, and only in recent years have studies begun to emphasize intrahousehold variation in social and cultural variables (Bentley and Pelto 1991).

The New Economics of the Family

Although hardly "new" any more, a different paradigm for studying family and household economic behavior emerged in the 1960s which shifted the traditional view of families as consumers of goods and services to one which redefined families as active producers of socially valued results such as child welfare and leisure time to enjoy the good life (Becker 1965, 1974, 1991). Families are viewed as making choices among an array of possible sources of satisfaction, such as having healthy children, valued material goods and enjoyment of leisure time activities. Variously termed the "new economics of the family" and the "new household economics," the new paradigm accorded greater attention to nonmonetary variables such as time and energy as important resources which families allocate to alternative goals and activities based on changing priorities and demands on the system. This model of the family as productive unit has gained increasing popularity within the social science research community as scholars discover its applicability to a wide range of problems in everyday life, including health-related issues, as discussed in the next section.

The new household economics framework has been criticized on a number of grounds (Berman, Kendall and Bhattacharyya 1994). Its applicability to impoverished populations has been questioned from the standpoint that choices are severely constrained under circumstances of economic deprivation. Moreover, and of particular relevance to anthropology, the new household economic models, like other economic models, accord little attention to cultural determinants of choice, nor are individual preferences adequately addressed. Finally, the extent to which households actually make decisions based on the common good of the aggregate group has been disputed. These problems with purely economic models of the household have stimulated the development of enlarged, more complex models of household production that incorporate a wider range of contextual factors.

The Household Production of Health

In recent decades the household production paradigm has undergone considerable development in the area of health-related studies which seek to explain variation in health status and behavior patterns of defined groups in terms of household social organization and allocation of resources for alternative ends (DaVanzo and Gertler 1990;

Grossman 1972; Schultz 1984). This view suggests that households combine purchased goods and services and use of time to produce health through mechanisms such as nutrition, child care, preventive health behavior and use of health services, a process sometimes referred to as the health production function (DaVanzo and Gertler 1990). Research in this tradition has focused on the determinants of decision-making regarding selection of behavioral inputs to maximize health and other valued goals (Schumann and Mosley 1994). Emphasis has been given to time allocation of family members, and particularly that of the mother, for both health care-seeking and health promotive activities (Coreil 1991). Another focus has been on the role of maternal education as a key factor which operates through various mediating variables such as child care practices.

A number of models have been proposed to guide research aimed at explaining differential rates of child mortality, and all of these models include household level variables as core elements in the system. One of the more influential of these models of child mortality is Mosley and Chen's (1984) analytic framework for the study of child survival in developing countries. This model attempts to order the variables affecting child mortality in terms of the degree to which they act directly or indirectly on health, that is, as proximate or intermediate determinants. Socioeconomic factors are conceptualized as distal determinants which are mediated through more direct health-related variables. Household-level variables are viewed as intermediate determinants that are largely conditioned by economic factors, or access to wealth, including the ability to acquire adequate food, water, clothing, housing, fuel, transportation, and health care.

Expanding on the Mosley and Chen framework, Millard (1994) presents a causal model of child mortality that incorporates a higher-order, political-economic dimension derived from world systems theory. Of interest to our present discussion, Millard accords a central role to household factors as intermediate pathways between the larger political and socioeconomic systems and the proximate determinants of child health such as exposure of children to pathogens and the adequacy of children's diets. Specific aspects of household situation included in the model are division of labor; decision-making for resource allocation; access to, distribution of, and preparation of food; and child care practices.

Research in nutritional anthropology has traditionally focused on the household as the unit of analysis for collecting data on diet, food patterns and nutritional status of defined populations. For the most part, however, these studies have lacked a coherent theoretical rationale for using the household as the locus of inquiry, and recent work has moved toward a household production model for studying nutritional outcomes (Bentley and Pelto 1991). For example, intrahousehold food allocation has received increased attention as a mediating variable between available household resources and individual food consumption (Pelto 1984; Van Esterik 1985; Gittelsohn 1991; Baer and Madrigal 1993).

Most recently, anthropologists have further refined the household production of health framework to address a variety of health problems (Schumann and Mosley 1994). Unlike the earlier economic models which stimulated this area of inquiry, anthropological studies of the household place greater emphasis on decision-making *processes* within the domestic group, cultural and social structural determinants of choice, and intrahousehold variation in preferences and influence on allocation of resources (Berman, Kendall, and Bhattacharyya 1994). Anthropological research also has highlighted new dimensions of the decision process such as social and psychological costs of health behavior (Coreil et al. 1994).

According to Berman, Kendall, and Bhattacharyya (1994:206), the household production of health conceptual framework can be defined as:

> A dynamic behavioral process through which households combine their (internal) knowledge, resources, and behavioral norms and patterns with available (external) technologies, services, information, and skills to restore, maintain, and promote the health of their members.

The authors identify three levels within this health maintenance process: the larger socioeconomic context which constrains household choices and opportunities; the behavioral choices affecting health made by households; and the health outcomes of these behavioral choices. It is noted that cultural patterns influence health-producing behavior, and that specific actions are not always explicitly linked to health goals. Finally, the authors argue against a disease-focused approach to research and program development, and for reorientation of social science studies of the household in terms of common categories of health-related behavior such as illness perception and labeling, health promotive behaviors, and patterns of help-seeking and resource allocation.

The Developmental Niche Framework

Harkness and Super's (1994) "developmental niche framework" is a particularly relevant theoretical formulation for this body of work. Derived from studies of children's behavior and development in different cultural contexts, Harkness and Super's model of the developmental niche offers useful guidelines for organizing ecological research on the household. The model builds on recent theoretical advances in anthropology, psychology and biological ecology, and reflects current thinking in developmental systems theory. In this view, the child and its environment are viewed as interactive systems, and "the household, as the center of early human life, is seen to be the focal mediator of this relationship, working largely through culturally constructed mechanisms" (Harkness and Super 1994:218). The developmental niche is conceptualized in terms of three integrated subsystems: the physical and social setting in which the child lives; culturally regulated customs of child care and child rearing; and the psychology of the caretakers.

It is Harkness and Super's elaboration on the physical and social settings of the household that is most useful to our task of constructing a model of household ecology of disease transmission. To illustrate how the physical and social environmental subsystem of the household can influence disease transmission, the authors present an analysis of dengue fever in Malaysia. The mosquito vector which transmits dengue, *Aedes aegypti*, breeds in and around urban houses in constructed receptacles containing clean, cool water. In the Malaysian setting, water is stored in large, open jars, drums, and cement tanks, thus providing ample breeding sites for the mosquitoes. Other breeding sites are created by the use of water-filled ant barriers placed underneath food storage cabinets. In the households of Chinese families, water and fruits are placed on an altar to the Goddess of Mercy, to remain for up to two weeks. Among Malay households in the study community, families often keep a jar of water in front of the house for members to wash their feet to prevent contamination of the house by evil spirits, which are believed to attach themselves to the soles of the feet outside. Furthermore, the authors suggest that the observed higher rate of dengue fever in women is probably related to their greater exposure to domestic mosquitoes because they spend more time at home than men. This example demonstrates how analysis of both the peridomestic environment and the social behaviors of people illuminate patterns of vector-borne disease transmission that are often overlooked.

Another application of the developmental niche framework illustrates the role of the physical and social environment in a study of acute respiratory infections among young children in Kenya and the United States by Super, Keefer, and Harkness (1994). In the Kenyan setting, where children spend the first two years of life in the home with siblings and parents, those children who were observed more frequently in the company of other young children were found through spot observations to have a higher rate of respiratory infections. This finding is consistent with research in the United States that documents a higher incidence of infectious illness among young children in group care compared to those who are cared for at home. The above two examples demonstrate the utility of studying the microenvironments of individuals within and between households for understanding differential exposure to infectious disease agents.

The Household in Water and Sanitation Studies

The final area of research which has bearing on the household ecology of disease transmission, and on dengue fever in particular, is that of water and sanitation. Domestic water handling and waste disposal are critical in the epidemiology of many infectious diseases such as diarrheal diseases, parasitic infections, and vector-borne diseases. Furthermore, access to adequate supplies of clean water plays an important role in domestic hygiene practices such as washing hands, clothing, and utensils, which can in turn affect respiratory infections and other communicable diseases. Because of the pivotal role women have as household water managers, research and intervention in this arena has become increasingly focused on the domestic sphere (Elmendorf and Iseley 1983; Melchior 1989; Steering Committee for Cooperative Action for the International Drinking Water Supply and Sanitation Decade 1990; Wijk-Sibesma 1987). Patterns of collection, storage, use, and disposal of waste water, and customs for handling solid waste in the home have been studied to help design improved water and sanitation systems for communities. Women perform the bulk of tasks related to household water supply and disposal of human waste; therefore, the relationship between gender roles and domestic work must be addressed. Likewise, women's domestic roles and their perceptions figure importantly in their receptivity to directed change programs in this area.

A MODEL OF THE HOUSEHOLD ECOLOGY OF DISEASE TRANSMISSION

In this section we present a general model for studying the household as a dynamic ecosystem which structures specific behaviors related to risk of disease transmission. The model, shown in Figure 6.1, identifies three types of disease-related behavior (risk behavior, transmission behavior, and risk protection) which are influenced by aspects of the domestic environment, here grouped into three conceptual domains (biophysical environment, social environment, and culturally constructed environment).

The model assumes that there are known, specific risk, transmission, and protective behaviors that can be identified for study as outcome measures of the transmission process. For example, known risk behaviors for a variety of infectious diseases in developing countries include early weaning of infants and infrequent hand-washing after handling soiled garments. Transmission behaviors for infectious disease, on the other hand, might include the sharing of eating utensils and use of contaminated water in food preparation, such as bottle-feeding. Risk protection behaviors include all practices that decrease

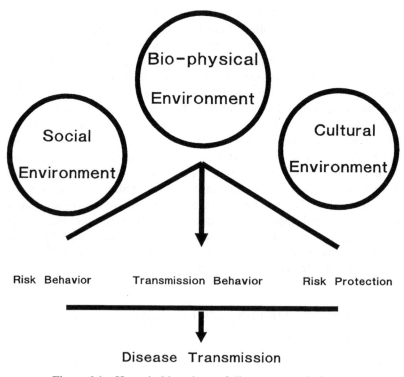

Figure 6.1 Household ecology of disease transmission.

the likelihood of an individual being exposed to an infectious agent, such as breastfeeding of infants, use of latrines, and bednets to prevent mosquito bites.

On the household environment side of the model (Table 6.1), the three domains are broken down into subcomponents which cover a range of relevant variables, but which are not intended to represent an exhaustive listing of all possible factors. Within the biophysical environment, we

Table 6.1

Subcomponents of the Household Ecological System

Biophysical Environment
Microclimate
Pathogens, vectors
Vegetation, animals
Dwelling, enclosures
Use of space
Water collection and storage
Waste accumulation and disposal

Social Environment
Household size
Household composition
Gender and age roles
Allocation of resources
Organization of domestic activities
Temporal cycles of household tasks
Linkages to larger social structures

Culturally Constructed Environment
Ethnoscientific models
– explanatory models of illness
– ethnoecology
– ethnoentomology
Symbolic elements
Value system
Technology

have included the following subcomponents, with examples in parentheses: microclimate (temperature, humidity); pathogens, vectors and their habitat (rodents, flies, pets); vegetation and animals; dwelling and adjacent enclosures (house construction, animal pens); use of space (yards, proximity to neighbors); water collection and storage (container size, covers); and waste accumulation and disposal (latrines, garbage, infant feces).

The social environment encompasses those aspects of domestic social structure and organization which have bearing on matters of health and illness. Within the social environment, we have identified the subcomponents of household composition (adults, children); gender and age roles (responsibilities, income-generation); organization of domestic activities (cooking, cleaning, child care); temporal cycles of household tasks (daily, weekly, seasonal); and linkages to larger social structures (community vector control programs, government services, employment patterns, political-economic conditions in the larger society).

The culturally constructed environment is conceptualized as those aspects of shared household beliefs, symbols and values that influence behavior. In this model we include ethnoscientific models such as explanatory models of illness, ethnoecology, and ethnoentomology. Ethnoecological research by anthropologists has concentrated on local cultural constructions of the physical and biological environment, particularly ethnoscientific knowledge related to use of plants, animals, and agriculture (Conklin 1969; Johnson 1974; Posey et al. 1984). However, ethnoecology also encompasses perceived disease risks linked to environmental conditions (Salazar 1993). Salazar (1993:33–34) notes that because human ecosystems include cultural components, we can "look upon the ecosystem, as experienced by its human inhabitants, as a social construct built on the basis of a given understanding of the physical and biological environment." He refers to this construct as an ethnoecosystem. Moreover, Salazar notes that the emic concept of an ethnoecosystem includes not only material aspects but intangible elements such as spirits, plants with magical powers, sacred places, and perceptions of natural elements such as the air being harmful or beneficial to health (Salazar 1993:37). A specific domain within ethnoecology is ethnoentomology (Posey 1981), or local understanding of the insect populations which inhabit the natural environment, including knowledge of mosquitoes, their breeding patterns and their role in disease transmission (Kendall 1990). The culturally constructed environment also includes symbolic elements (status symbols, religious belief and ritual), value system (relative importance of health, wealth, education), and technology (storage containers, washing facilities, insect repellents).

Depending on the kind of disease problem addressed, different aspects of the household environment will figure more or less importantly within the model of household ecology of disease transmission. For example, for understanding diarrheal disease transmission, food handling and waste disposal play a major role, while acute respiratory infections especially involve social organization patterns which regulate proximity and contact between household members. With dengue fever, on the other hand, it is water collection and storage that have primary importance in disease transmission. In the next section, we illustrate the applicability of the household ecology model in a study of dengue fever in the Dominican Republic.

DENGUE FEVER IN THE DOMINICAN REPUBLIC

The Study Community: Villa Francisca

Fieldwork for the project was conducted in 1989 in a poor barrio of Santo Domingo called Villa Francisca. This community is an older barrio on the southeastern edge of the capital city, inhabited by 35,000 people living in single family homes, multifamily (*multifamiliares*) apartment complexes, and crowded tenement compounds called *patios* that open out onto a communal yard. A commercial center located within the barrio brings a great deal of vehicular traffic through its narrow paved streets. The warm temperatures, frequent and plentiful rain, and unscreened living places create a favorable environment for mosquitoes. Moreover, the lack of a reliable piped water supply in the community makes it necessary for residents to store water in a variety of containers, ranging from small jars to 55-gallon drums, thus providing ideal breeding grounds for *Aedes aegypti*. Surveys of vector densities in neighborhoods adjacent to Villa Francisca documented extremely high rates of *A. aegypti* infestation (Tidwell et al. 1990).

The population of Villa Francisca is relatively older; two-thirds of survey respondents were 36 years or older. The educational level was typical for urban areas of the Dominican Republic, with a mean level of eight years of schooling completed. Although a poor neighborhood, residents span a wide range of socioeconomic levels. Our community survey showed that about 23% of the men work in professional or semiprofessional occupations, 39% at skilled jobs, 25% in unskilled work, and the remainder either unemployed or doing work that did not fit the above categories. About three-fourths of the women surveyed (77%) did not work for wages outside the home, 11% were skilled workers, 7% were professionals or semiprofessionals, 2% were unskilled workers, and 2% fell in the other category.

Research Methods

In designing the study, we framed our research questions around the known proximate determinants or risk factors for dengue fever transmission. In this case the important parameters centered on water, mosquitoes, and exposure prevention practices. To use the terminology of the household ecology model, we were interested in *risk behaviors* which favored the breeding of mosquitoes in domestic spaces (e.g., storage of water in uncovered vessels), *transmission behaviors* which brought people into contact with mosquitoes (e.g., time spent in the home), and *protective behaviors* which either decreased mosquito density or reduced exposure of individuals to mosquito bites (e.g., use of vector barriers).

The research followed a community study design and integrated ethnographic methods and a small-scale survey to address the three objectives stated above. Ethnographic methods included review of relevant documents, community mapping, structured observation within households, key informant interviews, and in-depth interviews with a small sample of men and women. The qualitative data collected in the ethnographic component helped design a structured questionnaire that was administered to a random sample of 100 adults in Villa Francisca. Ethnographic data were also used to complement, amplify, and give context to the quantitative results of the survey.

In the early stages of fieldwork, official documents and the scientific literature were reviewed to determine past and present policies and programs related to vector control, and to identify previous ethnographic research on dengue in Latin America and the Dominican Republic. Research reports and government documents helped to design initial drafts of data collection protocols. Community and household areas also were mapped in the early phases of the project to establish geographic and environmental parameters of the barrio, to map private and public spaces of activity, to identify major household spatial domains, and to determine common sources of mosquito breeding.

The next phase of data collection involved direct observation in nine households selected to represent a range of socioeconomic levels and household size. Following a semistructured guide, the project field director spent one day in each of the nine households observing the social and physical environment of the household, noting in particular those aspects having a bearing on mosquito breeding, such as water-handling, waste disposal, and barriers to vector circulation.

Insights gained through direct observation helped structure the content of in-depth interviews with a small sample of adults and key informants. The focus of the in-depth interviews with adults was eliciting explanatory models of dengue, the ethnoecology of the illness, including its relationship to mosquitoes and water, and local perceptions regarding alternative dengue control measures. Ten men and ten women were selected for in-depth interviews based on age, education, occupation and length of residence in the community. The interviews followed an open-ended topical guide. Nine key informants were selected based on their knowledge and involvement within the community, and their interest in serving in this capacity. These individuals were questioned on multiple occasions throughout the study to expand on critical issues, define key concepts, and provide background to explain local perceptions and attitudes.

The small-scale survey collected structured data on sociodemographic characteristics of the population, ethnomedical models of fevers, including dengue, household patterns of water use, ethnoecology of dengue, mosquitoes and water, and attitudes toward alternative approaches to prevention and control of dengue fever. A random sample of 100 households was selected based on a mapping of the community. The map was constructed by enumerating residential units within a defined geographic area. Households were selected based on a fixed interval sampling strategy. One adult per household was interviewed, resulting in a gender breakdown of 56 men and 44 women. Each responded to a 64-item interviewer-administered questionnaire that covered the topics noted above.

Data-analysis procedures included content analysis, statistical inference and cross-comparison of ethnographic and survey results. Content analysis of qualitative data relied on ethnosemantic techniques and identification of recurrent themes and patterns of belief and behavior. Survey data were analyzed for descriptive statistics and measures of association between selected variables. Ethnographic and survey findings were compared to assess concurrent validity, and juxtaposed to construct a robust picture of the household context of dengue.

   In the following sections we present examples of the kinds of data collected in the conceptual areas of the biophysical, social and culturally constructed environment of Villa Francisca in order to illustrate the applicability of the model for studying the household ecology of disease transmission. Selected findings are highlighted to show the importance of particular household variables for dengue fever transmission. The household environmental factors are discussed in relation to their influence on dengue-specific risk behaviors (creation of mosquito breeding sites); transmission behaviors (exposure to the vector); and risk protection (source control). A more detailed presentation of findings is reported in Whiteford and Coreil (1991) and Salazar (1993).

The Biophysical Environment of Dengue

The main components of the biophysical environment studied were housing types, microclimate, use of domestic space, water handling practices, waste disposal and vector breeding conditions. These factors were analyzed in relation to their influence on risk and transmission behaviors for dengue fever, that is, practices which facilitate the breeding of mosquitoes in the domestic environment and expose household members to the disease vector. Features of the biophysical environment which relate to risk protection for dengue were also noted. Most important among the foregoing factors were local customs for collection, storage, and disposal of water. These customs varied by housing type. Within the multifamiliares which represented the best housing within the community, one finds piped water and sewage and waste water drains connected to the municipal sewage system. Piped water can also be found in some of the individual houses, but in many cases the system is useless because of broken public mainlines. Moreover, tap water is often brackish and unsafe for drinking, so residents must buy purified water. The poorest dwellings, the patios or tenements, have no piped water to individual units, and only a minority of compounds have a communal tap. They must collect rain water and walk to the nearest public tap to obtain water.
   The public water supply is irregular at best, because of intermittent shortages of electricity which powers the pumps, as well as frequent mechanical breakdowns of equipment. Hence all households, even those fortunate enough to have indoor plumbing, must store water for domestic use. Collecting and storing water is an integral part of daily life in the community. Eighty percent of the households in our survey

had to collect water from sources outside the home. This involves transporting water from the local tap to the home, and pouring into household containers for later use. Rain water is similarly collected and stored for drinking and cooking. The patio inhabitants draw brackish water from the communal tap, and days may elapse with no water flowing. Thus, the common use of 55-gallon drums, called *tanques*, for water storage; these are frequently infested with mosquito larvae. The smaller storage containers also serve as breeding grounds. Some containers are covered, others are not. Households which did not have to collect water outside the home had the advantage of being able to manage with storage of less water than households which relied on communal water sources, thereby reducing the availability of vector breeding grounds.

Waste water disposal is a problem everywhere in the barrio. The municipal sewage system serves only a limited number of households, and in many places it is broken. People throw out waste water into the streets or ditches near their homes. When it rains, flooding is common.

Mosquitoes are ubiquitous in Villa Francisca. They thrive in discarded water that is relatively clean, in pools of rain water, in household containers, in latrines, and in building sites where workers store water for mixing concrete. Risk protective features of the domestic environment are quite limited; none of the homes have screens on windows, so mosquitoes circulate freely within living quarters and communal areas, exposing people to the *Aedes aegypti* vector on a daily basis. Some households use fans to blow away mosquitoes and some spray with insecticides, but these manipulations of the physical environment are not affordable for widespread use and have a limited impact on vector density.

The Social Environment of Villa Franciscan Family Life

Investigation of the social environment focused on household composition, employment patterns, allocation of household tasks, with particular attention to water handling, gender and age-related role differentiation, patterns for sick care, and attitudes toward community participation in disease prevention. Attention was focused on these factors because they have a direct bearing on risk behavior for dengue transmission as well as receptivity to taking risk protective actions at the household level. Our research documented that performance of water handling tasks within a given domestic unit was determined by household composition, gender roles, and family resources. As in most of the developing world, women are responsible for the bulk of domestic work and child care, although men and women both collect water. Men carry the heavy, large water vessels used to store brackish water used for washing and bathing, while women and girls are primarily responsible for food-related water activities.

In the barrio the senior woman of the house has the major responsibilities for household maintenance. It is she who controls the household money, the house and the commons, and to a lesser extent, minding the children. If there are no other adult men or women in the household, the senior woman takes responsibility for collecting water, if she is physically able. If she cannot handle the heavy hauling herself, she may pay someone to do it for her or enlist the assistance of non-household relatives (5% of households paid outsiders to carry water). Both male and female Villa Franciscans identified senior women as responsible for preparing the morning, midday, and evening meals. Dominicans enjoy their main meal at midday, and the senior women in the our survey report expending about two and a half hours every morning securing the foodstuffs and preparing the meal. In addition to the preparation of other daily meals, these women spend another hour and a half cleaning the house and the common area (often with help from younger women in the household), and they also report spending another hour each day carrying water.

While it appears that senior women and men of the household are deeply involved in collecting water daily, so is just about everyone else. Survey responses suggest that all members of the household spend some time in the collection, transport, storage, or disposal of water for domestic use. Both young men and women report spending an hour and a half each day carrying water; older men and young men together report that water carrying consumes an hour and a half of their day as well. Somewhat surprisingly, senior males were involved in as much as 20% of all the reported cases of water handling, a percentage that increases to 29% when both junior and senior males are included. The assignment of responsibility to men for transport of brackish water is attributed to the physical strength required to hauling large containers of water.

The sweet drinking water stored in small containers is overseen by women, is used daily, and is covered. The brackish water stored in large containers is used for domestic hygiene, is left uncovered and is not overseen by the women. Because the large vessels are left uncovered, mosquito larva are found in greater abundance in these containers. The large containers filled with public water for common uses may represent a domain outside the women's perceived boundaries. While this idea needs further documentation, it suggests that attention be paid to who is responsible for water collected from different sources and stored in different vessels. Interventions programs might focus on assignment of responsibility within families for the cleaning and covering of large storage vessels, possibly to men since they maintain the water supply in these containers.

During the day, women and children are in the living quarters of the community. Most of the men work away from home, and the majority of women do not. Also, over half of the households surveyed were headed by women who were either separated, divorced, widowed, or unmarried. While both men and women handle water, women are responsible for domestic cleaning and cooking and child care; therefore, they spend more time inside the house, and are exposed to vectors more often than men. Thus, as in the Malaysian setting discussed previously, women and children appear to have greater exposure to the *Aedes aegypti* vector in the home. By the same token, women who work outside the home, and children who attend school, have less exposure to the vectors than women and children who spend more time at home. On a related note, many of the families in this barrio sent their young children to live with relatives who lived in rural areas, and the children only spent short-term visits within the urban households of their parents, thus reducing their exposure to the urban-dwelling dengue vector.

Household size affects the amount of water that must be stored within the family living quarters. The more people there are to feed and keep clothed and clean, the more water that must be stored for these uses, and therefore the larger the potential reservoir for proliferation of mosquito vectors. Also, people who live in multifamily patios have the added exposure to vectors which breed in the stored water of communal household units. Thus, the size and structure of the domestic unit has a direct bearing on exposure to disease risk.

Perceptions of the larger social environment also figure importantly in relation to dengue transmission. In particular, the perceived locus of responsibility for risk protection was placed clearly in the political arena of government services. In this regard, a noteworthy finding was the salience of a local concept of community cooperation for the common good, referred to as *buena union*. Discussions of community participation in disease prevention programs generally, and vector control measures in particular, frequently invoked this notion, or more precisely the lack of buena union (*mala union*) in Villa Francisca, which local people perceived to be a barrier to effective mobilization of collaborative efforts. Local perception of the social environment was clearly one of a political space controlled by government and elected officials. Eighty-two percent of survey respondents stated that they expect the mosquito problem in Villa Francisca to be solved by the "authorities," that is, by representatives of the political and administrative system of the country. Key informants expressed the opinion that the reason there are so many mosquitoes in the area is because the authorities do not care enough. The reasons officials are expected to take responsibility for the problem are that they have the means to do it, they are prepared to do it and know how to do it, it is their responsibility, and it is the custom for them to do it. Yet despite this expectation for the government to do something about the mosquito problem, there was little evidence of state-supported source control within this community. Thus, no organized risk protection activities were undertaken outside the household arena.

The Culturally Constructed Environment of Dengue Fever

In studying the cultural construction of dengue fever, we sought to describe ethnomedical models of fevers and dengue in particular, patterns of treatment for dengue, the ethnoecology of the disease and its vector, and attitudes and perceptions related to prevention and source control. These factors have a direct bearing on residents' risk behavior, transmission behavior and risk protective actions. We found that the folk model of dengue transmission is a fairly complex mix of folk and biomedical etiologies. The incorporation of biomedical elements probably stems from exposure to educational messages about dengue incorporated into various community awareness campaigns undertaken by the government in recent years. According to Villa Franciscans, the disease is transmitted by contact (with larvae), by injection (mosquitoes) and through microbes. Children are perceived to be most at risk of infection. Although there is widespread name recognition for the disease (Sp. *dengue*), its symptomatology is not clearly distinguished from malaria (*paludismo*). People describe dengue as a type of *gripe*, characterized by fever, severe headaches, muscular pains, and sometimes gastrointestinal symptoms. It is thought to be a serious illness, potentially fatal if the person does not get proper medical care, and is considered particularly dangerous for those in weakened health or for infants who are vulnerable to all illness. Although some respondents mentioned symptoms associated with dengue hemorraghic fever (bleeding, blood in stool or urine), the folk model does not distinguish this more serious type of infection. A variety of treatment options were mentioned as appropriate for someone with dengue, including self-care, patent medicines, professional health care, special diet, and changes in hygiene.

In the ethnoecology of dengue, environmental factors figure prominently in perceived etiology. People believe that mosquitoes breed in garbage and dirty areas, and deposit their larvae in water. No distinction is made among different species of mosquitoes. Some informants noted that vegetation and humidity attract mosquitoes. Survey respondents identified four main categories of disease causation: mosquitoes (62%), standing water (31%), garbage (23%), and lack of hygiene (10%). The general theme of environmental contamination was expressed often in discussions of the origin of the problem of dengue. Some people also recognize a humoral etiology (temperature changes) or a contagious mode of transmission.

Mosquito breeding patterns are associated with different types of water, with four cultural categories recognized: "sweet" water (*agua dulce*), or tap water purified from rivers; brackish water (*agua salada*) drawn from wells with a high saline content; rain water collected mainly from roofs; and commercial water purified at plants and then bottled and sold. Only sweet water and purified water are used for cooking and drinking. Sweet water is stored in small containers because less is needed than water for washing. People think it is important only to cover water intended for family consumption; less care is given to covering the other types of water, hence greater opportunity for infestation.

In response to questions about protecting oneself from dengue, taking preventive measures, and controlling the sources of the disease (waste, mosquitoes, water), residents of Villa Francisca expressed generally fatalistic attitudes. People think there is not much that they, as individuals, families or as a community, can do about the dengue problem. The aspects of environmental contamination noted above are considered beyond their control. Most residents believe that it is the responsibility of government authorities to control the mosquito and standing water problem. Environmental sanitation in clearly viewed as a political problem, with little expectation for community involvement.

DISCUSSION

In this chapter we have presented a rationale for applying an ecological approach to the household unit as a basis for studying the process of infectious disease transmission. We began by reviewing the conceptual development of household studies in anthropology and related disciplines, highlighting recent work within the area of the household production of health. Next we presented a framework for research on the household ecology of disease transmission, and illustrated its applicability to the study of dengue fever in the Dominican Republic. In this final section we address some issues and questions regarding the utility of the household ecology model for anthropological research on infectious disease.

In examining the applicability of the household ecology model to a wider range of research questions, it is useful to consider the kinds of disease problems that might be amenable to the type of analysis outlined above. We would argue that not all research on infectious disease lends itself to an ecological approach, nor to a household-level focus. The epidemiology of a number of tropical diseases, such as malaria, schistosomiasis, and river blindness, for example, would require a more community-based research strategy because the vectors for those diseases breed in large bodies of water shared by whole communities. Likewise, the household context has less relevance for infectious diseases that primarily affect special risk groups, such as AIDS, because transmission behaviors are influenced heavily by factors outside the domestic environment. The key factors to consider in assessing the appropriateness of a household focus are the extent to which the proximate determinants of risk behavior, transmission behavior and protective behavior are influenced by household-level variables. We have already shown how dengue fever fits these criteria; other types of infections that might also fit the model include diarrheal diseases, respiratory infections (both acute and chronic such as tuberculosis), intestinal parasites, trachoma, and guinea worm. These latter infections can be controlled, at least partly, by behavioral and technological changes within domestic units.

We should note that although our discussion has focused on disease-specific studies, the household ecology model is not limited to research on singular infections, nor it is applicable only to infectious disease transmission. The conceptual approach to the household environment in terms of biophysical, social, and culturally constructed subsystems might be adapted to more broadly defined research questions such as general child health outcomes and aggregate family health. Another profitable line of inquiry along the lines suggested by Berman, Kendall, and Bhattacharyya (1994) would be to compare research results from similar household subsystems across studies of different health problems, such as, for example, the effects of the social organization of water handling on a variety of health outcomes.

It is important to note that a household context for research on disease transmission does not always dictate that the corresponding locus for planned intervention should be limited to the domestic sphere. While risk behaviors may be rooted in household patterns, strategies for behavioral change might effectively be aimed at individuals or the community. In practice most intervention programs require a multi-level strategy that integrates household level components with community and clinic-based activities. Moreover, a basic tenet of the ecological approach is the embeddedness of analytic systems within higher and lower order systems. Thus it would be reductionistic to constrain our research to the household unit while ignoring the effect of macrolevel systems which impinge on household organization and functioning. A number of theoretical models have been developed which situate the household within larger biocultural and political economic spheres, some of which were mentioned earlier in this chapter. Our elaboration of the household context as an ecological system is intended to augment these broader models, and to amplify the complexity of the household system which heretofore has been treated in a comparatively simplistic, undifferentiated way.

A good illustration of the foregoing points is provided in a study of trachoma transmission and control in Tanzania (McCauley, West, and Lynch 1992). A survey had revealed that children with unclean faces were at increased risk for the eye infection, so the focus of the project became one of determining ways to encourage more frequent face-washing of children in the home. Since mothers were responsible for this child care function, women were identified as the primary targets for behavior change. Through focus groups and interviews the women demonstrated a good understanding of contagion, hygiene and the relation of eye disease to poor sanitation. When asked about constraints to face washing they often stated that they did not have enough extra water to do this regularly. Moreover, because women were responsible for food production, their work in the fields was given high priority and they could not justify allocating more time to water collection and face-washing. They feared being criticized by the rest of the community for being negligent of their proper duties. This perception was corroborated by other community members who voiced the opinion that a woman was only justified in spending time on keeping her home and children clean if it did not interfere with her work in food production and preparation. In designing a program to promote face-washing, therefore, it was necessary to take a community-based approach that involved men, older women, and local leadership. The women were willing to adopt the new practices, "but they needed the support of the household and community, and expected agreement on changed norms to originate in recognized village authority structures" (McCauley, West, and Lynch 1992:823).

Households are constrained by the resources available to them; removing the constraints almost invariably requires political action at the community and national levels. Our study of dengue fever in the Dominican Republic demonstrated that while disease transmission was largely a function of household water storage practices, modification of these practices would require access to a more reliable supply of clean water, a change beyond the control of individual households. Given the current situation of low commitment of barrio residents to community participation in health development, coupled with meager government action in the area of dengue prevention, a household-focused intervention would require considerable external bolstering for any hope of success.

The household ecology of disease framework provides critical information about disease transmission, risk behavior, and risk protection. Investigation of these behavioral domains broadens our understanding of the interstices among the biophysical, social and culturally constructed environments as they shape health practices. Furthermore, this model offers a means to evaluate a community's readiness to participate in household- and community-based intervention projects, an important step in achieving project sustainability. Of the various disciplines involved in the study of infectious diseases, anthropology has the strongest potential for developing the household ecology framework, because of its ability to integrate concepts and methods from the related fields of biocultural ecology, ethnomedicine, household economics, ethnoecology, and family organization. Furthermore, in keeping with the ecological paradigm, as well as the discipline's contextual orientation, anthropological studies of the household and infectious disease are not likely to lose sight of the larger social and biological systems which affect household processes. Expanding our understanding of the domestic sphere will illuminate the unique aspects of disease transmission at this level yet also allow one to demonstrate points of articulation with higher- and lower-order systems. Anthropological methods allow navigation of these multiple levels even when the focus of analysis is a single domain such as the household. In this way, risk behavior can be understood in its fullest social and cultural context.

REFERENCES

Baer, R. D. and L. Madrigal. 1993. Intrahousehold Allocation of Resources in Larger and Smaller Mexican Households. Social Science and Medicine 36(3):305–310.

Becker, G. S. 1965. Theory of the Allocation of Time. Economic Journal 75:493–517.

Becker, G. S. 1974. Is Economic Theory with it: On the Relevance of the New Economics of the Family. The American Economic Review 64(2):317–319.

Becker, G. S. 1991. Treatise on the Family (Enlarged edition). Cambridge, Massachusetts: Harvard University Press.

Bentley, M. E. and G. H. Pelto. 1991. The Household Production of Nutrition: Introduction to Special Issue. Social Science and Medicine 33(10):1101–1102.

Berman, P., C. Kendall, and K. Bhattacharyya. 1994. The Household Production of Health: Integrating Social Science Perspectives on Micro-Level Health Determinants. Social Science and Medicine 38(2):205–215.

Conklin, H. C. 1969. Ethnoecological Approach to Shifting Agriculture. *In* Environment and Cultural Behavior. A. P. Vayda, ed. Pp. 221–233. Garden City, New York: The Natural History Press.

Coreil, J. 1991. Maternal Time Allocation in Relation to Kind and Domain of Primary Health Care. Medical Anthropology Quarterly 5(3):221–235.

Coreil, J. et al. 1994. Social and Psychological Costs of Preventive Child Health Services in Haiti. Social Science and Medicine 38(2):231–238.

DaVanzo, J. and P. Gertler. 1990. Household Production of Health: A Microeconomic Perspective on Health Transitions. A Rand Note, Jan.

Dewalt, B. R. and P. J. Pelto. 1985. Microlevel/Macrolevel Linkages: An Introduction to the Issues and a Framework for Analysis. *In* Micro and Macro Levels of Analysis in Anthropology. B. R. Dewalt and P. J. Pelto, eds. Pp. 1–21. Boulder, Colorado: Westview.

Elmendorf, M. L. and R. B. Isely. 1983. Public and Private roles of Women in Water Supply and Sanitation Programs. Human Organization 42(3):195–204.

Gittelsohn, J. 1991. Opening the Box: Intrahousehold Food Allocation in Rural Nepal. Social Science and Medicine 33(10):1141–1154.

Gordon, A. 1989. Cultural Factors in *Aedes aegypti* and Dengue Control in Latin America: A Case Study from the Dominican Republic. International Quarterly of Community Health Education 10(3):193–211.

Grossman, M. 1972. On the Concept of Health Capital and the Demand for Health. Journal of Political Economy 80:223–255.

Halstead, S. B. 1980. Dengue Haemorrhagic Fever – A Public Health Problem and a Field for Research. Bulletin of the World Health Organization 58(1):1–21.

Johnson, A. 1974. Ethnoecology and Planting Practices in a Swidden Agricultural System. American Ethnologist 1:87–101.

Kendall, C. 1990. Exploratory Ethnoentomology: Using ANTHROPAC to Design a Dengue Fever Control Program. Cultural Anthropology Newsletter, May:11–12.

McCauley, A. P., S. West, and M. Lynch. 1992. Household Decisions among the Gogo People of Tanzania: Determining the Roles of Men, Women and the Community in Implementing a Trachoma Prevention Program. Social Science and Medicine 34(7):817–824.

McElroy, A. 1990. Biocultural Models in Studies of Human Health and Adaptation. Medical Anthropology Quarterly 4(3):243–265.

Melchior, S. 1989. Women, Water and Sanitation. PROWWESS Technical Series Involving Women in Water and Sanitation: Lessons, Strategies, Tools. New York: United Nations Development Programme.

Millard, A. V. 1994. Causal Model of High Rates of Child Mortality. Social Science and Medicine 38(2):253–268.

Moore, L. G. et al. 1980. The Biocultural Basis of Health. St. Louis: C. V. Mosby.

Mosley, W. H. and L. C. Chen. 1984. An Analytical Framework for the Study of Child Survival in Developing Countries. Population and Development Review 10(supp.):25–40.

Netting, R. M., R. R. Wilk, and E. J. Arnould. 1984. Households: Comparative and Historical Studies of the Domestic Group. Berkeley: University of California Press.

Pelto, G. 1984. Intrahousehold Food Distribution Patterns. *In* Malnutrition: Determinants and Consequences. G. Davis, ed. Pp. 285–293. New York: Alan R. Liss, Inc.

Pelto, P. J. and G. H. Pelto. 1975. Intra-cultural Diversity: Some Theoretical Issues. American Ethnologist 2(1):1–18.

Posey, D. A. 1981. Ethnoentomology of the Kayapo Indians of Central Brazil. Journal of Ethnobiology 1(1):165–174.

Posey, D. A., J. Frechione, J. Eddins, L. F. Da Silva, et al. 1984. Ethnoecology as Applied Anthropology in Amazonian Development. Human Organization 43(2):95–107.

Salazar, D. R. 1993. Folk Models and Household Ecology of Dengue Fever in an Urban Community of the Dominican Republic. Doctoral Dissertation, University of South Florida.

Schumann, D. A. and W. H. Mosley, eds. 1994. The Household Production of Health. Introduction to Special Issue of Social Science and Medicine 39(2):201–204.

Schultz, T. P. 1984. Studying the Impact of Household Economic and Community Variables in Child Mortality. Population and Development Review 10(Supp.):215–235.

Steering Committee for Cooperative Action for the International Drinking Water Supply and Sanitation Decade. 1990. The IDWSSD and Women's Involvement. Geneva: World Health Organization.

Super, C. M., C. H. Keefer, and S. Harkness. 1994. Child Care and Infectious Respiratory disease during the First Two Years of Life in Kenya and the United States. Social Science and Medicine 38(2):227–229.

Tidwell, M. A. et al. 1990. Baseline Data on *Aedes aegypti* Populations in Santo Domingo, Dominican Republic. Journal of the American Mosquito Control Association 6(3):514–522.

Van Esterik, P. 1985. Intrafamily Food Distribution: Its Relevance for Maternal and Child Nutrition. *In* Determinants of Young Child Feeding and Their Implications for Nutritional Surveillance. Cornell International Nutrition Monograph Series, No. 14.

Whiteford, L. M. and J. Coreil. 1991. Household Ecology of *Aedes aegypti* Control in the Dominican Republic. Unpublished project report.

Wijk-Sijbesma, C. V. 1987. Drinking Water and Sanitation: Women Can Do Much. World Health Forum 8:28–32.

Wilk, R. R., ed. 1989. The Household Economy: Reconsidering the Domestic Mode of Production. Boulder, Colorado: Westview Press.

Wilk, R. R. 1991. Household Ecology: Economic Change and Domestic Life Among the Kekchi Maya in Belize. Tucson: University of Arizona Press.

Wilk, R. and R. M. Netting. 1984. Households: Changing Form and Function. *In* Households: Comparative and Historical Studies of the Domestic Group. R. Netting, R. Wilk, and E. Arnould, eds. Pp. 1–24. Berkeley: University of California Press.

CHAPTER 7

Infertility, Infection, and Iatrogenesis in Egypt: The Anthropological Epidemiology of Blocked Tubes

Marcia C. Inhorn and Kimberly A. Buss

HIND'S STORY

Hind,[1] the second of four daughters of a farmer who had migrated to Alexandria, Egypt, in search of work, was widely considered within her poor, urban neighborhood to be a young, voluptuous beauty. Despite the twelve-year-old Hind's protestations, her father gave her in marriage to another rural migrant, who Hind felt treated her like "his donkey." When Hind became pregnant after a brief but socially defined and stigmatizing period of infertility, her husband beat her with a boot in her pregnant belly. This, Hind believes, caused her

Reproduced, with permission, from **Medical Anthropology**, Volume 15, Marcia C. Inhorn and Kimberly A. Buss, "Infertility, Infection, and Iatrogenesis in Egypt: The Anthropological Epidemiology of Blocked Tubes," pp. 217–244, ©1993 by Gordon and Breach Science Publishers, a member of the Gordon and Breach Publishing Group.

The authors wish to thank Mary-Claire King for her encouragement and guidance in conducting this anthropological–epidemiological study and for the computer and other logistical support she provided in the data analysis phase. Without her support, the analysis of the data reported here would not have been possible.

future postpartum complications. When the baby was delivered by the *daya*, or midwife, he had pus in his eyes and could not open them. Hind herself experienced severe pelvic pain for three months. When she recovered, her son developed boils over his entire body and, shortly after his first birthday, succumbed to a fatal respiratory infection. Abused and miserable, Hind successfully pleaded with her father to help her obtain a divorce. Unfortunately, as a divorcee, Hind was a burden on her poor family even though she served as a surrogate mother and wetnurse to her two infant sisters.

At the age of sixteen, Hind was married again – this time to a handsome young man named Rayda. The marriage of Hind and Rayda – which has survived twelve years against all odds – has been plagued with difficulties, the most important of which is the couple's inability to have children. Hind, in a desperate "search for children," as she calls her quest for infertility therapy, has subjected her body to numerous costly, painful, and according to her, revolting therapies, some performed by traditional healers and some by physicians.

Inhorn wishes to thank the organizations that provided funding for this research, including the National Science Foundation (Doctoral Dissertation Research Improvement Grant #BNS-8814435), the Fulbright Institute of International Education, the U.S. Department of Education Fulbright-Hays Doctoral Dissertation Research Abroad (DDRA) Program, and the Soroptimist International Founder Region Fellowship Program. In addition, she wishes to thank the administration and staff of Shatby Hospital of the University of Alexandria, Egypt, who made this study possible, and especially Mohamad Rizk and Soad Farid, who secured permission for the study. Likewise, the chlamydial antibody component of this study would not have been possible without the help of a number of physicians at Shatby Hospital, including most notably Mohammed Mehanna, as well as the support and technical assistance of Julius Schachter, director of the Chlamydia Laboratory at San Francisco General Hospital, where antibody testing of serum samples from Egypt was carried out. In addition, Inhorn wishes to thank Janet Daling and Beth Anne Mueller of the Fred Hutchinson Cancer Research Center and the University of Washington for providing her with copies of the questionnaires utilized in case-control studies of infertility and ectopic pregnancy in King County Washington; these questionnaires were used as templates for constructing the semistructured questionnaire used in this study.

Finally Inhorn wishes to thank her four Egyptian research assistants, Shayma Hassouna, Rosie Kouzoukian, Hassanat Naguib, and Azza Hosam Shaker, and, most of all, the Egyptian women, infertile and fertile, who participated in her research and entrusted her with the most intimate details of their lives. Her gratitude to these women is profound.

Traditional ethnogynecologists, for example, have performed *kasr*, or cupping, on Hind's lower body until she turned black and blue; have inserted *ṣūwaf* or herbal suppositories, deep into her vagina, causing huge amounts of liquid to gush "from down," as the genitals are known; and have made her wash her body with water in which a preserved, miscarried fetus has been placed. For their part, biomedical gynecologists have performed numerous painful, invasive "therapies" on Hind, including *kayy*, or electrocauterization of her cervix with a heated metal instrument, and *nafq*, or tubal insufflation, a procedure in which carbon dioxide is insufflated, or pumped, into the uterine cavity to supposedly "open up" blocked fallopian tubes. In Hind's case, the problem was that none of the four physicians who independently performed *nafq* on her verified that she suffered from *anābīb masdūd*, or blocked tubes, as infection-scarred fallopian tubes are called in Egypt.

Eventually Hind found her way to the university hospital in Alexandria, hoping to learn something meaningful about the cause of her childlessness. There, the doctor told her that she needed *ṣūra ashiʿa bi ṣibghā*, or an X-ray by dye (i.e., hysterosalpingography or HSG) to assess the status of her fallopian tubes. After Hind underwent the HSG, the young doctor told her that she must have had an infection in the past that damaged both of her fallopian tubes beyond repair and rendered her infertile. Despite Hind's distress, which caused her to faint in his office, he urged Hind to "Give up and let God take care of you."

Later, when Hind consulted an older physician in the same hospital, he told her, "I can help you by doing an operation." When Hind explained that she had already had many operations, he asked, "Did these gynecologists open your belly?" Hind replied, "No, they were from down (i.e., vaginal)." The doctor responded, "The thieves! To open your tubes you need an operation to open your abdomen. They just stole your money and did nothing for you." Eventually, Hind under-went tubal surgery – surgery which she was told by a young resident has a success rate of only 5%. Unfortunately, despite powerful medicines administered postoperatively to "keep the tubes open," Hind was not among the lucky 5%.

Today, Hind is a candidate for in vitro fertilization (IVF), or the creation of a so-called baby of the tubes. Although eight months have passed since Hind was told about IVF she is still far from undergoing the procedure. In vitro fertilization is very expensive, even at the public university hospital, and it will be affordable to Hind only if she can convince her husband Rayda to sell the television and stop smoking two packs of cigarettes a day. This, she concedes, will never happen. So, she must discover some other way of obtaining the necessary money. Although Rayda has been good to Hind and says he will never "remarry for children," Hind worries about his commitment to her, given the pressures from his family to replace her with another wife. For Hind, the future is the source of uncertainty and fear, but she hopes that IVF may someday provide her with the solution to the infertility she suffers because of her blocked tubes.

THE ANTHROPOLOGICAL–EPIDEMIOLOGICAL NEXUS

Hind's case is typical of the thousands of Egyptian women who suffer from tubal-factor infertility (TFI), known in Egypt as *anābīb masdūd*. Tubal-factor infertility involves postinflammatory damage to the fallopian tubes (i.e., complete or partial obstruction) or to the surrounding pelvic structures, causing pelvic adhesions that adversely affect tubal function. Tubal changes do not occur normally; rather they result from upper genital-tract infections (also known as pelvic inflammatory disease, or salpingitis). Given the significant rates of TFI found in recent clinical studies of infertile women in both Cairo (Serour 1991) and Alexandria (El-Gezery 1988; Mehanna 1989), we found it necessary to examine the causal factors that place poor, urban Egyptian women at risk of sterilizing infection.

We argue that identifying causal factors requires a merging of medical anthropological and analytical epidemiological perspectives – perspectives that share a fundamental concern with the causes of poor health. Although many medical anthropologists approach illness causation from the perspective of ethnomedicine (e.g., Foster 1976; Young 1976, 1991; Ngokwey 1988), in recent years, a number of scholars have pointed to the merits of an interdisciplinary anthropological–epidemiological approach to the study of health problems (e.g., Janes, Stall, and Gifford 1986; Robert, Bouvier, and Rougemont 1989; Myntti 1991; True 1990).

Essentially, epidemiology seeks the origins and patterns of disease within given populations and investigates populations' exposures to disease-causing risk factors. In fact, epidemiology is often defined as the study of the distribution and *determinants* of diseases and injuries in human populations (Mausner and Kramer 1985). This emphasis on determinants is crucial to this discussion. While early epidemiologists focused their attention on describing patterns of disease prevalence, transmission, and spread, studies conducted during epidemiology's "boom period" (Rothman 1981) of the past 40 years tend to focus on identifying the determinants, or causes, of disease in defined populations (Kelsey, Thompson, and Evans 1986). Analytical epidemiology is the branch of epidemiology specifically concerned with discovering the underlying causes of diseases in various populations, especially populations manifesting levels of disease higher than statistically normal (Kelsey, Thompson, and Evans 1986).

These causal factors may be of many types. Most early epidemiological studies were concerned with "single-agent, single-disease" theories of causation and focused particularly on infectious agents and their interactions with human and animal "hosts" within particular environments (Dunn and Janes 1986; Trostle 1986). Over the years the definition of "agent" has been expanded to include a number of disease-producing factors, in addition to the infectious agents. Furthermore, epidemiologists now realize that a single agent rarely serves as a sufficient cause of a given disease, especially chronic diseases. Rather, causal forces of many types – biological, chemical, physical, behavioral, and psychological – interact in what various theorists have termed "causal webs" (MacMahon and Pugh 1960), "causal wheels" (Mausner and Bahn 1974), or "causal assemblages" (Dunn and Janes 1986).

Given the recognition of the variety of causative factors, epidemiologists have largely abandoned the term "agent" of disease and replaced it with "risk factor." The purpose of analytical epidemiology is to identify risk factors and to quantify their effect on disease causation (Kelsey, Thompson, and Evans 1986). As analytical epidemiology recognizes, culturally prescribed behaviors may serve as risk factors. In fact, epidemiology like anthropology is behaviorally oriented; according to Dunn and Janes, this focus on human behavior is the "basis of the complementarity of the two disciplines." They note:

> It is the goal of epidemiology to identify and measure the relative importance of factors within the causal web of a disease or disorder. Because all diseases are caused, at least in part, by the behavior of individuals, groups, or communities, epidemiology must be a behavioral science... Whereas epidemiology may be concerned primarily with determining the relationship of behavior to disease, medical anthropology most often focuses on the social and cultural correlates of behavior, or on the contexts of such behavior. The point of greatest possible complementarity and practical collaboration thus lies in exploring the

nexus between the health consequences of behavior and the social and cultural correlates of that behavior (Dunn and Janes 1986:3).

Anthropology's and epidemiology's mutual interest in human behavior – especially behavior that places human beings at risk of disease – has been noted by a number of medical anthropologists, many of whom have specified culturally prescribed human behaviors that may be deleterious to human health (Fabrega 1974; Dunn 1976; Helman 1984; Heggenhougen and Shore 1986; Nations 1986; Brown and Inhorn 1990; Inhorn and Brown 1990). Heggenhougen and Shore (1986:1235) muse, "We need only read Fabrega's 1974 volume *Disease and Social Behavior* and scan its 30 pages of references to be convinced that behavior and disease prevalence and incidence are interconnected."

Thus epidemiology and medical anthropology have an important task in examining the behavioral component of health problems. As Dunn and Janes (1986) note, medical anthropology's contribution in this process is the exploration of social and cultural contexts in which health-demoting behaviors are maintained.

In this chapter, we examine the case of TFI in urban Egypt, applying both anthropological and epidemiological methods of data collection and analysis to identify behavioral risk factors for TFI. In addition to identifying these risk factors, we explore the cultural norms which support "risky" behaviors leading to TFI, as well as the historically determined, political-economic context in which TFI-producing cultural practices are encouraged.

Following an introduction to the study we will focus on significant findings. Our results suggest that iatrogenesis (Illich 1976), or the health-demoting consequences of putative health-promoting practices, is significantly associated with TFI in the urban Egyptian setting. We will examine the specific practices associated with iatrogenic TFI in both the biomedical and ethnomedical realms in Egypt, arguing that, in the biomedical realm, practices intended to "treat" infertility may in fact produce more cases of TFI than they cure. In addition, we will focus on sexual practices leading to sexually transmitted diseases (STDs). A significant proportion of women with TFI in this study had serum antibody evidence of past sexually transmitted genital chlamydial infection. We argue that in order to understand STD seroprevalence data among urban Egyptian women, it is necessary to examine the political-economic history of male labor migration from Egypt and the contemporary context in which STDs are introduced into the urban Egyptian female population.

BACKGROUND TO THE STUDY: EGYPT'S ANTHROPOLOGICAL–EPIDEMIOLOGICAL LACUNA

Although anthropology and epidemiology are well established in the West, their disciplinary reproduction in academic circles in non-Western settings, especially those of the Third World, has yet to transpire fully. Egypt, despite its ancient and well-established university system and its young but flourishing biomedical one (Gallagher 1990; Kuhnke 1990; Sonbol 1991), lacks well-defined disciplines of either anthropology or epidemiology. Anthropology, or *'ilm il-insān* (the science of man), is a branch of knowledge that is recognized by some Egyptian universities but by few Egyptians, including the educated. The struggling discipline of epidemiology is subsumed within the marginal biomedical branch of "preventive and social medicine" (i.e., family and community medicine) or within public health institutes which are also marginal. In other words, although anthropologists and epidemiologists do exist in Egypt, they are few in number and poor in influence; their disciplines lack both the power and prestige of the other "human sciences" (Foucault 1973), especially biomedicine.

Because of the underdevelopment of epidemiology and the associated field of biostatistics in Egypt, as well as substantial differences in the ways in which Egyptian (as opposed to American) epidemiology is practiced,[2] reliable descriptive epidemiological data on most health problems – including such major public health problems as schistosomiasis, tuberculosis, neonatal tetanus, and diarrheal illness – are lacking. Not surprisingly little statistical data exist on the problem of infertility in Egypt, especially given the preoccupation of the Egyptian government and donor countries with Egypt's purported "overpopulation problem" (Mitchell 1991).

Nevertheless, data on the "infertility problem" have begun to emerge from Egypt's southern neighbors – nations that comprise the STD-induced, tubal-factor "infertility belt" of sub-Saharan Central Africa (Population Reports 1983; World Health Organization 1987; Collet et al. 1988). As part of a WHO-sponsored effort to trace global infertility patterns, especially those of Africa, a general estimate of infertility rates in Egypt has been made (Farley and Belsey 1988). However, according to a preeminent Egyptian infertility researcher (Serour 1989), the estimate that 8% of all married Egyptian couples are infertile is probably low by several percentage points.

Despite the lack of statistical information, most Egyptian gynecologists who treat infertility perceive it to be a significant problem in their practices. For example, two gynecologists practicing in Alexandria, who participated as informants in this study estimated that a third of their patients are infertile women; one of these gynecologists kept computer-based records to confirm this. Similarly in the university ob/gyn teaching hospital in which this study was based, several staff physicians estimated the population of infertile women desiring treatment to be at least as large as the population of fertile women desiring contraception.[3] According to gynecologists' perceptions, the problem of infertility in Alexandria, Egypt, is neither statistically nor socially insignificant, despite the frustrating "lack of statistics" on morbidity and mortality patterns in their country.

In addition to this absence of epidemiological surveillance of infertility prevalence and incidence in Egypt – due in part to problems inherent in collecting reliable data of this type in Egypt and other Third World settings (Fabrega 1974; Heggenhougen and Shore 1986) – little is known about causal factors associated with infertility here. In the West, tremendous research efforts have been made over the past two to three decades to reveal the various factors associated with the etiology of male and female infertility. However, comparable studies from the Third World have yet to emerge.

Given this scenario, one of us (Inhorn) decided to undertake an anthropologically informed, analytical epidemiological study of infertility causation in Egypt, with special focus on the problem of TFI. This study was conducted as part of a larger ethnographic research project on infertility among Egyptian women. The study lasted 15 months (October 1988 to December 1989) in the infertility clinic of the University of Alexandria's Shatby Hospital, the public ob/gyn teaching hospital serving the northwestern Nile Delta region of Egypt.

Prior to Inhorn's study an Egyptian physician, Mohamed El-Gezery, completed a study of infertility causation among women in the same hospital (El-Gezery 1988). That study represents the first analytical epidemiological study of infertility causation for this region.[4] El-Gezery's study, however, is substantially different from ours; he focuses on a much narrower range of potential risk factors, largely excluding those involving culturally prescribed behaviors specific to Egyptian women. Differences between the two studies also reflect El-Gezery's status as an Egyptian, male physician and Inhorn's status as an American, female anthropologist. As a physician, El-Gezery was more interested in the association between various biomedically defined risk factors and infertility (e.g., history of vaginitis), whereas Inhorn was more interested in cultural patterns of behavior and their relation to infertility (e.g., practices of female circumcision). As a woman, Inhorn was also able to obtain much more specific information on matters of sexuality and infertility. Egyptian women are often reluctant to discuss sexual behaviors and problems with male physicians.[5] Many religiously conservative women deem discussion of intimate matters with or examination of their bodies by a male physician to be sinful – a view that is becoming increasingly prevalent as a result of the contemporary rise of Islamic fervor in Egypt.

Because of her gender and status as an anthropologist, Inhorn was able to collect, through in-depth, formal and informal interviewing and observation, detailed information on culturally based behavioral risk factors for infertility among a population of predominantly lower- to lower-middle-class Egyptian women. Anthropological insights were crucial in all three stages of this epidemiological study including: (1) the design of the standardized, semistructured epidemiological questionnaire, which utilized knowledge of Egyptian culture and behavioral practices; (2) collection of data, by orally administering the questionnaire in Egyptian colloquial Arabic; and (3) interpretation of the epidemiological results in light of previous and ongoing ethnography in urban Egypt.

THE STUDY: DESIGN, POPULATION, AND DEFINITIONS

This was a case-control study in which 190 women representing the patient population of Shatby Hospital were selected to participate. They were lower- and lower-middle-class women primarily from Alexandria; however, some were from the provincial cities outside Alexandria and the outlying rural areas of the Nile Delta. One hundred of the women were infertile cases, and 90 were fertile controls. A comparative demographic profile of cases and controls is presented in Table 7.1.

Of the 100 infertile women, 56 were primarily infertile (i.e., they had never conceived following at least one year of unprotected intercourse). Thirty-seven women were secondarily infertile (i.e., they had failed to become pregnant following a previous pregnancy). Seven women were "possibly" secondarily infertile (i.e., they suspected they had been pregnant and spontaneously aborted, although the spontaneous abortions were unconfirmed). Of these cases of proven and possible secondary infertility 11 women had at least one living child; the other 33 women had no children. Of those without children, nine had delivered

Table 7.1

Comparative Demographic Profile of 100 Infertile Cases and 90 Fertile Controls

	Cases (n = 100) (%)	Control (n = 90) (%)
Age		
0–19	2	2
20–29	41	47
30–39	49	40
40+	7	11
Marital Duration (years)		
0–4	20	25
5–9	40	30
10–14	22	23
15–19	14	12
20+	4	10
Ethnicity		
Lower Egyptian	64	77
Upper Egyptian	32	21
Bedouin	2	2
Nubian	2	0
Religion		
Muslim	94	98
Christian	6	2
Residency		
Urban	62	65
Transitional	25	22
Rural	13	13
Education		
None	32	27
Primary	43	46
Preparatory	4	12
Secondary/Vocational	17	11
University/Graduate	4	4

Table 7.1 (*continued*)

	Cases ($n = 100$) (%)	Control ($n = 90$) (%)
Literacy		
Illiterate	51	40
Partial	20	27
Literate	29	33
Employment		
Never	62	53
Ever	18	30
Current	20	17
Combined Monthly Income (in Egyptian pounds, $1 = LE 2.5)		
0–49	7	8
50–99	30	26
100–199	35	37
200+	26	24
no information	2	5

stillborn or live infants that had later died; the remaining 24 spontaneously aborted at various stages of gestation.

Based on their biomedical records, women in this study were categorized according to types of infertility or infertility "factors," as shown in Table 7.2. It is important to note that women's records were subject to error, along with missing information. Most of the women in this study had undergone a full range of diagnostic tests, by virtue of their participation as patients at the university hospital. Many of these women, furthermore, were participants in another unrelated infertility study being conducted by a Shatby staff physician, who made his own careful records available to Inhorn. Thus, complete information on infertility factors could be ascertained by Inhorn for the majority of the women in the study. However, a few women were new patients to the infertility clinic and had not yet undergone the full range of infertility diagnostic tests available at Shatby Hospital. These women had

Table 7.2

Infertility Factors by Biomedical Type in Study Sample of 100 Infertile Egyptian Women*

Male Factors:	40/87 = 46%
Female Factors:	82/100 = 82%
Ovarian	49/87 = 56%
Tubal	41/89 = 46%
Cervical	25/56 = 45%
Uterine	19/100 = 19%
Miscellaneous	10/100 = 10%
Unknown Factors:	6/100 = 6%
Coital Factors:	13/100 = 13%

*These percentages do not equal 100 percent because many couples were affected by more than one factor.

usually been tested in various ways by other physicians, whose records were made available to Inhorn by study subjects. However the comprehensiveness of their diagnoses remains uncertain. Thus, the information on definitions of "disease" (i.e., infertility factors) presented in Table 7.2 reflects what was known about the entire population of 100 infertile women and their husbands at the conclusion of this study.

Fertile controls were selected for the study if they had living children and were free from infertility problems, as defined by them. Most of these women were outpatients seeking contraception or treatment for minor gynecological complaints. Others were receiving prenatal care or were hospitalized for deliveries, hysterectomies, post-miscarriage care, or IUD removals. Although fertile controls were not formally matched to infertile cases on possible confounding variables, an attempt was made to ensure that all controls, like cases, were women of reproductive age (in this case between 15 and 45 years of age).

Each fertile and infertile woman selected for the study agreed to participate in a confidential interview in which information about a wide range of potential risk factors for infertility was obtained. The complete list of potential risk factors considered in this study is shown in Table 7.3; relatively few of these factors appeared to be significantly related to TFI outcomes, as will be shown in the next section.

Information about both women and their husbands was obtained by interviewing women alone and was not based on interviews with their husbands or structured observations of behaviors.[6] Husbands were not formally interviewed in this study for two major reasons: (1) the vast

Table 7.3

Potential Risk Factors for Infertility in Egypt

Contraceptive Practices
  Oral contraceptive usage
  Intrauterine device usage
  Other contraceptive practices

Genital "Purification" and Hygiene
  Female circumcision (type, practitioner)
  Douching with device
  Manual douching
  Postcoital manual douching
  Use of genital depilatories
  Use of female hygiene sprays, other substances

Sexual Practices
  Number of sexual partners (husband, wife)
  Age at first intercourse (husband, wife)
  Use of prostitutes (husband)
  Sexual frequency
  Sexual infrequency due to absent husband (labor migration, marital separation)
  Sexual intercourse during menses
  Anal-to-vaginal intercourse
  Male sexual dysfunction (impotence, premature ejaculation, etc.)
  Female sexual dysfunction (vaginismus, coitus interfeminium, etc.)
  Lack of knowledge of fertile period
  History of sexually transmitted disease (STD) (husband, wife)
  History of recurrent vaginal infections (wife)
  History of recurrent urinary tract infections (UTIs) (husband, wife)

Table 7.3 (*continued*)

History of chronic prostatitis
Serum chlamydial antibodies (wife)

Nutritional and Consumption Practices

Obesity, husband/wife
Diabetes, husband/wife
Consumption of raw beef
Caffeine consumption (tea, coffee, soft drinks; husband, wife)
Cigarette smoking (husband, wife)
Waterpipe smoking (husband)

Iatrogenesis

Previous delivery (biomedical, traditional)
History of postpartum infection
Induced abortion
Appendectomy
Splenectomy
Dilatation and curettage (D&C)
Tubal insufflation
Reproductive surgery
Cervical electrocautery

Marriage Practices

Cousin marriage between husband/wife
Two generations of cousin marriage

Occupational Exposures

History of schistosomiasis (husband, wife)
History of pesticide exposure (husband)
History of occupational chemical exposure (husband)
Occupational heat exposure (husband)

Miscellaneous

Exposure to cats (i.e., toxoplasmosis)

majority of husbands did not accompany their wives to the hospital for infertility treatment, because infertility is widely perceived as a woman's rather than a couple's problem in Egypt and because most husbands were working during hospital hours; and (2) the gender of the anthropologist would have been an obstacle to obtaining personal information from men of this social class in this sex-segregated society. As a result, all epidemiological information regarding husbands was secondarily obtained through interviews with wives, and is thus less reliable. On the other hand, because of the rapport established by the anthropologist with most of the women in the study (see Inhorn 1991), the strict privacy of the interview setting, and the careful attention given to maintaining confidentiality, interview bias was minimized. In most cases, women appeared very comfortable talking about matters of sexuality and about their husbands' behaviors. Furthermore, most were eager to explain their histories in the biomedical system, as well as their gynecological health profiles.

Nevertheless, this and other possible sources of bias – defined as any process at any stage of inference which tends to produce results or conclusions that differ systematically from the truth (Sackett 1979) – must be recognized. Other possible sources of bias include: (1) nonrandom sampling, which may affect our ability to make inferences beyond the sample; (2) prevalence-incidence sampling, wherein we may be unable to confirm exposure to a risk factor before the onset of disease; (3) misclassification, wherein a case or control was misclassified according to exposure to the risk factor, due to the "nonblindness" (and subsequent potential bias) of the investigator, the difficulty of operationalizing some behavioral risk factor variables, or the exaggerated recall of exposure to risk factors among cases. Furthermore, small subdivided infertility type samples may not be able to show a significant association when one is, in fact, present. Although biases and problems of small sample size may be present in this study, it is important that studies such as this one be carried out, given what can be learned about possible associations between risk factors and health outcomes.

RESULTS: INFERTILITY, INFECTION, AND IATROGENESIS

In this study, 41 of the 87 infertile cases (46%) who underwent diagnostic evaluation for fallopian tubal pathology (through either diagnostic laparoscopy or HSG) had evidence of TFI. Given that nearly half of all cases in this study were diagnosed with TFI, it is important to understand the factors that place lower-class, urban Egyptian women at risk of sterilizing pelvic infection.

Of the potential risk factors listed in Table 7.3, those significantly associated with TFI in this study are all iatrogenic, including "ethno-iatrogenic." In other words, infections leading to TFI are likely to be induced by physicians or traditional healers. Although these procedures are intended to *promote* the health of women – including, ironically, to "treat" the problems of infertile women – their unintended consequence may be the production or exacerbation of TFI.

Although TFI-inducing iatrogenesis has been considered in numerous studies in the West – including studies of IUD usage (Daling, Weiss, Voight, Moore et al. 1985; Daling, Weiss, Metch et al. 1985), prior induced abortion (Daling et al. 1981; Daling, Weiss, Voight, Spadoni et al. 1985), appendectomy (Mueller et al. 1986, 1987), and gynecological surgery (ovarian cystectomy, wedge resection of the ovaries, and operative correction of uterine retroversion) (Trimbos-Kemper, Trimbos, and van Hall 1982) – the potential association between TFI and reproductive practices in Egypt has never been adequately examined.

For this reason, we evaluated a number of potentially iatrogenic practices as risk factors for TFI. In the discussion that follows, biomedical and ethnomedical practices that were found to be significantly associated with TFI are considered separately, and the context in which these practices are maintained in Egypt is explored.

Biomedical Iatrogenesis: Infertility "Treatments"

In Egypt, most of the invasive procedures commonly employed by gynecologists to *treat* infertility, usually in the absence of a definitive diagnosis of TFI or other types of infertility, potentially produce TFI in women without this condition. This occurs when infectious agents are introduced into the upper genital tract. Although a detailed critique of infertility management in Egypt is beyond the scope of this chapter (see Inhorn 1991), the three major biomedical procedures used in Egypt to treat infertility are potentially iatrogenic, as acknowledged by many university-based gynecologists.[7] These include tubal insufflation, an obsolete diagnostic procedure which has been used therapeutically in Egypt to "blow open" the fallopian tubes; dilatation and curettage, or D & C (*tausī 'wi kaht*), involving the "cleaning" of the uterine cavity through removal of the endometrial lining, a procedure that is also obsolete in the treatment of infertility in the West; and cervical electrocautery (*kayy*), another obsolete procedure in which the purportedly "eroded" cervix is thermocauterized. Additionally, the widespread practice of reproductive surgeries, including ovarian cystectomies, wedge resections of the ovaries, uterine fibroid tumor removals, and tubal surgeries, is another potential source of pelvic infection.

Given this rather "untherapeutic" environment for Egyptian women, we attempted to assess the TFI-related consequences of potentially iatrogenic biomedical procedures performed here. To do this, we examined only the population of infertile women, comparing those with TFI ($n = 40$) to other cases (i.e., all those with non-TFI-related infertility, $n = 49$), in order to determine whether undergoing procedures with iatrogenic potential leads to a significantly increased risk of TFI.

The results of bivariate analyses of individual risk factors that appear to be significantly associated with TFI are shown in Table 7.4 and unadjusted and adjusted odds ratios (ORs) are shown in Table 7.5. When considered independently, only tubal insufflation appears to be significantly associated with TFI as shown in Table 7.4. Moreover, the increase in risk of TFI with increasing numbers of insufflations performed on a woman's body (many women undergo two or more insufflations) is significant ($X^2 = 8.67$; $p = 0.03$), although the relationship is not linear as determined through logistic regression.

However, given that many infertile Egyptian women undergo multiple invasive procedures, often simultaneously, these potentially iatrogenic procedures (i.e., insufflations, D&Cs, and various reproductive surgeries) are considered together as a composite "iatrogenic" risk factor in a logistic regression model,[8] as shown in Table 7.5. An adjusted and unadjusted OR of 1.3 indicates that, with each additional iatrogenic procedure, the risk of TFI increases by 30%.

According to many university-based Egyptian gynecologists, iatrogenic potential in Egypt is great, with many Egyptian women being subjected to multiple reproductive procedures that may be complicated by TFI-producing infection. In both biomedical and ethnomedical settings in Egypt, the Western cultural ideal of "sterile technique," based on notions of "germ theory," is often lacking. Instead, techniques are often septic.

In the area of reproductive health, most Egyptian women over the course of their lifetimes are subjected to one or more potentially septic procedures. Ethnogynecological procedures may include female circumcisions, traditionally induced abortions, deliveries by traditional midwives, and a variety of vaginally invasive procedures used by traditional healers to treat infertility (Inhorn 1991). Although Egyptian

Table 7.4

Bivariate Associations in Tubal-Factor Infertility (TFI)

Risk factor	TFI Cases (40) N(%)	Controls (90) N(%)	X^2	(p-value)
Type of female circumcision				
excision	26(66.7)	44(51.1)		
clitoridectomy	13(33.3)	42(48.8)	2.62	(0.11)
Type of female circumciser				
traditional	33(84.6)	60(71.4)		
medical	6(15.5)	24(28.6)	2.51	(0.11)
Composite of circumcision risk				
both excision and traditional	23(59.0)	31(36.9)		
either excision or traditional	13(33.3)	41(48.8)		
neither excision nor traditional	3(7.7)	12(14.3)	4.71	(0.03)

	TFI cases (40) N(%)	Other cases (49) N(%)	X^2	(p-value)
Number of tubal insufflations				
more than two	9(23.7)	3(6.4)		
two	0(0.0)	5(10.6)		
one	15(39.5)	19(40.4)		
none	14(36.8)	20(42.6)	8.67	(0.03)

gynecologists are often quick to point to *dāyāt* (traditional midwives) as the primary contributors to problems of sepsis in women, many university-based Egyptian gynecologists also acknowledge the significant problem of sepsis produced in biomedical settings. For example, virtually all university-based gynecologists interviewed believed septic infection to be the major cause of secondary infertility in Egypt. Included among the possible biomedical sources of sepsis cited by them were hospital and clinic (private and public) deliveries, both vaginal and cesarean; intrauterine fetal deaths and miscarriages followed by

Table 7.5

Multivariate Associations in Tubal-Factor InFertility (TFI). Unadjusted and Adjusted Odds Ratios and 95% Confidence Intervals

Risk factor	Unadjusted OR (95% CI)	Adjusted OR (95% CI)
Excision vs clitoridectomy (TFI cases vs controls)	1.9(0.9, 4.2)	1.9(0.8, 4.2)[a]
Traditional vs medical circumciser (TFI cases vs controls)	2.2(0.8, 5.9)	2.1(0.8, 5.7)[b]
Composite of circumcision risk (TFI cases vs controls)	2.0(1.1, 3.6)	2.0(1.1, 3.7)[c]
Composite of iatrogenic risk (increasing number of procedures) (TFI cases vs other cases)	1.3(1.0, 1.9)	1.3(0.9, 2.5)[d]

[a] Adjusted for type of circumciser, marital duration, and wife's age.
[b] Adjusted for type of circumcision, marital duration, and wife's age.
[c] Adjusted for marital duration and wife's age.
[d] Adjusted for marital duration, wife's age, wife's education, and wife's literacy.

D&C; so-called criminal abortions by physicians (abortions are illegal in Egypt); IUD insertions; and unindicated abdominal surgeries, especially appendectomies and urinary tract operations undertaken for complications of schistosomiasis.

In addition, many of these physicians pointed to the septic potential of practices used in the putative treatment of infertility in Egypt. In their discussion of these potentially harmful procedures, they identified two major reasons why these invasive procedures continue to be practiced on a widespread basis throughout the country. First, iatrogenic infertility treatments are performed by many gynecologists as money-making ventures in a climate of stiff competition for paying clientele. Because Egypt is a poor country with a "stalled" economy (Ansari 1986); because an ill-coordinated national health policy has led to the training of excessive numbers of Egyptian physicians, most of whom want to practice in urban areas (USAID 1979); and because women desperate to become pregnant are willing to subject their bodies to costly invasive procedures and may even request these procedures from physicians (Inhorn 1991), Egyptian gynecologists are under considerable pressure to perform invasive infertility treatments as a source of significant income and as a means of attracting patients. Indeed, many gynecologists interviewed for this study described the considerable pressure they feel to "do something" for their infertile patients (and their struggling practices), even when the treatment is not indicated or is against the best interest of the patient. Second, these procedures are deemed standard practice throughout most of Egypt. In fact, tubal insufflation, D&C, and cervical electrocautery constitute the "traditional" treatment triad of long lines of Egyptian gynecologists, beginning with the now deceased university professors who introduced these practices decades ago. As one university-based gynecologist lamented:

> [These procedures are] very commonly done because of money. Some doctors do [them] because they believe this is the treatment. If you open a book written by [a professor] thirty years ago, you will find it. But things change. If this was a good treatment thirty years ago, it doesn't have to be kept because a professor mentioned it in a book. People here are sensitive about this; they say, "We are insulting our professor." Because here there is no democracy at any level ... In places like the United States and England, these are democratic countries, and any young doctor will question anything which is not logical.

Thus, to some degree, biomedicine has been reproduced in Egypt without concomitant Western, Enlightenment-inspired notions of "progress" and "modernity." Because biomedical "traditions" are upheld, old biomedical customs die slowly in Egypt. Some even "trickle down" to the ethnomedical community, where traditional healers can be found to practice antiquated forms of biomedical therapy once practiced by Egyptian physicians (Millar and Lane 1988).

As it now stands, women in Egypt who go to physicians hoping to receive help in becoming pregnant, whether or not they are actually infertile, may be at significant risk of irreparable, infertility-producing tubal damage through procedures currently used to treat them. The irony of this situation is not lost on many university-based Egyptian gynecologists, who decry the current state of affairs in their country. However, as they also acknowledge, even with the coming of new conceptive technologies to Egypt's urban areas, the current climate of "irrationality" and iatrogenesis in Egyptian infertility management is unlikely to change substantially without radical transformations in

Egyptian biomedical education and the elimination of the physician glut that has promoted truly "unhealthy" competition.

Ethnomedical Iatrogenesis: Female Circumcision

Physicians in Egypt are not solely responsible for TFI-linked iatrogenesis. As the results of this study show, the deleterious effects of female circumcisions performed by traditional practitioners in Egypt can be considered a form of ethnogynecological iatrogenesis, given that traditional practitioners intend to make women healthy and "normal" through circumcision rather than to harm them.

The risk of post-circumcision infection leading to TFI has been noted by a number of biomedical investigators working with Sudanese women (e.g., Shandall 1976; Rushwan 1980). Likewise, in Egypt, the possibility of infertility-producing, post-circumcision infections in Egyptian girls has been mentioned by the Cairo Family Planning Association (1983). Pubescent Egyptian girls who undergo circumcision by traditional practitioners may be at an increased risk of post-circumcision infections leading to TFI through subcutaneous, parasalpingial spread of these infections to the internal reproductive organs, resulting in pelvic infection.

It is important to note that, in Egypt, female circumcision, called *tahára* (meaning both circumcision and cleanliness) actually refers to three different procedures, including: (1) clitoridectomy, in which the clitoris or only the prepuce of the clitoris are removed, leaving the labia minora and majora intact; (2) excision, in which usually the clitoris and part or all of the labia minora are removed, leaving the labia majora intact; and (3) infibulation ("Sudanese" or "pharaonic" circumcision), in which all of the external genitalia are removed and the two sides of the vulva are sutured together, leaving only a tiny opening for the passage of urine and menstrual blood (Koso-Thomas 1987a).

Throughout most of Egypt, only clitoridectomy and excision are performed, although infibulation is found in the southernmost region of Egypt, especially among the Nubians. According to the findings of this study, Bedouins are the only ethnic group in Egypt who do not practice female circumcision routinely. As the Cairo Family Planning Association (1983) has also pointed out, female circumcision is a distinctively class-based phenomenon; it is not practiced by most middle- and upper-class Egyptians, who are generally unaware of the extent of the procedure among the general population.

In this study, virtually all of the 190 women interviewed were *muṭahharīn*, or circumcised (also meaning pure). Only six women, or 3% of the entire study population, were not circumcised – in most cases, because of their employment as childhood domestic servants in the homes of upper-class Egyptians, who disallowed the procedure. The rest of the women were circumcised: 42% by clitoridectomy, 53% by excision, and 2% by infibulation. The vast majority of the women in this study – 160 of 190, or 82% – had been circumcised by a traditional practitioner, either a *dāya* (midwife), *ghagarīya* (gypsy woman), or another woman specializing in circumcision. The remainder had been circumcised by a medical practitioner, either a physician, nurse, or nurse's aide, all of whom had charged fees for their services.[9]

Given this background and the fact that the association between female circumcision and TFI in Egypt has never been systematically explored, we decided to include female circumcision and type of circumciser as possible risk factors for TFI in this study. Bivariate results are shown in Table 7.4; it is clear that women with TFI (67%) are more likely to have undergone the more extensive form of excision than are fertile controls (51%). Likewise, women with TFI (85%) are more likely to have been circumcised by a traditional practitioner than are controls (71%). A composite chi-square analysis of circumcision risk – in which women who had had both excision and a traditional circumciser are compared to those who had had either an excision or a traditional circumciser and to those who had had neither – shows a statistically significant association with TFI ($X^2 = 4.71$; $p = 0.03$).

When the individual circumcision risk factors are considered independently in a logistic regression model, the strength of the associations remains, as shown in Table 7.5. Women who had undergone excision are at 1.9 times greater risk of TFI than are women who had undergone clitoridectomy, while women who had been circumcised by a traditional practitioner are at 2.1 times greater risk of TFI than are women who had been circumcised by a medical practitioner. Additionally, we found that when the type of circumcision and circumciser are considered together, there is a significant association with TFI, as shown in Table 7.5. Women who had either an excision or a circumcision by a traditional practitioner are at 2.0 times greater risk of TFI than are women who had neither, and women who had both an excision and a traditional practitioner are at four times greater risk of TFI than are women who had neither.

Interestingly, most women in this study did *not* believe that female circumcision is harmful in any way, despite the reported trauma of the circumcision event itself. In terms of the latter, women who had undergone traditional circumcisions had usually not been anesthetized nor had the sterility of the procedure been ensured. Circumcision was typically performed with a razor blade, knife, or scissors, and post-circumcision bleeding was often controlled by the application of oven ashes to the wounded area. Although most women in this study reported that their post-circumcision healing was uneventful, a few women recalled post-circumcision hemorrhaging and infection that resulted in their hospitalization.

Despite the pain and potential complications of circumcision, the vast majority of women in this study supported the procedure and were astonished to learn that it was not practiced uniformly on women worldwide (including the American researcher), and planned to circumcise their pubescent daughters. Common rationales for circumcision cited by these women included: (a) *sexual concerns*: the need to control the girl's sexuality, thereby protecting her honor by preventing her from making a "mistake" with a man, and the need to control the married woman's sexuality, thereby reducing her sexual insatiability and preventing her from making unreasonable sexual demands on her husband; (b) *religious concerns*: the need to follow the perceived Islamic mandate of female circumcision (even though Islamic scriptures do not prescribe this practice); (c) *health concerns*: the need to ensure a girl's pubertal maturation and health and the need to "purify" the genital region, given that the uncircumcised genitalia are thought to be unclean and to grow over time (becoming elongated like a penis or hanging out of the vulva like leaves or a "rooster's comb"), causing irritation and even blockage of the vaginal opening; and (d) *aesthetic concerns*: the need to make the genitalia "pretty" so that a husband will not be repulsed by his wife.

Given this normative support among lower-class urban and rural Egyptian women, it is not surprising that the practice of female circumcision continues unabated in Egypt today – despite legal prohibition, campaigns by Egyptian and international health organizations to eradicate it,[10] and the growing awareness among lower-class Egyptian women that female circumcision is neither uniformly practiced in Egypt nor in the rest of the world.

What remains to be done is to convince Egyptian women of the health consequences of female circumcision – especially its effect on a teenaged girl's fertility. If the results of this study are correct, Egyptian girls who undergo traditional circumcisions are at significant risk of subsequent TFI, an iatrogenic outcome that can literally destroy a woman's reproductive and marital future. If this message can be effectively delivered to Egyptian women, including the traditional practitioners who perform the bulk of female circumcisions on pubescent girls, then perhaps the practice of female circumcision, as well as its health-demoting consequences, can be avoided.

Sexual Practices and STDs

Biomedical and ethnomedical iatrogenic practices are not the only potential behavioral risk factors for TFI in urban Egypt. In studies around the world, the relationship between TFI and sexual practices leading to contraction of sterilizing STDs, especially gonorrhea and genital chlamydial infection, is well established (Population Reports 1983; Maybe et al. 1985; Millar 1987; WHO 1987; Collet et al. 1988; Sellors et al. 1988; Dixon-Mueller and Wasserheit 1991). Over the past decade, studies have emerged from the Alexandria vicinity that show STDs – which are often asymptomatic in women[11] – are not only present among married women at rates similar to those found in the West (Kotkat 1978; Ah 1980; El Ghazzawy 1980; Kholeif 1980; Basha 1981; EI-Latiff 1982; Elhefnawy 1985; Amer 1987), but also are associated with pelvic infections in women and the sterilizing sequelae of these infections (Fathalla 1986; Ghamri 1986; El Lakany 1988; Mehanna 1989).

Given this scenario, we attempted to investigate the relationship between sexual practices (of both women and their husbands), STDs, and TFI among Egyptian women. As shown in Table 7.3 , we considered as possible risk factors for TFI (1) sexual practices themselves (e.g., number of reported sexual partners of both wife and husband, husband's use of prostitutes); (2) medical histories indicative of possible STDs (e.g., history of vaginal infections, urinary tract infections of both husband and wife); (3) sexual infrequency due to extended marital separation (i.e., periods of possible extramarital sexual activity); and (4) serum antibody evidence of sexually transmitted genital chlamydial infection among women.

With regard to the last factor, blood samples for serum antibody investigation were drawn from 153 of the 190 women who participated in this study. Unfortunately, due to a lack of (a) adequate provisions for the separation of blood samples, (b) their storage in well-sealed vials, and (c) constant refrigeration in the Egyptian setting, 20 of the sera samples were degraded or spilled in transit to the United States, resulting in a total of 133 sera samples for investigation (33 TFI, 50 non-TFI, 50 controls). Furthermore, because of possible degradation, serum antibody titers were not as high as expected, and it was difficult at times to determine whether samples were positive for genital chlamydial infection or trachoma, a blinding eye disease common to Egypt that is caused by the same bacterium.

Nevertheless our results suggest a significant presence of genital chlamydial infections. Among women with TFI, 33% were positive for serum chlamydial antibodies, indicating possible past or present genital chlamydial infection among these women. Surprisingly, the prevalence of chlamydial antibodies among fertile control women was also high – 30%. As a result, the association between the presence of serum chlamydial antibodies and TFI could not be demonstrated statistically. Nevertheless, these seroprevalence data suggest that sexually transmitted genital chlamydial infections are present, and even common, among Egyptian women, and that they may lead to TFI in those cases that ascend to the upper genital tract.

This information presents another question: How might Egyptian women contract these infections? Either Egyptian women are contracting infections from sexual activity with infected pre- or extramarital partners, or Egyptian women's husbands are becoming infected through pre- or extramarital sexual activity and then infecting them. In all likelihood, husbands are the primary reservoir of infection in this setting.

In Egypt, especially among the rural and urban lower classes, women's sexuality is the source of great anxiety; a girl's virginity and a woman's marital fidelity are the main source of her natal family's *sharaf* (also known as *'ird*) or honor. Because *sharaf* infractions are the cause of great shame to the extended family, the sexuality of female members is strictly guarded. Girls are circumcised to "calm" their budding libidos and prevent them from "making mistakes." Proof of their virginity, in the form of a bloodied cloth known simply as *sharaf*, is expected by most families on or shortly after the wedding night. Postmarital behavior is also subject to scrutiny by both family and community members. Indeed, there is little opportunity for women to "go astray," given these direct social controls and the indirect threat of severe physical, social, and spiritual punishment should a woman deviate from these standards.

Men, on the other hand, have much greater sexual liberty. Although virginity at marriage and marital fidelity are also cultural ideals for men, it is widely expected that young men may deviate from these standards, especially before marriage, when they attempt to "gain experience." Marital fidelity is the stronger of these ideals, given the sinfulness of adultery in Islam. Yet, Egyptians acknowledge that men are likely to veer off the "straight path" of Islam, especially during periods of prolonged separation from their wives, as is the case during male labor migration.

Given these sexual standards, women in this study were questioned about their own sexual experiences and those of their husbands. As expected, all women who had been married only once (92.0%) said that they had had only one sexual partner: i.e., their husbands. Indeed, the implications of a situation different from this were so unthinkable to these women that many of them were openly incredulous at being asked such a question. However, it is important to note that Inhorn's status as a foreigner was a distinct advantage during this phase of the questioning. Essentially, her informants forgave her for asking such impertinent questions and often reasoned aloud that "foreigners like you" are allowed to have free sexual relations, which they had surmised from watching the American television serials, *Dallas, Dynasty, Knots Landing*, and *Falcon Crest*, all of which had been popular evening television fare in Egypt.

When asked about their husbands' sexual behavior, however, women's reactions were quite different. The majority were quite certain and even adamant that their husbands had been virgins at marriage and faithful in marriage, even if they had been married previously which was true of 14.0% of husbands. Many women noted additionally that their husbands were "religious," implying that religious faith would prevent them from sinning in this way. However, a significant proportion of both infertile and fertile women believed that their husbands had had premarital or extramarital sexual experiences with prostitutes or other "bad women." In several cases, women had been told this by their husbands or had discovered this themselves. For example, one secondarily infertile woman's labor-migrant husband of twelve years informed her "I've had more women than hairs on your head." At least one of these women had given him a genital chlamydial infection, which he unwittingly transmitted to his wife.

Interestingly, STDs, contracted by husbands and transmitted to wives, were discounted as "rare" or "not so common" in Egypt by all but two of the seventeen gynecologists who participated as informants in this study. Most of these physicians pointed to Egypt's status as a religiously conservative "Muslim community" and to the lack of clinical cases of STDs, especially gonorrhea, in their gynecological practices as evidence to support their contention that STDs are uncommon in Egypt. In short, whether or not STDs are present in Egypt and whether or not they are a major factor in the numerous TFI cases in Egypt are issues that the Egyptian gynecologists in this study were loath to consider.

Only two were candid about what they perceived to be the significant problem of STD-induced infertility in their country. As one of them stated:

> [Sexually transmitted disease] is, I think, the major factor [in TFI]. Many of these husbands get some sort of practice before marriage. Many times, it is a eunuch [i.e., homosexual] practice! He may take some sort of antibiotic or chemotherapy, but this is not enough to overcome the infection, and he can't go to a doctor and tell him he is practicing [i.e., sex], so the infection becomes chronic in his prostate. A real factor in primary infertility in our community is husbands who have chronic prostatitis. The first night [i.e., the wedding night], they inject the pus, or organism, into the vagina of their wives, causing ascending infection, which destroys the tubes. After some time, the doctor discovers the cause [i.e., TFI]. The man can be treated and sometimes he is OK. So he's the origin. And many of the wives lost their fertility and their marital life while they were just innocent and didn't know.

> Before marriage, many things should be put on the table – if he had an infection, by semen analysis, and any hereditary disease. From the wife's side, if there is a major fault regarding menstruation – for example, primary amenorrhea – this should be explained to the husband before marriage. But you know theoretical ideas cannot always be put into practice! If a father is responsible for his newly married daughter, he should ask for a semen analysis to be sure [about STDs], because [her husband] can destroy her tubes from the first night.

Although most of the Egyptian gynecologists interviewed tended to attribute the TFI problem to factors other than STDs, the widespread problem of TFI is probably tied to Egyptian male labor migration and the resultant introduction of STDs. Given the contemporary economic climate in Egypt – marked by low wages, spiraling inflation, un- and underemployment, inflated housing prices, and occasional "bread riots" over the increasing cost of subsidized foodstuffs (El-Sokkari 1984; Ansari 1986) – it is not surprising that many Egyptian men choose or are forced to migrate abroad. For example, 30% of informants' husbands had migrated abroad – 79% during the post-marital period and, in almost every case, without their wives.

Studies from around the world and from Africa in particular have shown that male labor migration brings with it a variety of social ills, one of the primary ones being infertility-producing and even life-threatening STDs, including AIDS. In a recent anthropological review of infectious disease problems (Inhorn and Brown 1990), the triad of migration, prostitution, and STD was linked to the serious sociomedical problem of infertility in populations in Africa and other parts of the Third World.

In Egypt, the vast majority of men migrate within the Muslim Middle East, especially to the Arab Gulf, Libya, and, before the recent Gulf War, to Iraq. Although information about prostitution in the religiously conservative nations of the Middle East is limited, both male and female prostitution is said to exist in most Arab countries, including the urban areas of Egypt. Egyptians claim that women who become prostitutes are forced to do so because of economic circumstances beyond their control or situations of coercion. For example, stories abound in Egypt of unfortunate Egyptian girls from poor families who are taken as brides by men from petro-rich Arab countries, only to find themselves serving as prostitutes in the homes of their supposed "husbands." Furthermore, following the Iran–Iraq war, women widowed or abandoned by the deaths of Iraqi soldiers were said by Egyptians to be entering prostitution out of economic desperation. Egyptian men, thousands of whom were living as migrants in Iraq before the Gulf War, were said to make up a large part of the clientele of these women.

Although the extent of prostitution, both male and female, is difficult to determine and the information presented here is based on unsubstantiated information from women who participated in this study, as well as their husbands and other informants, prostitution most certainly exists in this environment. It is also likely that changing sexual expectations on the part of Egyptian men have increased their use of prostitutes in recent years. Because of a thriving black market in pornographic videos from Western countries, Egyptian men are exposed to sexual practices that are culturally prohibited among the Egyptian lower classes (e.g., oral-genital sex, anal sex). When asked, their wives are often unwilling to engage in such practices, so Egyptian men may resort to prostitutes in order to experiment. Moreover sexual practices encountered during visits to prostitutes may also lead some men to request these practices from their wives. Either way, that Egyptian men are interested in what Egyptian women deem to be sexually "abnormal" and even sinful is apparent from the reports of many women informants, who said that they had refused their husbands' requests for fellatio in particular.

Thus, the migration–prostitution–STD triad found in sub-Saharan Africa and other parts of the Third World may operate in Egypt as well. That it is linked to STD-induced TFI is likely, given the findings of recent studies from Alexandria (Mehanna 1989). Yet, in the study reported here, few women had ever heard of "sexually transmitted diseases" or the Arabic terms for syphilis and gonorrhea, although many of them pointed in a different context to the problem of "pus" in their husbands' urine or semen analyses (for which their husbands had often sought treatment). Moreover, when women in this study mustered the courage to ask their physicians, "Why are my tubes blocked?," they were often informed of an "infection" that they never knew they had contracted. That their husbands may have transmitted the infection to them is a possibility that few Egyptian women or their physicians appeared to realize. That these infections may have been contracted by husbands during periods of economically forced labor migration is a political-economic reality that likely underlies the TFI problem in Egypt.

CONCLUSION

We began this chapter with the case of Hind, a poor, urban Egyptian woman whose infertility is due to TFI, or infection-scarred "blocked tubes." In Hind's case, the source of the pelvic infection that has literally scarred her for life is unclear; but it may have been due to any of a number of factors, including the complications of her early delivery by a traditional midwife, an STD given to her by one of her two husbands, or the numerous invasive ethnomedical and biomedical procedures to which she has subjected her body over the years in her attempt to become pregnant.

Arguing that Hind's case is typical of Egyptian women suffering from TFI, we have posed the question: What places poor, urban Egyptian women like Hind at risk of sterilizing infection?

This chapter has attempted to answer that question, through an integrative anthropological–epidemiological exploration of various behavioral risk factors leading to TFI outcomes among urban Egyptian women. Numerous potential, culture-specific risk factors for TFI were identified through preliminary ethnographic research. However, epidemiological analysis of case-control study data collected through in-depth, formal interviewing allowed us to identify which potential risk factors appear to be significantly associated with TFI. Of the factors shown in Table 7.3, only the iatrogenic biomedical procedures used in the putative treatment of female infertility and the ethno-iatrogenic practice of female circumcision appear to be significantly associated with TFI outcomes. In addition, epidemiological seroprevalence data demonstrate relatively high rates of serum chlamydial antibodies among women in this study population, indicative of sexually transmitted genital chlamydial infection, a known risk factor for TFI. Ethnographic data concerning sexual practices among this population suggest that Egyptian women may contract potentially sterilizing STDs from their husbands, who may have contracted these infections during periods of labor migration.

Together, anthropology and epidemiology have a crucial role in identifying factors, especially culture-specific behavioral factors, that place populations at risk of health problems such as TFI. Anthropological research designs, methods of ethnographic data collection, and forms of qualitative data analysis may be extremely useful in generating testable, analytical epidemiological hypotheses about the relations between potential behavioral risk factors and disease outcomes (Nations 1986). However, alone, anthropological approaches are insufficient to sort out from the myriad possibilities which behaviors, identified through ethnographic research, place groups of individuals at most significant risk of disease. Identifying significant factors is necessary to prioritize needs in behavioral intervention programs; this is where epidemiological approaches to risk assessment become necessary. Conversely, epidemiology is certainly not ethnography and hence lacks the ability to identify the many potential, culturally embedded risk factors that require further investigation in most cross-cultural studies. Most important, epidemiology is useful in identifying the most significant risk factors, but falls short in interpreting the social, cultural, and political-economic context in which these risk factors are found, maintained, and even encouraged at the population level.

It is in this interpretive arena that anthropology, with its methodological tradition of intensive ethnography, has perhaps the most important role to play in integrative anthropological–epidemiological research. Through ethnography focusing on the social, cultural, and political-economic correlates of behavior, anthropology can provide epidemiology with interpretations of the causes of poor health leading to understandings which are greater than the sum of either disciplines' individual contributions.

Thus, we urge the continuing development of a synthetic "anthropological epidemiology" through interdisciplinary training and collaboration.

Through such efforts, we can achieve superior understanding of the causes of poor health and begin to develop meaningful strategies for intervention.

NOTES

1. All names used in this article are pseudonyms.
2. For example, computers and software are in short supply in Egypt, even among epidemiologists, who must therefore perform much of their data management and analysis by hand. The substantial national divergences in the practice of epidemiology have been noted by Spruit and Kromhout (1987).
3. Because the hospital did not keep standardized records on outpatients, including those presenting for infertility services, accurate statistics on these populations of infertile and fertile women were not available. This lacuna is related to a general problem of medical record-keeping in Egypt.
4. An informative study of possible etiological factors in infertility has been carried out by Serour (1991) for Cairo. However, Serour's study does not employ an analytical epidemiological research design.
5. In the study to be discussed, Inhorn was often asked by her female informants to relay information of a particularly intimate nature (e.g., about sexual problems) to the mostly male physicians treating these patients for infertility. Informants were embarrassed to discuss such matters with male physicians themselves, but felt comfortable telling Inhorn and then encouraging her to transmit the information to those in charge of treatment. In this way, Inhorn served as a sort of clinical liaison.
6. However, informal interviews with a number of husbands were conducted outside of the hospital in informants' homes.
7. There tends to be a substantial difference between "town and gown" (i.e., community-based versus university-based) gynecologists in Egypt. Gynecologists at universities have better access to current literature, current technology, and opportunities for innovation. Although some community-based gynecologists attempt to keep "up to date" with innovations in the field, they do so on their own and at their own expense. Egypt lacks continuing medical education (CME) requirements of any kind, professional associations that meet regularly, or a system of malpractice litigation. As a result, there is very little regulation of, or peer pressure upon, physicians in the community. However, university-based gynecologists tend to be critical of many of the features of community-based infertility management (Inhorn 1991).
8. Logistic regression is a powerful statistical tool for studying the association between multiple risk factors and a disease outcome. Logistic regression

allows the confounding effects of other variables to be controlled simultaneously, while the relationship of a potential risk factor and a disease outcome is assessed through the estimation of an odds ratio (OR). In analytical epidemiological studies, the OR offers a means of estimating the so-called relative risk of contracting the disease under study, given past exposure to the risk factor. The calculation of the OR is based on the assumption that the disease being studied is relatively rare. If that is true, then the ratio of the odds in favor of exposure to the risk factor among the cases to the odds in favor of exposure among the controls – i.e., the OR – provides an estimate of the risk of becoming a case given exposure to the risk factor.

9. Because female circumcision is so common in Egypt, some medical personnel believe they are meeting an important need by performing less painful, less extensive circumcisions with the aid of local anesthetics and antiseptics. Although physicians who perform female circumcisions are certainly in the minority in Egypt, it is interesting to note that most of the gynecologists who participated as informants in this study and who had seen thousands of *fertile* circumcised women during their careers as practitioners agreed that female circumcision as it is practiced in Egypt (i.e., clitoridectomy or excision) is *not* damaging to women's fertility, despite its negative effects on women's sexuality.

10. The scholarly and semischolarly literature on female circumcision, much of it propagandizing against this practice, continues to grow. See, for example, Hayes 1975; Shandall 1976; Lowenstein 1978; Cook 1979; Baasher 1979; Taba 1979; Assaad 1980; Hosken 1980; McLean 1980; Giorgis 1981; Hall and Ismail 1981; Paige and Paige 1981; Gruenbaum 1982; Assaad 1982; El Dareer 1982; Cloudsley 1984; Al Naggar 1985; Koso-Thomas 1987a, 1987b; Paige 1987; Boddy 1989; and Gordon 1991. Furthermore, two of the W. H. R. Rivers Prize Essays in medical anthropology have been devoted to this subject – Gruenbaum's in 1982 and Gordon's in 1991. Gordon's is accompanied by five commentaries by anthropologists, all women, either working in Egypt or Sudan or interested in issues of gender and health. The reader is referred to this issue of *Medical Anthropology Quarterly* for a recent, provocative discussion of female circumcision by medical anthropologists.

11. One gynecologist reported that cervical smears taken from more than 1000 Alexandrian women participating in an internationally sponsored study of contraceptive methods showed gram-negative gonorrhea unaccompanied by clinical symptoms in 20.0% of cases. This gynecologist, who was in charge of the study, said he believed that the cultural practice of at least twice-daily manual vaginal douching by most Egyptian women was responsible for the asymptomatic nature of most gonorrhea cases in women in Egypt.

REFERENCES

Ali, O. 1980. Non Specific Urethritis Due to *Chlamydia trachomatis*. M.A. Thesis, University of Alexandria, Egypt.

Al Naggar, A. 1985. Islam and F. C. Cairo: Cairo Family Planning Association.

Amer, A. 1987. *Chlamydia trachomatis* and *Neisseria gonorrhoeae* in the Cervices of Women of the Child Bearing Age from the Egyptian Rural Community. M.A. Thesis, University of Alexandria, Egypt.

Ansari, H. 1986. Egypt: The Stalled Society. Albany, New York: State University of New York Press.

Assaad, F. 1982. The Sexual Mutilation of Women. World Health Forum 3:391–394.

Assaad, M. 1980. Female Circumcision in Egypt: Social Implications, Current Research, and Prospects for Change. Studies in Family Planning 11:3–16.

Baasher, T. 1979. Psychological Aspects of Female Circumcision. *In* Traditional Practices Affecting the Health of Women and Children: Female Circumcision, Childhood Marriage, Nutritional Taboos, etc. Pp. 71–105. Alexandria, Egypt: WHO Regional Office for the Eastern Mediterranean.

Basha, N. 1981. *Chlamydia trachomatis* Infection of the Cervix with Contraceptive Pills and Intrauterine Devices. M.A. Thesis, University of Alexandria, Egypt.

Boddy, J. 1989. Wombs and Alien Spirits: Women, Men, and the *Zar* Cult in Northern Sudan. Madison: University of Wisconsin Press.

Brown, P. and M. Inhorn. 1990. Disease, Ecology, and Human Behavior. *In* Medical Anthropology: A Handbook of Theory and Method. T. Johnson and C. Sargent, eds. Pp. 187–214. New York: Greenwood Press.

Cairo Family Planning Association. 1983. Facts about Female Circumcision. Cairo: Cairo Family Planning Association.

Cloudsley, A. 1984. Women of Omduran: Life, Love and the Cult of Virginity. London: Ethnographica.

Collet, M., J. Reniers, E. Frost, R. Gass, F. Yvert, A. Leclerc, C. Roth-Meyer, B. Ivanoff, and A. Meheus. 1988. Infertility in Central Africa: Infection is the Cause. International Journal of Obstetrics and Gynecology 26:423–428.

Cook, R. 1979. Damage to Physical Health from Pharaonic Circumcision (Infibulation) of Females: A Review of the Medical Literature. *In* Traditional Practices Affecting the Health of Women and Children: Female Circumcision, Childhood Marriage, Nutritional Taboos, etc. Pp. 53–69. Alexandria, Egypt: WHO Eastern Mediterranean Regional Office.

Daling, J., L. Spadoni, and I. Emanuel. 1981. Role of Induced Abortion in Secondary Infertility. Obstetrics and Gynecology 57:59–61.

Daling, J., N. Weiss, B. Metch, W. Chow, R. Soderstrom, D. Moore, L. Spadoni, and B. Stadel. 1985. Primary Tubal Infertility in Relation to the Use of an Intrauterine Device. New England Journal of Medicine 312: 937–947.

Daling, J., N. Weiss, L. Voight, D. Moore, and B. Stadel. 1985. IUDs and Infertility. New England Journal of Medicine 313:636.

Daling, J., N. Weiss, L. Voight, L. Spadoni, R. Soderstrom, E. Moore, and B. Stadel. 1985. Tubal Infertility in Relation to Prior Induced Abortion. Fertility and Sterility 43:389–394.

Dixon-Mueller, R. and J. Wasserheit. 1991. The Culture of Silence: Reproductive Tract Infections among Women in the Third World. New York: International Women's Health Coalition.

Dunn, F. 1976. Human Behavioural Factors in the Epidemiology and Control of *Wuchereria* and *Brugia* Infections. Bulletin of the Public Health Society, Malaysia 10:34–44.

Dunn, E. and C. Janes. 1986. Introduction: Medical Anthropology and Epidemiology. *In* Anthropology and Epidemiology: Interdisciplinary Approaches to the Study of Health and Disease. C. Janes, R. Stall, and S. Gifford, eds. Pp. 3–34. Dordrecht: D. Reidel.

El Dareer, A. 1982. Woman, Why Do You Weep? Circumcision and its Consequences. London: Zed Press.

El-Gezery, M. 1988. Epidemiological Features of Infertile Women Attending El-Shatby University Hospital. Ph.D. Thesis. Faculty of Medicine, Alexandria University, Alexandria, Egypt.

El Ghazzawy, E. 1980. Isolation of *Herpes simplex* Virus from the Cervix of Normal Females. M.A. Thesis, University of Alexandria, Egypt.

Elhefnawy, A. 1985. Characterization of *Neisseria gonorrhoeae* Isolated from Cases of Urethritis. M.A. Thesis, University of Alexandria, Egypt.

El Lakany, H. 1988. Prevalence of Genital Mycoplasmas and Chlamydiae in Infertile, Pregnant and Aborted Women. Ph.D. Thesis, University of Alexandria, Egypt.

El-Latiff, S. 1982. Non Specific Urethritis in Males due to *Herpes simplex* Virus. M.A. Thesis, University of Alexandria, Egypt.

El-Sokkari, M. 1984. Basic Needs, Inflation and the Poor of Egypt, 1970–1980. Cairo Papers in Social Science 7:1–103.

Fabrega, H. Jr. 1974. Disease and Social Behavior: An Interdisciplinary Perspective. Boston: MIT Press.

Farley, T. and M. Belsey. 1988. The Prevalence and Aetiology of Infertility. Paper Presented at the International Union for the Scientific Study of the Population, African Population Conference, Dakar, Senegal, November 1988.

Fathalla, F. 1986. Study of Different Risk Factors for the Development of Pelvic Inflammatory Disease. M.A. Thesis, University of Alexandria, Egypt.

Foster, G. 1976. Disease Etiologies in Non-Western Medical Systems. American Anthropologist 78:773–782.

Foucault, M. 1973. Madness and Civilization: A History of Insanity in the Age of Reason. New York: Vintage.

Gallagher, N. 1990. Egypt's Other Wars: Epidemics and the Politics of Public Health. Syracuse, New York: Syracuse University Press.

Ghamri, L. 1986. Isolation of Microbial Agents from Adult Females Suffering from Salpingo-oophoritis. M.A. Thesis, University of Alexandria, Egypt.

Giorgis, B. 1981. Female Circumcision in Africa. Addis Ababa, Ethiopia: U.N. Economic Commission for Africa Research Series.

Gordon, D. 1991. Female Circumcision and Genital Operations in Egypt and the Sudan: A Dilemma for Medical Anthropology. Medical Anthropology Quarterly 5:3–14.

Gruenbaum, E. 1982. The Movement Against Clitoridectomy and Infibulation in Sudan: Public Health Policy and the Women's Movement. Medical Anthropology Quarterly 13:4–12.

Hall, M. and B. Ismail. 1981. Sisters Under the Sun: The Story of Sudanese Women. London: Longmans.

Hayes, R. 1975. Female Genital Mutilation, Fertility Control, Women's Roles, and the Patrilineage in Modern Sudan: A Functional Analysis. American Ethnologist 2:617–633.

Heggenhougen, H. and L. Shore. 1986. Cultural Components of Behavioural Epidemiology: Implications for Primary Health Care. Social Science and Medicine 22:1235–1245.

Helman, C. 1984. Culture, Health and Illness. Bristol: Wright.

Hosken, F. 1980. Female Sexual Mutilations: The Facts and Proposals for Action. Lexington, Massachusetts: Women's International Network News.

Illich, I. 1976. Medical Nemesis: The Expropriation of Health. New York: Bantam.

Inhorn, M. 1991. Umm Il-Ghayyib, Mother of the Missing One: A Sociomedical Study of Infertility in Alexandria, Egypt. Ph.D. Thesis, University of California, Berkeley.

Inhorn, M. and P. Brown. 1990. The Anthropology of Infectious Disease. Annual Review of Anthropology 19:89–117.

Janes, C., R. Stall, and S. Gifford, eds. 1986. Anthropology and Epidemiology: Interdisciplinary Approaches to the Study of Health and Disease. Dordrecht: D. Reidel.

Kelsey, J., W. Thompson, and A. Evans. 1986. Methods in Observational Epidemiology. New York: Oxford University Press.

Kholeif, L. 1980. Chlamydia trachomatis in Cervices of Women in Late Pregnancy. M.A. Thesis, University of Alexandria, Egypt.

Koso-Thomas, O. 1987a. The Circumcision of Women: A Strategy for Eradication. London: Zed Press.

Koso-Thomas, O. 1987b. Female Circumcision and Related Hazards. *In* Report on the Seminar on Traditional Practices Affecting the Health of Women and Children in Africa. Pp. 65–67. Addis Ababa, Ethiopia: Inter-African Committee.

Kotkat, A. 1978. A Study of the Prevalence of *Trichomonas vaginalis* among Gynaecological Patients Attending Shatby Hospital. M.A. Thesis, High Institute of Public Health, Alexandria, Egypt.

Kuhnke, L. 1990. Lives at Risk: Public Health in Nineteenth-Century Egypt. Berkeley: University of California Press.

Last, J. 1983. A Dictionary of Epidemiology. New York: Oxford University Press.

Lowenstein, L. 1978. Attitudes and Attitude Differences to Female Genital Mutilation in the Sudan: Is There a Change on the Horizon? Social Science and Medicine 12:417–421.

MacMahon, B. and T. Pugh. 1960. Epidemiologic Methods. Boston: Little, Brown.

Mausner, J. and A. Bahn. 1974. Epidemiology – An Introductory Text. Philadelphia: W. B. Saunders.

Mausner, J. and S. Kramer. 1985. Epidemiology – An Introductory Text. Philadelphia: W. B. Saunders.

Maybe, D., G. Ogbaselassie, J. Robertson, J. Heckels, and M. Ward. 1985. Tubal Infertility in the Gambia: Chlamydial and Gonococcal Serology in Women with Tubal Occlusion Compared with Pregnant Controls. Bulletin of the World Health Organization 63:1107–1113.

McLean, S., ed. 1980. Female Circumcision, Excision and Infibulation: The Facts and Proposals for Change. London: Minority Rights Group.

Mehanna, M. 1989. Prevalence of *Chlamydia trachomatis* Infection among Cases of Tubal Infertility and Tubal Ectopic Pregnancy. M.A. Thesis, University of Alexandria, Egypt.

Millar, M. 1987. Genital Chlamydial Infection: A Role for Social Scientists. Social Science and Medicine 25:1289–1299.

Millar, M. and S. Lane. 1988. Ethno-ophthalmology in the Egyptian Delta: An Historical Systems Approach to Ethnomedicine in the Middle East. Social Science and Medicine 26:651–657.

Mitchell, T. 1991. America's Egypt: Discourse of the Development Industry. Middle East Report 21(2):18–36.

Mueller, B., J. Daling, D. Moore, N. Weiss, L. Spadoni, B. Stadel, and M. Soules. 1986. Appendectomy and the Risk of Tubal Infertility. New England Journal of Medicine 315:1506–1508.

Mueller, B., J. Daling, D. Moore, N. Weiss, L. Spadoni, B. Stadel, and M. Soules. 1987. Appendectomy and the Risk of Infertility. New England Journal of Medicine 316:1662.

Myntti, C. 1991. The Anthropologist as Storyteller: Picking Up Where Others Leave Off in Public Health Research. *In* The Health Transition: Methods and Measures. J. Cleland and A. Hill, eds. Pp. 227–236. Canberra: Health Transition Centre, The Australian National University.

Nations, M. 1986. Epidemiological Research on Infectious Disease: Quantitative Rigor or Rigormortis? Insights from Ethnomedicine. *In* Anthropology and Epidemiology: Interdisciplinary Approaches to the Study of Health and Disease. C. Janes, R. Stall, and S. Gifford, eds. Pp. 97–123. Dordrecht: D. Reidel.

Ngokwey, N. 1988. Pluralistic Etiological Systems in Their Social Context: A Brazilian Case Study. Social Science and Medicine 26:793–802.

Paige, K. 1987. Patterns of Excision and Excision Rationales in Egypt. Unpublished manuscript.

Paige, K. and J. Paige. 1981. The Politics of Reproductive Ritual. Berkeley: University of California Press.

Population Reports. 1983. Infertility and Sexually Transmitted Disease: A Public Health Challenge. Population Reports Series L 8:L113–151.

Robert, C., S. Bouvier, and A. Rougemont. 1989. Epidemiology, Anthropology and Health Education. World Health Forum 10:355–364.

Rothman, K. 1981. The Rise and Fall of Epidemiology, 1950–2000 A.D. New England Journal of Medicine 304:600–602.

Rushwan, H. 1980. Etiologic Factors in Pelvic Inflammatory Disease in Sudanese Women. American Journal of Obstetrics and Gynecology 138:877–879.

Sackett, D. 1979. Bias in Analytic Research. Journal of Chronic Disease 32:51–63.

Sellors, J., I. Mahony, M. Chernesky, and D. Rath. 1988. Tubal Factor Infertility: An Association with Prior Chlamydial Infection and Asymptomatic Salpingitis. Fertility and Sterility 49:451–457.

Serour, G. 1989. Infertility as a Health Problem in Egypt. Paper Presented at the National Meeting on Research Priorities in Human Reproduction, Cairo, Egypt, Dec. 21–23, 1989.

Serour, G. 1991. Infertility: A Health Problem in the Muslim World. Population Sciences 10:41–58.

Shandall, A. 1976. Circumcision and Infibulation of Females. Sudan Medical Journal 5:178–212.

Sonbol, A. 1991. The Creation of a Medical Profession in Egypt, 1800–1922. Syracuse, New York: Syracuse University Press.

Spruit, I. and D. Kromhout. 1987. Medical Sociology and Epidemiology: Convergences, Divergences and Legitimate Boundaries. Social Science and Medicine 25:579–587.

Taba, A. 1979. Female Circumcision. *In* Traditional Practices Affecting the Health of Women and Children: Female Circumcision, Childhood Marriage, Nutritional Taboos, etc. Pp. 43–52. Alexandria, Egypt: WHO Regional Office for the Eastern Mediterranean.

Trimbos-Kemper, T., B. Trimbos, and E. van Hall. 1982. Etiological Factors in Tubal Infertility Fertility and Sterility 37:384–388.

Trostle, J. 1986. Early Work in Anthropology and Epidemiology: From Social Medicine to the Germ Theory, 1840 to 1920. *In* Anthropology and Epidemiology: Interdisciplinary Approaches to the Study of Health and Disease. C. Janes, R. Stall, and S. Gifford, eds. Pp. 35–57. Dordrecht: D. Reidel.

True, W. 1990. Epidemiology and Medical Anthropology. *In* Medical Anthropology: A Handbook of Theory and Method. T. Johnson and C. Sargent, eds. Pp. 298–318. New York: Greenwood Press.

USAID. 1979. Health in Egypt: Recommendations for U.S. Assistance. Washington, D.C.: USAID.

Young, A. 1976. Internalizing and Externalizing Medical Belief Systems. Social Science and Medicine 10:147–156.

Young, A. 1991. Internalising and Externalising Medical Belief Systems: An Ethiopian Example. *In* Concepts of Health, Illness and Disease: A Comparative Perspective. C. Currer and M. Stacey, eds. Pp. 139–160. New York: Berg.

World Health Organization. 1987. Infections, Pregnancies, and Infertility: Perspectives on Prevention. Fertility and Sterility 47:964–968.

CHAPTER 8

Key Informants, Pile Sorts, or Surveys? Comparing Behavioral Research Methods for the Study of Acute Respiratory Infections in West Bengal

Karabi Bhattacharyya

As the attention of the public health community turns toward changes in individual behavior for health improvement, demand for explanations of certain behaviors that persist and how they can be changed will increase. Most health interventions today seek to change behavior by changing the decisions people make about their health. Examples include deciding whether or not to take a child for immunizations; whether or not to ask your sexual partner to wear a condom; and whether or not to go to a health care provider. Social and behavioral scientists are increasingly asked to apply their skills to public health problems and to explain why people behave the way they do. This expanding need for social and cultural information has been accompanied by much debate over the best way to collect this information.

Social scientists have investigated local beliefs and practices with two methods: KAP (knowledge, attitudes, practices) surveys and ethnography. Much debate has surrounded the value of data generated by quantitative surveys versus qualitative ethnographies. Knowledge,

The comments made by the anonymous reviewers were very helpful. The West Bengal study was funded by the Ford Foundation Epidman Network.

Attitude, Practice surveys have been criticized for providing misleading and invalid data while ethnographies have been described as too subjective and time consuming. This debate has led to two new research methods: rapid ethnographic assessment, which is intended to provide data specific to program needs in a short period of time, and triangulation, which uses data from an ethnography or a rapid ethnographic assessment to develop KAP survey instruments.

This chapter critically examines methodological approaches to behavioral research, using the example of acute respiratory infection (ARI). The first part reviews the debate over behavioral research methods, and the second part presents some results from a recent study in West Bengal, India, which compared the use of a survey, a Focused Ethnographic Study (FES), and an ethnography to investigate local beliefs and practices related to the management of acute respiratory infections (for a complete description of this study, see Bhattacharyya 1993). The chapter concludes with the argument that methods need to be assessed within a specific research agenda and that the criteria used to determine the value and the utility of the data produced should be reexamined.

THE METHODS DEBATE

Table 8.1 summarizes the advantages and limitations of each research method: KAP surveys, ethnographies, and RAPs and FESs.

KAP Surveys

Typically, a KAP survey involves asking a predetermined set of questions to a randomly selected group of respondents. Survey instruments tend to be highly structured with no flexibility in the order or wording of questions, and responses are often precoded. Although surveys have been shown to produce invalid and misleading results in developing countries (Bulmer and Warwick 1983; Chambers 1983; Kroeger 1983a, 1983b; Stone and Campbell 1984), KAP surveys are still the main source of information about local conditions to program planners (Manderson and Aaby 1992a). A great deal has been written about the limitations of KAP surveys, especially in developing countries (cf., Bulmer and Warwick 1983). The discussion in the literature focuses on three main concerns: logistical problems, interviewer biases, and reporting biases.

Table 8.1

Major Advantages and Limitations of Behavioral Research Methods

	Advantages	Limitations
KAP Surveys	– Allows statistical generalizability if a probability sample – Provides "hard" numbers which can show a change – Relatively easy to train interviewers – Often local capacity exists	– Logistical problems – Interviewer biases – Reporting biases – Assumes survey context is representative of all other contexts of interaction
"Traditional" Ethnography	– Provides detailed descriptive data – Places illness within the larger social, cultural, economic context – Inductive approach which allows exploration of unexpected results	– Prolonged data collection period, not timely enough for program planning – Highly subjective – Not generalizable – Data not focused to program needs
FES/RAP	– Triangulates multiple data sources – Rapid data collection and analysis – Focused to program needs	– Limited generalizability – Seasonal issues are not addressed – Reported behavior may not reflect actual lived behavior – Does not address intracultural variations in illness management – Gives limited attention to the social dynamics of illness and treatment seeking

It is often extremely difficult to conduct a survey in a developing country due to logistical problems, as reviewed by Ross (1984). The sampling frame (a list of the population units from which a sample is drawn), which is necessary for a random sample, is rarely available. If a random sample is not used, the statistical generalizations one can make are threatened. Furthermore, households selected to be part of the sample may be remote or difficult to reach which increases the time needed in the field. Moreover, the production of the survey instrument is subject to many logistical problems primarily due to differences among local languages and dialects. It is difficult to develop and translate questions in several different languages and still maintain the same meanings, all the while constructing questions enabling comparison to results from other parts of the world. Additionally, interrupted power supplies and the lack of an institutional infrastructure mean that data entry, cleaning, and analysis must be done far from the field site. Perhaps the greatest logistical problem for survey research is finding staff who know the relevant languages and who have experience in training, supervising, sampling, and other innumerable skills required for survey research. These logistical problems often eliminate the possibility of standardized procedures, making comparisons with other research difficult, if not meaningless (Ross and Vaughan 1986). Chambers (1983:53) has described the "survey slavery" of research institutions and universities in response to the need to keep field staff employed and attract funding agencies. The difficulties of collecting, coding, processing, and analyzing the data cause the survey to become "a juggernaut pushed by and pulling its researcher slaves, and sometimes crushing them as it goes."

A second limitation of KAP surveys results from biases due to the interactions between the respondent and interviewer. In most cases, interviewers are strangers to the respondents and the interaction will be influenced by social norms relating to outsiders and guests. Most developing countries are highly stratified societies and "since status tends to be ascribed, ... sex, age, marital status, caste, religion, nationality, language, and color are among the characteristics which can be of decided relevance" (Stycos 1983:58). A mother may not feel comfortable discussing her child with a male interviewer or someone much older (or younger) than she. In most cultures, surveys are an unfamiliar way of exchanging information. Thus, when a stranger approaches someone to ask questions, many respondents become suspicious of the interviewer and either refuse to participate or provide misleading information (Kroeger 1983b; Smith and Radel 1976). On the other hand, respondents may produce a "courtesy bias" by wanting to please the interviewer (as one pleases a guest). Their responses will be influenced by what is perceived as the "right answer" to please the interviewer and to avoid being scolded for giving an incorrect answer. This is especially difficult in areas where intervention programs may have included health education components. Finally, both interviewers and respondents may become frustrated by the highly structured nature of a survey interview. Interviewers may want to explain a question or change a particular term when a respondent does not understand. Such a "highly structured" interaction violates norms of discourse, often making respondents unclear of their role.

Finally, KAP surveys are subject to reporting biases. How people answer the questions may be influenced by recall bias, seasonal bias, and bias of the incongruence of reported behavior and actual behavior. Recall bias (difficulty in correctly remembering events) is related to the amount of time that has elapsed and the significance of the event. For example, in research on acute respiratory infection (ARI), it is almost impossible to determine the severity of past ARI episodes. If the mother did not feel the episode was serious, she may not be able to remember whether the child had specific signs and symptoms. A seasonal bias occurs when responses given at one time during the year are used to represent conditions throughout the year. In most communities, the amounts of cash, food, illness, and time varies throughout the year. In addition, the ways in which events are interpreted are often seasonal. For example, in West Bengal, the way that winds are interpreted varies by season: sometimes they are harmful and sometimes beneficial.

Biases in reported behavior occur when actual behavior and re-ported behavior differ. Reported behavior often reflects normative or the socially accepted behavior. This may be related to the perception of the interviewer or the influence of others present during an interview. For example, a mother may be reluctant to mention that she took her child to a traditional healer to an interviewer who is perceived as a "modern" person. In the West Bengal study, one mother did not mention that she had been to a traditional healer because she assumed that everyone knew that one always goes to a healer before an allopathic provider.

There is an additional bias in cross-cultural survey research which is due to misinterpretation of questions or culturally sensitive questions. Stone and Campbell (1984:31) conducted a study to determine the relative effects of sampling and nonsampling error using the World Fertility Survey in Nepal. By talking to respondents of the survey in unstructured interviews, they found large discrepancies between survey responses and actual knowledge or use of various birth control methods. This was due not only to the highly sensitive topic of birth control in this community but also to the fact that respondents had "reinterpreted the question ... to make the question far more threatening than it was intended to be." Another type of reporting bias is the assumption of survey research "that what people say in the interview context can stand as an accurate representation of what they say (and do) in all other contexts" (Stone and Campbell 1984:32). On the contrary, what people say in the context of an interview may not reflect what they say in another context, such as a clinic.

Ethnography

Ethnographies, by using the exploratory methods of key informant interviews and participant observation, can provide in-depth information on the local beliefs and practices in a variety of contexts. However, ethnographies have rarely been used by program planners for several reasons. First, ethnographers traditionally spend one to two years in a community and another one to two years writing up the study, by which time the information may be out of date for a program planner. Ethnographers tend to study topics which are not relevant to public health interventions. If relevant, the data are often inaccessible to program planners. As Chambers (1983:60) states:

> Through great struggles a few papers are forced out at intervals; but sometimes their erudition is matched only by their practical irrelevance and their inaccessibility to policy makers, who might not understand them even if they knew the journals and had time to read them.

The prolonged period of data collection which is essential for collecting in-depth information and understanding seasonal issues makes ethnography of little use to a program planner who must develop and implement a program in a constrained time frame.

Second, and more important, ethnographies are considered to be "soft science" because they do not provide "hard" numbers and lack the rigor of standardized surveys. Ethnographies are usually conducted by one person, so the data are dependent on highly idiosyncratic skills and personal characteristics of the ethnographer. Almost by definition, an ethnography involves an in-depth study of a fairly localized area which may not be generalizable to a larger population. Ethnographies are considered unscientific because they have "no hard-and-fast rules of procedure; design and method for data collection and analysis are not specified in advance, and variables do not appear to be either measurable or defined in operational terms. ... The entire process is vague, sloppy, and unsystematic" (Borman, LeCompte, and Goetz 1986).

Triangulation

For a long time, the methods debate centered on the quantitative KAP surveys and the qualitative ethnographies. Then scholars called for "triangulation" of these two methods. This triangulation of methods usually involves a one to two month (sometimes as little as two weeks) phase of "formative research" or in-depth study. The results of this phase are used to develop a more valid survey instrument and not to identify important topics to be investigated.

Triangulation of methods refers to the use of several different methods to increase the validity of data. The need to employ a variety of qualitative and quantitative research methods is increasingly advocated for health interview surveys (Huntington, Berman and Kendall 1989; Kroeger 1983a; Ross and Vaughan 1986; Stone and Campbell 1984). Household interview surveys in developing countries are increasingly preceded by ethnographic studies (some using a FES or Rapid Assessment Procedures [RAP]) which are used to develop the survey instruments. These methods are considered complementary, each making up for the limitations of the other (Whyte and Alberti 1983). Since ethnographies are not generalizable, one combines them with surveys which can be generalized to a larger population. Since surveys often result in interviewer biases, the use of qualitative data improves the framing of questions.

Focused Ethnographic Studies and Rapid Assessment Procedures

Anthropologists have responded to the limitations of both surveys and traditional ethnographies by developing ethnographic protocols which are highly focused and intended to produce systematic data in a short period of time. The intention of these protocols is to generate data which are easily accessible to planners. The first of these protocols, the *Rapid Assessment Procedures* manual developed by Scrimshaw and

Hurtado (1987), was designed to investigate the impact of primary health care on nutrition. More recently, manuals have been developed for the Focused Ethnographic Study of various health topics. Focused Ethnographic Studies differ somewhat from Rapid Assessment Procedures by being very focused to specific program needs. Presently, there are RAP or FES manuals for ARI (WHO 1993), women's health (Gittelsohn ct al. 1993), sexually transmitted diseases (Helitzer-Allen and Allen 1993), two for diarrheal diseases (Herman and Bentley 1993; Pelto personal communication), AIDS (Scrimshaw et al. 1991) and epilepsy (Long, Scrimshaw, and Hurtado 1988). As some scholars have remarked, there seems to be an "epidemic" of these manuals (Manderson and Aaby 1992a).

Since these protocols are relatively new, there are only a few articles which discuss their potential limitations and biases. Some of the limitations are similar to surveys. These include seasonal biases and the reliance on reported behavior, "which may be idealized or subject to poor memory recall" (Bentley et al. 1988:113). Other limitations are similar to those of ethnographies, specifically that the results are not generalizable or replicable. Manderson and Aaby (1992a, 1992b) in two papers have provided the most comprehensive review of FES and RAP to date. Their papers raise important concerns about the data produced by these protocols. Specifically, they stress the need for RAP and FESs to explore contradictions in order to document the variability of behaviors. Second, they state that "while the emphasis is currently on cultural concepts rather than the social and class context of health problems, both perspectives are important" (Manderson and Aaby 1992a:844). That is, these manuals tend to focus on cognitive taxonomies of illness more than on distribution of resources within a community or household. Nichter and Nichter (1994:371) have also pointed out that in these manuals it is difficult to assess "the social relational dimension of illness negotiation and health care-seeking [which] is responsible to gender and generation relations, social status, and moral-identity issues."

For ARI specifically, the World Health Organization developed a protocol for Focused Ethnographic Study.[1] The main objectives of this protocol were to assist national ARI Program managers to modify the WHO recommendations on home care advice, select terminology for appropriate communication with mothers or other caregivers with small children, specify the potential constraints to care-seeking, and suggest ways to adapt the ARI household morbidity and treatment survey instrument. The protocol uses formal and informal anthropological methods (including free listing, pile sorts, narratives of current and past ARI episodes, hypothetical scenarios and paired comparisons[2]) over a five to seven week period to investigate the local beliefs and practices related to ARI.

THE PROBLEM OF ARI

The World Health Organization has recognized the need for better research on ARI because it is a major cause of infant and child mortality in developing countries, causing the deaths of 4.2 million children under five each year (UNICEF 1990; Monto 1989; Parker 1987; Berman and McIntosh 1985; Stansfield 1987) or 11,000 children each day (Pio 1988).[3] Deaths due to ARI constitute 30% of all childhood deaths (UNICEF 1990), and in many countries, ARI is the leading cause of childhood mortality, while in most other countries it is surpassed only by diarrheal disease (Stansfield 1987). Studies have shown that though the incidence of ARI is comparable in developed and developing countries (Pio 1988; Steinhoff and John 1983), its duration and severity are much greater in developing countries, resulting in higher mortality.

In developed countries, mortality due to respiratory infections declined rapidly with improved living conditions – including clean water, sanitation, better housing, and better food – even before the introduction of antibiotics (Graham 1990). While the improvements in living conditions will undoubtedly decrease ARI mortality in developing countries, this remains the long-term solution. In the short term, the World Health Organization recommends three approaches to control ARI morbidity and mortality: (1) improved case management; (2) health education; and (3) strengthening immunizations for diphtheria, pertussis, measles, and tuberculosis (Pio 1986; WHO 1984). Since vaccine-preventable diseases account for only 15–25% of ARI deaths (Pio 1988), programs must rely on case management and health education to prevent the other 85% of ARI deaths.

The central component of the WHO's ARI control program is case management. In 1983, the WHO developed a decision flow chart for the case management of ARI in children under five years. These guidelines were revised in 1989 to include three different respiratory rates for three age groups with children less than two months old treated separately. The revised guidelines also emphasize the diagnosis of pneumonia based on the presence of fast breathing and chest indrawing. The guidelines are intended for community health workers, nurses, and physicians who classify and treat ARI.

Although community-based studies have shown a reduction in mortality due to case management by auxiliary health workers with antibiotics (Sazawal and Black 1992), little is known about the actual household processes which resulted in this reduction. Intervention studies have not evaluated specific household processes, such as symptom recognition or care-seeking which resulted in the reduction of mortality. With a better understanding of these processes, intervention programs could take advantage of what households are already doing, target specific practices which may be harmful, as well as target specific households whose practices may place children at greater risk. Since the case management strategy is completely dependent upon the recognition of disease and "compliance" with the treatment algorithm, it is imperative that these processes be understood.

The control of ARI mortality is somewhat different from other disease control programs in its reliance on antimicrobial treatment and hospital referral. Unlike interventions for the control of diarrheal diseases, there is no identified home care procedure which could prevent morbidity and mortality. Unlike sugar–salt solution (used to prevent dehydration among those suffering from a diarrheal disease), preventing ARI deaths usually involves going outside the home to see a health care practitioner, purchase antibiotics, or visit a hospital. The central issue for ARI control is promoting the decision to seek treatment outside the home. Thus, understanding how these decisions are made becomes central to any ARI control program.

Behavioral Research Agenda for ARI

The debate over the utility of various research methods has paralleled shifts in the ARI behavioral research agenda. The methodological debate, for the most part, has taken place outside of explicit discussion of the research questions. This section briefly outlines the behavioral research agenda for ARI.

As with most applied behavioral research, the ARI research agenda is set by the questions that program planners need to answer. Initially, program planners focused on health service utilization and wanted to know (1) do caregivers recognize the key symptoms of fast breathing and chest indrawing, and (2) do caregivers seek care for those symptoms. Typically, a KAP survey was conducted before and after an intervention in order to show a change in both symptom recognition and health service utilization. Recently, there has been a shift in the research agenda from a focus on symptom recognition to a fuller understanding of the local illness classification system and how this influences care-seeking behavior.

The behavioral research agenda that has been developed by the WHO is in the form of a series of questions that an ARI program manager would need to answer before developing and implementing an ARI intervention. These questions focus on six main areas of investigation:

(1) recognition and interpretation of ARI signs and symptoms;
(2) ARI household management practices;
(3) patterns of care-seeking;
(4) maternal expectations concerning ARI treatment and compliance;
(5) practitioner information and perspectives on maternal recognition and care-seeking; and
(6) communication with mothers.

These questions are answered by understanding the local conceptual models or "cognitive maps" of illnesses which are related to ARI. Specifically, this involves understanding the language used to describe ARI signs and symptoms, how illnesses are categorized, and notions of causality and appropriate treatments. The manual for a Focused Ethnographic Study was developed specifically to address these issues.

Until recently, there were very few published studies that described the investigation of local conceptions of illness in relation to ARI (Tupasi et al. 1989; Wilson and Kimane 1990). A recent issue of *Medical Anthropology* (15[4] 1994) was devoted to articles discussing much of the behavioral research on ARI and included some accounts of FESs (Hudelson 1994; Kresno et al. 1994). These studies showed that the interpretation of the main symptoms of pneumonia, (fast breathing and chest indrawing,) varied greatly among cultures. In one part of India, fast breathing was interpreted to be "the stomach moving up and down" (Bhattacharyya 1994b); while in Honduras, fast breathing indicated "tiredness" (Hudelson 1994). Similarly, in Indonesia, the presence of chest indrawing did not influence the illness label or its perceived severity (Kresno et al. 1994). All of the studies in the issue describe a conceptual model or taxonomy of ARI with an emphasis on symptom recognition, illness labeling, and perceived causes. These studies describe an ideal model but few of the studies investigate how these conceptual models of illness are used within specific social and economic contexts during actual illness episodes to make treatment decisions.

Nichter (1994:322) sets out a research agenda which moves beyond illness classification systems to a focus on "how illness is conceptualized and responded to in real life." Some of the questions that Nichter highlights are as follows:

(1) intracultural variation in illness labeling in different settings (home, clinic, interview) and as associated with caretaker characteristics and illness experience;
(2) role of commercial medicines in illness labeling and treatment, role of marketing;
(3) social relations surrounding illness reporting and treatment seeking;
(4) children's characteristics including how a child's chances of survival are estimated and differences in illness recognition and treatment by age; and
(5) role of both traditional and cosmopolitan practitioners [1994: 322–326].

Researchers and practitioners need to recognize the ambiguity of illness labeling and the processes of negotiation within households. These negotiations take place within a social, conceptual, and material context. Labeling of an illness is not always based solely on the presence of physical signs and symptoms, but often involves the manipulation of power and authority. For example, a father may be reluctant to label a serious illness in his child because he does not have or want to spend the money for treatment. In addition, the ARI behavioral research agenda should include an understanding of the roles of "outsiders" (health care providers, relatives from another village, researchers, etc.) in changing the context of illness labeling and treatment. Since the control of ARI depends on contact with outsiders (health care professionals who will appropriately diagnose and treat ARI), we need to understand how the outsiders are perceived by local communities.

WEST BENGAL ARI STUDY

The West Bengal ARI study had two objectives: (1) to understand the process of decision making for treatments for children suffering from ARI; and (2) to compare the use of three methodological approaches, a

KAP survey, a FES, and an interpretive ethnography, in their ability to investigate the local beliefs and practices related to ARI. Some of the findings from the second objective are reported here.

The study was conducted in affiliation with the Child in Need Institute (CINI), which is located 17 kilometers south of Calcutta, West Bengal, India. West Bengal is located in eastern India and shares borders with the Indian states of Bihar, Orissa, Sikkim, and Assam and the foreign countries of Nepal, Bhutan, and Bangladesh. Although it is the third smallest state in India, it ranks fourth in population with 68 million people (Government of India 1991). It is the second most densely populated state in India with 766 people per square kilometer. Despite its role as a major industrial center, 74% of West Bengal's population live in rural areas and work in agriculture (Roy Choudhury 1984). Like the rest of India, West Bengal is culturally diverse including Hindu, Muslim, and tribal populations as well as migrants from other parts of India, Nepal, and Bangladesh. Culturally, West Bengal is dominated by Bengali Hindus.

The Child in Need Institute is a nongovernmental organization which provides outreach services to a population of 87,000 people living in 48 villages in the South 24 Parganas District of West Bengal. The institute's activities include the provision of maternal and child health services through village-based clinics run by women's groups. The institute also runs a 15-bed emergency ward and a nutrition rehabilitation center. Although precise mortality statistics are unavailable, the most common causes of death in children under five years are ARI, diarrhea, neonatal tetanus, and measles. During the study, there was no ARI intervention underway, with the exception of a measles immunization program.

The study was conducted over a 12-month stay between 1991 and 1992. Most interviews were conducted in Bengali. Two agricultural communities were selected from the CINI project area. The villages Nandigram and Sherpur (pseudonyms) were selected purposefully through field visits and interviews with CINI staff. Nandigram is off the main road and Sherpur more interior. Nandigram is half Hindu and half Muslim while Sherpur is 100% Hindu. Both villages took about an hour to reach from CINI and neither was participating in another research study. Nandigram had a total population of 2481 (491 households) and Sherpur 817 (152 households). Almost all the Hindus of both villages belonged to lower castes. The distribution of occupations varied widely between Sherpur and Nandigram. In Sherpur, 29% of people cultivated their own land as opposed to only 3% in

Nandigram. In Nandigram, 42% of people worked as daily wage laborers; 19% in Sherpur. Literacy also varied greatly; among both men and women over 15 years old, in Nandigram, 31% of women and 69% of men were literate as opposed to Sherpur where 57% of women and 86% of men were literate.

The study was conducted in three phases. The first phase involved a complete census of the two villages and a survey of the knowledge, attitudes, and practices related to ARI management. The instrument used for the survey was adapted from the survey instrument developed by UNICEF for a study in six states in India of the knowledge and practices related to ARI, which is being used to develop India's national ARI program. The second phase of the study followed the methods and guidelines of the FES protocol. The FES involved a series of data collection techniques including key informant interviews, formal ethnographic techniques (such as pile sorts and paired comparisons), interviews with health providers, and mothers responding to a WHO videotape which shows children exhibiting the signs and symptoms of ARI. The third phase of the study, the ethnography, had two parts: clinic-based interviews and community-based interviews. The clinic-based interviews involved semistructured interviews with caregivers for children with a current ARI episode. The community-based interviews included key informant interviews, unstructured interviews with families who had experienced the death of a child in the past year, and in-depth case studies of twelve families.

Each of the three data sets is analyzed and written up independently using the appropriate statistical and ethnographic analytic techniques. The methods were compared based on the type of data produced and the experiences using the methods. There was no "gold standard" for comparison among the three methods because each method makes different theoretical assumptions about human behavior (see, Bhattacharyya 1994a). The comparison of the three methods constituted a case study. The results, like all case studies, illustrate important features but cannot be generalized to all settings. The results comparing the three methods are presented in three sections: the type of data provided, cost and logistics, relationship to the community.[4]

Type of Data Provided

Table 8.2 shows some of the conclusions one draws from each of the methods for issues relevant to program planning. All three methods reveal that mothers recognize fast breathing, but the ethnographic results show that some illnesses are not defined by physical signs and

Table 8.2

Comparison of Selected Results from the Three Methods

	Symptom recognition	Triggers for treatment seeking	Delays in receiving treatment
KAP Survey	– Recognize FB* and CI* but never experienced symptoms	– Cough and cold should be treated by a doctor – Cough and FB are common and nothing to worry about	– Economic constraints – May not recognize seriousness of FB
FES	– Recognize FB and CI but FB is not of concern	– Any symptoms should be seen by a doctor – Triggering symptoms include wheezing, bad cough, not eating, diarrhea	– Arrange for money – May not be concerned with FB
Ethnography	– Recognize FB and CI but more concerned with breathing difficulty and wheezing	– Label of "measles" means no treatment is sought – Triggering symptoms include "worse at night", bad cough, unable to breathe – Treatment seeking is socially negotiated	– Arrange for money which may involve a redefinition of the illness – May not recognize the severity – Providers refer from one place to another

* FB means fast breathing, CI means chest indrawing.

symptoms. This means that recognition of fast breathing is of less importance for treatment seeking than the label the illness is given. Illnesses are labeled as a result of social negotiations which consider previous illness experiences, the stigma of an illness, as well as specific physical signs and symptoms. In the second column, triggers for treatment seeking, both the FES and the survey results provide contradictory information. Survey respondents report that a simple cough and cold should be treated by a doctor but then report that "a cough and fast breathing are common and nothing to worry about."

Similarly, the FES respondents reported, for all of the hypothetical scenarios, that the children should be taken to a provider, but mothers did not actually bring their children to a provider for each of the illnesses mentioned in the scenarios. Finally, all three methods show that economic factors cause delay in seeking appropriate treatment. The ethnography found additional delays caused by referral from one provider to another even when families sought care promptly.

Many of the differences can be accounted for by comparing reported behavior with actual behavior and looking at behaviors in context. Table 8.3 ranks procedures according to how much context the method provides and whether actual or reported behavior was recorded. The more unstructured methods, participant observation, and in-depth interviews provide the best opportunity to see behaviors in the larger sociocultural context. Both structured and semistructured interviews

Table 8.3

Ranking of Specific Methodological Procedures:
Type of Data Provided

Procedure	Contextualization	Reported behavior	Actual behavior
Structured Interview[s]	−	++	−
Semi-structured Interview[f,e]	+	++	−
Free Listing[f]	+	+	−
Videotapem[f]	+	++	−
Hypothetical Scenarios[f]	+	+	−
Paired Comparisons[f]	+	+	−
Illness Sorting[f]	+	+	−
Severity Rating[f]	+	+	−
Medicine Inventory[f]	−	+	++
In-depth interviews[f,e]	++	++	+
Participant Observation[e]	++	++	++

[s] Used in survey   − Not at all
[f] Used in FES   + Some
[e] Used in ethnography   ++ A lot

by definition establish a question and answer pattern and often inhibit a respondent from "telling the whole story."

Comparing Costs and Logistics

A comparison of the staff and time requirements and the costs of the KAP survey, the FES, and ethnographic phase of this study is shown in Table 8.4. The FES is by far the least expensive and least time-consuming to conduct. These studies take only seven weeks from start to finish compared with 17 weeks for the survey and 27 weeks for the ethnography. They also cost less than half as much as either the survey or ethnography, primarily due to reduced staff time.

Table 8.4

Comparison of Time, Staff, and Costs of the KAP Survey, FES, and Ethnography

	KAP Survey*	FES	Ethnography
Time			
Development	6 weeks	1 week	1 week
Field	3 weeks	5 weeks	18 weeks
Analysis	8 weeks**	1 week	8 weeks**
Total Time	17 weeks	7 weeks	27 weeks
Staff*	PI, RA, 4 Interviewers	PI, RA	PI, RA
Cost			
Staff[+]	Rs.9205 ($307)	Rs.4375 ($146)	Rs.11875 ($396)
Transportation	Rs.7635 ($255)[++]	Rs.921 ($31)	Rs.2517 ($84)
Supplies	Rs.629 ($21)	Rs.384 ($13)	Rs.351 ($12)
Total Cost	Rs.17,469 ($583)	Rs.5680 ($190)	Rs.14,743 ($492)

* Including the census.
** Estimate.
*** Three levels of staff: PI – Doctoral student; RA – BA, bilingual; Interviewers – Higher secondary, from study villages.
[+] Excluding PI.
[++] Main component is the hired car.

Table 8.5 ranks the methodological procedures by the skills needed by a data collector, the time needed to collect the data including development of questionnaires or field guides, and the time for data analysis. Data collector skills are directly correlated to the degree of structure of the procedure: the less structured a procedure (e.g., participant observation), the better data collector skills required since data collectors must discern what is important to record. The ethnographic and survey methods require the most time in data collection and analysis.

Relationship to the Respondent

The type of relationship that is established has both long- and short-term implications. In the short term, the relationship affects the establishment of rapport and future data collection activities. In the long

Table 8.5

Ranking of Specific Methodological Procedures: Logistic Criteria

Procedure	Data collector skills	Time in data collection	Time in data analysis
Structured Interview [s]	+	++	++
Semi-structured Interview [f,e]	+	++	++
Free Listing [f]	++	+	+
Videotape [f]	+	+	+
Hypothetical Scenarios [f]	++	+	+
Paired Comparisons [f]	+	+	+
Illness Sorting [f]	+	+	+
Severity Rating [f]	+	+	+
Medicine Inventory [f]	+	+	+
In-depth Interviews [f,e]	++	++	++
Participant Observation [e]	++	++	++

[s] Used in survey
[f] Used in FES   + Some
[e] Used in ethnography   ++ A lot

term, the relationship may influence how the community perceives and reacts to "outsiders."

Table 8.6 ranks procedures according to the respondent's interest in the activity, flexibility of the procedure and whether the respondent was able to learn anything during the interaction. Some procedures were tedious and frustrating for respondents. The sorting task and severity ratings were designed to be conducted using cards with illness terms written on them. For an illiterate population, each term must be read out for each illness so that respondents can match symptoms with illnesses and rank severity. Thus, for each of five illnesses, 10 to 15 symptom terms are read out. Many respondents found this very tedious. Paired comparisons were also tedious. The flexibility in the procedure relates closely to the possibility of a respondent learning from the procedure. Flexible procedures can often be more interactive, allowing for an exchange of information.

Table 8.6

Ranking of Specific Methodological Procedures: Relationship to Respondent

Procedure	Respondent interest	Flexibility in procedure	Respondent learns
Structured Interview[s]	+	−	−
Semi-structured Interview[f,e]	+	+	−
Free Listing[f]	++	++	−
Videotape[f]	++	+	−
Hypothetical Scenarios[f]	+	+	−
Paired Comparisons[f]	−	+	−
Illness Sorting[f]	−	+	−
Severity Rating[f]	−	+	−
Medicine Inventory[f]	+	+	−
In-depth Interviews[f,e]	++	++	+
Participant Observation[e]	+	++	+

[s] Used in survey   − Not at all
[f] Used in FES   + Some
[e] Used in ethnography   ++ A lot

According to the rankings, the free listing and use of the videotape were clear winners. Both procedures require medium interviewer skills, medium time in collection and low time in analysis. Yet respondents enjoy and are very interested in both methods, and a wealth of data is provided.

Free listing (of illnesses, providers, remedies) is a very good way to start an interview. If informants and questions are properly selected, the free listing questions will put informants at ease and assure them that they can answer the questions. Free listing tends to generate many new terms, each of which must be explored in greater depth later. However, when listing illnesses, informants tended to think of the more unusual or serious illnesses often forgetting the common ones. For example, three informants did not even mention the common cold during the free listing. In addition, some illnesses were not mentioned because they are not associated with nontraditional practitioners. For example, no one mentioned *batash lagano* (literally "touched by the wind"), which must be treated by traditional healers, until informants were asked if there were any healers in the village. When asked if there were any traditional healers, informants typically replied "Oh, you mean for batash lagano? Yes, there are five." To compensate for possibly incomplete lists, free listing should be used in combination with other methods.

The videotape[5] provided data that were not available through other procedures. Despite its length, respondents were very attentive throughout the video and often gave a running commentary of everything they observed. Interviewers are easily trained in using the data collection forms. The two purposes of the video were to identify local terms for illnesses with fast breathing or indrawing and to study maternal recognition of these symptoms. However, there are many other potential uses for the video. In addition to observing physical signs and symptoms, mothers watched to see if the child was "playing" and observed the coloring of the child – some lighter-skinned children were thought to have a nutritional deficiency. Thinner children were sometimes thought to be sicker than chubby ones. The video could also be used to observe treatment negotiations within a household. For example, the video could be shown to a mother, father, and grandmother and they could then discuss the diagnosis of the illness and the appropriate treatment. Interviewers could be trained (though this would increase the level of skill needed) to observe these interactions in order to understand the negotiation process.

The least valuable procedure in the West Bengal study was the hypothetical case scenarios used in the FES. While the scenarios varied according to whether or not the child had fast breathing, mothers were more concerned about whether or not the child had a fever. In general, most of the respondents thought that the children in all the scenarios should go to a doctor and that the doctor would give medicine. Compared with the narratives of past episodes, the scenarios provided very superficial information about treatment seeking, and little new data were obtained using this procedure.

CONCLUSIONS

In the West Bengal study, most of the differences in the type of data produced were not due to inherent limitations of various methods but rather to differences in the research questions being addressed. The methods debate must take place within a specific research agenda. The underlying assumptions, or theoretical frameworks, about culture and behavior must first be articulated since these assumptions shape the collection and analysis of data, leading to different conclusions. With an explicit model of culture, researchers can adapt and triangulate methods in ways that will further the goal of understanding a particular cultural system.[6]

Among the KAP survey, the FES, and the ethnography, it is clear that the wealth of data, combined with the time, cost and logistical advantages of the FES make it a powerful tool. Its strong focus on issues relevant to program planners as well as its extremely short time between data collection and final report make it a highly effective tool for obtaining information on local beliefs and practices. However, the FES is not without limitations. The FES investigates the conceptual models of illness but fails to address the social dynamics of illness management within and among households. Some modifications are needed to address these issues. Although it is a relatively short time period, the FES could include some case studies of families based on repeated interactions over six weeks. During the peak ARI season, it is highly likely that children will develop an ARI which would allow observation of the decision making process within the household. Case studies could provide in-depth investigations of the relative authority and responsibility of household members. More attempts should be made to identify children in the community who suffer an ARI. By increasing the unstructured time spent with families in the community, the ability to observe behaviors and interactions is increased. Hence the normative rules discovered through pile sorts, scenarios, and rankings could be contrasted with the actual behavior of families when confronted with an illness. The contradictions between observed and reported behavior could then be explored.

This study begs the question of what are the most appropriate criteria by which to evaluate the value of data produced by various methods. Research methods are usually assessed in terms of their validity, reliability, and objectivity. Some scholars have begun to question the utility of such criteria across philosophical paradigms (Bednarz 1985; Lincoln and Guba 1985). These scholars argue for an understanding of the underlying ontological and epistemological assumptions of each of these concepts before using them to compare methods. Bednarz (1985) argues that qualitative and quantitative methods have developed out of completely different philosophical paradigms and that meaningful comparisons can only be made within a particular paradigm. For instance, the notion of reliability implies a static and closed system (or culture) that has no endogenous sources of change. Many social scientists would disagree with this view of culture and emphasize the need to understand historical processes and recognize the fluidity of community and cultural boundaries. The notion of objectivity assumes that there is a distance between the researcher and the study area which allows the two to be analytically separate. This concept has been questioned by scholars who argue that those who research social processes are always shaping that which they are studying (cf., Giddens 1984). Johannsen (1992) states that research should be considered a type of intervention and should involve people in that intervention.

Lincoln and Guba (1985) have developed an alternative set of criteria to determine the "trustworthiness" of data within the naturalistic paradigm which makes different ontological and epistemological assumptions. Lincoln and Guba (1985) develop the concept of trustworthiness of data as a way to assess the value and worth of data. The criteria of trustworthiness is developed out of the naturalist paradigm which makes assumptions about the nature of reality and causality that differ from a "rationalist" paradigm. The components of trustworthiness are truth value (credibility), applicability (the "transferability" from one context to another), consistency (dependability), and neutrality.[7] It is beyond the scope of this chapter to assess Lincoln and Guba's criteria; however, two additional criteria are suggested. First, there must be a realistic comparison of the cost and logistical requirements of different methods. Second, the type of relationship that is established between the researcher and researched, both as individuals and communities, must be a criteria for selecting methods. If one acknowledges that research is an intervention and that it will influence future relationships between communities and researchers (who are often affiliated with service providers), then the power dynamics of different methods must be taken into consideration. This is especially important when health service institutions conduct research since the relationships established during the research process often influence health service utilization. The use of participatory research methods in behavioral research has great potential in this respect. These methods use primarily visual diagrams (e.g., village maps, ranking procedures, seasonal diagramming, body mapping) created by local participants. Not only do people enjoy them but they often learn something about their own community since the analysis of the diagram is done as a group.

Anthropologists have an increasingly important role to play in establishing behavioral research questions and in developing appropriate research methodologies for a wide variety of public health problems. Anthropologists must continue these discussions while refining the ability to articulate our unique perspective to others. Focused Ethnographic Study manuals are already being used for many infectious disease problems. However, the way questions are framed within a biomedical disease category affects the type of data collected. Anthropologists and others must move beyond research questions within specific disease categories to questions which cut across these categories, e.g., care-seeking processes, treatment "compliance," intrahousehold resource allocation. With such a re-orientation, we would begin to be able to understand illness the way that it is experienced in households and communities around the world.

NOTES

1. For a description of the development of the FES, see Gove and Pelto (1994). Focused Ethnographic Studies in the WHO Programme for the Control of Acute Respiratory Infections, *Medical Anthropology*, 15(4):409–424.

2. Free listing is a way to obtain the local terms used to describe ARI. It follows a semi-structured format where informants are asked to list all the childhood illnesses they know. Through careful probing and interviews with several informants, a comprehensive list of terms for ARI illnesses, signs and symptoms is developed. Responses are then tabulated and listed by frequency of response. The free listing procedure was used to develop lists of terms of illnesses, cough or breathing signs and symptoms, other signs and symptoms, home remedies, causes and treatments of illnesses, and practitioners.

The narrative of a past ARI episode was conducted with both key informants and interviews with mothers in the community. The purpose of this was to understand home management practices and timing of care seeking. These were unstructured interviews conducted without any questionnaire. The manual suggested 12 topics that should be covered in the interview, including illness recognition, home care including food and liquid intake, and experience with providers. The information was then recorded and tabulated using standardized forms.

Hypothetical case scenarios were developed to determine whether mothers recognize the severity of illness, how mothers respond to respiratory infections at home or by seeking treatment, and expectations of treatment. Six scenarios were developed which included a child with and without signs of pneumonia in each of three age categories: neonate, 6 months, and 2 years. Each mother responded to three scenarios where two of them were children of the same age. This followed a semi-structured format where the respondents were presented with the scenario and then asked what the mother should do, what illness the child has and other signs to watch for, what home remedies should be given and whether treatment should be sought from a provider. These results were then tabulated.

Paired comparison of providers is a structured task designed to determine the preferred choice of providers. Six local providers are chosen from the free listing data. These six providers are then listed randomly in all possible pairs giving a total of fifteen pairs. The providers included both traditional and allopathic providers. The respondent is referred to one of the scenarios of a child with pneumonia and asked for each pair which provider they would choose if those were the only two providers available. After a provider is chosen, the respondent is asked why that choice was made. The procedure continues until all fifteen pairs are completed. The results are then tabulated to show the percentage of times a specific provider was selected. The reasons for the choices are also tabulated and categorized into economic reasons, convenience, belief in modern or traditional medicines, and certain positive or negative qualities of the providers.

In order to understand the relationships among illness names and specific signs and symptoms, respondents were asked to place cards labelled with symptom terms together with cards labelled with illness terms (pile sorting). The terms are selected based on the key informant interviews. This procedure was done differently among literate and non-literate respondents. For literate respondents, cards with terms written in Bengali were used. The respondent is given an illness card and asked to place all the symptom cards that go with that illness. This procedure continues until all illnesses have been finished. The procedure for non-literate respondents involves asking, for each illness, whether each of the symptoms goes with that illness. Summary sheets and cross tabulations are tabulated to determine the percentage of respondents placing a specific symptom with a specific illness.

3. This is probably an underestimate (Leowski 1986).

4. Tables 8.3 and 8.5 used a modification of a format developed by Joel Gittelsohn.

5. The videotape used was one developed by the World Health Organization to assess maternal recognition of ARI signs and symptoms. The videotape shows 20 children under 4 years old who exhibit different signs and symptoms of ARI, including fast breathing, chest indrawing, wheezing and stridor.

6. The West Bengal study in fact employed three different models of culture because each methodological approach defined culture differently and made different assumptions about the relationship of culture to behavior. The survey views culture as the sum of individual attributes, the FES views culture as a set of cognitive rules, while the ethnography used an interpretive model of culture where culture provides a context for the creation of meaning. In a separate paper (1994a), I have described the three (implicit) models of culture and behavior in greater detail.

7. For a full discussion of trustworthiness, see Chapter 11 in Lincoln and Guba (1985).

REFERENCES

Bednarz, D. 1985. Quantity and Quality in Evaluation Research: A Divergent View. Evaluation and Program Planning 8:289–306.

Bentley, M. E., G. H. Pelto, W. L. Straus, D. A. Schumann, C. Adegbola, E. de la Pena, G. A. Oni, K. H. Brown, and S. L. Huffman. 1988. Rapid Ethnographic Assessment: Applications in a Diarrhea Management Program. Social Science and Medicine 27(1):107–116.

Berman S. and K. McIntosh. 1985. Selective Primary Health Care: Strategies for Control of Disease in the Developing World. XXI. Acute Respiratory Infections. Reviews of Infectious Diseases 7(5):674–691.

Bhattacharyya, K. 1994a. Methods or Models? Comparison of a KAP Survey, a Focused Ethnographic Study and Ethnography. Submitted to Social Science and Medicine.

Bhattacharyya, K. 1994b. The Marathi "Taskonomy" of Respiratory Infections in Children. Medical Anthropology 15(4):395–408.

Bhattacharyya, K. 1993. Understanding Acute Respiratory Infections: Culture and Method. Doctor of Science dissertation, Johns Hopkins School of Hygiene and Public Health.

Borman, K. M., M. D. Le Compte, and J. P. Goetz. 1986. Ethnographic and Qualitative Research Design and Why It Doesn't Work. American Behavioral Scientist 30(1):42–57.

Bulmer, M. and D. P. Warwick (eds.). 1983. Social Research in Developing Countries. New York: John Wiley and Sons, Ltd.

Chambers, R. 1983. Rural Development: Putting the Last First. New York: Longman Scientific and Technical.

Giddens, A. 1984. The Constitution of Society. Berkeley: University of California Press.

Gittelsohn, J., P. J. Pelto, M. E. Bentley, K. Bhattacharyya, J. Russ, and M. Nag. 1993. A Protocol for Using Ethnographic Methods to Investigate Women's Health. Unpublished Manuscript.

Gove, S. and G. Pelto. 1994. Focused Ethnographic Studies in the WHO Programme for the Control of Acute Respiratory Infections. Medical Anthropology 15(4):409–424.

Government of India. 1991. Census of India. 1991. Provisional Population Totals Series 26.

Graham, N. M. H. 1990. The Epidemiology of Acute Respiratory Infections in Children and Adults: A Global Perspective. Epidemiologic Reviews 12:149–178.

Helitzer-Allen, D. and H. A. Allen. 1993. Targeted Intervention Research on Sexually Transmitted Illnesses. Fieldtest Version #1.

Herman, E. and M. Bentley. 1993. Rapid Assessment Procedures (RAP): To Improve the Household Management of Diarrhea. Boston, Massachusetts: International Nutrition Foundation for Developing Countries (INFDC).

Hudelson, P. 1994. The Management of Acute Respiratory Infections in Honduras: A Field Test of the Focused Ethnographic Study (FES). Medical Anthropology 15(4):435–446.

Huntington, D., P. Berman, and C. Kendall. 1989. Health Interview Surveys for Child Survival Programs: A Review of Methods, Instruments and Proposals for Their Improvement. Institute for International Programs Occasional Paper No. 6, June, 1989.

Johannsen, A. M. 1992. Applied Anthropology and Post-Modernist Ethnography. Human Organization 15(1):71–81.

Kresno, S., G. G. Harrison, B. Sutrisna, and A. Reingold. 1994. Acute Respiratory Infections in Children Under Five Years in Indramayu, West Java, Indonesia: A Rapid Ethnographic Assessment. Medical Anthropology 15(4):425–434.

Kroeger, A. 1983a. Anthropological and Socio-Medical Health Care Research in Developing Countries. Social Science and Medicine 17(3):147–161.

Kroeger, A. 1983b. Health Interview Surveys in Developing Countries: A Review of Methods and Results, International Journal of Epidemiology 12(4):465–481.

Leowski, J. 1986. Mortality from Acute Respiratory Infections in Children Under 5 Years of Age: Global Estimates. World Health Statistical Quarterly 39:138–144.

Lincoln, Y. S. and E. G. Guba. 1985. Naturalistic Inquiry. Newbury Park, California: Sage.

Long, A., S. Scrimshaw, and E. Hurtado. 1988. Epilepsy Rapid Assessment Procedures (ERAP): Rapid Assessment Procedures for the Evaluation of Epilepsy Specific Beliefs, Attitudes and Behaviors. Epilepsy Foundation of America, Landover, Maryland.

Manderson, L. and P. Aaby. 1992a. An Epidemic in the Field? Rapid Assessment Procedures and Health Research. Social Science and Medicine 37(7):839–850.

Manderson, L. and P. Aaby. 1992b. Can Anthropological Procedures be Applied to Tropical Diseases? Health Policy and Planning 7(1):46–55.

Monto, A. S. 1989. Acute Respiratory Infections in Children of Developing Countries: Challenge of the 1990s. Reviews of Infectious Diseases 11(3):498–505.

Nichter, M. 1994. Introduction. Medical Anthropology 15(4):319–334.

Nichter, M. and M. Nichter. 1994. Acute Respiratory Illness: Popular Health Culture and Mother's Knowledge in the Philippines. Medical Anthropology 15(4):353–375.

Parker, R. L. 1987. Acute Respiratory Illness in Children: PHC Responses. Health Policy and Planning 2(4):279–288.

Pio, A. 1988. WHO Programme on Acute Respiratory Infections. Indian Journal of Pediatrics 55:197–205.

Pio, A. 1986. Acute Respiratory Infections in Children in Developing Countries: An International Point of View. Pediatric Infectious Disease 5(2):179–183.

Ross, A. S. 1984. Practical Problems Associated with Programme Evaluation in Third World Countries. Evaluation and Program Planning 7:211–218.

Ross, D. A. and J. P. Vaughan. 1986. Health Interview Surveys in Developing Countries: A Methodological Review. Studies in Family Planning 17(2):78–94.

Roy Choudhury, P. 1984. Left Experiment in West Bengal. New Delhi: Patriot Publishers.

Sazawal, S. and R. E. Black. 1992. Meta-analysis of Intervention Trials on Case-Management of Pneumonia in Community Settings. The Lancet 340:528–533.

Scrimshaw, S., M. Carballo, L. Ramos, and B. Blair. 1991. The AIDS Rapid Anthropological Assessment Procedures: A Tool for Health Education Planning and Evaluation. Health Education Quarterly 18(1):111–123.

Scrimshaw, S. and E. Hurtado. 1987. Rapid Assessment Procedures. Los Angeles: UCLA Latin American Center Publications.

Smith, S. A. and D. Radel. 1976. The KAP in Kenya: A Critical Look at Survey Methodology. *In* Culture, Natality, and Family Planning. J. F. Marshall and S. Polgar, eds. Pp. 263–288. Chapel Hill, North Carolina: Carolina Population Center, University of North Carolina.

Stansfield, S. K. 1987. Acute Respiratory Infections in the Developing World: Strategies for Prevention, Treatment, and Control. Pediatric Infectious Disease Journal 6:622–629.

Steinhoff, M. C. and T. J. John. 1983. Acute Respiratory Infections of Children in India. Pediatric Research 17:1032–1035.

Stone, L. 1992. Cultural Influences in Community Participation in Health. Social Science and Medicine 35(4):409–417.

Stone, L. and J. G. Campbell. 1984. The Use and Misuse of Surveys in International Development: An Experiment from Nepal. Human Organization 43(1):27–37.

Stycos, J. M. 1983. Sample Surveys for Social Research in Underdeveloped Areas. *In* Social Research in Developing Countries. M. Bulmer and D. P. Warwick, eds. New York: John Wiley and Sons, Ltd.

Tupasi, T. E., C. A. Miguel, V. L. Tallo, T. M. P. Bagasao, J. N. Natividad, L. B. Valencia, M. E. G. De Jesus, S. Lupisan, and F. Medalla. 1989. Child Care Practices of Mothers: Implications for Intervention in Acute Respiratory Infections. Annals of Tropical Paedeatrics 9:82–88.

UNICEF. 1990. The State of the World's Children. New York: Oxford.

Whyte, W. F. and G. Alberti. 1983. On the Integration of Research Methods. *In* Social Research in Developing Countries. M. Bulmer and D. P. Warwick, eds. Pp. 299–312. New York: John Wiley and Sons, Ltd.

Wilson, R. and I. Kimane. 1990. Mother's Perception of ALRI: A Case Study in Lesotho. *In* ALRI and Child Survival in Developing Countries. Baltimore: Johns Hopkins University, Institute for International Programs.

World Health Organization. 1993. Focused Ethnographic Study for Acute Respiratory Infections. ARI/93.2. Geneva, Switzerland.

World Health Organization. 1984. A Programme for Controlling Acute Respiratory Infections in Children: A Memorandum from a WHO Meeting. Bulletin of the World Health Organization 62(1):47–58.

Part Four

Ethnographies

CHAPTER 9

"Digestive Worms": Ethnomedical Approaches to Intestinal Parasitism in Southern Ethiopia

Norbert Vecchiato

INTRODUCTION

Ascaris lumbricoides, the large intestinal roundworm of humans, constitutes a global health hazard. More than a billion people are estimated to be affected with ascariasis, an infection of the small intestine triggered by roundworm infestation (Stephenson 1987:3). Typically, the disease is contracted by ingestion of infective eggs from soil contaminated with human feces or uncooked vegetables contaminated with soil containing infective eggs. Worldwide dimensions of helminthic infection points to serious repercussions on the health and the nutritional status of rural and urban communities in developing

This chapter expands on a paper presented at the 1992 Annual Meeting of the Society for Applied Anthropology, Memphis, Tennessee. The fieldwork on which this research is based benefitted from the invaluable assistance of the Comboni Institute (Rome and Addis Ababa). I wish to thank my Sidama informants and specialists for disclosing the complexities of their ethnomedical system. I am grateful to experienced African botanist Rev. Giuseppe Calvi MCCJ for the identification of the anthelminthic plants used by the Sidama. I am also indebted to Professors David Crompton, Celia Holland, Helmut Kloos, and the editors of this volume for the useful comments they offered on previous drafts of this chapter. All errors are mine.

countries (Holland 1991; Stephenson 1994). Specifically, worm burden has been blamed for impaired learning abilities in children (Kvalsvig, Cooppan, and Connolly 1991; Nokes and Bundy 1994) and the loss of productivity in adults (Morrow 1984).

The intensity and prevalence of helminthic parasites in humans are related to a variety of ecological, behavioral, immunological, and demographic determinants (Bundy and Medley 1992:S105–S119). Worm transmission is enhanced by poor socioeconomic conditions, deficiencies in sanitary facilities, improper disposal of human feces, insufficient supplies of potable water, poor personal hygiene, substandard housing, and lack of health education (Holland et al. 1988). These factors correlate with poverty and underdevelopment, and in that sense intestinal parasitoses can be labeled "diseases of poverty" (Cooper 1991). They are, nonetheless, inextricably linked to, and shaped by, culturally determined perceptions and practices concerning health, hygiene, and disease. Medical anthropologists have argued that infectious diseases do not simply result from the concatenation of ecological and physiological determinants; rather they are precipitated by deliberate and non-deliberate behaviors which are influenced by culturally determined beliefs, practices, and social expectations (Brown and Inhorn 1990; Dunn and Janes 1986; Inhorn and Brown 1990). Sociocultural determinants of infectious disease transmission can be divided into three main areas of analytical importance: (1) culturally determined behaviors affecting infectious diseases; (2) ethnomedical beliefs about infectious disease; and (3) ethnomedical practices involving prevention and treatment.

First, the spread of communicable diseases is enhanced by culturally reinforced behaviors. These involve daily individual and community activities. In particular, attention should be focused on the household role in disease transmission (Berman, Kendall, and Bhattacharyya 1994). Households engage in a wide range of behaviors which promote the transmission of infectious ailments particularly to its younger members, as in the case of hydatid disease and the role of domestic dogs in infant care (Brown and Inhorn 1990:207). Similar attention should be devoted to household hygiene and sanitation behavior patterns, particularly in reference to infant care and helminthic infections.

Second, health and disease fostering behaviors are influenced by culturally determined beliefs and attitudes. These are generally incorporated into disease explanatory theories which form an integral part of ethnomedical systems (Nichter 1992). In the context of helminthiases special emphasis should be given to indigenous nosological theories and perceived degrees of severity ascribed to worm infestation. Human intestinal helminths are often viewed as minor ailments when compared to other health problems afflicting a developing community. A community's perceptions of helminths have important epidemiological and health planning ramifications (Kamunvi and Ferguson 1993; Rousham 1994).

Third, in most cultures the ethnobotanical lore includes remedies against infectious diseases including intestinal parasites. Traditional anthelmintic remedies are often taken following self-diagnosis and in conjunction with commercial drugs. Since the latter are generally more expensive than traditional remedies, their use may increase in time of economic crisis, as a study in a Guatemalan community demonstrated (Booth, Johns, and Lopez-Palacios 1993). Local medical beliefs and practices related to the transmission of intestinal worms should be identified in order to elicit active community participation in control measures, improve disease surveillance, and adapt health education programs to relevant sociocultural and cognitive parameters.

In Ethiopia, intestinal helminthiases are a major health hazard to both urban and rural communities.[1] These parasites are the second overall leading cause of out-patient morbidity in the country (Ministry of Health 1986, 1991). *A. lumbricoides* constitutes the most prevalent species of nematode parasite (Kloos and Tesfa-Yohannes 1993). Public health interventions by the Ethiopian Ministry of Health to control *A. lumbricoides* and other helminthic infections have been sporadic and mostly treatment-oriented through mass drug programs (Tesfa-Yohannes 1990). Little is known of the behavioral and cultural components of ascariasis in Ethiopia. Yet, the magnitude of this health problem calls for an integrated approach to its control with particular attention to transmission-fostering traditional practices and prevailing indigenous perspectives. This chapter examines the behavioral and cultural dimensions of helminthic parasite management in a rural southern Ethiopian community. Morbidity rates are juxtaposed to indigenous explanatory models, prevailing ethnophysiological concepts, and traditional treatment practices. Ethnomedical versus biomedical differential perceptions of their consequences on human health will be highlighted in reference to health education and control programs.

RESEARCH SETTING AND METHODS

Population and Subsistence

The anthropological research on which this study is based was conducted among the Sidama, a Cushitic-speaking people inhabiting the southern Ethiopian Rift Valley at an elevation ranging from 1400 to 2800 meters. They are estimated at 1.5 million occupying a territory of 6793 square kilometers (Government of Ethiopia 1986:23). Their traditional social organization includes a number of patrilineal exogamous clans intersected by an age-grade system wherein circumcised male elders occupy a preeminent moral and legislative role (Hamer 1987).[2] The religious belief structure postulates the existence of a supreme being and creator, Maganu, and a host of spirits (*sheitanna*). These are ascribed an important role in disease causation and propitiated through possession healing ceremonies (Vecchiato 1993a). Magical forces such as evil eye (*buda*), sorcery (*gojo*), and curse (*rumo*) are also considered potential sources of ill health.

The Sidama are sedentary, subsisting on a farming and cattle-raising economy. Although their diet has been recently supplemented with new crops (maize, legumes, and coffee), their staple food consists of the porridge derived from the "false banana" plant (*Ensete ventricosum Ch.*). The final edible product is obtained following a series of processing stages carried out by women during which food-soil contact and exposure to flies and other insects constantly occur, thus possibly transmitting parasites to humans. Furthermore, cattle-raising is an important economic activity and an indicator of social status. Cattle and other domestic animals are penned in a special area inside the circular Sidama hut at night. This close proximity probably relates to the spread of zoonoses, namely diseases communicable from animals to man.

Research Methods

The main research area was the farming community of Dongora located approximately 10 kilometers northwest of the town of Aletta Wondo. Comparative data were also gathered in other localities of the Sidama district. The fieldwork on which this research is based was carried out during 1982 and 1983 and in 1987.[3] The research focused on the identification of the main features of the Sidama ethnomedical system and sociocultural determinants of health behavior. Research methods included ethnographic interviews, participant observation, and a health status survey. Through ethnographic interviews with traditional medical practitioners, patients, and other selected informants; prevailing illness etiologies, ethnophysiological concepts, and indigenous perspectives on *A. lumbricoides* and other diseases were unraveled. Data concerning traditional remedies and materia medica related to parasitic infections and other ailments were also gathered. In addition, sanitation and hygiene practices were recorded through participant–observation techniques and their significance discussed with informants and protagonists. Finally, a survey was conducted in order to ascertain both quantitative patterns of therapeutic choice in a pluralistic medical setting and community attitudes toward diseases prevalent in the area. The present study will focus primarily on the prevailing indigenous approach to worm infection.

Morbidity Rates

As in the rest of Ethiopia, intestinal helminths in Sidamaland constitute a major health hazard. Large-scale morbidity surveys, worm burden rates, and reliable clinical data concerning helminth infections are lacking for the Dongora area. Useful morbidity rates, however, were obtained from the Dongora Catholic Clinic. Staffed by biomedically trained Ethiopian and expatriate medical personnel, approximately 30,000 Sidama patients are treated at this health facility every year. During the 1981–1982 period 12.5% ($n=1219$) of all new outpatients ($n=10,703$) sought treatment for helminthiases. A breakdown by disease type shows that ascariasis led with 9.3% ($n=916$), followed by taeniasis (i.e., tapeworm infestation) which afflicted 3.1% of new health-seekers ($n=303$) (Vecchiato 1985:331).

More recent morbidity statistics for the 1990–1991 period show that 25% ($n=2617$) of all new outpatients ($n=10,222$) were diagnosed with helminthiases at the same facility, representing a 12.5% increase from 1981–1982 (Table 9.1). Research is needed to ascertain whether this significant difference over a ten-year period indicates an actual increase in helminth infections or an increase in the number of Sidama resorting to modern vermifuges (i.e., agents for expelling intestinal worms) which may have become more accessible to rural health seekers. The latter explanation should not be excluded, since preference for modern drugs over traditional medicines was noted in the treatment of other diseases such as malaria (Vecchiato 1991). Yet, given widespread under-reporting and universal reliance on traditional vermifuges, the number of outpatients who sought biomedical treatment may be a small fraction of all cases.

Children are the primary victims of helminth infections. At the Dongora Clinic 70% of all outpatients treated for helminthiases were children under fourteen years of age; the one- to four-year-old group

Table 9.1

Top 12 Diagnoses of All New Out-Patients, Dongora Clinic, Sidamo District (1991–92)

Disease name	(*n*)	(%)
1. Helminthiases	2617	25.6
2. Skin problems	1004	9.8
3. Upper respiratory infections	807	7.8
4. Rheumatism	787	7.7
5. Malnutrition	629	6.1
6. Gastritis	547	5.3
7. Eye problems	418	4.1
8. Anemia	365	3.6
9. Diarrhea	356	3.5
10. Pulmonary tuberculosis	350	3.4
11. Malaria	256	2.5
12. Otitis and other ear diseases	176	1.7
Subtotal	8312	81.3
Other ailments	1908	18.7
Total	10220	100.0

Source: Dongora Clinic, unpublished data.

appeared to be the most susceptible (34%) to worm infection (Table 9.2). In the same age group, males (20.5%) surpassed females (13.5%) in infection rates. The gap narrowed, however, in the subsequent, 5 to 14 years age group, making it difficult to establish statistically significant sex-related differences in worm infection. Ostensibly, only 28.7% of all treated cases were adults over 15 years of age. Further research is needed to ascertain whether this reduction in treatment-seeking reflects a decrease in worm burden typically occurring in adult life (Keystone 1989), or whether mature Sidama tend to rely more on traditional vermifugal remedies than on modern anthelminthic (i.e., worm-expelling) drugs.

Table 9.2

Age and Sex Differences in Ascariasis Infection
Rates among Out-Patients, Dongora Clinic, Sidama

Age	Males		Females		Total	
	(*n*)	(%)	(*n*)	(%)	(*n*)	(%)
<1 year	80	8.5	77	8.2	157	16.7
1–4 years	192	20.5	127	13.5	319	34.2
5–14	84	8.9	106	11.3	190	20.3
15–44	77	8.2	102	10.9	179	19.2
45–65	33	3.5	23	2.4	56	5.9
66+	11	1.1	23	2.4	34	3.6
Total	477	(51%)	458	(49%)	935	100.0

Source: Dongora Clinic, unpublished data, 1981–82.

Attitudes toward Intestinal Parasites:
Quantitative Patterns

While morbidity rates point to the threat helminthiases pose to the
health of the Sidama especially in the case of a heavy worm burden,
research was needed to determine how the Sidama community viewed
helminthic infections within the framework of their cultural hierarchy
of disease severity. In the effort to answer this question, 217 people,
112 men (52%) and 104 women (48%), were selected through quota
sampling procedures aimed at securing an even representation of the
population in terms of sex and age. While highly desirable, the
selection of respondents through random sampling techniques was
unfeasible due to the political unrest affecting the area at the time of
research. Respondents were interviewed by trained Sidama-speaking
research assistants through a health questionnaire. The questionnaire
schedule and full results of the survey are reported elsewhere
(Vecchiato 1985). Among the various questions, respondents were
asked: "What do you consider the ten most serious diseases afflicting

Table 9.3

Disease Ranking by Perceived Degree of
Severity among the Sidama

Disease	(n)	(%)
1. Tuberculosis	63	29.0
2. Hepatitis	32	14.7
3. Malaria	30	13.8
4. Cold	13	6.0
5. Helminthiases	11	5.6
6. Headache	10	4.6
8. Gonorrhea	9	4.1
9. Gland swelling	7	3.2
10. Rheumatism	6	2.8
11. Cough	3	1.4
12. Other	33	15.2
Total	217	100.0

Source: Fieldnotes (Adult Health Status Questionnaire).

the community?" Table 9.3 shows that helminthiases ranked fifth in perceived seriousness although they are the most commonly reported ailment for which patients sought treatment at the Dongora Clinic. Tuberculosis, hepatitis, malaria, and the common cold were regarded as more severe health threats than helminths. An explanation for the difference between the high morbidity rates versus their relatively low perceived degree of gravity may be found in the community perception that intestinal helminths are not life-threatening and also in the widespread ethnomedical belief that some categories of worms carry out useful functions in human digestive processes, as discussed later.

Ecological Factors

The distribution of *A. lumbricoides* in Ethiopia correlates with climate, altitude, and seasons. The abundant moisture of the Ethiopian highlands (1500–2700 meters) appears to offer conditions ideal for the embryonation and long-term survival of *A. lumbricoides* eggs and larvae (Tedla and Ayele 1986). Moreover, *A. lumbricoides* was found more prevalent (8.1%) at the beginning of the rainy season (June) and less prevalent (4.3%) at the climax of the dry season (December–January) (Tesfa-Yohannes 1983). Geoclimatic and altitudinal factors also play a fundamental role in the survival and transmission of helminths in Sidamaland. With the exception of lacustrine sedimentary areas around Lake Awasa and Lake Abaya, the preponderant geological configuration of the Sidama District is characterized by reddish-brown lateratic soils. Combined with a highly moist climate, dense vegetation, and a mean temperature of 24–26° C, these clay soils appear to present an ideal environment for *A. lumbricoides*. Moisture and vegetation are guaranteed by average precipitation rates exceeding 1500 millimeters annually (Vecchiato 1985). Environmental factors alone, however, would probably not explain the high rates of *A. lumbricoides* in Sidamaland which may be enhanced by culturally conditioned practices.

BEHAVIORAL DETERMINANTS OF HELMINTH INFECTION

The health threat *A. lumbricoides* poses to human communities is better understood when its infection avenues are clarified. Ascariasis is a nematode infection of the upper small intestine by *A. lumbricoides*. In the transmission cycle, ascarid eggs reach the soil in the feces. They subsequently undergo embryonation and remain infective for months or years in favorable soil and climatic conditions (Benenson 1994). Following human ingestion, the embryonated eggs hatch in the intestines, while the larvae reach the lungs by way of the circulatory system. From the lungs, larvae ascend the trachea and are swallowed into the small intestine, where they mature, mate, and lay eggs 45 to 60 days after ingestion. The eggs are discharged in feces.

The transmission cycle of intestinal parasites is facilitated by a variety of components in the human ecology and health behavior of a community. The Sidama culture and health model encompasses expectations and practices of hygiene pertaining to areas including bodily cleanliness, disposal of human and animal excreta, food preparation, collection and storage of water, and insect control (Vecchiato 1985:307–310). However, health and disease do not appear to be clearly linked to cleanness and sanitation. Behavioral components possibly related to the spread of helminths and other parasites concern three main areas of the Sidama cultural–ecological environment: (1) human waste disposal, (2) housing and food-processing, and (3) water supply.[4]

Human Waste Disposal

As explained earlier, a major avenue of helminth transmission is the fecal-oral route. Cairncross and Feachem (1983) noted that rates of helminth prevalence are greatly affected by the method of disposal of human feces by a community or household. The Dongora Sidama generally do not use pit latrines, although their construction was enforced by numerous peasant associations of the now defunct socialist government (Teka 1993).[5] While indiscriminate defecation is socially unacceptable, the inner recesses of the thick ensete grove surrounding the thatch-roofed homesteads are routinely used as a latrine. Feces are generally not buried unless evacuation ensues following the ingestion of traditional vermifuges; rather, they are left to dry in the open.

Hazards may derive from this open-air defecatory custom. Since most Sidama go barefoot, contact with infected feces and soils is likely to occur especially in the transmission of hookworm (Gilles 1986). Additionally, while among adults post-defecatory cleaning is carried out predominantly with a rolled up piece of dry ensete leaf *(hashuccho)*, unsupervised children tend to use their hands which generally remain unwashed. In a study by Okubagzhi (1988) in Northern Ethiopia, 30% of a sample population of school children were found positive for ova of *A. lumbricoides*, the left-hand fingers being significantly more contaminated than the right-hand fingers due to the pervasive Ethiopian custom of left-hand post-defecatory anal cleaning. Among the Sidama *A. lumbricoides* larvae and ova content in children's fingernails may similarly be ingested while eating, since food is generally brought to the mouth with one's hand rather than with utensils and children do not follow strictly the custom of eating with one's right hand.

Additionally, the close proximity of defecatory areas to habitation should also be considered because of the role played by flies in spreading the helminth infective stage to inhabitants. Studies clearly indicating the common house-fly as a carrier of intestinal helminths are lacking for Ethiopia. However, Umeche and Mandah (1989) showed in their Nigerian study that *Musca domestica* is able to transmit various helminth parasites, including *A. lumbricoides*, to humans and animals through its vomitus or excreta or mechanically through its appendages. Most Sidama appear to regard flies as a nuisance rather than a potential health hazard. This apparent lack of concern was manifested in various instances observed by this author when thick layers of flies were allowed, undisturbed, to cover entirely the face of toddlers in a kind of dark, grotesque mask.

According to Sidama toilet-training practices, children are taught early in childhood not to defecate inside or in front of the house. Violations to this rule may be met by parental corrective action. However, involuntary defecation by children occurs frequently in or around dwellings. Moreover, excreta left around by chickens and cattle pose a major health threat to unsupervised toddlers with the ever-present possibility of coprophagy or the ingestion of contaminated soil. Additionally, children and adults defecate amid bushes disseminated in the communal grazing areas while tending cattle thus increasing the possibility for the transmission of geohelminthiases (i.e., soil-transmitted worm-infection), and *Taenia saginata*. The latter is passed to humans through ingestion of infected meat.

Housing and Food-Processing

It has been observed that worm infections in children can be universally attributed to ingestion of contaminated soil (Wong, Bundy, and Golden 1991:91). In this regard, increasing attention should be given to housing quality and the presence or absence of a dirt floor. In Mexico, Forrester and colleagues (1990) found a statistically significant relationship between household infection with *A. lumbricoides* and the presence of a dirt floor. Additionally, Schulz and Kroeger (1992) identified the presence of helminth eggs in the dust of Brazilian houses. Similarly, Taticheff, Abdullahi, and Haile-Meskal (1981) noted that children who experience most morbidity from ascariasis in Ethiopia are believed to contract it through contact with ascarid eggs in the soil while playing around the house or through feces and water contamination.

In Sidamaland, huts are almost universally built on a dirt floor which women are supposed to sweep daily. Their daily chores also include removing fresh dung accumulated overnight in the animal pen (*hadiro*) of the hut by hand-filling a basket and taking it to the dungheap adjacent the house or directly into the fields. These basic cleaning activities are probably not sufficient to eliminate the helminth larvae and ova harbored in the dirt floor and intradomiciliary dust.

Toddlers face the greatest risk of infection because they frequently sit naked on the floor and touch their buttocks without subsequent hand-washing with soap.

Ensete fermentation pits are additional areas likely to transmit helminthic parasites among the Sidama. The processing of the ensete plant requires a fermentation stage (Besrat, Mehansho, and Bezuneh 1979). This takes place in a 50 centimeter deep earth-pit dug inside the house, where the ensete pulp is interred for one to six months. Although carefully wrapped in banana leaves prior to its placement in the pit, the prolonged contact with the soil may facilitate helminth contamination and should be considered as a heretofore largely unexplored avenue of parasite transmission. Household surveys and laboratory tests are needed to verify this potential hazard. Findings would be relevant to a large number of people in Ethiopia since in excess of 10 million Ethiopians rely on the coarse flour obtained from the ensete plant as their primary or secondary source of food (Bekele, Wolde-Gebriel, and Kloos 1993).

Water Supply and Hygiene

As in other parts of rural Ethiopia (Kitaw 1980; Teka 1993), difficulty in obtaining clean water is a fundamental threat to the health of the Sidama. While most homesteads in the Dongora area have private, hand-dug wells, these are generally seasonal. During the dry season people are forced to fetch water from distant rivers and ponds shared by surrounding villages for water-provisioning, laundry, and cattle-watering. A typical late afternoon scene at one pond includes people washing clothes, cattle drinking and defecating in the water, children swimming and playing in close proximity to the cattle, and women and girls filling claypots with the same water for their family's needs. Being unfamiliar with germ theory, traditional Sidama are unaware that both protozoan and helminth parasites can be transmitted via water. In particular, ascarid embryonated eggs passed through feces can survive in the water in excess of three weeks, thus constituting an additional avenue of infection transmission (Keystone 1989:351). The practice of boiling drinking water, taught through health education programs, may offer some protection against this hazard, although it may not be practical for households short of fuel wood.

As far as personal hygiene is concerned, soap is seldom used notwithstanding the fact that it can be purchased at local open-air markets and urban stores. Morning and evening ablutions are carried out by most Sidama on a daily basis. However, a complete bath is virtually unknown due largely to the total absence of indoor plumbing and limited water supply. Thus, inadequate personal hygiene may be in part imputed for the high prevalence of helminthic infestation. Some hygienic improvements such as the use of soap are noticeable in educated adults. This underscores the importance of mass health education as a crucial prerequisite for effective health programs and the overall improvement of a community's health status.

ETHNOPHYSIOLOGICAL PERSPECTIVES

Indigenous Health Model

Health maintenance constitutes a major personal and social concern for the Sidama. Like other Ethiopian ethnicities (Bishaw 1991; Vecchiato 1993b), the Sidama define health in terms of a holistic balance. The predominant Sidama term for health, *keranchimma* (adj. *kerancho*), denotes a state of equilibrium, which is preserved through: (1) watchfulness over one's physiological cycles (digestion, evacuation, and "blood level" maintenance); (2) guarded interaction with natural forces (weather, climate, fauna, and flora); (3) quality of personal acts (control of emotions, moderation in drinking and commonplace activities); (4) harmony with fellow human beings (quarrel avoidance); and (5) ritual propitiation of, and magical control over, supernatural forces (God, spirits, evil eye, and sorcery).

Following the above axioms, ethnomedical theories of disease can be subdivided into the naturalistic and supernaturalistic. Most infectious diseases are explained naturally although their treatment may involve magical remedies. Rather than possessing a systematic explanatory model to account for the onset of infectious diseases, the Sidama ethnomedical system includes etiologies for specific communicable ailments. Causal theories are, however, characterized by intracultural variation rather than by homogeneous models. For instance, malaria is mainly thought to be triggered by inhaling the pollen of blooming maize, but it may also be ascribed to exposure to bad weather (Vecchiato 1991). Additionally, following pan-Ethiopian beliefs hepatitis is often thought to be caused by contact with bat droppings, although some informants thought that hepatitis may ensue following excessive ingestion of sugar cane or that it may be related to excessive

blood in one's body (Vecchiato 1985). Similarly, tuberculosis is generally associated with overworking, fatigue, and undernutrition (Vecchiato
1994). A naturalistic explanatory model is advocated also for ascariasis
and other helminthiases, which should be understood within the framework of prevailing ethnophysiological concepts concerning the structure and functioning of the human body.

The human body is regarded as the main locus of health and
comprises twelve named parts (*tonalame billite*), in contrast to the
thirty-three attributed to bovine anatomy. An important feature attributed to the stomach (*salto*) and intestines (*helle*) is the presence of
hamasho (lit.: worm, snake). In the Sidama conceptualization of human
physiology, the hamasho refers to nematode roundworms, which are
distinguished from tapeworm (Sid. *matallo*, *soyccho*) and other intestinal parasites (e.g., hookworm, whipworm) prevalent in the region. The
latter are collectively referred to as *da'mulle*. While roundworm is
associated with important digestive functions, tapeworm and other
worms are considered a health hazard and managed through traditional and biomedical remedies.

Digestive Worms

A fundamental Sidama concept postulates that every human being is
born with hamasho and that a man born without hamasho cannot
survive. The main function of hamasho is to digest food, which is
thought to be carried out through five main stages: (1) receive food that
reaches the stomach; (2) crush it into a fine poultice; (3) separate good
and bad food substances; (4) transmit nutrients to heart, liver, and
lungs; and (5) pass the rest to the lower intestines to be later transformed
into excreta and evacuated. The digestive properties of hamasho are
considered vital.

A body's original hamasho is regarded as a father (*hamasho anni*),
which endlessly generates hamasho-children, namely tapeworm and
other worms. To rid the body of excessive worms one should take
traditional or modern vermifugal remedies with regularity. The ultimate purpose of this practice, however, is not the total elimination of
worms, but rather the maintenance of a numerical balance. A complete
annihilation of hamasho is considered fatal since it would destroy the
digestive process.

The success of hamasho's digestive activities depends on the quality
and quantity of the food one eats. When one's hamasho is satisfied,

digestion proceeds normally, the body functions properly, and a person is well. Conversely, an unhappy or famished hamasho will rebel and cause ill health. Consequently, watchfulness must be exercised to avoid abdominal pains resulting from hamasho's rejection of unacceptable food. In this context, the Sidama exercise precautions while traveling, that is, when the possibility of being exposed to potentially harmful foods increases. Informants explained that one's hamasho grows used to a certain type of food and finds it difficult to adjust to strange substances.

The Sidama involve hamasho in the context of a variety of digestive functions. The digestive experience is accounted for in terms of hamasho's reaction to ingested food, which is monitored through various signs. A regular rumbling sound (*waamanno*) experienced in the abdominal region signifies that hamasho is carrying out its digestive activities in a normal way. Similarly, when it is felt moving around (*milli yanno*), it is believed that hamasho is distributing the processed food substances to various parts of the body. Conversely, if the above-mentioned signs are not noticeable, it is feared that something may be wrong with the ingested food and hamasho may have rejected it. Abdominal pains and other symptoms such as nausea, diarrhea, lassitude, heartburn, abdominal cramps, and indigestion are generally ascribed to hamasho's displeasure with the food eaten by the human host. Additionally, infant diarrhea is often explained in terms of hamasho's presence in the stomach and its rejection of ingested food (*hamashu givinosi*). When a gravely ill person is unable to eat, it is believed that the starving hamasho is forced to leave the stomach in search for food. Ultimately, it will surface through the patient's esophagus into his or her mouth, as biomedical personnel routinely witnessed while assisting dying Sidama patients. The Sidama perceive this process as irreversible and fatal because once the hamasho has left the stomach it will be unable to find its way back.

Pan-Ethiopian Dimensions

The above outlined Sidama helminthic model is characterized by a bipartite distinction between digestive (or useful) versus excessive (or harmful) helminths. According to this model, health is secured if at least the following elements are in place: (1) careful selection and ingestion of edible foods; (2) regular food-processing functions by digestive worms; and (3) maintenance of an ideal worm population through worm-expelling remedies. While the history of the Sidama exposure to helminthiases may never be known, endemic helminthiases have contributed to the cultural development of a utilitarian model of worm burden, which enabled the population to cope with the health problem.

Similar ethnophysiological concepts are reported elsewhere in Ethiopia. Young (1970) noted that among the Amhara, *wesfat* (ascaris) are ethnomedically conceived as forming a colony inside the human stomach that carries out important digestive functions. Human health is thought to be secured by wesfat's satisfaction with the received food. Conversely, wesfat are thought to rise up to bite the stomach causing pain, fever, and lassitude, if offensive food is ingested by the human host. This belief was confirmed by Bishaw (Bishaw 1991:194) who suggested that the prevailing Ethiopian ethnomedical model of human health postulates a numerical balance of ascaris worms and that the "Amhara believe that some wesfat worms (ascaris) are needed to help digest food."

The similarities in ethnophysiological concepts of ascaris were ascertained among two prima facie geographically and culturally diverse Ethiopian ethnic groups, the Semitic-speaking Amhara and the Cushitic-speaking Sidama. It is probable that ethnophysiological models of the human body including the digestive functions attributed to ascaris are shared throughout the Ethiopian highlands by several other culturally affinal populations. Further group-specific research is needed to verify this. Such research would aid in planning and implementing national control programs.

TRADITIONAL ANTHELMINTHIC TREATMENT

Travel diaries, missionary accounts, and medico-magical treatises reveal the historical importance of traditional vermifugal remedies in the Ethiopian ethnomedical system (Pankhurst 1969; Strelcyn 1965). As Tesfa-Yohannes and Kloos (1988) noted, both ascariasis and taeniasis are so widespread in Ethiopia that most people seek biomedical treatment from hospitals, clinics, and rural pharmacies only when these infections cause major discomfort. Instead they rely mostly on the utilization of traditional medicinal plants upon noticing segments of tapeworm in the feces or when experiencing abdominal discomfort. *Kosso* (*Hagenia abyssinica*), a powerful taenicide traditionally used primarily against *Taenia saginata*, persists as the most popular remedy.[6]

Seventeen other types of vermifugal plant derivatives were reported by Lemordant (1971) and 15 by Pankhurst (1969). Additionally, a survey by Kloos of 13 markets in Central Ethiopia revealed that most vendors sold a variety of vermifugal remedies including *Embelia schimperi V.* (Amh. *enkoko*), *Croton macrostachys H.* (Amh. *bisanna*), and *Glinus lotoides* (Amh. *mettere*) (Kloos 1976–77).

Among the Sidama, traditional remedies remain the most popular form of helminth management. Preliminary surveys reveal that the Sidama ethnobotanical repertoire comprises a wide number of liquid anthelminthic remedies (Table 9.4).[7] These may be self-procured or purchased from an herbalist or at the marketplace. As children the Sidama master significant portions of their surrounding botanical environment, including well-known vermifugal plants which are routinely utilized by most households. Alternatively, more powerful remedies may be bought from traditional herbalists (*taghissancho*) who specialize in a number of ethnobotanical recipes, including potent taenicides. Finally, marketplaces provide an important source of modern and traditional medicines. Health-seekers can purchase traditional anthelminthic remedies as needed from one of the open-air markets that operate within a radius of a two- to three-hour walk. Different parts of the plant (roots, seeds, leaves, bark, juice) are utilized either to reduce the colony of helminths or to soothe abdominal pains attributed to hamasho.[8]

As in the rest of Ethiopia, taking traditional vermifuges in Sidama has over-arching social ramifications. Particularly in the case of kosso-taking (Sid. *soyccho*), the patient is conferred the status of a sick person and exempted from social obligations in order to recover from the debilitating effects of such a powerful vermifuge.[9] Empathy and support are expressed through visits by food-bearing relatives, neighbors, and friends. The actual act of drinking taenicides is surrounded by practical prescriptions and magical precautions. Sidama ethnomedical wisdom advises the patient to take the remedy early in the morning and to jump up and down to ensure that it will reach the stomach. Additionally, the ingestion of the medicine is considered a dangerous act that places the patient in a vulnerable position and a potential victim of evil-eye bearers (*budakko*). Consequently, the patient is supposed to hide in the most remote part of the house or behind the leaves of the ensete plants. The Sidama believe that the gaze of an evil-eye bearer would prevent the medicine from "falling down" (*di ubbanno*) properly into the stomach. It could instead revert against the patient who would consequently become seriously ill.

Table 9.4

Preliminary Taxonomy of Sidama Anthelminthic Remedies

Sidama	Scientific term	Utilized parts
1. Afududa	Nigella sativa	Fruits
2. Abay Qu'ne	Papyrus sp.	Roots
3. Bakula	Cucurbita pepo	Seeds
4. Bursa	Carduus sp.	Bark
5. ekkata	Cassia sieberiana	Roots
6. Duwancho	Syzygium guineense	Leaves
7. Ennare	Artemisia absinthium	Leaves
8. Ghidincho	Discopodium penninervium	Fruits
9. Goddiccho	Ekebergia senegalensis	Fruits
10. Gotilcho	n/a	Leaves
11. Hamararo	Datura erborea	Roots
12. Janjivelo	Zingiber officinale	Roots
13. Kalala	Thunbergia alata	Roots
14. Kire	Momordica foetida	Leaves
15. Masincho	Croton macrostachys	Bark
16. Otilcho	Carissa edulis	Fruits
17. Qanqo	Embelia schimperi	Fruits
18. Soyccho	Hagenia abyssinica	Fruits
19. Sunkurta	Ruta graveolens	Fruits
20. Surua	Cucurbitacea fam.	Fruits
21. Tayccho	Aeschonomene pfundi	Roots
22. everakko	Bersama abyssinica	Leaves
23. Tontono	Stachys aethiopica L.	Leaves
24. u'naye	Solanum nigrum	Fruits
25. Wajjo barzafe	Eucalyptus globosus	Leaves
26. Wajjo tuma	Alium officinale	Fruits

Source: Fieldnotes.

IMPLICATIONS FOR CONTROL

The anthropological data examined in this study point to the fundamental differences noticeable between the biomedical and ethnomedical perspectives on worm infection and their attributed health consequences in a rural southern Ethiopian community. On one side, biomedicine emphasizes the serious ramifications that helminth infections have on the health of children and adults and the need for their control. On the other side, the Ethiopian ethnomedical paradigm envisions positive functions for roundworms and, while advocating a numerical control of other intestinal worms, it rejects their total annihilation. Hence, although helminthiases constitute the most widespread source of morbidity in the area, they are not regarded as the most serious health hazard.

Such a fundamental discrepancy between the two systems points to some of the sociocultural and behavioral factors identified in this chapter that should be considered by health planners before implementing control programs. First, while the high number of Sidama patients seeking treatment for helminthiases at the Dongora Clinic attests to the fundamental openness of the community to biomedicine, mass chemotherapeutic programs aimed at total deworming are bound to encounter resistance given the prevailing beliefs that some worms are necessary for human digestion. Second, the persisting practice of peridomestic defecation may contribute to the persistence of endemic helminthiases even if mass drug programs were to be implemented. Third, the inadequate provision of clean water and sanitation pose a major obstacle to the implementation of control programs that presuppose basic hygienic standards (Teka 1993). Fourth, the neglect by public health officials of prevailing ethnophysiological concepts related to intestinal parasites and indigenous approaches to hygiene may preclude a full understanding of program objectives on the part of the community. The persisting beliefs and practices indicate that little will be accomplished without the implementation of extensive, culturally grounded health education campaigns.

Additionally, it has been observed that helminthic infections have generally received low priority in the implementation of control measures by national governments (Arfaa 1986). In Ethiopia, the apparent governmental disinterest may be due to: (1) the low mortality rates associated with helminthiases; (2) the great costs involved in mass chemotherapy and environmental sanitation; and (3) the pervasiveness of transmission-fostering cultural beliefs and practices. However, the well-documented adverse health consequences of worm infection compel a revision of planning priorities. Increased funding may be needed in order to implement mass health education programs, to improve sanitation and water supply, and to provide modern taenicides. In the meantime, most health-seekers will undoubtedly continue to rely on the use of traditional taenicides, which are relatively inexpensive and readily accessible to both urban and rural communities.

Short-term reduction in prevalence can be achieved through mass distribution of anthelmintic drugs and the implementation of waste disposal and water supply improvement programs (Esrey et al. 1991). Researchers, however, attest to the overall failure of control measures which were not accompanied by the full understanding and long-term participation of the target community and the integration of social and biomedical control strategies (Holland 1989:409). Conversely, the social and behavioral patterning of parasite burden suggests the need for control programs grounded in the sociocultural environment of the community and an understanding of indigenous versus biomedical differences in the perceived harmfulness of parasitic infections.

Ascariasis control programs will be fruitless unless the community sanctions the behavioral modifications that are fundamental for inter-rupting transmission and takes an active part in their implementation. Full community participation, accompanied by the support of local associations, government agencies, NGOs, schools, and media, is needed for long-term control of ascariasis and other communicable diseases (WHO 1987; Winch, Kendall, and Gluber 1992). Medical anthropologists have emphasized that traditional beliefs and customs need not be considered an "obstacle" to such programs (Kendall et al. 1991; Stone 1992). Rather, detailed awareness of local knowledge and prevailing indigenous coping strategies as illustrated in this study may facilitate the communication process with health-seekers, improve disease surveillance (Brieger and Kendall 1992), and contribute to the control of infectious diseases in developing countries.

NOTES

1. The prevalence rates of helminthiases, as well as other diseases, increased following the implementation of forced resettlement and villagization programs on the part of the defunct socialist government of Ethiopia (Kloos, Bedri, and Addus 1991).

2. Following the incorporation of the Sidama society into modern Ethiopia (1893), judicial and administrative functions in Sidamaland were taken over by the central government and its provincial branches. Additionally,

during the socialist era (1974–1991) like the rest of the country the Sidama were organized into "peasant associations" led by officials and committees elected by the local community. These sociopolitical changes greatly reduced the authority of the elders. However, they retain a great deal of moral authority in local affairs ranging from dispute settlement to medical decision making.

3. I previously worked among the Sidama in educational and development capacities from 1972 to 1977. During this period, I had the opportunity to study and use both Amharic, the national language of Ethiopia, and Sidama, the language predominantly spoken in the Dongora community. This prolonged stay among the Sidama greatly facilitated my subsequent anthropological fieldwork.

4. It is beyond the scope of this research to provide quantitative data concerning the behavioral components of Sidama sanitation and hygiene practices. It is hoped that the qualitative observations reported in this section will provide a basis for additional quantitative research in the area of parasitic transmission.

5. Informants argued that pit latrines remained unused because they smelled, attracted flies, and were hard to maintain given the friability of the soil. They were also considered dangerous for small children. Most people preferred their traditional defecatory practices in the "false banana" grove conveniently located in the backyard. Current research is needed to verify patterns of current construction and use of pit latrines in the area and their possible ramifications for helminthic control.

6. Kosso is botanically classified as a dioecious tree (i.e., the male and female flowers grow separately on different trees). Dried female flowers are ground into powder, mixed with cold water, and left to macerate overnight. The liquid is strained and then consumed in the morning on an empty stomach. The worms are expelled within six hours. The ether and water extracts of Hagenia abyssinica contain four active principles: kossotoxin, protokossin, kossidin, and α and β kossins, all phloroglucinol derivatives (Arragie 1983). Ingested orally, *H. abyssinica* can cause diarrhea and mild to severe forms of poisoning manifested by dizziness, blurred vision, and tachycardia.

7. The ethnobotanical remedies used by the Sidama against worms were collected by this author with the help of informants. The plants were then scientifically identified by botanist Rev. Giuseppe Calvi MCCJ and compared to existing national collections.

8. It is beyond the scope of this chapter to analyze in detail the cultural criteria according to which certain plants are considered efficacious against worms. However, most informants agreed that ethnobotanical anthelmintic remedies must contain a high degree of bitterness in order to be effective.

9. Taking kosso is generally described as a debilitating experience characterized primarily by severe abdominal cramps, vomiting, and prostration

lasting several days. Most users are aware of some of the consequences of kosso overdose, such as exhaustion, excessive diarrhea, and even death (Kloos 1976). However, the potential toxicity of anthelmintic remedies and their side effects, including blindness and changes in the respiratory, cardiovascular, and central nervous systems, may go unrecognized by the general population (Arragie 1983; Low et al. 1985).

REFERENCES

Arfaa, F. 1986. Ascariasis and Trichuriasis. *In* Strategies for Primary Health Care. J. A. Walsh and K. S. Warren, eds. Pp. 178–188. Chicago: The University of Chicago Press.

Arragie, M. 1983. Toxicity of Kosso (Hagenia Abyssinica). Ethiopian Medical Journal 21:89–93.

Bekele, A., Z. Wolde-Gebriel, and H. Kloos. 1993. Food, Diet, and Nutrition. *In* The Ecology of Health and Disease in Ethiopia. H. Kloos and Z. Ahmed Zein, eds. Pp. 85–102. Boulder, Colorado: Westview Press.

Benenson, A. S., ed. 1993. Control of Communicable Diseases in Man. Washington D.C.: The American Public Health Association.

Berman, P., C. Kendall, and K. Bhattacharyya. 1994. The Household Production of Health: Integrating Social Science Perspectives on Micro-level Health Determinants. Social Science and Medicine 38:205–215.

Besrat, A., H. Mehansho, and T. Bezuneh. 1979. Effect of Varietal Difference and Fermentation on Protein Quantity and Quality of Ensete. Nutrition Reports International 20:245–259.

Bishaw, M. 1991. Promoting Traditional Medicine in Ethiopia: A Brief Historical Review of Government Policy. Social Science and Medicine 33:193–200.

Booth, S., T. Johns, and C.Y. Lopez-Palacios. 1993. Factors Influencing Self-Diagnosis and Treatment of Perceived Helminthic Infection in a Rural Guatemalan Community. Social Science and Medicine 37:531–539.

Brieger, W. R. and C. Kendall. 1992. Learning from Local Knowledge to Improve Disease Surveillance: Perceptions of the Guinea Worm Illness Experience. Health Education Research 7:471–485.

Brown, P. J. and M. C. Inhorn. 1990. Disease, Ecology, and Human Behavior. *In* Medical Anthropology. Contemporary Theory and Method. T. M. Johnson and C. F. Sargent, eds. Pp. 187–214. New York: Praeger.

Bundy, D. A. P. and G. F. Medley. 1992. Immuno-Epidemiology of Human Geohelminthiasis: Ecological and Immunological Determinants of Worm Burden. Parasitology 104:S105–S119.

Cairncross, S. and R. G. Feachem. 1983. Environmental Health in the Tropics: An Introductory Text. New York: John Wiley and Sons.

Cooper, E. S. 1991. Intestinal Parasitoses and the Modern Description of Diseases of Poverty. Transactions of the Royal Society of Tropical Medicine 85:168–170.

Dunn, F. L. and C. R. Janes. 1986. Introduction: Medical Anthropology and Epidemiology. *In* Anthropology and Epidemiology: Interdisciplinary Approaches to the Study of Health and Disease. C. R. Janes, R. Stall, and S. M. Gifford, eds. Pp. 3–34. Dordrecht: D. Reidel Publishing Company.

Esrey, S. A., J. B. Potash, L. Roberts, and C. Shiff. 1991. Effects of Improved Water Supply and Sanitation on Ascariasis, Diarrhoea, Dracunculiasis, Hookworm Infections, Schistosomiasis, and Trachoma. Bulletin of the World Health Organization 69:609–621.

Forrester, J. E., M. E. Scott, D. A. Bundy, and M. H. N. Golden. 1990. Predisposition of Individuals and Families in Mexico to Heavy Infection with Ascaris lumbricoides and Trichuris trichiura. Transaction of the Royal Society of Tropical Medicine and Hygiene 84:272–276.

Gilles, H. M. 1986. Hookworm Infection and Anemia. *In* Strategies for Primary Health Care. J. A. Walsh and K. S. Warren, eds. Pp. 119–126. Chicago: The University of Chicago Press.

Government of Ethiopia. 1986. Ethiopia: Statistical Abstract. Addis Ababa: Central Statistical Authority.

Hamer, J. H. 1987. Humane Development: Participation and Change among the Sadama of Ethiopia. Tuscaloosa, Alabama: The University of Alabama Press.

Holland, C. V. 1989. Man and His Parasites: Integration of Biomedical and Social Approaches to Transmission and Control. Social Science and Medicine 29:403–411.

Holland, C. V. 1991. Helminth Infections, Impact on Human Nutrition. Encyclopedia of Human Biology 4:113–122.

Holland, C. V., D. L. Taren, D. W. T. Crompton, M. C. Nesheim, D. Sanjur, I. Barbeau, K. Tucker, J. Tiffany, and G. Rivera. 1988. Intestinal Helminthiases in Relation to the Socioeconomic Environment of Panamanian Children. Social Science and Medicine 26:209–213.

Inhorn, M. C. and P. J. Brown. 1990. The Anthropology of Infectious Disease. Annual Review of Anthropology 19:89–117.

Kamunvi, F. and A. G. Ferguson. 1993. Knowledge, Attitudes and Practices (KAP) of Human Intestinal Helminths (worms) in two Rural Communities in Nyanza Province, Western Kenya. East African Medical Journal 70:482–490.

Kendall, C., P. Hudelson, E. Leontsini, P. Winch, L. Lloyd, and F. Cruz. 1991. Urbanization, Dengue, and the Health Transition: Anthropological Contributions to International Health. Medical Anthropological Quarterly 5:257–268.

Keystone, J. S. 1989. Ascariasis. *In* Tropical Medicine and Parasitology. R. Goldsmith and D. Heyneman, eds. Pp. 350. Norwalk, Connecticut and San Mateo, California: Appleton and Lange.

Kitaw, Y. 1980. Water Supply in a Small Village in Western Ethiopia. Ethiopian Medical Journal 18:165–169.

Kloos, H. 1977. Preliminary Studies of Medicinal Plants and Plant Products in Markets of Central Ethiopia. Ethnomedizin 4:63–104.

Kloos, H., A. Bedri, and A. Addus. 1991. Intestinal Parasitism in Three Resettlement Farms in Western Ethiopia. Ethiopian Journal of Health Development 5:51–56.

Kloos, H. and T. Tesfa-Yohannes. 1993. Intestinal Parasitism. *In* The Ecology of Health and Disease in Ethiopia. H. Kloos and Z. Ahmed Zein, eds. Pp. 223–235. Boulder, Colorado: Westview Press.

Kvalsvig, J. D., R. M. Cooppan, and K. J. Connolly. 1991. The Effects of Parasite Infections on Cognitive Processes in Children. Annals of Tropical Medicine and Parasitology 85:551–568.

Lemordant, D. 1971. Contribution à L'Ethnobotanique Ethiopienne. Journal d'Agriculture Tropicale et de Botanique Appliquée 18:1–35, 142–179.

Low, G., L. J. Rogers, S. P. Brumley, and D. Ehrlich. 1985. Visual Deficits and Retinotoxicity caused by the Naturally Occurring Anthelmintics, *Ambelia ribes and Hagenia abyssinica.* Toxicology and Applied Pharmacology 81:220–230.

Ministry of Health. 1986. Comprehensive Health Services Directory. Addis Ababa: Ministry of Health.

Ministry of Health. 1991. Comprehensive Health Services Directory. Addis Ababa: Planning and Programming Department.

Morrow, R. H. 1984. The Application of a Quantitative Approach to the Assessment of the Relative Importance of Vector and Soil Transmitted Diseases in Ghana. Social Science and Medicine 19:1039–1049.

Nichter, M. 1992. Ethnomedicine: Diverse Trends, Common Linkages. *In* Anthropological Approaches to the Study of Ethnomedicine. M. Nichter, ed. Pp. 223–259. Amsterdam: Gordon and Breach Science Publishers.

Nokes, C. and D. A. P. Bundy. 1994. Does Helminth Infection Affect Mental Processing and Educational Achievement? Parasitology Today 10:14–18.

Okubagzhi, G. 1988. Ova, Larvae and Cysts in Fingernail Contents. Ethiopian Medical Journal 26:33–35.

Pankhurst, R. 1969. The Traditional Taenicides of Ethiopia. Journal of the History of Medicine and Allied Sciences 24:323–334.

Rousham, E. K. 1994. Perceptions and Treatment of Intestinal Worms in Rural Bangladesh: Local Differences in Knowledge and Behavior. Social Science and Medicine 39:1063–1068.

Schulz, S. and A. Kroeger. 1992. Soil Contamination with Ascaris Lumbricoides Eggs as an Indicator of Environmental Hygiene in Northeast Brazil. Journal of Tropical Medicine and Hygiene 95:95–103.

Stephenson, L. S. 1987. The Impact of Helminth Infections on Human Nutrition. New York: Taylor and Francis.

Stephenson, L. S. 1994. Helminth Parasites, a Major Factor in Malnutrition. World Health Forum 15:169–172.

Stone, L. 1992. Cultural Influences in Community Participation in Health. Social Science and Medicine 35:409–417.

Strelcyn, S. 1965. Les Écrits Médicaux Éthiopiens. Journal of Ethiopian Studies 3:82–108.

Taticheff, S., Y. Abdullahi, and F. Haile-Meskal. 1981. Intestinal Parasitic Infection in Pre-School Children in Addis Ababa. Ethiopian Medical Journal 19:35–40.

Teka, G. A. 1993. Water Supply and Sanitation. *In* The Ecology of Health and Disease in Ethiopia. H. Kloos and Z. Ahmed Zein, eds. Pp. 179–190. Boulder, Colorado: Westview Press.

Tedla, S. and T. Ayele. 1986. Ascariasis Distribution in Ethiopia. Ethiopian Medical Journal 24:79–86.

Tesfa-Yohannes, T. 1983. Intestinal Helminthiasis Among the Out-patients of Zway Health Centre, Central Ethiopia. Ethiopian Medical Journal 21:155–159.

Tesfa-Yohannes, T. 1990. Effectiveness of Praziquantel Against Taenia Saginata Infections in Ethiopia. Annals of Tropical Medicine and Parasitology 84:581–585.

Tesfa-Yohannes, T. and H. Kloos. 1988. Intestinal Parasitism. *In* The Ecology of Health and Disease in Ethiopia. Z. Ahmed Zein and H. Kloos, eds. Pp. 214–230. Addis Ababa: Ministry of Health.

Umeche, N. and L. E. Mandah. 1989. Musca Domestica as a Carrier of Intestinal Helminths in Calabar, Nigeria. East African Medical Journal 66:349–352.

Vecchiato, N. L. 1985. Culture, Health, and Socialism in Ethiopia: The Sidama Case. Unpublished Doctoral Dissertation. Los Angeles: University of California Los Angeles.

Vecchiato, N. L. 1991. Ethnomedical Beliefs, Health Education, and Malaria Eradication in Ethiopia. International Quarterly of Community Health Education 11:385–397.

Vecchiato, N. L. 1993a. Illness, Therapy, and Change in Ethiopian Possession Cults. Africa 63:176–196.

Vecchiato, N. L. 1993b. Traditional Medicine. *In* The Ecology of Health and Disease in Ethiopia. H. Kloos and Z. Ahmed Zein, eds. Pp. 157–178. Boulder, Colorado: Westview Press.

Vecchiato, N. L. 1997. Sociocultural Aspects of Tuberculosis Control in Ethiopia. Medical Anthropology Quarterly 11(2):1–19.

Winch, P., C. Kendall, and D. Gubler. 1992. Effectiveness of Community Participation in Vector-borne Disease Control. Health Policy and Planning 7:342–351.

Wong, M. S., D. A. P. Bundy, and M. H. N. Golden. 1991. The Rate of Ingestion of Ascaris Lumbricoides and Trichuris Trichiura Eggs in Soil and Its Relationship to Infection in Two Children's Homes in Jamaica. Transaction of the Royal Society of Tropical Medicine and Hygiene 85:89–91.

World Health Organization. 1987. Prevention and Control of Intestinal Parasitic Infections. Technical Report Series 749. Geneva: World Health Organization.

Young, A. 1970. Medical Beliefs and Practices of Begemder Amhara. Unpublished Doctoral Dissertation. Pennsylvania: University of Pennsylvania.

CHAPTER 10

Illness Semantics and International Health: The Weak Lungs–Tuberculosis Complex in the Philippines

Mark Nichter

INTRODUCTION

Tuberculosis (TB) remains a leading cause of mortality and morbidity in the world despite the fact that most cases are curable.[1] It is estimated that somewhere between one-third and one-half of the world's population is infected with *Mycobacterium tuberculosis*. There are some 30 million cases of active tuberculosis worldwide, with 8–10 million new cases occurring annually. Approximately half of these cases are contagious. Between 10–20% of new cases are in children. An estimated 2.9 million people die from tuberculosis each year, of which 98% are from less-developed countries. This makes the disease the largest cause of death from a single pathogen. In less-developed countries, tuberculosis accounts for an estimated 6.7% of all deaths and 18.5% of deaths among adults between the ages of 15 and 59. Notably, the

Reprinted from **Social Science of Medicine**, Volume 38, Mark Nichter, "Illness Semantics and International Health," pp. 649–663, ©1994, with permission from Elsevier Science Ltd., The Boulevard, Langford Lane, Kidlington 0X5 1GB, UK.

Western Pacific Region (including the Philippines as demarcated by the World Health Organization) has the greatest number of people infected with the *M. tubercle bacillus* (574 million), the highest number of new tuberculosis cases (2.56 million), and the second largest number of deaths attributed to the disease.

In this chapter, I will discuss the findings of an ethnographic study of tuberculosis which followed a detailed study of acute respiratory infection (ARI) on the Island of Mindoro in the Philippines (Nichter and Nichter 1994). During the previous study, popular perceptions of linkages between tuberculosis and ARI emerged from an examination of the illness category "weak lungs" (*mahina ang baga*). Attention is presently directed to what I will term the "weak lungs–tuberculosis complex." Weak lungs is a specific ambiguous illness category (Nichter 1989) pervasive in the popular health culture of the Philippines as well as fostered by its practitioners of biomedicine. Arguing that the semantics of illness have important public health significance, I will illustrate how popular understanding of weak lungs has: (1) influenced perceptions of the purpose of tuberculosis medications leading to drug misuse and possibly drug resistance; and (2) fostered false expectations of tuberculosis medications, contributing to delays in health care seeking for ARI in cases of children taking tuberculosis prophylaxis medications.

First, however, let me briefly present some background data on tuberculosis transmission and its prevalence in the Philippines, disease control and treatment regimes, and drug resistance.[2] This information will clarify why an ethnographic assessment of tuberculosis is of vital importance to international health.

TUBERCULOSIS TRANSMISSION AND SUSCEPTIBILITY

Pulmonary tuberculosis is a contagious disease transmitted by *Mycobacterium tuberculosis*. Infection results when a host inhales tubercle bacilli in small airborne droplets.[3] Bacilli harbor in the apices of the lungs if not eliminated by the immune system. The body develops an immune response to the bacilli at the site of infection (primary focus). The course of the lesion depends on the relationship between bacillary multiplication and host defense. If host defense is good, slow fibrosis and calcification occurs over 12–18 months and the infection is rendered dormant. In this dormant state, the bacilli constitute an asymptomatic infection, not a disease.[4] Few people (an estimated 5–15%)

infected with the bacilli will actually develop the disease over the course of their lives.

Tuberculosis reactivates when host immunity is depressed by any one of several host-dependent factors. Among these, poor nutrition, crowding, and adverse working conditions have been identified as alterable risk factors. For this reason tuberculosis constitutes a good index of a population's general health (Dubos and Dubos 1987 [1952]; McKeown 1979; Packard 1989; Pope and Gordon 1955; Riley and Moodie 1974; Wolff 1940).

Tuberculosis control measures include finding and treating cases, chemoprophylaxis of those at high risk, vaccination, and improvement of socioeconomic conditions. In terms of biotechnical interventions, the most effective general control measure is preventing active cases from infecting new hosts through drug therapy which renders the bacillus inert (Rodrigues and Smith 1990). Experts estimate that each sputum positive case will infect ten new cases a year. Identifying active cases entails laboratory investigation of sputum samples or X-ray examination of the lungs. Control measures include both passive case finding (testing symptomatics who consult clinicians) and active surveillance which entails screening for likely cases in the community (mass screening and tracing of likely contacts).

TUBERCULOSIS PREVALENCE, TREATMENT, AND DRUG RESISTANCE IN THE PHILIPPINES

Tan (1991) estimates that of the 60 million inhabitants of the Philippines, some 396,000 are sputum positive (infectious) for tuberculosis. In 1988, tuberculosis ranked as the fourth leading cause of death in the Philippines accounting for 8% of reported deaths. The rate of tuberculosis in Oriental Mindoro, the site of this study, is above the national average and the highest in Region Four (a national subdivision) which is composed of eleven provinces.

Both short-course chemotherapy (isoniazid, pyrazinamide, and rifampicin) recommended by the World Health Organization for sputum-positive cases of tuberculosis, and standard long-term tuberculosis regimen (streptomycin and isoniazid) recommended in cases of tuberculosis reinfection and drug resistance to short-course therapy, are theoretically available free of charge to Filipino citizens. These medications are supposed to be distributed at local *barangay* health stations (BHS) throughout the Philippines, but in many areas of the country supplies of short-course drugs are wanting and patients are treated with streptomycin injections. Short-course therapy is the preferred treatment. It is administered for a period of six months, while the long-term regime is administered for twelve months, but with less compliance (DOH 1988). Parents of children suspected of having tuberculosis primary-complex on the basis of a family medical history, failure to thrive, and other signs and symptoms (e.g., cough and low-grade fever of long duration, swollen lymph nodes) are advised to administer isoniazid to their children for a year. Sometimes health workers also recommend the purchase of rifampicin suspension from the pharmacy.[5]

Many people afflicted by weak lungs–tuberculosis seek care from private practitioners. The National Tuberculosis Prevalence Survey (DOH 1988) carried out between 1981 and 1983 found that of those individuals who had bacteriologically confirmed cases of tuberculosis and had sought medical assistance, 34% consulted private doctors, 25% health centers, and 21% hospitals.[6] The survey also found that 39% of tuberculosis patients reported engaging in self-medication. A more recent study by Sarmiento (1990) reported that 31% of tuberculosis patients engaged in self-treatment. Neither report specified the type(s) of medicine utilized or duration of self-treatment.

Drug resistance is the primary factor underlying multiple drug therapy strategies in tuberculosis control. Resistance to a medication needs to be viewed both epidemiologically and anthropologically. Resistance may reflect patterns of pharmaceutical misuse related to: over-the-counter drug use for self-medication or self-regulation of prescription drugs; poverty (the inability to afford recommended treatment beyond symptomatic relief); local interpretations of tuberculosis and expectations from drugs; the compliance of private practitioners with public health guidelines given practical contingencies; and the availability and accessibility of drugs for effective chemotherapy. A high prevalence of resistance often suggests inefficient arrangements for the treatment of tuberculosis (Mitchison 1984). Drug-resistant tuberculosis is on the rise globally (Iseman 1989) and constitutes a major obstacle to successful treatment in the Philippines.

THE WEAK LUNGS–TUBERCULOSIS COMPLEX: AN ETHNOGRAPHY

Sample and Methods

A four-month ethnographic study of tuberculosis-related behavior was conducted in a rural coastal area of central Oriental Mindoro. Oriental

Mindoro (population 560,215: 1988) is 160 kilometers south of Manila and is separated from Luzon by the Sulu Sea. It is the seventh largest island in the Philippines. The site selected for study, some 50 kilometers from the region's capital, is largely inhabited by Christian Tagalogs who engage in rice agriculture and fishing. An opportunistic sample of 50 lower-class, literate mothers was drawn from a population whose children attended community creches in two adjacent hamlets (*barangay*). Mothers were interviewed about their perceptions of and experiences with weak lungs–tuberculosis and types of illness and other factors predisposing one to tuberculosis.

In addition, twenty informants participated in illness attribute recognition interviews wherein a deck of cards naming illness attributes gleaned from the open-ended interviews and enriched by several opposing attributes (e.g., dry cough: productive cough) were used to prompt associations. Ten informants had already participated in open-ended (nonprompted) interviews a month or two before and another ten informants (matched for age, education, and number of children) participated in only this form of interview.

A series of 13 focus groups was also conducted with five participants per group. The groups consisted of mothers 30 years old and younger, mothers over 30 years old, grandmothers, men between 30 and 45 years old, and men over 45 years old. Participatory rural appraisal techniques maximizing visual cues were utilized to assess community perceptions of weak lungs–tuberculosis prevalence and severity when compared to other local illnesses. During these exercises, informants constructed crude histograms of prevalence and severity out of seeds and stones, and then debated the order of magnitude constructed. Three focus groups were held with men to explore perceived relationships between personal habits (smoking, drinking, sexual behavior) and ill health. An additional three focus groups centering on social stigma and medicine-taking behavior were held with former weak lungs–tuberculosis patients. Finally, two focus groups were held with government midwives to discuss their experiences related to tuberculosis and ARI management, the health care seeking behavior of villagers, and medicine default.

Weak Lungs

"Weak lungs" (*mahina ang baga*) is an ambiguous illness term which commonly surfaced in discussions of tuberculosis as well as ARI. The term is used by doctors as well as the lay population. During interviews with several private and government doctors, physicians reported that they told some patients who were sputum or X-ray positive for tuberculosis (but not coughing up blood) that they had weak lungs, "to reduce social stigma." Children suspected of having primary-complex tuberculosis were also told they had weak lungs. These findings confirmed data collected in the community. Individuals taking anti-tuberculosis drugs were asked what illness their doctors told them they had. All children and most adults taking antituberculosis medicine reported weak lungs as their diagnosis.

Weak lungs also describes acute respiratory infections. During a previous ARI study in Mindoro (Nichter and Nichter 1994), several cases were documented in which doctors had told parents of children experiencing recurrent or prolonged respiratory tract infections that their child had weak lungs. A variety of medicines were prescribed for these children (e.g., amoxicillan suspension, salbutomol prepara-tions for wheeze, expectorants and cough suppressants, and isoniazid). Primary-complex tuberculosis has diffuse symptoms which may over-lap with ARI.

In popular health culture, "weak lungs" can apply to states of ill health in which a child experiences recurrent or prolonged cough and cold, loss of weight and lack of appetite, fatigue and restlessness, and low-grade "inside fever" (nangingilalim ang lagnat). Under such condi-tions people imagine either: (1) that the lungs are coated with mucus (plema) as a result of previous illnesses (usually associated with ARI); or (2) that a child is predisposed to weak lungs manifested by wheezing (hapo) or a history of tuberculosis in the family. Among adults, if a person is unable to work hard, weak lungs is suspected. The symptoms associated with weak lungs are similar to those associated with tuberculosis (see below) except for "coughing up blood."

When asked about the relationship of weak lungs to tuberculosis (n = 50), 76% of informants stated that weak lungs develops into tuberculosis if not cured, 12% said the two illnesses were the same, and 12% said there was no connection. Notably, 18% of informants stated that tuberculosis was an illness which only affected adults. According to these informants, children who suffered from weak lungs were likely to develop tuberculosis later if not cured. In response to the question of what the chances were that someone with weak lungs would develop tuberculosis, 50% of informants believed they would, while the other 50% thought that their chances of getting the disease were about even.

To obtain information on perceptions of the incidence of weak lungs, informants were asked what they thought the chances were that someone in their own household would develop weak lungs. Thirty-two percent of informants said that someone in their household either had weak lungs now or in the last three years ($n = 16$, 8 children and 8 adults). The remainder were unwilling to speculate about the chances of weak lungs occurring in their houses. When asked to speculate on ten neighboring households, however, a median of 5.5 out of 10 households was cited. Perceived incidence was high, in large part because of the wide range of health problems encompassed by the term "weak lungs." Fifty-six percent of the sample reported that someone having weak lungs had spent time (at least three days) in their house in the past two years.

LOCAL PERCEPTIONS OF TUBERCULOSIS

In Oriental Mindoro, tuberculosis and *pulmonya* (an illness category encompassing adult pneumonia) routinely emerged as two of the three most serious causes of adult morbidity identified during participatory rural appraisal focus groups (Chambers 1990). An ill person is spoken of as having tuberculosis only after being diagnosed by a doctor as having tuberculosis or when they have been seen coughing up blood. Taking short-course tuberculosis medication did not necessarily label one as a "tuberculosis patient" because this medication is thought to be useful in the treatment of weak lungs, an antecedent illness.

Tuberculosis is not openly spoken about; initially mothers disclaimed much knowledge of it. Reluctance to discuss the illness has been cited as evidence of social stigma in the government reports on tuberculosis (DOH 1988; Ortega, Meniado, and Tobias 1991; Sarmiento 1990). Our interviews initially focused upon health problems in the community. Following informants' mention of tuberculosis or weak lungs, they were asked a number of open-ended questions. This approach proved more productive and less threatening than a structured interview narrowly focusing on tuberculosis.

Table 10.1 documents symptoms associated with tuberculosis. Persistence of these symptoms was cited as a reason to consult a doctor to see if a person had weak lungs–tuberculosis. Informants spoke more about factors predisposing one to weak lungs–tuberculosis than specific etiology. Factors predisposing one to tuberculosis are presented in Table 10.2

Tuberculosis is perceived to result from factors seriously weakening or shocking the body; modes of etiology involving pathogens, contagion

Table 10.1

Symptoms Associated with Weak Lungs– Tuberculosis in Adults:

Pain in back and chest	+++
Becoming thin, poor appetite	+++
Weakness/fatigue	+++
Cough:	
productive	+
dry	++
continuous	++
with blood	+++
noisy breathing	+++
Intermittent fever, morning and afternoon	++
Hot feeling in back and chest, fever in lungs	++
Paleness	+
Dislike cold water bath	+

$n = 50$
+++ = > 61% of informants.
++ = 31–60% of informants.
+ = 14–30% of informants.

and heredity; and illnesses which progress and transform into tuberculosis. Several factors are thought to place one at risk for tuberculosis by weakening one's general health. Among these are hunger and "lack of vitamins;" exposure to the elements especially during changes of climate; overwork; and excessive habits including smoking, drinking, and sex. Hunger, smoking, and drinking are interlinked in that they disrupt well-being established by the routine consumption of rice which is considered necessary. This results in a condition referred to as *pasma sa guton*. Poverty prohibits the purchase of rice, while excessive consumption of alcohol leads to a loss of appetite for rice and untimely eating. Men who drink eat rice sporadically, to some degree because while drinking alcohol they snack on finger foods (*palutan*), generally fried fish or meat eaten in small quantities. Cigarette smoking is

Table 10.2

Risk Factors for Weak Lungs–Tuberculosis

Factors predisposing one to weak lungs–TB	Open–ended Interview ($n = 50$)	Attribute Recongnition Interview ($n = 20$)
Microbyo, germs	+	++
Fatigue, overwork	++	++
Carelessness of body	+	+
Unsanitary environment	++	++
Poverty	+++	+++
Too little food	+++	+++
Untimely eating	++	+
Sleeping on cold floor, exposure to fan, or wind, sweat drying on back	++	++
Plegma dried on lungs	++	++
Pilay, blocked flow within body	+	+
Excess smoking	++	+++
Excess drinking	+++	+++
Lack of vitamins	+	++
Develops from other ARI related illnesses when not cured (*Bronkitis, Pulmonya*)	++	+++
Hereditary	+++	+++
Contagious		
Tuberculosis	+++	+++
Weak lungs	++	+

+++ = 61% of informants.
++ = 31–60% of informants.
+ = 14–30% of informants.

associated with tuberculosis not only because it is considered harmful for the lungs, but also because smoking is observed to reduce the appetite of some, though not all smokers. For smokers who maintain or gain weight, the habit of smoking is deemed less harmful and is described as compatible (*kasundo*) for their bodies.

Overwork and exposure to the elements as well as excessive sexuality are perceived to weaken the body not just through fatigue, but by shocking the body through dramatic changes of hot–cold. This state is also referred to as *pasma*. Exposure to the elements, especially the hot sun followed by cold rain or wind, is linked to several illnesses in Mindoro, especially those associated with ARI. Overwork is associated with excessive sweating which may dry on the back, a commonly cited risk factor for the illness pulmonya. Pulmonya is an illness many informants think weakens the lungs, predisposing them to tuberculosis.

Male informants associated "excessive sexuality," especially sex with a "new girl," with overheating the body. This appeared to be a gender-specific perception. The focus group of 40- to 60-year-old men articulated the fear that sex places them at risk for tuberculosis because having intercourse several times in one evening causes the body to become very hot. Then, as one informant noted, "After sex one often exposes the body to the night air or the wind produced by a fan in a hotel room. This is very unhealthy." No female informant listed excessive sexuality as a risk factor for tuberculosis. However, one woman whose husband was undergoing treatment for tuberculosis cited hot–cold reasoning in yet another way:

> He has a small *sari sari* (provisions) shop so he hasn't had to do hard
> work in the hot sun and he doesn't smoke or drink, but he has the habit
> of sleeping with the fan on!

In terms of specific etiology, during open–ended interviews only 14% of informants noted that tuberculosis was associated with germs (*microbyo*). These data match the findings of Ortega, Meniado, and Tobias (1991), who surveyed a rural population elsewhere in Region Four of the Philippines and an urban Metro Manila population. During the illness attribute interviews we conducted, however, recognition of microbyo increased. Fifty-five percent of the mothers presented with a deck of 80 possible illness attributes identified microbyo as a "risk factor or cause of tuberculosis." Of the ten informants who had previously participated in open–ended interviews and not mentioned microbyo as a cause of tuberculosis, six associated microbyo with tuberculosis during the illness attribute exercise.

Two interpretations of the data are possible. First, mothers may have known that microbyo caused tuberculosis, but did not recall this association. Second, they may have been identifying health education messages to gain social status (i.e., appear educated and modern).

Follow-up interviews with those informants who had chosen microbyo during attribute recognition exercises revealed that microbyo was rarely cited as the specific etiology of tuberculosis. Microbyo was primarily associated with tuberculosis in discussion of treatment.

Data generated by three other research questions asked during lengthy open–ended interviews ($n = 50$) about weak lungs–tuberculosis provide further insights into how and when microbyo are thought about in relation to this illness complex:

Q1. *Is tuberculosis curable and if so how?* Ninety percent of informants thought tuberculosis was curable. All of these informants believed that to be cured it was necessary to take doctors' medicine, not just rest and eat good food. When asked why, many (42%) stated that doctors' medicine cured diseases caused by microbyo. Here we have an example of an illness interpreted in relation to the medicine deemed effective to cure it. Microbyo emerged as an attribute of tuberculosis when informants were asked questions about medicines needed to cure it, but not when asked about the illness as an objectified construct.

Q2. *Is tuberculosis preventable, and if so, how?* Sixty-four percent of informants thought tuberculosis was preventable, 22% thought it was not, and 14% had no opinion – expressing confusion about the issue. When asked how tuberculosis was preventable, 48% of informants mentioned immunization (*bakuna*) and 16% mentioned better food or vitamins. Notably, not one of the 24 informants citing immunizations as a means of preventing tuberculosis specifically mentioned Bacille Calmette-Guerin Vaccine (BCG).[8] Of these 24 informants, 11 thought there was a specific immunization for tuberculosis while 13 thought that immunizations made children healthy thereby preventing all serious disease. While some people had heard of microbyo, they did not know whether one type of microbyo caused one or many illnesses, or whether vaccinations only prevent specific illnesses or promote health in general.

Q3. *Is tuberculosis contagious?* Ninety-six percent of informants stated that tuberculosis was contagious. However, 56% believed that only a person coughing blood was contagious. Of the ten informants who had participated in both the open–ended and attribute-identification interviews, all stated that tuberculosis was contagious regardless of whether they identified microbyo as a risk factor.

To the question "How is tuberculosis contagious?" several modes of transmission were noted (Table 10.3).

Discussion revealed that perceptions of contagion (*nanakahawa*) were as much based upon contiguity (where contact with blood, saliva, food or breath placed one in a contiguous relationship with the disease), as were notions of microbyo as body-invading pathogens. Irrespective of how contagion was conceptualized, knowledge of transmission pathways may influence medicine compliance. For example, Conanan and Valeza (1988) found that 85% of tuberculosis patients who finished the full course of their medications knew transmission pathways as compared to 62% of defaulters.

Contiguous relationships with the disease exist in time as well as space. Seventy percent of informants stated that tuberculosis was a hereditary disease transmitted through the blood of either the father or mother. Content analysis of tuberculosis discourse revealed that the notion that tuberculosis was hereditary extended beyond parents' references to grandparents, uncles, and aunts having tuberculosis. An assessment of discourse among family members and neighbors of those afflicted with tuberculosis found both marked (specific) and unmarked (open–ended, general) references to tuberculosis "running in the family."[9]

Another factor commonly associated with tuberculosis is a previous illness or state of ill health. In four of fifty households, a family member

Table 10.3

Modes of Tuberculosis Transmission

Through the air: breathing, coughing	+++
Contact with the afflicted's body (touch, intimate relations)	++
Contact with food the afflicted has touched	++
Contact with a glass, fork, spoon, plate the afflicted has used	+++

$n = 50$
+++ = 61% of informants.
++ = 31–60% of informants.
+ = 14–30% of informants.

had a history of tuberculosis. In two households tuberculosis was associated with a previous illness, while in another two, tuberculosis was described as hereditary. Among twelve people participating in three focus groups of former tuberculosis patients, eight linked their illness to previous illness states, most notably pulmonya and weak lungs. This corroborated with the impressions provided by the sample as a whole. Twenty-eight percent of informants stated that those at greatest risk for tuberculosis were those who had previously experienced pulmonya, and 76% identified weak lungs as a common antecedent illness.[10]

Social Stigma

Most knowledge, attitude, practice surveys of tuberculosis conducted in the Philippines have called attention to social stigma. When we asked informants to describe what people thought about tuberculosis in general, they commonly used phrases such as *batik sa pamilya* (bad mark to family), and *nakakahiya* (shameful). The attributes *habag* (pity) and *inuwasan* (avoidance) were included in the illness attribute deck presented to 20 informants participating in the illness attribute recognition interviews. A majority (70%) identified both of these terms as associated with tuberculosis. In open–ended interviews and focus groups, informants indicated that greater confidentiality should be exercised by health staff when discussing sputum tests and tuberculosis medicine with community members. Several informants stated that distribution of tuberculosis medicines should be more secretive so that "neighbors would not talk against people afflicted with tuberculosis."

While talk of stigma was certainly common when the subject of tuberculosis was raised during interviews, observation in the community revealed that talk about the shame of affliction was more common than the practice of social avoidance among kin and close neighbors. Tuberculosis patients were not outcasts, and having a parent or sibling who suffered from tuberculosis was not reported to reduce the chances of other family members finding a marriage partner or job. Ninety-six percent of informants said that the social shame of having tuberculosis was not as strong as that for sexually transmitted diseases. Many stated that one had little control over the former, but considerable control over the latter.

Social stigma for tuberculosis was more extrafamilial than intrafamilial. That is, family members who were afflicted with tuberculosis were not alienated by other household members or extended kin. Asked whether the stigma associated with tuberculosis was the same for weak lungs, 96% of informants said no. The vast majority of informants expressed concern when a tuberculosis patient visited their home. However, only 24% stated that they would be "very concerned" if someone with weak lungs visited their home. If the person was a child there was even less concern. Eighty-eight percent of informants stated that they would let their children play with a neighbor child who had weak lungs. Ninety-eight percent of informants stated that regardless of their concerns, a relative or friend arriving at their home with *either tuberculosis or weak lungs* would be treated as a guest and not asked to leave. Debts of gratitude (*utang no loob*) and the norms of reciprocal exchange as well as Christian charity and compassion (*awa, malasakit*) took precedence over fears of physical risk.

Concern expressed about tuberculosis and weak lungs varied considerably. Does this reflect differences in perceptions about contagion and prevention? Asked the general question "is weak lungs contagious?" 38% of informants said yes, 44% said no, and 18% were unsure. To probe whether age was a factor influencing contagion, we asked whether a child with weak lungs could cause an adult to fall sick with the illness. Eighty-four percent of informants said no, although 66% stated that an adult with weak lungs could cause a child to become ill.

The two most common means of transmitting weak lungs were "through the air" and through contact with an ill person's eating utensils, the same two factors held responsible for transmitting tuberculosis. People afflicted with weak lungs–tuberculosis are commonly given separate plates and utensils in their own homes as well as the homes of relatives. Informants commonly voiced the opinion that there was little one could do to prevent either illness without avoiding the afflicted, which was against cultural norms.[11] A national survey conducted in 1987 (Ministry of Health of the Philippines 1990) reported that 76% of respondents stated that the way to prevent tuberculosis was to avoid contact with those ill with the disease. This is probably not feasible given the social dictates of Filipino culture.

TREATMENT OF WEAK LUNGS AND TUBERCULOSIS

Ninety percent of informants reported that weak lungs and tuberculosis were curable by doctors' medicine. It was generally known that tuberculosis treatment required the taking of several medicines for an extended period of time, there being some confusion over duration of treatment and when injections (streptomycin) are necessary. Injections appeared to mark the severity and dangerousness of an illness.[12] Blister packs of short-course tuberculosis therapy have recently been introduced by the Philippine health ministry. Some informants had the impression that those who were really ill with tuberculosis required injection therapy, while those having weak lungs were placed on tablet medications. A few informants went so far as to state that X-rays were a necessary part of treatment (not diagnosis) of tuberculosis. When asked how long tuberculosis patients needed to take medication *until they were no longer contagious*, 68% of informants said they had no idea while 24% thought nine to twelve months of treatment were necessary. Only 4% thought that a tuberculosis patient would always be contagious, even after treatment.

With respect to treatment for weak lungs, a general impression was that *vitamin sa baga*, vitamins for the lungs, were necessary to strengthen the lungs. The impression that vitamins were required to cure this ailment is connected to the marketing strategies of manufacturers of isoniazid (Tan 1994). More than two dozen isoniazid products are on the market. Some of these products prominently display the words "vitamins" (e.g., *odinah*) on the label of the product, while others have given their products names which suggest that they are vitamin products (e.g., Trisofort, Trisovit).[13] The term "vitamin sa baga" is commonly used in illness discourse about weak lungs and was mentioned by 16 informants who reported a family member having a history of weak lungs.

The range of medicines described as vitamin sa baga among this subsample varied considerably. Asked what type of vitamin sa baga the afflicted had consumed, five informants specifically mentioned drugs containing the antibiotic rifampicin plus isoniazid, while the remainder cited only an isoniazid preparation. Informants were then asked how long the afflicted had taken vitamin sa baga. Four people were presently taking the medication. Of the remaining twelve people, the median duration for taking isoniazid was three to four weeks, four of the twelve having taken isoniazid for two weeks or less. Ten of those ill with weak lungs had also taken rifampicin, four labeling it as vitamin sa baga, two labeling it as an antibiotic, and four as a medicine for tuberculosis. Of the ten, the median duration of medicine consumption was three to four weeks. This coincides with the amount of time it generally takes for symptomatic relief of nonadvanced tuberculosis to occur and is only one-sixth the amount of time recommended by the WHO for the clinical management of active tuberculosis.

The data presented above as well as in Table 10.4, which summarizes the drug-taking behavior of 13 other people afflicted with weak lungs–tuberculosis, illustrate that medication taken for weak lungs–tuberculosis often falls short of recommended courses of therapy. Irrespective of whether or not an ill person had a bacteriologically confirmed case of active tuberculosis or primary complex, the taking of either isoniazid or rifampicin for short durations creates a set of conditions conducive to the development of drug-resistant bacteria.

Five of the 16 informants (noted above) and five out of 13 members of the focus groups summarized in Table 10.4, all people reporting a history of weak lungs, secured tuberculosis medications directly from a pharmacy. In order to get a sense of how difficult it was to secure tuberculosis drugs over-the-counter, a drugstore confederate study was conducted in two towns. One town was eight kilometers from the study site while the other was a larger market town an hour away by jeep. Attendants at eight chemist shops were presented an illness scenario by my research assistant. In the scenario she stated that she was the mother of a four-year-old child. She then explained that her sister suspected her daughter had weak lungs because she had a cough and "inside fever" for over a month. An *arbolaryo* (local herbalist) had been consulted and he suggested that she purchase vitamin sa baga. The advice she received from pharmacists or their assistants is presented in Table 10.5.

The Mindoro data suggest that pharmacists and their attendants commonly offer isoniazid preparations to clients who request vitamin sa baga. They ask few questions when selling this medication and offer little unsolicited advice. Duration of treatment is often left unspecified. Rifampicin, by comparison, rarely appears to be sold over-the-counter unless asked for specifically by name.[14]

If isoniazid is perceived to strengthen the lungs, do people having a stock of vitamin sa baga share it with other family members? If so, for what types of complaints? Six out of the 16 informants having experience with isoniazid stated that on one or more occasions they had shared a stock of vitamin sa baga with another family member or neighbor. In five instances isoniazid was shared with a child who had a bad cough or wheeze, while in one case medicine was shared with a child who exhibited general signs of weakness and poor appetite. In only one case was rifampicin shared. Informants expressed a fear of sharing an antibiotic with another person until compatibility with the medicine was established following a doctor's prescription. In the one case recorded, rifampicin prescribed for one child was offered to

Table 10.4

Medication History of 13 Members of 3 Focus Groups*

Diagnosis	Isoniazid	Rifampicin	Streptomycin	Other antibiotic	Other
TB (private doctor)	+2 months	–	+2 months	–	–
Weak lungs (self)	+2 types, 1 month	–	–	–	+Solmox **, Broncho
Weak lungs (Gov. Dr.)	+2 months	–	+1 month	–	–
Weak lungs (private doctor)	+1 month	–	+2 weeks	+fucidin, 2 weeks	+Ventolin **, 1 month
Weak lungs (Gov. Dr.)	+3 months	+3 months	–	–	–
Weak lungs (self)	+2 weeks	–	–	–	+check for pilay
Weak lungs (self)	+3 weeks	–	–	–	+Solmux **, Broncho
TB (private doctor)	+9 months	+9 months	+2 weeks	+Bactrim, 3 months	+Asmalin**, 1 year
Weak lungs (private doctor)	+1 month	–	+1 month	–	–
Weak lungs (self)	+3 weeks	–	–	–	+Ventolin**, 2 months
Weak lungs (self)	+5 weeks	–	–	–	–
Weak lungs (Gov. Dr.)	+6 months (SCC)	+6 months (SCC)	–	+Additional brand name Rifampicin-periodic	+Cough syrup Ventolin**
Weak lungs (Gov. Dr.)	+2 months	–	+2 injections	–	–

* The 13 members of 3 focus groups *identified themselves or their children* as having had tuberculosis or weak lungs during the last 2 years. All of the afflicted ($n = 8$ men, 5 women) consumed isoniazid.
** Antiasthmatic preparations (salbutomol or theophylline).

Table 10.5

Drugstore Confederate Study (*n*=8 shops). What did the Shop Attendant Recommend or Do?

	Drug shop No.							
	1	2	3	4	5	6	7	8
More details of case requested?	no	no	no	no	no	no	no	—
Customer told to consult a doctor?	no	no	yes	no	yes	no	no	—
Isoniazid preparation recommended?	yes	yes	yes	yes	no	yes	yes	+
Duration of medicine noted No/Yes	Y 1 mo	N	N	Y 4 mos	N	Y 6 mos	N	N
Rifampicin recommended	no	no	no	yes	no	no	no	—
Seen by: *Pharmacist (P) *Shop attendant (A)	A	A	P	A	P	P	A	A

another with a bad cough and fever by a mother who had no money to purchase antibiotics recommended by a midwife.

ADDITIONAL TREATMENT ISSUES

Six additional issues related to treatment practices emerged out of focus groups and case studies. First, when asked under what circumstances it would be inadvisable to take medicines for weak lungs–tuberculosis, several women voiced the opinion that such medicine should not be taken during pregnancy or lactation. One case was documented in which a woman found to be sputum positive in 1988 discontinued her treatment after two months when she found out that she was pregnant. During an interview she stated that she wished to continue therapy, but was waiting until her child was weaned for fear that the medicine might dry up her milk or harm her baby. She was poor and noted that should her milk dry up she would not be able to afford to feed her child "canned milk." Given that many women are pregnant or lactating for a significant part of their lives in the Philippines, ideas about the appropriateness of tuberculosis treatment during this condition should be explored in greater depth.

A second issue emerged from a re-analysis of an ARI data set collected in Mindoro in 1989, prompted by an in-depth household case study of weak lungs in which a child taking isoniazid developed pneumonia. The family's delay in seeking health care was linked to the child being on tuberculosis medication.[15] During the 1989 ARI study, a series of interviews had been conducted with the caretakers of 17 children afflicted with pneumonia. The cases were opportunistic and collected from a variety of hospital, private clinic, and community settings. In four cases, a mother had delayed seeking health care for her child because she noted that the child was already taking medicine for weak lungs. In each case the child's parents were poor and isoniazid was considered a medicine which strengthened the lungs and prevented serious illness and mucus drying on the lungs (a lay explanation for difficult breathing).

The pattern suggested by these data was not recognized until the last month of the 1991 study. A focus group was held with a group of five experienced public health midwives. They were asked to reflect on the health care seeking behavior of mothers whose children were taking medicines for weak lungs. An unprompted discussion of ARI cases ensued with three of the midwives citing cases of mothers who had delayed treatment for acute lower respiratory illness.

A third issue involved medication default and the cost of medicines in the private sector among those diagnosed by doctors as having weak lungs. During individual interviews and focus groups, people who reported taking medication for weak lungs were asked how long they had taken medication and why they discontinued medication against the recommendations of their doctor. Those who defaulted tended to claim either that they were now healthy (e.g., no longer as weak, their appetite had returned) or that the medicine did not suit them. Reports of incompatibility with medications prompted data collection on side effects. Notably, side effects listed in medical texts were infrequently reported.

Cost of medication was probed as a factor influencing duration of medicine consumption. When asked if the cost of medications played a role in their decision to discontinue use, all informants purchasing rifampicin on the open market said yes. This included patients who had consulted private doctors as well as patients of government doctors who did not have available supplies of medication. The market price of a daily adult dose of rifampicin is between peso 18–20 per day

(U.S. $80). This is several times the cost the government pays for generic medication and about one-third of a poor household's daily food expenditure. For children, rifampicin suspension is less costly (5–8 peso a day), but purchasing bottles of suspension often costs more than impoverished parents can pay. Several informants stated that their economic condition precluded spending money on medicine except when a family member was acutely ill.

A double bind was noted. Poor diet resulted in shock to the body (pasma sa guton) predisposing one to weak lungs–tuberculosis. If one spent money on medicine and not food then how could one remain healthy? And what of one's family? Among the poor, spending money on medicine for one individual is known to negatively affect the general health of the household. Money spent on medicine meant less money was available for fish, frying oil, sugar, and cans of milk for young children.

A fourth issue involved alcohol and medicine taking. Alcohol is not only thought to predispose one to tuberculosis, but many doctors make it clear that medicine and alcohol consumption are incompatible.[16] Two male informants reported taking weak lung medication only until serious symptoms abated because they found it too difficult to give up drinking. Those who are addicted to alcohol are at high risk both for tuberculosis and for defaulting on tuberculosis medication. Drinking serves an important social role among Filipino men in Mindoro. Abstaining from drinking marks one as seriously ill.

A fifth issue involves add-on drugs during tuberculosis treatment. Many informants held the opinion that government drugs are inferior in quality to medicines available in the private sector. Cases were documented of patients taking government supplied regimes of tuberculosis drugs plus medicines procured from pharmacists. In one case an elderly man was taking government-issued tuberculosis short-course therapy, periodic doses of a brand name rifampicin–isoniazid preparation, an antibiotic, salbutomol (a medicine for wheeze), a mucolytic, and an expectorant. No one in the health system had asked him what other medicines he was taking, even when he complained to his doctor of side effects.

The sixth issue to emerge concerns relapse once weak lungs–tuberculosis has been treated. The possibility of relapse was voiced during focus groups held with former weak lung–tuberculosis patients, by defaulters of medicine courses as well as "graduates of treatment programs." Concern reflected unrealistic expectations from treatment associated with popular perceptions of weak lungs and tuberculosis medications. Some informants expressed the expectation that once their condition was treated they would no longer suffer from respiratory problems. Others perceived medications as strengthening the lungs or removing the dried mucus which rendered them vulnerable to respiratory illness. When an episode of ARI was experienced they feared relapse and wondered whether they needed to go back on medication for weak lungs. In an impoverished population, this fear is compounded by high rates of anemia. The symptoms of anemia (fatigue, reduced appetite, paleness) overlap symptoms of tuberculosis. In one case, fear of relapse led a man to request three sputum tests over the course of one year. Lack of trust in negative test results prompted this individual to privately purchase isoniazid over-the-counter.

DISCUSSION

Fifteen findings of this study are highlighted for their applied relevance:

1. The illness category "weak lungs" is broad and covers a variety of symptom states. In the population at large, some people equate weak lungs with tuberculosis, but many others do not. The latter tend to think of weak lungs as a condition which may develop into tuberculosis over time. Tuberculosis is equated with coughing up blood.

2. It is widely believed that weak lungs is caused by phlegm drying on or sticking to the lungs. This is the same image people have of illness categories which encompass forms of ARI.

3. Use of the term "weak lungs" is propagated by clinicians who wish to minimize stigma associated with the disease tuberculosis, employ the term to label persistent or recurring respiratory conditions, or employ the term to call attention to a patient's state of vulnerability or risk.

4. Many people who perceive tuberculosis as contagious do not perceive weak lungs as contagious.

5. Tuberculosis is thought about more in terms of predisposing factors than causative agents.

6. While most people do not think of microbyo as causing weak lungs, they link microbyo to tuberculosis through an association with doctor's medicine. Faith in biomedicine is strong and belief in biomedical fixes extends beyond cure to prevention.

7. Most people are not familiar with Bacille Calmette-Guerin Vaccine (BCG) and are unsure whether there is a specific immunization against tuberculosis. They believe, however, that immunizations are generally good for health and therefore may prevent tuberculosis.

8. Many people are aware that tuberculosis is spread through the air and not just through contact with eating utensils. In everyday life, however, their practice of preventive health is directed to isolating eating utensils and pouring boiling water on them. These actions provide a token sense of control befitting Filipino culture which precludes the social isolation of kin with weak lungs or tuberculosis.

9. While tuberculosis is stigmatized in general, interactions with afflicted relatives and close friends do not seem to alter much. The issue of stigma emerges in the population's desire for privacy in how sputum is collected, test results reported, and medicine distributed.

10. Weak lungs is often self-diagnosed and self-treated. Pharmacists comply with consumer demands for weak lungs medication by distributing isoniazid. Little advice is given about the length of time isoniazid should be taken.

11. Isoniazid is thought to contain vitamins which strengthen the lungs. It is not only purchased over the counter, but shared with kin suffering from ARI.

12. Many people taking isoniazid alone or in combination with rifampicin continue medication for only a month until symptoms abate. For those purchasing drugs from the market, the cost of medicine is an important factor influencing medicine default.

13. There is considerable confusion among midwives concerning what advice they should give pregnant and lactating mothers who are sputum positive. Pregnant women fear that the medicine will cause miscarriage and lactating mothers fear the medicine will dry up their milk or harm their baby.

14. Among mothers of children routinely taking weak lungs medication, some (especially the poor) delay taking their children to health care providers in cases of ARI. They are under the impression that their child is already taking medicine for the lungs, and thus, do not need further treatment.

15. There is considerable confusion among former patients regarding tuberculosis relapse. Short course "graduates" fear that their

illness has relapsed when they develop ARI and anemia-related symptoms.

CONCLUSION

Much of the health social science research on tuberculosis has been decontextualized in the sense that tuberculosis is studied in isolation from other lung diseases. As a result, little is known about how tuberculosis is conceptualized in relation to other types of sickness, the extent to which other illnesses are recognized as predisposing one to tuberculosis, and how perceptions of causality influence treatment practices. In addition, little attention has been focused on the marketing of tuberculosis medicines in less-developed countries and how this influences perceptions of illness, over-the-counter drug use, and medicine sharing. Research reports have suggested that tuberculosis is associated with stigma in some cultural contexts. Yet, little is known about the illness semantics of tuberculosis: how this illness is and is not spoken about, by whom, in what contexts, and for what reasons. Further, little is known about how the stigma of tuberculosis influences the health care seeking process, household health behavior, and social support. While studies of tuberculosis medication compliance are commonplace, few studies have considered how the cost of paying for tuberculosis medications influences default following the reduction of symptoms.

This ethnographic account of tuberculosis-related behavior in Oriental Mindoro has illustrated practical reasons for investigating these issues. Special attention has been drawn to the study of illness semantics. Numerous studies of illness taxonomies have been conducted during the past decade, many sponsored by international health agencies. In some cases, the utility of these studies beyond providing background knowledge about local health culture has been questioned. Some point out that consensus in the use of illness terms is often not established, leading health experts to question the sensitivity and specificity of local terms to identify acute states of disease.

A few studies stand out as demonstrating the importance of ethnosemantic studies. Yoder (1989), in a study of diarrheal disease in Zaire, illustrated that a morbidity study which only asked informants to report on "diarrheal disease" would miss more than 50% of cases of diarrhea in the community and that differences in oral rehydration solution use varied as much as 400% by illness category. Chowdhury and Vaughan (1988), in a study of oral rehydration solution utilization patterns in Bangladesh, have likewise documented that patterns of health care seeking behavior and oral rehydration solution use were illness specific. Notably, they illustrated that it was prudent to evaluate health programs along the lines of local (emic) illness categories.

Both of the studies cited above involve taxonomic studies of illness categories demarcated by sets of definitive attributes. The case of weak lungs–tuberculosis illustrates why studies of illness semantics which attend to ambiguity and social relational dimensions of the language of illness are important to international health. "Weak lungs" is a "specific ambiguous" illness term (Nichter 1989). It is used to: (1) identify a state of ill health associated with a variety of attributes ranging from failure to thrive among children and weakness in adults, to chest or back pain, low-grade fever, or wheeze; (2) label an ARI condition which is persistent or recurrent; (3) describe a state of perceived weakness or vulnerability; and (4) call attention to a state of ill health linked to tuberculosis while deflecting attention from the stigma of this disease. Multiple agendas underscore use of the term "weak lungs" by doctors and the lay population alike.

Weak lungs is linked to a complex of illnesses in Oriental Mindoro which encompasses ARI, tuberculosis, and possibly lung cancer (Alonzo et al. 1991). Weak lungs is linked to environmental and climatic change, perceived to develop out of any one of several illnesses associated with ARI, be it hereditary, or caused by excessive habits such as smoking or drinking. It is considered by most people to pre-dispose one to tuberculosis. Yet, a majority do not consider weak lungs contagious, except possibly to children. It is a condition which does not carry the stigma of tuberculosis, due in part to the wide range of conditions indexed by the term. For this reason, "weak lungs" is a comfort-able term for clinicians to use when talking to patients testing positive for tuberculosis without the telltale sign of "coughing up blood."

While the sensitivity of clinicians in the Philippines to social stigma is laudatory, use of the term "weak lungs" has important public health consequences which extend beyond the issue of perceived contagion. Weak lungs is not deemed as serious an illness as tuberculosis. For this reason, the poor may be less likely to comply with recommendations to take six-month courses of medication once symptoms are managed. This would particularly be the case where they are required to pay for medication. Broad usage of the term "weak lungs" also affects self-treatment practices and over-the-counter purchase of tuberculosis medications. Medications prescribed to one person with weak lungs by a doctor are deemed useful for other health problems also labeled weak lungs in popular health culture. Over-the-counter isoniazid purchases and isoniazid sharing for persistent cough are evidence of this. It is not just doctors who foster such practices. The pharmaceutical industry has capitalized on marketing isoniazid preparations as vitamins for the lungs. This association leads people to think that the medication is useful for all illnesses which weaken the lungs, even if taken for just a few weeks.

These practices have serious ramifications. Attention has been drawn to the manner in which inappropriate use of tuberculosis medication increases the chances of drug resistance. This is a real possibility in the Philippines. Health care seeking delays among mothers of children prescribed vitamin sa baga and rifampicin constitutes another ramification of popular thinking about weak lungs. Impoverished mothers believe isoniazid strengthens lungs and rifampicin helps to expel phlegm from the lungs. Given such perceptions, delays in treating ARI are predictable.

A third ramification has to do with expectations from treatment regimes for weak lungs–tuberculosis. Graduates of tuberculosis short-course treatment, as well as defaulters perceiving themselves to be cured, maintain a set of expectations of their medication which is unrealistic. Linking weak lungs and tuberculosis to respiratory tract infections leads some patients to expect that they will not experience episodes of ARI. When they do, they fear relapse to their former condition and set about a range of activities including repeat sputum tests and purchase of weak lung medicines over-the-counter. Based on the drug store confederate study conducted, there is good reason to suspect that anyone wanting tuberculosis medications will have their demands met in Oriental Mindoro without much screening on the part of pharmacists or their attendants.

The case of weak lungs–tuberculosis illustrates why it is important to study the semantics of illness labeling and the semiotics of medicine advertising, lay interpretations of and expectations from medicines, as well as the role doctors and pharmacists play in fostering popular representations of illness. Medical anthropological studies of infectious (and noninfectious) disease are clearly needed if we are to better understand how health care resources are accessed and when and in what manner they are used. Studies of illness semantics add social relations of illness perspective to health service research which tends to focus on studies of health care seeking and medicine compliance. As noted in this chapter and elsewhere (Nichter 1995), the social relations of illness influence how illness identities are negotiated by members of one's therapy management group, inclusive of practitioners sensitive to the stigma carried by various diagnoses. While epidemiological and public health studies of disease point out trends in illness incidence and prevalence, compliance, etc.; anthropological studies help us appreciate why specific ambiguous classifications of illness persist, and the importance of social risk which often overrides concerns for physical risk.

Anthropological studies of illness semantics provide insights into self-medication as well as the marketing strategies of pharmaceutical companies which play off and influence popular ideas about illness. Given the importance of self-help and medicine self-regulation, anthropological studies of illness semantics and pharmaceutical practice (e.g., Nichter and Vuckovic 1994) are needed to contextualize public health studies which tend to focus on the public sector while acknowledging the importance of the private sector and self-help practices in less-developed countries.

NOTES

1. Data on global rates of tuberculosis mortality and morbidity are taken from Dannenberg (1982); Kochi (1991); Murray, Styblo, and Rouillon (1990); Raviglione, Snider, and Kochi (1995); Riley (1980); and Styblo (1989). Beyond the scope of this chapter is a consideration of HIV infection as an activator of previously inactive tuberculosis (Harries 1990; Perriens, Mukadi, and Nunn 1991; Styblo 1988) and tuberculosis drug resistance associated with human immunodeficiency (DeCock et al. 1992; Iseman 1993, 1994; Ryan 1993). Given the rising rate of HIV infection in the Philippines, these issues demand future consideration. Studies have found that between 25–50% of AIDS patients in other regions have experienced tuberculosis during the course of their HIV infection (Raviglione, Snider, and Kochi 1995). In the United States, most cases of multidrug-resistant tuberculosis have occurred in persons having HIV infection.

2. This brief overview of tuberculosis is based on Bloom and Murray (1992); Comstock (1975); Dannenberg (1980); Murray, Rouillon, and Styblo (1990); Riley (1980); and Styblo (1989).

3. Transmission of *M. tuberculosis* by sputum, saliva, or urine is very rare. Small droplets may remain suspended in the air for many hours unless removed by ventilation. Individual risk to infection is associated with: (1) competence of one's immune system; (2) the concentration of organism-bearing particles exhaled by the source; (3) rate of ventilation; and (4) duration of exposure. The environment plays a key role in rates of infection.

4. Resistance to tuberculosis is not stable and increased exposure to the bacillus does not result in increased resistance.

5. Primary-complex tuberculosis is particularly difficult to diagnose among infants and young children as it manifests in a range of symptoms which overlap with other childhood diseases.

    Acute respiratory infection and primary-complex tuberculosis are commonly confused.

6. In two other studies of tuberculosis patients identified with and without bacterial confirmation, only 21–24% sought assistance at government health units and 6–10% at hospitals (DOH 1988; Sarmiento 1990).

7. A recent review of unpublished Filipino studies (UPPGH 1991) reported drug-resistant tuberculosis bacilli to isoniazid in 25–89% of cases examined in a variety of clinical and community contexts. Notably, studies reporting rates at the higher end of the resistance continuum were community- as opposed to clinic-based. Rates for streptomycin resistance were also high (19–50%). Resistance to rifampicin has been reported to be as high as 7.6%, leading some researchers to recommend quadruple drug regimens by adding ethambutol to the standard short course of isoniazid, rifampicin, and pyrazinamide.

8. Bacille Calmette-Guerin Vaccine does not prevent tuberculosis overall, only severe forms of tuberculosis in children. Its reported rate of efficacy has varied considerably.

9. A detailed case study was conducted of one family in which a child became ill following the extended stay of an aunt described as having "weak lungs" (Nichter 1995). The family's reference to weak lungs–tuberculosis as hereditary served to deflect responsibility from the aunt onto a less immediate agent of causality. This constituted a coping strategy in a poor household where concern about the risk of disrupting social relations superseded concern about physical risk.

10. *Pulmonya* is an illness associated with fever, labored noisy breathing, and chest and back pain. It is thought to manifest suddenly as well as progress from a cough which is not cured. This illness category sometimes, but not always, corresponds to the biomedical disease pneumonia.

11. When asked this question directly, many of these informants had earlier stated that immunizations prevented tuberculosis.

12. A study by Mata (1985) in Honduras found that the perceived seriousness of tuberculosis was determined by the sophistication of the technology needed to diagnose it.

13. Isoniazid is supplemented with vitamins because long-term use can lead to vitamin B6 deficiencies and decreases in niacin stores leading to pellagra.

14. A second confederate drug store study was conducted elsewhere in the Philippines. Ten pharmacies were visited in Legaspi and Tobaco cities in

Bicol Province, Luzon, a region with an active tuberculosis education program. In only two drug stores were attendants willing to sell isoniazid preparations over-the-counter. In six others, my research assistant was told to visit a doctor.

15. The child's mother was previously in the habit of purchasing amoxicillan suspension for her child if a fever and cough lasted more than three days. If the illness did not subside within five to six days, a doctor was consulted. Once rifampicin and isoniazid were started, the child was no longer self-treated with other forms of antibiotics. The mother reported waiting longer before consulting a doctor for symptoms of ARI.

16. Alcohol consumption is contraindicated during isoniazid treatment and is associated with hepatitis.

REFERENCES

Alonzo, F., R. Desales, D. Diaz, et al. 1991. The Concepts, Attributes and Beliefs of the Filipino on Lung Cancer. Philippine Journal Internal Medicine 29:255–271.

Banerji, D. and S. Anderson. 1963. A Sociological Study of Awareness of Symptoms among Persons with Pulmonary Tuberculosis. Bulletin of the World Health Organization 29:655–683.

Bloom, B. and C. Murray. 1992. Tuberculosis: Commentary on a Reemergent Killer. Science 257(5037):1055–1064.

Chambers, R. 1990. Rapid but Relaxed and Participatory Rural Appraisal: Towards Applications in Health and Nutrition. Paper presented at the International Conference on Rapid Assessment Methodologies for Planning and Evaluation of Health Related Programs. PAHO, Washington, D.C. 12–15 November.

Chowdhury, A. M. R. and J. P. Vaughan. 1988. Perception of Diarrhea and the Use of a Home Made Oral Rehydration Solution in Rural Bangladesh. Journal of Diarrheal Disease Research 6(1):6–14.

Comstock, G. W. 1975. Frost Revisited: The Modern Epidemiology of Tuberculosis. American Journal of Epidemiology 101:363–382.

Conanan, E. C. and F. S. Valeza. 1988. Factors Affecting Completion Rate in Tuberculosis Short-Course Chemotherapy. Journal of the Philippine Medical Association 64(1):11–14.

Dannenberg, A. M. Jr. 1980. Pathogenesis of Tuberculosis. In Pulmonary Diseases and Disorders (Vol. 2). Alfred P. Fishman, ed. Pp. 1264–1281. New York: McGraw-Hill.

Dannenberg, A. M. Jr. 1982. Pathogenesis of Pulmonary Tuberculosis. American Review of Respiratory Disease 125:125–129.

DeCock, K., B. Soro, I. Coulibaly, and S. Lucas. 1992. Tuberculosis and HIV Infections in Sub-Saharan Africa. JAMA 268:1581–1587.

Department of Health. 1988. Manual of Procedures for the National Tuberculosis Control Program. Review of 1983 National TB Prevalence Survey. Republic of the Philippines, Manila.

Dubos, R. and J. Dubos. 1987. (1952) The White Plague: Tuberculosis, Man and Society. Reprint, New Brunswick, New Jersey: Rutgers University Press.

Haram, L. 1991. Tsuana Medicine in Interaction with Biomedicine. Social Science and Medicine 33(2):167–175.

Harries, A. 1990. Tuberculosis and Human Immunodeficiency Virus Infections in Developing Countries. Lancet 335:387–390.

Iseman, M. D. 1989. Drug-Resistant Tuberculosis: New Threat From an Old Disease. Postgraduate Medicine 86(2):109–114.

Iseman, M. D. 1993. Treatment of Multidrug-Resistant Tuberculosis. New England Journal of Medicine 329(11):784–791.

Iseman, M. D. 1994. Evolution of Drug-Resistant Tuberculosis: A Tale of Two Species. Proceedings of the National Academy of Sciences of the United States of America 91(7):2428–2429.

Kochi, A. 1991. The Global Tuberculosis Situation and the New Control Strategy of the World Health Organization. Tubercle 72:1–6.

Madico, G., R. Gilman, W. Checkly, L. Cabera, I. Kohlstadt, K. Kacena, J. Diaz, and R. Black. 1995. Community Infection Ratio as an Indicator of Tuberculosis Control. Lancet 345(8947): 416–419.

Mando, F., F. Tan, and J. Sbarbaro. 1990. Community-based Short-course Treatment of Pulmonary Tuberculosis in a Developing Nation. Initial report of an eight month, largely intermittant regimen in a population with a high prevalence of drug resistance. American Review of Respiratory Disease 142:1301–1305.

Mata, J. I. 1985. Integrating the Client's Perspective in Planning a Tuberculosis Education and Treatment Program in Honduras. Medical Anthropology 9:57–64.

McKeown, T. 1979. The Role of Medicine: Dream, Mirage, or Nemesis? Oxford: Basis Blackwell.

Ministry of Health of the Philippines. 1990. National Health Study of 1987, Department of Health.

Mitchison, D. A. 1984. Drug Resistance in Mycrobacteria. British Medical Bulletin 40(1):84–90.

Murray, C. J. L., K. Styblo, and A. Rouillon. 1990. Tuberculosis in Developing Countries: Burden, Intervention and Costs. Bulletin of the International Union Against Tuberculosis 65(1):2–20.

Murray, C, A. Rouillon, and K. Styblo. 1990. Tuberculosis. *In* Disease Control Priorities in Developing Countries. D.T. Jamison and W.H. Mosley, eds. pp. XXX. Washington, D.C.: Population, Health and Nutrition Division, The World Bank.

National Health Service (NHS), Republic of the Philippines. 1990. National Health Survey 1987.

Ndeti, K. 1972. Sociocultural Aspects of Tuberculosis Defaultation: A Case Study. Social Science and Medicine 6:397–412.

Nichter, M. and M. Nichter. 1994. Acute Respiratory Illness: Popular Health Culture and Mothers' Knowledge in the Philippines. Medical Anthropology 15(4):353–374.

Nichter, M. 1989. Anthropology and International Health: South Asian Case Studies. Dordrecht: Kluwer Academic Press.

Nichter, M. 1995. The Social Relations of Therapy Management. Unpublished manuscript. Department of Anthropology, University of Arizona.

Ortega, A. R., M. V. Meniado, and M. C. Tobias. 1991. Comparative Study on the Knowledge, Attitudes, and Practices on Tuberculosis of Low Income Groups in a Rural and Urban Community in the Philippines. Bicutan: PCHRD.

Packard, R. 1989. White Plague, Black Labor. Berkeley: University of California Press.

Perriens, J., Y. Mukadi, and P. Nunn. 1991. Tuberculosis and HIV Infection: Implications for Africa. AIDS 5c (Suppl. 1):S127–S133.

Pope, A. S. and J. E. Gordon. 1955. The Impact of Tuberculosis on Human Populations. The American Journal of the Medical Sciences 230:317–353.

Raviglione, M., D. Snider, and A. Kochi. 1995. Global Epidemiology of Tuberculosis: Morbidity and Mortality of a Worldwide Epidemic. Journal of the American Medical Association 273(3):220–226.

Republic of the Philippines Department of Health. 1988. Manual of the National Tuberculosis Control Program. Manila: DOH.

Riley, R. L. 1980. The Changing Scene in Tuberculosis. *In* Pulmonary Diseases and Disorders (Vol. 2). Alfred P. Fishman, ed. pp. 1229–1233. New York: McGraw-Hill.

Riley, R. L. and A. S. Moodie. 1974. Infectivity of Patients with Pulmonary Tuberculosis in Inner City Homes. American Review of Respiratory Diseases 110:810–812.

Rodrigues, L. and P. Smith. 1990. Tuberculosis in Developing Countries and Methods for its Control. Transactions of the Royal Society of Tropical Medicine and Hygiene 84:739–744.

Ryan, F. 1993. The Forgotten Plague. Boston: Little and Brown.

Sarmiento, A. G. 1990. Operational Assessment of the Case Finding and Treatment Aspects of the Strengthened National Tuberculosis Control Program. Manila: DOH.

Science. 1995. WHO Calls for Action Against TB. Science 268:1763.

Styblo, K. 1986. Overview and Epidemiological Assessment of the Current Global Tuberculosis Situation with an Emphasis on Tuberculosis Control in Developing Countries. Bulletin of the International Union Against Tuberculosis: 39–44.

Styblo, K. 1988. The Potential Impact of AIDS on the Tuberculosis Situation in Developed and Developing Countries. Bulletin of the International Union of Tuberculosis and Lung Disease 63:25–28.

Styblo, K. 1989. Overview and Epidemiologic Assessment of the Current Global Tuberculosis Situation with an Emphasis on Control in Developing Countries. Review of Infectious Disease 2 (Suppl. 2):S339–S346.

Tan, M. L. 1991. Philippine Health Matters. Health Alert. Special Issue 7:116–117.

Tan, M. L. 1994. The Meaning of Medicines: Examples from the Philippines. *In* Medicines: Meanings and Contexts. Nina Etkin and Michael Tan, eds. Pp. 69–81. Quezon City: Health Action Information Network.

Teklu, B. 1984. Reasons for Failure in Treatment of Pulmonary Tuberculosis in Ethiopians. Tubercle 65:17–21.

University of the Philippines, Post Graduate Hospital (UPPGH). 1991. Review of Infectious Diseases 1991, unpublished report from the files of the Clinical Epidemiology Unit, University of the Philippines.

Van der Veen, K. 1987. Private Practitioners and the National Tuberculosis Programme in India. Journal of Research and Education in Indian Medicine 6:3–4, 59–66.

Wiese, H. J. C. 1974. Tuberculosis in Rural Haiti. Social Science and Medicine 8:359–362.

Wolff, G. 1940. Tuberculosis Mortality and Industrialization. The American Review of Tuberculosis 42:1–27, 214–242.

Yoder, S. 1989. Cultural Conceptions of Illness and the Measurement of Changes in Morbidity. Working paper No. 115. Annenberg School of Communications, University of Pennsylvania.

CHAPTER 11

The Sitala Syndrome:
The Cultural Context of
Measles Mortality in Pakistan

Dorothy S. Mull

INTRODUCTION

> Count your children after the measles has passed.
> —Middle Eastern proverb, cited by Morley (1973:212)

In industrialized nations, measles is commonly regarded as a relatively minor childhood illness, but in the developing world, it often takes a severe form that can be fatal. The fever is very high and the rash becomes confluent, giving a deep red color to the skin. Changes also occur on the surface of the intestines, causing malabsorption of nutrients and predisposing the child to severe, sometimes bloody diarrhea and subsequent dehydration and death. Pneumonia accompanying or following the rash is another common complication (Morley 1973).

Because malnutrition and crowding increase the severity of the disease, it takes its greatest toll in the poorest countries. Case-fatality rates have been reported from 3% to higher than 15% in the

The author wishes to thank Nina Gera and the many Karachi families who shared their homes and stories to make this study possible. Ann Millard, Dennis Mull, two anonymous reviewers, and the editors of the present volume provided much-appreciated suggestions for revision of the manuscript.

developing world, and rates are even higher if delayed deaths are counted in (Cutts 1990). The youngest are particularly vulnerable; in The Gambia, one community study showed a case-fatality rate of 64% in infants under a year old (Williams and Hull 1983). In contrast, the fatality rate in the United States has in recent years averaged well below 1 per 1000 cases (Walsh 1986).

Current estimates are that measles and its devastating sequelae accounts for well over a million child deaths worldwide – more than all other immunizable diseases combined (World Health Organization 1994). After pneumonia and diarrhea, measles is the third most common killer of children (Grant 1994:1), and this is true despite the fact that an effective vaccine has been available for more than 30 years. Proverbs collected in developing countries such as "Count your children after the measles has passed" (Middle East) and "If your child has not had measles you do not have a child yet" (Africa; cited in Imperato 1969:779) reflect popular recognition of the extreme seriousness of the disease.

This chapter is an attempt to move beyond impersonal "measles mortality" statistics to present information from detailed interviews with women in Pakistani squatter settlements. Anthropological inquiry reveals the existence of a constellation of beliefs, many very ancient, that discourage both optimal home management and expeditious biomedical treatment of measles. Although most fully trained physicians are not aware of these beliefs, unlicensed practitioners are and build on them to attract business during measles epidemics.

Three case histories of children who died after contracting the disease highlight the close relationship between measles, pneumonia, and diarrhea – a connection largely ignored in highly focused international health campaigns. Further, they demonstrate how familial stress, maternal demoralization, and competition for scarce resources influence decisions about medical care. Close examination of the circumstances surrounding measles death provides powerful insights into the fatal interaction between cultural concerns and other important issues within the household – issues ultimately linked to macrolevel forces perpetuating poverty and injustice.

PREVENTION OF MEASLES: A LONG-RANGE GOAL

Eventually, immunization campaigns may make household studies such as this unnecessary. Vigorous initiatives are underway, and the goal of the World Health Organization's Expanded Programme on

Immunization is to reduce measles incidence to 10% of pre-1980 levels by 1995 (Cutts 1990:5). However, global control of measles by immunization is likely to be extraordinarily difficult for several reasons. First, the disease is so contagious that virtually all susceptible individuals must be immunized to prevent its resurgence – a daunting task (Markowitz and Orenstein 1990:620). Current estimates are that only about half of the children in the developing world who should be immunized have been reached (Cutts et al. 1991). The main problem is difficulty of access to vulnerable populations and vaccine failure.

The measles vaccine is a live-virus vaccine that loses potency when not kept cold, and children must be immunized during the interval between their loss of maternal antibodies sometime during the first year of life and their exposure to the disease itself, which is usually a very brief interval in developing countries (Walsh 1986). New high-dose vaccines that can provide protection at a very young age were tried, but there were safety problems (World Health Organization 1994). Further, the present vaccine has long been known to have a failure rate of at least 5% even in the United States, where the vaccine can usually be stored properly and administered to children at a time when it is maximally effective (Emergency Medicine 1991:97).

In the developing world, where refrigeration is often unavailable and children are typically immunized whenever they can be reached, presumably the failure rate is much higher than 5%. Anecdotal reports from physicians and mothers in many developing countries where measles deaths occurred after immunization campaigns strongly suggest this. A recent study has shown that even apparently high levels of vaccine coverage in The Gambia did not prevent a serious outbreak of the disease in subsequent years (Mulholland 1995).

MANAGEMENT OF MEASLES IN THE HOME

Because of all these difficulties, global eradication of measles through immunization is not now feasible, and effective home management of the disease and its complications continues to be of great importance. This is an area in which local practices have long been known to have a strong influence on child mortality, although most previous reports from the field have been brief. In contrast to the present chapter, none of these reports have included detailed ethnographic material illuminating the household reasoning underlying such practices, and none have documented their existence in Pakistan.

An early, unpublished study of traditional measles beliefs and behaviors was initiated by David Morley in the 1960s (Morley et al. n.d.). Surveying physicians worldwide, Morley found that in many societies, measles was regarded as a dangerous but necessary event that all children must experience, a natural part of growing up, and that frequently a god or a devil was thought to cause it. Since the emergence and fading of the rash signaled that the disease had run its course, people focused on "getting the rash out" at all costs.

Morley notes that some of the practices surrounding these beliefs – while of deep cultural significance – were also detrimental to health. For instance, children with measles were often kept hidden from virtually everyone, and doctors and allopathic medicines were especially avoided in the belief that they would cause harm. Dietary restrictions were very common, with predictable ill effects on already malnourished children. In some countries, it was thought that the child must be kept warm to force the rash to emerge, so overwrapping and withholding of fluids were also practiced, resulting in severe dehydration. In others, laxatives or enemas were given to cause or worsen diarrhea and thus get the disease "out."

More recent reports by Imperato (1969), Kakar (1977), Wakeham (1978), Maina-Ahlberg (1979), Shahid et al. (1983), Werner (1986), Adetunji (1991), Edward (1991), and Nichter and Nichter (1994) have independently confirmed the existence of such practices in Mali, India, Afghanistan, Kenya, Bangladesh, Mozambique, Nigeria, Uganda, and the Philippines, respectively.[1] Even in the United States, during the 1989–1991 epidemic there were reportedly cases where dehydration accompanying measles proved fatal when the child was not taking fluids and the parents did not seek prompt treatment (Los Angeles Times 1989).

From a biomedical standpoint, maintaining hydration, encouraging nutrient intake, and reducing fever with acetaminophen (Lancet 1991) are centrally important in the appropriate home management of measles. Further, prolonged diarrhea – associated with changes on the intestinal surface, as noted above – can be very dangerous because it causes life-threatening dehydration. Thus, in a study population in Bangladesh where 73% of measles episodes were accompanied by diarrhea, the case-fatality rate among children experiencing sustained diarrhea was 12% – six times the fatality rate when there was no diarrhea or only brief diarrhea (Koster et al. 1981).

It has been noted, also, that if there is diarrhea with measles and a child is not adequately fed, this can easily lead to a loss of 10% of body weight (Black 1984:589) and weaken the child's resistance to other infections. Throughout the disease process, the child needs careful monitoring to determine whether a physician should be consulted. Special attention must be paid to behavior changes such as difficult breathing and lethargy, since they may signal an urgent need for medical treatment of encephalitis or measles-related pneumonia.

In recent years in California, one-fourth to one-third of measles victims have required hospitalization for complications, chiefly pneumonia or dehydration from diarrhea (Los Angeles Times 1990), and the percentage of severe cases is certainly even greater in the developing world. Thus, it is clear that beliefs and behaviors surrounding measles deserve continuing investigation. The present study, conducted in urban squatter settlements of Pakistan, illustrates both the acute need for such research and the complex forces affecting household management of the disease.

MEASLES IN PAKISTAN

It is estimated that in Pakistan, more than 35,000 children die each year of measles (Government of Pakistan and UNICEF 1988:44). That people in urban squatter settlements and rural villages know the disease in its severe form is evidenced by their recounting of recent deaths, some in children who were supposedly immunized. As in many other developing countries, immunization coverage is relatively low. Although the official estimate is that 76% of children in Pakistan have been vaccinated against measles (Grant 1994:68), this figure is almost certainly optimistic and in any case it does not take into account the probability of widespread vaccine failure.

Names for the disease that I have encountered in various areas of Pakistan include *khasra* (Urdu and Punjabi; the most widely used term), *surkh* (Baluchi; literally, "red," denoting the skin color), *choti mai* or *choti mata* (Hindi; literally, "the smaller mother" – as opposed to *bari mai* or *bari mata*, "the greater mother," a phrase used for smallpox), *sharay* (Pashto), and *nissiko lihazi* (Khowar; literally, "the coming-out disease," referring to the rash). It should be noted that in some people's usage, these terms encompass pox diseases other than measles, e.g., chickenpox.

DESIGN OF THE PRESENT STUDY

In the spring and summer of 1987, I was engaged in a household study of childhood diarrhea and malnutrition in squatter settlements of

Karachi, a multiethnic city of some 10 million people. I was assisted by a female Urdu–English interpreter and by speakers of regional languages as needed. The informants were 150 mothers of malnourished children under five years old whose families lived in catchment areas served by outreach clinics set up by The Aga Khan University. These clinics provided simple curative care and also sent community health workers to visit the families on a weekly basis; their role was to monitor health status and furnish basic preventive health education. For example, they weighed babies, instructed mothers about oral rehydration therapy, and distributed sample packets of oral rehydration salts (ORS).

Most of the 150 informants were chosen because their children had recently been seen at the clinics for diarrhea and community health workers could easily remember who they were and direct me to their homes. They were technically a nonrandom sample of squatter settlement mothers in Karachi, although in practice I found them to be virtually indistinguishable from their neighbors, most of whom had children who had also been seen for diarrhea at the clinics but perhaps not as recently.

As I moved from house to house during the pilot phase of the study, mothers remarked that a measles epidemic was then in progress and that three children in the settlements had just died of the disease. Knowing that measles is commonly associated with diarrhea in the developing world (Morley 1973; Shahid et al. 1983), I decided to visit the homes of those three children to inquire about the circumstances of the deaths. I also added to my structured interview guide a few questions about the cause, preventability, and proper management both of measles and of measles-related diarrhea.

In talking with mothers, I spent between two and three hours in each home and took note of family interactions, child care practices, and foods and medicines available in the house. Given the frequently sensitive nature of the questions, some of which probed reasons for a child's severely malnourished state (Mull 1991), it was crucial to build rapport with informants. Hence the pace was relaxed – no more than three interviews were done on any given day – and the interpreter and I participated in ongoing household activities as much as possible.

HOUSEHOLD INTERVIEW RESULTS

Presented below is a general sociodemographic profile of the 150 informants, followed by a summary of their views about measles diarrhea, the spiritual dimensions of the disease, isolation and wrapping of the child, feeding practices, and avoidance of allopathic medicines.

Sociodemographic Data

The women interviewed were young (mean age = 28); most were illiterate; and they were very poor – the average monthly income for a family of six or seven people was about U.S. $64. Many mothers had already lost children to disease. They lived in crowded conditions surrounded by raw sewage and garbage heaps. Half-starved dogs roamed the dusty streets; flies were everywhere; water was scarce. In this traditionally patrilineal, patrilocal society, 55% of the women were living in households with their husbands' kin. Where present, the mother-in-law, older sister-in-law, or both often had a great deal of input into the interview responses.

Most of the major ethnic and religious groups of Pakistan were represented in the sample. Fifty percent of the women were Muslims, including – in order of their numbers – Mohajirs whose families had migrated from India after Partition in 1947, Baluchis from Baluchistan, Punjabis from Punjab, Pathans from North West Frontier Province, Sindhis from the area near Karachi, Kashmiris from Kashmir, and one Bengali woman whose forebears had come from Bangladesh. Thirty-nine percent were Punjabi Christians, mainly from families who had converted from Hinduism in the early part of the twentieth century, and 11% were Hindus.

Measles Diarrhea

Questioning of the 150 mothers revealed that in Karachi, the basic belief about measles is that the rash represents internal "heat" and "dirt" that must come out at all costs or the child will die. This parallels views in India (Kakar 1977; Nichter 1989) and Bangladesh (Shahid et al. 1983).[2] Thus all treatment or lack of treatment is aimed at bringing out the rash. Measles is classed as a "hot" disease character-ized by fever and by an inner force trying to expel heat and dirt from the body. Nothing must be allowed to interfere with this process. Thus many mothers said that if diarrhea accompanied measles, it was desirable since it was another manifestation of the same expulsive force that produced the skin rash and it would "help the spots come out."

(Only one mother was unfamiliar with the phenomenon of measles-related diarrhea.)

Overall, 50% of the 150 mothers interviewed said that measles diarrhea benefitted the child, and 30% said that they didn't know. Only 20% of mothers – including only one of the 17 Hindu informants – said that it could be dangerous. There was a striking emphasis on the "dirt" and "rubbish" that would come out in the measles diarrhea, and one person even reported that the stool had a foul odor denoting the presence of "dirt." Typical comments were "It's very good for the child to have diarrhea at this time," and "There's hope for the child if he does have diarrhea." People had strong fears that in the absence of diarrhea, the heat present in the stomach – which was the body organ regarded as the seat of the disease – might affect the eyes permanently or go to the brain and cause convulsions.[3]

Mothers in the "pro-diarrhea" group said that loose stools should continue at least until the rash had fully emerged, which they said could take up to nine days following its first appearance. (Since oral rehydration solution was widely believed to affect the natural flow of stool, its use was precluded during that period, and it was also avoided as an allopathic therapy inappropriate for use in measles; see discussion below.[4]) Some women even felt that diarrhea should continue until the rash had faded away completely, a process that could take an additional week or more.

Notably, these clinically important findings would have been missed if – as originally planned – only diarrhea in general had been asked about during the household visits. To the questions "Is diarrhea dangerous?" and "Should oral rehydration solution be used when a child has diarrhea?" virtually 100% of mothers responded in the affirmative. It was only when they were asked about measles *specifically* that their special perceptions of measles diarrhea became evident. Reliance on broad survey-type questions would have produced highly misleading data because of the imperfect fit between biomedical and ethnomedical categories.

Informants stated that if diarrhea was absent, the "measles spots" (i.e., the rash) might stay on the lungs or intestines and cause pneumonia, fever, and eventual death. As one woman put it, "When the spots stay hidden inside the body, you know that the person's doomed." To prevent this, six mothers, all Muslim, said that they gave their children humorally "hot" foods designed to make the spots come to the surface of the skin – foods like cow's milk with unrefined sugar (*gur*) dissolved in it, or figs or large dried grapes (*munakka*), either eaten plain or boiled in water or milk and then mashed. These foods were also viewed as purgatives.

Even among the 20% of mothers who thought measles diarrhea was undesirable, three gave as a reason that "if there is no diarrhea, the heat has to come out through the skin as a rash and that's good." They said that "doctors" had told them this, illustrating accommodation of allopathy to the traditional belief system. (Estimates are that at least half of the allopathic practitioners in Pakistan are uncredentialed.) One mother, a Mohajir Muslim, commented that the child should have "only a high fever," not diarrhea, to make the spots come out, and went on to list various herbal teas she gave to heighten the fever.

Spiritual Dimensions of the Disease

One informant, a Punjabi Christian, said that measles would cause a child to become "dark and scared." It is important to note two aspects of this statement: the accurate observation that the rash often appears to be dark red in serious cases (generally, the darker the color, the greater the severity) and the idea that fright is associated with the disease. One Baluch mother showed how she had tied amulets around her child's neck and goat's hair around his ankle to keep him from being "frightened" by measles; she added that Hindus traditionally used tiger's hair or bear's hair instead. This emphasis on fright ties to a view of measles as being caused by forces in the spirit world.

Indeed, talismans against fright and evil spirits were mentioned by informants from all three religious groups. Punjabi Christians said that leaves of the *neem* tree (*Azadirachta indica*) and rose petals should be strewn on the child's bed, and that a red *dupatta* (woman's scarf) should also be placed on it; they added that the latter was "a Hindu custom." Rose water should also be sprayed around the room. Gold or silver wedding rings should be steeped in water and the water given to the child to drink (cf. Shahid et al. 1983:155). Neem leaves were supposed to be used to "brush" the rash and were sometimes also strewn on the floor of the child's room; Hindus placed them over the entryway to the house.

Hindus added that a can of wet cow dung should be kept at the door of the child's room, and people should put their feet in the dung before entering the room. When asked why, they said that the dung was "pure" (*pak*) and would cleanse anyone who was "impure" (*napak*). Sindhis said that an herb known as *kala dana*, also used for illness caused by evil eye (*Urdu nazar*), should be thrown into the fire, as its smoke was "good for measles" and would help the rash to come out; Hindus recommended the burning of incense. A bystander, a Punjabi Christian midwife, said that elephant dung should be burned instead, since "measles comes from Kali Devi and Ganesh is her son." (The reference is to the Hindu goddess Kali and the elephant god Ganesh.)

The Hindu informants themselves referred to measles as *choti mai* or *choti mata* ("the smaller mother") as contrasted with *bari mai* or *bari mata* ("the larger mother," i.e., smallpox). This group understood the disease in explicitly religious terms. They said that measles was caused by a goddess called Sitala – literally, "the cool one" – and they pointed out the tiny shrine dedicated to her in their neighborhood.

Sitala, a North Indian village goddess, was associated with smallpox before it was eradicated in the 1970s, but today she is commonly linked with measles (Nicholas 1981:40). Her name, somewhat paradoxical for the representative of a "hot" disease, reflects the fact that she loves coolness, and at her festivals, only cold foods, cooked the day before, are served (Wadley 1980). According to legend, Sitala is one of a band of seven sisters who bring epidemic diseases and who live in the neem tree. Several women said that beliefs surrounding Sitala and measles were carryovers from a time when smallpox was a major killer.

Although Sitala is by nature cool, when she is angry she becomes heated and attacks with pox diseases, overheating her victims as well. Excess heat in the body then causes the skin rash to appear (Wadley 1980:35). The idea is that the disease of measles is the goddess and that when measles occurs, the goddess herself is within her victims, burning them.[5] From this it follows that measles victims themselves are in something resembling a "godlike" state and that it is appropriate for them, and their families, to follow a restricted "purification" diet while the disease is in progress.

Like many Indian goddesses, Sitala is simultaneously regarded as protective and destructive. To placate her, Hindu informants said that on about the fifth day after the rash appeared, the parents would take the child – well-wrapped in a white cloth – to the temple (*mandir*) for a blessing. Then, on returning home, the mother would use wet cow dung to make sacred symbols, shaped roughly like an upside-down U, on the wall of the house compound; I photographed several of these (Figure 11.1(a–d)). She would stick bits of white cotton on the dung at regular intervals and would place a dot of red powder used in worship (*puja*) ceremonies in the middle of each bit of cotton, saying a prayer in the child's name "to make Sitala happy."[6]

Figure 11.1(a–d) Worship (puja) symbols photographed during a measles epidemic in Karachi, Pakistan, 1987. Mothers in Hindu squatter settlements placed the symbols, fashioned from cow dung and cotton, on the walls of their homes to appease the measles goddess. See text for discussion.

It was noted that the mother must make the puja symbols when she was completely alone, and their design was also used to worship the Hindu goddess Kali. The intent was to minimize the wrath of the goddess by indicating that the family had done all it could to honor her. (It seems clear, too, that a parent who had performed the ritual would experience less guilt if a child suffered serious complications of the disease.) Muslim informants who were familiar with this Hindu practice related it generally to the custom of making vows at Muslim shrines – vows signaled by a piece of thread or yarn left tied onto a wall grating there. In other words, people emphasized the propitiatory aspect of the mother's actions.

However, Hindu informants added that the worship symbol was meant to be seen by neighbors as well as by Sitala, partly to keep them away from the house while the child had measles. (The symbols that I saw were about a foot high.) Thus the cow dung design appears to be one of a semiotically interesting group of devices that have a double purpose – warning people away as well as marking the occurrence of an important life event. In Punjabi squatter settlements, these polysemic devices include the leaves of the sheree tree that are put up over doorways in celebration and warning when a male child is born (Figure 11.2) – something not done for female children (see Mull 1991:187).

Christian and Muslim informants did not place symbols on their houses or refer to a disease goddess; most said they did not know what caused measles or simply attributed it to "God's will." Nevertheless,

Figure 11.2 Mother with sheree leaves placed over her doorway to mark the birth of a male child in a squatter settlement, Karachi, Pakistan, 1987. Like the measles symbols shown in Figure 11.1, the leaves warn away the ritually impure as well as commemorate an important life event.

they and the Hindu informants reported many of the same beliefs and practices, undoubtedly reflecting the close association between Hindus and non-Hindus before Partition in 1947. As described above, the privileging of measles diarrhea as a beneficial cleansing was common to all religious groups. Other features of what I term the "Sitala syndrome" – a constellation of traditional measles beliefs and behaviors potentially affecting the outcome of the disease – are described below.

Isolation and Wrapping of the Child

All three groups said that it was important to keep the child isolated in a clean, darkened room and well wrapped in cloths or blankets. When questioned as to the rationale, mothers denied that this practice was intended to prevent the spread of the disease to other children; indeed, 74% stated that measles could not be prevented, whether through immunization or otherwise. Rather, they said, the child was isolated and wrapped for three other important reasons.

First, wrapping the child was designed to increase perspiration and hasten the skin eruption, a procedure recommended by the Arab physician al-Razi (Rhazes) as early as 900 A.D. (see Nicholas 1981:26). Mothers said that for the same reason – to permit emergence of the rash – measles victims were not to be bathed until the rash was completely gone. At that point, when the danger was past, they were ceremonially washed with water in which neem leaves had been boiled. This water was carefully discarded because it was considered dangerous to others.

Second, wrapping the child was thought to prevent pneumonia, which was greatly feared as a common complication of measles and was regarded as caused by exposure to cold (cf. Mull and Mull 1994). One Muslim mother said that children with measles should be given a bead or "pearl" (*moti*) to swallow, coated with sugar or flour, in order to keep them warm inside as well. There was general agreement that even after the rash had faded, a child should be kept indoors for at least a week lest he or she get a "breathing problem." One informant added that Sitala and her sisters had a brother god who caused the gasping for breath seen in severe pneumonia, a comment suggesting that the measles-pneumonia connection is embedded in Hindu mythology.

Finally, mothers said that isolating and wrapping would protect the child against contact with a pregnant woman or with anyone who might be in a state of ritual impurity. When asked to give examples of people who were impure, they variously mentioned a mourner, a sweeper, a person with leprosy, or an "unclean woman" (Urdu *napak aorat*) – the latter phrase referring to a woman who was menstruating or had had sexual intercourse without taking a ritual bath afterward.

The nearly universal belief among all religious groups was that such individuals would arrest the emergence of the rash, an idea most understandable if one postulates – as Topley (1970) has suggested for Hong Kong – that the victim is somehow seen as being in a "sanctified" state of transition as outlined by van Gennep (1960:12) in his seminal discussion of *rites de passage* (1960:12).[7] Hindus thought that the measles goddess would become angry because of the disrespect shown to her by ritually polluted people coming into her presence, and would make the illness worse. Whatever the precise formulation, the elaborate precautions taken to protect the child from harmful influences show that people regard the experience of having measles as a highly significant life event rather than as a routine disease process in the biomedical sense.

Dietary Restrictions

Isolation of the child in a clean environment obviously has beneficial aspects, and wrapping the child would not be harmful unless the many layers of cloth overheated an already feverish child. However, a not so innocuous belief shared by nearly all informants was that the child's diet should be very restricted – basically only sweetened milk, herb tea, and softened biscuits or bread (*roti*). Further, there should be absolutely no frying in the house, no lentils cooked, and especially no meat prepared. Women in all religious groups emphasized that beef was particularly dangerous.[8] The Hindus said that frying and meat-eating would offend the measles goddess, Sitala, who would retaliate with a more severe attack of the disease.[9]

One Hindu informant added that the child should be given no food at all for seven days following the appearance of the rash, "even though he'll get very thin, like your picture" (I had shown a photograph of a child with third-degree malnutrition), "because if you give food the child will get worse." Pakistan is a country in which more than 60% of children are estimated to be undernourished, 7% severely so (Government of Pakistan and UNICEF 1988:53). In a situation like a measles episode, where already malnourished children are likely to have poor appetites and frequently have diarrhea as well, withholding food could clearly have serious consequences – as it did in one of the cases of child death described below.

Avoidance of Medicines

Seventy percent of mothers also said that no doctor should be consulted, and no medicines should be taken, while the rash was emerging – which, depending on the informant, was thought to take between seven and nine days. Even simple fever medications were regarded as threats to the child's welfare. So, also, was oral rehydration solution – not only because of its association with allopathy but also because it supposedly inhibited the full course of the disease. Hindus said that such nontraditional treatments offended the measles goddess, who was herself present in the child's body, but the idea of avoiding excursions to doctors and all allopathic therapies at least until the rash began to fade was present in every religious group. People thought that modern medicine might kill the child. One knowledgeable health worker living in the squatter settlements confirmed that people acted in accordance with this belief. He said that in his Punjabi Christian area, a child was normally taken to a doctor if diarrhea lasted more than two or three days, but this was not done for diarrhea associated with measles; therefore dehydration could become very severe before medical help was sought. Indeed, in a prior study among Sikhs in India, Kakar (1977:14) found that none of 18 measles victims was taken to a doctor; three of the 18 died.

CASE HISTORIES

In the Pakistani population described here, three children died from the complications of measles when food was not given and diarrheal dehydration or pneumonia went untreated for too long. All three belonged to families living in areas served by Aga Khan University clinics and were registered there for continuing care; all had supposedly been immunized against measles. Mothers of all three had been visited by community health workers who had tried to educate them about oral rehydration therapy and the importance of continued feeding during diarrhea. Yet home management of measles was (from a clinical perspective) inadequate. The reasons were revealed when households were visited and a history of the child's illness was obtained. This history was furnished mainly by the mother, but details were added by her relatives and neighbors, and to a lesser extent by local health workers.

Collection of such jointly constructed narratives differs from collection of "verbal autopsies" (Bang et al. 1992) in that its purpose is not merely to determine the clinical cause of death: pneumonia, dysentery, neonatal tetanus, and so on. Rather, the intent is to explore as many of the circumstances preceding the death as possible, the actions taken (or not taken) to treat the illness, and attitudes surrounding the events that occurred. In the present study, the overriding goal was to identify the cultural, economic, social, and psychological factors that place particular children at special risk of dying.

The three cases described here are obviously atypical in that these children were among the relatively small percentage of measles victims who die in any given outbreak in the developing world. However, as Myntti (1993) has pointed out in her study of "at risk" families in Yemen, analysis of extreme cases – both the ones with very good and the ones with very bad outcomes – often results in insights that are obscured if one looks only at "average" women and children.

Among the fatal cases I investigated, one child was a Hindu, one was a Punjabi Christian, and one was a Baluch Muslim. One was a boy and two were girls. There were some striking similarities, however: all three children were between one and a half and two years old; all had been weaned from the breast a few months before they died; all were said to have eaten virtually nothing during measles; and all belonged to extremely poor families under severe stress, where the mother was illiterate and had had three or even four children under the age of five to care for. In two of the three cases, there had already been another child death in the family.

The Case of Vijay

The first child, Vijay (all names are pseudonyms), was a Hindu boy who died at age two of diarrhea and dehydration following measles. When I visited, his puja symbol, dried out and crumbling, was still visible on the wall. His mother had had no schooling. She had three other children under the age of five, including a healthy four-year-old boy, a moderately malnourished three-year-old girl, and a two-month-old baby boy. Another child, a girl, had died of diarrhea (described by the mother as caused by "water in the spinal cord") at the age of one and a half.

The mother said she had stopped breastfeeding Vijay when she knew she was pregnant with the last baby, i.e., about six months before he died. (The reason for this is a belief, common worldwide, that breastmilk becomes "bad" as a result of a new pregnancy; see Mull 1992.) Since then, Vijay had existed on biscuits and tea and, according to a community health worker, his mother had failed to feed him during measles, giving most of her attention to her new baby instead. Privileging the newborn is a behavior appropriate in some ways (Harkness and Super 1994), but in this case it proved fatal to the displaced toddler.

Ironically, Vijay had been featured as a model of a fat, healthy child in a nutrition education booklet put out by the Aga Khan University clinics the previous year. On inquiry, I learned that his parents believed that this attention had led to evil eye being directed at Vijay out of envy and had also caused the father – who had a wild-eyed look suggesting mental disturbance – to lose his job as a shoemaker. At the time of Vijay's death, the father had been out of work for five months and his entire family, along with 14 other people in the house compound, was being supported by one of his brothers.

The parents had taken Vijay to a Hindu spiritual healer (*guru*) for an evil eye cure, and various objects associated with such cures could be seen in the home, still in use because the father thought that with Vijay's death, the evil eye was now directed exclusively at him. After Vijay developed diarrhea with measles and became even more emaciated, he had also been taken – well-wrapped – to a self-trained "doctor" in the squatter settlement where he lived and finally to the Aga Khan University outreach clinic, but only after his diarrhea had continued for two weeks.

The community health worker said that following this visit, Vijay's mother finally gave him oral rehydration solution for 15 days but for unknown reasons she made it double strength, using two packets of powder per liter of water. Vijay died while being rushed to a hospital with malnutrition and severe dehydration resulting from his month-long bout with diarrhea – dehydration probably made worse by the overly strong oral rehydration fluid.

The Case of Parveen

The second measles victim was Parveen, a Punjabi Christian who died at the age of one and a half of diarrheal dehydration and vomiting. Her mother had had two years of formal education but could not read or write. Besides Parveen, she had three children under the age of five to care for. A three-year-old boy was said to have previously died of *jadu* (sorcery) after the house was bewitched by a jealous sister-in-law who had no sons of her own. (That child's symptoms reportedly included fever, vomiting, and bloody diarrhea.)

Parveen's family lived alone, without any of the father's kin, in a tiny one-room house located essentially on a garbage dump. Sanitary facilities were nonexistent and a neighborhood privy was used, a sign of extreme poverty in this population (the father was a rubbish collector). As with Vijay, the mother had stopped breastfeeding Parveen six months before the child died – not because she was pregnant but because she was "ill" (see Mull 1992 for a discussion of this term). The mother said that Parveen "stopped eating" when she became sick with measles. She had given homemade oral rehydration solution but not until after the rash faded, and she had made it much too weak: two teaspoons of sugar and a pinch of salt for a liter of water. Further, she had administered it in too-small quantities as if it were a medicinal tonic (cf. Mull and Mull 1988).

Like Vijay, Parveen had been taken to a self-trained "doctor" in the squatter settlement, but only during the last 10 days of her illness, after she had already had diarrhea for two weeks. It was this practitioner who had recommended the rehydration fluid, though he had conveyed the wrong instructions for making and giving it. Parveen was never taken to the Aga Khan University clinic. In the mother's view, which she said was shared by the local "doctor," Parveen died because all of the measles spots did not come out – some stayed inside her body and caused her death. The mother sadly related how the child had been allowed to go out to play because the danger seemed to be past, but she soon returned to the house, lay down silently, and never got up again.

The Case of Karima

The third child was Karima, a Baluch Muslim who died at age two of diarrhea and pneumonia following measles. The mother had had no schooling. At the time of the death, she had three other children under age five and was eight months pregnant. Five of her six children were girls, and Karima was the youngest daughter (frequently an ominous position because of son preference in South Asia). The house was very poor, there were many flies, and children's feces were lying on the ground, a feature which I learned to associate with maternal demoralization, inadequate child care, and poor health status. Two of the husband's brothers, and their families, also lived in the house compound. All of the brothers were day laborers who could find only sporadic employment.

As with Vijay, the mother had stopped breastfeeding because of pregnancy, so since the age of one and a half Karima had been surviving on biscuits and tea. Reportedly she had eaten virtually nothing during her month-long illness, which had been characterized by fever as well as diarrhea throughout. Her mother seemed very depressed and was hesitant to offer details. However, she did say that she had been more worried about the fever than about the diarrhea, and that she even regarded the diarrhea as good because she thought it would help the rash to erupt. Hence the diarrheal dehydration was not treated.

At the end, as the rash faded and Karima's condition worsened, she was taken to two self-trained "doctors" and twice to a Muslim religious leader (*molvi*) as well, but she was not given oral rehydration fluid until finally a neighbor brought a packet of salts to the house on the day before she died. By then, pneumonia had set in and the child was unable to swallow the fluid or even to breathe. This neighbor said that she had wanted to come earlier, but by "custom" no one outside the immediate family was to visit a child with measles for fear of worsening the disease. Finally, however, she decided to come anyway because she and Karima's mother were "as close as sisters."

In this case, as in Parveen's, neighbors commented that if a child died of measles, all of that child's medicines must be thrown away – quite contrary to the usual thriftiness in poor areas of Karachi – because any child taking them in the future would die. This indicates once again that measles is considered to be a spiritually caused condition (cf. Mull 1991:181n.). Although the overt connection with a goddess is made only by Hindus, the "Sitala syndrome" embracing very limited feeding, wrapping, avoidance of allopathic medicines, and tolerance of persistent diarrhea is found in all religious groups. Throughout her illness, Karima was never taken to the Aga Khan clinic located half a mile from her home, and clinic workers were unaware that she had died until I told them.

IMPLICATIONS OF THE CASE HISTORIES

Several points are illustrated by these three cases. First, pre-existent malnutrition due to sudden weaning and inadequate supplemental foods was a major factor in the deaths. Better-nourished children might have survived the measles outbreak despite withholding of food and prolonged diarrhea, but the health of these three was already so compromised that they could not withstand the assault of the disease. Second, severe family stress related to the father's unemployment or underemployment and maternal overload (too many children to care for) underlay the mother's seemingly "neglectful" child care practices, i.e., demoralization played a part.[10]

Third, in two of the families a child had already died of diarrhea, suggesting that certain households are at special risk (Mull 1991; Myntti 1993). Finally, self-trained allopathic practitioners – locally known as *chota* ("smaller") doctors – were approached much more readily than qualified Aga Khan University personnel for measles treatment, even though treatment by the latter was available at a comparable or even lesser cost (five rupees, then about the equivalent of U.S. 30 cents).

This may have been partly because the self-trained allopaths showed a much greater willingness to adapt to traditional beliefs and practices than did fully trained physicians. Questioning of 10 mothers and three unlicensed practitioners in the same Karachi squatter settlements during follow-up research in 1990 revealed that these practitioners were sympathetic to people's interest in bringing out the measles rash. They also understood their positive attitude toward diarrhea. Some even gave injections during measles, which is forbidden by tradition in many parts of South Asia (cf. Morley et al. n.d.), but they presented these injections not as "treatments" for the disease but rather as ways to speed up emergence of the rash and to mark the conclusion of a natural process.

In 1990, details were elicited about how various "doctors" treated measles. Six of the 10 mothers said that practitioners prescribed medicines such as elixirs and suspensions (*sharbats*) as "hot" medicines that would force the spots to erupt more quickly. One woman said that practitioners gave an injection of a "hot" medicine (apparently an antibiotic) when the child had fever but the rash had not yet appeared, charging five to 15 rupees for this service. Another said that two "private doctors" (actually compounders, i.e., drug dispensers) each gave a series of three measles injections for 10 rupees: one injection to make the rash appear, one to make it fade, and one to make it disappear completely. It was apparent that such practices were gaining acceptance, even among Hindus, despite long-established customs mandating avoidance of allopathic medicines during measles.

Importantly, licensed practitioners were largely unaware of the nature and strength of traditional beliefs about many types of disease, not just measles. As in other parts of the developing world, most physicians in Pakistan are drawn from the upper classes and tend to distance themselves from folk beliefs, which they regard as unscientific nonsense (Mull 1991:187). In contrast, the unlicensed allopaths were very familiar with these beliefs as well as with people's financial burdens, and they adjusted their therapies accordingly.

For example, women who were afraid to take prenatal vitamins because they were humorally "hot" and might cause abortion were told to eat "cold" foods such as yogurt afterward to counteract the hotness. People who had very little money were given only enough medicine for one day (typically four doses of a suspension), in their own bottles; some were even sold just one tablet or capsule and were told to return if they needed more (cf. Mull and Mull 1994). In one case an enterprising "doctor" showed how he divided a packet of oral rehydration salts into four parts so that he could sell individual doses wrapped in newspaper; he instructed patients to mix each dose in one glass of water.

Similarly, people were warned not to "waste time" going to a lay midwife (*dai*) to have her raise a fallen fontanel if an infant had diarrhea and fever (in Pakistan, as in Mexico, diarrhea is thought to be caused by a fallen fontanel, which is believed to be connected to the palate; cf. Mull and Mull 1988). Instead, the "doctors" often appropriated this function for themselves by putting glycerin on a cotton ball, holding the cotton with forceps, and pressing up on the child's palate more or less as a midwife might do with her forefinger. One such practitioner confided that he knew this was fraudulent but he was trying to save the child's life by preventing treatment delay.

In short, marginally qualified practitioners were much more adept at allaying people's anxieties than were fully trained physicians. Although foreign to biomedically oriented health care providers, such practices are worthy of study because they so effectively bridge the gap between traditional and allopathic medicine. When – as in measles – prompt treatment of complications is essential, flexibility on the part of the physician can mean the difference between life and death. Knowledge of traditional beliefs and concerns is a sine qua non of such flexibility.

DISCUSSION

Each year, more than a million children die of measles and its associated sequelae, primarily diarrheal dehydration and pneumonia. Until immunization brings about global eradication of the disease, which will be very difficult, effective home management of measles remains essential. Such management would ideally include continued feeding and administration of fluids to the child – including oral rehydration solution when necessary – and expeditious consultation with trained allopathic practitioners if the child's condition worsens. Though biomedicine is itself a cultural system (Rhodes 1990) and no panacea, the fact is that in the case of measles diarrhea or pneumonia, rehydration and antibiotics can have an enormous impact on child mortality at very little cost.

Yet household interviews of 150 mothers carried out in urban squatter settlements in Pakistan showed that only 20% felt that diarrhea associated with measles was dangerous, and 70% said that no doctor should be consulted, and no medicines should be taken, at least until the rash was fading. The reason was embedded in centuries-old beliefs, particularly associated with Hinduism but not limited to Hindus, emphasizing the importance of bringing out the rash as a means of ridding the child's body of accumulated "heat" and "dirt."

Though measles was viewed as a "hot" disease, cooling remedies were not used to restore balance as would be expected in the humoral system. Instead, humorally hot foods and drinks were given and the child was kept well-wrapped in the belief that this would create more heat and thus force the rash out of the body to the surface of the skin. For the same reason, diarrhea (a "hot" symptom) was not only tolerated but in many cases welcomed as a further sign that "heat" and "dirt" were leaving the body. Although trained health workers had visited all 150 homes to explain how oral rehydration therapy should be used to prevent diarrheal dehydration, rehydration fluid was said to be avoided in the case of measles in the belief that it, like antifever medicines, would arrest the process by which heat and dirt were expelled.

In three cases, diarrheal dehydration (in one instance accompanied by pneumonia) was the proximate cause of a child's death. The three families were visited and carefully observed; detailed histories of the child's final illness were also taken. It was evident that macrolevel forces fostering selective poverty and disempowerment had a role in the deaths (cf. Millard 1994). At the household level, severe financial stress, maternal demoralization, and competition for scarce resources had interacted with strongly held cultural beliefs – the "Sitala syndrome" – to have a devastating impact on management of measles. Oral rehydration solution was eventually given, but ineffectively and much too late. Further, despite the fact that all three families were registered at university outreach clinics where the child could have received appropriate therapy at very low cost, all three children were taken to unlicensed or traditional practitioners instead. The likely reasons for this were explored in follow-up research and were found to be related to those practitioners' sensitivity to their patients' ethnomedical beliefs concerning measles.

NEEDED RESEARCH AND IMPLICATIONS FOR INTERNATIONAL HEALTH

Despite a few preliminary studies, we know very little about how licensed and unlicensed practitioners worldwide respond to patients' traditional beliefs about disease. A major reason is that such information is very difficult to gather. In addition, most practitioners are located in or near cities, and historically, very little medical anthropological research has been carried out in urban areas (Nichter and Kendall 1991). However, study of the practices of local doctors in treating measles and other infectious diseases could add much to our understanding of the way in which biomedicine is transformed in different cultural settings in response to economic and other pressures – a subject of considerable theoretical interest.

In the case of measles, modification of strict bioscientific principles is not limited to practitioners in the developing world. It also occurs in the United States, where, for example, it has been pointed out that some physicians delay giving measles vaccine until the optimal time period has passed because Medicaid reimbursement practices make it more profitable for them to give it singly rather than along with other immunizations (Emergency Medicine 1991:106). In other words, as anthropologists have long recognized, biomedicine is everywhere a more flexible entity than it appears to be at first glance (Lock and Gordon 1988).

Studies of unlicensed practitioners could also be very useful in the planning of international health initiatives. Because these "doctors" are numerous, accessible, sensitive to traditional beliefs, and trusted by local people, they constitute a largely unexamined resource that could be used to save children's lives. Although they are often disparaged, actual observation of their practices indicates that the merely greedy are outnumbered by those who genuinely want to heal their clients but lack sufficient expertise to do so (Mull and Mull 1994). Their existing knowledge of danger signs could be reinforced through educational interventions and they could be encouraged to recommend ORS in a more effective manner. Incentives could take the form of posters for their offices and free samples of oral rehydration salts, for example.

The fact that in the present study, one such practitioner did recommend homemade oral rehydration fluid, even though his recipe was wrong, is a hopeful sign. It would be worth knowing how this "doctor" persuaded the family to use such a therapy in a situation in which diarrhea is considered beneficial. Perhaps he presented it as a way to cleanse the body of impurities. The dangers inherent in appearing to recommend purgatives for diarrhea must of course be borne in mind (cf. Mull and Mull 1988). On balance, however, it seems unwise to ignore the positive contribution that these practitioners could make to child health if they were properly trained.

Whether the audience is practitioners or mothers, the present study shows that comprehensive views of disease should be stressed. The household data summarized here make it clear that measles has been inappropriately segmented off from diarrhea and pneumonia in "vertical" international health initiatives that are narrowly focused on one specific problem. As Nichter has pointed out (1994:325), children frequently have more than one illness more or less concurrently. We need to identify and address cultural concerns in order to be sure that each illness is being appropriately treated.

Thus, in diarrhea education campaigns, the danger of withholding fluids during measles and ignoring persistent diarrhea should be prominently mentioned. Further, the value of oral rehydration therapy in preventing dehydration during measles – even before the rash begins to fade – should be emphasized. Similarly, in ARI (acute respiratory infection) initiatives, people's existing awareness of pneumonia as a major complication of measles should be validated and built on. The fact that measles, diarrhea, and pneumonia form a deadly triad should be stressed. The algorithm recently developed by the World Health Organization to promote integrated case management of childhood illness is a step in the right direction.

THE IMPORTANCE OF
THE ANTHROPOLOGICAL PERSPECTIVE

Measles must be appropriately contextualized in other ways as well. To this end, homes should be visited and careful observations made. The anthropological method of participant observation, with its traditional emphasis on holistic perspectives, is ideally suited to such tasks.

Recent work focusing on what actually goes on in the household unit (e.g., Bentley 1988; Harkness and Super 1994) indicates that this line of inquiry will be extremely productive. More and more, it is recognized that despite doctors' arrays of powerful medicines, "diseases occur – and interventions must operate – under social conditions beyond the control of the biomedical scientist" (Schumann and Mosley 1994:203).

In the present study, the walls were virtually crying out for attention with their worship symbols; in other studies, bunches of herbs hung up to dry or numerous half-empty bottles of antibiotics have spoken of other health-related issues (Mull and Mull 1990, 1994). Research carried out in a central meeting area with groups of unrelated women can never capture the lived experience of an illness, and artifacts often tell an important part of the story. Similarly, family tensions influencing health status often reveal themselves only in the home.

Collection of illness histories by anthropologically oriented observers visiting families should be part of any attempt to understand and combat high child mortality rates from whatever cause. As the present study shows, such histories often encapsulate contextual factors that influence management of the illness – not only cultural beliefs, but intrahousehold competition for scarce resources (Nichter and Kendall 1991:198), maternal stress, and so on. They also have the potential to advance our understanding beyond that of the researcher who records them, since they allow for the possibility of reinterpretation by people with more, or different, knowledge. The difference between survey results and case histories is the difference between fragmentation and linkage, between knowing that an event occurred and beginning to understand its meaning for the participants.

It is worth remembering that informants, while commenting on disease episodes, are drawing on contexts in ways that the researcher may not guess. I was struck by this while talking with a mother living in a squatter settlement with a child mortality rate of close to 20%. Always interested in the possibility of cross-cultural parallels, I asked whether she had ever heard the proverb used as an epigraph for this chapter. "No," she replied. "We don't say 'Count your children after the measles has passed.'" Then she paused, thought for a moment, and added, "But we do say something else. We say, 'Don't count your children at all.'"

In other words, death in childhood is an all-too-common event for people in the developing world; but in the press to avert those deaths, health planners must be careful not to overlook nuances and details that could subvert their well-intentioned efforts.[11] One of the best-known illustrations in the literature comes from Honduras, where diarrhea associated with the folk disease empacho was not considered undesirable and therefore oral rehydration therapy was not used in such cases (Kendall et al. 1984). Similarly, the present study shows that in Pakistan, diarrhea accompanying measles is seen as different from most diarrheas – beneficial rather than dangerous. Combined with the "Sitala syndrome" emphasis on keeping the child very warm and the restriction of feeding and fluids, this privileging of measles diarrhea can and does lead to dehydration and death. As the Honduras experience demonstrated, massive public education campaigns urging people to use oral rehydration solution "when your child has diarrhea" will fail to persuade if the diarrhea is seen as a special case and that special case is not mentioned.

International health initiatives frequently ignore the particular and exceptional in their drive to popularize universalistic remedies. Financial constraints and time pressures are a large part of the reason. Yet the present study shows that a truly cost-effective approach to health promotion must include attention to culturally meaningful categories while resisting inappropriate aggregation. Wherever children still needlessly perish, we need to know the local interpretation of what happened and why. This is precisely the strength of anthropologically oriented inquiry.

NOTES

1. Kamende Edward's letter from Uganda (1991) is illustrative: "People in the Toro Kabarole District of Western Uganda say that if your child gets measles do not give any medical treatment otherwise you will kill the child...It is said that if the child gets much diarrhea then that is good because he or she is passing more measles virus in the stool. If a child gets a high temperature use more blankets." Note the fusion of the biomedical concept of a virus with traditional ideas.

2. A similar notion has been documented in Hong Kong and Taiwan, where the heat is thought of as a "hot poison" acquired in the womb that eventually emerges as the measles rash (cf. Topley 1970:425 and Gould-Martin 1978:41). Furth (1987) cites parallels in 18th century Chinese medical texts.

3. In Pakistan, many people think that even under non-illness conditions, heat "rises" in the body and that normal body heat escapes through the cranial sutures.

4. In Bangladesh, Shahid et al. (1983) found that 68% of children with measles had associated diarrhea, but 84% of those children were not treated with oral rehydration therapy even though their mothers ordinarily used it for diarrhea. Fifty-three percent of the mothers said that diarrhea associated with measles was "normal" and another 30% thought it was caused by harmful wastes and so was beneficial and should not be interfered with.

5. See Wadley 1980:55 and Nuckolls 1991:68 for similar ideas surrounding smallpox.

6. For the symbolic significance of red and white colors in Indian ritual, see Beck 1969.

7. Topley reports a proscription against contact between a child with measles and a pregnant woman in Hong Kong, and I have personally encountered it not only in Pakistan but in a remote village in Nayarit, Mexico. Topley suggests (p. 427) that the underlying idea may be that contact between two individuals in a similarly "transitional" state is dangerous; her informants said that not only would emergence of the measles rash be checked, but the pregnant woman would be unable to give birth. However, more naturalistic interpretations are also possible.

   Aside from the well-known risk to the fetus if a pregnant woman contracts measles, the anthropologist Peter Aaby has found increased perinatal mortality among babies delivered to mothers who have already had measles but have been reexposed during pregnancy (Aaby et al. 1988). Thus a so-called "folk belief" may actually be based on very astute observation (cf. Mull 1991:179n.). There is a parallel involving the smallpox goddess Mariamman. Egnor (1984:31–33) points out that pregnant woman who got smallpox experienced high rates of fetal wastage and neonatal death, and that even today, Mariamman is said to "hate" pregnant women.

8. One informant, a Punjabi Christian, added that people in the house should refrain from sexual intercourse while the child was ill (cf. Imperato 1969:778). To reduce temptation, hair should remain uncombed and cosmetics should not be used.

9. See Odebiyi 1989:988–989 for similar ideas about diet and the measles god in Nigeria; cf. also Maina-Ahlberg 1979:143.

10. How far these mothers had distanced themselves emotionally from their children, so that the deaths in fact constituted a form of (possibly unconscious) passive infanticide, is debatable and beyond the scope of the present study. However, Scheper-Hughes (1992) has described such a dynamic in a Brazilian community characterized by similar levels of poverty and stress. Where there is severe scarcity, terrible choices must often be made (Mull 1991).

11. The importance of identifying local disease classifications is reinforced by a recent study conducted in the Philippines by Nichter (this volume). There, some people with tuberculosis regarded themselves as having "weak lungs" instead – a condition viewed as less serious than tuberculosis. Because "weak lungs" sufferers were unlikely to finish the complete course of tuberculosis medication, the development of drug resistant strains of the disease was a very real threat.

REFERENCES

Aaby, P., J. Bukh, I. M. Lisse, E. Seim, and M. C. de Silva. 1988. Increased Perinatal Mortality Among Children of Mothers Exposed to Measles During Pregnancy. The Lancet 1:516–519. March 5.

Adetunji, J. A. 1991. Response of Parents to Five Killer Diseases Among Children in a Yoruba Community, Nigeria. Social Science and Medicine 32(12):1379–1387.

Bang, A. T., R. A. Bang, and the SEARCH Team. 1992. Diagnosis of Causes of Childhood Deaths in Developing Countries by Verbal Autopsy: Suggested Criteria. Bulletin of the World Health Organization 70(4):499–507.

Beck, B. E. F. 1969. Colour and Heat in South Indian Ritual. Man (N.S.) 4:553–572.

Bentley, M. E. 1988. The Household Management of Childhood Diarrhea in Rural North India. Social Science and Medicine 27(1):75–85.

Black, F. L. 1984. Measles. *In* Tropical and Geographical Medicine. K. S. Warren and A. A. F. Mahmoud, eds. Pp. 586–593. New York: McGraw-Hill.

Cutts, F. T. 1990. Measles Control in the 1990s: Principles for the Next Decade. WHO/EPI/GEN/90.2. Geneva: World Health Organization.

Cutts, F. T., R. H. Henderson, C. J. Clements, R. T. Chen, and P. A. Patriarca. 1991. Principles of Measles Control. Bulletin of the World Health Organization 69(1):1–7.

Edward, K. 1991. Traditional Beliefs and Measles [letter]. Community Eye Health 8:10.

Egnor, M. T. 1984. The Changed Mother, or What the Smallpox Goddess Did When There Was No More Smallpox. Contributions to Asian Studies 18:24–45.

Emergency Medicine. 1991. Countering the Measles Epidemic. Pp. 97–106. October 15.

Furth, C. 1987. Concepts of Pregnancy, Childbirth, and Infancy in Ch'ing Dynasty China. Journal of Asian Studies 46(1):7–35.

Gennep, A. van. 1960. The Rites of Passage. London: Routledge and Kegan Paul.

Gould-Martin, K. 1978. Hot Cold Clean Poison and Dirt: Chinese Folk Medical Categories. Social Science and Medicine 12:39–46.

Government of Pakistan and UNICEF. 1988. Situation Analysis of Children and Women in Pakistan. Karachi: UNICEF.

Grant, J. P. 1994. The State of the World's Children 1994. Oxford: Oxford University Press [for UNICEF].

Harkness, S. and C. M. Super. 1994. The Developmental Niche: A Theoretical Framework for Analyzing the Household Production of Health. Social Science and Medicine 38(2):217–226.

Imperato, P. J. 1969. Traditional Attitudes toward Measles in the Republic of Mali. Transactions of the Royal Society of Tropical Medicine and Hygiene 63(6):768–780.

Kakar, D. N. 1977. Folk and Modern Medicine. Delhi: New Asian Publishers.

Kendall, C., D. Foote, and R. Martorell 1984. Ethnomedicine and Oral Rehydration Therapy: A Case Study of Ethnomedical Investigation and Program Planning. Social Science and Medicine 19(3):253–260.

Koster, F. T., G. C. Curlin, K. M. A. Aziz, and A. Haque. 1981. Synergistic Impact of Measles and Diarrhoea on Nutrition and Mortality in Bangladesh. Bulletin of the World Health Organization 59(6):901b–908.

Lancet, The. 1991. Management of Childhood Fever. Vol. 338, p. 1049. October 26.

Lock, M. and D. R. Gordon, eds. 1988. Biomedicine Examined. Boston: Kluwer Academic Publishers.

Los Angeles Times. 1989. Poor and Immigrants' Ignorance of Medical System Can Be Deadly. April 7, Part II, p. 3.

Los Angeles Times. 1990. Measles Epidemic Worsens. March 31, p. B9.

Maina-Ahlberg, B. 1979. Beliefs and Practices Concerning Treatment of Measles and Acute Diarrhoea among the Akamba [Kenya]. Tropical and Geographical Medicine 31:139–148.

Markowitz, L. E. and W. A. Orenstein. 1990. Measles Vaccines. Pediatric Clinics of North America 37(3):603–625.

Millard, A. V. 1994. A Causal Model of High Rates of Child Mortality. Social Science and Medicine 38(2):253–268.

Morley, D. 1973. Paediatric Priorities in the Developing World. London: Butterworth and Co., Ltd.

Morley, D., I. Allen, and W. J. Martin n.d. Preliminary Results of a World Wide Enquiry into Beliefs Associated with Measles. London: Institute of Child Health.

Mulholland, K. 1995. Measles and Pertussis in Developing Countries With Good Vaccine Coverage. The Lancet 345:305b–307. February 4.

Mull, D. S. 1991. Traditional Perceptions of Marasmus in Pakistan. Social Science and Medicine 32(2):175–191.

Mull, D. S. 1992. Mother's Milk and Pseudoscientific Breastmilk Testing in Pakistan. Social Science and Medicine 34(11):1277–1290.

Mull, D. S. and J. D. Mull. 1988. Mothers' Concepts of Childhood Diarrhea in Rural Pakistan: What ORT Program Planners Should Know. Social Science and Medicine 27(1):53–67.

Mull, D. S. and J. D. Mull. 1990. The Anthropologist and Primary Health Care. In Anthropology and Primary Health Care. *In* Anthropology and Primary Health Care. J. Coreil and J. D. Mull, eds. Pp. 302–322. Boulder, Colorado: Westview Press.

Mull, D. S. and J. D. Mull. 1994. Insights from Community-Based Research on Child Pneumonia in Pakistan. Medical Anthropology 15:335–352.

Myntti, C. 1993. Social Determinants of Child Health in Yemen. Social Science and Medicine 37(2):233–240.

Nicholas, R. W. 1981. The Goddess Sitala and Epidemic Smallpox in Bengal. Journal of Asian Studies 41(1):21–44.

Nichter, M. 1989. Anthropology and International Health: South Asian Case Studies. Dordrecht: Kluwer Academic Publishers.

Nichter, M. 1994. Introduction to Special Issue on Acute Respiratory Infection. Medical Anthropology 15:319-334.

Nichter, M. and C. Kendall. 1991. Beyond Child Survival: Anthropology and International Health in the 1990s. Medical Anthropology Quarterly 5(3):195–203.

Nichter, M. and M. Nichter. 1994. Acute Respiratory Illness: Popular Health Culture and Mother's Knowledge in the Philippines. Medical Anthropology 15:353–375.

Nuckolls, C. W. 1991. Becoming a Possession-Medium in South India: A Psychocultural Account. Medical Anthropology Quarterly 5(1):63–77.

Odebiyi, A. I. 1989. Food Taboos in Maternal and Child Health: The Views of Traditional Healers in Ile-Ife, Nigeria. Social Science and Medicine 28(9):985–996.

Rhodes, L. A. 1990. Studying Biomedicine as a Cultural System. *In* Medical Anthropology: A Handbook of Theory and Method. T. M. Johnson and C. F. Sargent, eds. Pp. 159–173. New York: Greenwood Press.

Scheper-Hughes, N. 1992. Death Without Weeping: The Violence of Everyday Life in Brazil. Berkeley: University of California Press.

Schumann, D. A. and W. H. Mosley. 1994. Introduction to The Household Production of Health. Social Science and Medicine 38(2):201–204.

Shahid, N. S., A. S. M. Mizanur Rahman, K. M. A. Aziz, A. S. G. Faruque, and M. A. Bari. 1983. Beliefs and Treatment Related to Diarrhoeal

Episodes Reported in Association with Measles. Tropical and Geographical Medicine 35:151–156.

Topley, M. 1970. Chinese Traditional Ideas and the Treatment of Disease: Two Examples from Hong Kong. Man (N.S.) 5:421–437.

Wadley, S. S. 1980. Sitala: The Cool One. Asian Folklore Studies 39(1):33–62.

Wakeham, P. F. 1978. Severe Measles in Afghanistan. Journal of Tropical Pediatrics and Environmental Child Health 24:87–88.

Walsh, J. A. 1986. Measles. *In* Strategies for Primary Health Care. J. A. Walsh and K. S. Warren, eds. Pp. 60–70. Chicago: The University of Chicago Press.

Werner, D. 1986. Report Concerning Diarrhea Control in Mozambique. Palo Alto, California: The Hesperian Foundation.

Williams, P. J. and H. F. Hull. 1983. Status of Measles in The Gambia, 1981. Reviews of Infectious Disease 5:391–394.

World Health Organization. 1994. [Global Programme for Vaccines.] Role of Mass Campaigns in Global Measles Control. The Lancet 344:174–175. July 16.

CHAPTER 12

Knowing Pneumonia:
Mothers, Doctors, and
Sick Children in Pakistan

Sara H. Cody, J. Dennis Mull, and Dorothy S. Mull

INTRODUCTION

Acute respiratory infection (ARI), chiefly in the form of pneumonia, kills an estimated four million children every year (Leowski 1986). A comprehensive review (Graham 1990) indicates that the severity of the disease rather than the incidence of infection explains the striking differences in mortality among various regions of the world. In developing countries, death rates from ARI are 20 to 50 times higher than elsewhere (WHO 1984). Since most pneumonia in these countries is believed to be of bacterial origin (Stansfield 1987), such deaths would

The authors would like to thank Dr. M. Z. Malik Kundi, Professor and Chair of the Department of Paediatrics at Rawalpindi General Hospital, and Dr. Muhammad Anjum, also of the Department of Paediatrics, for facilitating this study. Ms. Kausar Shahdin went far beyond the usual interpreter's role to provide cultural insights with generosity and good humor. We are very grateful, too, to the many women whose willingness to share their stories made this study possible. Dr. Cody also wishes to think the Wilbur Downs International Health Committee at Yale University for grant support that enabled her to undertake the project.

be preventable if the disease were promptly diagnosed and treated with antibiotics according to standard case management protocols.

In the developing world, where reliable X-rays and laboratory tests are often impossible to obtain, researchers have determined that accurate diagnosis of pneumonia is best achieved by assessing children's breathing rates (Leventhal 1982; Gove and Kumar 1988; Shann 1988). Fast breathing – defined by the World Health Organization (1990) in different ways for different age groups – is the best single indicator of the presence of pneumonia as opposed to the common cold. Chest indrawing, or observable depression of the chest as the child tries to breathe in with lungs stiffened by infection, indicates that the pneumonia is severe.

Following diagnosis, pneumonia should be treated with antibiotics, but antibiotics should not be given for simple coughs and colds. Not only will they be ineffective in such cases, but their indiscriminate use may create strains of drug-resistant bacteria. The initial focus of ARI campaigns worldwide has thus been on teaching health personnel (usually physicians in government clinics) not only to recognize fast breathing but also to avoid the inappropriate use of antibiotics. In some countries, efforts are currently underway to teach mothers directly via the mass media.

The Role of Anthropology in ARI Programs

In undertaking these ARI initiatives, the World Health Organization has attempted to draw on lessons learned from the diarrhea campaigns of the last decade (summarized by Nichter 1993). Most notably, it has involved anthropologists from the start by funding a large-scale research effort, the Focused Ethnographic Study (FES) initiative, which is charged with gathering baseline data on ARI beliefs and practices worldwide (Gove and Pelto 1994). Although FESs have not been carried out in Pakistan, a large body of data has emerged from this effort, some of which has been published in a special issue of Medical Anthropology (Volume 15[4] 1994) along with other first-generation research on ARI.

As Nichter (1994) points out in his introduction to this special issue, the call for medical anthropological research has grown as many health initiatives have failed in the absence of adequate baseline knowledge. To cite an example from our own experience, in Pakistan an international agency's effort to promote tetanus injections during pregnancy was initially unsuccessful because unknown to the health planners, mothers-in-law considered such injections to be "hot" and therefore dangerous as possible abortifacients (Dr. Hector Traverso, personal communication 1991).

Indeed, ignorance of socioeconomic, cultural, and behavioral factors linked with illness and disease has been called the "Achilles heel" of attempts to improve health status in the developing world (Ramalinga-swami 1989), and some have argued that studies of these factors should have priority in countries with limited resources (WHO 1984; Pio 1986). Others have pointed out the special need for anthropological studies of ARI as an emerging area of concern. For example, there is a paucity of information on ARI treatment patterns among practitioners in both the traditional and the biomedical sectors (Nichter 1993, 1994).

The present chapter is an attempt to supplement existing ethno-graphic research on ARI by presenting an extensive body of illness histories gathered from caregivers (mainly mothers) of 103 children with confirmed pneumonia in Pakistan. These histories illuminate diagnostic and treatment practices both within and outside the home.

Mothers and ARI

We focused on talking with mothers because of their crucial role in influencing children's health through the quality of their caregiving: feeding, nurturing, noticing that a child is ill. Anthropological and public health studies have repeatedly shown that a mother's degree of autonomy within the family has a positive effect on child survival (Caldwell 1979; Doan and Bisharat 1990; Ren 1994). Women who are able to assert themselves can urge that their sick children be taken to a doctor, can stand up to a mother-in-law's possibly harmful ideas about illness management, and can ensure that female children are well fed.

Relatively powerless women, on the other hand, are less likely even to know what health care facilities are available, since their mobility outside the home is restricted. They can easily become so demoralized that their effectiveness as caregivers is severely compromised. At least two recent studies (Mull 1991; Myntti 1993) have identified maternal demoralization as a very significant factor influencing child morbidity and mortality independent of the effect of economic deprivation.

Even in a country such as Bangladesh, where – as in Pakistan – most young mothers have low status within the household, an observa-tional study has shown that mothers with more education have more healthful child feeding practices (Guldan et al. 1993 [household wealth was controlled for]). The authors of that study postulate that maternal assertiveness and attentiveness to feeding may be a major route by which women's education translates into decreased child morbidity and mortality. Another researcher (Griffiths 1990) has also noted that a woman's sense of personal control seems crucial in that fatalistic attitudes negatively affecting child health are thereby avoided.

Because of the mother's worldwide primacy in caregiving, almost all international health initiatives aimed at the family have focused on reaching women. Recently, however, some writers have suggested that mothers are being inappropriately held responsible for their children's welfare and illogically blamed when they fall ill. As Santow (1995:158) puts it, "noticing illness is not the same as dealing with it, and the power of mothers to intervene when a child is sick may be very limited." A study carried out in rural South India has shown, for example, that even though grandparents in extended families were increasingly yielding control over health care decision-making to the child's parents, mothers were less likely than fathers to make these decisions (Caldwell, Reddy, and Caldwell 1983).

In the present study, therefore, we were interested in looking at the dynamic of mothers' interactions with other family members, both by observing it directly in the hospital and by inferring it from their accounts of the child's illness. Among our areas of concern were any constraints on the mother that might limit her ability to obtain adequate health care for the child, her style of interaction with other family members, and her general degree of assertiveness. Recent anthropological studies focusing on what has become known as "the household production of health" (Berman, Kendall, and Bhattacharyya 1994) have underlined the importance of such issues (Clark 1993).

Pakistan: ARI and ARI Research

Pakistan came into existence in 1947 as a result of division of the Indian subcontinent at the time of independence from Britain. Founded as a homeland for Muslims, it remains a predominantly Islamic state. Its 130 million inhabitants, most living in rural areas, include 17 major linguistic and ethnic groups. In 1985, literacy was estimated at 43% for men and 18% for women. The infant mortality rate, while officially 110 per 1000 live births, is twice this in impoverished areas (National Institute of Population Studies 1992). As in much of the developing world, accurate disease-specific mortality figures are unavailable, but pneumonia is believed to account for at least 80,000 child deaths each year (United States Agency for International Development 1988).

With assistance from several international agencies, Pakistan initiated a much-needed national ARI control program in 1989. The primary goals were to reduce the incidence and severity of ARI and to promote the rational use of antibiotics in treating respiratory disease. At the time the program was begun, there were no national-level data about ARI, although an important interventional study had been completed in a rural region (Khan et al. 1990). In that intervention, pneumonia case-finding and education of families by community health workers succeeded in reducing ARI mortality by more than half.

Aside from the study just mentioned, the earliest pneumonia work in Pakistan dealt mainly with the etiology and epidemiology of the disease. For example, research conducted as part of a multi-country initiative demonstrated a high rate of bacterial isolates in the blood of children with pneumonia (Ghafoor et al. 1990), indicating that those pneumonias were bacterial rather than viral and therefore amenable to antibiotic therapy. A related study (Mastro et al. 1991) showed that in the test-tube, 97% of bacterial isolates were resistant to at least one antimicrobial drug and 31% were resistant to cotrimoxazole – a worrisome finding because the latter is currently the World Health Organization's antibiotic of choice for uncomplicated bacterial pneumonia in the developing world.

When the first national workshop on ARI in Pakistan was held in late 1989, plans were made to conduct a country-wide study of attitudes and behaviors related to respiratory illness. After the Gulf War broke out in the winter of 1990–1991, international agency funding was cut and these plans were abandoned. However, a handful of studies addressing ARI beliefs and practices were carried out over the next few years (Faisel, Shafi, and Mian 1990; Khan et al. 1992; Kundi et al. 1993; Mull and Mull 1994; Mull et al. 1994). These studies – along with an ARI review article summarizing unpublished as well as published research findings (Marsh et al. 1993) – provide a preliminary indication of some of the problems likely to be faced by pneumonia initiatives in Pakistan.

First, it is widely believed that most doctors in the country, and virtually all unlicensed health practitioners, do not count the respiratory rate when assessing respiratory infections, nor do they prescribe antibiotics according to World Health Organization recommendations.

Partial confirmation was provided by two of the present authors, who observed several unlicensed practitioners in their offices and noted that they did not count breaths, use a stethoscope properly, or know how to look for chest indrawing (Mull and Mull 1994).

Similarly, an investigation undertaken to determine why government health centers reported an extremely high incidence of respiratory illness severe enough to require antibiotics found that the government doctors essentially made the diagnosis fit the medicine they dispensed. These young physicians lacked confidence in the World Health Organization case management protocol and felt it difficult to resist patients' requests for particular medicines, especially antibiotic injections. Some stated that since doctors in large government hospitals and other specialists were also willing to abandon rational antibiotic use and prescribe according to patient demand, they did not see any reason not to follow suit (Faisel, Shafi, and Mian 1990). The extent to which families consult government doctors when their children are ill is a question that itself merits further study. As noted above, the training of such doctors is central to the national ARI program. These doctors, most of whom are assigned to rural areas, are charged with providing basic primary health care to the Pakistani people. However, there is evidence that a majority of families go elsewhere when their children are ill. For example, a national survey carried out in 1982–1983 determined that only 15.7% of the population patronized government health facilities (Federal Bureau of Statistics 1986). Reasons reportedly include the perceived nonavailability of effective medicines and frequent absenteeism of the medical staff (Government of Pakistan and UNICEF 1988:40).

Rationale for the Present Study

Our study was conceived as an attempt to confirm and extend some of these preliminary findings by eliciting detailed illness narratives from caregivers (predominantly mothers) of children diagnosed with pneumonia in a major teaching hospital in Pakistan. We elected to focus not only on ethnomedical beliefs about the cause and proper treatment of pneumonia but also on home remedies actually used, types of health care providers actually consulted, diagnostic and treatment practices of these care providers as reported by mothers, adequacy of those practices from a biomedical standpoint, and the dynamics of therapy management in families faced with a child's serious illness.

A detailed description of the study population, including statistical correlations between sociodemographic characteristics, health-seeking behaviors, and severity of illness, is presented elsewhere (Cody 1993). In this chapter we focus on findings of a practical nature that might inform and guide a national pneumonia training program. Where appropriate, we also draw attention to general patterns of health-care seeking illuminated by the mothers' stories.

THE SETTING

The study was conducted at Rawalpindi General Hospital, a 507-bed government hospital serving a poor population living in and around the city of Rawalpindi in Punjab Province. As in many such facilities in Pakistan, mothers of hospitalized children stayed in the ward, sleeping in the bed with the ill child or on a nearby wooden bench. Meanwhile, various other family members camped out in the corridors, going to the market to obtain medications or food for the mother and child as needed. Such items were purchased and paid for by the families. Nurses were few and usually too busy to provide much in the way of individual attention.

The hospital was clean but spartan, with few amenities of the type taken for granted in industrialized nations. More than once, we saw bleeding patients on gurneys being hurriedly trundled down crowded staircases (there were no elevators) on their way to the surgical suite. Electrical outages were common; sanitary facilities were few and basic; rudimentary patient records – mainly attendance and mortality figures – were kept stacked in enormous Dickensian ledgers. Such figures were summed each day without benefit of so much as a hand-held calculator.

DESIGN OF THE STUDY

Interviews were conducted by one author (SHC) almost daily from January through March 1992, during the cool, rainy winter season when the majority of children with respiratory infections enter the hospital (Ghafoor et al. 1990). The interpreter present in all interviews was a highly intelligent local woman born in Punjab who was fluent in English and Urdu as well as Punjabi and was completely familiar with the hospital setting. In a few cases, speakers of regional languages other than Punjabi were recruited to help interpret.

Our informants were caretakers (mainly mothers) of 103 children under the age of five with clinically diagnosed pneumonia who had been admitted to the hospital. The interviews averaged 45 minutes to an hour each and were conducted in a leisurely fashion so that people had an opportunity to tell as much as they wished. Where present, family members other than the mother often had a great deal of input into the conversation; the mother's mother-in-law was likely to be particularly vocal to the point of dominating the discussion.

The majority of the interviews took place on the inpatient pneumonia ward; the remainder were conducted in the outpatient clinic just after the pneumonia diagnosis was made by hospital physicians. Many of these physicians were participating in a concurrent study of the clinical efficacy of cotrimoxazole sponsored by the Centers for Disease Control in Atlanta. They had received careful training for that study, and our personal observation confirmed that their criteria for diagnosing pneumonia were both internally consistent and consistent with World Health Organization guidelines (1990). The severity of illness among children in the present study ranged from mild to very severe. Three of the children (two boys and one girl) died while the study was underway.

The interview was semistructured and was guided by a questionnaire designed to elicit sociodemographic data as well as a detailed description of the course of the illness before the child was brought to the hospital. Mothers were asked to recount what happened from the time they first noticed their child to be ill to the time of the interview, including whom they had consulted and why.

For each reported visit to a health care provider, they were asked specifically about the provider's use of a thermometer and stethoscope and they were questioned about any activity that might have been an effort to take a respiratory rate (use of a watch, looking at the chest for a long time, etc.). We hypothesized that use of a thermometer was a proxy for some degree of commitment to scientific diagnostic procedures. Respondents were also asked to say what they thought had caused the child's illness and to describe their use of home remedies, if any.

The Sample: Strengths and Weaknesses

The advantage of this hospital-based study was the assurance that the children had clinical pneumonia rather than upper respiratory infection, malaria, tuberculosis, asthma, or some other disease that could have had overlapping symptoms. We were also able to ask mothers what they did do rather than a hypothetical what they would do if their children were ill with pneumonia. However, it is well known that in any hospital-based sample the behaviors described may not represent the community at large but rather be particular to those people who (a) consider the hospital an acceptable place to receive care and (b) have sufficient resources to attend an institution located at often considerable distance from their homes (transport, family consent, etc.).

On the first point, conversations with hospital staff and comments by mothers in this study indicated that some people in the surrounding community associated the hospital with death.[1] Thus hospital attendees might well have been bolder, or have had more faith in modern medicine, than mothers in the general population. It should be noted, however, that most of the fear had to do with hospitalization, not with simply bringing a child to the outpatient clinic.

Many families came thinking that they were making a clinic rather than a hospital visit, i.e., they did not expect their children to be hospitalized. (Because of the need for subjects in the concurrent Centers for Disease Control study, physicians were admitting children with mild pneumonia who might otherwise have been treated on an outpatient basis.) Nevertheless, the fact remains that in the present study, as in most hospital-based studies, the sample is very unlikely to be representative of the population at large, especially because about 90% of the people in Pakistan live in rural areas and our informants were largely urban. Results must be interpreted with this possible source of bias in mind.

Sampling difficulties such as these, though often glossed over in both anthropological and nonanthropological research reports, are basically unavoidable in any study in which time and resources are limited. In the case at hand, we make no claim of epidemiological impeccability (cf. Nations 1986) but simply present our findings as a carefully elicited body of illness histories obtained from caretakers of children with confirmed pneumonia. To our knowledge, it is the largest body of such histories gathered in a single country as yet described in the literature. Given the status of pneumonia as a major killer of children worldwide, we feel it important to report this information, since it not only provides insights of immediate clinical significance but may serve to guide future researchers with greater resources at their disposal.

RESULTS

The Study Sample

As noted above, we interviewed caretakers of 103 pediatric patients who presented with pneumonia during the study period. The sex distribution of these patients (61.2% male, 38.8% female; $p < 0.005$) was not significantly different from that of all 218 children who came to the hospital with pneumonia during the same time frame (63.7% male, 36.3% female).[2] Ages ranged from 2 to 54 months, but the majority of the children (67%) were 12 months old or younger. Though the difference did not reach statistical significance, males were younger with a mean age of 9.4 months as opposed to 13.6 months among females. Most children were being breastfed.

Comparison with figures from the National Institute of Population Studies (1992) showed that families of study patients resembled those in the general population in terms of size and the percent that were extended as opposed to nuclear in structure. Further, the level of parental education within the study group, while higher than that for Punjab Province as a whole, was essentially identical to that found in major cities in the country. Thus in terms of these broad demographic indicators, the study sample appeared to be similar to the general or the general urban population of Pakistan.

As indicated above, patients included in the study came mainly from urban areas near the hospital (83.3% from Rawalpindi or the nearby capital city of Islamabad), and from extended families (64.1%). Such families were typically patrilineal and patrilocal, usually consisting of the husband, wife, and children; the husband's parents; and sometimes the husband's brother or brothers and their own families. In a few cases, however, the mother was living with her own parents, especially if she had just given birth (cf. Berman, Kendall, and Bhattacharyya 1994:207).

Most of the respondents spoke Punjabi as their first language. A minority (11%) spoke Pashto, one of the major languages of North West Frontier Province, a region of Pakistan located between Punjab and Afghanistan. Urdu was spoken by 86.1% of mothers as a second language. Interviews were conducted primarily in Punjabi, sometimes in Urdu, and three or four times in Pashto and Punjabi with the aid of a Pashto-speaking bystander.

The income reported by patients' families averaged 2456 rupees per month ($98 at an exchange rate of 25 rupees per U.S. $1). This average was somewhat skewed by a few families with unusually high incomes;

the median income was 1900 rupees per month (U.S. $76). Fathers' jobs were typically semiskilled or unskilled, ranging from shopkeeper to clerk to day laborer to rickshaw driver. Notably, 92% of respondents reported the family's income to be irregular. Most mothers did not work outside the home. They generally had only minimal formal education, having completed an average of 3.9 years of school; nearly half (47.6%) had had no formal education at all. Fathers, on the other hand, had had an average of 7.4 years of schooling.

Mothers' Perceptions of the Cause of Pneumonia: "Coldness"

Regardless of their educational level, mothers reported overwhelmingly that they believed that exposure to "cold" caused pneumonia (Table 12.1). Only a few volunteered responses related to supernatural forces,[3] and even fewer mentioned contagion or a predisposing illness.

Table 12.1

Cause Number of Responses

Child was in contact with cold temperature	**70 (64%)**
– cold weather (rain, snow, cold wind, cold morning or evening air, mountain air, child rode on motorbike without a cap, no electricity in home)	53
– exposure from bathing (child was bathed in cold water after birth, bathed on a rainy day, bathed while sick, exposed to cold air while being bathed)	5
– exposure to drafts during too-frequent diaper or clothing changes	4
– other (child sat on cold floor, drank cold milk, mother touched child with cold hands, child was exposed to drafts from frequent door-opening by other children)	8
Mother was cold and child nursed "cold" breastmilk	**13 (12%)**
– washed clothes/floors/dishes	8
– hands were wet	2
– drank lassi (humorally cold yogurt drink)	1
– recently bathed	1
– was weak and breastmilk was not strong enough	1

Table 12.1 (*continued*)

Rapid decrease in temperature (*garam–saard*)	**15 (14%)**
– child went from warm indoors to cold outdoors or cold room	9
– perspiring/febrile child contacted cold air	2
– crying/perspiring child contacted cold air	1
– child went from heated bus to cold taxi	1
– child went from warm climate to cold mountain area	1
– mother bathed after intercourse, then nursed child	1
Supernatural cause	**2 (2%)**
– "could be" evil eye (*Urdu nazar*)	2
Contagion	**2 (2%)**
– neighbor coughed on child	1
– mother and father had colds and kissed child	1
Predisposing illness	**2 (2%)**
– woke up with a cold	1
– had measles	1
Don't know	**4 (4%)**
Total responses	**108**

Cold was described primarily as a temperature state, although we could see vestiges of an underlying humoral classification ultimately derived from ancient Greek tradition.

The child might be affected directly by coldness, as in the case of exposure to cold weather, cold water, cold drafts, or too-frequent bathing. Alternatively, informants said that coldness could sometimes be transferred to the child from the mother via "cold" breastmilk if she herself was in a "cold" state, e.g. if she had become chilled while washing clothes, dishes, or floors. An abrupt change from hot to cold (Urdu garam–saard) was seen as more dangerous than simple coldness, leaving the body in a particularly vulnerable "shocked" condition.

Sixteen of the 103 families identified ways in which pneumonia could perhaps be prevented. Breastfeeding mothers avoided foods thought to be humorally cold such as oranges, sour foods, pickles, yogurt, and rice and tried to eat more eggs and other foods felt to be humorally hot. Some mothers said they never removed their children's shoes. Five mothers were reluctant to give baths for fear of the child's contracting pneumonia; these children went without a bath for 10 to 30 days or until the head itched.[4]

Several mothers volunteered ideas of how cold had entered the body and caused the congestion they observed in their children. Of particular concern was the production of phlegm (Urdu *raysha*), thought to originate in the brain and to flow out through the nose, especially if this flow of raysha were blocked, described as a cause of significant pain. The feet, even with shoes on, were believed to be a vulnerable port of entry for cold. Cold weather was also thought to cause raysha as the cold air went into the body with each breath. Just as cold milk was thought to produce raysha, hot green tea was thought to melt it.

An aura of maternal culpability surrounded many discussions of the cause of pneumonia; occasionally a mother-in-law present during an interview would openly accuse her daughter-in-law of some supposedly negligent behavior. Perhaps the child's mother was not careful to dry and warm her hands after washing dishes or clothes and before breastfeeding, or perhaps she exposed the child to cold drafts while changing the diaper, or let the older children take the younger one outside, or did not keep the doors closed. Whatever the behavior was, one sensed that family members felt that the mother should have known enough to have avoided it. The following example is illustrative.

During a relatively calm period on the ward when no adult males were present, a mother-in-law described exactly how her only grandson had contracted pneumonia while she had been away visiting relatives. She related that, against strict orders, her daughter-in-law had had sexual intercourse with her son, necessitating a bath as dictated by the Holy Quran. Because the daughter-in-law had been in a "hot" state (having received "heat" from her husband's semen), and had then undergone a rapid cooling via contact with cold water, she was particularly vulnerable to *garam-saard*, a sudden temperature change thought to shock the system as described above.

The baby cried soon thereafter and the mother breastfed during this dangerous time, passing the cold from her body to his via her milk. When the mother-in-law came home the next morning, she found her grandson seriously ill with a respiratory infection and blamed her daughter-in-law (cf. Stewart et al. 1994:390 for a report of a similar belief in Bangladesh). The mother-in-law added that before this incident, she had been sleeping between her son and his wife to prevent just such an occurrence.

This narrative illustrates the powerful social pressures experienced by young women in a traditional society who are held accountable for the health of their children. There was no course of action available to this young mother that would have simultaneously placated her mother-in-law, her husband, and her child. We explored the issue further with several other mothers to understand whether they might consider withholding breastmilk under some circumstances. Few women volunteered that they had avoided nursing for fear of transmitting coldness, but many did express worry that breastfeeding under "cold" conditions might be harmful. This is an issue that warrants further exploration, since malnutrition worsens the prognosis in ARI (Tupasi et al. 1990). Breastmilk also conveys passive immunity to the child, potentially protecting against respiratory infection.

Home Treatments

In 70% of the cases, mothers used home treatments for the respiratory infection before seeking care outside the household. Typically, these treatments were initiated with the first symptoms and were continued throughout the illness episode. In other words, the home remedies were not necessarily stopped when a practitioner was consulted but rather were used as a complement to the practitioner's medicines.

About a quarter of the remedies consisted of over-the-counter drugs or leftover medicines that had been purchased for someone else. Those drugs that could be identified included antibiotics such as Amoxil drops ($n=2$), Ampiclox ($n=1$), and Septran ($n=1$); fever medications such as Paracetamol ($n=6$), Panadol ($n=1$), Ponstam ($n=1$), and Calpol ($n=2$); and decongestants such as Phenargan or Tixylix.

The other home remedies were largely traditional – teas, oils, humorally hot foods, chest wraps, and the like. These were given to restore heat and provide comfort to the child, and were basically intended to counter the physical coldness that had supposedly caused the illness. Among the more unusual remedies were opium (used as a sedative and painkiller) and powdered deer horn, a "hot" medicine thought to be potent against many serious ailments (Table 12.2). Occasionally, if a supernatural as well as a physical cause was suspected, the child would also wear a special *taveez* (amulet) containing appropriate passages from the Holy Quran to protect against fear, excessive crying, or vulnerability to illness.

It was clear that many home remedies described were part of an oral tradition that had been passed from generation to generation. Women

TABLE 12.2

Home Remedy	Number of Responses
Teas	**40**
– green tea (plain, with cardamom, with cardamom and cinnamon, or with other combinations of the following: cardamom, cinnamon, fennel [Urdu *saunf*], mint [Urdu *podina*], a spice made from ajowa seed, *Trachyspermum ammi* [Urdu *ajwain*], cloves, and peppercorns)	28
– black tea (plain or with various combinations of milk, fennel, cardamom, cinnamon, cloves, ajwain, and sugar)	9
– other herbal teas (joshanda [a commercially packaged collection of herbs], plain fennel, mint, or ajwain)	3
Ointments or oils applied to child's chest, throat, or back	**40**
– Vicks	20
– mustard oil (plain or with turmeric)	10
– Iodex	8
– ghee (clarified butter)	1
– asafoetida [Urdu *heeng*] in oil	1
Eggs	**25**
– soft-boiled (plain, with buffalo milk, or with green tea)	12
– raw (plain or yolk only, beaten in cup of warm milk, mixed with tea and spices, or mixed with milk and sugar)	9
– hard-boiled (whole, yolk only, or white only)	4
Steam inhalation	**16**
Chest wraps	**7**
– Chest tied with *dupatta* (mother's scarf), a practice known *as sina bunno* ("chest-binding") in Urdu	2
– egg yolk from wild hen rubbed on chest under wrap	1
– warm ashes tied in cloth and placed on chest	1
– cotton material warmed and wrapped around chest	1
– banakshah flowers boiled, strained, tied on chest while warm	1
– betel nut leaves placed on chest	1

Table 12.2 (*Continued*)

Home Remedy	Number of Responses
Other	**19**
– honey	5
– cloves	3
– *ajwain*	2
– brandy, one drop in milk or water	2
– opium, plain or in green tea	2
– deer horn (Urdu *bara singa*), ground and mixed with water	2
– ginger	1
– asafoetida	1
– chicken soup	1
Total responses	**147**

have traditionally been the "carriers of knowledge" with respect to children's illness (Sharp 1986). However, modern media were also a potent source of information, for several mothers volunteered that they had given the child a chest massage with Vicks or Iodex ointment after seeing the product advertised on television.

Most home remedies used probably did no harm, and some – such as inhalation of steam and vapors from hot teas – may have provided symptomatic relief. Warming the nose by inhaling hot humidified air has been shown to decrease symptoms and improve the course of the common cold (Tyrrell, Barrow, and Arthur 1989). However, a few home therapies, albeit reported by very few mothers, may have actually worsened the illness. One such therapy is the giving of opium, which can severely depress the respiratory rate and decrease the level of oxygen in the blood. In fact, one of the three children in the study who died was a three-month-old boy who had been given green tea with opium by his paternal grandmother "to give a warm effect and relieve the pain."

Another risky remedy is "tying the pain" (Urdu: *dard nu bunno*), which, though reported only twice by caretakers, is a well-known practice in Pakistan (Khan et al. 1993). "Tying the pain" consists of tightly binding the chest with a cloth to limit movement in an attempt to reduce the chest pain that is occasionally associated with severe pneumonia. Such practices may further increase respiratory distress; one recent study of infants in Turkey showed that babies who had been swaddled for at least three months were four times as likely as others to develop radiologically confirmed pneumonia (Yurdakok, Yavuz, and Taylor 1990).

Many mothers in the present study responded to respiratory illness by wrapping the child in multiple layers of clothing. While not as hazardous as opium or chest-binding, such overwrapping is worrisome because it may exacerbate fever and distress the child (Berman and McIntosh 1985). It also reduces the chance that the mother will detect fast breathing or chest indrawing associated with severe pneumonia (Khan et al. 1993). The practice continues, of course, because mothers want to negate the "coldness" thought to have caused the child's illness.

The perception that exposure to cold causes pneumonia is not limited to illiterate mothers in developing countries. Worldwide, it is shared by highly educated people, including all types of health care providers. At the 1989 ARI workshop in Pakistan, for example, a representative from the World Health Organization called for the reduction or elimination of "chilling" as a risk factor for ARI. In the present study, mothers reported that practitioners often warned them to dress their children warmly; one advised a family not to bring the child back to him for follow-up care if it was raining. Indeed, we noted that the number of visits made to Rawalpindi General Hospital and consequently the number of children admitted with pneumonia dropped precipitously on rainy days.

Numerous studies (Nichter 1987; Pool 1987), some done in Pakistan (Hunte and Sultana 1992; Kundi et al. 1993), have documented the widespread belief that coldness is the primary or even the only cause of respiratory illness; this is an idea that permeates many otherwise disparate cultures and has endured for centuries. It is true, of course, that respiratory infections are more common in winter (Wilder 1963). As noted above, Rawalpindi General Hospital records show that ARI cases always peak in December and January when the temperature is coolest (Ghafoor et al. 1990). Thus an apparent "folk belief" could well have a scientific basis, though the precise mechanism remains unclear.[5]

The Process of Seeking Care Outside the Home

The following five case histories illustrate the complex trajectories preceding children's ultimate arrival at the hospital for care. While they were selected for their variety and interest, they are also representative of the entire body of study cases in many important ways. First and most obvious, three of the five case studies (60%) involve boys, who constituted 61% of the study sample. Second, four (80%) of the families were living temporarily or permanently in or around Rawalpindi, vs. 83% of the families in the entire sample. Third, in terms of family structure, four of the five families were extended and involved the father's kin, while 64% of the study cases were in this category. Fourth, both in the sample as a whole and in this sample of five, home remedies were tried by most mothers – 80% here, 70% in the main group – usually as a first resort.

Fifth, in the entire sample of 103 children, family members made 194 visits to health care practitioners before bringing children to the hospital, or a mean of 1.9 practitioner visits per child; here, 10 visits were made on behalf of five children, or a mean of two per child. Further, the average interval between the family's awareness of the child's illness and arrival at the hospital was roughly similar: 6.7 days in the larger sample, 4.8 days in this sample of five. Of note, the shortest delay – two days – was reported by a mother who had had prior experience with pneumonia (Case 2).

It is somewhat surprising that in the five cases, there was only one reported use of an over-the-counter drug (Calpol). However, the kinds and numbers of home treatments used were otherwise typical of those listed in Table 12.2 for the entire study sample. Mothers described three uses of teas (fennel, cardamom, and joshanda), two chest massages with Iodex, one throat massage with mustard oil, one feeding with egg yolk, and one feeding with ajwain – eight uses of home remedies for five children (1.6 per child) vs. 147 such uses for 103 children in the group as a whole (1.4 per child).

The single most atypical feature of these five cases is one family's resort to a *pir* (Muslim holy man), which was the only reported instance in the entire sample. The case is included here as a demonstration of the mother-in-law's still-powerful influence on patterns of health care seeking and the survival of traditional ideas of illness causation. It should be noted, however, that the pir was not consulted for the pneumonia diagnosis itself but for a predisposing condition: evil eye disease.

Besides their value as a fair sampling of the entire data set, the histories humanize the information presented elsewhere in this chapter in tables, graphs, pie charts, and lists. Reading through them, one can easily see the forces arrayed against a mother's taking a child directly to the hospital – distance, time, various pressures from other family members – as well as the family's growing sense of urgency as the child's condition worsens despite attempts at treatment. (In the following accounts, all names are pseudonyms.)

Case 1: Asif A 20-year-old mother of two boys noticed that her younger son Asif, ten months old, had a fever and cough. She had been born in Rawalpindi but was living with her husband and his parents in a village about 175 miles from the city. Initially, the young couple took Asif to an unlicensed, self-trained practitioner in their village whom they had visited many times before; he gave an injection and a day's supply of a red syrup. They administered the syrup for a day but the child showed no improvement.

Because it was raining the next day and the first doctor's office was located at some distance from their home, the father decided to take Asif to a dispenser (similar to a pharmacist's assistant) who was within walking distance. In that way the child did not have to be exposed to the rain for a long period. The dispenser gave a one-day supply of a dark pink syrup and three crushed tablets. However, Asif still did not improve, so the mother-in-law began giving him throat massages with mustard oil, an egg yolk a day, and joshanda, a commercial tea.

On the eighth day of Asif's illness his maternal grandfather came to visit and suggested that the child be taken to a hospital in Rawalpindi. All members of the family agreed. The grandfather took Asif back to Rawalpindi that night and brought him to the hospital the next morning. More than a week had passed since his symptoms were first noticed.

Case 2: Karim A 30-year-old mother of four living with her husband at some distance from the city was visiting her mother in Rawalpindi. When her four-month-old son Karim awoke one morning with what she believed to be a fever and a "cold," she sent her mother to the market to buy Calpol, a fever medicine. Later that night she noticed Karim having difficulty breathing. She said that his ribs were "lifting up" and that he looked like her other son had when he had had pneumonia.

The grandmother wanted Karim to be taken to a doctor in private practice where he could get one or two injections and be "cured," but the mother did not agree. Instead, at 9:30 that night she insisted that she and the grandmother take the child to the Rawalpindi General Hospital emergency room because she had heard that the hospital was a good one. Karim was admitted to the pneumonia ward with severe disease, at which time the grandmother went home to call the child's father to notify him about what had occurred. This was on the second day after Karim's mother first observed his fever and respiratory distress.

Case 3: Amina   A 26-year-old mother of two noticed that her six-month-old daughter Amina had developed fever, cough, and chest congestion with phlegm. She was living in an extended family with her mother-in-law and brother-in-law while her husband worked temporarily as a taxi driver in Saudi Arabia (a fairly common situation in Pakistan). During the first three or four days of illness, she fed Amina ground roasted ajwain with sugar and rubbed Iodex on her chest.

The brother-in-law then sent Amina and her mother to see a doctor friend who lived close by. The doctor gave one injection and three syrups. The child seemed no better the next day, however, and so the family stopped giving the syrups after the morning dose. They could not take the child to another private physician because it was Friday (the Muslim holy day) and everything was closed. Since the mother-in-law was familiar with Rawalpindi General Hospital, having recently been admitted there, the mother and brother-in-law decided to bring Amina to the emergency room. About six days had passed since her symptoms were first noted.

Case 4: Fareed   A 16-year-old mother living in an extended family became concerned when her three-month-old son Fareed suddenly refused to nurse and cried excessively. She and her husband decided to take the baby to a doctor whose office was located near their home. That doctor prescribed a pink syrup which they were to give hourly for a day and told them to return the next morning for an injection. But the syrup did not relieve Fareed's symptoms.

Since the young couple had lost faith in the first doctor, the next day they took the baby to another one located farther away who had treated other children they knew. The second doctor dispensed a one-day supply of syrups and administered an injection but gave no instructions. The mother was dissatisfied, commenting to us that "there were nurses and other doctors and he was busy gossiping."

The couple went home and massaged Fareed's chest with Iodex as recommended by a neighbor. That night the child cried all night and kept the whole extended family awake. The next morning, the mother-in-law said that the reason the medicines were not working was that Fareed had contracted *nazar* (evil eye) "because the other children think the baby is very cute and they pick him up." At her suggestion, early that morning the whole family took Fareed on a five-hour drive to see a pir (Muslim holy man), who gave the child a taveez (amulet). On the way home from visiting the pir, the family stopped to consult yet another doctor who had evening hours at the bazaar. That doctor told them that Fareed was seriously ill with pneumonia and should be taken to a hospital. The mother-in-law agreed with this and the parents immediately brought him to the hospital emergency room. Three days had elapsed since Fareed's mother had first noticed his symptoms.

Case 5: Nasreen   A 35-year-old mother of five living with her husband's extended family noticed that her 21-month-old daughter Nasreen had fever and phlegm (raysha). She gave Nasreen fennel and cardamom teas in an attempt to drain the raysha from the brain so it could go out the child's mouth, but there was no improvement.

The next day her husband described Nasreen's symptoms to an unlicensed doctor in a dispensary adjacent to the government office where he worked as a typist. Without actually examining the child, this practitioner suggested that Nasreen's fever be treated with a powder dissolved in warm water. (Such "second-hand" diagnosis is common in Pakistan as elsewhere in the developing world.) The following day the child was still ill, however, so one of her older brothers took her to a neighborhood doctor who gave one injection, three crushed tablets, and a yellow syrup.

That day and the next, Nasreen still failed to improve. The mother became angry at the second doctor's failure to cure the child and argued strenuously that she should not be taken back to him. This caused an argument with her husband, who told her, "You are illiterate, you don't know anything, we must go back to the same doctor." Unaccompanied by his wife, he did take Nasreen back to that doctor, who gave the same medicines as before to no effect. The next day – the fifth day after onset of illness – the mother took the child to Rawalpindi General Hospital with her husband's permission.

These illness narratives raise several issues which need further exploration. How are health care decisions made? Which health care providers are used and why are their services discontinued? Why do people consult Rawalpindi General Hospital physicians? Do local practitioners count the child's respiratory rate and examine the chest? What are the implications of their diagnostic and prescribing habits? What about costs? How do mothers view medicines? In the discussion below, we summarize findings from the entire body of 103 illness histories to answer these questions.

Decision-making

As is suggested by the five case studies, many members of the family typically participated in the decision to seek care and ultimately bring the child to the hospital. This was true for both nuclear and extended families. Thus no one person made decisions alone; rather, there was a dynamic, engaged, and constantly changing "therapy management group," to use a term drawn from Janzen's classic study (1978).

As primary caregivers for their young children, the mothers were almost always the first to notice the symptoms and to suggest that medical attention was needed. However, in patrilineal extended families the mother-in-law or older sister-in-law often exerted tremendous influence or even directed care. In all families, relatives other than the mother, and sometimes even landladies and neighbors, joined in assessing the child and making the decision to seek medical care outside the home.

Of note, mothers almost never visited practitioners on their own. They were usually accompanied by their husbands or other male relatives, less often by older female family members. In 44% of the cases, mothers secured permission from their husbands before bringing the child to the hospital or before allowing the child to be admitted; if the husband was absent, they most often sought permission from another member of his family or from their own parents if they happened to be visiting them. It was clear that few women would have acted alone without the consent of their husbands or other family members.

When considering the implications of such consent-seeking, one must remember that 53% of women in Punjab are married to a first cousin and another 12% are married to a second cousin or other relative (National Institute of Population Studies 1992). So when a woman asks her husband for permission to do something, she may be asking a first cousin whom she has known since infancy; when she asks her father-in-law, she may be asking her own uncle.

Also, although a majority (68%) of mothers reported that they had sought permission from their husbands or in-laws before bringing their children to the hospital, further comments revealed that it was actually a process of consensus, bargaining, and notification. The case studies illustrate how many mothers were not as passive as the phrase "sought permission from husband" would suggest. In-depth interviews like those carried out in the present research can capture nuances of this type that are missed when respondents are simply asked survey-type questions by a person with a checklist.

Choice of Provider

As shown in Figure 12.1, the 103 families made a total of 194 visits to health care providers between onset of illness and arrival at Rawalpindi General Hospital. Some practitioners were seen more than once. The providers were categorized as accurately as possible on the basis of the mother's description. In practice, however, these descriptions were sometimes quite difficult to interpret.

In particular, mothers were often unsure whether the "doctor" that had been seen was a fully trained physician with an M.B.B.S. degree (Bachelor of Medicine, Bachelor of Surgery – a designation derived from the British system) or an unlicensed, self-trained allopathic practitioner, popularly known as a chota ("small" in Urdu) doctor. The "?M.B.B.S." category shown in Figure 12.1 is intended to reflect this uncertainty. Overall, 68% of the visits (132/194) were to these private allopathic practitioners.

Several other categories represented in the figure need to be clarified. First, dispensers (sometimes called compounders) are similar to pharmacists' assistants in the United States. Some work with chota or M.B.B.S. doctors and some are solo practitioners operating out of a shop of their own. As in other developing countries (Whyte 1992), some have considerable medical knowledge while others are mere vendors and a few are charlatans. Dispensers may or may not represent themselves as doctors, but in practice they are addressed as such by patients.

Characteristics of homeopaths and *hakims* are described in detail elsewhere (Mull and Mull 1994). Briefly, homeopaths diagnose mainly by history, dispense medicines in tiny amounts, and adhere to the concept – developed in 18th-century Germany – of "like cures like." Hakims base their therapies on the ancient humoral theory of Hippocrates. Traditionally they have diagnosed by feeling the pulse and have relied on herbs for treatment, but many now use allopathic medicines

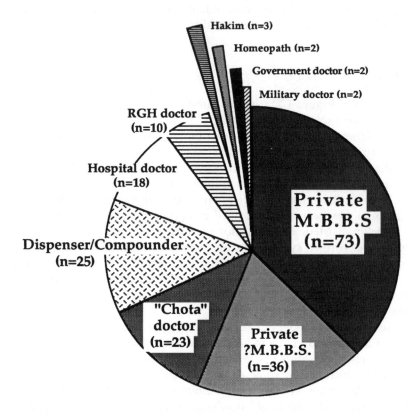

Figure 12.1   194 visits made by 103 families between onset of illness and admission to Rawalpindi General Hospital.

(even injections) as well. In Pakistan, both homeopaths and hakims tend to specialize in treating chronic conditions.

In Figure 12.1, a distinction is made between "RGH doctor" and "hospital doctor" because a handful of mothers used the outpatient clinic at Rawalpindi General Hospital as their main source of care, returning there for treatment by an "RGH doctor" until the child became so ill as to require admission. Some families used other hospital clinics in this way and then came to Rawalpindi General Hospital if specifically referred by personnel at those clinics ("hospital doctors").

Importantly, only two of the 194 visits reported by mothers were to a doctor in a community-based government clinic (Rural Health Center or Basis Health Unit). This may be partly due to the nature of our study population, which was largely urban and thus may not have been familiar with the four or five periurban Basic Health Units – essentially bare-bones clinics with a few hospital beds – nearby. However, as noted above, underuse of such facilities has been previously documented by the Government of Pakistan itself. Especially in life-threatening pneumonia cases, a public perception that appropriate medicines might not be available there would naturally lead people to bypass such sites.

The most commonly expressed reason for consulting a particular practitioner new to the family was that "the neighbors go there." The number of different providers consulted and the number of visits made before the child was diagnosed with pneumonia at Rawalpindi General Hospital varied tremendously. On average, however, mothers made 1.9 visits to various practitioners during an average of 6.7 days of illness (see discussion of "delay" below). More than three-quarters of the families (78%) made only one visit to any given provider before turning to the next one or bringing the child to the hospital. The illness narratives contain frequent comments such as, "The child didn't improve so we went to another doctor."

In contrast to findings reported previously from the same hospital (Kundi et al. 1993), there was no unvarying or even normative pattern ("hierarchy of resort") evident in these consultations. As Figure 12.1 shows, however, the majority of mothers in this study did not patronize hakims or homeopaths, who are not often used for acute life-threatening illness in Pakistan. Overall, 97% of the pre-hospital consultations (189/194) were with trained or untrained allopaths rather than with more traditional health care providers.

Delay in Coming to the Hospital

As noted above, mothers reported a mean of 6.7 days of illness elapsed between the time they first noted the child's respiratory symptoms and the time when the child was admitted to the Rawalpindi General Hospital. This is considerably longer than the mean of 3.8 days reported by Kundi et al. (1993) in their study of 50 children with pneumonia brought to the same hospital. The discrepancy is partly accounted for by the fact that children with pneumonia severe enough to require hospitalization were excluded from the Kundi study; thus the sample was different. However, other factors may have come into play.

First, there could well have been an interviewer effect on mothers' responses, since the interviewer in the 1993 study was a busy physician with a friendly but brisk manner while the interviewer in the present study was (then) a senior medical student with considerably fewer demands on her time. She had the leisure to establish rapport with mothers and to convey her interest in hearing their complete stories. We noted that when respondents were asked careful follow-up questions, they often recalled an earlier onset of illness – and thus a longer delay – than they had at the beginning of the conversation. Also, mothers' definitions of "onset" may well have differed according to whether they were thinking of the onset of respiratory symptoms or the onset of symptoms that they recognized as serious. As Nichter and Nichter have pointed out (1994:368), elicitation of detailed illness histories can clarify these and many other issues.

In the present study, the number of days of delay before coming to the hospital was positively correlated with the amount of money spent on treatment ($p < 0.0001$), though there was no statistically significant correlation with family income as a whole. Delay was also positively correlated with the age of the child ($p < 0.001$; i.e., younger children were brought sooner) and with the number of children at home, the latter perhaps reflecting the mother's difficulty in securing child care ($p < 0.01$). Importantly, less educated mothers also reported greater delay ($p < 0.01$).

In contrast to findings from other research (Kundi et al. 1993; Mull et al. 1994), in this study mothers who had prior experience caring for a child with pneumonia or who lived in extended families were not significantly more likely to bring their children to the hospital sooner than other mothers. Boys were not brought any earlier than girls and there was no significant correlation between length of delay and the severity of the child's illness on admission.

As the five case studies suggest, mothers and other family members had many good reasons for not coming to the Rawalpindi General Hospital as soon as they noticed the child was ill. Neighborhood practitioners were familiar and easily reached, and visiting them was usually much less costly than traveling to the hospital. Obtaining care for other children was a serious concern, especially since hospitalization might be needed. Men might have to take time off from their work to accompany the mother to the hospital and then to fetch food for the mother and medicines for the ill child.

Further, most of these children were being breastfed and we observed more than once that mothers were very embarrassed at having to nurse in a public setting, e.g. in the outpatient clinic where the diagnosis was made and where many male strangers were present. Kendall (1990) has described a related reluctance to bring illnesses from the private to the public sphere. Considering all of these deterrents, it is not surprising that many families delayed in the apparent hope that the odds were in their favor and the child would recover without needing to be taken to the hospital.

Why Come to Rawalpindi General Hospital?

The reason most commonly given for choosing this particular health care facility was that it was conveniently located either near the mother's home or near a bus route. Many women also said that they felt some personal tie to the hospital because a child had been born there, a relative had been successfully treated there, or a friend or family member was employed there (such employment included any job on the hospital grounds no matter how far removed from the delivery of medical care).

Some respondents stated that they had come to this particular hospital because they knew the charges at the outpatient clinic were minimal and they had used up most of their money going to private doctors. (A visit to the clinic costs only one rupee – less than a nickel in U.S. currency.) As suggested above, however, people knew that hospitalization was not cheap and many delayed coming to Rawalpindi General Hospital (or any other hospital) for precisely that reason.

Diagnostic and Prescribing Habits of Providers

Because a major goal of the study was to investigate whether practitioners could correctly diagnose and treat pneumonia, a large part of the interview was devoted to eliciting mothers' descriptions of what happened in the practitioners' offices. Figure 12.2 depicts mothers' recollections of the physical examinations performed by four different categories of providers.[6] As the white spaces indicate, data were occasionally missing because some mothers could not remember what had happened or had not been present during the visit.

Mothers reported that hospital-based doctors counted respirations 46% of the time, private office-based M.B.B.S. doctors 12% of the time, and chota doctors, homeopaths, and hakims never. If hospital-based doctors are broken down into Rawalpindi General Hospital doctors specially trained for the Center for Disease Control study and doctors from other hospitals (not shown in figure), it becomes clear that almost

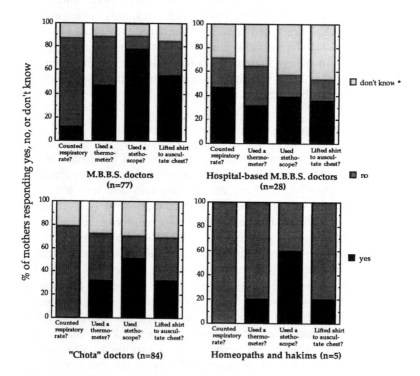

Figure 12.2 Comparison of physical exams performed by different provider types, as reported by mothers. M.B.B.S. doctor includes private M.B.B.S., government, and military doctors; Hospital-based doctor includes RGH and other hospital doctors; "chota" doctor includes dispenser/compounder, ?M.B.B.S., and "chota" doctor. *"Don't know" may mean mother did not notice or that she was not present when the child was examined.

all of those counting breathing rates were in the former group. As mentioned previously, an increased respiratory rate is the single best clinical sign of pneumonia as yet identified. Judging from mothers' reports, few other doctors knew how to take a respiratory rate or recognized its importance.

Most providers reportedly used stethoscopes, a powerful medical accoutrement in Pakistan (Mull and Mull 1994). Fewer, however, lifted the child's shirt, which is essential for accurate interpretation of chest sounds while listening with the stethoscope (a process known as auscultation). The hospital-based doctors were the least likely to use a stethoscope (the World Health Organization pneumonia protocol discourages it), but when they did they almost always lifted the shirt. In this way they were also able to look for chest indrawing and to observe the child's breathing more closely.

We attempted to validate the accuracy of mothers' reports in two ways. First, we asked them to describe the diagnostic practices of the Rawalpindi General Hospital physicians. Since we knew that these doctors were counting breaths and lifting shirts but avoiding the use of stethoscopes, we could get a rough idea of the mothers' reliability as observers by comparing their reports with what we knew to be the case. At least with respect to these particular physicians, they were very reliable – correct more than 90% of the time.

Second, as a further check we visited the offices of several allopathic practitioners near the hospital. All were fully trained M.B.B.S. physicians. Their "offices" were more like storefronts, typically consisting of one dimly lit room that was very sparsely furnished, usually with a compounder visible behind a screen in one corner. There were no examining tables or examining rooms and no facilities where people could disrobe.

In one such office, we saw patients waiting on benches until they were summoned to a chair next to the doctor's desk. We observed that he placed his stethoscope briefly on each patient's body in an essentially symbolic fashion without appearing to listen and without moving it around; in one case, he put it on top of the patient's head. Virtually no conversation took place, but after a minute or two he scribbled out something on a piece of paper and handed it to the patient, who then presented this "prescription" to the compounder to be filled. Doctors at Rawalpindi General Hospital reported that this practitioner and other physicians in the area frequently prescribed cortisone "to bring the fever down fast" in pneumonia and other ailments, a very dangerous practice since the drug reduces resistance to infection.

Thus, while second-hand accounts must always be interpreted with caution, we are inclined to accept mothers' reports that most physical examinations by local practitioners were inadequate. (See Mull and Mull 1994 for corroborative observations made in Karachi, another major city Pakistan.)

Medicines and Mothers' Attitudes Toward Them

Based on mothers' reports, the dispensing and prescribing habits of private office-based M.B.B.S. doctors were almost indistinguishable from those of chota doctors except that that chota doctors tended to dispense more medicines (Figure 12.3). More than half of both private M.B.B.S. and chota doctors gave injections, while hospital-based clinic doctors rarely did so. Hakims and homeopaths were more likely to dispense tablets than were chota doctors, who in turn outstripped licensed allopathic practitioners in this regard. Hospital-based doctors almost never prescribed or dispensed tablets.

The average cost of a visit to a chota doctor, including medicines, was 16 rupees as compared with an average of 23 rupees for a visit to a licensed private physician (Figure 12.4). Thus, visits to chota doctors were 30% less expensive than visits to office-based M.B.B.S. doctors. The highest cost of any visit was 100 rupees (U.S. $4), for a private physician. The traditional healers – the hakims and homeopaths – charged very little. The pir consulted by one family is not represented in the figures because he was treating a disposing condition, evil eye, rather than pneumonia itself, but in any case he charged nothing, simply accepting a donation for his services in traditional fashion.

Mothers' comments revealed a far greater interest in medicines and rapid cure than in the credentials of any given health care provider. The medicine in fact seemed to be the crucial part of the transaction between doctor and patient. The practitioner's reputation was essentially based on the medicines dispensed, and families usually allowed no more than a day or two for a medicine to work before consulting a new practitioner. In part because they changed health care providers so frequently, many families amassed a large number of bottles of different drugs, each containing a one- or at most a two-day supply. Figure 12.5 shows a not atypical collection left over from just one illness episode.

In keeping with previous reports (Mull and Mull 1994), we found that most providers dispensed only a one-day supply of medicines. Mothers said that this was partly because if the family was paying for the drugs, a one-day supply was all that could be afforded. If, on the

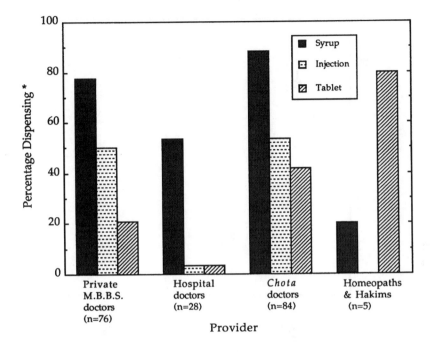

Figure 12.3 Comparison of syrups, tablets, and injections dispensed by different providers types, as reported by mothers.

other hand, the practitioner was including medication as part of the price of the consultation, he could keep down his own cost by dispensing only what would be used. Practitioners knew that most people would give the medicines for only a day or two. Mothers explained the reasons for this. If the medicine was not working, they said, why should we keep giving it? And if the medicine did work and the child was better, why continue? In other words, money was limited and people did not understand the importance of completing a full course of treatment (see Whyte 1992 and discussion below).

While mothers often did not know whether a health care provider was a specialist or a generalist, a licensed physician or a chota doctor, they could with few exceptions describe the medicine dispensed in exquisite detail (color, consistency in the case of a syrup, size in the case of a tablet, amount, and cost) in much the same way as they could

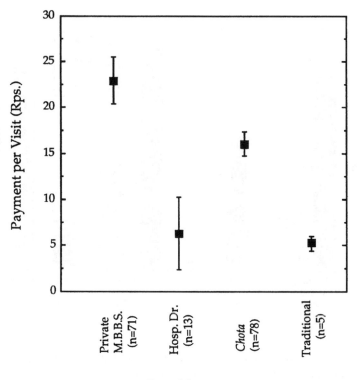

Figure 12.4   Comparison of mean cost ($+/-$ S.E.) of visit (in Rupees), including consult fee and medicines dispensed, by different provider type, as reported by mother.

describe recipes for home remedies. They almost never knew what these medicines actually were (e.g. an antibiotic, a fever medicine; they simply knew that they were "good for pneumonia" or "good for cough.") (See Dua, Kunin and White 1994:719 for similar findings among clients interviewed in pharmacies in India.)

In many cultures, it has been shown that the less educated tend to regard the form of the medicine as much more important than its content (Reeler 1990). However, the present study suggests that mothers have little choice but to focus on the appearance of medicines because they have been told nothing about them. Consultations with health care providers were usually very brief and conversation was limited.

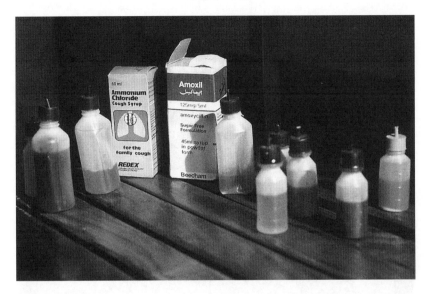

Figure 12.5 This is the collection of medicines that one family had accumulated while seeking treatment for one child with pneumonia. They had brought all of the medicines with them into the hospital.

In some cases there may even have been intentional mystification of the treatment process. For example, Figure 12.6 shows an encrypted prescription collected from a mother in Rawalpindi (not an informant in the present study) in January 1992. Instead of the medicines being named, codes are used that can be read only by the doctor's dispenser: "C + C_{111}" and so on. One of the medicines is clearly an injection, however, since the notation "Im" (intramuscular) appears.

Mothers were not asked specifically about injections, but four informants volunteered a strong desire for them. Among their comments were, "The child will not get well if the doctor does not give an injection," "Injections work faster," and "The child can be cured with an injection." There has been much discussion of the overuse of injections in the developing world, supposedly because patients demand them (Reeler 1990; Wyatt 1992). However, one study from Togo showed that although 69% of providers perceived that a mother would want an injection for her child, only 10% of mothers actually said that they did (Deming 1984). Whether the extensive use of injections documented in the present study (more than half of all doctors gave them) was actively desired by mothers is unclear, but

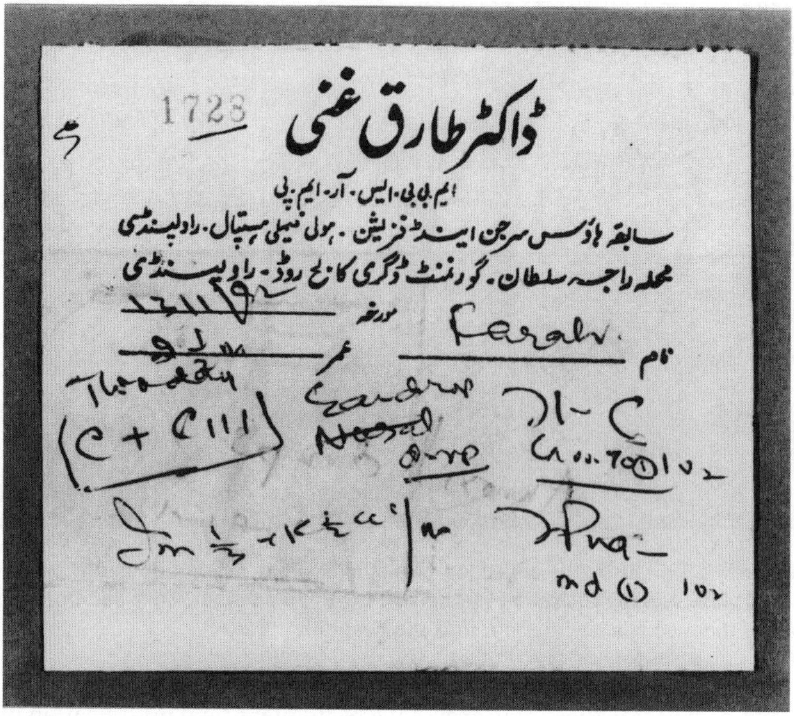

Figure 12.6   A coded prescription for injections and suspensions given by a licensed physician, Rawalpindi, Pakistan, 1992.

prior research conducted in the same hospital indicates that 40% of mothers did think they should be given for pneumonia "in order to cure it faster" (Kundi et al. 1993).

The panoply of medicines amassed during each illness episode is of great concern. For one thing, the poor may actually spend more than the rich on any given illness episode, i.e., scarce resources are wasted (Ali 1990). Further, it is certain that many of the tablets, syrups, and injections described and shown to us by mothers were antibiotics, since they are widely available in the developing world without prescription (Kunin et al. 1987; van der Geest 1987; Kunin et al. 1990). Multiple one-day dosing with different antibiotics courts bacterial resistance and could well lead to a future public health disaster in which certain strains of pneumonia would be difficult or impossible to cure. In fact, as noted above, resistance to antibiotics among certain respiratory pathogens has already been documented in Rawalpindi (Mastro et al. 1991). Unfortunately, we found little evidence that private practitioners – let alone mothers – had any understanding of this problem.

DISCUSSION

Like many people in other parts of the world, mothers interviewed in the present study believe that physical coldness causes pneumonia, and their home remedies – mainly designed to "warm" the child – follow from this belief. Their choice of practitioners shows that they view pneumonia as an illness requiring allopathic care. However, detailed histories elicited from mothers reveal that most of the practitioners consulted, both licensed and unlicensed, neither performed adequate diagnostic procedures nor dispensed medicines appropriately. Further, the data show that families almost never consulted community-based government doctors, so that an educational campaign aimed solely at training government doctors will almost certainly be insufficient. Moreover, it is doubtful that even government doctors' behavior will be easily altered.

A recent study carried out in Egypt (Langsten and Hill 1995) illustrates some of the problems involved. Mothers in 12 rural villages were questioned about health care providers' management of more than 2,000 episodes of respiratory infection. Both government clinic doctors and private practitioners were available in the area; in fact, the authors make the important point that almost all of the government doctors were in private practice after hours to supplement their incomes (this is also true in Pakistan).

Judging from mothers' reports about how different types of practitioners treated the children's respiratory infections, only about 58% of those infections were appropriately managed (Langsten and Hill 1995:176). More than half of the mild, uncomplicated coughs were treated with antibiotics while these drugs were not given to almost a quarter of the children with fast or difficult breathing, indicators of serious infection. (Mothers themselves classified the infections as "mild" or "severe" – a limitation of the research design.)

Halfway through the study, the Egypt Child Survival Program coincidentally provided the government physicians with a two-day didactic training course on the proper diagnosis and management of ARI. Despite this, there was only minimal improvement in the government physicians' treatment practices (slightly fewer coughs and colds

were treated with antibiotics), while the private physicians' performance actually worsened (i.e., more such cases were inappropriately
treated with antibiotics). The authors conclude that training alone is
unlikely to improve treatment very much, and that what is needed is
better supervision of doctors in government facilities and educational
campaigns aimed directly at mothers.

As important as this study is, it raises more questions than it
answers. Were the private physicians who gave more antibiotics the
same people as the government doctors who appropriately withheld
them? If so, why were their prescribing patterns so different in the two
venues? Were antibiotics withheld from the government facilities to
discourage their use? Could the doctors have pilfered such medicines
from the government facilities so that they could sell them to private
patients after hours?

Further, why did the training course have so little effect? Did the
government doctors not understand, or not want to understand, the
message, and in each case, why? Were mothers' demands responsible
for the increased inappropriate use of antibiotics in the private sector,
and if so, why did mothers want these drugs for their children with
uncomplicated coughs?

As the authors themselves note (Langsten and Hill 1955:179), they
have no data to answer these questions – to provide additional details
and especially to illuminate the reasons for these medically inappropriate behaviors. Here is where anthropological techniques of participant
observation and low-key inquiry could have helped. Anthropologists
are noted – some would say notorious – for incessantly asking "Why?"
and it is this perspective that is too often absent from even very solid
and important international health research. Clearly, we must know
what is currently done and the reasons for it before we can begin to
effect change, and this is as true of pneumonia management as it is of
anything else.

In the present chapter we have tried to elucidate the "what" and
have investigated the "why" as far as our resources allowed. We
conclude that while mothers' beliefs about the cause and proper
treatment of pneumonia are occasionally detrimental to health (unwill-
ingness to venture to the doctor on rainy days, opium use, tight
wrapping of the child's chest), most of the barriers to proper care are
not under their control.

Poverty, low status within the family, and lack of education all too
frequently lead women to delay seeking care outside the home, and
when they do seek such care, to rely on poorly trained health care

providers unable to diagnose and manage the disease properly. In fact, who could be surprised if mothers demand antibiotics for all cases of respiratory infection in a setting in which they cannot be sure of practitioners' diagnostic skills? The answer, then, seems to us to lie both broadly in the expansion of formal education for women and narrowly in mass-media educational campaigns targeting health care providers and mothers alike.

NOTES

1. There is certainly good reason to associate the hospital with death; records kept at the institution show, for example, that 10% of the children admitted to the pediatric ward in 1990 and 1991 died.

2. Some writers on ARI in Pakistan have suggested that such marked sex differentials probably reflect a greater cultural valuation of boys (Marsh et al. 1993:19). Of note, in a recent study carried out in India where the severity of the respiratory infection was controlled for, it was still found that boys with ARI received better and more costly medical care than girls (Ganatra and Hirve 1994). However, such privileging of boys was not supported by results of the present study. No more money was spent on boys' care than on girls' and boys were in fact brought to the hospital slightly later than girls, on average. Further, it must be remembered that young males have a greater biological susceptibility to pneumonia (Glezen and Denny 1973). For further discussion and a review of world literature, see Cody 1993.

3. Note that some of the categories in Table 12.1 do not accurately express the way mothers think about illness causation. For most people, for example, a "natural vs. supernatural" distinction is not meaningful. Thus, if evil eye is seen as different from cold air, it is not because it is viewed as supernatural but because it involves human rather than environmental agency. Further, at least one mother (Case 5) saw it in the same way as measles or the common cold in the sense that it could be a "predisposing condition" for pneumonia. Similarly, in this culture the phenomenon of a mother bathing after intercourse and then nursing a child would have pollution as well as hot–cold implications (cf. Mull 1991). Although we here use Western categories as a shortcut, maternal thinking about ARI causation is much more complex than the table indicates.

4. Our interpreter explained that many less educated Pakistanis believe that Westerners from cold countries do not fall ill as often as people from South Asia because they take fewer baths. She said that this idea has been passed down through generations of families since the 1800s, when the British in India were observed to bathe relatively infrequently by Indian standards (both Hinduism and Islam require ritual bathing).

5. No one questions the fact that cold weather promotes increased crowding, close contact between people, a greater chance for respiratory droplets to spread, and a consequent increase in the incidence of respiratory infections. However, there is indirect but difficult to disregard evidence that cold temperature in itself affects the natural history of respiratory infection in humans. Rodbard, Wachslicht-Rodbard, and Rodbard (1980) reviewed more than 200 papers and hypothesized that body temperature is a critical factor in determining host susceptibility and thus the natural history of disease, including infectious disease. These authors note that bacteria have temperature niches that make them more virulent in particular parts of the body, and that temperature can also affect host resistance by affecting the function of immune cells. Since viruses responsible for the common cold prefer cooler temperatures, an airway chilled by cold air might be more conducive to the growth of these pathogens.

6. In this figure, categories of practitioners shown in Figure 12.1 are conflated as follows: "private MBBS doctors" includes private MBBS doctors ($n = 73$), government doctors ($n = 2$), and military doctors ($n = 2$); "hospital-based MBBS doctors" includes hospital doctors ($n = 18$) and RGH doctors ($n = 10$); and "chota doctors" includes "private ?MBBS doctors" who may or may not have been licensed physicians but are assumed here to have been unlicensed ($n = 36$), chota doctors ($n = 23$), and dispensers/compounders ($n = 25$).

REFERENCES

Ali, R. 1990. Cure Now, Pay Later. Newsline 141–142. August–September.

Berman, P., C. Kendall, and K. Bhattacharyya. 1994. The Household Production of Health: Integrating Social Science Perspectives on Micro-Level Health Determinants. Social Science and Medicine 38(2):205–215.

Berman, S. and K. McIntosh. 1985. Selective Primary Health Care: Strategies for Control of Disease in the Developing World. Reviews of Infectious Disease 7(5):674–691.

Caldwell, J. C. 1979. Education as a Factor in Mortality Decline: An Examination of Nigerian Data. Population Studies 3:395–413.

Caldwell, J. C., P. H. Reddy, and P. Caldwell. 1983. The Social Component of Mortality Decline: An Investigation of South India Employing Alternative Methodologies. Population Studies 37(2):185–205.

Clark, L. 1993. Gender and Generation in Poor Women's Household Health Production Experiences. Medical Anthropology Quarterly 7(4):386–402.

Cody, S. H. 1993. Perceptions of Childhood Pneumonia in Pakistan: Health-Seeking Behaviors of Mothers of Hospitalized Children. M.D. Thesis, Yale University School of Medicine.

Deming, M. 1984. Foreign Trip Report (Togo). Evaluation and Research Division, International Health Project Office. Atlanta: Centers for Disease Control.

Doan, R. M. and L. Bisharat. 1990. Female Autonomy and Child Nutritional Status: The Extended-Family Residential Unit in Amman, Jordan. Social Science and Medicine 31:783–789.

Dua, V., C. M. Kunin, and L. V. White. 1994. The Use of Antimicrobial Drugs in Nagpur, India: A Window on Medical Care in a Developing Country. Social Science and Medicine 38(5):717–724.

Faisel, A., S. Shafi, and U. K. Mian. 1990. Study of Implementation and Utilization of Standard Treatment Guidelines for Acute Respiratory Infections and Blood in Stool in Sindh, Pakistan. Islamabad: Primary Health Care Project.

Federal Bureau of Statistics. 1986. Statistical Pocket Book of Pakistan. Karachi: Government of Pakistan.

Ganatra, B. and S. Hirve. 1994. Male Bias in Health Care Utilization for Under-Fives in a Rural Community in Western India. Bulletin of the World Health Organization 72(1):101–104.

Ghafoor, A., N. K. Nomani, Z. Ishaq, S. Z. Zaidi, F. Anwar, M. I. Burney, A. W. Qureshi, and S. A. Ahmad. 1990. Diagnoses of Acute Lower Respiratory Tract Infections in Children in Rawalpindi and Islamabad, Pakistan. Reviews of Infectious Diseases 12(8):S907–S914.

Glezen, W. P. and F. W. Denny. 1973. Epidemiology of Acute Lower Respiratory Disease in Children. The New England Journal of Medicine 288(10):498–505.

Gove, S. and V. Kumar. 1988. Simple Signs and Acute Respiratory Infections. Lancet 626–627. September 10.

Gove, S. and G. H. Pelto. 1994. Focused Ethnographic Studies in the WHO Programme for the Control of Acute Respiratory Infections. Medical Anthropology 15(4):409–424.

Government of Pakistan and UNICEF. 1988. Situation Analysis of Children and Women in Pakistan. Karachi: Elite Publishers Ltd.

Graham, N. M. 1990. The Epidemiology of Acute Respiratory Infections in Children and Adults: A Global Perspective. Epidemiologic Reviews 12:149–178.

Griffiths, M. 1990. How to Improve Child Well-Being? First, Improve Mothers' Self-Confidence. Development Communication Report 70:7–8,18.

Guldan, G. S., M. F. Zeitlin, A. S. Beiser, C. M. Super, S. N. Gershoff, and S. Datta. 1993. Maternal Education and Child Feeding Practices in Rural Bangladesh. Social Science and Medicine 36(7):925–935.

Hunte, P. A. and F. Sultana. 1992. Health-Seeking Behavior and the Meaning of Medications in Balochistan, Pakistan. Social Science and Medicine 34(12):1385–1397.

Janzen, J. M. 1978. The Quest for Therapy in Lower Zaire. Berkeley: University of California Press.

Kendall, C. 1990. Public Health and the Domestic Domain: Lessons from Anthropological Research on Diarrheal Diseases. *In* Anthropology and Primary Health Care. J. Coreil and J. D. Mull, eds. Pp. 173–195. Boulder, Colorado: Westview Press.

Khan, M. A., S. A. Qazi, G. N. Rehman, A. Bari, and D. S. Mull. 1992. ARI Concepts of Mothers in Punjabi Villages: A Community-Based Study. Presentation at the 11th Biennial International Conference of the Pakistan Paediatric Association, Karachi, February 4.

Khan, A. J., J. A. Khan, M. Akbar, and D. G. Addiss. 1990. Acute Respiratory Infections in Children: A Case Management Intervention in Abbottabad District, Pakistan. Bulletin of the World Health Organization 68:577–585.

Kundi, M. Z., M. Anjum, D. S. Mull, and J. D. Mull. 1993. Maternal Perceptions of Pneumonia and Pneumonia Signs in Pakistan. Social Science and Medicine 37:649–660.

Kunin, C. M., K. S. Johansen, A. M. Worning, and F. D. Daschner. 1990. Report of a Symposium on Use and Abuse of Antibiotics Worldwide. Reviews of Infectious Diseases 12(1):12–19.

Kunin, C. M., H. L. Lipton, T. Tupasi, T. Sacks, W. E. Scheckler, A. Jivani, A. Goic, R. R. Martin, R. L. Guerrant, and V. Thamlikitkul. 1987. Social, Behavioral and Practical Factors Affecting Antibiotic Use Worldwide: Report of Task Force 4. Reviews of Infectious Diseases 9(Supplement 3): S270–S285.

Langsten, R. and K. Hill. 1994. The Effect of Physician Training on Treatment of Respiratory Infections: Evidence from Rural Egypt. Health Transition Review 4:167–182.

Leowski, J. 1986. Mortality from Acute Respiratory Infections in Children Under 5 Years of Age: Global Estimates. World Health Statistics Quarterly 39:138–144.

Leventhal, J. M. 1982. Clinical Predictors of Pneumonia as a Guide to Ordering Chest Roentgenograms. Clinical Pediatrics 21(12):730–734.

Marsh, D. R., I. ul-Haq, A. F. Qureshi, Q. Noorani, and R. Noorali. 1993. Childhood Acute Respiratory Infection in Pakistan. Journal of the Pakistan Medical Association 43(1):14–20.

Mastro, T. D., A. Ghafoor, N. K. Nomani, Z. Ishaq, F. Anwar, D. M. Granoff, J. S. Spika, C. Thornsberry, and R. R. Facklam. 1991. Antimicrobial Resistance of Pneumococci in Children with Acute Lower Respiratory Tract Infection in Pakistan. Lancet 337:156–159.

Mull, D. S. 1991. Traditional Perceptions of Marasmus in Pakistan. Social Science and Medicine 32:175–191.

Mull, D. S. and J. D. Mull. 1994. Insights from Community-Based Research on Child Pneumonia in Pakistan. Medical Anthropology 15(4):335–352.

Mull, D. S., J. D. Mull, M. Z. M. Kundi, and M. Anjum. 1994. Mothers' Perceptions of Pneumonia in Their Own Children: A Controlled Study in Pakistan. Social Science and Medicine 38(7):973–987.

Myntti, C. 1993. Social Determinants of Child Health in Yemen. Social Science and Medicine 37(2):233–240.

National Institute of Population Studies. 1992. Pakistan Demographic and Health Survey 1990/1991. Islamabad: Demographic and Health Surveys, IRD/Macro International Inc.

Nations, M. K. 1986. Epidemiological Research on Infectious Disease: Quantitative Rigor or Rigormortis? Insights from Ethnomedicine. *In* Anthropology and Epidemiology: Interdisciplinary Approaches to the Study of Health and Disease. C. R. Janes, R. Stall, and S. M. Gifford, eds. Pp. 97–120. Dordrecht: D. Reidel.

Nichter, M. 1987. Cultural Dimensions of Hot, Cold, and Sema in Sinhalese Health Culture. Social Science and Medicine 25(4):377–387.

Nichter, M. 1993. Social Science Lessons from Diarrhea Research and Their Application to ARI. Human Organization 52(1):53–67.

Nichter, M. 1994. Introduction. Special Issue on Acute Respiratory Infection. Medical Anthropology 15(4):319–334.

Nichter, M. and M. Nichter. 1994. Acute Respiratory Illness: Popular Health Culture and Mother's Knowledge in the Philippines. Medical Anthropology 15(4):353–375.

Pio, A. 1986. Acute Respiratory Infections in Children in Developing Countries An International Point of View. Pediatric Infectious Disease 5(2):179–183.

Pool, R. 1987. Hot and Cold as an Explanatory Model: The Example of Bharuch District in Gujarat, India. Social Science and Medicine 25(4):389–399.

Ramalingaswami, V. 1989. Perspectives on Research and Diseases of the Tropics: An Asian View. Annals of the New York Academy of Sciences 569:25–35.

Reeler, A. V. 1990. Injections: A Fatal Attraction? Social Science and Medicine 31(10):1119–1125.

Ren, X. S. 1994. Infant and Child Survival in Shaanxi, China. Social Science and Medicine 38(4):609–621.

Rodbard, D., H. A. Wachslicht-Rodbard, and S. Rodbard. 1980. Temperature: A Critical Factor Determining Localization and Natural History of Infectious, Metabolic, and Immunological Diseases. Perspectives in Biology and Medicine (Spring):439–471.

Santow, G. 1995. Social Roles and Physical Health: The Case of Female Disadvantage in Poor Countries. Social Science and Medicine 40(2): 147–161.

Shann, F. 1988. Clinical Signs of Pneumonia in Children. Lancet:792–793. October 1.

Sharp, S. 1986. Folk Medicine Practices: Women as Keepers and Carriers of Knowledge. Women's Studies International Forum 9:243–249.

Stansfield, S. K. 1987. Acute Respiratory Infections in the Developing World: Strategies for Prevention, Treatment and Control. Pediatric Infectious Disease Journal 6(7):622–629.

Stewart, M. K., B. Parker, J. Chakraborty, and H. Begum. 1994. Acute Respiratory Infections (ARI) in Rural Bangladesh: Perceptions and Practices. Medical Anthropology 15(4):377–394.

Tupasi, T. E., N. V. Mangubat, E. S. Sunico, D. M. Magdangal, E. E. Navarro, Z. A. Leonor, S. Lupisan, F. Medalla, and M. G. Lucero. 1990. Malnutrition and Acute Respiratory Tract Infections in Filipino Children. Reviews of Infectious Diseases 12(8):S1047–S1054.

Tyrrell, D., I. Barrow, and J. Arthur. 1989. Local Hyperthermia Benefits Natural and Experimental Common Colds. British Medical Journal 298:1280–1283.

United States Agency for International Development. 1988. Project Paper No. 391–0496: Pakistan Child Survival. Washington.

van der Geest, S. 1987. Self-Care and the Informal Sale of Drugs in South Cameroon. Social Science and Medicine 16:2145–2153.

Whyte, S. R. 1992. Pharmaceuticals as Folk Medicine: Transformations in the Social Relations of Health Care in Uganda. Culture, Medicine and Psychiatry 16:163–186.

Wilder, C. S. 1963. Acute Respiratory Illnesses Reported to the U.S. National Health Survey During 1957 to 1962. American Review of Respiratory Diseases 88:521–630.

World Health Organization. 1984. A Program for Controlling Acute Respiratory Infections in Children: Memorandum from a WHO Meeting. Bulletin of the World Health Organization 62:47–58.

World Health Organization. 1990. Acute Respiratory Infections (ARI) Case Management Charts.

Wyatt, H. V. 1992. Mothers, Injections and Poliomyelitis. Social Science and Medicine 35(6):795–798.

Yurdakok, K., T. Yavuz, and C. E. Taylor. 1990. Swaddling and Acute Respiratory Infections. American Journal of Public Health 80(7):873–875.

Part Five

Political Economies

CHAPTER 13

"Prostitution," "Risk," and "Responsibility": Paradigms of AIDS Prevention and Women's Identities in Thika, Kenya

Karina Kielmann

Our background has made us think we should be Christians and see the women as immoral. But there was no prostitution before; we had polygamy [Kenyan health worker, January 1991].

A poster produced by the Kenyan Ministry of Health depicts a man following a shapely figure clad in a red mini dress and high heels. Against the backdrop of a city at night, only we can see the frontal view of the skeletal figure, the mask of Death, and a caption reading: "WHAT YOU SEE IS NOT WHAT YOU GET – AIDS KILLS."

The research on which this chapter is based was supported through an award from the Canadian Society for International Health as well as a travel grant from the Faculty of Graduate Studies, McGill University, in conjunction with the Social Sciences and Humanities Research Council (SSHRC). I also gratefully acknowledge the receipt of a McGill Major Fellowship for the year 1990–1991, which contributed to preparation of the project. Fieldwork in Thika, Kenya was undertaken with the approval of the Scientific Steering Committee, Kenya National AIDS Control Program and under the auspices of the Department of Community Health, University of Nairobi.

The poster was one of the first educational efforts undertaken by the Ministry of Health and the Red Cross in 1986 to inform the Kenyan public about AIDS. Two years later, the Kenyan National AIDS Control Program launched an impressive campaign including radio and television broadcasting of educational messages, distribution of printed educational materials, and lectures and seminars open to the public. At the same time, direct education and counseling activities were geared towards what were considered core groups[1] in the spread of the HIV-infection, specifically prostitutes.

From as early as 1983, an authoritative Western medical paradigm of "African AIDS" crystallized the identities of "prostitutes in Africa" by defining the female subjects of epidemiological studies primarily through their main risk attribute, namely promiscuous sexuality. This paradigm shaped public and media discourses on AIDS in Africa, and partly directed research and interventions which identified women as a locus of infection, and therefore the target population for health education and condom distribution activities in various sub-Saharan African countries, including Kenya (D'Costa et al. 1985; Katsivo and Muthami 1991; Kreiss et al. 1986; Piot et al. 1987; Plummer et al. 1983; Simonsen et al. 1990; Van de Perre et al. 1985).

One of the locations chosen was Thika, an industrial town located approximately fifty kilometers northeast of Nairobi. Between March and December 1989, a team of nine health workers, attached to Thika Hospital, was actively involved in educating and counseling 450 women who were contacted in bars, restaurants, and hair salons in town as well as in homes in the surrounding low-income residential areas. In addition to being administered a KAP (Knowledge, Attitudes, and Practices) survey evaluating prior knowledge of STDs and AIDS as well as sexual practices and any precautions adopted to prevent STDs, the women were individually counseled, provided with basic information about AIDS transmission, and given condoms as well as a "green card" to allow free and confidential access to a weekly STD clinic, especially set up for the purpose.

The representation of prostitutes in the medical discourse on AIDS in Africa fixed certain assumptions about the women's social and sexual identity, their risk status and their responsibility in AIDS prevention. These assumptions and their implications for the impact of an STD–AIDS prevention program in Thika, Kenya form the subject of this chapter. By contrasting the medical discourse with the lay meanings attributed to prostitution and risk by the women targeted through the program, I wish to critically highlight the very premises upon which the program was based. These include: (1) prostitutes in Thika form a readily identifiable group of women, homogeneous with respect to their social characteristics; (2) these women are at risk because of their sexual behavior; (3) by providing the women with information about AIDS and condoms, the program's intervention will lead to (a) greater awareness of risk and responsibility in prevention, and subsequently (b) a change in behavior and thus, a reduction in STD and HIV-infection among both the women and their sexual partners.

In challenging the paradigm of prostitution and AIDS which informs the Thika program, it is not my intention to deny or downplay the rates of STD and HIV-infection among the women in question, but rather to raise some questions concerning intervention guidelines. I shall argue that the efficacy of prevention programs aimed at changing behavior is limited as long as medical knowledge, with its fixed definitions of identity, behavior, risk and health, is imposed on lay populations for whom these categories fluctuate with the social context and subjective content of individual lives and self-perceptions.

METHODOLOGY

This chapter is based on fieldwork that I conducted in Thika from January to April 1991 with the participation and assistance of health workers involved in the STD–AIDS education program based at Thika Hospital, and a sample of 60 women who had been originally educated through the program.[2] During the initial month of fieldwork, I carried out semistructured interviews with the nine members of the education program who were actively involved in educational and counseling activities during March and December 1989. The questionnaire elicited information on personal motivations, interaction with the target group, ideas on the implementation of program objectives, and knowledge of the role of prostitution in the spread of STD–AIDS. All interviews were conducted in English.

The following three months were spent interviewing 60 women with the help of a semistructured questionnaire and two field assistants. Fifty-two of these women had been directly educated through the program while eight women claimed second-hand knowledge, derived through word-of-mouth from colleagues or friends educated directly. Women were interviewed at home ($n = 32$) and at places of work ($n = 28$) including bars, restaurants, clubs, hair salons, and one sweet factory in town.

The questionnaire used for the interviews elicited socioeconomic data including age, marital status, level of formal education, number and age of children, and place of origin. We also attempted to gain an understanding of how women perceived their health status by asking questions relating to illness experiences and patterns of resort for these during the past year. The women were further asked to describe their interaction with program members, their knowledge and ideas on STDs and AIDS and their perceptions of the program's impact. Additionally, life histories were elicited from three women in order to gain further insight into the socioeconomic and cultural context of women's identities in the community, and their experience of risk for STDs and AIDS. The interviews and life histories with the women were conducted mainly in Kiswahili or Kikamba, depending on their ethnic origin or on the common language established among those present. Some points should be made concerning my interaction and interviews with the 60 women. The sample was initially selected based on the time available, the average length of interviews, and the willingness of women to spare time to talk to us, rather than randomness. The data were drawn from the first 60 completed interviews of women who agreed to participate in the study and the interviews were fairly evenly distributed in 10 locations in and around Thika.[3] With respect to certain socioeconomic characteristics such as age, marital status, and educational level, the selected sample was representative of the 450 women who were originally educated through the program in 1989, at the same time, the criterion of representativeness was complicated by two factors. The extremely high job mobility of women, especially among those working in town bars and other establishments, made it difficult to find the women later. More fundamentally, though, the category of "prostitution" is in itself mobile, fluctuating with the women's movement within the informal sector of Thika, and their own changing perceptions of their social position and possibilities to earn a living.

I shall first give a brief account of the Thika STD–AIDS prevention program and examine the construction of a Western medical paradigm of prostitution and AIDS which led to the development of the program. The epidemiological paradigm and the assumptions it entails are contrasted with a portrait of the women targeted through the program, as well as through the meanings the women attach to their relationships with men, and their notions of risk and AIDS. The final section discusses the implications of these incongruities for an evaluation of the program's social impact.

FOUNDATIONS OF A MEDICAL ICON OF PROSTITUTION IN AFRICA

In Kenya, STD and AIDS education efforts with prostitutes derive in part from the extensive studies that have been carried out by a joint Canadian–Belgian–Kenyan medical research team in the settlement of Pumwani near Nairobi. The location was chosen as the site of an AIDS prevention and education scheme after initial research had been carried out on the incidence of sexually transmitted diseases among women of the community. The Pumwani program is widely quoted in the medical literature as being successful in demonstrating that the more intensively prostitutes are "followed," in other words, educated and treated for STDs, the greater the likelihood of their sexual partners using condoms, and subsequently, the lower their risk of infection. In fact, women who had been educated through the program and who reported that their partners used condoms were associated with a threefold reduction in risk of sero-conversion (Ngugi et al. 1988). These findings prompted the identification, in 1989, of outreach sites, including Thika, for the replication of the Pumwani health education and condom promotion activities.

The outreach programs in Thika and elsewhere in Kenya were established on the basis of conclusions drawn from the Pumwani data, which were widely represented in publicized discussions of AIDS and prostitution in Africa. Studies carried out since 1981 in the context of the Pumwani STD clinic maintained that prostitutes were the "most frequently named source contacts" of 57% of 300 men with *Haemophilus ducreyii* culture-positive chancroid attending the clinic (Plummer et al. 1983), were major "reservoirs" of STDs (D'Costa et al. 1985); were "sensitive indicators for the presence of HIV in Nairobi" (Kreiss et al. 1986:417); in short, a "high frequency STD transmitter core group" (Moses et al. 1991:407); and therefore the most logical and cost-effective target of behavioral interventions and control programs (Mann, Tarantola, and Netter 1992; Moses et al. 1991).

The Pumwani studies created a medical icon that was uncritically adopted in the media discourses on AIDS in Africa and as the guideline for prevention strategies. Tacitly assuming a Western definition of prostitution, the researchers of these studies lead one to believe that prostitutes in urban Kenya, indeed throughout Africa, constitute a homogeneous group with respect to their social identification with an explicit profession and status. At the same time, the terminology used effectively objectifies the women in question through bodily categories of risk and infection. They lack both identity and voice; their physicality is implicated through the presence of disease.

The extrapolation of the Pumwani data and the implications drawn for intervention priorities are problematic on a number of grounds. First, the women of Pumwani referred to do not form a homogeneous group, nor one that can be said to represent the rest of Kenya. As one of the oldest settlements of Nairobi, Pumwani was established in 1922 by the colonial government as a "Native Location." Its importance is documented in colonial records as "a first measure towards the controlling of native prostitution."[4] Pumwani also has a unique history of association with Tanzanian migrant women (Bujra 1975; White 1986). The historical background of the settlement is reflected in the predominantly non-Kenyan origin of the women said to be practicing prostitution in Pumwani, a fact pointed out by various researchers (Piot et al. 1987:1109; Simonsen et al. 1990:140).

Second, the first clinic for venereal diseases was set up in 1932, and may be seen as a forerunner of the present STD clinic. This suggests that Pumwani women have a history of exposure to institutional interventions. As members of a community founded as a measure of social control, they are acutely aware of their social status as prostitutes and their medical status as subjects of epidemiological studies dating back to 1981. While this background may constitute a factor that helps to account for the success of the education program in Pumwani, it is not one shared by women in the other outreach sites including Thika.

Third, within the literature on prostitution and AIDS in Kenya, different rates of STD and HIV infection are recorded for prostitutes from lower, middle, and upper socioeconomic strata. These categories are marked by differences in the average number of sexual partners, earnings, and clientele (D'Costa et al. 1985; Kreiss et al. 1986; Simonsen et al. 1990). Yet there is no evidence about differences in the social and economic possibilities open to the women, the types of relationships they have with men, with the community in general – including institutional authorities, or their general health status. These factors could have an important influence on the women's self-perceptions of being at risk for STDs and HIV infection, their access to, and use of, health care facilities and their response to health education interventions.

The epidemiological model of AIDS in this setting explicitly specifies the women's sexual activity as risk behavior for HIV infection. Among the lower-class prostitutes in the above mentioned studies, higher frequency of "sexual exposure," in particular to clients from areas of high infection, are linked to higher rates of STD infection (including vaginal discharge, genital ulcers and gonorrhea; see D'Costa et al. 1985) and an increase in the risk of HIV infection. Sixty-six percent of the 64 prostitutes were found to be HIV-positive as compared with "only" 31% of the 26 prostitutes of higher socioeconomic status (Kreiss et al. 1986).

While the rates of infection recorded are alarmingly high, the implicit claim that the women in these studies are vectors of the infection may be challenged. Female to male transmission of the virus remains significantly lower than vice versa (Cameron and Padian 1990:100; Padian 1988:416) and the Pumwani findings, as reinterpreted by Standing (1992), could just as well point toward an alternative risk group of men from Central African countries.[5] A review of medical literature on the role of prostitutes in the global spread of HIV infection points out that the cultural differences in the prevalence of prostitution, the willingness to report prostitute contact, and the heterogeneity in the prostitute population makes it difficult to evaluate cross-cultural data effectively (Padian 1988:414). Given the heterogeneity of both the prostitute and the client population even within the urban Kenyan setting, the evaluation of "risk groups" and "risk behavior" becomes less evident.

The priority ranking given to sexual activity as a behavioral risk factor and the focus on prostitutes as a core group have some important consequences for intervention guidelines. First, the focus on a research paradigm of sexual transmission limits efforts to explore alternative avenues of transmission of the HIV infection. Packard and Epstein (1991) and Minkin (1991) draw attention to the high levels of background infection, malnutrition, the use of unsterilized needles and other unsafe medical practices as neglected areas of research which may explain increased susceptibility to HIV infections among certain populations in Africa. These factors imply a structural shift in priorities, and clearly indicate the need to consider wider political and economic factors affecting the quality of general health and health care provision.

Second, an overemphasis on the role of prostitution in the spread of HIV infection coexists with a neglect in research on male transmission of the disease (De Bruyn 1992:251). In Kenya, research and intervention efforts geared toward men remain scarce, despite the indication that 75% of those who visit so-called prostitutes are married men (The Daily Nation 1989). Finally, the medical definition of female prostitutes as a "risk group" presupposes their social identification as "prostitutes." Interventions are based around the assumption that prostitutes, because of the nature of their relationship with men, have the control and the incentive to assume responsibility for prevention. The problem with this is that the label "prostitute," one of sexual identity,[6] not only constrains women's perceptions of being at risk for HIV infection, but also masks the very conditions that place them in an insecure social and economic position over which they have little control, and which render them vulnerable to STDs and HIV infection.

The problems in translating a medical paradigm into socially feasible guidelines for prevention are illustrated in the remainder of this chapter. My focus is on the women targeted through the Thika STD–AIDS education program. By providing a context for the women's position in Thika, their relationships with men, and their experiences of risk and disease, I wish to show how, and why, their medical status as a risk group has to be reconceptualized within the framework of social dimensions and in relation to other risks.

"THE BEER IS ALWAYS SWEETER WHEN SERVED BY WOMEN"[7]: A PROFILE OF THIKA BARWOMEN AND *CHANGA'A* SELLERS

Local Meanings of "Prostitution"

In attempting to understand the ambiguities in the meaning and context of "prostitution" in sub-Saharan Africa, in particular Kenya, I have found the political economy approach to prostitution more useful than cultural and demographic explanations of the phenomenon (Caldwell et al. 1989). Social historians including Hake (1972), Dawson (1988) and Hunt (1988) point to the legacy of political and economic structures inherited from the colonial economy and demand for labor in Kenya, notably the presence of migrant labor systems favoring a skewed sex ratio in industrial towns. Writing about the early history of Nairobi, Hake (1972:65) quotes colonial records as late as 1940 observing a ratio of one female to eight males. In conjunction with inadequate housing to accommodate families in the city, settlements like Pumwani, established by the colonial government as a native location in 1922, came to harbor primarily single men and women seeking their means of subsistence on the fringe of the economy.

While men tended to oscillate between rural home areas and Nairobi, the break with rural home areas was more definitive for women (Thadani 1978–9:72). Motives to leave home areas frequently involved situations which were not tolerated in the rural home setting, such as a woman's infertility, widowhood, or quarrels with her husband or family. With little education or training, the most lucrative means of subsistence for single women were limited to the illegal brewing and selling of maize beer, and participation in various forms of sexual relationships involving an exchange of "services" which varied in durability and the extent of commercialization (Nelson 1992).

The nearly exclusive female monopoly of these activities provided the women with some means to gain bargaining power and property. Independently organized, some women were able to gain an increasingly advantageous economic position and became active and integrated participants in the local community (Bujra 1975; White 1986). At the same time, these illicit activities actually served the colonial economy as tools for maintaining a cheap male labor force.

During the early post-colonial period, however, a public discourse critical of "de-Africanization" emerged in Kenya and other East African countries. The polarization of rural traditional, African and "good" values, as opposed to urban, Western, and corrupted values, was embodied in perceptions of the single woman in the city, who became a figure of public controversy over both visible transformations as the adoption of Western dress, cosmetics, and hairstyles as well as gradually changing sexual, marriage, and childbearing patterns (Van Amelsvoort 1976; Wipper 1972)..

The "prostitute" became a symbol, not necessarily linked to sexuality, of a wider discourse on "cultural prostitution" and its negative impact on women's "traditional" social status, and Kenyan society in general. This hypothesis is supported by the sparse ethnographic material on women during this period. Scobie (1960:51 in Thadani 1979:77), for example, suggests that many so-called prostitutes were women who had not been formally betrothed, in other words, for whom the traditional Kikuyu brideprice *ruracio* had not been paid. Further, Nelson (1979) maintains that women's casual and commercialized sexual relationships in Mathare Valley were not considered immoral per se, but because they tended to be separated from procreation for the patrilineage.

In urban Kenya today, in particular Nairobi, Ngugi (1988) confirms that for many single women, alcohol-brewing and various forms of independently organized partial prostitution coincide with unemployment, poor housing, and overcrowding in slum areas and squatter settlements. These women operate in an insecure and difficult environment, and as Nelson (1979, 1987) shows in the case of beer-brewers in Mathare Valley, they occupy an ambivalent position in the face of city authorities. Treated in a derogatory manner in public institutions such as hospitals, they are also subject to frequent raids by policemen and indirect harassment by politicians and clergy.

The changing position of women and the emergence of a local definition of "prostitution" is closely tied to modernization and urbanization in Kenya and the accompanying polarization of urban versus rural and modern versus traditional values. At the same time, the position and the perceptions of single women have also been influenced by the strong presence of Christian fundamentalism in Kenya. Early mission societies had a key role in undermining Kikuyu sexual morality and the position of women in the regulation of sex and reproduction. The phenomena of partial prostitution and "town wives," emerging in urban areas directly as a result of the colonial labor demands, were ironically regarded by the colonialists and missionaries as abhorrent African cultural practices.

In Kenya today, the appeal and popularity of Christian evangelism remains widespread. As I found among many of the female health workers I interviewed in Thika, religious affiliation was an important means of defining themselves and their relationships to the women participating in the program. Activities such as drinking, smoking, sexual promiscuity, polygyny, adultery, and ancestor worship were recast, especially for women, as sins to be atoned. Here, then, the identity of "prostitute" becomes one associated with the rejection of Christian morals, reinforcing the boundary between middle-class, married, and "saved"[8] women versus low-income, single, and not "saved" women.

The development of a local complex of meanings surrounding "prostitution" may thus be traced to historical and cultural changes in Kenya that directly altered women's positions in society and indirectly modified local perceptions of women. Urbanization, the development of periurban shanty towns, and the growth of the informal sector have contributed to the social and legal marginalization of single, low-income women in urban areas. Simultaneously, the introduction of Western values of modernity and religious fundamentalism have led to a conceptual and moral redefinition of gender roles, sexuality, and relationships between men and women.

In the following sections, I focus on single, low-income women involved, to varying degrees, in commercial sex work in Thika. I show that ambiguities in public perceptions of these women and their positions were brought into sharp relief through the Thika STD–AIDS prevention program. While a Western understanding of prostitution was not shared, nor necessarily linked to the risk of HIV by the women I interviewed, the majority of them were in a position of socioeconomic and legal marginality which in turn, negatively affected their health conditions and their envisaged control over personal health and welfare.

Prostitution in Thika

Thika is a densely populated industrial town in the heart of Kikuyu land, lying just off the main route to the Mount Kenya area. Its location, and the presence of many factories there, have favored a preponderance of single male workers as well as large numbers of truck, bus, and *matatu* (public taxi) drivers who frequently make the town a stopover on long-distance trips. As in many other sub-Saharan African towns, this situation has fostered the existence of various forms of quasi-commercialized sexual relationships, of which essentially three broad types are found in Thika.

A number of bars and so-called nightclubs in the town center employ women as barmaids, many of whom practice the most commercialized type of sexual relationships found in the area.[9] They develop short-term liaisons with men they meet in the bar and may spend the night with them in the attached lodging facilities, earning about 100 to 150 KSH (4 to 6 USD; exchange rate in January 1991) per night. While barmaids are bound to a tight working schedule, and have to answer to bar managers with respect to their working shifts and pay, their involvement in prostitution is more or less independently organized.

Independent organization is also characteristic of "unemployed" sex workers, who may merely use a particular bar or restaurant, which does not have lodging facilities, to attract customers and then move to a rented lodging elsewhere. As the client must pay for the accommodation, as well as the company of the women, these women tend to make less money.

Finally, a third type of quasi-commercialized relationship is practiced by women working in low-income residential areas who are frequently involved in the brewing and selling of *changa'a*, a local gin produced from millet husks. The alcohol is brewed along the river and sold wholesale to the women, who then resell it from their homes. Customers coming to drink at the homes of these women often become regular partners.

The characteristics of bar employment as opposed to informal sector activity in Thika may be shown by a consideration of the different settings, activities and relationships the women have with clients or customers as well as with the authorities. The majority of the women I interviewed in Thika fall into one or more of the above categories, with just over half of the women being "formally" employed. However, the coexistence of formal and informal sector employment may account for the extremely high spatial job mobility among women working in town, as confirmed in the present study.

Most bars and nightclubs in Thika town are relatively uniform in appearance. The external facade of the bar often distinguishes itself from the adjacent houses and shops through colorful walls and hand-painted signs and murals. The entrance, often a curtain rather than a door, opens to reveal a rather dark room with a bar counter and a few scattered tables and chairs. In some bars, a second door at the back of the room leads to an inner courtyard with a few more tables and chairs, and occasionally umbrellas. About half of the bars visited had attached lodging facilities, rooms sparsely furnished with one or two beds, sheets, a blanket, and a towel. A few bars with attached butcheries are famous for their *nyama choma*, meat roasted on an open grill in the courtyard.

A limited number of bars may be classified as more sophisticated than others and this is reflected in the appearance and behavior of the women employed in them. Unlike their colleagues working in other bars, or for that matter, low-income women in Thika generally, they are often dressed in Western-style clothing and wear hairpieces and wigs, closely parodying Kenyan middle-class women.[10] Additionally, many openly smoke and drink bottled beer, activities rarely seen among women outside of bars like these.

The women work irregular shifts, with the bulk of activity during the morning and from the late afternoon until around 11 pm. Morning activities consist of cleaning rooms, sweeping or washing the court-yards with water, preparation of food (meat stew, *irio* [a mixture of potatoes and vegetables], and *chapatis* [a flat, unleavened bread]), and loading the cases of empty beer and soft drink bottles from the previous night on to trucks. Afternoon and evening activities are divided between serving at the bar counter and waiting tables. It was my impression that as long as these duties were fulfilled, the women employed in a bar were free to drink and entertain male customers during working hours.

Whether employed or not, all of the women interviewed live in either low-income residential plots or shanty towns outside of Thika. This is the sphere where most informal sector activity takes place. The semisquatter settlement of Pole-Pole is composed of temporary, often makeshift, housing constructed from wood scraps and reinforced with mud. Women interviewed in this area live, in general, in self-constructed, one-room dwellings divided into a sleeping area and a kitchen area and housing up to five people, usually a single mother with her young children. Water is collected from a central pump and transported to homes in jerry cans. There are a small number of *dukas*, small informal shops, selling necessities including fruit, vegetables, milk, matches, tea, and cooking fat. Other services include a few tailors, a carpentry shop, and a bicycle repair man.

Most of the women working in low-income semisquatter areas like Pole-Pole make a living through informal means, such as the sale of changa'a, cooked food, or charcoal on their premises. In part, they are supported by the male customers with whom they have relationships. Women interviewed in this setting maintain that they had a number of "boyfriends" who provide for them by supporting household costs, protecting them, and sometimes acknowledging paternity of children by assisting the women with school fees and other costs. This form of support and attachment contrasts with the short-term relationships witnessed in bar settings, especially in the town of Thika.

Women who make a living through informal means based in their home areas confront a number of daily risks. At the time of the interviews, the land upon which Pole-Pole was constructed was being reallocated and the squatters faced imminent eviction. Additionally, because of the concentration of illicit activity in slum and squatter areas, women who live there face the threat of raids from the Municipal Council, police, or Kenya African National Union youthwinger patrols.[11]

During one of my visits to Pole-Pole, I found the entire area strangely empty and the dwellings locked from the outside. When I finally met with Wambui, one of my informants, I found her extremely distressed. She proceeded to tell me that the *askaris* (watchmen) had been making raids and many of the women were hiding in the tall grass and bushes so that they would not be caught red-handed with changa'a in their houses. At a later date, I met Wambui in town as she and a few other women were accompanying a friend who had been summoned to court due to possession of the liquor and subject to a fine of KSH 1800 (approximately 72 USD at the time). Others had been able to avoid the court fine, but were forced into paying bribes to the askari, many of whom came to drink regularly in the women's houses. Marjorie, an older informant, claimed she had been jailed over a hundred times since she began selling changa'a.

In some ways, then, women who are involved in informal sector activity appear to be at a greater socioeconomic disadvantage than women employed formally or semiformally in town who gain a higher and more secure form of income. The apparent security of formal employment is, however, less evident when we consider the relationships among the women themselves and between bar managers and their employees. Partly as a result of the risks they face and their living conditions, women in Thika's shanty towns have developed strong networks of solidarity to protect and assist each other in times of difficulty and financial need. This tends to be less the case among women who work in bars and nightclubs, possibly due to the high rate of mobility in employment. The reasons given for changing place of employment frequently revolve around the poor relationship among women working in the same bar and the relationship to the manager of the bar. Women who had recently changed their place of work complained of being overworked, of being accused of stealing from the cash box and of bar managers who paid the women irregularly.

This general description of "prostitution" in Thika shows that there are variations in the social relations and environments of the women interviewed. These can account for the different understandings of prostitution in this context, both from the point of view of the outsider, as well as that of the women themselves. At the same time, it is clear that the majority of the women share a socioeconomically disadvantaged status and an ambiguous relationship with institutional authorities. In the next section, I consider the effect of these shared characteristics on the health of the women interviewed in the study.

Socioeconomic and Medical Profile of Women Interviewed

The majority of the 60 women interviewed were under the age of 30, single, and had completed primary education. Nearly two-thirds (63%) of the women were between 21 and 30 years old. Both the health workers and the older women interviewed maintained that many women above 30 got married; or exclusively sold changa'a, or became hawkers, and thus did not rely on men to support them. The educational level of this age bracket is the highest among the women interviewed, and corresponds to the figures recorded for women in this district as a whole (Government of Kenya 1991). Compared to men of the same age, the women interviewed had relatively less education, partly because of their families' inability to pay school fees and associated costs, but also because of the lower value accorded to higher schooling by the families of the women. Informants left school at an early age in order to help their mothers at home, take care of their siblings, or to assist in family businesses, for example, brewing and selling alcohol, or selling produce from the *shamba*, the family home-garden.

The high number of single women (64%) closely reflects the pattern of population influx to Thika. Out of the 60 women interviewed, only 21 came from Thika. Twenty-eight women had migrated from areas less than 50 kilometers outside Thika, while 11 came from locations more than 50 kilometers outside Thika. The majority of the 39 women whose origin was outside Thika came on their own to seek employment ($n = 19$); because of disputes with their spouses ($n = 5$); or due to financial troubles ($n = 4$). Seven women had come to Thika accompanying their husbands or family or for concrete employment opportunities in Thika's numerous industries.

Two-thirds of the women (67%) had fewer than two children. The relatively large number of childless women includes women who experienced stillbirths and abortions, and may also indicate an unusually high level of sterility due to recurrent sexually transmitted infections, as will be discussed below. While infertility is a source of great anxiety and distress, those women with children struggle to meet extra costs and are often forced to leave their children with relatives or friends in the "reserves," rural home areas.

Health: Access, Knowledge, and Control

Information about the health status of the women was gained through discussions with the women, with program health educators, and with hospital staff. One of the indicators chosen to introduce a discussion of health issues was the number of hospital visits during the past year.[12] Over two-thirds of the women interviewed had been to the hospital at least once. The five main reasons expressed by the women for going to the hospital were the following: illness of children (most commonly diarrhea, pneumonia, malaria); reproductive health (fertility, childbirth, STDs); abdominal pains; malaria; and infected cuts and sores.

As revealed in women's accounts of their experiences of hospital visits, however, the true incidence of ill health is not reflected in hospital statistics. While more women than men went to the hospital,[13] it was more frequently for the health of their children. Because sexually related health problems carry considerable social stigma, women tended to avoid the government services available nearest to them for problems related to reproductive health (Raikes 1989; Maina-Ahlberg 1991). Many of the women I interviewed confirmed their preference for private treatment in the case of STDs for quick attention and privacy. They feared that government hospitals, in contrast, would ask them to disclose the names of their sexual partners or that information about their illness would be made public resulting in possibly being fired from their jobs. A number of my informants drew my assistants, experienced public health nurses, aside to ask for advice or medicine for symptoms such as burning sensations when urinating, vaginal discharge and stomach cramps. Njeri, an older woman from Pole-Pole, came to the hospital to find a cure for her infertility and was discouraged because she was told to bring her husband. Jane, another woman working in a bar outside of town, was in an advanced state of pregnancy and suffering from an STD when we first spoke to her. A week later, when we met up with her in another bar, she told us that she had lost the child.

Maternal and Child Health (MCH) and Family Planning (FP) clinics are underutilized because they fail to adequately meet the needs of women. This is due not only to technical obstacles including shortage of supplies and manpower, but also to the increasing medicalization of sex and reproduction. Traditional mechanisms of fertility control have been supplanted by Western models which have had a generally low impact in Kenya partly because they are poorly understood (Maina-Ahlberg 1991:9). The many queries addressed to us concerning STDs, pregnancy, family planning methods and their side effects reveal the health concerns of many women, and the insufficiency of knowledge which is provided to them.

At the same time, women's choice in reproductive matters is often limited by factors other than lack of access or knowledge, as illustrated in the case of Susan, a young woman who sought our advice. Having felt dizzy and nauseated for some time, Susan suspected that she was pregnant. Her boyfriend had not allowed her to take the pill, but upon hearing that she might be pregnant insisted on taking her to a clinic in Nairobi for an abortion. She was scared of having an abortion but could not return home with a baby as she would be ostracized by her family.

Other aspects of ill health which are either absent from hospital statistics or detected at a late stage include the effects of alcoholism, related malnutrition, self-neglect, as well as domestic violence. In the course of fieldwork, I was able to observe signs of long-term alcohol consumption and malnutrition particularly in women who were experienced changa'a brewers and sellers. In addition to the loss of control over health in connection with alcohol consumption, women claimed that when they drank with their customers, they were less likely to resist the advances of men, or to be cautious about with whom they slept. Some changa'a brewers commented on the violence experienced when they had refused to pay bribes to the local watchmen.

As suggested above, the loss of control over health must be seen in connection with changing social patterns which affect women's relationships with men. Migration patterns, for example, have had a significant impact on gender relations. In the postcolonial period, the increased numbers of women seeking work in urban areas independently had to adjust to changes in patrilineal structures, the extended family, and conventional marriage (Nelson 1992). The frequently negative impact of these changes is illustrated in the narrative of Grace Mugore, a 38-year-old woman who lives in the low-income residential area of Majengo. In order to pay for the monthly rent for two rooms (250 KSH each, roughly 10 USD) for herself and her three children, she sells changa'a. In addition to Kiswahili and Kikuyu, she has an impressive command of idiomatic English.

> I was born in 1953 in Majengo, the first of nine children. My father was a casual laborer for the Europeans, and my mother sold vegetables. I went to school until 1961, Standard 7 [age 12], then I was discouraged by my mother from continuing; she said 'if you can cook and wash, what else do you need? You'll be married and your husband will provide for you.' My three brothers following me were able to continue school. I left home at 18 and went to Kitui to work for Ushinde Photo Studios, stayed there for a year, married and moved with my husband to Garissa, where I worked in another studio as a shop assistant. In 1971, my first child, Moses, was born. In Garissa there were more women than men; the women were chasing men and my husband ran off with another woman. My husband and I quarreled a lot during this period and I decided to leave with the child. I then went to Tana River with Moses, and the husband stayed on in Garissa with Kennedy [second child, date of birth not given]. I stayed in Tana River until the death of the father of my children then had to go to court in order to fight for custody of the children (1975) whom the father's family were attempting to retain control over.

Grace won the court case and stayed in Tana River working at another photo studio. When she came back to Majengo, she moved into a rented house with another woman. Initially, her mother helped

her with food and other costs; later, she quarreled with her mother and
took on odd jobs which did not pay off. Her situation then became
quite desperate, since the children were growing up fast (she noted
ironically: "what fertilizer were they taking?") and she needed to pay
school fees. She became acquainted with a man who "kept me as a
mistress." After the birth of her last-born child in 1986, the father of
the child left:

> At that point, I started to drink heavily and I became quite violent
> towards the children. They refused to sleep in the same room as me. I
> myself refused to eat, I lost a lot of weight and became white-skinned.
> It was during this period that I also started to sell changa'a in order to
> survive. Some of the men who came to drink offered me money to play
> sex with them. There were two types of men – some stayed for the night
> if they appreciated the house and my company, and others were only
> there for 'shorts.' One day, I realized that my children were scared of me
> and that I could not do anything without alcohol. I asked my son to take
> me to the hospital to [clinical officer] whom I know very well. I was
> admitted to the Rehabilitation Centre for one week and was also tested
> for HIV infection during this period. Thank God I was found to be
> negative.

From this time on, Grace said she started to recover and to regain
strength. She also became "saved" and openly spoke of her conversion
to Christianity. My field assistant confirmed that Grace had put on
weight and looked much healthier than a year ago. Grace continued
to sell changa'a and told us that she had to bribe the askaris in order
to survive. She still drank, but said she could control it, and had also
become more "careful with men" because of her fear of AIDS.

By emphasizing the role of external constraints that place women
like Grace in a socially marginalized position, the narrative helps to
relate the concepts of risk, control, and social identity in the Thika
setting. The risk of HIV infection must be situated in the context of
other risks: poverty, violence, social isolation. Similarly, the category
"prostitution" should be placed within the context of social and
economic patterns which leave single, low-income mothers with few
choices over their and their children's personal welfare and health. In
contrast to what is assumed in the Western literature, the use of the
term "prostitute" in Kenya tells us much less about the sexual activity
of the women interviewed than it does about the ambiguous position
they occupy in local, Kenyan perceptions of single, urban women. Let
us now turn to the women's knowledge concerning AIDS and AIDS
prevention.

"A RISKY BUSINESS": HOW WOMEN IN THIKA SITUATE THEMSELVES IN THE DISCOURSE ON PROSTITUTION AND AIDS

Sources of Knowledge on AIDS in Thika

A triangulation of hospital records, health workers' observations, and women's narratives confirms that AIDS has a definite presence in Thika, in both actual numbers of cases and in people's conceptual frameworks. The Thika Hospital laboratory technician's reports covering a 7-month period of HIV surveillance among STD and antenatal cases indicated roughly 6% (46 out of 746) HIV positivity for this population. At this hospital, patients with AIDS are no longer the exception. The nurses and the clinical officer mentioned between 13 and 15 patients on the wards, approximately half of whom were in terminal phases of AIDS. These reported numbers acquired social meaning in the statements of the interviewed women, who closely associated AIDS cases with the hospital.

> One girl who was working with me at Community [bar] got sick and died at the hospital. People said it was AIDS because she was wasted and she had been a mobile girl. Her boyfriend ran away after giving her AIDS.

> I heard about a woman who went to the hospital for a blood transfusion. She became sick soon after and died. They did not even allow her own people to bury her.

> When he [a truck driver from Pole-Pole] was admitted to the hospital, people talked about him and went to see him one by one. They became suspicious of the girls working in the bars that he used to drink in. It seems his body was put in a polythene bag after he died at Kenyatta [Kenyatta National Hospital in Nairobi].

For women who recalled AIDS cases in their vicinity, the most disturbing aspects of the deaths were the isolation of the person from the community, the estranged burial, and the prospect of leaving motherless children behind. The extent to which these fears are shared, the specific targeting of women in the AIDS education program, and women's primary concern for their children are factors which contributed to substantial awareness about AIDS among women at the time of the study. In the view of one informant:

> Women are better informed about AIDS than men; they set the climate for fear. It is more of a public shame to the community to die of AIDS as a mother with children.

The Thika STD–AIDS education program was a systematic and comprehensive step to inform the women about AIDS. In order to determine its impact on the level of official information on STDs and AIDS among the 60 women, I asked the women the following general questions:

(1) Can you tell me what AIDS is?
(2) In what ways is AIDS different than STDs?
(3) How is the disease transmitted?
(4) Who is at risk for contracting the disease?
(5) How can the disease be prevented? (How can you protect yourself?)

Overall, the responses demonstrated a relatively high level of "factual" knowledge about AIDS transmission and prevention.[14] Reflecting the goals of the program, all women knew that the AIDS virus was transmitted sexually. In fact, nearly half of the women mentioned sexual transmission as the only mode of transmission. Likewise, all women mentioned condom use as a means of prevention, and over half additionally referred to reducing the number of sexual partners. All but two women knew that most STDs were identifiable and could be treated, whereas AIDS was not curable; many referred to it as a "killer disease." Although it was not altogether clear to women how the AIDS virus acted upon the body, most women mentioned "symptoms" of wasting, loss of appetite, mouth rashes, coughs, and the recognition that "even if you catch a common cold, you do not get better." Approximately one-third of the women suggested that you could be infected with AIDS, but appear healthy. In general, no distinction was made between HIV infection and AIDS.

Although a significant source of official information, the program was not necessarily uniform in its impact, either in terms of the women's response to the program or the actual information acquired. Before examining how women interpreted the formal knowledge they acquired through the program, let us briefly consider what the women's level of formally reproduced knowledge tells us about the program objectives.

It is clear from both the health workers' statements and the responses of the women to the above questions that the education program as well as information disseminated through the Kenya National AIDS Control program emphasized sexual transmission and prevention of sexual transmission of AIDS. What remains unexplained in both sets of responses, however, is the actual mechanism of the virus and its transmission through the exchange of bodily fluids. Thus, the women made the association between sexual activity and AIDS, but were not sure why sex was risky, nor what AIDS had to do with the number of sexual partners, or with condoms. Also, while condom usage was technically explained to the women by the health workers, the women were unclear as to *who* was being protected from the "disease" by the condom, and *how* using a condom lowered the risk of exposure to the virus.

In addition to these gaps in information, a wealth of informal knowledge affected the women's understanding of AIDS. In looking for the sources of informal knowledge on AIDS, we have to bear in mind that the program did not descend upon a void of information, but rather on ground fertile with speculations about AIDS. The majority of the women interviewed had heard about the disease before 1989, that is before the program activities commenced, most commonly through rumors and the radio. The contents of this initial information tended to revolve around the "symptoms" of people afflicted with AIDS, the modes of transmission, and the origins of AIDS:

> I first heard about AIDS on a Kikuyu station. They were saying it comes through sexual misbehavior like prostitution and creates divisions in the family.

> At the time they were saying that when whites brought the disease, they already knew the cure and would make money off it!

> I remember that the lorry drivers were saying that it had come from outside of Kenya; you could get it from a woman and only become sick and die after two years.

> Some people in the plot were claiming that AIDS was just a family planning con trick.

Much of this early, often inaccurate, information remained intact, despite the coexistence of formal knowledge about AIDS disseminated through the program. This is because informal communication, such as gossip, was and is a major channel for exchanging rumurs and reinterpreting "facts" on AIDS. Women's acquisition of formal knowledge about AIDS should therefore not be seen merely as a process whereby false or no information was replaced by accurate information, but a process involving choice and assimilation of fragments of information depending on their envisaged utility and meaning in a given social context.

Gossip revolving around the questions "what is AIDS?", "where does it come from?" and "who is at risk?" illustrated the role of informal knowledge about AIDS in creating and maintaining socially meaningful boundaries. Women perceived AIDS as a foreign "germ" which entered the human body through sexual contact or through the bloodstream and proceeded to "eat" the body, make it weak, make "fat people thin." Indeed, the extreme weight loss experienced by many AIDS patients was understood to be a "symptom" of the disease, thereby creating widespread suspicion toward anyone who displayed apparent weight loss. As one informant summarized:

> AIDS is talked about so much now that even if you lose weight, you can be suspected of having the disease; men openly reject women who have lost a lot of weight.

The idea that AIDS was a foreign germ was supported by the overwhelming belief that the disease was introduced into Kenya through the presence of *wasungus*, white foreigners:

> AIDS comes from wasungus who came in through the Mombasa port. When tourists come to visit, they have too much money and pay for sex with women and spread the killer disease.

These rumors were reinforced in women's narratives linking foreign and familiar elements:

> When my brother was at University, in Nairobi, he befriended a *musungu* [white foreigner] lady who had the AIDS virus. He also got sick...and died in 1988. They were saying he got AIDS because he went to the Kenya–Uganda border to trade – he was the manager of a large shamba – he had a girlfriend there.

> One of my relatives who sells secondhand clothing that comes from America was suspected of having AIDS.

The association of the disease with external sources also involved a delimitation of the local, familiar community, which had important implications for the women's perceptions of risk. While over half of the women knew that one way to prevent the risk of infection was to reduce their number of sexual partners, most of the above interpreted this precaution as avoiding men from outside the local area. This interpretation did not necessarily imply that men from outside were more likely to carry the virus, but that sexual trespassing of social boundaries was, in itself, a dangerous activity. Thus, in the case of Wambui, a young woman with a sickly and listless baby in Pole-Pole, it was rumored among other women in the settlement that the infant had AIDS because the semen of too many different men had "mixed," and was coming through the mother's milk.

The observation that sexual trespassing of social boundaries is risky was closely tied to the women's perceptions of their identity in the community. Women living and working in the low-income residential areas distinguished themselves from the women working in Thika bars, not only through appearance, but also in their mutual appraisals. The women who did not work in town saw themselves as unified through their socioeconomic vulnerability and the common risks they faced in their position on the fringe of Thika mainstream society and economy. They did not, however, identify their illicit means of coping as a possible source of social stigmatization or of risk to their health. On the other hand, social deviance and the risk of contracting AIDS were commonly connected to "real" prostitution, seen as more likely to take place in a context of anonymity:

> The prostitute is the one in a risky business! She has so many partners whom she does not know.

> Street girls who are unmarried are at risk; those who go out and sit on the streets waiting for any men to make money.

The divergences in self-perceptions of the women played a role in the women's perceptions of risk. It was interesting to find that the women's notions of risk did not necessarily correspond to my biomedical understanding of risk as a status somewhere between health and illness. Roughly a third of the women recalled that they had been surprised when informed through the health workers that they were considered a high risk group, and interpreted it as a moral rather than a medical judgement. It is important to situate this reaction within local perceptions of prostitution in Kenya, as discussed above. In the eyes of the Thika health workers, the women are at risk not only because they have multiple sexual partners, but because they occupy an ambiguous position on the fringe of society, failing to fit into either "traditional" or "modern" typecasting for Kenyan women.

Women working in bars tended to be aware of their status as a risk group, possibly due to the fact that many had undergone testing for HIV infection through a survey of bar personnel in selected towns in 1986. Some of these women noted changes in the public's, in particular, men's behavior toward them since awareness about AIDS had become widespread.

> Men have different attitudes now. They come to drink beer and go home – or they come with their girlfriends.

> Barmaids are hated because they are thought to spread disease. Anyone who is mobile is now called a prostitute.

On the other hand, the same women saw themselves as having an advantage over women working in slum areas because they were obliged to undergo regular medical check-ups (which do not include surveillance for STDs or HIV) by their employers.

Overall, however, the question of which population groups were particularly at risk for infection was most often met with the response that all sexually active single men and women could become infected. At the same time, women frequently commented, tongue-in-cheek, that married women were just as liable to become infected since they were often unaware of, yet equally vulnerable to the consequences of, their husbands' philandering. The irony of one informant's claim – that one way to prevent AIDS was to "stick to a married man as you can assume he will not move around as much" – reveals the perceived divergence between ideally expected behavior and actual behavior of married individuals. The underlying premise is a recognition of male promiscuity:[15]

> You have to pray that your man is not moving around, as you can't keep him in your pocket all day long!
>
> Men are not trustworthy!
>
> If he comes continuously, you can suspect he's not going elsewhere for satisfaction!

The explicit social division of male and female worlds, combined with conceptual boundaries including local : external, slum area : town, and married : single, provide a framework of meaning in which the sources and the risk of AIDS infection are understood by the women. Furthermore, I would argue that a coherent explanatory model of AIDS does not exist for the women I interviewed, for a number of reasons. First, as we have seen, the women share a fairly high degree of factual knowledge about AIDS transmission and prevention, yet the extent to which this knowledge makes sense, and is understood in terms of bodily processes, is much less apparent. This is not due to the women's lack of comprehension, but evidently to the type of information provided, which concentrates nearly exclusively on prevention guidelines. Second, AIDS is perceived as a "foreign," and a "new" disease, and there appears to be, understandably, some reluctance to attribute a local meaning or definition to it. Finally, the threat of AIDS is relative to many other risks that the interviewed women face in their lives, and occupies, possibly, a much less important position in the women's perceptions of health and illness than we are led to believe.

Having looked at how formal knowledge on AIDS is acquired and interpreted by the women, the question remains: Does the increased knowledge have an impact on decision making and behavioral choices in the women's everyday lives? It would appear that the extent to which knowledge on AIDS prevention can be put into practice is less a matter of knowledge, than one of women's perceived relationships with men, and their possibilities for subsistence as single, independent women. The feasibility of AIDS prevention guidelines can thus only be evaluated in the light of women's informal strategies and options in relationships with men, and in coping with situations perceived as risky.

Paradigms of Prevention and Women's Identities in Thika

The prevention guidelines promoted through the Thika education program included reducing the number of sexual partners, condom use, and control and early treatment of STDs. As I have suggested earlier, a number of premises underlie this model of AIDS education, including the assumption that the women targeted through the program could (and should) bear the responsibility for prevention of AIDS, because of the nature of the relationships they have with men. In concrete terms, this implies that women have the choice and control over the number of sexual partners, and the power to insist that the latter use condoms. Here, I maintain that the feasibility of realizing each of the above guidelines cannot be taken for granted precisely because of women's perceptions of control in relationships with men and in generally risky situations.

The shared assumption that men are more sexually mobile, and the often ambiguous position they occupy in the interviewed women's lives as lovers, customers, clients, as well as figures of authority and social control, contribute to a strong sense of female solidarity involving mutual support, protection, and exchange of knowledge. One mechanism of dealing with the ambivalent status of men is to exchange information about them. Especially for women employed in bars or those women who frequent bars to pick up men, sharing information about "new" as opposed to regular customers, keeping an eye on each other, and sometimes approaching men in pairs is a way of avoiding unwanted and risky situations. Similarly, women who work and live in the low-income areas have strong informal communication networks which involve, for example, warning each other of difficult customers and being on the look-out for police raids.

There are indications that women evaluate their position vis-a-vis men differently, according to their socioeconomic situation and to the type of relationships maintained. Women working in bars are more frequently involved in paid sexual encounters with men they do not know, which they refer to as being "kept by a man." On the other hand, women working in their homes often declared their marital status as "keeping a man." They perceive of themselves as being more in control of their relationships with men than are women who work in bars, partly because they can decide with whom to do business in their homes. As Wanjiko, a single mother who sells changa'a from her house in Pole-Pole, recalls:

> Before, we used to go to bars to catch men, and we would share a beer between three or four of us so that they could not throw us out. In those days, it was bad; we couldn't say no to an offer. Men kept us and often beat us. Now, I can choose which man to keep in my house!

On the other hand, the financial situation of women in low-income areas like Pole-Pole is more precarious than that of women employed in bars, and may constrain the choice of sexual partner. The same informant admitted that when she was drunk with changa'a, she became less discriminate about her "boyfriends" and would not let an opportunity to make 30 KSH (1.20 USD) go by.

The constraints to women's control over sexual relationships become evident when we consider the queries women had concerning STDs and AIDS, and their response to the question of condom use. Women saw themselves as having little powers to negotiate in sexual matters, and little control over their partners' movements with other women:

> If a man really wants you and has AIDS, how can you protect yourself?

> If you have a husband who moves around with many women, how can you convince him to use a condom?

> Does a female condom exist?

While all women had mentioned condom use as a means of reducing the risk of STD–AIDS infection, actual practice remained largely restricted to persuading men they did not know to use a condom. With "friends," and regular boyfriends, condom use was rare because of the men's mistrust and the association of condoms with prostitution and disease:

Men suspect you're sick if you offer them a condom.

If I asked my boyfriend to use a condom, he would accuse me of moving around with other men.

It is difficult to convince men; they ask if you have an STD and may become violent if you insist on them using a condom.

Some women resorted to indirect means in order to convince a man to use a condom:

When you try to get the man to use a condom, you should use the language of family planning rather than disease.

If a man looks like he won't understand, I tell him I have some strange symptoms and he has to protect himself if he wants me.

My somewhat naive suggestion that the women could speak to their partners about mutual protection, responsibility, and care was often met with incredulous laughter. One of the married informants commented:

For us, it is not possible to speak freely about such matters! We don't discuss sex like you people do... If I even suggested using a condom, my husband would accuse me of moving with other men.

The women also cited a number of other reasons condoms were unacceptable, or at best, disliked. These included lack of pleasure, the fear that the condom would get lost in the vagina during intercourse, and impracticality; a number of women who sold changa'a explained that when they got drunk, they became forgetful. Additionally, condoms are probably generally unpopular because they are unfamiliar; even as a contraceptive measure, they are not widely used in this area.

A further guideline set by the Thika program for the prevention of AIDS involves the early detection and treatment of STDs. Although few women knew that having genital lesions from other STDs increased the risk of transmission of the AIDS virus, most were familiar with symptoms and treatment of common STDs like syphilis and gonorrhea. Women pointed out, however, that men and women contracted STDs differently, and therefore had differential means of controlling them:

When a man gets an STD, his wife may take a long time before realizing that she has the infection;

A man will take three days, a woman three weeks to know they have gonorrhea.

Some of the women interviewed had developed informal means of "detecting" an infected partner, which ranged from examining the male genital area (strictly in bar encounters with unfamiliar partners) to speculations, on the basis of unusual behavior in the men:

> Women pass on information about men who are potentially sick; they sometimes make jokes about AIDS–STDs with the men to test their reaction.

and in bars:

> If a man is sick with an STD, you can instinctively tell by the high amount of money he is willing to pay and the facial expression.

Although the AIDS prevention program had installed a weekly confidential clinic for investigation and treatment of STDs, some women still feared that they would be asked to disclose their sexual partners, or that they would be looked down upon or abused verbally if they asked for condoms or pills. At the same time, the women explained that men who had contracted an STD were more likely to pay for private treatment to "hide their shame," and would only attend a government hospital "if they are very weak."

Women's reactions to the possibility of free testing for HIV infection were mixed. As previously mentioned, some women had undergone testing in 1986 and were bitter about the procedure as they had never been informed of their serological status. Nearly all of the women who had not been previously tested said they would not object to being tested if they suspected they were infected. Yet the majority saw no reason to voluntarily undergo a test if apparently healthy, as they foresaw both a psychological burden, as well as social stigma:

> People are scared of being tested. They don't want to be told they're dying if there is no cure – and they know they will be isolated and feared.

> If one was tested and found to be positive, you might die faster because of the psychological stress you live with, worrying about the future of your children.

> AIDS is a form of death like any other – I can die tomorrow in a matatu [public taxi] accident! Why should I know?

DISCUSSION: ANTHROPOLOGIES OF RISK AND RESPONSIBILITY

I have established that although the women I interviewed who were targeted through the Thika program display awareness, and a certain degree of knowledge about AIDS, they do not necessarily subscribe to the dominant medical model, nor to an identifiable, alternative cultural explanatory model of AIDS. Information about AIDS is derived from both informal and formal means, whereby one body of knowledge does not supplant the other. There are reasons the women interviewed do not necessarily translate the knowledge they acquire about AIDS into terms of personal risk, or responsibility. I argue that these reasons are likely to be located in a set of Western biomedical assumptions which inform the program in Thika, and indeed many AIDS education programs elsewhere.

First, the hopes for success of health education programs are often based on the conviction that scientific, that is medical knowledge, somehow transcends cultural knowledge and that medical definitions of health, illness and risk can stand on their own as absolute and universal indicators. Both health professionals as well as numerous social scientists who have become interested in AIDS prevention have tended to perpetuate predetermined and static categories of risk, risk behavior and risk group, while sociocultural context is presented as a constraint to full comprehension of the prevention guidelines.[16] As Watney (1991) points out, much previous research has largely accepted epidemiological models which reinforce the ideological categories of "prostitution," "homosexuality," and "drug abuse" as given because:

> academic methodology is *threatened* by what we learn from the study of the epidemic: that sexual and drug-using behaviors are not immutably fixed and stable within clearly defined and identifiable social groups; that the categories of sexual 'science' constitute a complex biopolitics which is perhaps the most fundamental level at which social life is managed, organized, and 'thought'; and that the meaning of 'sex' and sexual categories is not natural, but cultural [Watney 1991:9].

In contrast, although women in Thika are aware of AIDS as a "killer disease," this does not mean that AIDS is prioritized as a health risk. Indeed, the idea of risk, even in the context of AIDS, is socialized, rather than medicalized, and informal knowledge about AIDS reflects concerns with social boundaries of gender, social status, and community. When women in Thika share knowledge about AIDS, they draw on both official and informal sources. There are certain associations made about AIDS: a socially estranged death, its "foreignness," and its primarily sexual transmission. Thus, women who earn money in bars, who dress in Westernized, urbanized fashions, and who frequent men "they don't know" are seen as being at risk by other women who live and work in the shanty town. Yet, the women interviewed share various factors which render them vulnerable: poverty, social isolation, violence, but also dependency and insecurity in their relationships with men.

These observations, while tentative, contribute to a growing body of literature on the medical "anthropology of risk" (Douglas 1986; Frankenberg 1994; Glick Schiller et al. 1994). The empirical work that has been carried out to date points to the ambiguity in institutionally defined states of risk and suggests that epidemiological and medical concepts of risk need to be conceptually placed in relation to lay perceptions of risk that have their own terms of reference. Gifford (1986), for example, shows how epidemiological and clinical models of statistical risk for breast cancer differ substantially from women's personal experience of risk as a state of being. Similarly, Kaufert and O'Neil (1994), in discussing childbirth in northern Canada, contrast clinical conceptions of risk with Inuit women's subjective perceptions, which derive, they argue, from "Inuit assumptions about the general 'riskiness' of human existence" (1990:33).

Specifically with respect to perceptions of "risk" and "risk behavior" relating to HIV infection, anthropologists have indicated the importance of recognizing and understanding the distinction between medical and lay concepts of risk. Ankrah (1991) points out that Ugandan women perceive themselves being more susceptible to infection because of their lack of decision-making power in matters of sex and because of their husbands' multiple partners rather than from their own sexual behavior. Another carefully documented and important study from the United States looks at drug users' perceptions of AIDS risk in Massachusetts (Connors 1991).

The risk of contracting HIV is seen in relation to and ranked accordingly with other risks encountered in procuring, and using hard drugs. Ironically, activities considered risk behavior in the medical model, for example, sharing needles, are seen by some drug users as a means to avoid other risks.

Second, the translation of epidemiological findings into core and target groups creates and consolidates identities, indeed "communities," with little consideration for the heterogeneity in social characteristics of the individuals involved. While in Thika various forms of relationships between men and women are maintained as a means of security, the extent to which they are conceived of as "prostitution" by the women involved is open to question. Women *are* at risk, because of an overall poor health status, untreated STDs, and as they themselves emphasize in relation to their sexuality, *because they are women* and often "pay the price" for men's polygamous nature.

Third, the language of health education which derives from epidemiological findings is grounded in disease prevention and control. As such, it is often technical, sterile and divorced from the social reality of the populations it is intended to reach. At the same time, given that information about issues like family planning and AIDS prevention is often couched in terms of moral and social responsibility, there is much less emphasis on explanations of what is happening in individual bodies. Yet, for the women of Thika, to know, or not to know, how the contraceptive pill works on the body, what its side effects are, how HIV works, and why condoms can act as a barrier are clearly issues that render the question of control and responsibility over one's health problematic.

Finally, health education programs are based on the recognition that it is ultimately the individual who is responsible for, and in control of, his or her health, or risk status, a notion that assumes free choice over lifestyle, and the material and social conditions determining it.[17] Yet for women in Thika the question of choice and control over these conditions is highly arguable. The extent to which knowledge about AIDS prevention can be put into practice is less a question of responsibility, or of will, than one of envisaged options, most importantly, the ability to negotiate sexual relationships with men, and the access to, and appeal of health services provided for reproductive health issues.

When I asked the women what changes they wished for in their lives, many expressed the desire to change their social status, to: "find a good man"; "marry and settle down"; "set up a small duka, and be independent"; "have a child"; "cultivate my own shamba." One may hypothesize that the desire for social mobility and security needs to be fulfilled to some degree before health and responsibility over health can become feasible goals.

CONCLUSIONS

How can the information gained on the social context of prostitution and the risk of HIV infection for low-income women in Thika be incorporated in practical recommendations for this and other AIDS education programs? The experience of the Thika program suggests that anthropological insight can be integrated at all three levels of an AIDS education program, that is, the planning, the implementation, and the evaluation stages. Interventions are usually planned on the basis of epidemiological data drawn from selected population studies.

These data have to be situated in both their narrow context (who are the participants of the study?) and the broader context to which findings may be extrapolated (who are the study participants with respect to the general population?). Similarly, the risk factors under study have to be accorded a relative significance in relation to other co-risk factors (included and not included) in the study. In a consideration of risk factors, and especially in the planning of interventions which aim to modify risk behavior, we have to look at how a so-called target population evaluates risk, and risk behavior subjectively, and to what degree the concepts of "risk" and "health" are of subjective importance, if at all.

In Thika, the observations of health workers and women alike underline the necessity of developing a means to approach and educate men in the area of STD–AIDS prevention, rather than concentrating on a defined set of women. If, in fact, it is men who are, medically, transmitting HIV more "effectively" than women,[18] health education activities with men should ideally be paralleled by efforts to make condoms more widely available, more familiar, and more appealing to the public. Provided an adequate supply is ensured, this would involve their distribution in places other than the hospital and pharmacies, and a gradual incorporation of them in general educational messages to lessen the negative current associations.

In the implementation of programs, the generally prescriptive style of health education communications reinforces a relationship of active, dominant expert versus passive, dependent client (Farrant and Russell 1986). In practice, this can be avoided by diversifying not only the type of knowledge provided, but the channels and means of disseminating information. In Thika, while the hospital seemed the obvious choice as a base for a health education program, the study has shown that it is not necessarily the first choice for patients, or clients. If the hospital remains the last resort for treatment of STD and AIDS-related symptoms, its association with incurable diseases and death may hinder its potential as an AIDS education and prevention center. By widening the forum for education on AIDS and STD, and integrating information into already existing channels (schools, *barazas* [public meetings], church gatherings), population groups currently neglected by the educational activities could be more effectively reached.

The value of taking AIDS education out of the hospital and into the community has been demonstrated through the Thika program, notably through the appointment of group leaders for distribution of condoms, and to a lesser extent, passing on information about

STD–AIDS. The present study suggests that informal communication channels could be utilized to a far greater degree than they are currently. Among the women interviewed, there is no doubt that informal knowledge plays a far greater role in their lives than formal knowledge. This is related to women's poorer access to education, as well as their lower exposure to media communication, but also to the great importance of informal communication and solidarity among women who live in an overtly insecure environment.

The evaluation of health education programs is often seen in terms of the "measurement" of a defined end product: modifications in awareness, knowledge, or behaviors. In the case of the Thika program, a measurement of acquired knowledge and condom use among men would possibly lead to false conclusions, and in any case, be rather discouraging. It seems essential that evaluation be seen as a process, rather than an outcome. In this approach, the participation of both health workers and women in a two-way exchange of information could create a "buffer zone" around the formal information transmitted, in which the issues surrounding the limits to formal knowledge, and the constraints to putting knowledge into practice, could surface, and be taken into account.

There are socioeconomic and political factors beyond control of the women influencing the extent to which knowledge about AIDS prevention can be applied. For the women currently involved in commercialized sexual relationships, the alternatives to ensuring an income are scarce and fraught with other difficulties. While in recent years, employment in the urban informal sector has mushroomed, the measures to quell illicit and "unsightly" forms of deriving income have become increasingly oppressive. Squatter areas and shanty towns have been bulldozed, and the many individuals involved in informal sector activities harassed, their "businesses" confiscated or destroyed. With this recognition, it is imperative that single, low-income women are not further marginalized and inculpated through a medical allocation of risk and responsibility.

NOTES

1. Core groups are defined as: "segments of the population who are high frequency transmitters of STDs" (Mann et al. 1992:174).
2. All personal names and names of residential areas have been changed to ensure anonymity of the participants.

3. The catchment area around Thika included one semisquatter settlement, five low-income residential areas, the town center, the market area, a residential settlement built for workers in a tannery, and two bars along the main road out of Thika.

4. See Bujra (1975:87). The creation of a native reserve at a distance from the living areas of the Europeans was justified by the colonial authorities as a public health measure against the threat of syphilis to the European soldiers stationed in Nairobi.

5. "The study found that for the women, there was no correlation between HIV status and age, duration of prostitution or number of sexual encounters... It did, however, find a correlation with the extent of sexual exposure to men of different African nationalities, notably from Uganda and central Africa and with exposure to other STD (Standing 1992:477)."

6. The targeting of prostitutes has, for example, led women who occasionally engage in sexual relationships for pay to refrain from condom use in order to avoid being identified as prostitutes (De Bruyn 1992:231).

7. Kikuyu saying, as related to me by one of my field assistants in Thika.

8. The new Christian fundamentalists divide between those who are "born again" or "saved" and those who are not, but who offer the possibility of instant conversion through public testimony and proclamation of commitment to Jesus.

9. It should be noted that commercialized sexual relationships which come closest to a Western stereotype of prostitution developed primarily in Nairobi and Mombasa as a specific response to the high foreign presence, initially of soldiers, later of tourists in these cities. Women involved in these relationships are denoted by the Swahili term *malaya*, "prostitute."

10. In most other bars, women are dressed traditionally with a head kerchief and *khangas*, printed cloths.

11. League of young men affiliated to the dominant political party who have assumed patrolling functions.

12. Free governmental medical services in Kenya have been available since 1966.

13. Men prefer, and are more likely to be able to pay for, private clinics.

14. Other concurrent, although less direct, "formal" sources of knowledge on AIDS transmission and prevention include radio spots and printed materials disseminated through the Kenya National AIDS Control Programme. The impact of these sources on women remains relatively limited as they are geared towards an urban population literate in Kiswahili or English.

15. The term "promiscuity," as I use it, is equated with "polygamy," as used by some of the women interviewed, and without censure, the culturally licensed sexual involvement of men with multiple partners.

16. See Kinnell 1991; Larson 1989; Scrimshaw 1990; Ulin 1992.
17. See Farrant and Russell 1986; Rodmell and Watt 1986.
18. It is now generally accepted that male to female sexual transmission is more likely than vice versa, because of the different sensitivity of genital tissues, and possibility of abrasions in sexual intercourse.

REFERENCES

Ankrah, E. 1991. AIDS and the Social Side of Health. Social Science and Medicine 32(9):967–980.

Bujra, J. 1975. Women "Entrepreneurs" of Early Nairobi. Canadian Journal of African Studies 78(4):213–234.

Caldwell, J.C. et al. 1989. The Social Context of AIDS in Sub-Saharan Africa. Population and Development Review 15(2):185–233.

Cameron, D. and N. Padian. 1990. Sexual Transmission of HIV and the Epidemiology of Other Sexually Transmitted Diseases. AIDS 4(1):S99–S103.

Connors, M. 1991. Risk Perception, Risk Taking, and Risk Management among Intravenous Drug Users: Implications for AIDS Prevention. Social Science and Medicine 34(6):591–601.

The Daily Nation, Nairobi. 1989. December 12.

Dawson, M. 1988. AIDS in Africa: Historical Roots. *In* AIDS in Africa: The Social and Policy Impact. N. Miller and R. Rockwell, eds. Pp. 57–69. New York: The Edwin Mellor Press.

D'Costa, L. et al. 1985. Prostitutes are a Major Reservoir of Sexually Transmitted Diseases in Nairobi, Kenya. Sexually Transmitted Diseases June: 64–67.

De Bruyn, M. 1992. Women and AIDS in Developing Countries. Social Science and Medicine 34(3):249–262.

Douglas, M. 1986. Risk Acceptability According to the Social Sciences, London: Routledge and Kegan Paul.

Farrant, W. and J. Russell. 1986. The Politics of Health Information. London: Institute of Education.

Frankenberg, R. J. 1994. The Impact of HIV/AIDS on Concepts Relating to Risk and Culture within British Community Epidemiology: Candidates or Targets for Prevention. Social Science and Medicine 38(10):1325–1336.

Gifford, S. 1986. The Meaning of Lumps. *In* Anthropology and Epidemiology, C. Janes, R. Stall, and S. Gifford, eds. Pp. 213–246. Dordrecht: D.Reidel.

Glick Schiller, N. et al. 1994. Risky Business: The Cultural Construction of AIDS Risk Groups. Social Science and Medicine 38(10):1337–1347.

Government of Kenya. 1991. Population Census for Kiambu District.

Hake, A. 1972 African Metropolis: Nairobi's Self-Help City. London: Sussex University Press.

Hunt, C.W. 1988. Africa and AIDS: Dependent Development, Racism and Sexism. Monthly Review, February.

Katsivo, M. and L. Muthami. 1991. Social Characteristics and Sexual Behavior of Women at High Risk of HIV Infection in a Town in Central Province of Kenya. East African Medical Journal 68(1):34–38.

Kaufert, P. and J. O'Neil. 1994. Analysis of a Dialogue on Risks in Childbirth: Clinicians, Epidemiologists, and Inuit.

Kinnell, H. 1991. Prostitutes' Perceptions of Risk and Factors Related to Risk-taking. *In* AIDS: Responses, Interventions and Care. P. Aggleton, G. Hart and P. Davies, eds. Pp. 79–94. London, New York, Philadelphia: The Falmer Press.

Kreiss, J. et al. 1986. AIDS Virus Infection in Nairobi Prostitutes: Spread of the Epidemic to East Africa. New England Journal of Medicine 314: 414–418.

Larson, A. 1989. Social Context of Human Immunodeficiency Virus Transmission in Africa: Historical and Cultural Basis of East and Central African Sexual Relations. Review of Infectious Diseases 11(5):716–731.

Maina-Ahlberg, B. 1991. Women, Sexuality, and the Changing Social Order: The Impact of Government Policies on Reproductive Behavior in Kenya. Philadelphia, Reading: Gordon and Breach.

Mann, J., D. Tarantola, and T. Netter (eds.). 1992. The Global AIDS Policy Coalition. Cambridge, Massachusetts, London, U.K.: Harvard University Press.

Minkin, S. 1991. Iatrogenic AIDS: Unsafe Medical Practices and the HIV-epidemic. Social Science and Medicine 33(7):786–789.

Moses, S. et al. 1991. Controlling HIV in Africa: Effectiveness and Cost of an Intervention in a High-Frequency STD Transmitter Core Group. AIDS 5:407–411.

Nelson, N. 1979. Women Must Help Each Other: The Operation of Personal Networks among Buzaa Beer Brewers in Mathare Valley, Kenya. *In* Women United, Women Divided. P. Caplan and J. Bujra, eds. Pp. 77–98. Bloomington: Indiana University Press.

Nelson, N. 1987. "Selling her Kiosk": Kikuyu Notions of Sexuality and Sex for Sale in Mathare Valley, Kenya. *In* The Cultural Construction of Sexuality. P. Caplan, ed. Pp. 217–239. London and New York: Tavistock.

Nelson, N. 1992. The Women Who Left and Those Who Stayed Behind: Rural–Urban Migration in Central and Western Kenya. *In* Gender and Migration in Developing Countries. S. Chant, ed. London: Belhaven Press.

Ngugi, E. et al. 1988a. Health Outreach and Control of HIV-infection in Kenya. Journal of Acquired Immune Deficiency Syndromes 1(6):566–570.

Ngugi, E. et al. 1988b. Social, Cultural and Economic Aspects of Prostitution in Developing Countries. WHO consultation paper.

Packard, R. and P. Epstein. 1991. Epidemiologists, Social Scientists and the Structure of Medical Research on AIDS in Africa. Social Science and Medicine 33(7):771–794.

Padian, N. 1988. Editorial Review: Prostitute Women and AIDS; Epidemiology. AIDS 2:413–419.

Piot, P. et al. 1987. Retrospective Sereoepidemiology of AIDS Virus Infection in Nairobi Populations. Journal of Infectious Diseases 155(6):1108–1112.

Plummer, F. et al. 1983. Epidemiology of Chancroid and Haemophilus Ducreyi in Nairobi, Kenya. The Lancet (December 3):1293–1295.

Raikes, A. 1989. Women's Health in East Africa. Social Science and Medicine 28(5):447–459.

Rodmell, S. and A. Watt (eds.). 1986. Politics of Health Education: Raising the Issues. London: Routledge and Kegan Paul.

Scrimshaw, S. 1990. HIV/AIDS Rapid Assessment Procedures: Rapid Anthropological Approaches for Studying AIDS-related Beliefs, Attitudes, and Behavior. World Health Organization: Global Program on AIDS.

Simonsen, et al. 1990. HIV Infection among Lower Socioeconomic Strata Prostitutes in Nairobi. AIDS 4:139–144.

Standing, H. 1992. AIDS: Conceptual and Methodological Issues in Researching Sexual Behavior in Sub-saharan Africa. Social Science and Medicine 34(5):475–483.

Thadani, V. 1979. Women in Nairobi: The Paradox of Urban "Progress." African Urban Studies 3:67–83.

Ulin, P. 1992. African Women and AIDS: Negotiating Behavioral Change. Social Science and Medicine 34(1):63–73.

Van Amelsvoort, V. 1976. Medical Anthropology in African Newspapers. Oosterhout, Holland: Anthropological Publications.

Van de Perre, P. et al. 1985. Female Prostitutes: A Risk Group for Infection with Human T-cell Lymphotropic Virus Type III. The Lancet (July 14):524–526.

Watney, S. 1991. AIDS: The Second Decade: "Risk," Research and Modernity. *In* AIDS: Responses, Interventions and Care. P. Aggleton, G. Hart and P. Davies, eds. Pp. 1–18. London, New York, Philadelphia: The Falmer Press.

White, L. 1986. Prostitution, Identity, and Class Consciousness in Nairobi During World War II. Signs: Journal of Women in Culture and Society 11(21):225–273.

Wipper, A. 1972. African Women, Fashion and Scapegoating. Canadian Journal of African Studies 6(2):329–349.

CHAPTER 14

Ethnography, Social Analysis, and the Prevention of Sexually Transmitted HIV Infection Among Poor Women in Haiti

Paul Farmer

Social scientists and physicians alike have long known that the socioeconomically disadvantaged have higher rates of disease than do those not hampered by such constraints. But by what mechanisms and processes might social factors be transformed into personal risk? How do forces as disparate as sexism, poverty, and political violence become embodied as individual pathology? These and related questions are key not only to medical anthropology, but to social theory in general.

These questions are posed acutely in considering HIV infection, as AIDS may soon become the leading cause of young adult deaths

Especially warm thanks to the World AIDS Foundation, which supported UCAP, and also to FPIA, which supports our work with women's groups in central Haiti. Editorial suggestions, in one form or another, have been garnered from Marcia Inhorn, Haun Saussy, Jim Yong Kim, and from the members of the Group d'Etude sur Sida et la Classe Paysanne, especially Maxi Raymonville. For Clinical and laboratory work, I am indebted to Simon Robin, Therese and Poteau Joseph, and all the members of Proje Sante Fanm. Special thanks to Didi Bertrand, who helped transcribe the interviews cited here, to Marie-Flore Chipps, and to the participants in the IHSJ seminar, "Women, Poverty, and AIDS." This essay is offered in memory of Marie-Andree Louihis.

throughout the world. As HIV advances, it is becoming clear that, in spite of a great deal of epidemiological and ethnographic research, we do not yet understand risk and how it is structured. Who is likely to become infected with HIV? Recent trends in the pandemic should undermine the falsely reassuring – and inappropriately stigmatizing – notion of discrete "risk groups" to be identified by epidemiologists.

Increasing incidence of HIV disease among women is a case in point. In a sobering report, the United Nations (1992) observed that, "for most women, the major risk factor for HIV infection is being married. Each day a further three thousand women become infected, and five hundred infected women die. Most are between 15 and 35 years old."

It is not marriage, however, that places women at risk. Throughout the world, most women with HIV infection are living in poverty. The study of the dynamics of HIV infection among poor women affords a means of examining the complex relationships between power, gender, and sexuality. To rephrase the above questions: How, precisely, do social forces (such as poverty, sexism and other forms of discrimination) translate into risk for infection with HIV?

Although many observers would agree that forces such as these are the strongest enhancers of risk for infection, this subject has been neglected in both the biomedical and anthropological literature on HIV disease to the benefit of a narrowly behavioral and individualistic conception of "risk."[1] Take, for example, Ellerbrock and colleagues' investigation of heterosexually transmitted HIV infection in "rural" Florida. The study revealed that fully 5.1 % of 1082 women attending a public prenatal clinic in rural Florida have antibodies to HIV. What "risk factors" might account for such high rates of infection? Ellerbrock et al. reported a statistically significant association between HIV infection and having used crack cocaine, having had more than five sexual partners in a lifetime, or more than two sexual partners per year of sexual activity. Also associated with seropositivity to HIV were histories of exchanging sex for money or for drugs or of having had sexual intercourse with a "high-risk partner." The study concludes that, "in communities with a high seroprevalence of HIV, like this Florida community, a sizeable proportion of all women of reproductive age are at risk for infection through heterosexual transmission" (Ellerbrock et al. 1992:1708). The paper's title announces that this community is a "rural" one.

It may be argued that these are not, in fact, the most significant conclusions to be drawn from such a study. In settings with an even higher seroprevalence of HIV, such as New York City, it is now clear that not all women of reproductive age are at increased risk for HIV infection: poor women, who are usually women of color, are the ones at high risk. But nowhere in this article does the word "poverty" appear, even though the authors mention that over 90 % of the women who knew their incomes belonged to households earning less than $ 10,000 per year. Nowhere in the article do we see the words "racism," even though in Florida, as elsewhere, African-American and Hispanic communities bear the brunt of the epidemic. The terms "sexism," "despair," and "powerlessness" are also absent from the discussion. And yet one might as easily conclude by arguing that, in Palm Beach County – a district more notable for its harsh juxtaposition of extreme wealth and poverty than for its "rurality" – women who are "at risk" of attending a public prenatal clinic are statistically at higher risk of acquiring HIV; these are mostly unemployed women of color who are more likely to have unstable sexual unions or to exchange sex for drugs or money.

How representative of the biomedical literature is the above paper, which was published in the *New England Journal of Medicine*? "To date," note Krieger and co-workers (1993:86) in an important review of the epidemiological literature, "only a small fraction of epidemiological research in the United States has investigated the effects of racism on health." They report a similar dearth of attention to the effects of sexism and class differences; non-existent are those studies that examine the conjoint influence of these social forces.[2] Navarro (1990:1240), noting growing class differentials in mortality rates in the United States, was able to deplore "a deafening silence on this topic." In an even more recent review of changes in mortality rates, Marmot (1994:197) observes wryly that such trends are "of much interest to demographers but, judging by papers in the major medical journals, of little interest to doctors."

Why might this be so? Granted, canonical issues are pertinent in explaining this silence: Most epidemiological and biomedical journals do not consider racism, sexism, and class differentials to be subjects of polite discussion. But significant theoretical and methodological difficulties also impede investigation of these issues (as does, perhaps, a sense of helplessness about the practical implications of careful examination of such issues). Some of these difficulties are perennial: how broadly must the net be cast if we are to capture both the large-scale forces structuring risk and the precise mechanisms by which these forces affect the lives of individuals?

A nascent anthropology of infectious disease suggests that the net must be cast widely. In a recent review of this subject, Inhorn and

Brown (1990:98–99) argue that "any anthropological study that hopes to shed light on the etiology and transmission of infectious disease must ultimately adopt both a macrosociological perspective... and a micro-sociological perspective." A decade of research on AIDS among the Haitian poor has led me to agree, and to argue for a "responsible materialist" approach to a disease that has run along the fault lines of an international order linking "remote" Haitian villages to, say, cities in the United States (Farmer 1992).

Many issues of individual agency are illuminated only by examining the gritty details of biography; life stories must be embedded in ethnography if their representativeness is to be understood. These local understandings are to be embedded, in turn, in the larger-scale historical system of which the fieldwork site is a part.[3] This approach must thus be geographically broad and historically deep, and must include critical rereadings of relevant data from epidemiology, history, and political economy. Only through such a broad approach will the role of "structural violence" – the degree to which a society (itself a problematic concept, as we shall see) is characterized by economic inequity, say, or sexism and racism – come into view.[4] I would like to examine the relationship between poverty, gender, and HIV disease by presenting data from Haiti, which currently serves, sadly, as a natural laboratory for the ill-effects of poverty and oppression on the health of a population. In keeping with the views detailed above, I present these data by telling one woman's story, and then continue by discussing first a study of HIV infection among poor women from rural Haiti and, second, an intervention that attempts to incorporate the results of this and other research in efforts to prevent AIDS. In so doing, one moves from biography to the structual violence that to no small extent shapes biography by constraining options available to women living in poverty.

HIV, GENDER, POVERTY: GUYLENE'S STORY

Guylene Adrien[5] was born in Bois Joli, a dusty village in the middle of Haiti's infertile central plateau. Like other families in the region, the Adriens fed their children by working a small plot of land and selling produce in regional markets. Like other families, the Adriens were poor. Guylene was the third of four children, a small family by Haitian standards. It was to become smaller still: Guylene's younger sister died in adolescence of cerebral malaria. Guylene's oldest sister, embittered by the loss of all four of her children, eventually left for the Dominican

Republic, where she works as a servant. Guylene's other sister, the mother of two, lives with her own mother; together they work the family plot of land for ever-diminishing returns.

Guylene recounts her own conjugal history in the sad voice reserved for retrospection. When she was a teenager – "perhaps 14 or 15" – a family acquaintance, Occident Dorzin, took to dropping by to visit. A fairly successful peasant farmer, Dorzin had two or three small plots of land in the area. In the course of these visits, he made it clear to Guylene that he was attracted to her. "But he was already married, and I was a child. When he placed his hand on my arm, I slapped him and swore at him and hid in the garden."

Dorzin was not so easily dissuaded, and in short order approached Guylene's father to ask for her hand, not in marriage, but in *plasaj* (a potentially stable sexual union widespread in rural Haiti).[6] Before she was 16, Guylene moved, with a man 20 years her senior, to a village about an hour away from her parents. She was soon pregnant. Occident's wife, who was significantly older than Guylene, was not at all pleased, and friction between the two women eventually led to dissolution of the newer union. In the interim, however, Guylene gave birth to two children, a girl and then a boy.

After the break with Dorzin, Guylene and her nursing son returned to her parent's house. She remained in Bois Joli for five months, passing through the village of Do Kay on her way to the market in Domond or to visit her daughter, who remained in Occident's care. It was in these travels that she met a young man named Osner, who worked intermittently in the city as a laborer or a mechanic. One day he simply struck up a conversation with Guylene as she visited a friend in Do Kay. "Less than a month later," she recalled, "Osner sent his father to speak to my father. My father was in agreement." Leaving her toddler son in her parents' household, Guylene set off to try conjugal life a second time, this time in Do Kay.

The subsequent months were difficult ones. Guylene's father died later that year, and her son, cared for largely by her sister, was often ill. Guylene was already pregnant with her third child, and she and Osner lacked almost everything that might have made their new life together easier. Osner did not have steady work in the countryside. After the baby was born, in 1985, they decided to move to the city: Osner would find work as a mechanic, and Guylene would become involved in commerce. Failing that, she could always work as a maid. In the interim, Osner's mother would care for the baby, as Do Kay was felt to be safer for an infant than Port-au-Prince.

Osner and Guylene spent almost three years in the city. These were
hardscrabble times. Political violence was resurgent, especially in the
slum areas. The couple was often short of work: he worked in a garage;
she split her time between jobs as a maid and selling fried food on the
wharf in Cite Soleil, a notorious slum north of the capital. Guylene
much preferred the latter:

> Whenever I had a little money, I worked for myself selling, trying to
> make [her capital] last as long as I could. When we were broke I worked
> in ladies' houses... If the work is good, and they pay you well, or the
> person is not too bad...you might stay there as long as six or seven
> months. But if the person treats you poorly, you won't even stay a
> month. Perhaps you only go for a single day and then you quit.

When asked what she mean by decent pay, Guylene stated that the
equivalent of $20 a month was passable, as long as you were able to
eat at work.

In 1987, three "unhappy occurrences" came to pass in quick succes-
sion. A neighbor was shot, fatally, during one of the military's regular
nighttime incursions into the slum; bullets pierced their own thin walls,
too. A few weeks later, Guylene received word that her son had died
"abruptly." And, finally, Osner became gravely ill. It started, Guylene
recalled, with weight loss and a persistent cough. He returned to Do
Kay a number of times in the course of his illness. In a young man
returning from Port-au-Prince with tuberculosis, it was routine practice, in the Do Kay clinic, to consider HIV infection in the differential
diagnosis, and it was suggested as a possibility at that time. Osner
reported a lifetime total of seven sexual partners, including Guylene.
With one exception, each of these unions had been monogamous, if
short-lived, and four of them were with women from urban Haiti.

When he did not respond, except transiently, to biomedical interventions, many of the villagers also began to raise the possibility of
sida, as AIDS is termed in Haiti. At his death in September 1988, it
was widely believed, in the Kay area, that he had died from the new
disease; his physicians concurred. Guylene subsequently returned to
Bois Joli, to a cousin's house. She tried selling produce in local markets,
but could not even support herself, much less the child she had left in
the care of Osner's mother. She was somewhat humiliated, she said, by
having to ask Osner's mother for financial assistance, even though she
informed her that she was pregnant with Osner's child.

Finally, a full year after Osner's death, the fetus "frozen in her
womb" began to develop.[7] It was, she insisted, Osner's baby (however,

a man from her hometown of Bois Joli was identified by one of my co-workers as the child's father). She had the baby, a girl, in November of 1989. Osner's mother always referred to the child as her grand-daughter.

A month after her confinement, Guylene returned to Bois Joli with the baby. The young widow was unemployed; her mother and sister were barely making ends meet. Guylene and others in the household were often hungry at this time. Feeling as if she were a burden, Guylene finally went to the coastal town of Saint-Marc, where she had cousins. She worked as a servant in their house until the baby became ill; Guylene, too, felt exhausted. Since medical care was freely available only in Do Kay, she returned again to Osner's mother, who said she would take the child. Guylene's and Osner's first child had already started school at the Ecole Saint-Andre, and Osner's mother, who worked at the school, allowed she could always find food for one more.

By early June, Guylene was ill: she had lost weight, had amenor-rhea, and felt short of breath on exertion. But it was her child's symptoms – abdominal pain, irritability, poor food intake – that brought her, on June 18, 1992, to the clinic. The child's physical exam was unremarkable except for pallor and a slightly enlarged liver. Dr. Dessalines heard both stories with some alarm. Yes, Guylene had heard of AIDS; some had even said that Osner had died from it, but she knew it was not true. After reviewing Osner's chart, the physician suggested that she be tested for HIV. She was leaving for Port-au-Prince, Guylene informed him, but would return for the results. The child was treated, empirically, for worms and also for anemia, and sent home to her grandmother.

The next day, Guylene returned to Port-au-Prince, then in the throes of its worst economic depression in recent decades. She worked a few days as a maid, but found the conditions intolerable. She tried selling cigarettes and candy, but remained hungry and fatigued. "I was," she said, "ready to try anything." Shortly thereafter, Guylene's baby died quite suddenly of cardiac failure, presumed secondary to HIV cardiomyopathy. Although the child had never been tested for antibodies to the virus, Guylene's test had come back positive a few days prior to the tragedy.

Guylene was informed of her positive serology on the day following her return; she listened impassively as the possible significance of the test was explained. Careful physical examination and history suggested that Guylene had not yet had a serious opportunistic infection. Her manifes-tations of HIV infection at that time were severe anemia (the cause of most of her symptoms), weight loss, amenorrhea, occasional fevers, and generalized lymphadenopathy. Guylene was placed on prophylactic isoniazid, protein supplements, iron and folate, and multivitamins.

Guylene did not return to Port-au-Prince, but rented a house with financial aid she received through the clinic. Although she soon experienced significant improvement in her symptoms, she remained depressed and withdrawn. A young man named Rene had been visiting her, but Guylene discouraged him and he disappeared – "he went to Santo Domingo, I think, because I never heard from him again." In mid-November, however, Guylene responded to the advances of a soldier stationed in Peligre. A native of a large town near the Dominican border, with a wife and two children there, the soldier had only been in the region about a month. Although residents of Peligre said that he had a *menaj*, a girlfriend, in that village as well, Guylene insists that she was his only partner in the region:

> He saw me here, at home. He saw me only a couple of times, spoke to me only a couple of times, before announcing that he cared for me. After that, he came to visit me often. I didn't think much of it until he started staying over. I got pregnant at about the time they announced that he was being transferred back to [his home town]. He said he'd be back, but I never saw or heard from him again.

Because Guylene's physicians had gone to some trouble to prevent her from having unprotected sexual intercourse, we were of course anxious to know how our conversations about this subject may have figured in her decision – if decision is the term – to conceive another child.[8] That Guylene understood what it meant to be an asymptomatic carrier of HIV seemed clear from a metaphor she used to describe herself:

> You can be walking around big and pretty, and you've got a problem inside. When you see a house that's well built, inside it's still got ugly rocks, mud, sand – all the ugly, hidden things. What's nice on the outside might not be nice on the inside.

Guylene understood, too, that her child might well be sick with HIV infection. But she was impatient with questions, tired of talking about sadness and death: "Will the baby be sick? Sure he could be sick. People are never not sick. I'm sick ... he might be sick too. It's in God's hands. I don't know."

Currently, Guylene draws to the close of her fifth pregnancy, which may well culminate in another death. Two of her children are dead; two others have long looked to a father or grandmother for the bulk of their parenting. Guylene's own sisters are dead, missing, or beaten into submission by the hardness of Haiti. Few of her nephews and nieces have survived to adulthood. Guylene assures her physicians that she is without symptoms, but seems inhabited by a persistent lassitude.

LINKING MICRO TO MACRO

When compared to age-matched North Americans with AIDS, Guylene, like other rural Haitians with AIDS, has a sparse sexual history. Although Pape's and co-workers (see Pape and Johnson 1988) case-control study suggested that urban Haitian men, at least, had more partners than did patients in rural settings, research conducted in Guylene's neighborhood in Port-au-Prince suggests that her case is not as unusual as it would seem:

> the high seropositivity rate (8%) found in pregnant women 14 to 19 years of age suggests that women [in Cite Soleil] appear to acquire HIV infection soon after becoming sexually active. Moreover, this age group is the only one in which a higher seropositivity rate is not associated with a greater number of sexual partners. Women with only one sexual partner in the year prior to pregnancy actually have a slightly higher prevalence rate (although not significantly so) than the others. This suggests that they were infected by their first and only partner (Desvarieux and Pape 1991:275).

In fact, there is little about Guylene's story that is unique; it is recounted in some detail because it brings into relief many of the forces that effectively constrained not only her options, but those of most Haitian women.

Such, in any case, is my opinion after caring for dozens of poor women with HIV disease. There is a deadly monotony in their stories: young women – or teenaged girls – driven to Port-au-Prince by the lure of an escape from the harshest poverty; once in the city, each worked as a domestic; none managed to find the financial security so elusive in the countryside. The women I interviewed were straightforward about the non-voluntary aspect of their sexual activity: In their opinions, they had been driven into unfavorable unions by poverty.

Over the past several years, the medical staff of the clinic on Do Kay has diagnosed dozens of cases of HIV infection in people presenting to the clinic with a broad range of complaints. With surprisingly few exceptions, however, those so diagnosed shared a number of risk factors, as a small-scale case-control study suggests (Table 14.1). The study was conducted by interviewing the first 17 women diagnosed

Table 14.1

Case-Control Study of HIV Infection in
34 Rural Haitian Women

Patient Characteristics	HIV Disease (N 17)	Control (N 17)
Number of Sexual Partners	2.7	2.2
Partner of Truckdriver	9	1
Partner of Soldier	7	0
Partner of Peasent Only	0	15
Port-au-Prince Residence	14	4
Worked as Servant	11	0
Years of Education	4.8	4
Received Blood Transfusion	0	1
Used Illicit Drugs	0	0
Received > 10 IM injections	11	13

with symptomatic HIV infection (most had full-blown AIDS) who were residents of Do Kay or its two neighboring villages. Their responses to questions posed during the course of a series of open-ended interviews were compared with those of 17 age-matched, seronegative controls. In both groups, ages ranged from 17 to 37, with a mean of about 25 years. None of these 34 women had a history of prostitution; none had used illicit drugs; only one, a member of the control group, had a history of transfusion. None of the women in either group had more than six sexual partners. In fact, four of the afflicted women had had only one sexual partner. Although women in the study group had (on average) more sexual partners than controls, the difference is not striking. Similarly, there was no clear difference between the study and control group vis-a-vis the number of intramuscular injections received or years of education.

The chief risk factors in this small study group seemed to involve not the number of partners in a lifetime, but rather the professions of these partners. Fully 14 of the women with HIV disease had histories of sexual contact with soldiers or truckdrivers. Two of these women reported having only two sexual partners: one a soldier, one a truck-driver. Of those women diagnosed with HIV disease, none had a history of sexual contact exclusively with peasants. Among the control group, only one woman had as a regular partner a truckdriver; none reported contact with soldiers, and most had only had sexual relations with peasants from the region. Histories of extended residence in Port-au-Prince and work as a domestic were also strongly associated with a diagnosis of HIV disease.

Conjugal unions with non-peasants – salaried soldiers and truck-drivers who are paid on a daily basis – reflect these women's quest for some measure of economic security. In this manner, truckdrivers and soldiers have served as a "bridge" to the rural population, just as North American tourists seem to have served as a bridge to the urban Haitian population (Farmer 1992). But just as North Americans are no longer important in the transmission of HIV in Haiti, truckdrivers and soldiers will soon no longer be necessary components of the rural epidemic. Once introduced into a sexually active population, HIV will work its way into those with no history of residence in the city, no history of contact with soldiers or truckdrivers, and no history of work as a domestic.

The research presented here underlines the importance of social inequalities of the most casual, everyday sort in determining who is most at risk for HIV infection. In Haiti, HIV is sexually transmitted, and sexual unions are clearly made and unmade by the factors and forces so evident in Guylene's experience. Several years of participant observation by the author, and also a critical review of existing epidemiological data from urban Haiti and the rest of the Caribbean, do not suggest that additional factors ("voodoo practices" including animal sacrifice and ritualized sex had been suggested in both the popular and scientific literatures in North America) are involved in the transmission of HIV in Haiti.[9]

When ethnographic and clinical-epidemiological research are linked to unflinching social analysis, the contours of a rapidly changing epidemic – and the forces promoting HIV transmission – come into focus. Concluding that, in Haiti, "poverty and economic inequity serve as the most virulent co-factors in the spread of this disease" (Farmer 1995:24), it is possible to identify seven other socially conditioned forces enhancing rates of HIV transmission among Haitian women. These include:

1. gender inequality, especially concerning control of land and other resources;
2. traditional patterns of sexual union, such as plasaj (in which sexually-transmitted pathogens are much more likely to be shared among three or more persons);

3. emerging patterns of sexual union, such as the serial monogamy described by Guylene and by most of our patients (many of whom implicate poverty in the undermining of these unions);

4. prevalence of STDs and other genital-tract infections (such as trichomoniasis or infections causing mucosal lesions) and, perhaps more significantly, lack of access to treatment for them;

5. lack of timely response by public-health authorities, a delay related not merely to lack of resources but the persistence of a political crisis;

6. lack of culturally appropriate prevention tools;

7. political violence, much of it state-sponsored and directed at poor people.[10]

Each of these factors and forces was relevant in Guylene's experience, and they are relevant in the lives of most of our patients. These are the "givens," the structural violence of their country and, indeed, of the larger historical system in which it is ensnared.[11] Of all the millions of persons on the losing end of the system, few are more trammeled by punitive constraints than are Haitian women living in poverty. For poor Haitian women, often enough, the structures are more like strictures.

For reasons I hope to explore in the remainder of this chapter, these are not factors regularly discussed in the medical journals that publish epidemiological studies of HIV infection. Yet there is ample reason to believe that similar factors help to determine the epidemiology of HIV infection in wealthier countries too, especially those characterized by high indices of economic disparity, such as the United States.[12]

One reason social forces are not candidly discussed in the biomedical press may be related to the way AIDS research funds have been doled out. Quick to associate anthropology with studies of exotic animal sacrifice, say, or ritual scarification, those in control of funds ask anthropologists to perform "rapid ethnographic assessments" of settings with high rates of HIV transmission. And, medical anthropologists have too often assented, restricting their inquiries to "delineating the cultural component" of illness. Because culture is merely that, a component, such research has been the object of legitimate critiques:

> Medical anthropologists and sociologists have tended to elevate the cultural component into an omnibus explanation. The emphasis is on cultural determination. Even when social relations receive more than reflexive recognition, medical social scientists restrict the social relations

to small 'primary' group settings, such as the family, and factions at the
micro unit... Little or no attempt is made to encompass the totality of
the larger society's structure (Onoge 1975:221).[13]

In my view, obscuring "the totality of the larger society's structure"
(including its place in international systems) is all too often the mission
of anthropological assessment when the goal of such assessment is to
assign origins or vectors for disease in such "barbaric" practices as
animal sacrifice and blood ritual. In the vast majority of settings in
which anthropologists work, HIV is transmitted through much more
mundane mechanisms.

Finally, such "exotic" practices are out of the ordinary, isolated, and
to a large extent voluntary. By associating them with AIDS, do we not
silently reassure ourselves that the disease we study is equally voluntary, exceptional, and experience-distant? If that is the profile of
medical anthropology in the AIDS pandemic, Haiti has a lesson to
teach it.

ETHNOGRAPHY, SOCIAL THEORY, AND EPIDEMIOLOGY: BRINGING IT ALL TOGETHER IN AIDS PREVENTION

If the chief forces promoting HIV transmission are powerful political
and economic currents, what meaningful interventions might be made
on the local level? If one of the chief reasons poor women like Guylene
engage in sexual relations is to conceive a child, what are the chances
of promoting condom use? In a setting of political upheaval and
violence against community organizers, what hope is there of seeing
projects through to fruition?

Two community-based organizations, one Haitian and one North
American, have attempted to incorporate insights gained from ethnographic, epidemiological, and clinical work in an AIDS-prevention
project in rural Haiti. In early 1992, Partners in Health and Zanmi
Lasante received funds from the World AIDS Foundation in order
to inaugurate "Une Chance a Prendre" (UCAP), a comprehensive,
community-based response to a rapidly advancing epidemic. The
project includes efforts to prevent transmission of HIV and other
sexually transmitted pathogens, and it also introduces training programs for Haitian health workers. A significant component of UCAP
attempts to improve clinical care for those already infected with HIV,

and to enhance providers' abilities to diagnose opportunistic infections (and other complications of HIV infection) in a timely fashion.

In spite of a very adverse political climate – a coup d'etat took place months before the project was initiated, crippling the team's ability to work outside of the Zanmi Lasante catchment area – each of these aspects of UCAP was inaugurated and most of them completed as planned. I will focus here, however, on one small project within UCAP, as it demonstrates both the utility and the limits of culturally appropriate efforts to prevent HIV transmission among the poor.

Zanmi Lasante is the parent organization for a large and vibrant women's health project, one sponsoring interventions ranging from women's literacy to screening for cervical disease. A group of women involved in these efforts decided to create, in the context of UCAP, a series of AIDS-prevention tools for women like themselves: poor, landless, and subject to discrimination at many levels. HIV-positive women also participated in the project, which has led, we believe, to the first prevention tools designed by and for poor Haitian women.

Because most rural Haitians do not read or write, and because UCAP had funds for a video recorder and portable generator, the women's group settled on making a video. Basing their script on the life story of the first woman from Do Kay to die of AIDS, the women created *Chache Lavi, Detwi Lavi.* The expression (which is literally rendered as "Looking for Life, Destroying Life") is used whenever someone dies in the course of honest efforts to make a living – for example, when a market woman dies in a truck accident while transporting her produce to market. Many people in rural Haiti feel the expression is apposite to the stories of young women who are infected with HIV in the course of their struggle to survive.

The half-hour program tells the story of Jocelyne, a young woman who loses her family land to a hydroelectric dam – and, shortly thereafter, her mother to tuberculosis. Soon she is responding to the overtures of a truck driver. Jocelyn hopes that, through him, she can pull her family out of poverty. After she gives birth to a child, she finds herself alone and again penniless. Jocelyne sees work in the city as her only hope of surviving, and the only hope for a brighter future for her daughter.

What happens to Jocelyne in the city is typical of the lot of poor women in Haiti, as the case study and our clinical experience, summarized above, suggest. Her next sexual union is with a second truck driver who promises to help her find a job. Soon, Jocelyne is working as a servant for a pittance and, unbeknownst to her employer, is pregnant. She is fired abruptly when this becomes evident, but the truck driver is no longer around to help. Her next – and final – liasion is with a soldier, with whom she conceives twins. Sick and beaten down by her experience, she returns to Do Kay. There she is diagnosed with AIDS.

Marie, one of the seropositive actors who has since died of AIDS, offered the following observations in an interview conducted as the video was being edited:

> There are so many people who think that you get AIDS by being promiscuous (*nan vilib*), but through this story we are able to show what's really happening in Haiti. People like Jocelyne are everywhere – there's nothing for them, so they have to put themselves in peril to feed their children. Perhaps if she had known what was waiting for her, she could have taken precautions.

It is not clear, of course, that Jocelyne would have been able to alter her course had she been better informed, but the video has other merits, as well. A Haitian nurse who directs a women's clinic in Port-au-Prince had the following to say upon viewing the video:

> The video really shakes you to your core, because it takes a hard look at the real culprits in this epidemic. It's so easy to say that poverty and oppression are to blame, and it's true. But when you see how Jocelyne's life is squashed at every turn by these forces... It's so commonplace, it's banal – and yet why is this not part of our discussions of the disease?... The video also helps to denounce a series of 'myths' – that you can stop AIDS by merely circulating condoms, that you can stop AIDS by educating people, that AIDS is a result of promiscuity, et cetera.

In spite of the many forces conspiring to make a video irrelevant among the Haitian poor – who have no electricity, much less televisions with VCRs – *Chache Lavi, Detwi Lavi* is proving to be more durable than might be expected. The video's narrator has since become a skilled facilitator, and has presented the group's work in many settings, sometimes with the help of a portable generator and projector. More recently, the video has twice been shown on national television (which has, admittedly, limited reach among those most at risk). Other community groups have petitioned Zanmi Lasante; they would like to make AIDS-prevention videos, too.

UCAP has also been instructive in its failures. These have included fall-out from the coup d'etat (from expulsion of two project coordinators to threats from soldiers who quite correctly saw our work as "anti-military"); problems among the professional staff ("burn-out" due to high patient load, a problem dramatically worsened by the breakdown of the public-health sector after the coup); and a lack of passion for some aspects of UCAP (e.g., repetitive community meetings). There have also been worse-than-anticipated shortages of materials, and unanticipated bureacratic barriers that slowed down the training component of the project.

What possible effects might such a modest project have had in the face of such overwhelming odds? It is not possible to prove that *Chache Lavi, Detwi Lavi* has prevented a single case of HIV transmission. But it is possible to argue that tens of thousands of Haitians have heard their first candid discussions of these issues in hearing the story of Jocelyne Gracia. It is possible to observe that the relationship between AIDS and gender inequality has become, as a result of UCAP, the subject of sustained community discussions. It is possible to speculate that "people who can name the source of their problems may be better off than those who are uncomprehending or silent" (Krieger et al. 1993:103).[14]

Although a realistic analysis should lead one to a more pessimistic assessment of the value of preventive efforts in a setting like Haiti, perhaps the last words should go to the women who made the video. Convinced their efforts will not be in vain, members of the group repeatedly express the hope that women elsewhere can use the ideas present in *Chache Lavi, Detwi Lavi* to make their own AIDS-prevention tools. To cite Marie again: "We're telling this story to show how the circumstances of our lives have forced us to enter into bad situations like [Jocelyne's]. As poor women, we are committed to sharing what we've learned with other women like ourselves, especially those who don't have the means to create a video like this one."

CONCLUSIONS: POVERTY AND POWERLESSNESS AS CO-FACTORS

Poverty and powerlessness can serve as powerful co-factors in the spread of HIV. An anthropology of infectious disease that is more than mere ethnography – one that plumbs social and political-economic analysis in an effort to discern the forces that structure risk – would certainly seem to buttress this assertion. Do these insights hold for infectious diseases other than HIV infection? Piecemeal evidence would suggest that poverty and inequality (including gender-based discrimination) is a significant risk enhancer for most sexually transmitted diseases, including chlamydia, syphilis, gonorrhea, lymphogranuloma venereum, hepatitis, and syndromes such as pelvic inflammatory disease (see Aral and Holmes 1991; Goeman, Meheus and Piot 1991; Muir and Belsey 1980). Because human papilloma virus is similarly influenced by social forces, perhaps even cervical cancer can be said to be a disease of poverty – in some developing countries, it is the leading neoplasm in women (Paavonen, Koutsky and Koviat 1990; Reeves, Rawls and Brinton 1989; Standaert and Meheus 1985). Surely a majority of parasitic diseases – including amebic dysentery, malaria, schistosomiasis, trypanosomiasis, and onchocerciasis – are similarly disproportionately distributed among the poor.

Studies spanning time, geographical space, and cultural diversity all point to an important thesis: poverty and inequality put people at risk for infectious diseases. With regard to certain diseases in specific settings, such as tuberculosis in the poor countries of the southern hemisphere, it may be that absolute poverty, with its attendant malnutrition and immunosuppression, is responsible for striking mortality differentials among those with reactivation disease (see Farmer et al. 1991). Regarding other diseases, such as HIV infection, it seems that multiple inequities are to blame: As Guylene's story would suggest, steep grades of inequity (gender-based, economic, environmental) seem to put the disempowered at risk of AIDS as a sexually transmitted disease. Social discrimination and the violation of human rights have also been strongly implicated as risk factors for exposure to HIV (Mann 1991).[15]

These tentative conclusions have a number of implications for further anthropological research on infectious disease. When behavior is strongly constrained by social forces, as was the case with Guylene, it is not illuminating to lump these forces under the catch-all category of "behavioral factors." As Mann (1991:555) has commented, "the study of the behavioral determinants of risk behavior, using standard concepts and classical methods, may have reached its limit." A new research agenda would do more than stress the importance of socioeconomic status; surely this has been well-enough established. Rather, it would seek to explore the translation of large-scale forces – here I have focused on poverty and gender, but other factors may be equally important – into risk for populations and for individual patients.

In order to exploit fully the fruits of basic research, we now need large-scale investigations that would allow us to understand both the dynamics of infectious diseases within certain populations and the precise mechanisms by which social forces become embodied as risk for infection. The idea, here, would not be to "control" or "adjust" for socioeconomic status or "race," but to study their effects on the distribution and course of infectious disease. Such research, based on prospective studies and sociocultural analysis, would attempt to ascribe relative weights to various social factors – a critical epidemiology that would link variations in incidence or prevalence ("risk") to socioeconomic status, gender, and factors such as discrimination, sexism, and political upheaval.

These variables have always proven difficult to measure, and anthropologists could help bring important contextual considerations to the center of the large-scale epidemiological projects that will be necessary to bring these mechanisms into relief. Krieger and co-workers – whose magisterial review of epidemiological studies of the health effects of racism, sexism and social class should be read by all medical anthropologists – outline an alternative research agenda for an epidemiology that would address such questions, underlining four key elements and assumptions: (1) Patterns of disease, whether in individuals bodies or in populations, are the result of "a dynamic interplay between exposure and susceptibility;" (2) The processes of both exposure and susceptibility are themselves structured over time and "conditioned by history;" (3) The social forces and relations manifest in racism, sexism, and social class will influence, one way or another, the exposure and suseptibility of those whose lives are defined by these relations; and (4) The mechanisms by which these social forces affect the health of populations include the shaping of exposure and susceptibility to both pathogens (and pathogenic processes) and protective factors, events, and processes; the degree of access to, and type of, health care; and the shaping of health research and health policies (Krieger et al. 1993:100).

Research would also examine the rate of disease progression in the light of these and other factors, linking them to nutritional and immunological status. The explanatory power of models stemming from such research would be enhanced by their ability to account for variation over time and across geographical and cultural divides, and would thus be informed by history and political economy. Although ethnography tends to bring life to the often arid studies of economists and historians, I am not convinced that the maintenance of disciplinary boundaries between economics, history, sociology, and anthropology is helpful. Immanuel Wallerstein (1987:312) pushes this line of thought even further: "The question before us today is whether there are any criteria which can be used to assert in a relatively clear and defensible way boundaries between the four presumed disciplines of anthropology, economics, political science, and sociology. World-systems analysis responds with an unequivocal 'no' to this question. All the presumed criteria – level of analysis, subject-matter, methods, theoretical assumptions – either are no longer true in practice or, if sustained, are barriers to further knowledge rather than stimuli to its creation."

Such cross-disciplinary research has been inaugurated at times in the past, both in anthropology and in related fields. Indeed, exemplary studies were conducted in the earlier part of this century, when, for example, Goldberger, Wheeler, and Sydenstricker (1920) examined the occurrence of pellagra, whose etiology had not yet been revealed, in seven cotton-mill villages in South Carolina. Although the received wisdom was that high rates of this disorder among the poor were due to "poor hygiene" (or, among blacks, to innate "racial weakness"), Goldberger and co-workers disproved these notions with a careful study that included not merely the study of household diets and income, but also the ways in which incomes and foodstuffs were obtained and seasonal variation affecting access to food and capital. Their research suggested that income alone did not determine rates of pellagra in these towns; instead, susceptibility to pellagra was related to the degree of dependency on cash cropping for cotton, thus linking the disorder to the larger political economy. Because Goldberger – who later discovered that niacin-deficiency was the etiologic factor in pellagra – called for changes in the southern economy that would result, he argued, in lower rates of pellagra among these groups, he was vilified by many of his contemporaries in the medical field.

Today, Goldberger's work is regarded as exemplary public-health research, but, as Krieger and co-workers (1993:99) note, "it is hard to imagine present U.S. epidemiologic studies explicitly testing detailed hypotheses about the social production and political economy of disease, as Goldberger and Sydenstricker once did." And why not? The authors speculate that there exists within epidemiology a certain reluctance "to discuss uncomfortable subjects or to tackle issues whose remedies could lie outside the bounds of traditional public health interventions."

While this is true, I doubt that this reluctance is in any way native to epidemiology. Nor is it the province of medicine, although it may be, as Gifford (1986:239) suggests, that "greater control on the part of the medical profession over the diagnosis and treatment of risk . . . has diverted attention away from translating epidemiologic knowledge into population level interventions and has allowed the focus to be directed towards the medicalization of risk within individuals."

In anthropology, similarly, Brown's study of malaria control in Sardinia "emphasizes the need to understand the political economic

variables which influence both the rates of disease and development"
(Brown 1983:6). Other researchers in the social sciences – including
Schoepf (1988) in anthropology, Turshen (1984) in political science,
and Packard (1989) in history – have reached very similar conclusions
in examining modern epidemics. And yet all deplore a recurrent
tendency, noted in each of these fields, to divert attention from the
obvious conclusions of investigations of the patterning of disease,
similar to my critique of epidemiology at the outset of this chapter.

The obvious conclusions are that risk for most diseases is structured
in large part by social – political and economic – forces. If the distribution of these diseases is to be altered, it will be done so by social –
political and economic – responses. It is only appropriate to recall that
sound anthropological research on infectious diseases is by no means
among the most important task at hand for those seeking to diminish
the suffering of the destitute sick. Nor is it being called for by the sick
themselves. For the mechanisms of the uneven distribution of the
world's resources – including the fruits of technology and science – are
no longer obscure, if indeed they ever were. Sound research should be
embedded in efforts to make available to people like Guylene the
resources and information already available to the more fortunate. If
anything redeeming might be said to have come from this latest plague,
it might be that it has thrown into relief the vast disparity in resources
available to people caught in the same web of social and economic
relations.

Even the pessimists involved in the Haitian AIDS prevention efforts
described above – those who doubt that educational efforts could have
much of an effect on a rapidly advancing epidemic – share the women's
group's hopes that their example will inspire other women to organize
their communities in order to promote a broader program of social
justice. For all the project participants agree that educational programs
are not enough to prevent AIDS: Poor women, no matter how dignified
or well-informed, will remain at risk as long as they are not liberated
from the myriad conditions, large-scale and local, that keep them
dependent and vulnerable.

NOTES

1. This is true, as well, of the AIDS megaconferences held each year. Of the
   thousands of epidemiology-track posters and abstracts presented at the
   VIIIth International Conference on AIDS, only three used "poverty" as a
   key word.

2. Krieger and co-workers (1993:99) conclude their review with a sharp reproach: "The minimal research that simultaneously studies the health effects of racism, sexism, and social class ultimately stands as a sharp indictment of the narrow vision limiting much of the epidemiological research conducted within the United States."

3. The term "historical system" is used following Wallerstein (1987:317), whose world-systems analysis "substitutes for the term 'society' the term 'historical system.' Of course, this is a mere semantic substitution. But it rids us of the central connotation that 'society' has acquired, its link to 'state,' and therefore of the presupposition about the 'where' and the 'when.' Furthermore, 'historical system' as a term underlines the unity of historical social science. The entity is simultaneously systemic and historical." The argument for application of a world-systems approach to a "responsible materialist" investigation of AIDS in Haiti is made in *AIDS and Accusation* (Farmer 1992:13, 256–262).

4. What is intended, here, by the term "structure? I would agree with Turner (1987:179) who reminds us that "structure is a process, not a thing" and "refers to the ordering of interactions across time and in space." By structural violence, then, I refer to the processes, historically given and often economically driven, by which human agency may be constrained, whether through ritual, routine, or the hard surfaces of life. For some, including many of my informants and patients, life is structured by racism, sexism, *and* grinding poverty.

5. The names of informants and patients are pseudonyms, as are those of the villages in central Haiti.

6. For more information about *plasaj*, see Farmer (1995), Lowenthal (1984), and Vieux (1989). A detailed review of the constraints placed on Haitian women is available in the study by Neptune-Anglade (1986).

7. Pregnancies are said to last significantly longer than nine months – up to several years – when women are "in perdition," a construct examined in some detail by Murray (1976).

8. I was both Guylene's physician and the person who conducted the interviews cited in this paper. The term "we" refers to the team of physicians responsible for patient care.

9. Both the research and review are in *AIDS and Accusation* (Farmer 1992; see Chapters 7–14, and 19).

10. Indeed, the evacuation of several urban slums – such as Cite Soleil, with its alleged 10% seropositivity rate – meant that many with asymptomatic HIV infection returned to low-prevalence home villages to wait for the violence to subside. No research has addressed the means by which political violence thus changes the equations that might describe the rates of HIV transmission in Haiti.

11. As Wallerstein (1987:318) has noted, "by the late nineteenth century, for the first time ever, there existed only one historical system on the globe. We are still in that situation today." I have examined Haiti's "fit" into this system in a recent study, which also examines how this "political economy of brutality" comes to have its effects in the lives of poor women (Farmer 1994).

12. In the United States, the fastest-growing subepidemic is among those who contract HIV heterosexually, a group consisting largely of poor African-American and Hispanic populations. For example, St. Louis and co-workers (1991) found that 3.2 % and 3.7 % of similarly disadvantaged teenagers applying for work in the U.S. Jobs Corps were already seropositive for HIV. See also the reviews of "Women, Poverty, and AIDS" in the issue of *Culture, Medicine and Psychiatry* (volume 17, issue 4, 1993) devoted to this subject.

13. As Brown (1983:3) has noted, anthropology "is particularly well adapted to meet such a challenge because the holistic approach provides the 'big picture' of interacting cultural, demographic, economic and political variables which might evade other social scientists." Unfortunately, the big picture has all to often evaded anthropologists, as well. See also Gifford's (1986:239) discussion of the "medicalization" of the concept of risk, and also her warning: "we should be wary that social and cultural processes do not become reduced to factors which are translated *only* into individual health promotion." For a critical discussion of the cooptation (theoretical, methodological, and moral) of anthropology by the AIDS establishment, see also Farmer (1991, 1995) and Farmer and Kim (1991).

14. Krieger and co-workers (1993) are referring to a small literature examining hypertension among African-Americans living in the United States. There are as yet no data suggesting that naming the sources of one's oppression (or dignity in the face of oppression) can alter the nature of risk in settings such as Haiti. Such research is certainly called for.

15. It may be true that, in many instances, *setting*, and not type of infection, is the most important determinant of mortality. In a recent review of national trends in morbidity and mortality, Wilkinson (1994:63) notes that the relationship between per capita GNP and mortality "peters out in the developed world. Apparently there is some minimum level of income (around $5,000 per capita in 1990) above which the absolute standard of living ceases to have much impact on health." It is important to add that any nation-based study has limitations in those adopting a broader systems approach.

REFERENCES

Aral, S. and K. Holmes. 1991. Sexually Transmitted Diseases in the AIDS Era. Scientific American 264(2):62–69.

Brown, P. 1983. Introduction: Anthropology and Disease Control. Medical Anthropology 7:1–8.

de Bruyn, M. 1992. Women and AIDS in Developing Countries. Social Science and Medicine 34(3):249–62.

Centers for Disease Control. 1990. AIDS in Women-United States. Morbidity and Mortality Weekly Report 39:845–846.

Deschamps, M.-M., J. Pape, P. Williams-Russo, S. Madhavan, J. Ho, and W. Johson. 1993. A Prospective Study of HIV-Seropositive Asymptomatic Women of Childbearing Age in a Developing Country. Journal of Acquired Immune Deficiency Syndromes 6(5):446–451.

Desvarieux, M. and J. Pape. 1991. HIV and AIDS in Haiti: Recent Developments. AIDS Care 3(3):271–279.

Dunn, F. 1984. Social Determinants in Tropical Disease. *In* Tropical and Geographic Medicine. K. Warren and A. Mahmoud, eds. Pp. 1086–1096. New York: McGraw Hill.

Dunn, F. and C. Janes. 1986. Introduction: Medical Anthropology and Epidemiology. *In* Anthropology and Epidemiology. C. Janes, R. Stall, and S. Gifford, eds. Pp. 3–34. Dordrecht: D. Reidel.

Ellerbrock, T., S. Lieb, P. Harrington, et al. 1992. Heterosexually Transmitted Human Immunodeficiency Virus Infection among Pregnant Women in a Rural Florida Community. New England Journal of Medicine 327(24): 1704–1709.

Farmer, P. 1992. New Disorder, Old Dilemmas: AIDS and Anthropology in Haiti. *In* Social Analysis in the Time of AIDS. G. Herdt and S. Lindenbaum, eds. Pp. 287–318. Beverly Hills: Sage Publications.

Farmer, P. 1992. AIDS and Accusation: Haiti and the Geography of Blame. Berkeley: University of California Press.

Farmer, P. 1994. The Uses of Haiti. Monroe, Maine: Common Courage Press.

Farmer, P. 1995. Culture, Poverty, and the Dynamics of HIV Transmission in Rural Haiti. *In* Culture and Sexual Risk: Anthropological Perspectives on AIDS. H. ten Brummelhuis and G. Herdt, eds. Pp. 3–28. New York: Gordon and Breach.

Farmer, P. and J. Kim. 1991. Anthropology, Accountability, and the Prevention of AIDS. The Journal of Sex Research 28(2):203–221.

Farmer, P., S. Robin, St.-L. Ramilus, and J. Kim. 1991. Tuberculosis, Poverty, and "Compliance": Lessons from Rural Haiti. Seminars in Respiratory Infections 6(4):254–260.

Gail, M., P. Rosenberg, and J. Goedert. 1990. Therapy May Explain Recent Deficits in AIDS Incidence. Journal of the Acquired Immune Deficiency Syndromes 3:296–306.

Gifford, S. 1986. The Meaning of Lumps: A Case Study of the Ambiguities of Risk. *In* Anthropology and Epidemiology. C. Janes, R. Stall, and S. Gifford, eds. Pp. 213–246. Dordrecht: D. Reidel.

Goeman, J., A. Meheus, and P. Piot. 1991. L'Epidemiologie des Maladies Sexuellement Transmissibles dans les Pays en Developpement a l'Ere du Sida. Annales de la Societe Belge de Medecine Tropicale 71:81–113.

Goldberger, J., G. Wheeler, and E. Sydenstricker. 1920. A Study of the Relation of Family Income and Other Economic Factors to Pellagra Incidence in Seven Cotton-mill Villages of South Carolina in 1916. Public Health Reports 35:2673–2714.

Gorman, M. 1986. The AIDS Epidemic in San Francisco: Epidemiological and Anthropological Perspectives. In Anthropology and Epidemiology. C. Janes, R. Stall, and S. Gifford, eds. Pp. 157–174. Dordrecht: D. Reidel.

Inhorn, M. 1994. Medical Anthropology and Epidemiology: Divergences or Convergences? Social Science and Medicine 40(3):285–290.

Inhorn, M. and P. Brown. 1990. The Anthropology of Infectious Disease. Annual Reviews in Anthropology 19:89–117.

Janes, C. 1986. Migration and Hypertension: An Ethnography of Disease Risk in an Urban Samoan Community. In Anthropology and Epidemiology. C. Janes, R. Stall, and S. Gifford, eds. Pp. 175–212. Dordrecht: D. Reidel.

Krieger, N. and E. Fee. 1994. Social Class: The Missing Link in U.S. Health Data. International Journal of Health Services 24(1):25–44.

Krieger, N., D. Rowley, A. Herman, B. Avery, and M. Phillips. 1993. Racism, Sexism, and Social Class: Implications for Studies of Health, Disease, and Well-being. American Journal of Preventive Medicine (Supplement) 9:82–122.

Larson, A. 1989. Social Context of Human Immunodeficiency Virus Transmission in Africa. Reviews of Infectious Disease 11:716–731.

Lowenthal, I. 1984. Labor, Sexuality and the Conjugal Contract in Rural Haiti. In Haiti – Today and Tomorrow: An Interdisciplinary Study. C. Foster and A. Valdman, eds. Pp. 15–33. Landham, Maryland: University Press of America.

McBarnett, L. 1988. Women and Poverty: The Effects on Reproductive Status. In Too Little, Too Late: Death with the Health Needs of Women in Poverty. C. Perales and L. Young, eds. Pp. 55–81. New York: Harrington Park Press.

McBride, D. 1991. From TB to AIDS: Epidemics among Urban Blacks since 1900. Albany, New York: State University of New York Press.

Mann, J. 1991. Global AIDS: Critical Issues for Prevention in the 1990s. International Journal of Health Services 21(3):553–559.

Mann, J., D. Tarantola, and T. Netter, eds. 1992. AIDS in the World. Cambridge, Massachusetts: Harvard University Press.

Marmot, M. 1994. Social Differentials in Health Within and Between Populations. Daedalus 123(4):197–216.

Muir, D., and M. Belsey. 1980. Pelvic Inflammatory Disease and its Consequences in the Developing World. American Journal of Obstetrics and Gynecolology 138:913–928.

Murray, G. 1976. Women in Perdition: Ritual Fertility Control in Haiti. *In* Culture, Natality, and Family Planning. J. Marshall and S. Polgar, eds. Pp. 59–78. Chapel Hill, North Carolina: Carolina Population Center, University of North Carolina.

Nations, M. 1986. Epidemiological Research on Infectious Disease: Quantitative Rigor or Rigormortis? Insights from Ethnomedicine. *In* Anthropology and Epidemiology. C. Janes, R. Stall, and S. Gifford, eds. Pp. 97–124. Dordrecht: D. Reidel.

Navarro, V. 1990. Race or Class versus Race and Class: Mortality Differentials in the United States. The Lancet 336:1238–1240.

Neptune-Anglade, M. 1986. L'Autre Moitie du Developpement: A Propos du Travail des Femmes en Haiti. Petion-Ville, Haiti: Edition des Alizes.

Onoge, O. 1975. Capitalism and Public Health: A Neglected Theme in the Medical Anthropology of Africa. *In* Topias and Utopias in Health. S. Ingman and A. Thomas, eds. Pp. 219–232. The Hague: Mouton.

Paavonen, J., L. Koutsky, and N. Kiviat. 1990. Cervical Neoplasia and other STD-related Genital and Anal Neoplasias. *In* Sexually Transmitted Diseases. K.K. Holmes, et al., eds. Pp. 561–562. New York: McGraw Hill.

Packard, R. 1989. White Plague, Black Labor: Tuberculosis and the Political Economy of Health and Disease in South Africa. Berkeley: University of California Press.

Packard, R. and P. Epstein. 1991. Epidemiologists, Social Scientists, and the Structure of Medical Research on AIDS in Africa. Social Science and Medicine 33(7):771–794.

Pape, J. and W. Johnson. 1988. Epidemiology of AIDS in the Caribbean. Bailliere's Clinical Tropical Medicine and Communicable Diseases 3(1):31–42.

Reeves, W., W. Rawls, and L. Brinton. 1989. Epidemiology of Genital Papillomaviruses and Cervical Cancer. Reviews of Infectious Diseases 11(3): 426–439.

Rothenberg, R., M. Woelfel, R. Stoneburner, J. Milberg, R. Parker, and B. Truman. 1987. Survival with the Acquired Immunodeficiency Syndrome: Experience with 5833 Cases in New York City. New England Journal of Medicine 317(21):1297–1302.

St. Louis, M., G. Conway, C. Hayman, et al. 1991. Human Immunodeficiency Virus in Disadvantaged Adolescents. Journal of the American Medical Association 266:2387–2391.

Schoepf, B. 1988. Women, AIDS, and the Economic Crisis in Central Africa. Canadian Journal of African Studies XXII(3):625–644.

Political Economies

Simonsen, J., F. Plummer, E. Ngugi, et al. 1990. HIV Infection Among Lower Socio-economic Strata Prostitutes in Nairobi. AIDS 4:139–144.

Standaert, B. and A. Meheus. 1985. Le Cancer du Col Uterin en Afrique. Medecine en l'Afrique Noire 32:406–415.

Turner, J. 1987. Analytical Theorizing. *In* Social Theory Today. A. Giddens and J. Turner, eds. Pp. 156–194. Stanford: Stanford University Press.

Turshen, M. 1984. The Political Ecology of Disease in Tanzania. New Brunswick, New Jersey: Rutgers University Press.

United Nations Development Program (UNDP). 1992. Young Women: Silence, Susceptibility and the HIV Epidemic. New York: UNDP.

Vieux, S. 1989. Le Placage: Droit Coutumier et Famille en Haiti. Paris: Editions Publisud.

Wallerstein, I. 1987. World-Systems Analysis. *In* Social Theory Today. A. Giddens and J. Turner, eds. Pp. 309–324, Stanford: Stanford University Press.

Wilkinson, R. 1994. The Epidemiological Transition: From Material Scarcity to Social Disadvantage. Daedalus 123(4):61–77.

CHAPTER 15

"I'm Not Dog, No!": Cries of Resistance Against Cholera Control Campaigns

Marilyn K. Nations and Cristina G. Monte

CHOLERA'S FOOTHOLD IN LATIN AMERICA

The global epidemic of cholera – an ancient, acute bacterial enteric disease – continues to spread throughout the world, despite scientists' efforts to control its transmission (AHRTAG 1993:1–8). For the first time in this century, cholera is gaining a foothold in the Western hemisphere. In Latin America, the number of endemic cases now rivals those in Asia and Africa. This seventh cholera pandemic, which started in Asia in 1961, spread to Africa, Europe, and Oceania, but had spared the Western hemisphere. That was, however, before January 1991 when toxigenic *Vibrio cholera* O1, biotype El Tor and serotype Inaba,

Reprinted from **Social Science and Medicine**, Volume 43, Marilyn Nations and Christina Monte, "I'm Not Dog, No!," pp. 1007–1024, ©1996, with permission from Elsevier Science Ltd., The Boulevard, Langhorne Lane, Kidlington OX5 1GB, UK.

We thank the Instituto Conceitos Culturais and Medicina (CC&M) and Clinical Research Unit, UFC in Fortaleza, Brazil for supporting this work. To families in Gonçalves Dias and Conjunto Palmeiras, we are indebted for their privileged personal accounts of what it is like to be poor, sick, and discriminated against because of suffering "The Dog's Disease." Special mention must be made of Dona Jandira, spirited laundress, whose piercing social critique of cholera proved to "hold water." We are particularly grateful to our was reported for the first time in some 100 years in South America (Lima and Guerrant 1994:1–5). Appearing almost simultaneously in several coastal Peruvian cities, the epidemic of *V. cholera* O1 exploded with some 426,000 probable cholera cases and over 3300 deaths reported in Peru alone.

It then spread rapidly throughout the continent. Crossing the Andes, the disease swept aggressively eastward into Brazil. By April 1993, 70% of Brazil's 27 states and territories reported domestically acquired cases of cholera for a total of 27,374 cases, with an incidence of 5.5 per 100,000 of the population and case fatality rate of 1.6%. It was in the impoverished Northeast, however, that the epidemic flourished, reporting 87% of Brazil's total cases and an incidence of 16.9 per 100,000 of the population (Lima 1994:593).

For centuries this drought-stricken region has been scourged by misfortune, disease, and death. Both diarrheal disease attack rates (Guerrant et al. 1983:986–997; Victoria 1988) and infant mortality rates (UNICEF 1986:61–70) in Brazil's Northeast are among the highest reported in the world. Here, endemic poverty, faulty sanitation, contaminated water and food supplies, coupled with high rates of illiteracy and less access to effective health services means that in many northeastern communities, cholera will probably persist for many years to come. Unlike other outbreaks, this latest pandemic will not go away. Instead, cholera is expected to become endemic in the Americas, as it has in Africa.

Vibrio Cholera O1 causes disease by adhering to the mucosa of the upper small bowel, where it produces a potent enterotoxin which stimulates the secretion of isotonic water and electrolytes. While the majority (90%) of cholera cases are mild and many infected persons have no symptoms, they can be carriers and silently infect others. Far

COSSAH colleagues at Harvard University Medical School, Department of Social Medicine, for their comments on an earlier draft of this paper presented at a recent faculty meeting in Chiapas, Mexico (Dr. Paul Farmer's insights on the dynamics of accusations and AIDS and Dr. Steffan I. Ayora-Diaz's reference to Scott's work on hidden transcripts were especially helpful), Dr. Aldo Lima, M.D. (UFC) for his solicitation of a social diagnosis of cholera, and Maria Auxiliadora de Souza, M.D., MPH, Ph.D. for easing our entry into the homes and lives of women in Gonçalves Dias. Finally, special recognition to Mario R. de C. Martin, Carmozita Peixoto da Silva and Inacio de Noiola Gomes Fernandes who made possible our daily treks into the field, always emotionally and physically exhausting.

fewer (5–8%) experience mild to moderate diarrhea. Cholera's reputation as a killer is restricted to a relatively small proportion of people (2–5%) who develop "cholera gravis" (Lima and Guerrant 1994:2). In such classic cholera cases, infected persons experience severe and profuse watery diarrhea and vomiting resulting in the rapid and profound loss of fluid and electrolytes. So severe may be the losses of essential fluids, that the patient may lose the equivalent of his entire body weight over two to three days. These huge losses of liquid may, in extreme cases, lead to severe dehydration, shock in four to twelve hours, and death. But today, no one need die from cholera.

As with all diarrheal diseases, the successful treatment of cholera depends on rapid replacement of fluid and electrolyte losses through (preferably) oral or intravenous routes (Mahalanadis et al. 1974:82–87). Before the discovery of rehydration therapy, some 30–50% of severely infected persons died from cholera. These numbers have declined drastically to less than 2% with the discovery of rehydration therapy (Lima 1994:596). The key is oral rehydration therapy (ORT).

Oral rehydration therapy was first discovered in Britain in the 1830s, although it was not until the 1960s that the importance of sugar in the solution was discovered (Parker et al. 1980:44); glucose significantly increases the body's ability to absorb fluid (Morello 1983:32). In the 1970s and especially in the 1971 cholera epidemic in Bangladesh, the utility of ORT for treatment of diarrheal dehydration was conclusively demonstrated. *The Lancet* has called ORT "potentially the most important medical advance this century" and ranks it second only to the discovery of antibiotics in terms of lives saved (Morello 1983:32).

The idea is simple; to replace the fluids and electrolytes lost during cholera and other secretory diarrheas; to maintain the patient without attempts to cure the diarrhea itself. The treatment is administered in the form of oral rehydration solution (ORS), consisting of water with salts and sugar added. Oral rehydration solution is fed continuously to the patient during the diarrheal episode, obviating the need for intravenous rehydration, which is an effective therapy. The death rate from diarrhea in hospitalized populations has dropped below 1% due to intravenous rehydration (Parker 1980:43–44). But it is expensive and necessarily confined to use in hospitals by qualified personnel, whereas ORT can be prepared and administered at home.

The exact optimum combination of electrolytes in ORS is a matter of some debate, but the general composition is agreed upon. The World Health Organization promotes use of a packaged powder containing sodium chloride, sodium bicarbonate, potassium chloride, and glucose in proper proportion, ready to mix with water and use. This oral rehydration solution has been found effective and can be used by lay persons at home (e.g., Clements 1980; Clements et al. 1980; Egman and Bertan 1980:333–338; Ellerbrock 1979; Harland et al. Au: Harland et al. not in bib.1981:600–601; Kielman et al. 1977:197–201; Melamed and Segall 1978:1317–1318; Moran 1976:32–33; Nations 1982, 1983; Nations and Rebhun 1988; Nations et al. 1983, 1988; Pizzaro et al. 1979:983–986; Shields et al. 1981:839–841; Than-Toe Au: cf. spelling of Than-Toe to bib. Thane-Toe et al. 1984:581–589).

Some planners have argued that it is possible for lay persons to mix an acceptable ORS at home using common table salt and sugar with proper instruction (Clements 1980; Harland et al. 1981:600–601; Kielman et al. 1977:197–201; Shields et al. 1981:839–841) and in some cases it is preferable (Nations 1982; Nations et al. 1983:1612). Although homemade ORS tends to omit sodium bicarbonate and potassium chloride, accurate measures are possible in even the most impoverished households using readily available 1-liter carbonated beverage bottles (or other containers) to measure the water, and bottle caps to measure the salt (1 level capful) and sugar (7–8 heaping capfuls). Homemade ORS has the advantage of being less expensive than the packaged ORS and, because of its home preparation, of being more accessible to impoverished mothers. Even locally available crude brown sugar such as lobon-gur in Bangladesh has been found effective in such solutions and is, importantly, more accessible to impoverished families (Sack 1980).

Cereal-based ORT, in which glucose is replaced by cereal flour (rice, maize, sorghum, millet, wheat, or potato), not only may be more available and acceptable to families, but has the added advantage of reducing stool output (Molla et al. 1985:751–756; Molla and Molla et al. 1989:429–431). Despite the debates about fine points in the composition of the formula, ORT is now unanimously accepted by the international health community and actively promoted by the WHO for the treatment of diarrheal dehydration, including that associated with cholera. Its scientific basis is well-established (Hirshhorn 1983; Parker 1980) and its ability to save lives has been convincingly demonstrated. It is low-cost and low-tech, and, theoretically, this should make it accessible to impoverished families, the bulk of those who die from enteric infections, including cholera.

Antibiotics, while helpful are not essential in the treatment of cholera. Antimicrobial therapy reduces the total volume of fluid loss and shortens the duration of both illness and carriage of vibrion in the feces (Goodenough 1964:355–357). However, antimicrobial resistance has been a growing problem in some parts of the world. Family contacts of patients with cholera may be treated prophylactically with tetracycline or doxycycline to prevent illness, however, antibiotic treatment of an entire community, or mass chemoprophylaxis, has not been shown to limit the spread of cholera (Lima and Guerrant 1994:5).

Other common, but ineffective, prevention measures include vaccination, quarantine or restricting the movement of people and food imports from affected areas. Effective prevention methods are the same as for other forms of diarrhea: drinking uncontaminated water, handwashing, good home and environmental hygiene, and avoidance of potentially contaminated foods (e.g., raw seafood, shellfish, contaminated municipal water). But the real key to eliminating cholera, as for all diseases linked to underdevelopment, lies in improving the conditions which enable cholera to flourish: poverty, illiteracy, lack of knowledge, economic recession, discrimination against women, lack of safe water, and adequate sanitation systems.

ADVERSITY, ACCUSATIONS, AND INFECTIOUS AGENTS

Epidemics of particularly dreaded illnesses always provoke a popular outcry. When such adversity as cholera – a virulent, infectious agent which spreads capriciously and kills indiscriminately – strikes, people are quick to incriminate, and finger-pointing becomes a human passion. As Sontag (1990) says,

> Any disease that is treated as a mystery and acutely enough feared will be felt to be morally, if not literally contagious [Sontag 1990:6]... Demands are made to subject people to 'tests,' to isolate the ill and those suspected of being ill or of transmitting illness, and to erect barriers against the real or imaginary contamination of foreigners [Sontag 1990:168].

Punitive notions of disease have a long history, dating to at least 1882 and the discovery of tuberculosis, and more recently with cancer and AIDS. In such cases of mysterious malevolence, Sontag points out, accusations of culpability are commonplace. "Who cast the evil eye?" "Who threw the roots?" "Who pointed the bones?" "Who sent the *trabalho* (hex)?" "Who is guilty of transgressing social norms?" There is one burning desire: to identify who caused the suffering. That accusations and folk disease etiologies are interwoven is well documented in the anthropological literature (Kluckhohn 1944; Rubel 1960:795–814; Tinling 1967:483–490; Wintrob 1973:318–326). Only recently, however, have such twisted illness accusations been interpreted critically. Farmer (1992) in *AIDS and Accusations: Haiti and The Geography of Blame* makes a perturbing observation. Victims are doubly damned; they suffer first a debilitating illness followed by image-damaging discrimination.

In Latin America, pinning blame on victims is a pastime (Acheson 1972:1152–1169). The most glaring, recent example is Harrison's (1985) *Underdevelopment is a State of the Mind* essay. He places blame for lack of progress squarely on poor people's heads, on peasants' supposed fatalistic mentality. Enculturation into a "culture of poverty" (Lewis 1966:19–25), maintains Harrison, creates mind sets mired in the muck of helplessness, jealousy, and in-fighting. Thus trapped, peasants are seen as unwilling to try to succeed, to take advantage of the many opportunities knocking at their doors. Examples of "blaming the victim" as an explanatory principle are plentiful: penniless, peasant mothers are branded "neglectful" (Scheper-Hughes 1984:535–546; 1985:291–317); suffering HIV-infected Haitians are labeled AIDS "originators" (Farmer 1992); malaria-infected, malnourished, and massacred Ianomani Indians are said to "lack initiative," and the like.

Farmer critiques such accusatory interpretations of illness in rural Haiti by putting poverty first. His objections echo Valentine's (1968) and Acheson's (1972:152–169) which took to task Lewis (1966:19–25), Foster (1965:293–315, 1967:50–56, 1972:165–202), and others who link poverty to cognitive images of the poor (e.g., Image of Limited Good) and who underemphasize political economy and other structural factors (e.g., discrimination, racism, lack of access to health services and money to pay for care). We agree with Farmer that an interpretive anthropology which fails to consider prevailing political and economic forces is short-sighted, especially in impoverished countries where "the hard surfaces of life seem to underpin so much of experience" (Farmer 1992:529), resulting in a socially unjust interpretation. Taking the calculus of economic and symbolic power seriously, Farmer pushes the "cult of blame" analysis to its limits. He argues that faced with accusations, the weaker invent counter-accusations, voicing them in seemingly far-fetched conspiracy theories. Actually they are rhetorical defenses against aggressors' discriminatory and demeaning attitudes. According to Farmer (1992), such conspiracy theories pose explanatory challenges:

accusation impute(s) to human agency a significant role in the propaga-
tion of a dreaded sickness. . . conspiracy theories impute to the powerful
evil motives, either the desire to weaken the ranks of outcasts, or to
defame black (in reference to Haiti) people. In each case, then, one social
group attributes unsavory motives to another [Farmer 1992:234].

Such conspiracy theories are "weapons of the weak," according to
Scott (1985). They are part of a "hidden transcript" (Scott 1990)
expressing popular indignation at political and social domination.
Creating convincing conspiracy theories is an art, an art of resistance.
This "offstage" discourse is typically produced in response to practices
of domination and exploitation, of insults and slights to human dignity,
that elites routinely exercise over subordinates (Scott 1990:7). Hidden
transcripts are low-profile forms of a shared critique of power and
resistance that "dare not speak in their own name." They are implicit
protest, dissent, and subversive discourse of underdogs against their
worldly fate. Recognizing that elites have privileged access to power,
wealth, and health because of their dominate social position, subordinate groups have learned tactical prudence when protesting. Rarely do
they blurt out their hidden transcripts in public; elaborate forms of
disguise are employed. The public expression of insubordination of
subordinate groups is "sufficiently indirect and garbled that it is
capable of two readings, one of which is innocuous" (Scott 1990:157).

Cries of "I'm Not Dog, No!" and the creation of far-out cholera
conspiracy theories by poor Brazilians pose no direct threat or opposition to the authorized medical position on cholera. But at a deeper
level, it is apparent that the euphemisms, folktales, and plays-on-words
of popular culture encode and conceal double meanings from medical
authorities and contest the inequitable social order in northeastern
Brazil. This chapter explores the hidden transcripts or discourse –
gestures, speech, practices – about cholera that is ordinarily excluded
from the public transcript of the dominant, medical professionals. We
describe a rich folk disease taxonomy of cholera. We probe the
underlying accusations that provoke poor residents in Gonçalves Dias
and Conjunto Palmeiras to cry out "farce!" and resist well-intended
medical advice and medications. We describe hurtful, discriminatory
accusations which inflict suffering on infected persons and whose
originators, in retribution, become the target of popular cholera conspiracy theories. We describe how a positive cholera diagnosis results
in social stigmatization, prejudice, and discrimination against the
infected poor. We argue that conspiracy theories are rhetorical defenses – a kind of symbolic protest – against the crippling accusations

of elites. Moreover, we argue that so-called patiênt noncompliance – mocking cholera prevention messages, lashing out at medical authorities, threatening powerful politicians, shunning doctors' advice, spitting-up medication, and resisting hospital rehydration – is popular resistance against, not so much cholera care, but the more insidious social diseases of defamation and discrimination.

CHOLERA AND BLAME IN BRAZIL

During the recent cholera epidemic in Northeast Brazil, the damaging dynamics of blame were visible. In Ceará state, 16,325 cases were registered in 119 of 184 counties, resulting in 121 deaths in the first nine months of 1993 alone; 9336 cases have been reported in the capital of Fortaleza (*O Povo* 10–9–93:12a). These statistics represent only a fraction of all cases. Early in the epidemic, official diag nostic criteria for cholera required a positive laboratory confirmation. As numbers of suspected cases out-paced laboratory facilities, clinical and epidemiological evidence was accepted as sufficient to establish a positive diagnosis. Even so, many cases – Dona Lucimar's and Antonio's below – remained hidden from the "public transcript" of biomedicine. They suffered cholera's ravening clinical course at home, alone.

With confirmed cholera cases quickly mounting, Brazilian health authorities sounded an all-out alert to contain the spread of *V. cholera*. The disease now threatened not only millions of slum-dwellers in the Northeast, but, perhaps more important to politicians, the economic livelihood of the region (e.g., tourism, seafood export). By the spring of 1993, general panic had set in, particularly in the capital, Fortaleza (pop. 2 million), which reported the highest national cholera attack and mortality rates in the country. Prevention messages were continually broadcast over radio and television airwaves; private school children had daily hand washing drills; five-star hotel restaurants washed vegetables in bleach; and luxury, beach front apartment residents treated private wells with chloride. Overnight, the already dual-class society, sharply divided: cholera-infested and cholera-free. There were those living with cholera and those defending themselves. Imaginary walls quickly rose to seal off the wealthy enclave, Aldeota, from the cholera-infected poverty zones of the periphery. Upper-class residents quietly dismissed maids, cooks, laundresses, and nannies living in cholera-infested, lower-class neighborhoods. The rich prohibited their children from contacting poorer playmates, using public restrooms and eating in popular restaurants. Northeast bound tourists cancelled trips. Meanwhile, poor residents living in Fortaleza's 300 shanty towns came under intense scrutiny and government-sponsored cholera surveillance. Teams of well-intentioned sanitary workers mapped out high-risk cholera zones, treated community wells and in-home drinking water with chloride, tracked the number and appearance of residents' diarrheal stools, and administered prophylactic antibiotics to asymptomatic *V. cholera* carriers. In short, the stated intention of public health teams was to declare war against the rapidly spreading water-borne cholera bacillus (*A Guerra Contra Colera*). But according to *favela* residents, the sanitary workers' hidden strategy was to contain cholera in slums and prevent its spread to wealthier neighborhoods.

TWO FAVELAS, TOO POOR

During the cholera epidemic of 1993 in Fortaleza, Ceará, Brazil, we conducted an ethnographic study of cholera-related beliefs and behaviors among residents of two high-risk urban slums – Gonçalves Dias (pop. 2000) and Conjunto Palmeiras (pop. 20,000). Goncalves Dias is a painfully poor favela located only a few blocks from the Federal University of Ceará's (UFC) medical complex and the state's São José Infectious Diseases Hospital.[1] Some 30 years ago, Gonçalves Dias was an unpaved avenue on Fortaleza's outskirts, until landless peasants invaded one night and staked it out as home. Boring tenacious roots into the packed dirt of Avenida Gonçalves Dias, they built hovels, raised families, and constructed a community along the narrow street. Over the years, residents have been expelled four times from "The Avenida" and their homes, most recently during this project.[2] Pressured by wealthier neighbors, local politicians have ordered families to disassemble their cardboard, tin, adobe, and stick homes; pack-up; and resettle in government housing projects on the distant outskirts of the sprawling capital city. The resilient residents of "The Avenida" grudgingly obey the official mandates, only to return when eviction threats subside and the ruling politicians leave office. Today Gonçalves Dias consists of some 440 tightly packed houses with common walls and no privacy. The most common house construction is clay molded over stick frames forming two *vaos* or rooms, with mostly earthen floors. Pictures and posters of Catholic-saints, deceased relatives, soap opera stars, popular musicians, and political candidates adorn the otherwise drab walls. During the rainy season (December to March), tropical down-pours literally dissolve the protective clay walls. The larger vao, measuring some four square meters, doubles as a living room and bedroom, the second, smaller vao at the rear is the kitchen. As many as ten people sleep in the front vao by stringing up hammocks, criss-cross on three levels: low, medium, and high. Bed-wetting infants and cholera defecating adults sleep on the low rung. More than 80% of the houses have no sanitary facilities; raw sewage flows throughout the favelas in open gutters. Adults defecate in an empty tin can filled with dirt. At night they fling the contents in a vacant space. The children defecate anywhere convenient. Using old newspapers or banana leaves, mothers scoop up the feces and toss (*rebola*) them outside. Simple coal-burning fires heat the family's two cooking pots: one larger for simmering beans, and another smaller for preparing the baby's porridge (*mingau*) and boiling water to prepare coffee. Electricity is often tapped illegally from power lines servicing wealthier neighbors. Women's income as laundresses or maids in wealthier homes is more stable than their often sporadic male partners'. Children as young as five often care for newborns while mothers work. Exclusive breastfeeding is rare. The diarrheal attack rate in children less than five years is extremely high: 11.4 illnesses per year (Shorling et al. 1987:489). Sixty-eight percent of children aged three to five years presenting diarrhea have one or more parasitic infections (Pennie et al. 1995). Of 244 children born to 43 families (5.7 children per family) 24.6% had died when surveyed in 1983 (Guerrant et al. 1995); 52% died with diarrhea, 10% with pneumonia, and 7% with measles. On weekends Gonçalves Dias bustles with life: red-lipped adolescents, in glove-tight short-shorts and sensual, off-the-shoulder midriff blouses, jive to the pounding tropical Lambada, forró, and Axé rhythms, which drown-out the blasts of shotguns, screams of battered women, cries of hungry infants, bickering of neighbors, bartering of drug dealers, and violent arguments between a group of men who down shots of *cahaça*[3] at the local bar.

The second slum, Conjunto Palmeiras,[4] conjures up a romantic, tropical imagine at first. Palmerias refers to the clusters of lush, green palm trees that line Ceara's coastline, their trunks swaying rhythmically and their tattered fonds rustling in the soothing trade winds. But the idealistic image quickly gives way to another sobering reality. Conjunto Palmeiras is a planned resettlement community. It is an endless sea of identical, poorly constructed clay and brick row-houses which are home to some 20,000 people who relocated (often forcibly) from higher-priced city lots or migrated from the drought-stricken interior (*sertão*) in search of a better life. Conjunto Palmeiras is located on Fortaleza's periphery, just past Jangurursu, the municipal dump, where the garbage of some two million people is deposited, scavenged, saved, and sold daily. Like Jangurursu, Conjunto Palmeiras is a dump, only a human one, where it seems society's throw-aways are left to decompose. While potable water was installed in 1988 following requests by community leaders, no sewage network or public garbage collection service exists. There is only one paved street in town on which old buses run sporadically. A branch of the polluted Coco River borders on the south. Most community activities occur in a small square around which the main school, church, market, community radio, birth center, and day-care center are located. Animals roam freely in public places, where rubbish and feces often mix. Socioeconomic conditions, while generally poor, vary among residents (Monte 1993:69). Classified as "very poor," are 25.5% of families who live in mud homes with straw roofs, earthen floors, no sanitation and having a radio as the only appliance, if any. The majority (51.4%) are "poor" households of unplastered brick with straw roofs and cemented floors, always possessing a radio, sometimes a television, but very rarely a refrigerator. Most have access to piped water outside the house and some have pit latrines. "Less poor" households (23.1%) are brick structures, sometimes plastered with tile roofs and ceramic floors, with access to piped water (sometimes within the house), pit latrines, and having a radio, television and refrigerator. Some 50% of households have six or more members, with 93% having at least three children under five years of age. Children suffer frequent diarrhea; 30% of those under five years of age had experienced diarrhea with severe or moderate dehydration in the previous two weeks.[5] Male unemployment, burglary, drug abuse, mental stress, and violence against women (rape, domestic violence, murder) take their toll. But the demoralizing affliction in Conjunto Palmeiras is political abandonment and disenfranchisement. Families live on the periphery of modern life, shut-out of the opportunities and dreams of Fortaleza's better-off families.

These two favelas sadly reflect the conditions of many impoverished and forgotten Brazilian communities. Until very recently, there seems little hope for change. The first democratically elected president after some 20 years of military rule was entangled in scandal and eventually impeached by the Brazilian National Congress. The distribution of wealth – already the world's third most disparate – is widening, leaving the already privileged few (10%) even wealthier and the other 90% more destitute than ever (The World Bank 1990:236–237). The number of infants dying from preventable causes persists at disgraceful levels, despite increasing sophistication of modern medicine. Between 1980 and 1986 the infant mortality rate was 64.1, 98.8 in the underdeveloped Northeast and 44.6 in the affluent, industrial south; Fortaleza's infant mortality rate of 104.6 was far higher than Rio de Janeiro's (49.2) and São Paulo's (54.1) in the same year (UNICEF 1992). Violence and police brutality are at all time highs. In 1993 – during the cholera epidemic – the world was stunned by Brazil's brutal, police violence: the indiscriminate massacre of 111 prisoners in the Carandiru Prison in São Paulo, assassination of sleeping street children in the Candelária in Rio de Janeiro, and extermination of residents in Vigário Geral favela north of Rio de Janeiro. (Here, on August 30th, some 30 hooded Military Police invaded the favela at dawn and unmercifully executed 21 innocent residents – 20 workers and 1 student – in streets, bars, and homes (*Veja* 9–8–93:18–31).

GETTING BEHIND THE OFFICIAL CHOLERA STORY

Thus, the research upon which this chapter is based was "reality driven." Medical researchers at the Federal University of Ceará sensed "something was wrong" in Gonçalves Dias, where since 1985 they had surveyed households daily to detect diarrheal illnesses. Residents, normally cooperative, were now incredulous and resistant. They challenged – overtly and cryptically – researchers' authority to intervene and control cholera's spread. Behind the health workers' backs, residents dumped chlorinated water from their clay pots, spit out prophylactic antibiotic pills, falsely reported illness episodes, neglected to collect stool samples, refused hospital transfers, and sarcastically mimicked and distorted official cholera prevention slogans. It was apparent that some critical social forces were at play whose identification would be vital if cholera transmission was to be controlled in this community or others. University enteric diseases specialists, thus, summoned a team of social scientists with experience in infectious diseases in northeastern Brazil to gather privileged insights and commentaries on cholera from residents.

To begin we took a broad, holistic look at cholera. Our agenda was (deceptively) simple: to identify how social and cultural forces – at myriad levels – interact with *V. cholera*, infecting families living in urban poverty. We thought it essential to "see" cholera through the eyes of poor Brazilians who suffer most its consequences if our results were to be useful for rewriting the educational messages-gone-wrong. What is it like to be poor, hungry, and sick with cholera? What is it like to depend on inaccessible health professionals for your life? How does it feel to know what causes the suffering, yet be powerless against it? Penetrating local moral worlds of families living in poverty was the only way, we were convinced, to gain these insights into and commentaries on cholera as "lived-experience" (Kleinman and Kleinman 1986). Our search began knowing that such second-hand readings of suffering would never be complete. We aimed to probe the meaning-laden interior worlds of cholera-infected persons, while not losing sight of the political and economic forces that put them at risk in the first place. Given the epidemic nature and immediate need for social input in cholera control efforts, we worked quickly drawing heavily on Rapid Ethnographic Assessment (RAP) methodologies (Schimshaw and Hurtado 1987).

During two months (March–April 1993) at the epidemic's height, we conducted 80 in-depth, open-ended interviews with key informants living or working in Gonçalves Dias and Conjunto Palmeiras: poor mothers ($n = 33$); children ($n = 11$); persons sick with cholera ($n = 9$); community health agents ($n = 7$); community members in strategic positions to observe cholera-related behavior ($n = 7$); caretakers of cholera patients ($n = 6$); Afro-Brazilian *Umbanda* healers ($n = 2$); community leaders ($n = 2$); folk-Catholic healers ($n = 2$); and a traditional midwife ($n = 1$). Interview data were enriched and validated by observing in-home and community water use and storage practices, defecation, sewage disposal, food preparation, animal contact, community organization, medical compliance, self-care, healing rituals, and contact with hospitals and visiting health agents. Because we had conducted extensive ethnographic research in the two communities and maintained affective ties with many of the women and their families, rapport and immediate entry into the communities was eased. Our familiarity with the communities and ties of trust, allowed for immediate access to a far more difficult-to-reach arena: the "backstage" (Goffman 1959) and "hidden transcripts" (Scott 1990) of cholera.

We conducted all 80 interviews in Portuguese in either the homes of persons suffering cholera, at health posts, traditional healing centers (i.e., *terreiros* or Afro-Brazilian Umbanda centers), community wells or washing holes. Each interview lasted from one to three hours. All interviews were tape-recorded and then transcribed completely before translation. A series of techniques were employed to ensure validity and reliability. Questions were checked for adequacy during the pilot study and monitored during data collection. Triangulation (Denzin

1970) between informants, investigators, and within and between methods was used to validate the data collected. We analyzed the content in order to identify themes, which were then compared with accumulated anthropological research and knowledge. Three aspects of the interviews impressed us: (1) the frustration, anger, and revolt of adult informants when discussing cholera; (2) the severe physical suffering of cholera patients, many presenting classical, fulminating cases of infection; and (3) the resistance of cholera-infected persons to seek official medical care. Reluctant patients were often hauled – severely dehydrated or unconscious – to nearby emergency rooms by relatives and neighbors.

RITUAL RESISTANCE OF THE "DOG'S DISEASE"

Dona Zilnar,[6] traditional healer and mother of 22 children,[7] eyed suspiciously the printed paper reporting laboratory results of her feces exam collected by University of Ceará field researchers. "So what does it accuse?"[8] she pointedly queried. Unable to read the findings herself, her eldest daughter answered "P-o-s-i-t-i-v-e." "Positive for what devil thing? Dona Zilnar provoked. "*Vibrião cholera*" replied the community health worker, surprised by Dona Zilnar's unusual reaction. She continued aggressively:

> Hear me, this business of cholera doesn't exist. Here in Gonçalves Dias we don't have cholera, no! There doesn't exist anyone with cholera here! ... I'm not even going to speak with Our Lady Aparecida[9] about this thing because for her, there doesn't exist cholera. ... Somebody invented it! They are inventing it! And they are going to invent much more to come! [Dona Zilnar, traditional healer].

"I'm Not Dog, No!"[10] screamed Dona Zilnar uncontrollably as she wadded the paper with the laboratory results into a small ball and flung it at the feet of the now terrified health worker. "What do you think I am, some low-down *vira lata* (stray mutt dog)?"[11] Dona Zilnar's anger and frank denial of cholera alerted our attention: Why the upset? What in the cholera diagnosis set her off? Why a vira lata of all things? The medical team found curious not only her refusal to hear the community health workers' laboratory results, but the deeper, visceral revolt against her admirable intentions. Probing in greater depth the clinical histories of two individuals with cholera, Dona Lucimar and Antonio, we discovered painful stories of suffering. In severe cases of cholera, the intestine is infected with such rapidity and virulence that there is no time to resort to folk remedies, traditional healers and local pharmacy attendants. Even if there was, poor Brazilians know home-made teas are no weapon against such fulminant diarrhea and vomiting. Pragmatically, they seek intravenous rehydration at hospitals as the "only way out" (*o jeito*) in severe cases of "The Dog's Disease," (*doenca de cachorro*) as cholera is popularly called.

Case 1: Dona Lucimar, All Sucked Out From Inside by The Dog's Disease

Oh my God! I woke up with that fine pain...my guts ringing out dry, totally twisted inside... I prayed to Saint São Sebastião[12] that it wasn't cholera. I ran to the backyard ... it was only water...squirt, squirt, squirt...urinating out of my anus...all over my panties and new pants...shit, shit, shit and more shit! ... Oh! Doença de cachorro...humiliating, so awful. I was tempted to throw my pants away, but they were new! ... When dawn arrived I was very weak...a sour taste in my mouth...looked like I'd been sick for a week...all sucked out from the inside. I made a tea from orange peel, *goiabeira*[13] and *pitanga*.[14] My boy had four packets of oral rehydration solution... I don't even like the taste of ORS – but, I dissolved one quickly and drank it! I drank tea, drank ORS, drank tea, drank ORS, drank tea, drank ORS... I didn't have anyone to take me to the hospital... I don't like the hospital... I only went by force because of the attack...the taxi driver didn't take me... afraid I would die. They called an ambulance. My daughter was yelling and crying...when I woke up, I was in the Intensive Care Unit...all broken up and done in!

Case 2: Antonio, Cut Out The Death Robe

At about 10 p.m. Antonio threw open the door, ran right for the toilet...shitting and vomiting all night...burning with fever. He would sleep, run to the bathroom, cry, then pray, pray at the feet of the Padre Cicero[15] to stop it [diarrhea]... It's a really horrible disease...does away with one's meat [flesh]...very strong stomachache, leg pains so bad you can't stand up, vomiting. I said, Antonio, my son, let's go to the São Jose Hospital, boy. But he didn't want to go, he wanted a medicine for his headache. I said, 'my son, your medicine is the hospital!' I feed him orange peel tea, but he sickened. There wasn't any way out (*não tem jeito*). By 9 a.m. he couldn't stand up... white, white, white, and when a *morena*[16] is white... cut out the death robe. I hadn't a dime for a taxi, so I dragged him, walking and praying to Our Lady of Perpetual Help. São Jose Hospital is only two blocks away, but he sat down ten times. He couldn't walk anymore. When we arrived, I cut in front of the long line... He fell into the doctors' arms... his eyes rolled up... his pulse jumped up his arm... I went crazy, out of my mind. I grabbed the doctor and pleaded... For the love of God, don't let my son die. The next day I hunted for a hospital (to admit him)... only a mother would do this! There was nothing, no vacancy, nowhere... 'Give me the medicine,' I said, I'm taking him home because it's the same God at home as in the hospital!

THE GREAT CHOLERA INVENTION OR "PILING-ON-THE-ILLNESS"

Dona Lucimar's, Antonio's, and others' stories of suffering we collected are personal accounts of "experience-as-lived" and should be taken at face value. Even so, hard data verifying "real disease" exist: both Dona Lucimar and Antonio suffered laboratory-verified infections with *V. cholera*. Curious, then, are reactions of infected patients and families: they deny cholera and label it an imaginary illness, an "invention."

A closer look at our data shows that poor Brazilians in our study employed four strategies to negate the existence of this life-threatening cholera epidemic. First was flat-out denial, as Dona Lucimar's comments show and the following quotations reinforce:

> They did an exam... cholera. But it isn't so! It's really *cachaca*. The poor guy drinks a lot, you see. They invented that it's cholera! [daughter of 68-year-old cholera patient]

> The symptoms of cholera? I don't know, I don't even want to know. [mother]

> Half the people here don't believe cholera exists, even seeing my son, João, almost under the ground (dead). They think a person is behind it all... putting things in their head... they don't believe it!" [mother]

> We've had diarrhea all our lives... even before there existed this medicine thing... They invented it [cholera]. A mosquito bites and instantly it's malaria, yellow fever, dengue, this and that. They invented all this!

They just loaded this cholera thing on top of us...pile on that illness, that's it. [cholera patient]

At times during fieldwork we heard comical-sounding comments about cholera, despite its lethal nature. Health workers interrogated residents for detailed information about cholera, while residents responded by playing a curious hide-and-seek game. "Who was the first person you sought when the diarrhea began?" "I don't know what you're talking about." "When did you decide to go to the hospital for rehydration?" "Cholera is make-believe, an invention!" and so on. Below, a short excerpt from one such truncated and frustrating dialogue between a community health agent and a poor mother in Conjunto Palmeiras confirms this:

Q. Mrs. Sonia, have you heard any comments from people here about cholera?

A. Here? No.

Q. No one passing by here conversing, 'So-and-so is feeling this or that, with cholera?' Nobody talking about cholera, Sonia?

A. No, nobody talking about this, no.

Q. So many people gather here in front and nobody even comments much about this illness? Nobody says anything? Nobody is afraid?

A. No, we don't talk about this.

Q. Nobody feels anything, you know? Nobody comments anything, no?

A. No, here, no. Thanks to God, no. Thanks to God.

A second strategy was to deny outwardly that cholera exists, while fearing inwardly the illness. As with the virulent *Doença de Criança* (The Child's Disease) (Nations 1992:55–65), the mere mention or faintest vision could "call" the life-threatening illness to healthy bodies. Informants' denial of cholera could be construed as a culturally constructed protection against the unbearable, against the unspeakable. As seen in the following dialogue between a visiting nurse and a recuperating patient, even dreaming about cholera was forbidden.

Q. Do you talk about cholera with your friends?

A. No, converse, no.

Q. Why not?

A. Because I could dream, no? And then I will have it... For this reason I don't talk about it.

Q. If you dream, it can happen, ugh?
A. Yeah, the cholera.
Q. You don't talk about cholera, so you won't call it?
A. Yeah, if you say it, it will run after and grab you!

A third strategy was to render cholera trivial, commonplace and insignificant. Selective popular perceptions transformed virulent cholera into "ordinary diarrhea" or just about anything, so long as the word cholera was not uttered. Below we see how cholera was acknowledged, but assigned an amorphous identity like "the disease," or left nameless.

> I thought it was *the illness*, because it gives right away vomiting, fever, diarrhea, pains in the legs. [cholera patient]

> Exist, it exists. Only people don't have a name for it yet...lack of interest. [indigenous midwife]

Other informants trivialized cholera's virulence. A death-threatening infection was transformed into "a little annoyance," "a little thing," or "teething diarrhea" (*dentição*), a normal part of growing up. Said informants:

> My grandmother and my mother already talked about these illnesses. Exist, they exist...the common diarrhea that we've always had... What are you saying, that we can't have a little diarrhea? The person has a little diarrhea and the exam shows cholera. Invention! [traditional healer]

> When the girl comes with the exam results I'm going to fight with her because I don't believe it exists [cholera]...in the past they said everyone in the world had diarrhea, no?...now nobody can have it [diarrhea] and it is already this or that...this business of cholera. [mother]

> We never encountered an adult with cholera, more children, and even so the mothers would say, 'My child had diarrhea because of teething,' they would never say it was cholera. This is teething diarrhea, business of cutting teeth! [community health worker]

Informants also down-played cholera by equating it with clinically similar, yet far less virulent, dehydrating, and lethal, intestinal infections. Said one informant:

> There doesn't exist cholera, my daughter, no. There exists the name that they are calling it only. When you have diarrhea you lose a lot of liquid from your body, no?...you die in 24 hours...your intestine is eating your entire body...it's really only a profound intestinal infection, with

fever and headache that we feel. It isn't cholera, it's only an intestinal infection! [Umbanda healer]

Cholera's demotion by informants to a less virulent intestinal infection status was true even with confirmed laboratory results, as seen in the case of Dona Rita:

Q. Tell me about your cholera illness?

A. I didn't have cholera, no!

Q. No? Then did you see this type of illness in adults before?

A. No, with this name, no ... the illness I've seen.

Q. Without the name cholera?

A. Yes, without the name ... just diarrhea, acute diarrhea ... it gives hotness in the intestine, it's an intestinal infection.

Finally, a fourth popular strategy for denying cholera's existence was ridiculing the illness – to *leva na brincadeira* (to take it as a joke), as Brazilians say. Making cholera the brunt of jokes and teasing is what six teenagers, ages 10–15 years, did when we interviewed the group in Gonçalves Dias. Laughs, smirks, and elbow nudges emerged, and nobody had anything serious to say about cholera – until one of the boys bellowed out: "I don't know anything about cholera. I'm not a *favelado*.[17] I live in Aldeota (wealthy section of Fortaleza)!" Like dominos, the teens fell contagiously into uncontrollable fits of laughter, playfully back-slapping one other. "Hey, that's a good one!" "You said it, what a joke!" However, laughing off cholera was a strategy employed by all ages. A 34-year-old, severely ill patient from Gonçalves Dias joked:

I spent three days shitting without stopping. We just took it as a big joke. People in the street would tease, Hey, are you *Colorido*?[18] We would all start to laugh ... until yesterday ... I almost died, so skinny, all sucked-out from inside!

CHOLERA: MORE THAN MEETS THE EYE

The obvious question remains: why go to such culturally orchestrated lengths to deny a life-threatening disease like cholera? What hidden social forces trigger this (apparently) illogical reaction? Families in Gonçalves Dias and Conjunto Palmeiras believed there exists not cholera the disease, but rather cholera the conspiracy. They maintained that an organized plot exists to segregate rich from poor, or worse to "do in" poor people through massive genocide, thereby preserving the prevailing inequitable social structure. That the conspiracy threat was foremost on informants' minds was evident in the following passages:

> They are going to do away with us, creating illness and hunger. [cholera patient]

> There are many rich nearby that want to do away with this favela, for it to vanish. They say only thieves and drug addicts live here...now they've added cholera! They are even saying this! [mother]

> When I pass the alley they [better-off neighbor women] harass me, 'Hey woman, do you live in Gonçalves Dias?...it's only cholera... Hope your [anus is] all plugged up! They even made a petition to evict us... They want to do away with us! [laundress]

> Nobody wants to come close...when I took my nieces to nursery school, they said, 'Oh, no, for the love of God, leave them at home, they might have cholera and it could spread to the others! [aunt]

That cholera was invented as an excuse to "execute" the poor was reinforced, according to informants, by images used in the "War Against Cholera" Campaign of the Ceará State Health Department in early 1994. The official mass media campaign, like that described by Nichter (1990), was built upon an unfortunate metaphor: warfare. Along with soldiers from the Brazilian National Armed Services, the populace was called to "battle" against cholera (*lutar contra*), to "combat cholera" (*combater*), to form gangs (*arrastões*) (of delinquent youths) to "raid and loot" against cholera. But residents we interviewed perceived the battle and looting directed not against cholera, the water-borne bacillus, but against "we the cholera poor." Drawing upon a "battle" metaphor was especially inappropriate in 1993 for residents of Brazil's teeming favelas. The massacre at Carandiru Prison in São Paulo, the assassination of street kids in the Candelária in Rio de Janeiro, and the extermination of residents of Vigário Geral, were nightmares too recent in memory.

The official anticholera campaign poster showed a blindfolded man with a red "X" over his face. The caption read: "Cholera, Don't Close your Eyes to Life: Help Combat Cholera" (Figure 15.1). No more vivid and convincing evidence was needed, residents lamented, that the true "battle" ahead was against the "cholera poor"; they were being "identified during house-to-house searches, rounded-up, tested, blindfolded and "done-in." The blindfolded man depicted on the poster, we were told by informants, was "marked to die" and ready for execution with his

CÓLERA

não feche os olhos para a vida

AJUDE A COMBATER A CÓLERA

COMISSÃO DE PREVENÇÃO E CONTROLE DA CÓLERA

APOIO: PATROCÍNIO DESTE MATERIAL

b.b BANCO DO NORDESTE DO BRASIL S.A

DISQUE CÓLERA - 192187

Figure 15.1 Cholera campaign poster utilized to mobilize at-risk populations in Fortaleza, Brazil to control the spread of the disease. The word cholera, "X," and the subtitle beneath the image were highlighted in red ink.

Small subtitles announce that the State of Ceará supports this work and that the poster is financed by the Bank of the Northeast of Brazil.

hands bound behind his back, even though authorities had literally "covered-up the truth." Who was behind the sinister plot to spread cholera and exterminate the poor? When interpreting the poster, one 45-year-old semiliterate woman let her imagination roam. "The government was announcing that they would pay a ransom for anyone the community captured with cholera and turned in to authorities"! Why did she believe a ransom would be paid by authorities? To that question, the woman, without hesitation, pointed to the bottom right of the poster. It read: "This material was sponsored by the Northeast Bank of Brazil," accompanied by the bank's familiar logotype.

As Goffman (1963:46) has noted, "it is possible for signs which mean one thing to one group to mean something else to another group, the same category being designated but differently characterized." The soldiers, battles, raids, looting, blindfolded man, and red "X" meant one thing to State Secretary of Health Cholera Control workers and something quite different to families living in poverty. To authorities they were innocuous terms aimed at energizing the community; to poor families they were symbols of military, police, criminal, and drug lords' brutality – omnipresent in Brazil's favelas – which foreshadowed horror and death. Termed "stigma symbols" by Goffman (1963), such signs are "especially effective in drawing attention to a debasing identity discrepancy, breaking up what would otherwise be a coherent overall picture, with a consequent reduction in our valuation of the individual" (1963:43). The poster's "stigma symbols" are, thus, highly effective in transforming the poor cholera victim into a poor, cholera criminal who deserves justice: to be captured, blindfolded, and put before the firing squad.

Residents of Gonçalves Dias and Conjunto Palmeiras pinpointed as responsible wealthy bankers and financial institutions and implicated an amorphous "them," referring to the power elite in general (Freye 1963a, 1963b; Lipset and Solari 1967). They also earmarked the impeached ex-President of Brazil, Fernando Collor de Mello, as well as politicians, the pharmaceutical industry, land developers, doctors, foreigners, and visiting scientists. Revolted residents explained:

> There isn't research in rich houses, who wants to know if cholera is there? Nobody goes. They only visit poor favelas because it's the rich who are paying to know this information. [cholera patient]

> The government invented this cholera because it really isn't to help us. Better to forget, to write us off at once... like they say, the poor are only worth something buried. [cholera patient]

> Politicians have their reasons... they just want to win votes. [community leader]

> They say they are going to give the poor food, but they just invent illness like cholera so pharmacies can get rich selling us medicines instead. [community health worker]

Health care professionals were also implicated in the cholera conspiracy, with the exception of community doctors who were largely exonerated. Implicated were distant, alien doctors working in Rio de Janeiro or São Paulo:

> Doctors, not like Dr. A. (UFC project physician), no. But you can bet on ones from Rio de Janeiro and São Paulo...they're only interested in cholera so they can rise [advance in their careers].

The appearance of asymptomatic carriers of *V. cholera* added more fuel to the conspiracy fire: positive results without symptoms raised immediate suspicions that medical professionals were inventing the disease as part of the cholera conspiracy. That doctors failed to isolate an etiologic agent from diarrheal patients, reinforced an image of medical incompetence and duplicity. Said one women suffering from diarrhea but testing negative for cholera:

> The community health worker did the first exam, a second exam... nothing! What is it now, AIDS?, I asked. 'Are you crazy woman! It isn't AIDS!,' she said. Tell me, no worms, no nothing...well then, what devil of diarrhea is this anyway? [cholera patient]

If such down-home explanations fail to convince, a great global cholera conspiracy is entertained. Sontag (1990) in *AIDS and Its Metaphors*, suggests that "there is a link between imaging disease and imaging foreignness. It lies perhaps in the very concept of "wrong," which is archaically identical with the non-us, the "alien" (1990:48). Informants counterattack the highly industrialized and wealthy nations – Japan and the United States – as responsible for both inventing and planting cholera in the impoverished Northeast:

> There doesn't even exist cholera in São Paulo, no way. It was invented outside Brazil. [Traditional healer]

> It was a band of people over there that invented cholera. The same that invented dengue...the Japanese. It already came from there to here, cholera. They invented the robot...they work, do everything, equal to a person...even weave a hammock. So they invented robots so nobody will work. And invented cholera to do away with us because they can't raise our salaries. [mother]

> We all saw Dr. R., the American [doctor], help by putting medicine in the well water...but the other Americans with him, they only want women to stop having babies, to exploit us. [cholera patient]

THE MENACE OF METAPHORS

Let's assume, for now, that cholera was invented and introduced into Brazilian favelas as part of an elitists' conspiracy – a global conspiracy – to exterminate the poor. The next question is: how exactly do the

elite link impoverished Brazilians to the morally disgracing and disempowering imagery of cholera? Embedded in informant's narratives we
discovered one devastating way: metaphors. In *Metaphors We Live By*,
Lakoff and Johnson (1980:5) say "the essence of metaphor is understanding and experiencing one kind of thing in terms of another." This
is possible because the metaphor is built into the conceptual system of
the culture in which we live; it is embedded in our values, perceptions,
and systems of meaning. When making a direct association between
two domains is too abstract, unclear, difficult, or even risky – for
whatever reason – metaphors are used to define and assign meaning,
thus giving us a new understanding of our experience. First, the
metaphor highlights certain features while suppressing other aspects of
the concept that are inconsistent with metaphor. Second, the metaphor
does not merely entail other concepts, but it entails very specific aspects
of these concepts. Third, because the metaphor highlights important
experiences and makes them coherent while masking other experiences, the metaphor gives a new meaning. By highlighting and hiding,
can come to "see" humans living in poor housing conditions without
much to eat in terms of non-humans with animal motivations, actions
and characteristics. Without these channeling metaphors, but others,
we might just as well "see" *favelados* as devoted catholics, as working
mothers, as migrant laborers etc.

As harmless as metaphors – a simple figure of speech – may appear,
Ribeiro (1992) maintains that metaphors are the most powerful way to
communicate because they have "condensed power."

In the realm of disease, "nothing is more punitive than to give a
disease a meaning" (Sontag 1990:17). As Sontag explains:

> The subjects of deepest dread (corruption, decay, pollution, anomie,
> weakness) are identified with the disease. The disease itself becomes a
> metaphor. Then, in the name of the disease [that is, using it as a
> metaphor], the horror is imposed on other things. The disease becomes
> adjectival. Something is said to be disease-like, meaning that it is
> disgusting or ugly... Feelings about evil are projected onto a disease.
> And the disease (so enriched with meanings) is projected onto the world.
> [Sontag 1990:58]

From informants' perspectives, the elite in Brazil seem to have
a corner on using menacing metaphors. They are accused of sublimi-
nally (some may argue unconsciously, or even unwittingly) feeding into
pre-existing stereotypes, equating poor people with degrading and
humiliating cultural images and then playing on these potent metaphors

to link the poor directly to cholera. Two such culturally construed images are the *pessoa imunda* (filthy–dirty person) and *vira latas* (stray mutt dogs). Both are cognitive constructions of the defiling, repulsive, and repugnant. Both are common images in the everyday world of favelados. Both came to our attention because of the frequency with which they appeared in fieldnotes and transcriptions. We will now explore these two culturally forged images, showing how the favelado's identity, the Dog's Disease and cholera became inexorably bound.

FILTHY, DIRTY PERSON (PESSOA IMUNDA)

"We ARE the cholera!" pronounced 18-year-old Rosa in a matter-of-fact tone of voice, sending shivers through us. For after one month in the field, the force of a metaphor to spoil personal identity was becoming apparent. How had this young woman, recovering from a serious cholera infection, come to internalize that she, herself, her person, was equivalent to contaminated, polluted, dangerous, and feared feces?

Being physically dirty or lacking personal hygiene is particularly abhorred in Brazilian culture. Taking numerous baths per day, using deodorant and dousing oneself with cologne (from sweet smelling herbal water to imported French perfume, depending on class), wearing clean, pressed clothes and spotless shoes in public are valued across socioeconomic groups in Northeast Brazil. The "cult of cleanliness" is inculcated in young Brazilian children via such animated cartoon characters as *Sujismundo* (Dirty World) and *Cascão*, two filthy–dirty little boys, who because they never bathe are the brunt of jokes and teasing by playmates. Given this cultural abhorrence of poor personal hygiene, the dirty or the unkept are especially degrading and defiling images, spoiling one's identity.

We learned that prior to the current cholera epidemic, the favelado's image, in society's eyes, had already been firmly wedded to that of a pessoa imunda (filthy, dirty person).

> They nicknamed us favelados because we are poor, we live in a favela, we are imunda (filthy dirty), we don't have a salary, we don't have good nutrition. [12-year-old girl]

> It makes no difference, if I clean outside because my neighbor is so imunda. She raises pigs...her children walk without shoes...she throws the sewage on the street...and when it rains this dirtiness washes in front of my house. [mother]

Early in 1993, when cholera advanced quickly throughout Ceará, mass media prevention campaigns mentioned that fecal-oral contamination spreads cholera. What residents "heard" on radio and television, however, was a different and more damaging message: cholera is caused not by the water-borne bacillus but by miasmic *imundicie*, a popular word meaning "filthy squalor," the worst kind of dirtiness or pollution. The *mundo imunda*, the filthy world they were forced to live in "causes cholera." Urban squalor – *imundicie* – *was everywhere*: *"foul atmosphere," effusions (catinga)* from decaying pigs' feces and open sewage, decaying food from the nearby dump, garbage, rot, children playing with mud and walking without shoes, flies landing on feces then on food, proximity to the city's mortuary and bloody run-off water, homemade ice cream with decaying fly remains, and spoiled food scavenged from the dump. The generalizing of a specific infective process into an atmosphere found in urban slums – into imundicie and imundas (filthy, dirty) persons – was used to moralize cholera and to stigmatize infected persons by associating them with impurity, deviancy and disdain. Favelados were stigmatized as imundas persons; imundicie causes cholera; cholera is, therefore, favelados. Favelados are cholera.

It is no wonder, then, that an official national cholera campaign slogan in late 1992 – *Fora Colera*! (Get Out Cholera!) – did little to endear our informants to the government's control efforts. The slogan Fora Colera! is a subliminal play on the words Fora Collor! (Get Out [President] Collor!) which, just months before in September 1992, had been the rallying cry, chanted by millions of Brazilian citizens who took to the streets to demonstrate and force the impeachment of the then President of Brazil, Fernando Collor de Mello. Instead of "Get Out Cholera!" families heard, "Get out, you filthy–dirty crook! Get out, you worthless cholera-infected person." The official message, rather than mobilizing persons to eradicate *V. cholera* and, thus, protect themselves against infection, galvanized them against the (perceived) unscrupulous motives of the elite.

DOENÇA DE CACHORRO: THE DOG'S DISEASE

"Cholera, rabies, Doença de Cachorro." Dona Zilnar rambles the three words off so quickly, that they are hardly distinguishable. She has her reasons; in Portuguese the words are intimately related. *Colera* is a pseudonym for *raiva*, or rabies. According to the dictionary (*Novo Dicionário Aurélio da Lingua Portuguesa*), the word "colera," of Greek and Latin derivation means: (1) "a violent impulse against that which offends, wounds or causes us indignity; that angers or provokes raiva; (2) a ferocity of animals; (3) agitation; and (4) an infectious, acute, contagious disease, that can manifest as an epidemic, and is characterized in its classical presentation by abundant diarrhea, prostration and cramping." A *colerica* person is first a raivosa or angry person, and second a person infected with *V. cholera*. The dictionary defines the word "raiva," of Latin deviation, as first rabies, a viral disease that attacks mammals, and second as *V. cholera*. A raivosas person is one attacked by rabies and second one full of anger, full of cholera (*Novo Dicionário Aurélio da Lingua Portuguesa*).

In northeastern Brazil, people use the word cholera for rabies. Dogs foam at the mouth because of cholera. A colerico dog bites and passes raiva. People vaccinate their dogs against cholera. Given the linguistic resemblance of cholera and raiva, then, the metaphorical play that associates poor persons with vira lata dogs is fairly straightforward. Favelado is cholera is raiva is The Dog's Disease (as is cholera) is dog is vira lata (an especially scraggly, unkempt kind of dog who scavenges food from garbage cans). Metaphorically speaking, favelados are vira latas. In the eyes of the poor, how society treats a rabid stray mutt is also how it will symbolically treat a cholera-infected favelado.

STRAY MONGRELS (VIRA LATAS)

Thus, when Dona Zilnar screams "I'm not dog, no!," she is not referring to dog as Man's Best Friend – the pedigreed, pampered poodles rich Madames parade along Fortaleza's beachfront as Dona Zilnar begs money from tourists. The dogs Dona Zilnar refer to are another type: vira latas. They are the abandoned beasts that roam Fortaleza's favelas – hungry, diseased, unkempt, and unloved. Informants' colorful and degrading descriptions of vira latas would give anyone reason to revolt, if likened to them:

> Vira lata is a *bruto* (ugly, wild beast) animal, a stray mutt that runs loose in the four corners of the city, wild on the streets. Everybody who sees them wants the right to do something – kick, throw rocks, hit – do all sorts of violence to these vira latas because they don't even have an owner. [community health worker]

> Vira latas suffer a lot. They are born at home, but when they grow a little bit they must go to the streets. They scavenge garbage cans – turn them over – looking for any scrap of food. They are common animals like any other type (without pedigree). [12-year-old girl]

Vira latas don't have a place to stay...where they find someone to give a little scrap of food, they stay, but they are always an embarrassment to everyone (*desprezo de todos*). [cholera patient]

Vira latas are full of illness. You can almost get sick just looking at one. They are filthy–dirty...never vaccinated against rabies. If they are crazy and bite someone, this illness is very dangerous [for people]... They don't have anyone to do anything for them. They are brutos. They don't know anything. [community leader]

Given that being likened to a vira lata is bad enough, the term vira lata is also used derogatorily in everyday language to refer to female prostitutes. An English equivalent is "whore." The metaphorical implication is that prostitutes, like stray dogs, belong to no one and everyone, that they have no pedigree, no status, and no inherent rights. A vira lata girl is at ready disposal of anyone who desires to use and abuse her in exchange for leftovers – as little as 4.00–5.00 USD per sexual encounter in Fortaleza. The word dog or *cachorro* alone has multiple derogatory meanings in northeastern Brazil. "*Cachorro sem vergonha*"! loosely translates as "You low-down bastard without scruples"! Dictionary synonyms for the word cachorro include scoundrel (a mean, immoral, or wicked person or rascal) and wretch (a person who is despised or scorned) and its feminine version, cachorra, include shew, strumpet, and harlot (*Michaelis Dicionario Pratico*). A derivative form of cachorro, *cao*, also refers to a masculine dog, but according to the dictionary, the word cao alternatively mean "a contemptible person" (*Michaelis Dicionario Pratico*) and in popular usage it signifies the "demon" or "devil." The popular sayings, *Que o cao te carregue*! (May the devil carry you [to hell]!) or *Ele tem parte com o cao*! (He has a pact with the devil!) illustrates in common speech the diabolical connotation of the word cao or dog in Portuguese. A *banda de cachorros* or *cachorrada* literally refers to a pack of dogs; according to the dictionary, it also means a mob (a disorderly and lawless crowd or in slang, a gang of criminals) or alternatively, an ill-conceived, wicked and mischievous trick produced by cachorros (a low-down, dishonest person) (*Michaelis Dicionario Pratico*). A *cachorrice* is defined as a "wicked action" or "conduct," "dirty trick," "lowness," "meanness," "indignity" (*Michaelis Dicionario Pratico*). Furthermore, anyone living in one of Fortaleza's 300 favelas can tell the fate of a choleric vira lata dog suspected of rabies: dog catchers hunt it down, restrain the feisty animal with a leash and collar, muzzle and isolate it to keep it from biting innocent victims. In cases of bites, the stray is kept under keen observation. If the unfortunate victim develops symptoms of rabies, the dog is killed. Even in less extreme cases when dogs are not infected with rabies, many well-to-do residents prefer to see them eliminated and deliberately avoid all contact (particularly that of their children) with unvaccinated, stray mutts. As one informant emphasized:

> SUCAM (Government Infectious Disease Control Unit) must kill these vira latas. If not the city will be swarming with these mangy mongrels and this can't be permitted! [community leader]

As with the cholera eradication campaign poster, the State Secretary of Health's reported actions reinforced, in people's minds, the menacing metaphors. Headlines in the local newspaper of March 13, 1994 read: "Secretary of Health is Accused of Executing Dogs" (*O Povo* 3–13–94 p.25a). The International Association for the Protection of Animals filed suit against the Secretary of Health in neighboring Maracanaú, and two Health Post Veterinarians for indiscriminately capturing and killing dogs. "The workers from the Health Post capture dogs in the street without any respect for laws governing their sacrifice (all animals are entitled to an eight-day period after capture to locate the owner or process an adoption)," the article reported. The Health workers were accused of "extreme brutality" in sacrificing the animals: the captured dogs were hit over the head with a nail protruding from a two-by-four board and their throats slashed with a large knife.

To Dona Zilnar and her neighbor friends, the vira lata metaphor rings too close to home. Handing her a positive diagnosis for *V. cholera* was like symbolically screaming in her face: "You no good vira lata! You filthy, dirty stray mutt! How dare you bite us, you lowly mongrel! You worthless bitch! You cheap whore!" Through Dona Zilnar's eyes, identifying her as a *V. cholera* carrier was equivalent to branding her as an inferior, subhuman type only worthy of eating spoiled, leftover scraps of food (like those she scavenges from the garbage bins behind the São Sebastião Market every Friday). She has no pedigree, no family name worth weight. If she strays into well-to-do-neighborhoods, the dog catcher may catch, harness, muzzle and even "sacrifice" her. In the same way, when health authorities target endemic cholera enclaves, implement door-to-door disease surveillance, erect highly visible cholera treatment tents in town centers, and set up barricades to contain the disease's transmission, she feels like a huge dog collar is being tightened around the rabid, choleric community. Slowly it is cinched. Once the muzzle is fitted, the leash secured, the rabid, mad vira lata dog restrained, extermination proceeds.

METAPHORS, STIGMA, AND SPOILED IDENTITY

Through metaphors the identity of favelados is inexorably bound to morally repugnant cultural images of filth and stray mutts and, in certain instances, prostitutes. In Mary Douglas's (1966) *Purity and Danger* she argues that every culture is a means of ordering experience. However, every ordering system gives rise to anomalies and ambiguities, which it must be prepared to control when they violate principles of order by crossing some forbidden line. Labeling anomalies or violators as "impure," "polluting," or otherwise "dangerous" allows society to rid of them through destruction, banishment, or execution – either directly or symbolically. Because epidemic cholera flourishes in unsanitary favelas yet disregards socioeconomic barriers, favelados are perceived by wealthy Brazilians as one such "danger" which threatens the rigid class structure of Brazilian society. Order must be restored and violators controlled. One way, is to label favelados as impure, polluting, and dangerous, as we have witnessed in Conjunto Palmeiras and Gonçalves Dias. Moral sentiments support the rules of purity, according to Douglas. Favelados are not only polluting and dangerous, they are labeled as being morally inferior to upper-class elites. A vira-lata mutt is a bastard dog (or prostitute), a morally disgraceful identity in this largely Catholic country. The very idea of pollution occurring through, say, casual contact between the morally inferior poor and the upstanding elite, may suffice to preserve the sharply drawn class distinctions in Northeast Brazil, having one of the world's worst distributions of wealth (The World Bank 1990:236–237). Moreover, with the aggressive spread of the epidemic, the poor often come to be seen by elites as their adversaries that can attack, bite, hurt, steal (scraps of leftover food), and even kill. In keeping with the principle of purity and order, these enemies must be destroyed. Adversarial models of health interventions and education can be employed to "declare war," "target," "attack," "exterminate," "execute," those who threaten class order, temporarily upset (Nichter 1990).

Through such degrading and animalistic metaphors, favelados suffer contamination not only of their intestinal mucosa, but of their social identity. In his classic work on stigma, Goffman (1963) defines stigma as:

> An attribute that makes him different from others... of a less desirable kind...a person who is quite thoroughly bad, or dangerous, or weak. He is thus reduced in our minds from a whole and usual person to a tainted, discounted one. Such an attribute is a stigma, especially when its discrediting effect is very extensive. [Goffman 1963:2–3]

Cholera – like tuberculosis, leprosy, and HIV-AIDS – is a mysterious infectious disease that is not only acutely feared but is felt to be morally, if not literally, contagious. A moralistic judgement about the person accompanies the disease. Freidson (1979) notes that when a moralistic judgement of blame is made, the bearer may be held responsible for the illness. Medical problems may be stigmatized to the extent that by social taxonomy, the illness becomes a crime and the sick person a deviant deserving punishment in society's eyes. Even worse, stigma may spoil normal identity permanently (Ablon 1981:5–9; Boutte 1987:209–217).

> Stigma is so closely connected with identity that even after the cause of the imputation of stigma has been removed and the societal reaction has been ostensibly redirected, identity is formed by the fact of having been in a stigmatized role...one's identity is permanently spoiled. [Goffman 1963:74]

In this largely Catholic world where filth and sexual immorality are formally abhorred, the social labels of imunda or, worse, vira lata are weighty, image-destroying stigmas. Besides suffering the wrenching cramps of a *V. cholera* infected intestine, cholera patients are seen by many elites as immoral individuals, who are fully responsible for the epidemic. Their identities as mothers, workers, students are spoiled permanently. Even after the cholera epidemic is controlled, the images of imundicie and vira latas will remain.

Acquiescence to such social stigmatization, however, is seldom a popular response. Rather, labeling and stigmatization more often provoke acts of subtle resistance by peripheral people against the dominant (Comaroff 1977; Scott 1985, 1990). The highly stigmatized do not always accept the very norms that disqualify them. Explains Gussow and Tracy (1986):

> Surely there are other feasible modes of adaptation. One is the development of stigma theories by the stigmatized – that is, ideologies to encounter the ones that discredit them, theories that would explain or legitimize their social condition, that would attempt to disavow their imputed inferiority and danger and expose the real and alleged fallacies involved in the dominant perspective. [Gussow and Tracy 1986:317]

So it is with cholera. If poor people cannot confront the elite or revolt violently and vociferously against their unfair characterization and stigmatization, they dig in and brandish symbolic fists (Scott 1985, 1990). Why comply with medical advice? Why obey instructions? Why become a "dog"? Why be abused, kicked, muzzled or shot? Better to define cholera as an invention, fantasy, or conspiracy and shout out, "I'm Not Dog, No!" than to internalize its accusatory message. Better to suffer in silence than to assume "stray-dog status" and be buried in their weight of its prejudice. Noncompliance becomes a silent revolt against the injustices of everyday life. "It's rabies! It's cholera! Careful rich one, don't let us bite you!" bellows out Dona Beatriz, as two wealthier women pass by. Defiance serves to reverse estrangement and reconstitute the divided self. Bucking authorities, no matter how discreetly, becomes a survival strategy to keep one's identity and passionate human spirit in tact. The force and furor of the backlash churn beneath the surface largely invisible to the public eye.

In both communities we studied, examples abound of resistance, including noncompliance with recommended treatment and public health prevention efforts. Prophylactic antibiotics are expectorated and chloride for sterilizing water pots dumped out, once health workers leave. As informants explained:

> God help me! I'm not taking those pills. They look like rat poison, my sister, it was rat poison! [cholera patient]

> My green pills I threw over the wall. [mother]

> They brought me drops [chloride] to put in my water pot...it was nothing but bleach, common bleach, women! Thanks a lot, I said, because I have a little tiny pile of clothes to wash! [laundress]

Second, as we learned from Dona Zilnar and others the implications of the cholera-as-invention posture is that people "hide" their symptoms from health authorities and, hence, grossly underestimate their risk of infection from *V. cholera*. This is particularly true of asymptomatic carriers, because without symptoms it is easier to dismiss one's role in transmitting the disease, especially if cholera is "make believe."

Third, many informants experienced exaggerated confidence in supernatural protection. Only spiritual protection was 100% effective, informants often said. Sick and suffering cholera patients retreated into their homes, into the comfort of their private saints to whom they pray for forgiveness and salvation while self-treating with herbal remedies.

Fourth, we noticed both a marked resistance and delay in seeking biomedical services. Few informants sought out nearby São Jose Hospital for electrolyte replacement therapy and, then, only when nearly unconscious. Finally, we identified a strange, morbid sense of pending death experienced by cholera-infected persons. With the onset of profuse watery stools, they invariably begin bidding final farewells to horrified and frantic family members.

LESSONS FOR CHOLERA CONTROL

It is clear from the above that to control cholera in Northeast Brazil, it is necessary to "remove dog collars" – that is, to listen to people's opinions, to include them in the definition of educational messages, and to design and implement control strategies which are socially and culturally appropriate. Experience shows that poor people do participate in learning experiences when opportunity is present. In such a context, people's innate learning skills are stimulated and instructions make sense (Drummond 1975; Freire 1977; Rifkin 1983).

We see none of the crippling fatalism and myopic "Limited Good" vision so often ascribed to Latin American peasants in our informants' responses (Acheson 1972:152–169; Foster 1965, 1967, 1972; Harrison 1985; Lewis 1966; Ryan 1971; Scheper-Hughes 1984, 1985; Valentine 1968). On the contrary, residents in Gonçalves Dias and Conjunto Palmeiras have frustratingly down-to-earth ideas about what needs to be done to control cholera in their communities. What they lack is not the will, but the way to implement changes, as comments below attest:

> The government must come to see the situation here. They have been saying a lot about hygiene and we know by experience that any improvement in hygiene is good for health. Why don't they do something about sanitation? [mother of five young children]

> We have been trying to do something to improve the environment but we receive no support from any institution. [community leader]

> In my family nobody likes drinking chloride water but I force them to do it anyway. They say that cholera can kill us. I don't want to die. [mother]

Based on the above ethnographic findings, we can recommend to health authorities in Fortaleza, Brazil more generally, and, perhaps, other developing regions, the following strategies to control cholera:

1. Replace moralistic miasmic theories of the spontaneous generation of cholera with the destigmatizing germ theory of water-borne contagion;

2. Promote healthy hygienic practices (handwashing, feces disposal, in-home water treatment) as an integral part of people's daily life routine rather than an extraordinary cholera-linked measure;

3. Mobilize traditional healers and lay persons in early initiation of in-home rehydration with household fluids, herbal teas and oral rehydration salts as an alternative to hospital-based rehydration (Nations and Rebhun 1988:25–38; Nations et al. 1988:335–354);

4. Avoid earmarking specific communities or persons as foci of disease transmission; control measures should be applied across the board to all economic classes and all persons in endemic regions;

5. Avoid "high visibility" control interventions such as community "cholera tents" and community-wide testing in public places; private, discrete face-to-face instructions will probably be more effective;

6. Avoid fear-driven educational messages; mass media campaigns should speak to specific methods to prevent infection using popular terminology and cognitive images;

7. Most important, eliminate all menacing, stigmatizing metaphors which insidiously discriminate by linking cholera to the identity of the poor.

ANTHROPOLOGY'S CONTRIBUTION TO CHOLERA CONTROL

Because of the life-threatening nature and urgency of epidemics of infectious diseases such as cholera, medical assistance must be mobilized quickly and efficiently to control their spread. In the haste to deliver emergency medical services, the cultural beliefs, perceptions, attitudes and behaviors of threatened individuals are frequently overlooked. Suffering people are often dehumanized by health workers as "disease hosts," "carriers," or "sources of contamination," and their communities as a "target population" or "foci of disease transmission." Their human qualities are transformed, or worse, forgotten. Because anthropology treats humans holistically in their natural sociocultural setting and captures people's own representations of their day-to-day world, the discipline can help fill the conceptual gap left by medical teams studying infectious diseases. Grasping an emic perspective (Berreman 1966:346–354; Harris 1976), as we have seen in the case of cholera, is fundamental even in such trying, emergency situations. Control campaigns which ignore the anthropology of its "target population" at best achieve only stunted program effect, far below its full potential, and, at worse, provoke anger, resistance, revolt and rejection among infected individuals and their families.

The specific contributions of anthropology to the study of infectious diseases we identified based on our experience with cholera in Fortaleza, Brazil are as follows:

1. Key-informants' colorful descriptions of symptoms, onset, manifestations, and suffering associated with infection, drawing on cultural representations and embedded in local systems of meaning can speed the diagnostic process and provide invaluable insights for health professionals about the disease as "lived experience" (Kleinman and Kleinman 1986) which can differ from standard textbook accounts. Our rich descriptions of cholera episodes "lived" at home, for instance, paint a real life picture of suffering, generally not appreciated in decontextualized, biomedical accounts of enteric infections.

2. Knowledge of people's self-care practices and health-seeking behavior in relation to a specific infection, allows health professionals to identify culturally specific practices and resources in the community to help patients cope with illness at home. Based on this information, health professionals can prescribe interventions that are both accessible and feasible to practice. For instance, we discovered a strong resistance to the addition of bleach to household drinking water as a cholera control measure. Vinegar was identified during the ethnographic study as a more acceptable alternative. We also learned that cholera is treated at home with medicinal herbal teas and patients seek the advise of *rezadeiras*, or traditional folk catholic healers. Based on this ethnographic data, oral rehydration therapy can be successfully mixed with herbal teas and mild to moderate cases of cholera managed at home by rezadeiras, lay experts in diarrheal diseases (Nations and Rebhun 1988:25–38; Nations et al. 1983:1612; 1988:335–354).

3. In-household participant-observation of family members preforming daily chores can lead to the discovery of behavioral modes of disease transmission not previously imaged or identified by epidemiologist (Nations 1986:97–123). Preparation of homemade popsicle with cholera-infected water or the eating of feces-contaminated dirt (geophagia) by children, for instance, were two such behaviors we observed inside homes in Gonçalves Dias.

4. Anthropological analysis of symbolic behavior and hidden transcripts which gets behind the scenes of official presentations for health workers can lead to the important discovery of patients' "noncompliant" behavior and, more importantly, their rational for rejecting well-intentioned interventions, as we have discussed above.

5. Detailed linguistic and ethnographic data on lay terminology and cognition, and explanatory models of illness can help bridge sometimes fatal gaps in doctor-patient communication. Eliciting the metaphorical meanings of the "Dog's Disease," for instance, was essential for improved communication with cholera-infected individuals in Fortaleza. As a result, relationships between health care providers and communities, especially poor communities, can be improved.

6. Ethnographic data can guide the rewriting of educational messages gone wrong. By situating messages in the imaginary world of "target" populations, their meaning is more easily understood and, hence, acted upon. Images and terms that provoke anger, disapproval and rejection can be avoided.

7. Rapid ethnographic assessment, which gleans essential data about infectious disease beliefs, attitudes and behaviors, can give quick responses on how to control disease transmission. The quick turn around time from data collection to use by program managers, is a positive feature of RAP in emergency, epidemic settings. In such trying situations, program managers are pressed to design and implement control measures immediately. Using RAP methodology in Fortaleza, we were able to provide university enteric disease specialists with preliminary ethnographic observations and impressions after one week of fieldwork, highly focused on the in-household transmission and control of cholera. Simultaneous with data collection and on-going analysis, program managers were continuously updated regarding our ethnographic hypotheses and findings. Our general findings, presented here in greater detail, were incorporated into the emergency cholera control program in Gonçalves Dias long before tape-recorded interviews were completely transcribed and the final manuscript written. The quickness of RAP methodology together with numerous short cuts taken by the authors in organizing and processing data, permitted the anthropology of cholera victims and their communities to figure squarely in redesigning control efforts in Gonçalves Dias which were more sensitive to people's reality and proved instrumental in reducing the incidence of cholera in this favela [Dr. Aldo Lima, personal communication].

To conclude, an anthropological interpretation of contagious cholera, requires that researchers first understand the local worlds of people exposed to the water-borne, cholera-causing bacillus. Only with probing insights into this day-to-day reality can researchers and communities work together to identify possible strategies which can effectively control disease transmission within households. Without these key cultural insights, as we have clearly seen with cholera, it is difficult, if not impossible, to design highly effective educational interventions to prevent its spread and foresee the "collateral effects" such culturally blind messages may provoke. The morally disgracing, disgusting and disempowering illness imagery associated metaphorically with cholera-tainted, rather than cured, individuals and communities we studied. It is not so much the cholera-causing bacillus that is feared but the morally polluting stigmas that are dreaded. A positive cholera diagnosis debases one's identity. Although physically recovered from painful gastric cramping, explosive diarrhea and life-threatening dehydration, patients rarely heal completely from the wounds of social stigmatization. This "collateral effect" of cholera prevention campaigns, we have seen, can spark outrage and revolt on people's part, causing them to resist well-intended control measures.

Even if a new anthropologically sensitive approach can guard against the "collateral effects" of conventional educational interventions, we must never lose sight that there is a larger issue with which we must contend with equal urgency: the eradication of the true "Dog's Disease" in developing countries – that is, economic poverty in which families are forced to live.

NOTES

*   Authors' note: Except for several structures, the *favela* Gonçalves Dias no longer exists. In 1995 a major road was built through the community, dispersing the homeless families.

1.   State of Ceará's public hospital for infectious diseases notorious for its large case load of very sick patients, including HIV-infected individuals. Patients receiving treatment at Sao José Hospital are often stigmatized and feared as carriers of "dangerous" diseases.

2.   Recently, the 440 families of Gonçalves Dias were evicted for fourth time due to government plans to build a road through the favela. As appraisers valued homes for expropriation, one resident sobbed: "I've lived here 17 years! This is home. I was raised here. My kids were born here. Even my *anginho* (dead infant) is buried here. What *micheira* (spare change) do you think I'm going to get for my house of dirt and sticks? It will never pay for all of what is mine here!"

3.   The name of a popular and potent alcoholic beverage brewed from sugar cane.

4. A conjunto is a government-subsidized, planned resettlement community built on large tracks of cheap land distant from the city for displaced slum dwellers and migrants. Eviction, abandonment, and overcrowding of the small, identical box-like homes is common due to high fixed rents.

5. Obtained through personal communication with Dr. Aldo Lima, Director Clinical Research Unit, Federal University of Ceara.

6. All names of ethnographic informants are pseudonymous.

7. Of Dona Zilnar's 22 live births, only 15 of her children are alive today. Seven died during infancy from preventable diarrheal dehydration, measles, and malnutrition.

8. That informants use the verb "to accuse" to refer to findings of the medical examination, is indirect evidence that accusatory pressures are routinely exerted by medical professionals.

9. The terms refers to Brazil's patron saint and one of few *negra* (black) virgins recognized by the Roman Catholic church.

10. The phase "I'm Not Dog, No!" is the title of a popular song originally written by Euripides Waldick Soriano in Portuguese as *Eu Não Sou Cachorro Não!* and aired on country radio during the early 1970's, years of military rule and political repression. Recently the title was translated into English as "I'm Not Dog, No! and the song reinterpreted by *brega* (funky folk) singers, Falcão and Tarcisio Matos.

11. Portuguese term which literally translates as "turn can," vividly describing stray mutts or mongrels who roam streets in poor neighborhoods and favelas turning over garbage cans in search of food.

12. The term refers to the Catholic saint revered in Umbanda as protector against epidemics.

13. *Psidium guayava L.* is an oil extract from leaves used popularly to treat diarrhea.

14. *Stenocalyx micheli Berg* is a plant medicinal whose leaves are used to make tea to treat diarrhea.

15. Miracle-performing Catholic saint of Juazeiro do Norte, Ceará who is a central figure in popular folk healing in Northeast Brazil.

16. The term refers to a Brazilian of mixed African and European descent.

17. Term for an "inhabitant of a favela or urban slum," which is also used derogatorily to refer to someone poor and unhygienic. *Novo Dicionário Aurélio da Lingua Portuguesa*, 1986, P. 762, 2nd edition, Editor Nova Fronteira S.A.

18. This phrase is a clever play on words. "I'm Collorido," the catchy campaign slogan used by ex-President of Brazil Fernando Collor de Mello, loosely translates into English as "Color me Collor." The accompanying television image showed drab black and white photos coming alive when painted yellow, green and blue (Brazil's national colors).

Popular usage here refers to being infected with cholera, a pun since the National Congress of Brazil, in a historic and unprecedented action, impeached President Fernando Collor de Mello for corruption and ideological misrepresentation.

REFERENCES

Ablon, Joan. 1981. Stigmatized Health Conditions. Social Science and Medicine 15B:5–9.

Acheson, J. M. 1972. Limited Good or Limited Goods? Response to Economic Opportunity in a Tarascan Pueblo. American Anthropologist 74:1152–1169.

AHRTAG (Appropriate Health Resources and Technologies Action Group, Ltd.). 1993. Controlling Cholera. Dialogue on Diarrhea 52 (March–May): 1–8.

Berreman, G. D. 1966. Anemic and Emetic Analyses in Social Anthropology. American Anthropologist 68:346–354.

Boutté, M. I. 1987. "The Stumbling Disease": A Case Study of Stigma among Azorean-Portuguese. Social Science and Medicine 24:3:209–217.

Clements, M. L. 1980. Sudan Community-based Family Health Project: Trip Report 21 August–2 September. University of Maryland (Unpublished).

Clements, M. L. et al. 1980. Comparison of Simple Sugar/Salt Versus Glucose/Electrolyte Oral Rehydration Solutions in Infant Diarrhea. University of Maryland (Unpublished).

Comaroff, J. 1985. Body of Power Spirit of Resistance. Chicago: University of Chicago Press.

Denzin, N. K. 1970. The Research Act in Sociology. London: Butterworth.

Douglas, M. 1966. Purity and Danger. London: Routledge and Kegan Paul.

Drummond, T. 1975. Using the Method of Paulo Freire in Nutrition Education: An Experimental Plan for Community Action in Northeast Brazil. Cornell International Nutrition Monograph Series No. 3. Ithaca, New York: Cornell University Press.

Egeman, A. and Bertan, M. 1980. A Study of Oral Rehydration Therapy by Midwives in a Rural Area in Ankara. Bulletin World Health Organization 58(2):333–338.

Ellerbrock, T. V. 1979. Oral Replacement Therapy in Rural Bangladesh with Home Ingredients. Dacca, Bangladesh: Bangladesh Rural Advancement Committee. (Unpublished).

Farmer, P. 1992. AIDS and Accusation: Haiti and the Geography of Blame. Berkeley, California: University of California Press.

Foster, G. M. 1965. Peasant Society and the Image of Limited Good. American Anthropologist 67:293–315.

Foster, G. M. 1967. Peasant Character and Personality. *In* Peasant Society a Reader. M. Potter, M. Diaz, G. Foster, eds. Pp. 50–56. Boston: Little, Brown.

Foster, G. M. 1972. The Anatomy of Envy: A Study in Symbolic Behavior. Current Anthropology 13(3):165–202.

Freidson, E. 1979. Profession of Medicine: A Study of the Sociology of Applied Knowledge. New York: Dodd, Mead.

Freire, P. 1977. Pedagogy of the Oppressed. London: Penguin Books.

Freye, G. 1963a. The Masters and the Slaves. A Study in the Development of Brazilian Civilization New York: Knopf.

Freye, G. 1963b. The Mansions and the Shanties: The Making of Modern Brazil. New York: Knopf.

Goffman, E. 1959. The Presentation of Self in Everyday Life. Garden City, New York: Doubleday and Co., Inc.

Goffman, E. 1963. Stigma: Notes on the Management of Spoiled Identity. Cliffs, New York: Prentice-Hall.

Goodenough, W. B., R. S. Gordon, Jr., and I. S. Rosenberg. 1964. Tetracycline in the Treatment of Cholera. The Lancet 1:355–357.

Guerrant, R. L., L. V. Kirchhoff, D. S. Shields, et al. 1983. Prospective Study of Diarrheal Illnesses in Northeastern Brazil: Patterns of Disease, Nutritional Impact, Etiologies and Risk Factors. Journal of Infectious Diseases 148:986–997.

Guerrant, R. L., J. F. McAuliffe, and M. A. de Souza. 1996. Mortality among Rural and Urban Families: An Indicator of Development and Implications for the Future. *In* At the Edge of Development: Health crises in a Transitional Society. R. L. Guerrant, M. A. de Souza, and M. K. Nations, eds. Pp. 69–88. Durham, North Carolina: Carolina Academic Press.

Gussow, Z. and G. S. Tracy. 1986. Status, Ideology and Adaptation to Stigmatized Illness: A Study of Leprosy. Human Organization 27:316.

Harland, G. et al. 1981. Composition of Oral Solutions Prepared by Jamaican Mothers for Treatment of diarrhea. The Lancet 1:600–601.

Harris, M. 1976. History and Significance of the Emic/Etic Distinction. Annual Review of Anthropology 5:329–350.

Harrison, L. 1985. Underdevelopment is a State of Mind. Lanham, Maryland: University Press of America.

Hirshhorn, N. 1983. Oral Rehydration Therapy: The Scientific and Technological Basis. In Proceedings of the International Conference on Oral Rehydration Therapy, 7 June, 1983. Pp. 19–23. Washington, D.C.: U.S. Agency for International Development (USAID).

Kielman, A. A. 1977. Home Treatment of Childhood Diarrhea in Punjab Village. Journal Tropical Pediatrics Environmental Child Health 23:197–201.

Kleinman, A. and J. Kleinman 1986. Suffering and Its Professional Transformation: Toward an Ethnography of Experience. Paper presented at the first conference of the Society for Psychological Anthropology. "On Current Thinking and Research in Psychological Anthropology," San Diego, California. Oct. 6–8.

Kluckhohn, C. 1944. Navaho Witchcraft. Cambridge, Massachusetts: Harvard University Papers of The Peabody Museum 22:2.

Lakoff, G. and M. Johnson. 1980. Metaphors We Live By. Chicago: The University of Chicago Press.

Lewis, O. 1966. The Culture of Poverty. Scientific America 215:4:19–25.

Lima, A. M. 1994. Cholera: Molecular Epidemiology, Pathogenesis, Immunology, Treatment, and Prevention. Current Science 3:593–601.

Lima, A. M. and R. L. Guerrant. 1994. The Management of Cholera Today. Mediguide to GI Diseases 5:4:1–5.

Lipset, S. M. and A. Solari. 1967. Elites in Latin America. New York: Knopf.

Mahalanabis, D. et al. 1974. Use of an Oral Glucose-Electrolyte Solution in the Treatment of Paediatric Cholera: A Controlled Study. Journal Tropical Pediatrics Environmental Child Health 20:82–87.

Melamed, A. and Segall, M. 1978. Spoons for Making Glucose-Salt Solution (letter). The Lancet 1(8077):1317–1318.

Molla, A. M., A. Molla, S. K. Nath, et al. 1989. Food-Based Oral Rehydration Salt Solution for Acute Childhood Diarrhea. The Lancet 2:429–431.

Molla, A. M, et al. 1985. Rice-Based Oral Rehydration Solution Decreases Stool Volume in Acute Diarrhea. Bull. WHO 63:751–756.

Monte, C. M. G. 1993. Improving Weaning Food Hygiene Practices in a Slum Area of Fortaleza, Northeast Brazil: A New Approach. Ph.D. Thesis. p. 69. London School of Tropical Medicine and Hygiene. London, U.K.: University of London. (Unpublished)

Morello, T. 1983. A Spoonful of Sugar... Far Eastern Economic Review 119:8:32–17.

Moran, M. 1976. Oral Rehydration Therapy in Home and Hospital: Experience in Rural Nigeria. Pediatric Nursing 2:5:32–33.

Nations, M. K. 1982. Illness of the Child (Doenca de Crianca): The Cultural Context of Childhood Diarrhea in Northeast Brazil. Ph.D. Dissertation. Berkeley, California: University of California, Department of Anthropology (unpublished).

Nations, M. K. 1983. Spirit Possession to Enteric Pathogens: The Role of Traditional Healing in Diarrheal Diseases Control. Proceedings of the International Conference on Oral Rehydration Therapy. Washington, D.C.: U.S. Agency for International Development (USAID).

Nations, M. K. 1986. Epidemiologic Research of Infectious Diseases: Quantitative Rigor or Rigormortis? – Insights from Ethnomedicine. *In* Anthropology and Epidemiology. C. R. Janes, R. Stall, and S. M. Gifford, eds. Pp. 97–123. Boston, Massachusetts: D. Reidel Publishing Company.

Nations, M. K. 1992. The Child's Disease (Doença de Criança): Popular Paradigm of Persistent Diarrhea? Acta Paediatr Suppl 381:55–65.

Nations, M. K. and L. A. Rebhun. 1988. Mystification of a Simple Solution: Oral Rehydration Therapy in Northeast Brazil. Social Science and Medicine 27(1):25–38.

Nations, M. K. et al. 1983. Care Within Reach: Appropriate Health-Care Delivery in the Developing World. The New England Journal of Medicine 310(24):1612.

Nations, M. K. et al. 1988. Brazilian Popular Healers as Effective Promoters of Oral Rehydration Therapy (ORT) and Related Child Survival Strategies. Bulletin Pan American Health Organization (PAHO) 22(4):335–354.

Nichter, M. 1990. Vaccinations in South Asia: False Expectations and Commanding Metaphors. *In* Anthropology and Primary Health Care. J. Coreil and D. Mull, eds. Pp. 196–221. Springfield, Michigan: Westwood Press.

Parker, R. L. et al. 1980. Oral Rehydration Therapy (ORT) for Childhood Diarrhea. Population Reports, Series L: 2, November–December.

Pennie, R. A., R. D. Pearson, and M. I. McAuliffe, and R. L. Guerrant, 1996. The Illness Burden in Poor Rural and Urban Communities: Enteric Parasitic Infections. *In* At the Edge of Development: Health Crises in a Transitional Society. R. L. Guerrant, M. A. de Souza, M. K. Nations, eds. Pp. 149–159. Durham, North Carolina: Carolina Academic Press.

Pizzaro, D. et al. 1979. Evaluation of Oral Therapy for Infant Diarrhea in an Emergency Room Setting: The Acute Episode as an Opportunity for Instructing Mothers in Home Treatment. Bulletin World Health Organization (WHO) 57:6:983–986.

Ribeiro, L. 1992. Comunicação Global: A Magica da Influnca. Rio de Janeiro, Brazil: Editora Objetiva.

Rifkin, S. B. 1983. Planners' Approaches to Community Participation in Health Programs: Theory and Reality. Contact 75:6–13.

Rubel, A. J. 1960. Concepts of Disease in Mexican-American Culture. American Anthropologist 62:795–814.

Ryan, W. 1971 Blaming the Victim. New York: Vintage Press.

Sack, D. A. 1980. Lobon-Gur (Common Salt and Brown Sugar) Oral Rehydration Solution in the Diarrhea of Adults. Scientific Report 36. Dacca, Bangladesh: International Center for Diarrheal Diseases Research. (Unpublished)

Scheper-Hughes, N. 1984. Infant Mortality and Infant Care: Cultural and Economic Constraints on Nurturing in Northeast Brazil. Social Science and Medicine 19(5):535–546.

Scheper-Hughes, N. 1985. Culture, Scarcity, and Maternal Thinking: Maternal Detachment and Infant Survival in a Brazilian Shantytown. Ethos 13(4):291–317.

Schimshaw, S. C. M. and E. Hurtado. 1987. Rapid Assessment Procedures for Nutrition and Primary Health Care: Anthropological Approaches to Improving Programme Effectiveness. Reference Series, Vol. 11. Tokyo, Japan and Los Angeles, California. The United Nations University and University of California, Los Angeles (UCLA) Latin American Center Publications.

Scott, J. C. 1985. Weapons of the Weak: Everyday Forms of Peasant Resistance. New Haven: Yale University Press.

Scott, J. C. 1990. Domination and the Arts of Resistance: Hidden Transcripts. New Haven: Yale University Press.

Shields, D. S. et al. 1981. Electrolyte/Glucose Concentration and Bacterial Contamination in Home-Prepared Oral Rehydration Solution: A Field Experiment in Northeastern Brazil. Journal of Pediatrics 98:5:839–841.

Shorling, J. S., S. Shorling, J. McAuliffe, et al. 1987. Epidemiology of Prolonged Diarrhea in an Urban Brazilian Slum. Clinical Research 35:489A (Abstract).

Sontag, S. 1990. Illness as Metaphor and Aids and its Metaphors. New York, New York: Anchor Books, Doubleday. (Illness as Metaphor first published in 1977; Aids and its Metaphors first published in 1988).

Thane-Toe, et al. 1984. Oral Rehydration Therapy in the Home by Village Mothers in Burma. Transactions Royal Society Tropical Medicine and Hygiene 78:581–589.

The World Bank. 1990. Poverty: World Development Report 1990. Pp. 236–237. New York: Oxford University Press.

Tinling, D. C. 1967. Voodoo, Rootwork, and Medicine. Psychosomatic Medicine 29:483–490.

UNICEF. 1986. Perfil Estatistico de Criancas e Maes no Brasil: Aspectos Socio-Economicos de Mortalidade Infantil em Areas Urbans. Pp. 61–70. Rio de Janeriro, Brazil: Instituto Brasileiro de Geografia e Estatistica.

UNICEF. 1992. Crise and Infància no Brasil: O Impacto das Politicas de 1988 Ajustamento Econômico. Brasilia, D.F.: UNICEF.

Valentine, C. 1968. Culture and Poverty: Critique and Counter-Proposals. Chicago: University of Chicago Press.

Victora, C. G. and F. C. Barros. 1988. A Saúde das Crianças Cearenses: Um Estudo de 8,000 Familias. Brasilia, D.F.: UNICEF.

Wintrob, R. 1973. The Influence of Others: Witchcraft and Rootwork as Explanations of Behavior Disturbances. Journal of Nervous and Mental Disease 156:318–326.

INDEX

Aaby, P. with Manderson, L.
  on methodological survey in
  behavioral research, 218
Acquired Immunodeficiency
Syndrome (AIDS, also Human
Immunodeficiency Virus, HIV)
  "anthropology of risk"
  in, 402–5
  in Africa, 46
  blame/conspiracy, issues of,
  443–5
  case histories, 416–21, 391–2
  "Chache Lavi, Detai Lavi"
  (AIDS education video),
  426–8
  and changing value systems,
  383–4
  and coccidioidomycosis, 79
  condom usage, 400–2, 408
  as an emergent infection, 3
  epidemiology, 10, 15–16
  as an external threat, 395–6
  Farmer, Paul, on, 444
  In Florida, 414–5
  in Haiti, 27, 416–428,
  432–4, 444
  intervention programs, 375–7,
  378–82, 393–5, 399, 401–3,
  405–7, 425–8, 432
  in Kenya, 27, 375–408
  and marriage, 414
  and number of sex partners,
  422–3
  occupational incidence among
  men, 423
  and prostitution, 27, 375–7,
  378–8, 392–405, 407, 408

sexual activity as risk behavior,
  46–7, 380–1, 408
and sexually transmitted
  diseases (STDs), 389–90,
  400–2, 424
social perceptions of risk,
  395–9
social forces as risk factors, 27,
  382–5, 391–2, 396, 407,
  414–6, 421, 423–5, 428–9,
  432, 434
testing for, 402
Une Chance A Prendre
  (UCAP, AIDS prevention
  project), 425–8
in the United States, 47, 431
among women, 414–5,
  421–3, 432
and women's health issues,
  389–92
women's knowledge of, 393–9,
  402–3
women's paradigms for
  prevention, 399–402
Acute Respiratory Infections
(ARI) (see also Tuberculosis;
Pneumonia)
  antibiotics, use of, 332, 364–5
  in behavioral research, 220–2
  child mortality, 219, 331
  in Egypt, 365–6
  household ecology, 220
  intervention programs, 332–3,
  334–6, 219–220
  in Kenya, 152–3
  and measles, 322
  in Pakistan, 26, 332–6